European Union Non-Discrii
Law

EU equality law is multidimensional in being based on different rationales and concepts. Consequently, the concept of discrimination has become fragmented, with different instruments envisaging different scopes of protection. This raises questions as to the ability of EU law to address the situation of persons excluded on a number of grounds.

This edited book addresses the increasing complexity of European equality law from jurisprudential, sociological and political science perspectives. Internationally renowned researchers from Scandinavian, Continental and Central European countries and Britain analyse the consequences of multiplying discrimination grounds within EU equality law, considering its multi-dimensionality and intersectionality.

The contributors to the book theorise the move from formal to substantive equality law and its interrelation to new forms of governance, demonstrating the specific combination of non-discrimination law with welfare state models which reveal the global implications of the EU. The book will be of interest to academics and policymakers all over the world, in particular to those researching and studying law, political sciences and sociology with an interest in human rights, non-discrimination law, contract and employment law or European studies.

Dagmar Schiek is Jean Monnet Professor and holds the Chair in European Law at the University of Leeds, UK, and is Director of the Centre of European Law and Legal Studies.

Victoria Chege is a research assistant at the Carl von Ossietzky University of Oldenburg, Germany.

European Union Non-Discrimination Law

Comparative perspectives on
multidimensional equality law

**Edited by Dagmar Schiek and
Victoria Chege**

Routledge·Cavendish
Taylor & Francis Group
LONDON AND NEW YORK

First published 2009
by Cavendish Publishing

Transferred to digital printing 2008
by Routledge-Cavendish
2 Park Square,
Abingdon, Oxon, OX14 4RN

Simultaneously published in the USA and Canada
by Routledge-Cavendish
270 Madison Ave, New York, NY10016

*Routledge-Cavendish is an imprint of the Taylor & Francis Group, an
informa business*

Typeset in Times New Roman by

British Library Cataloguing-in-Publication Data
A catalogue record for this book is available from the British Library

Library of Congress Cataloging in Publication Data
European Union non-discrimination law : comparative perspectives on
    multidimensional equality law / Dagmar Schiek and Victoria Chege.
        p. cm.
    ISBN 978–0–415–45722–4
    1. Discrimination—Law and legislation—European Union
countries.   2. Equality before the law—European countries.
3. Discrimination—Law and legislation—Europe.   4. Equality before
the law—Europe.   I. Schiek, Dagmar.   II. Chege, Victoria.
    KJE5142.E97 2008
    342.2408′5—dc22

2008005771

ISBN10: 0–415–45722–X (hbk)
ISBN10: 0–415–47115–X (pbk)
ISBN10: 0–203–89262–3 (ebk)

ISBN13: 978–0–415–45722–4 (hbk)
ISBN13: 978–0–415–47115–2 (pbk
ISBN13: 978–0–203–89262–6 (ebk)

Contents

Preface

The inception of this book dates back to November 2004, when Dagmar Schiek presented a paper at a conference organised by Rikki Holtmaat (University of Leiden), focusing on how multiplying the 'discrimination grounds' affected women. The paper defended the thesis that a mere prohibition of sex discrimination would mainly benefit those women considered (*inter alia*) as white, belonging to a majority ethnicity and religion and as heterosexual and able-bodied (that is, a small minority of all women). Multiplying of grounds in EU non-discrimination law thus emerged as an advantage for the majority of women.

In November 2004, this seemed counter-intuitive. Multiplying of grounds had seemingly resulted in an upgrading of 'other equalities' at the expense of gender equality. A few days before the said conference, the European Commission had held an official conference on equality law, for which no one had considered it appropriate to include gender equality or experts in that field. This illustrated the institutional logic of going beyond gender equality: the 'other equalities' could only gain priority at the expense of gender equality, and gender equality could only hope to retain its status at the expense of the 'other equalities'.

Such an approach was highly questionable. Focusing on the 'other equalities' exclusively, the European Commission was bound to neglect the majority of the 'groups' circumscribed by these: women constitute the majority in each, and they are the ones suffering from discrimination on grounds of their ascribed gender in addition to or intersected with any other ground. Ignoring gender would lead to neglecting the situation of the majority of people altogether.

The question remained how EU equality law would digest the multiplication of grounds and approach intersectional discrimination. Thus, a proposal for a follow-up conference emerged, resulting in the 'First European Conference on Multidimensional Equality Law' (FEMCEL) in May 2007. FEMCEL did not phase out gender equality. In fact, most of the speakers were female, having gained experience in gender equality law before focusing on multidimensional aspects of EU equality law. From the conference discussions, the conceptual basis of EU non-discrimination law emerged as more important than ever and, at the same time, inextricably linked with the failing response to intersectionality by EU law. The result of all this is a book combining authors from the Czech Republic, Denmark, Finland, France, Germany, Iceland, the Netherlands, Norway and the UK. Drawn together, their contributions offer a coherent text on the conceptual state of EU non-discrimination law and its development towards a multidimensional equality law for Europe.

We need to acknowledge support for the process leading to this book. This extends to the main sponsor of the conference, the Fritz Thyssen Stiftung (Cologne), especially for stepping in after the DFG (German Research Council) and HWK (Hanse Institute for Advanced Study) had turned down the application. Further support came from the European Commission, which contributed towards the conference and language check for publication via its Jean Monnet programme. Our authors were patient with an editing process disturbed by Dagmar Schiek's migration from Oldenburg (Germany) to Leeds (UK). Special thanks are due to Dr Paul Skidmore (Berlin), who contributed to the editing process considerably beyond language-checking contributions of non-native speakers, based on his former work on equality law.

Dagmar G Schiek and Victoria A Chege   Leeds/Oldenburg, January 2008

List of illustrations

Figures

Tables

List of contributors

Dr Oddný Mjöll Arnardóttir is Professor of Law at Reykjavík University, Iceland. She is also a board member of the Icelandic Human Rights Centre.

Dr Susanne Burri is Senior Lecturer at the School of Law (Gender and Law), University of Utrecht, The Netherlands.

Victoria Chege (LLM, LLM (Eur)) is research assistant at the University Carl von Ossietzky of Oldenburg, Germany.

Sandra Fredman is Professor of Law and a Fellow of Exeter College at the University of Oxford, UK. She was elected Fellow of the British Academy in 2005.

Dr Morag Goodwin is Lecturer in Law at the University of Maastricht, The Netherlands, and a CLPE Visiting Fellow at Osgoode Hall Law School, Toronto, Canada.

Dr Kristina Koldinská is Lecturer in Law at the Charles University of Prague, Czech Republic.

Dr Sylvaine Laulom is Lecturer in Law at the University of St Etienne, France.

Dr Titia Loenen is Professor of Gender and Law at the University of Utrecht, The Netherlands.

Dr Ruth Nielsen is Professor of Law at Copenhagen Business School, Denmark.

Dr Kevät Nousiainen is Academy Professor for women's studies at the University of Helsinki, Finland, and Professor of Comparative Law and Legal Theory at the University of Turku, Finland. She is also a board member of the Christina Institute of Women's Studies.

Dr Michael Orton is Senior Research Fellow at the Institute for Employment Research, University of Warwick, UK.

Dr Sacha Prechal is Professor of European Law at the University of Utrecht, The Netherlands.

Dr Peter Ratcliffe is Professor of Sociology and Director of the Centre for Rights, Equality and Diversity at the University of Warwick, UK.

Dr Lynn Roseberry is Associate Professor of Law at Copenhagen Business School, Denmark.

Dr Ute Sacksofsky, MPA (Harvard) is Professor of Public Law and Comparative Law at University of Frankfurt aM, Germany, a director of the Cornelia Goethe Centrum für Frauenstudien und die Erforschung der Geschlechterverhältnisse (Centre for Women's and Gender Studies), and Public Advocate to the Hessian State Constitutional Court.

Dr Dagmar Schiek is Jean Monnet Professor and Chair of European Law and Director of the Centre of European Law and Legal Studies at the University of Leeds, UK.

Dr Hege Skjeie is Professor in Political Science at the University of Oslo, Norway, adjunct professor at the Faculty of Social Sciences, Aalborg University, Denmark, and a Member of the Norwegian Equality Tribunal.

Dr Iyiola Solanke is Lecturer in Law at the Law School, University of East Anglia, Norwich, UK. In 2007, she was awarded a Jean Monnet Fellowship at the University of Michigan Law School.

Dr Ulrike M Vieten is visiting Lecturer in Media and Cultural Studies at the University of East London and at the London Metropolitan University, UK.

Table of cases

International and Supranational Jurisdictions

Table of legislative instruments

Introduction

1 From European Union non-discrimination law towards multidimensional equality law for Europe

Dagmar Schiek

1.1 A multidimensional perspective on European Union discrimination law

This book offers a comprehensive approach towards developing a meaningful legal framework for equality in social reality. The point of departure is the rather fragmented body of EU non-discrimination law, which has moved towards multidimensionality in a number of ways in recent years.

1.1.1 Notion of multidimensionality

The reference to 'multidimensionality' is meant to capture both the present state of EU non-discrimination law and perspectives of developing it towards a body of equality law that will meet the challenges ahead. EU non-discrimination law is multidimensional in its conceptual approaches, which continue to oscillate between form and substance, individual and group, and equality of treatment and result.[1] It is also multidimensional in the number of exclusionary criteria addressed explicitly (now: sex, ethnic origin, race, age, disability, sexual orientation and religion and belief). The contributions to this book aim to further the conceptual debate as well as the practical use of EU non-discrimination law. The main challenges we identify are those posed by a lack of theoretical reflection on purposes and directions of equality law, reflected in EU non-discrimination law's fragmented nature, and by multiplying discrimination grounds. The notion of multidimensionality thus encompasses interrelations of different conceptions of equality law as well as intersections between discrimination grounds.[2]

1.1.2 Developing European Union non-discrimination law

EU non-discrimination law (often also termed 'EU Anti-Discrimination Law')[3] has been acknowledged as a field in its own right following legislation based on Art 13 of the EC Treaty (Art 13 EC). Inserting this provision into the Treaty by the Treaty of Amsterdam, the Heads of States may have employed less deliberation than the subject has conjured since then. They merely stated that the Council should be enabled to 'take appropriate action to combat discrimination based on sex, racial or ethnic origin, religion or belief, disability, age or sexual orientation', and subjected this new competence to a number of caveats.[4]

Contrary to negative premonitions of Art 13 EC as condemned to a perennial slumber,[5] the EU proceeded rather fast in proliferating provisions prohibiting discrimination. In the wake of a nationalist populist party forming part of the government of a small Member State,[6] and against the background of intense lobbying from a very well organised non-governmental organisation (NGO) since 1993,[7] a first anti-discrimination directive was passed as early as 2000. Prohibiting discrimination on grounds of race and ethnic origin only, Council Directive 2000/43/EC[8] went beyond the narrow confines of employment law and thus – arguably[9] – beyond the confines of social policy, elevating non-discrimination law towards a policy in its own right. From the start, there was some criticism relating to the overly simple regulatory approach.[10] The 'Framework Directive' (Council Directive 2000/78/EC)[11] endeavoured more daringly to prohibit discrimination on a number of grounds: religion and belief, sexual orientation, disability and age. Less daring, its scope of application remained within employment, at the exclusion of social security, which had always been covered by Community gender equality legislation.

Prior to 2000, Community law required equal treatment of persons[12] only in relation to gender and nationality. While Council Directives 2000/43/EC and 2000/78/EC exclude the ground of nationality,[13] they were soon complemented by new legislation on sex discrimination: Directive 2002/73/EC reformed Council Directive 76/207/EEC in the field of gender equality in employment;[14] and Council Directive 2004/113/EC constituted a more timid version of the Race Directive's 'non-employment-provisions', providing a narrower scope of protection against gender discrimination than Council Directive 2000/43/EC affords against racial discrimination.[15]

Although now the youngest addition to the legislative body, gender equality law had been a point of departure for doctrinal development of equal treatment of persons.[16] The conceptual debate on gender equality law highlighted the tension between formal and substantive equality,[17] the asymmetric character of discrimination in social practice[18] and shortcomings of enforcing individual rights to equal treatment,[19] leading to demands for effective remedies, institutional support and encouragement of associations.

By 2000, all these strands of critique had led to some cautiously progressive European Court of Justice (ECJ) case law developing the principle of effective remedies,[20] acknowledging pregnancy discrimination as sex discrimination,[21] allowing for some positive action[22] and to the implementation of a 'gender mainstreaming clause' into the EC Treaty (Art 3(2) EC). The legislative body of gender equality law was not consolidated in any way. The

Equal Treatment Directive (Council Directive 76/207/EEC)[23] still consisted of seven meagre articles, the wording of which was stretched far by dynamic interpretation on the part of the ECJ.

Council Directives 2000/43/EC and 2000/78/EC addressed some of the shortcomings of the Gender Equality Directives. They defined direct and indirect discrimination, and included harassment as a form of discrimination. They granted Member States some explicit discretion for positive action and obliged them to establish effective remedies as well as to engage in social dialogue and dialogue with non-governmental actors in order to enhance equal treatment in practice. Council Directive 2000/43/EC also obliged Member States to create at least one institution for the furtherance of equality. All these developments had passed by gender equality law, until Directives 2002/73/EC and 2004/113/EC were adopted.[24]

In the wake of discussions from the UK, reflecting the persistence of institutional racism against a long history of racial equality legislation,[25] a parallel discussion on how to overcome complaints-based approaches in favour of positive obligations for institutions developed. Ensuing legislative proposals are even given the credit of creating a fourth generation of equality law, which overcomes the shortcomings of the preceding three generations.[26] The main feature of the 'new generation' or the 'group justice model' is that it creates positive obligations (mostly on public actors) to establish institutional preconditions for equality in social reality. No such positive obligations exist as yet in Community law.

1.1.3 Fragmentation of European Union non-discrimination law

All these legislative and jurisprudential developments have resulted in a fragmented body of law. This first of all implies that the conceptual approach to non-discrimination and equality is not uniform, to the point of being contradictory.

The new directives, starting with the Race Directive, have been criticised for not proceeding towards the fourth generation of equality law in the UK, although otherwise attempting to transplant UK law to the continent.[27] Some elements of a third generation approach, which *inter alia* endorses effective enforcement and support by agencies, are contained in the directives. There are provisions on remedies, mirroring ECJ case law in gender equality. Member States shall provide some institutional support for those discriminated against, which goes beyond existing case law.

From a perspective beyond the UK, these directives – taken together with the ECJ case law – insufficiently mirror the move from formal towards substantive equality. The ECJ case law on gender equality in this respect is mirrored in the explicit provision declaring pregnancy discrimination as sex discrimination in Directive 2002/73/EC and Council Directive 2004/113/EC as well as in the general clause allowing Member States some scope for positive action, contained in all the directives. It is questionable, however, as to how far the narrow approach taken in the gender equality case law will continue to be applied.[28]

In particular, EU law hints towards an asymmetric conception of non-discrimination in providing limited scope for positive action and in acknowledging the especially vulnerable position of women.[29] It does not, however, adequately address the problem. Deceptively, the youngest Commission-sponsored study on multidimensional equality states: 'The answer to the question "who is vulnerable to multiple discrimination?" becomes simple: all individuals are potentially vulnerable'.[30] Nothing is further from the truth. Each single 'ground' delimitates categories of persons who are likely to suffer detriment in relation to that ground (for example, those ascribed ethnic minority status, the female gender or a non-heterosexual lifestyle) and those who profit from the same discrimination (for example, those accepted as part of the ethnic majority, as male or as heterosexual). To add to the complexity, a person may well combine personal traits that make her suffer from discrimination and profit from discrimination against others at the same time. Accordingly, an asymmetric approach is seen as a precondition for effectively endorsing a substantive conception of equality,[31] in particular where multiplying discrimination grounds is provided for.[32]

Second, EU non-discrimination law is fragmented in its response to different 'grounds' of discrimination. Its provisions are scattered about in four different legal instruments, protecting different grounds. This fragmented approach in itself is bound to lead to frictions. At the same time, the new body of law insufficiently reflects the interrelation between the grounds.[33] This is all the more serious if combined with the reluctance to endorse a substantive, asymmetric position to discrimination in social reality. The mere fact that different grounds are covered in different instruments may call for a ground specific interpretation as well as a teleological reading of all these different instruments as one body of law.[34] However, EU law itself offers only some hints as to how this interpretation should take place.[35]

1.1.4 Point of departure for this collection

This state of affairs poses a challenge for the further development of the field of EC non-discrimination law, especially if it is – as the title of this collection suggests – developing towards a body of equality law. This development will have to take place in the Member States, which had to implement most of the relevant legislation until the end of 2006.[36] As has been mentioned, EU equality law has tended not to be grounded in developments in and adapted to realities of national legal cultures.[37] This can be explained with reference to the special dynamics of European integration and the role of non-discrimination law therein.[38] However, if continuing to devise effective equality law for 27 Member States in a top-down mode, the European institutions will most probably not achieve any adequate ways to address complex phenomena such as multidimensional discrimination in different social circumstances.[39]

To date, EU non-discrimination law is modelled upon only a few jurisdictions, UK and Dutch influences being predominant.[40] Comparative legal reasoning beyond these jurisdictions would be required to offer roads for bottom-up development in the field of equality law.

In spring 2007, it seemed a good time to collect comparative approaches from different disciplines and legal traditions within Europe to contribute towards a sustained effort in addressing these issues. We address the intersections between different grounds, that is, a problem of any regime of equality law, as well as the intersections between different policy fields, as coloured by the specific dynamics of EU bureaucracy in the field. The latter is a specific issue of European equality law, which is based on the specific polity mix of the EU. Both facets of the multidimensionality theme shall be discussed in this introductory chapter, in order to form a background of further discussion of the single chapters.

1.2 Non-discrimination and equality law in the context of European integration

EU non-discrimination law is first and foremost part and parcel of European integration through law within the EU. As such, it is subject to specific dynamics, which are at best loosely connected with the socio-political aspirations of equality law as such. The European integration project has developed from a purely market-oriented endeavour towards a more integrated polity, which has taken a turn towards re-nationalisation in the recent 'constitutional debate' that has resulted in the Treaty of Lisbon,[41] not yet in force as these lines are being written. The EU is still competing with its Member States in most policy fields that are characteristic for establishing statehood.

1.2.1 Non-discrimination and social policy

This is particularly true for social policy. In this field, the competences of the EU have always been fragmented, for a number of reasons.[42] The integration project commenced as an economic project in the 1950s based on the optimistic belief that economic integration by establishing a Common Market would lead to social cohesion and a steady raising of living standards without any further Community policies and legislation. Although this belief was abandoned with the Treaty of Maastricht,[43] European integration continued to lean towards economic integration. As this tended to undermine the public support for the project,[44] the European Economic Community has from the start relied on social policies as well, however fragmented.

Non-discrimination and equality have always been an important parts of these. Arguably, this was due to the fact that none of the Member States (except the UK, and later Ireland) had comprehensive social-policy projects evolving around non-discrimination and equality,[45] but this was not the only reason. Establishing an Internal Market is contingent on equal treatment of some kind. In a very neo-liberal fashion, states could rely on equal treatment of products (that is, goods and services alone) and leave persons to compete on the basis of different 'social costs'.[46] The EU has always chosen a different road, on which equal treatment of persons accompanied free movement of labour and freedom of establishment instead.[47] Thus, what was conceptualised as a legal framework for market integration, slowly developed into a base for claims of individual citizens[48] to equal treatment on the labour market and in gaining access to different countries by having their qualifications acknowledged, to name but two examples.

1.2.2 Conceptions of citizenship and non-discrimination law

The culmination point of this development was the acknowledgement of EU citizenship with the Treaty of Maastricht, which also laid the basis for European economic and monetary union. The next step towards a fully integrated economy[49] – economic and monetary union – and the next step towards integrated statehood – EU citizenship – were both taken at the same time. The symbolism of this must not be underestimated. Its significance lies first and foremost in the close connection between citizenship law and social policy.[50]

Despite this importance, EU citizenship did not seem a significant development initially.[51] Arguably, only the ECJ case law, that linked the right to move freely within the territory of the Member States to the right not to be discriminated against[52] has freed up the potential of EU citizenship, opening a Pandora's box[53] containing *inter alia* access to welfare-state type rights for the economically inactive and residence rights for third country nationals as parents of EU citizens who are not yet of age[54] – both developments that were not to be expected from the meagre seven Articles in the EC Treaty.

EU Citizenship and EU non-discrimination law are often mentioned as being conceptually linked.[55] The obvious nominal link is the repetition of non-discrimination as a principle in Art 12 EC and Art 13 EC: the former has proven decisive for lending substance to citizenship law; the latter is the basis of EU non-discrimination law. The conceptual link stems from the interlocking nature of national and EU citizenship: this conception must lead to equal treatment between citizens of different nationalities as the main element of EU citizenship. EU citizenship is thus cited as an example of a multiple identity, within which equalising of rights gains prime importance[56] as well as managing diversity and promoting integration.[57]

Both citizenship and non-discrimination law are thus important contributions to legitimising the EU. Both fields of law show a development from market integration law towards a more integrated approach. While the notion of EU citizen was regarded as inherent in embryonic state in the 1957 EEC Treaty,[58] the citizen before the Treaty of Maastricht could only exercise rights in relation to his or her market citizen status. The Treaty of Maastricht established wider implications for non-market citizens. Arguably, non-discrimination law is a necessary compound of the cosmopolitan citizenship status.[59] A citizen who is not discriminated on grounds of her nationality, but on grounds of her ethnic origin and sexual orientation, is just as unable to realise this cosmopolitan ideal as someone excluded from the territory of a Member State on grounds of nationality. Accordingly, non-discrimination law contains rights typical for the EU and its citizenship.

The field of EU discrimination law does go beyond citizenship law, however. Although the non-discrimination directives stress that they do not cover differential treatment on grounds of nationality in matters of immigration, they certainly convey rights upon third country nationals. Once legally resident in the Member States (and arguably even when illegally so) they can rely on the body of law granting them equal treatment irrespective of all the six grounds. Thus, the third country national, just as any EU citizen, must be protected against discrimination on grounds of his religion or her perceived disability. There are even good reasons to derive from Council Directive 2000/43/EC a certain degree of protection against ethnic discrimination in immigration procedures in favour of third country nationals.[60] Frictions between EU citizenship law on the one hand and EU non-discrimination law on the other hand will certainly arise. When discussing the mixture of ethnic and religious discrimination arising from the use of the hijab in this book, Lynn Roseberry and Hege Skjeie touch upon this friction.

1.2.3   *Human rights and non-discrimination law*

Alongside EU Citizenship, the Treaty of Maastricht also introduced a first explicit reference to human rights protection into the EU legal framework (Art 6 EU). Again, the coincidence of finally accepting fundamental rights explicitly as an element of EU law with the taking of a decisive step further towards an integrated economy was of relevance for enhancing the integrationist pull of the polity. It has also been considered as decisive for Constitutionalism ever since.[61] Of course, fundamental rights have been protected long before the founding of the EU, again by ECJ case law. Beyond the narrow confines of internal market law,[62] the field of gender equality has been a source of developing the doctrines of Community fundamental rights law.[63] As citizenship law and fundamental rights law, EU discrimination law is based on a rights' discourse. Thus, the three fields may seem to have very much in common.

However, there are also potential frictions. Some have hinted at possible conflicts between discrimination law and protection of certain human rights.[64] Especially when discussing the 'hijab enigma' in this book, Ruth Nielsen, Titia Loenen, Lynn Roseberry and Ute Sacksofsky all point towards the possibility of justifying direct discrimination on grounds of religion and indirect ethnic discrimination by reference to the combat against gender inequality. More seriously, human rights protection in the EU remains fragmented. The ECJ is not bound by the European Convention on Human Rights (ECHR), but rather considers it as 'source of inspiration' for fundamental rights protection in the EU. While the European Court of Human Rights (ECtHR) and the ECJ have developed a co-operative relationship in their case law,[65] there is still the potential of frictions between the two legal orders. As equality norms within the ECHR and in the ECtHR case law are less developed than within the EU, this may prove problematic for the field.

As it happens, this is even more so for cases of intersectional discrimination. Three contributions in this book discuss this issue: Titia Loenen finds that the ECJ will most probably take a different road in assessing a headscarf ban than the ECtHR, and is seconded in this view by Lynn Roseberry. Oddny Arnardóttir analyses the case law of the ECtHR for any potential of addressing intersectionality in a sensible way, and reveals some interesting discoveries.

1.2.4 From non-discrimination towards equality and 'new governance'

While the EU has so far preferred to use the negative concept of prohibiting discrimination in its legislation, policy development has progressed towards the concept of equality. The relation between these two concepts has never been fully clarified. Some authors consider anti-discrimination legislation as being based upon a 'set of negative obligations, focusing on actions that (one) must refrain from',[66] while equality law regimes are described as including prohibitions of harassment and victimisation as well as positive obligations.[67] From this perspective, EU non-discrimination law would already tend towards equality law, as it prohibits harassment and victimisation. Using a comparative perspective, it seems less convincing to make a distinction in that manner. Equality as a positive term is more usual in Continental constitutional norms than in UK legislation.[68] If equality law was the more far-reaching concept, one would expect the body of equality law in countries such as France, Italy or Germany to be more comprehensive than that of UK non-discrimination law. This is, however, not the case.[69] It seems more adequate to view equality and discrimination as two different ways to approach the subject: equality mirrors the positive state of affairs one wishes to achieve by (*inter alia*) prohibiting discrimination.

A prohibition of discrimination is, of course, not the only way to enhance gender, racial, sexual and other equalities. EU gender equality policy has, in line with international developments, embraced the principle of gender mainstreaming, which was introduced into the EC Treaty by the Treaty of Amsterdam. Mainstreaming is not conceptually limited to gender mainstreaming.[70] The Reform Treaty (Treaty of Lisbon) extends the gender mainstreaming clause contained in Art 3(2) EC towards a general obligation to mainstream non-discrimination on a number of grounds.[71]

The principle of mainstreaming departs from a non-discrimination approach. Instead of targeting certain behaviour of individuals, it aims at changing policy contents in general. It is defined as '(re)organisation, improvement and evaluation of policy processes, so that a ... equality perspective is incorporated in all policies at all levels at all stages, by the actors normally involved in policy making'.[72] The focus on informing policies rather than commanding certain actions has been compared to 'new governance' structures generally.[73] New governance, still not a settled concept, is usually understood to comprise processes operating differently from traditional command and control structures.[74] It comprises participatory processes geared to achieve policy aims more effectively than traditional hard law. Its main representative within the EU seems to be the Open Method of Coordination, which circumvents the necessity to pass binding EU legislation by convincing Member States to dedicate themselves to a process of developing best practices and to achieve aims voluntarily.[75] New governance mechanisms are being questioned in relation to enhancing the effectiveness of rights, while at the same time it is conceded that legislation is not the only or most effective way forward in relation to enhance equality in reality.[76]

It may well be that multiplying the grounds enhances the complexity of equality law to a degree that legal obligations become impractical. On the other hand, rights enforcement may be especially important for those finding themselves at the intersections of disadvantage. Whether a combination of enforceable rights and new governance structures is the way forward or whether new governance is likely to compromise rights is a decision not easy to make.

Unsurprisingly, our authors tend towards different answers: Sandra Fredman stresses the advantages of positive obligations, while Kevät Nousiainen exposes the disadvantages of over-reliance on a gender mainstreaming discourse as opposed to a rights discourse. Ruth Nielsen demands to 'gendermainstream' EU non-discrimination law in order to adequately protect women from inequality.

1.3 Challenges of multiplying grounds

One of the foci of this collection is the question whether and if so, how, EU law was able to respond to the challenge of multiplying grounds on which discrimination is prohibited. As Ruth Nielsen rightly mentions, the two traditional dimensions of Community discrimination law, gender and nationality, tended to intersect as well. However, with more grounds, EU non-discrimination law is more likely than ever to cover situations in which discrimination on more than one ground occurred.

1.3.1 The intersectionality debate and its relevance for Europe

Of course, such situations are typical for any social situation in which different exclusionary mechanisms are at work. As Ulrike Vieten and Iyiola Solanke argue in more detail in their contributions, the interrelation of different dimensions of exclusion in the social situation of women from ethnic minorities or of non-standard lifestyle was first discussed in the 1980s both in the US and in Europe. As most of our authors reference the US origins of the concept of intersectionality, a short summary may suffice here.

In the US, black feminist legal scholars criticised feminist and anti-racist politics as well as campaigns for anti-discrimination law for the denigrating effect that their essentialist position had on the situation of black women: whereas anti-racism politics were focused on the situation of black men, feminism tended to essentialise the experience of white middle class women as being universal for all women. The degree of ignorance about women of colour within the feminist movement of the 1970s and 1980s is deftly illustrated by a scene reported in a 1982 publication: when asked why an exhibition of works of women artists did not include any exhibit by a black woman, a white feminist replied: 'It's a women's exhibit!'.[77] At the same time, the anti-racist movement was criticised for negating any kind of subordination of black women by black men.[78] Against the background of these discourses, K. Crenshaw succeeded in establishing what is today known as the concept of intersectionality.[79] Starting from black women's employment experiences[80] and their exposure to sexual violence,[81] Crenshaw argued that these specific situations should be clearly identifiable and remediable by legal instruments, lest black women would only enjoy effective protection by law to the extent that their experiences coincided with those of either white women or black men.[82]

Today, the intersectionality debate among legal scholars usually takes Crenshaw's theory as a starting point, while extending the argument to situations of women other than 'black',[83] and to international law,[84] UK law[85] or Canadian law and practice.[86] Of course, the issue of localising oppression on different grounds is not necessarily a legal question. It has been addressed by a variety of disciplines, and most frequently by social and political theory.[87]

Several contributions to this book add a specifically European perspective to this wealth of literature. Morag Goodwin and Kristina Koldinska reflect on the situation of the Roma in Eastern Europe. Goodwin stresses the interrelation of ethnic discrimination and poverty, whereas Koldinska addresses specific experiences by Roma women in the second part of her article on the Czech and Slovak Republic. Kevät Nousiainen highlights, *inter alia*, the ethnic dimensions of sex work and the specific situation of women of native and migrated ethnic minorities in Finland. Ulrike Vieten questions whether a discourse developed predominantly in the US is capable of being transposed to a European context without modifications for different cultural contexts.

1.3.2 *Between additions and intersections in European Union law*

Focusing more narrowly on legal questions, most authors find it important to distinguish between different forms of how diverse discrimination grounds interrelate. A usual distinction is that between additive and intersectional discrimination. Additive discrimination[88] is mostly used for the interplay of separate, distinct criteria, while intersectional discrimination[89] involves an invisible interaction of grounds that specifically disadvantages persons at the intersection of grounds. Terminology is not uniform (yet) here. In this book, the notion multiple discrimination or multidimensional equality is used as an overarching notion. Some also refer to additive discrimination as multiple discrimination.[90] The term 'compound discrimination' is used for intersectional discrimination[91] as well as for additive discrimination (see Nielsen, Chapter 2, in this book).

Obviously, additive discrimination is less difficult to address than intersectional discrimination, as the former 'only' involves experiences made by 'all' ethnic minority persons and 'all' women, which coincide in one person. There is some doubt whether there is a purely additive experience, however.[92] Intersectional discrimination is experienced only by persons at the intersection of several grounds, and is as such more difficult to embrace by legal concepts. The more legally oriented debate from the US, the UK and Canada has stressed that it is difficult to have courts accept situations characterised by intersectional experience. As will be repeated throughout several articles here, US courts are considered particularly timid in addressing intersectional claims,[93] whereas Canadian courts are often considered as more innovative in this respect.[94] However, in both jurisdictions demands to further develop the (positive) law to embrace intersectionality are being made.[95]

For the European experience, these discussions are widely referenced.[96] Arguments are made concluding from the inability of the US courts to accept that a teleological reading of Title VII would lead to acknowledging true intersections instead of just 'additional categories'.[97] If one remains within the confines of this approach, the exhaustive list of grounds in the EU non-discrimination directives (and in Art 13 EC) would lead to the conclusion that intersectionality can never be addressed by EU law.[98] If that is so, the ECJ's decision in *Chacón Navas*,[99] which found that the list in Art 13 is indeed exhaustive, would constitute a definite barrier towards acknowledging intersectional claims under EU law. This would not do justice to the references to intersections in the legislation itself.[100]

Several authors in this book arrive at more optimistic conclusions for EU law, although the present state of affairs, with underdeveloped case law on the non-discrimination directives, is as yet far from satisfactory. Ruth Nielsen proposes a teleological reading of the directives to capture intersectional discrimination, warning against the limiting effect of different scopes of application. The latter reservation is shared by Sandra Fredman, who nevertheless sees good ground for developing positive policies embracing intersectional situations in EU law. Titia Loenen and Lynn Roseberry, in analysing the 'headscarf enigma', both conclude that the ECJ, using its bespoke method of dynamic interpretation, could very well accept discrimination on grounds of the headscarves as cases of intersectional discrimination. Hege Skjeie proposes to categorise these cases as gender discrimination, while developing some arguments on how to integrate different female identities into gender equality law, using the Norwegian example.

1.3.3 Interdisciplinary challenges

One of the challenges, that has not been addressed very much in past discussion on intersectionality at all, is the intersection between disciplines. Intersectionality theory is not inherently jurisprudential, although one of its best-known proponents is a lawyer. The literature in other disciplines is actually wider. The challenge of accommodating intersectional claims in EU law (and its implementations in national law) is thus also a challenge of accommodating other disciplinary approaches into legal reasoning.

These frictions are discussed by Ulrike Vieten, who concludes that not all social theory approaches to intersectionality are digestible to legal discourse. She stresses that anti-discrimination legislation remains reliant on identifiable grounds, and proposes a way to distinguish the grounds from the identities that partly inform them. Iyiola Solanke, writing as a legal scholar, also identifies the grounds as the main problem. Concerned that intersectional legal theory may lead to an unidentifiable mass of grounds, she proposes the new category of 'stigma' to better capture experiences with discrimination in reality legally. Morag Goodwin is equally concerned with grounds – or rather the lack of protection against poverty and social exclusion in law. She questions whether a litigation strategy based on non-discrimination (as pursued by the European Roma Rights Centre (ERRC)) is really the best way to enhance the situation of severely disadvantaged people such as the Roma. Peter Ratcliffe and Michael Orton demonstrate how implementation of a legal-administrative framework based on a single-ground approach can lead to multidimensional policies in practice. They warn, however, that positive action plans nurtured by contract compliance theory have a limited capacity to positively impact on intersectional disadvantage only.

1.3.4 Issues not addressed in this book: multiple remedies

There are some challenges by intersectional discrimination that have not been addressed in the present book. Above all, this is the quest for adequate remedies in cases of intersectional discrimination, which is only briefly mentioned in Ruth Nielsen's contribution. Views on the question whether additive or intersectional discrimination must lead to higher indemnity diverge. In the Canadian debate, it has been argued that the lack of higher remedies is actually a reason for persons not to bring forward intersectional cases.[101]

In different national jurisdictions, different solutions to the problem have been developed. From the US, Areheart, a protagonist of intersectionality, argues that recognising intersectional claims does not entail a right to greater redress[102] whereas Reynosso argues for the need to develop appropriate remedies in relation to such cases.[103] In Canada, Duclos argues that remedies should reflect the disadvantage suffered.[104] In Austria, Rebhahn and Windisch-Graetz defend the view that injuries sustained in multidimensional cases will usually be more severe than in single ground discrimination cases.[105] From Germany, the same view is upheld. Kocher proposes this view particularly in relation to additive discrimination. Intersectional cases must, in her opinion, be assessed on case-by-case basis to determine whether or not injuries are higher or more severe.[106] Däubler argues for higher remedies in both additive and intersectional discrimination cases, for multidimensional discrimination encroaches more in the private sphere than single ground discrimination.[107]

These issues certainly need to be considered more carefully, against the background of more experience, which is the reason why detailed exploration must wait for later publications. Initially, the latter view may seem more convincing, if one considers that intersectional cases tend to remain invisible.[108] The primary focus of law and policy should hence be to make visible those at the intersections. Also, when the social context of discrimination is examined, the structural background of those at the intersections could reveal a more vulnerable situation caused by an interplay of ground related aspects of discrimination, and prevailing economic, historic, social factors.[109] In that respect therefore, injuries suffered by the persons at the intersections could be higher. Justice L'Heureux-Dube has argued:

> No one should dispute that two identical projectiles, thrown at the same speed, may nonetheless leave a different scar on two different types of surfaces. Similarly, groups that are more socially vulnerable will experience the adverse effects of a legislative distinction more vividly than if the same distinction were directed at a group which is not similarly socially vulnerable.[110]

1.4 The structure of the book

As has become apparent from the foregoing discussion, discussing multidimensional European non-discrimination law with a focus on intersectionality does not lend itself to separated approaches in any one contribution. It was thus impossibly to restrict each author into one drawer, discussing only one section of one of these problems. All of our authors touch upon different aspects. Notwithstanding this, the book is organised in a way that allows readers to proceed from general issues towards more specific problems.

The contributions to the first part discuss how legal frameworks relate to multi-ground prohibitions of discrimination. Nielsen opens the part with a discussion of the EU legal framework. She exposes the reluctant approach of Community institutions to multiple and intersectional discrimination. Discussing several instances of substantive discrimination, she comes to the conclusion that EC sex discrimination law has always had the potential to cover intersectional cases, although this was not mirrored in ECJ case law.

She demands to develop this potential in the future, lest the Community institutions would fall short of adhering to the principle of gender main-streaming. Arnardóttir investigates the ECHR framework of protection against discrimination, which differs from that of the EC *inter alia* because it does not address specific discrimination grounds in specific ways. Arnardóttir demonstrates how the openness of Art 14 of the ECHR, often seen as a detriment, can become an asset when addressing cases of additive and inter-sectional cases. For instance, the ECtHR does not use a strict comparator test to define discrimination. While it has not embraced the concept of inter-sectionality (yet), Arnardóttir views its general approach as well suited to meet this challenge. From the tendency to purposeful and contextual reading she derives the potential of ECHR doctrine to better respond to challenges of multidimensionality than EC law. Fredman combines the issue of developing positive equality duties against a background of a substantive concept of equality law and the intersectionality issue. She comes to the (surprising) conclusion that positive duties may better embrace specific intersectionalities, as they open up the opportunity to employ a positive duty in favour of – for example – disabled ethnic minority people or Roma women. She concludes that positive duties may better target specific situations, finding positive duties and intersectionality strategies to be ideal partners in the quest for equality.

In the second part, intersectionality as a concept is discussed from different disciplinary perspectives, as detailed above.[111] Vieten analyses sociological conceptions of intersectionality from their origin in the US towards their specific transformations to the European context. She goes on to question in how far these concepts can be used in strategies based on law. She submits that empirically grounded views on intersectionality may be more helpful for use by discrimination lawyers than others. Her focus on class as an important category coincides with Goodwin's demand to not ignore social exclusion when applying discrimination law. Similarly, Solanke argues in favour of not diluting grounds towards the meaningless. She offers the category of stigma to distinguish equalities that matter from others. In this way, she is able to capture the specific discrimination against young black men, without taking recourse to intersectionality theory. Goodwin discusses how the deprived and excluded situation of the Roma in Central and Eastern Europe could be ameliorated. She contrasts a litigation strategy, based on race discrimination law, with a policy strategy embracing different aspects of the situation. Besides stressing the necessity of taking levels of poverty into account when applying discrimination law, her article also criticises a certain approach to this field for its polarising potential, which may not enhance social integra-tion. Goodwin's and Solankes' focus on race discrimination is shared by Ratcliffe and Orton, who insist that racial inequality should remain an important focus of equality measures. At the same time, they analyse the effects of policy instruments developed to combat racism in a setting which is sensitive to multiple discrimination. Their result is that proactive strategies such as contract compliance have effects beyond the single-ground approach under which they were introduced.

The third part then turns to comparative perspectives. Adding to the mass of literature comparing different approaches from different Anglo-American jurisdictions, the contributions explore Czech, Dutch, Finnish, French and Norwegian approaches to equality law, varying from a focus on gender (by Burri and Prechal) to a focus on a variety of grounds, including gender (by Laulom, Koldinska, Nousiainen and Skjeie). All contributions in the comparative part have an additional focus beyond a mere comparison. Nousiainen's contribution starts the part, as it needs to be read in context with Fredman's contribution. She presents a comparison of Finnish and EU equality law in the areas of gender equality on the one hand and ethnic equality on the other hand, discussing in how far these do justice to situations of intersectional discrimination. Besides contrasting Fredman's positive view of mainstreaming,[112] she details how a less rights-oriented approach to gender equality creates a particular bias for the situation of ethnic minority women. Their ethnic discrimination is focused upon under a 'boost of rights', whereas sex discrimination remains rather invisible. Nousiainen exemplifies the dangers of group-focused theories and an economic mainstreaming agenda using examples as different as sex work of women from different ethnicities and childcare needs of Sami and Roma women. Burri and Prechal consider whether a rich conception of equality informs EU gender equality law and in how far this conception is mirrored in French, Dutch and Czech law. They conclude that the results vary *inter alia* on grounds of different national traditions. Koldinska starts her contribution with a report on implementing EU non-discrimination directives in two former socialist countries, the Czech and Slovak Republics, not concealing that there is a discrepancy between the wording of statutes and immersion of equality law in social reality. It is with this in mind that she turns towards the situation of Roma women. She analyses their situation in employment and education as well as forced sterilisation, the latter being an example of intersectional discrimination in her view. Her conclusion illustrates how EU law fails to address the latter phenomenon adequately, *inter alia* due to the limited scope of application of gender equality law. Laulom offers a detailed analysis of French law's approach to intersectionality. She submits that the French approach to equality law may seem particularly receptive to intersectional cases, as different discrimination grounds are contained within the same framework. Relying on quantitative and qualitative research on equality cases before French courts and her own analysis of cases before the HALDE, the French independent body, Laulom concludes that a single ground approach prevails, except in cases brought by trade unions which seem to insist that their members are discriminated on grounds of their union membership as well as on any other ground relevant to the case. In her conclusion, she points to recent developments that may lead to more sensibility towards intersectional cases, including the Charter for diversity by some social partners and recent legislation to actively further gender pay equality. The final contribution in the comparative part comes from Norway. Skjeie focuses on the effect of merging different, ground specific agencies into overarching ones.[113] In the first section she introduces the institutional framework for supervising equality law in Norway, consisting of two levels: the Ombud and the newly created Equality Tribunal. She then evaluates whether this framework initiates a new approach to discrimination and equality, evaluating the frequency of intersectional cases. She concludes that Norway is typical in that equality agencies prefer a single ground view. As an illustration of the effects of such a view, she analyses how the Ombud institution deals with headscarf cases. Her conclusion is sobering: the Gender Equality Ombud considered the intersectionality issues inherent in the headscarf dilemma even more effectively than the new multi ground Ombud. Thus, her conclusion is cautious as to the viability of the new framework.

Skjeie's contribution leads over to the last part of the book, which is dedicated to the issue of the headscarf. Loenen starts this part with a contribution that is, at the same time, comparative: she evaluates the ECtHR case law on the headscarf, and attempts to predict future case law of the ECJ, using case law of the Dutch equal treatment commission as an example. This contribution also poses an interesting contrast to that by Arnardóttir, in that it arrives at a less positive evaluation of ECtHR case law. Roseberry, again working comparatively, gives an overview on the Danish case law on headscarf cases. She then contextualises the result with discourses on intersectionality, and also adds some analysis of EC legislation and ECtHR case law. She bases her analysis on a specific approach of racist and ethnic discrimination in Europe after September 11, within which discrimination against those perceived as Muslim may be qualified as racist discrimination. Ute Sacksofsky presents a very up-to-date accound of German headscarf cases: The Hesse Staatsgerichtshof, upon an application of Sacksofsky acting as prosecutor of the public interest, decided upon the new state legislation re religious gear in schools in late December 2007. Sacksofsky concurs with Roseberry in concluding that the reluctance to accept headscarves worn by Muslim women, by feminists and others, amounts to a new recourse of 'white womanism'.

All in all, this book can offer an overview of the current debates on European non-discrimination law, in which multiplying of grounds, new governance and the move from formal towards substantive equality have created a web of diverse approaches. Its different contributions and parts also demonstrate, that European non-discrimination law continues to be a highly interesting and demanding field of research and practice.

Notes

* Thanks to Victoria Chege who contributed a first draft towards section 1.3. The usual disclaimer applies.

1 See for an overview D Schiek, L Waddington and M Bell (eds) (2007) 'Introductory Chapter: A comparative perspective on non-discrimination law', in
   D Schiek, L Waddington and M Bell (eds) *Cases, Materials and Text on
   National, Supranational and International Non-Discrimination Law*, Oxford: Hart
   Publishing, pp 25–32 with further references.
2 See, D Schiek (2005) 'Broadening the scope and the norms of EU gender
   equality law: Towards a multidimensional conception of equality law',
   Maastricht Journal of European and Comparative Law, 12: 427–66.
3 See the title of E Ellis' encompassing treatise (2005) *EU Anti-Discrimination Law*,
   Oxford: Oxford University Press, and the published version of a PhD that originated at the European University Institute (M Bell (2002) *Anti-Discrimination Law
   and the European Union*, Oxford: Oxford University Press).
4 First, the Council needed to act unanimously; and second, the European
   Parliament was only to be consulted. That way, the bespoke pro-integrationist
   tendencies of the European Parliament were less influential. The European
   Parliament had supported a much wider version of Art 13, including direct effect
   (Parliamentary Resolution on Racism, Xenophobia and Anti-Semitism and on
   the Results of the European Year against Racism [1998] OJ C56/13, para 4).
   Third, the provision applied only 'without prejudice to the other provisions' of
   the EC Treaty and 'within the limits of the powers conferred by it upon the
   Community'. The last formula was unprecedented and elicited much legal
   argument on the potential for any meaningful EU non-discrimination law (see
   M Bell (1999) 'The New Article 13 EC Treaty: A sound basis for European
   anti-discrimination law?', *Maastricht Journal of European and Comparative
   Law*, 6: 5–28).
5 L Flynn (1999) 'The implications of Article 13 EC Treaty – After Amsterdam,
   will some forms of discrimination be more equal than others?', *Common Market
   Law Review*, 36: 1127–52.
6 C Barnard (2001) 'The changing scope of the fundamental principle of equality?' *McGill Law Journal* 46: 955–77, p 967 with fn 72.
7 It is no secret that the first legislative package, consisting of what is today Council
   Directive 2000/43/EC and 2000/78/EC plus an action plan providing for extensive
   funding opportunities (COM (1999) 564 final), was the result of intense lobbying
   of the Starting Line Group, founded as a co-operation of the UK Commission
   for Racial Equality, the Dutch National Bureau *tegen rasisme* and the 'Churches
   Commission for Migrants in Europe' (an EU non-governmental organisation
   domiciled in Brussels), which proposed a comprehensive anti-racism directive
   as early as 1993 (I Chopin (1999) 'The Starting Line Group: A harmonised
   approach to fight racism and to promote equal treatment', *European Journal of
   Migration and Law*: 111–29). Its main intellectual roots and campaigners being
   from the UK and the Netherlands, the Starting Line proposal relied on legal
   models from these states (A Geddes and V Guiraudon (2004) 'Britain, France
   and EU anti-discrimination policy; The emergence of an EU policy paradigm',
   West European Politics, 17: 334–53, at pp 340–4).
8 Council Directive 2000/43/EC implementing the principle of equal treatment
   between persons irrespective of racial or ethnic origin [2000] OJ L180/22.
9 Barnard defines the 'non-employment fields' covered by the Race Directive as
   being new social policy fields. See C Barnard (2001) 'The changing scope of the
   fundamental principle of equality?' *McGill Law Journal* 46: 955–77, at p 968.
10 D Chalmers (2001) 'The mistakes of the good European?', in S Fredman (ed)
   Discrimination and Human Rights: the Case of Racism, Oxford: Oxford University Press, pp 193–249.
11 Council Directive 2000/78/EC establishing a general framework for equal treatment in employment and occupation [2000] OJ L303/16.

12 Beyond that, the ECJ has accepted equal treatment as a general principle of Community law. This principle resembles the principle of equal treatment before the law and must be distinguished from equal treatment of persons, in that it applies to situations and non-human issues. In the Community law context, equal treatment of goods from different origins, or services provided from different countries of origin, are relevant examples. On the conceptual relevance of equal treatment of persons see D Schiek (2002) 'A new framework on equal treatment of persons in EC law? Directives 2000/43/EC, 2000/78/EC and 2002/73/EC changing Directive 76/207/EEC in context', *European Law Journal*, 8: 290–314. In contrast to this, R Nielsen (Chapter 2, in this book) analyses internal market law as part of non-discrimination law.

13 See Art 3(2) of Council Directive 2000/43/EC and Council Directive 2000/78/EC.

14 Directive 2002/73/EC amending Council Directive 76/207/EEC on the implementation of the principle of equal treatment for men and women as regards access to employment, vocational training and promotion, and working conditions [2002] OJ L269/15. Directive 2002/73/EC has now been 'recast' by Directive 2006/54/EC on the implementation of the principle of equal opportunities and equal treatment of men and women in matters of employment and occupation (recast) [2006] OJ L204/23. This Directive is to replace Council Directive 76/207/EEC by 15 August 2009.

15 For a critical analysis see D Schiek (2005) 'Broadening the scope and the norms of EU gender equality law: Towards a multidimensional conception of equality law', *Maastricht Journal of European and Comparative Law*, 12: 427–66, at pp 429–30.

16 See, on the development of gender policy in the EU, C Hoskyns (1996) *Integrating Gender: Women, Law and Politics in the European Union*, London: Verso. On comparative approaches towards implementing EU gender equality law see S Burri and S Prechal, Chapter 10, in this book.

17 See, for instance, S Fredman (2002) *Discrimination Law*, Oxford: Oxford University Press, pp 1–26; for a summary of different conceptions of equality and non-discrimination in law see D Schiek, L Waddington and M Bell (eds) (2007) 'Introductory Chapter: A comparative perspective on non-discrimination law', in D Schiek, L Waddington and M Bell (eds) *Cases, Materials and Text on National, Supranational and International Non-Discrimination Law*, Oxford: Hart Publishing, pp 25–32.

18 See for a summary A McColgan (2005) *Discrimination Law. Text, Cases and Materials*, Oxford, Oregon, OR: Hart Publishing, pp 24–32.

19 For a short summary see D Schiek, L Waddington and M Bell (eds) (2007b) 'Introductory Chapter: A comparative perspective on non-discrimination law', in D Schiek, L Waddington and M Bell (eds) *Cases, Materials and Text on National, Supranational and International Non-Discrimination Law*, Oxford: Hart Publishing, pp 31–2.

20 See C Tobler (2005) *Remedies and Sanctions in EC Non-Discrimination Law*, European Commission: Brussels, available at http://p30029.typo3server.info/fileadmin/pdfs/Reports/Remedies_and_Sanctions/remedies_en1.pdf (accessed 3 January 2008).

21 On ECJ case law on maternity and the less than contingent concept of family live conveyed therein, see T Hervey and J Shaw (1998) 'Women, work and care: Women's dual role and double burden in EC sex equality law', *Journal of European Social Policy*, 8: 43–63, and C McGlynn (2006) *Families and the European Union: Law, Politics, and Pluralism*, Cambridge: Cambridge University Press, Ch 4.

22 Cases C-450/93 *Eckard Kalanke v Freie und Hansestadt Bremen* [1995] ECR I-3051; C-409/95 *Helmut Marschall v Land Nordrhein-Westphalen* [1997] ECR

I-6363; C-158/97 *Georg Badeck et al* [2000] ECR I-1875; C-407/98 *Katarina Abrahamsson and Leif Anderson v Elisabet Fogelqvist* [2000] I-5539; C-476/99 *Lommers v Ministerie Landbouw* [2002] I-2891.

23 Council Directive 76/207/EEC on the implementation of the principle of equal treatment for men and women as regards access to employment, vocational training and promotion, and working conditions [1976] OJ L39/40.

24 On these see text accompanying nn 14 and 15 above.

25 HMSO (1999) *The Stephen Lawrence Enquiry*, Cm 4262-1, London: Her Majesty's Stationery Office.

26 B Hepple, M Coussey and T Choudhoury (2000) *Equality: A New Framework: Report of the Independent Review of the Enforcement of UK Anti-Discrimination Legislation*, Oxford: Hart Publishing. On positive obligations see also Fredman, Chapter 4, in this book. Similarly, some characterise this new mode as relying on a group justice model as opposed to an individual justice model (C McCrudden (2003) 'The new concept of equality,' *ERA Forum*, 4: 9–23).

27 B Hepple (2004) 'Race and law in Fortress Europe', *Modern Law Review*, 67: 1–15, at p 3.

28 For a wider approach in relation to racial and ethnic discrimination, but not race see D Caruso (2003) *Limits of the Classical Methods: Positive Action in the European Union after the New Equality Directives*, Boston University, School of Law, working paper no 03–21, available at www.bu.edu/law/faculty/scholarship/workingpapers/abstracts/2003/pdf_files/CarusoD090903.pdf (accessed 3 January 2008).

29 See Recital 3 and 14 of Council Directive 2000/78/EC and Council Directive 2000/43/EC respectively.

30 H Bielfeldt (2007) *Tackling Multiple Discrimination. Practices, Policies and Law*, Brussels: European Commission, September, available at http://ec.europa.eu/employment_social/publications/2007/ke8207458_en.pdf (accessed 3 January 2008), p 36.

31 See, for example, S Fredman (1997) *Women and the Law*, Oxford: Clarendon Press, pp 383–4, and her contribution to this book (Chapter 4, text preceding and following n 26 therein).

32 See D Schiek (2005) 'Broadening the scope and the norms of EU gender equality law: Towards a multidimensional conception of equality law', *Maastricht Journal of European and Comparative Law*, 12: 427–66, at pp 463–4.

33 The Recitals of Council Directives 2000/43/EC and 2000/78/EC refer to the fact that many people, and in particular women, will find themselves under impact of discrimination against them on a variety of grounds (see fn. 29).

34 For the latter perspective see D Schiek (2005) 'Broadening the scope and the norms of EU gender equality law: Towards a multidimensional conception of equality law', *Maastricht Journal of European and Comparative Law*, 12: 427–66, at pp 462–6.

35 For a comprehensive analysis of the approach of EU law in this respect see Ruth Nielsen, Chapter 2, in this book.

36 This was the implementation date for Council Directive 2004/113/EC, although Member States have the right to allow insurers to continue to discriminate on grounds of sex until 2008. Also, the implementation of the 'Recast Directive' is only due for August 2009.

37 On challenges of comparative discrimination law see D Schiek, L Waddington and M Bell (eds) (2007) 'Introductory Chapter: A comparative perspective on non-discrimination law', in D Schiek, L Waddington and M Bell (eds) *Cases, Materials and Text on National, Supranational and International Non-Discrimination Law*, Oxford: Hart Publishing, pp 13–24.

38 See below, text accompanying nn 42–48.

39 The European Commission seems to be convinced of the contrary. It has commissioned a study of over eight months aiming to devise policy recommendations for top-down regulations, based on interviews with as little as five individuals, and round table discussions with public servants from different Member States (H Bielefelt (2007) *Tackling Multiple Discrimination. Practices, Policies and Law*, Brussels: European Commission, September, available at http://ec.europa.eu/employment_social/publications/2007/ke8207458_en.pdf (accessed 3 January 2008)). The study was then presented to the public in a conference in early December 2007 in Copenhagen, recommending 'a uniform definition of multiple discrimination; in a new EU Directive, accompanied by a few funded research projects as the way forward.

40 See D Schiek (2007) 'Implementing non-discrimination Directives – Typologies for legal transplanting', *International Colloquia Europees Verzekeringsrecht – Colloques Internationaux de droit européen de assurance*, 5: 47–83, with further references. Despite Dutch approaches being part of the mainstream in EU non-discrimination law, it is equally true that they are being less reflected upon than Anglo-American approaches, as two of our Dutch authors stress (Burri and Prechal, in the introduction to Chapter 10, in this book).

41 Treaty of Lisbon amending the Treaty on European Union and the Treaty establishing the European Community, signed at Lisbon, 13 December 2007, [2007] OJ C306, 17 December 2007.

42 See C Barnard (2007) 'Social policy revised in the light of the constitutional debate', in C Barnard (ed) *The Fundamentals of the EU Revisited. Assessing the Impact of the Constitutional Debate*, Oxford: Oxford University Press, pp 109–51, at pp 110–17.

43 See D Schiek (2008) 'The European social model and the Services Directive', in U Neergaard, R Nielsen and L Roseberry (eds) *The Services Directive – Consequences for the Welfare State and the European Social Model*, Copenhagen: D\FV, para 3.2 with fnn 78 and 83.

44 This was clearly seen in the 1970s when M Shanks, then responsible for EU social policy pointed to the necessity of Europe being perceived as more than an opportunity for capitalists to exploit the Common Market in order for it to be accepted by its people (M Shanks (1977) 'The social policy of the European Communities', *Common Market Law Review*, 14: 375–83, at p 377). Recently, the French and Dutch negative referendum on the Constitutional Treaty was attributed *inter alia* to 'fears generated by . . . in particular it perceived excessive market liberalism' (C Barnard (2007) 'Introduction', in C Barnard (ed) *The Fundamentals of the EU Revisited. Assessing the Impact of the Constitutional Debate*, Oxford: Oxford University Press, p 1).

45 W Streeck (1995) 'From market making to state building? Reflections on the political economy of European social policy', in S Leibfried and P Pierson (eds) *European Social Policy: Between Fragmentation and Integration*, Washington DC: Brookings Institution, pp 389–431, at p 400.

46 This actually is upheld as a positive vision by some (see P Magnette (2007) 'How can one be European? Reflections on the pillars of European civic identity', *European Law Journal*, 13: 664–79, at p 672: 'non-discrimination did not serve a utilitarian purpose. To equalise the salaries and social rights of workers meant depriving migrant workers from their main economic advantage, their lower costs').

47 P Davies (1997) 'Posted workers: Single market or protection of national labour law systems?' *Common Market Law Review*, 24: 571–602, at p 588; C Barnard (2006) *EC Employment Law*, 3rd edn, Oxford: Oxford University Press, p 171.

48 S Besson and A Utzinger (2007) 'Introduction: Future challenges of European

citizenship – facing a wide-open pandora's box', *European Law Journal*, 13: 573–90, at p 585, fn 54.

49 On the different steps towards economic integration see W Molle (2006) *The Economics of European Integration: Theory, Practice & Policy*, 5th edn, Adlershot: Dartmouth, pp 10–11.

50 On a detailed account of the development of European citizenship from concerns to integrate social issues of migrant workers see W Maas (2008) 'The Evolution of EU Citizenship', in K McNamara and S Meunier (eds) *Making History European Integration and Institutional Change at Fifty: The State of The European Union*, vol 8, Oxford: Oxford University Press, forthcoming.

51 See, for instance, N Reich (2001) 'Union citizenship – metaphor or source of rights?', *European Law Journal*, 7: 4–23.

52 Cf D Kostakopoulou (2007) 'European Union citizenship: Writing the future', *European Law Journal*, 13: 623–46, at pp 634–41; F Jacobs (2007) 'Citizenship of the European Union – A legal analysis', *European Law Journal*, 13: 591–610.

53 That image is used by S Besson and A (2007) 'Introduction: Future challenges of European citizenship – facing a wide-open pandora's box', *European Law Journal*, 13: 573–90

54 For a summary of ECJ case law on citizenship see annex to F Jacobs (2007) 'Citizenship of the European Union – A legal analysis', *European Law Journal*, 13: 591–610 (compiled by A Thies).

55 M Bell (2000) 'Equality and diversity: Anti-Discrimination law after Amsterdam', in J Shaw (ed) *Social Law and Policy in an Evolving European Union*, Oxford: Hart Publishing, pp 157–69 (this is repeated in M Bell (2002) *Anti-Discrimination Law and the European Union*, Oxford: Oxford University Press, p 202)

56 P Magnette (2007) 'How can one be European? Reflections on the pillars of European civic identity', *European Law Journal*, 13: 664–79.

57 M Dougan (2004) *National Remedies Before the Court of Justice: Issues of Harmonisation and Differentiation*, Oxford: Hart Publishing, p 389.

58 F Jacobs (2007) 'Citizenship of the European Union – A legal analysis', *European Law Journal*, 13: 591–610, at p 592.

59 Again, this argument is made convincingly by D Kostakopoulou (2007) 'European Union citizenship: Writing the future', *European Law Journal*, 13: 623–46.

60 C Brown (2002) 'The Race Directive: Towards equality for all people of Europe?', *Year Book of EU Law*, 21: 195–217.

61 See A Williams (2007) 'Respecting fundamental rights in the New Union: A review', in C Barnard (ed) *The Fundamentals of the EU Revisited. Assessing the Impact of the Constitutional Debate*, Oxford: Oxford University Press, pp 71–107.

62 See on the interrelation of effects of Community law, in particular in the field of fundamental freedoms, and Constitutionalisation via accepting human rights S Prechal (2007) 'Direct effect, indirect effect. Supremacy and the evolving constitution of the European Union', in C Barnard (ed) *The Fundamentals of the EU Revisited. Assessing the Impact of the Constitutional Debate*, Oxford: Oxford University Press, pp 35–69, at pp 47–51.

63 See T Hervey (2005) 'Thirty years of EU sex equality law: Looking backwards, looking forward', *Maastricht Journal of Comparative and European Law*, 12: 307–26, at pp 319–21.

64 See R Wintemunte (2002) 'Religion vs. sexual orientation. A clash of human rights?', *Journal of Law & Equality*, 2: 125–54, discussing whether freedom of religion may justify discrimination against lesbian, bisexual, gay and transgender people.

65 Most notably, the recent Bosphoros decision of the ECtHR (ECHR App No

45036/98, *Bosphoros v Ireland* (2006) 42 EHHR 1) paved the way for a structured relationship of mutual respect
66 See M Bell (2002) *Anti-Discrimination Law and the European Union*, Oxford: Oxford University Press, p 148; S Prechal (2004) 'Equality of treatment, non-discrimination and social policy: Achievements in three themes', *Common Market Law Review*, 41: 533–51, at p 537.
67 Ibid, Bell, p 140.
68 See K Monaghan (2007) *Equality Law*, Oxford: Oxford University Press, p 29.
69 See on some reasons D Schiek (2007) 'Implementing Non-Discrimination Directives – Typologies for legal transplanting', *International Colloquia Europees Verzekeringsrecht – Colloques Internationaux de droit européen de assurance*, 5: 47–83.
70 See on a number of uses J Shaw (2005) 'Mainstreaming equality and diversity in European Union law and policy', *Current Legal Problems*, 58: 255–312, under 2 b.
71 The Treaty on the Functioning of the European Union shall contain the following Art 5a: 'In defining and implementing its policies and activities, the Union shall aim to combat discrimination based on sex, racial or ethnic origin, religion or belief, disability, age or sexual orientation'.
72 Council of Europe (1998) *Gender Mainstreaming. Conceptual Framework, Methodology and Presentation of Good Practices*, Strasbourg, available at www.coe.int/t/e/human_rights/equality/02._gender_mainstreaming/099_EG(1999)03.asp (accessed 13 September 2007), 15.
73 J Shaw (2005) 'Mainstreaming equality and diversity in European Union law and policy', *Current Legal Problems*, 58: 255–312, under 4.
74 G De Búrca and J Scott, 'Introduction', in G De Búrca and J Scott (eds) (2006) *Law and New Governance in the EU and the US*, Oxford, Portland, OR: Hart Publishing, p 2.
75 See V Hatzopoulos (2007) 'Why the open method of coordination is bad for you: A letter to the EU', *European Law Journal*, 13: 309–42.
76 G De Búrca (2006) 'EU race discrimination law: A hybrid model?', in G De Búrca and J Scott (eds) *Law and New Governance in the EU*, Oxford, Portland, OR: Hart Publishing, pp 97–120.
77 A Walker (1982) 'One child of one's own: A meaningful digression within the work(s) – an excerpt', in GT Hull, PB Scott and B Smith (eds) *All Women are White, All Blacks are Men, but Some of Us are Brave*, New York: Feminist Press, pp 37–47, at p 40.
78 See for example M Wallace, 'A black feminist's search for sisterhood', in Hull et al (eds), ibid, pp 5–12.
79 K Crenshaw (1989) 'Demarginalizing the intersection of race and sex: A black feminist critique of antidiscrimination doctrine, feminist theory and antiracial politics', *The University of Chicago Legal Forum*: 139–67 (cited from the reprint in DK Weisberg (ed) (1993) *Feminist Legal Theory: Foundations*, Philadelphia, PA: Temple, pp 383–95); K Crenshaw (1991) 'Mapping the margins: Intersectionality, identity politics, and violence against women of color', *Stanford Law Review*, 43: 1241–99.
80 Ibid, Crenshaw, 'Demarginalizing the intersection'.
81 K Crenshaw (1991) 'Mapping the margins: Intersectionality, identity politics, and violence against women of color', *Stanford Law Review*, 43: 1241–99
82 See K Crenshaw (2000) *Background Paper for the Expert Meeting on the Gender-Related Aspects of Race Discrimination*, Zagreb, Croatia, available at www.wicej.addr.com/wcar_docs/crenshaw.html (accessed 4 January 2008); K Crenshaw (1989) 'Demarginalizing the intersection of race and sex: A black feminist critique of antidiscrimination doctrine, feminist theory and antiracial politics', *The University of Chicago Legal Forum*: 139–67

83 V Wei (1996) 'Asian women and employment discrimination: Using intersectionality theory to address Title VII claims based on combining factors of race, gender and national origin', *Boston College Law Review*, 37: 771–845 and J Reynosso (2004) 'Perspectives on the intersections of race, ethnicity, gender, and other grounds: Latinas at the margins', *Harvard Latino Law Review*, 7: 63–73.

84 E.g. T Makkonen (2002) *Multiple, Compound and Intersectional Discrimination: Bringing the Experience of the Most Marginalized to the Fore*, Institute For Human Rights Åbo Akademi University, available at http://web.abo.fi/instut/imr/norfa/timo.pdf (accessed 4 January 2008).

85 E.g. S Hannett (2003) 'Equality at the intersections: The legislative and judicial failure to tackle multiple discrimination', *Oxford Journal of Legal Studies*, 23: 65–86; D Ashiagbor (1999) 'The intersections between gender and "race" in the labour market: Lessons for anti-discrimination law', in A Morris and T O'Donell (eds) *Feminist Perspectives on Employment Law*, London: Cavendish, pp 139–60; E Rooney (2006) 'Women's equality in Northern Ireland's transition: Intersectionality in theory and place', *Feminist Legal Studies*, 14: 353–75.

86 E.g. N Duclos (1993) 'Disappearing women: Racial minority women in human rights cases', *Canadian Journal of Women and the Law*, 6: 25–51; D Pothier (2001) 'Connecting grounds of discrimination to real peoples experience', *Canadian Journal of Women and the Law*, 13: 37–73.

87 E.g. N Yuval-Davis (2006) 'Intersectionality and feminist politics', *European Journal of Women's Studies*, 13: 193–209; M Verloo (2006) 'Multiple inequalities, intersectionality and the European Union', *European Journal of Women's Studies*, 13: 211–28; A Brah and A Phoenix (2004) 'Ain't I a woman? Revisiting intersectionality', *Journal of International Women's Studies*, 5: 75–86; A Ludvig (2006) 'Differences between Women? Intersecting voices in a female narrative', *European Journal of Women's Studies*, 13: 245–57; L McCall (2005) 'The complexity of intersectionality', *Journal of Women in Culture and Society*, 35: 1771–800.

88 See S Hannett (2003) 'Equality at the intersections: The legislative and judicial failure to tackle multiple discrimination', *Oxford Journal of Legal Studies*, 23: 65–86, fnn 11 and 12; L Roseberry (1999) *The Limits of Employment Discrimination Law in the United States and the European Community*, Copenhagen: DJ\F Publishing, pp 331–8.

89 K Crenshaw (2000) *Background Paper for the Expert Meeting on the Gender-Related Aspects of Race Discrimination*, Zagreb, Croatia, available at www.wicej.addr.com/wcar_docs/crenshaw.html (accessed 4 January 2008), and N Duclos (1993) 'Disappearing women: Racial minority women in human rights cases', *Canadian Journal of Women and the Law*, 6: 25–51; Hannett, ibid; Roseberry, ibid, p 331; D Ashiagbor (1999) 'The intersections between gender and "race" in the labour market: Lessons for anti-discrimination law', in A Morris and T O'Donell (eds) *Feminist Perspectives on Employment Law*, London: Cavendish, pp 139–60; D Schiek (2005) 'Broadening the scope and the norms of EU gender equality law: Towards a Multidimensional Conception of Equality Law', *Maastricht Journal of European and Comparative Law*, 12: 427–66, at pp 454–62.

90 T Makkonen (2002) *Multiple, Compound and Intersectional Discrimination: Bringing the Experience of the Most Marginalized to the Fore*, Institute For Human Rights Åbo Akademi University, available at http://web.abo.fi/instut/imr/norfa/timo.pdf (accessed 4 January 2008), pp 9–14.

91 EW Shoben, (1980) 'Compound discrimination: The interaction of race and sex in employment discrimination', *New York University Law Review*, 55: 793–835; N Duclos (1993) 'Disappearing women: Racial minority women in

human rights cases', *Canadian Journal of Women and the Law*, 6: 25–51; Makkonen, ibid, pp 9–14.

92 K Crenshaw (1989) 'Demarginalizing the intersection of race and sex: A black feminist critique of antidiscrimination doctrine, feminist theory and antiracial politics', *The University of Chicago Legal Forum*: 139–67

93 Cases cited as evidence for this reluctance include *DeGraffenreid v General Motors Assembly Div*, 413 F Supp 142 (US Federal Court of Appeal); *Lee v Walters* 1988 US Dist LEXIS 11336, at *1 (ED Pa 1988) and *Chaddah v Harris Bank Glencoe – Northbrook, NA*, 1994 US Dist LEXIS 2693 (NDIII 1994), aff'd 42 F 3d 1391 (7 Cir 1994).

94 Cases cited as evidence for this include *Law v Canada* (Minister of Employment and Immigration), [1999] 1 SCR 497, *Corbière v Canada* (Minister of Indian and Northern Affairs) [1999] SCR 203.

95 B Areheart (2006) 'Intersectionality revisited. Why Congress should amend Title VII to recognise intersectional claims', Express*O* Print series, paper 1289; D Gilbert (2003) 'Time to regroup. Rethinking section 15 of the Charter', *McGill Law Journal*, 48: 627–49.

96 See for references and a step towards a European approach V Chege (2007) 'The interaction of race and gender in eu equality law', in B Graue, A Mester, G Siehlman and M Westhaus (eds) *International-Europäisch-Regional*, Oldenburg: BIS-Verlag, pp 267–88.

97 It seems that the approach of the Canadian courts to acknowledge some cases of intersectional discrimination rests on the fact that the Constitutional equality clause is open ended (see A Bayefsky (1990) 'A case comment on the first three equality rights cases under the Canadian Charter of Rights and Freedoms: Andrews Workers' compensation reference, Turpin', *Supreme Court Law Review*, 1: 503–34, pp 518–21. L'Heureux-Dubé J in *Egan v Canada* [1995] 2 SCR 513 at 551–2, who attempts to develop a grounds-unspecific approach).

98 S Fredman (2005) 'Double trouble: Multiple discrimination and EU Law', *European Anti-Discrimination Law Review*, 2: 13–21.

99 Case C-13/05 *Chacón Navas v Eurest Colectividades SA* [2006] ECR I-6467.

100 Recitals 3 and 14 of Council Directives 2000/78/EC and 2000/43/EC respectively.

101 N Duclos (1993) 'Disappearing women: Racial minority women in human rights cases', *Canadian Journal of Women and the Law*, 6: 25–51; The Ontario Human Rights Commission has launched a systemic study on remedies in intersectional cases, which concluded that these have not necessarily lead to higher awards. Ontario Human Rights Commission (2005) *An Intersectional Approach to Discrimination: Addressing Multiple Grounds in Human Rights Claims, Discussion paper*, Queens Printer for Ontario, available at http://ohrc.on.ca/english/consultations/intersectionality-discussion-paper_1.shtml (accessed 4 January 2008).

102 B Areheart (2006) 'Intersectionality revisited. Why Congress should amend Title VII to recognise intersectional claims', Express*O* Print series, paper 1289, at p 52.

103 J Reynosso (2004) 'Perspectives on the intersections of race, ethnicity, gender, and other grounds: Latinas at the margins', *Harvard Latino Law Review*, 7: 63–73, at p 72.

104 See for example Duclos' assessment of *Olarte v DeFilippis and Commodore Business Machines Ltd* ((1983) 4 CHRR D/1705) in N Duclos (1993) 'Disappearing women: Racial minority women in human rights cases', *Canadian Journal of Women and the Law*, 6: 25–51, at p 39 f.

105 R Rebhahn, in R Rebhahn (ed) (2005) *Gleichbehandlungsgesetz. Kommentar*, Wien: Springer, § 3 no 52; M Windisch-Graetz (2005) 'Probleme der mehrfachen Diskriminierung in der Arbeitswelt', *Das Recht der Arbeit (Wien)*: 238–43.

106 E Kocher, in D Schiek (ed) (2007) *Allgemeines Gleichbehandlungsgesetz (AGG): ein Kommentar aus europäischer Perspektive*, Munich: Sellier, § 15, no 35; see also D Schiek, in Schiek (ed) ibid, § 4, no 9, 159.

107 W Däubler, in W Däubler and M Bertzbach (eds) (2006) *Allgemeines Gleichbehandlungsgesetz, Handkommentar*, Baden-Baden: Nomos, § 4, no 14.

108 See on this aspect Fredman, Chapter 4, in this book, p 84.

109 See for example K Crenshaw (1989) 'Demarginalizing the intersection of race and sex: A black feminist critique of antidiscrimination doctrine, feminist theory and antiracial politics', *The University of Chicago Legal Forum*: 139–67.

110 *Egan v Canada* [1995] 2 SCR 513, at 551–2.

111 See p 13, text between nn 100 and 101.

112 See p 11, text following n 76.

113 The discussion finds a parallel in the UK with the recent establishment of the CEHR (see C O'Cinneide (2007) 'The Commission for Equality and Human Rights: A new institution for new and uncertain times', *Industrial Law Journal*, 36: 141–62.

Part I

Assessing legal responses to multidimensionality

2 Is European Union equality law capable of addressing multiple and intersectional discrimination yet?

Precautions against neglecting intersectional cases

Ruth Nielsen

2.1 Issues

This chapter explores the development from single ground to multi-ground EU legal frameworks of gender equality by asking where and how concepts related to multiple discrimination are used in legal texts at EU level and in what contexts multiple discrimination is addressed. Multiple discrimination in EU equality law has mainly been addressed explicitly with a view to gender-mainstreaming the fight against other kinds of discrimination (discrimination on grounds of ethnic origin, age, etc). Finally, it is discussed to what extent the existing provisions on discrimination and positive action are applicable in multiple and intersectional discrimination cases and to what extent EU law offers effective means of redress in such cases.

2.2 Conceptualisation of multiple discrimination

In legal literature[1] the term multiple discrimination usually covers both compounded discrimination, that is, situations where different grounds for discrimination are added to each other[2] and intersectional cases where the combination of discrimination on various grounds produces something distinct from any one form of discrimination.

2.2.1 Added discrimination (double, triple, etc)

Different forms of discrimination, for example on grounds of nationality, ethnic origin and gender interact and may reinforce each other. It is, however, an open question how far the fight against various discriminations can reinforce each other – some aspects are common but there are also important differences. Protection of one equality right, for example religious freedom, may even be invoked as justification for restrictions of equality in regard to other criteria, for example gender, or vice versa, see for example *Leyla Sahin v Turkey*[3] in which the European Court of Human Rights (ECtHR) in a case about the Islamic headscarf in Turkey balanced the rights of women against the Islamic religion.

2.2.2 Intersectional discrimination

Recognition of multiple discrimination in the US has been pioneered by African American women who have demonstrated how sex discrimination law focuses on white women and race discrimination law on black men so that discrimination of black women is not properly covered.[4] An employer who allegedly discriminates against black women may justify his employment practices as not discriminatory on ethnic or gender grounds by showing that he employs many (male) blacks and that many (white) women make success-ful careers in the undertaking. The concept of 'intersectionality' has been developed to counteract this problem. Intersectionality may be defined as:[5]

> intersectional oppression [that] arises out of the combination of various oppressions which, together, produce something unique and distinct from any one form of discrimination standing alone.

Although an intersectional analysis is relevant to any combination of grounds, it has in particular been used in race or race-related cases.

2.2.3 Multidimensional equality/discrimination

In legal literature,[6] the term 'multidimensional equality' can encompass dif-ferent conceptions of equality (for example, formal and substantive equality) and a multitude of discrimination grounds.

2.2.4 European Union law

At the conceptual level EU law has not yet produced (binding) definitions of multiple and intersectional discrimination. The term 'multiple discrimin-ation' is today (2007) used in scattered provisions in EU legislation and EU soft law (see below), but it is – in contrast to other equality concepts such as direct and indirect discrimination, harassment and sexual harassment – not defined in binding legal texts at the EU level. In the case law of the European Court of Justice (ECJ) the term 'multiple discrimination' is not used, but a number of rulings in discrimination cases address the combination of age and gender. The term 'intersectionality' is not explicitly used in EU legislation, soft law or case law.

In the decision[7] establishing the 'European Year of Equal Opportunities for All (2007) – towards a just society', it is stated in the Preamble[8] that the European Year 'will also seek to address issues of *multiple discrimination, that is discrimination on two or more of the grounds listed in Art 13 EC*' (my emphasis). Council and Parliament are here close to defining multiple discrimination as added discrimination within the range of discrimination grounds listed in Art 13 EC, that is, discrimination based on: (1) sex; (2) racial or ethnic origin; (3) religion or belief; (4) disability; (5) age; or (6) sexual orientation. The European Year of Equal Opportunities for All (2007) will also seek to promote a balanced treatment of those six grounds of discrimination.

It is worth noting that nationality – which is one of the most important prohibited discrimination grounds in EU law generally – is not included in the above concept of multiple discrimination. It does also not address the other prohibited discrimination grounds listed in Art 21 of the Charter of Fundamental Rights, that is, social origin, genetic features, language, political or any other opinion, membership of a national minority, property or birth.

2.3 Where in European Union law are there provisions on (multiple) discrimination?

Provisions prohibiting discrimination on various grounds are spread around in EU law. There are both binding and soft law provisions.

2.3.1 Binding European Union law

2.3.1.1 Treaty provisions

Art 12 EC provides that within the scope of application of the EC Treaty any discrimination on grounds of nationality is prohibited. The general provisions of the EC Treaty on free movement of goods (Art 28 EC), persons (Art 39 EC on workers and Art 43 EC on freedom of establishment), services (Art 49 EC) and capital (Art 56 EC) also prohibit discrimination on grounds of nationality. According to Art 141 EC each Member State shall ensure that the principle of equal pay for male and female workers for equal work or work of equal value is applied.

Art 13 EC provides a legal base for secondary legislation to combat discrimination based on sex, racial or ethnic origin, religion or belief, disability, age or sexual orientation. In matters of employment and occupation Art 141(3) EC provides a legal base for adopting measures to ensure the application of the principle of equal opportunities and equal treatment of men and women.

According to Art 6 EU, the EU is founded on the principles of liberty, democracy, respect for human rights and fundamental freedoms and the rule of law, principles which are common to the Member States. It respects fundamental rights as guaranteed by the European Convention on Human Rights (ECHR) and as they result from the constitutional traditions common to the Member States as general principles of Community law.

2.3.1.2 The Article 13 Directives

Three directives have been adopted on the basis of Art 13 EC: the Directive on Ethnic Equality,[9] the Employment Framework Directive[10] and the Directive on Gender Equality in Access to and Supply of Goods and Services.[11]

In the Ethnic Equality Directive it is stated in the Preamble (emphasis added):

> 14. In implementing the principle of equal treatment irrespective of racial or ethnic origin, the Community should, in accordance with Article 3(2) of the EC Treaty, aim to eliminate inequalities, and to promote equality between men and women, especially *since women are often the victims of multiple discrimination.*

A similar provision is found in the Employment Framework Directive.[12] Here the EU thus requires gender mainstreaming of the fight against ethnic, age, religious, disability and sexual orientation discrimination.

The Directive on Gender Equality in Access to and Supply of Goods and Services does not mention multiple discrimination. In the Preamble to this directive it is stated:

> 3. While prohibiting discrimination, it is important to respect other fundamental rights and freedoms, including the protection of private and family life and transactions carried out in that context and the freedom of religion.

2.3.1.3 The gender equality directives in employment and occupation

There are a number of Directives on Gender Equality in employment and occupation.[13] With effect from 15 August 2009 the Directives on Equal Pay, Equal Treatment, Occupational Social Security and Burden of Proof will be repealed and replaced by the Recast Directive on Gender Equality.[14]

The Gender Equality Directives are single-ground directives. They do not mention multiple discrimination. In the 2002 amendment to the Equal Treatment Directive there is, however, a provision stating:[15]

> This Directive respects the fundamental rights and observes the principles recognised in particular by the Charter of Fundamental Rights of the European Union.

This reference to the Charter of Fundamental Rights is not repeated in the Recast Directive on Gender Equality.

2.3.2 Soft law

2.3.2.1 Article 21 of the Charter of Fundamental Rights

Art 21 of the Charter of Fundamental Rights provides under the heading Non-discrimination:

> 1. Any discrimination based on any ground such as sex, race, colour, ethnic or social origin, genetic features, language, religion or belief, political or any other opinion, membership of a national minority, property, birth, disability, age or sexual orientation shall be prohibited.
> 2. Within the scope of application of the Treaty establishing the European Community and of the Treaty on European Union, and without prejudice to the special provisions of those Treaties, any discrimination on grounds of nationality shall be prohibited.

The Charter of Fundamental Rights does not address multiple discrimination or the many possible intersections between the many prohibited grounds of discrimination.

2.3.2.2 Gender equality programmes

Council decision of 20 December 2000 establishing a programme relating to the Community framework strategy on gender equality (2001–5), which was prolonged for 2006,[16] it is stated in Recital 3 that:

> The persistence of structural, gender-based discrimination, *double- and often multiple-discrimination* faced by many women and persistent gender inequality justify the continuation and strengthening of Community action in the field and the adoption of new methods and approaches.

And in Art 3(b) that it aims:

> to improve the understanding of issues related to gender equality, including direct and indirect gender discrimination and *multiple discrimination against women*, by evaluating the effectiveness of policies and practice through prior analysis, monitoring their implementation and assessing their effects;

The above programme has been followed by the Roadmap for equality between women and men 2006–10[17] which has the following declared purpose of:

> *1.6. Combating multiple discrimination, in particular against immigrant and ethnic minority women.*

The EU is committed to the elimination of all discrimination and the creation of an inclusive society for all. Women members of disadvantaged groups are often worse off than their male counterparts. The situation of ethnic minority and immigrant women is emblematic. They often suffer from *double discrimination*. This requires the promotion of gender equality in migration and integration policies in order to ensure women's rights and civic participation, to fully use their employment potential and to improve their access to education and lifelong learning.

Here the focus is on the combination or intersection of gender and ethnic discrimination.

2.3.2.3 *Fight against discrimination in general*

The Council adopted a decision on establishing a Community action programme to combat discrimination[18] in 2000. It provided in Recital 4:

In the implementation of the programme, the Community will seek, in accordance with the Treaty, to eliminate inequalities and promote equality between men and women, particularly because *women are often the victims of multiple discrimination.*

and in recital 5:

The different forms of discrimination cannot be ranked: all are equally intolerable. The programme is intended both to exchange existing good practice in the Member States and to develop new practice and policy for combating discrimination, including *multiple discrimination.* This Decision may help to put in place a comprehensive strategy for combating all forms of discrimination on different grounds, a strategy which should henceforward be developed in parallel.

This programme, which was adopted at the same time as the Ethnic Equality and Employment Framework Directives, contains provisions similar to those found in these directives.

2.3.2.4 *Progress*

In its Social Agenda (2005–10),[19] the EU fixed as its overall strategic goal to promote more and better jobs and to offer equal opportunities for all. The realisation of the Social Agenda relies on a combination of instruments comprising EU legislation, the implementation of open methods of co-ordination in various policy fields and financial incentives such as the European Social Fund.

The period of the above programme to combat discrimination ended on

31 December 2006. For the 2007–13 programming period, the Commission decided to pursue further its efforts in this direction, proposing that the previous separate programmes be integrated into one framework programme, PROGRESS.[20] The overall aim of PROGRESS is to support financially the implementation of the objectives of the EU in the employment and social affairs area, as set out in the Social Agenda, and thereby contribute to the achievement of the Lisbon Strategy goals in these fields. It aims at supporting the core functions of the European Community towards fulfilling its Treaty-delegated tasks and powers in its respective areas of competence in the employment and social sphere. More specifically, PROGRESS will support (my emphasis):

> the implementation of the European Employment Strategy;
> the implementation of the open method of coordination in the field of social protection and inclusion;
> the improvement of the working environment and conditions including health and safety at work and reconciling work and family life;
> *the effective implementation of the principle of non-discrimination and promotion of its mainstreaming in all EU policies;*
> *the effective implementation of the principle of gender equality and promotion of its mainstreaming in all EU policies.*

It is divided into five policy sections which are: (1) Employment; (2) Social inclusion and social protection; (3) Working conditions; (4) Non-discrimination; and (5) Gender Equality.

2.3.3 From two prohibited grounds of discrimination to the six listed in Article 13 EC or more

In the EU, nationality and gender were the only equality issues on the legal agenda from the outset in 1958 and for about 40 years. Third-country nationals are often of a different ethnic origin than EU-nationals, so that there is some interaction between nationality and ethnic discrimination. Likewise different ethnic and religious groups experience gender inequality differently. Notwithstanding this, multiple discrimination was practically not discussed in official EU legal texts until the 1990s.

Today (2007), EU discrimination law addresses a wide spectrum of possible grounds of discrimination (nationality, gender, race, colour, ethnic or social origin, genetic features, language, religion or belief, political or any other opinion, membership of a national minority, property, birth, disability, age or sexual orientation). They are all covered by the Charter of Fundamental Rights.

There are specific directives on gender, race/ethnic origin, age, religion, disability and sexual orientation discrimination. As mentioned, in the decision[21] establishing the European Year of Equal Opportunities for All (2007)

– towards a just society, it is stated in the Preamble[22] that the European Year will also seek to address issues of multiple discrimination, that is discrimination on two or more of the six grounds listed in Art 13 EC (sex, racial or ethnic origin, religion or belief, disability, age or sexual orientation).

2.4 In what contexts are multiple discriminations addressed?

2.4.1 From an internal market to a fundamental rights perspective

Prohibition of discrimination both on grounds of nationality and gender was originally introduced in EU law as a means to develop the Internal Market.[23] Discrimination on grounds of nationality is still often addressed with a view to making the Internal Market more effective. Equality and discrimination on other grounds (gender, ethnicity, age, religion, etc) is, however, today mainly treated in a fundamental rights context. The EU respects, according to Art 6 EU, fundamental rights, as guaranteed by the ECHR and as they result from the constitutional traditions common to the Member States, as general principles of Community law. To the extent the ECtHR[24] has developed rules on multiple discrimination they also form part of EU law.[25] In *Prais*,[26] a Jewish applicant for a position with the Council relied on Art 9 of the ECHR in support of a claim that it was unlawful that a test took place on a day where she for religious reasons was unable to participate. The ECJ held that it is desirable that an appointing authority informs itself in a general way of dates which might be unsuitable for religious reasons, and seeks to avoid fixing such dates for tests. In *Prais* the appointing authority was not informed of the unsuitability of certain days until the date for the test had been fixed and was entitled to refuse to fix a different date when the other candidates had already been convoked.

In the proposal for a Directive on Equal Treatment of Men and Women in the Access to and Supply of Goods and Services,[27] the Commission explicitly stressed that the EU approach to gender equality has developed over time, so that the original emphasis on equal pay and on avoiding distortions of competition between Member States has been replaced by a concern for equality as a fundamental right. A similar development has taken place in case law. The ECJ has, since the ruling in *Defrenne* (3) in 1978, considered equality between men and women a fundamental right and a general principle of law.[28] In 1976, in *Defrenne* (2),[29] the ECJ took the view, as regards Art 141 EC on equal pay, that it pursues a twofold purpose, both economic and social. In *Schröder*,[30] the ECJ went further and held that the economic goals of avoiding distortion of competition underlying Art 141 EC are secondary to the social aims of that provision, which constitutes the expression of a fundamental human right.

There is a different historical development in Anglo-American and EU equality law.[31] In the US and the UK race/ethnic discrimination was one of the first equality/discrimination issues to be addressed in legislation and legal practice. Gender equality was taken up at about the same time, but not – as in the EU – a generation before the race/ethnic issue. In the US, a Civil Rights Act was adopted in 1964. It deals primarily with race discrimination, but also includes a ban on sex discrimination. In the UK, the first Race Discrimination Act was adopted in 1968. It was replaced by the Race Relations Act 1976. Sex discrimination was addressed in the Equal Pay Act 1970 and the Sex Discrimination Act 1975.

2.4.2 Scope of application of discrimination bans – employment and occupation and other fields of society

Discrimination law is generally most developed in regard to the labour market. Discrimination on grounds of nationality and all the grounds listed in Art 13 EC (sex, racial or ethnic origin, religion or belief, disability, age or sexual orientation) is prohibited in employment and occupation but only nationality, gender and racial or ethnic discrimination is – to varying degrees – prohibited outside the labour market.

As appears from the outline of EU provisions given above, the Roadmap for equality between women and men 2006–10 put particular emphasis on the combination of gender and ethnic minorities. The case law in EU Member States on headscarf cases has a similar focus. Gender discrimination is prohibited both in regard to employment and occupation[32] and in the access to and supply of goods and services,[33] but not at EU level with regard to social protection and education outside an employment/occupation context. Ethnic and racial discrimination is prohibited both in regard to employment and occupation, in the access to and supply of goods and services, and in regard to social protection and social advantages and education also outside an employment/occupation context.[34]

The fact that discrimination on some grounds, for example religion, is only prohibited with regard to the labour market under EU law, while the prohibition against gender and ethnic discrimination has a wider range, may reduce the possibility to invoke EU law to combat multiple discrimination.

2.4.3 Gender mainstreaming the fight against discrimination on other grounds than gender

The gender mainstreaming strategy is mainly addressed to the drafters of rules and policies at all levels in society, for example legislators, judges, organisations and businesses, and calls upon them to integrate the gender dimension into the design and implementation of all their rules and policies.

2.4.3.1 Concept of gender mainstreaming

The concept of gender mainstreaming is not clearly defined.[35] Many have used the metaphor of equality as something that flows in its own subsidiary stream. With the mainstreaming strategy equality is lifted into the mainstream understood as the ordinary organisational, political and legal system. In the Council of Europe's report on mainstreaming from 1998[36] it is defined in the following way:

> Gender mainstreaming is the (re)organisation, improvement, development and evaluation of policy processes, so that a gender equality perspective is incorporated in all polices at all levels and at all stages, by the actors normally involved in policy-making.

It is further explained that gender mainstreaming can mean that the policy process is reorganised so that ordinary actors know how to incorporate a gender perspective. It can also mean that gender expertise is made a normal requirement for policy-makers.

The mainstreaming principle was first applied in the context of international development aid where it has been used since the mid-1980s.

2.4.3.2   The European Union duty of gender mainstreaming

The EU has practised the gender mainstreaming strategy by means of soft law since the early 1990s in the field of employment and occupation and increasingly also in other fields such as development aid and research.[37] The first binding EU measure on gender mainstreaming was the Regulation on gender mainstreaming activities in the area of development co-operation.[38]

The Community's mainstreaming obligation was (as from 1 May 1999) reinforced by the Amsterdam Treaty which elevated it in the hierarchy of the sources of law to Treaty level and extended its material scope to all areas covered by Community competence. Under Art 2 EC, the Community shall have as its task to promote equality between men and women. Article 3(2) EC states that in the context of the activities referred to in Art 3(1) EC carried on for the purposes set out in Art 2 EC:

> The Community shall aim to eliminate inequalities, and to promote equality, between men and women.

Under Art 3(2) EC there is an obligation for all Community actors (legislator, judiciary, executive) to contribute to gender mainstreaming. There is reference to this provision in the Preambles to all the Equality Directives adopted since 2000. The amendment to the Equal Treatment Directive in 2002[39] extended the personal scope of the obligation to gender mainstream in matters of employment from Community actors to the Member States. In the Equal Treatment Directive as amended in 2002 the above Treaty provisions are summarised as follows (emphasis added):

> Equality between women and men is a fundamental principle, under

Article 2 and Article 3(2) of the EC Treaty and the case-law of the Court of Justice. These Treaty provisions proclaim equality between women and men as a 'task' and an 'aim' of the Community and impose a *positive obligation* to 'promote' it in all its activities.

In *Dory*[40] Advocate General Stix-Hackl argued that there is an obligation for the ECJ to interpret anti-discriminatory Community measures[41] in light of the mainstreaming provision in Art 3(2) EC; see the following:

> ... in my opinion, in interpreting the scope of Directive 76/207, Article 3(2) EC must now also be taken into account. That provision of primary law was not yet in force at the time when the directive was drawn up. However, the Community is now expressly required by that provision actively to promote equality between men and women. As regards the scope of Article 3(2) EC, it may be seen that it applies to the Community's 'activities referred to' in Article 3(1) EC. Community law concerning the equal treatment of men and women in access to employment may be regarded as 'social policy' within the meaning of Article 3(1)(j) EC. (48) As regards the 'activities referred to', Article 3(2) EC imposes an obligation on 'the Community'. That presumably includes the Court when dealing, in connection with a reference for a preliminary ruling, with the interpretation of secondary law in the field of social policy.

That principle will apply equally or *a fortiori* to the Equality Directives adopted after 2000,[42] that is, at a time when the gender mainstreaming strategy is well-known and at least some of the participants in the legislative process are very conscious about the mainstreaming perspective in the directive.

2.4.3.3 National courts' duty of gender mainstreaming as a matter of European Union law

In 1984, in *Colson*,[43] and *Harz*,[44] the ECJ laid down an obligation for all the authorities of the Member States, and especially the courts, to interpret national law in conformity with Community law. Advocate General Mancini, in *Jongeneel Kaas* described the national courts also as Community courts, see the following:[45]

> The general principles ... of Community law ... may be relied upon by individuals before the national court which, as is well known, is also a Community court.

Advocate General Léger in *Köbler*[46] similarly stated that the European Communities have been developed and consolidated essentially through law. Since the national courts have the function of applying the law, including

Community law, they inevitably constitute an essential cog in the Community legal order.

Because all national courts are, under EU law, also Community courts the national courts presumably have mainstreaming obligations similar to those of the ECJ.

2.5 Applying existing bans on discrimination in multiple and intersectional discrimination cases

2.5.1 Case law of the European Court of Justice: gender and age

Many ECJ rulings on sex discrimination are concerned with factual situations where there is a combination of gender and age. That is for example true of the three *Defrenne* cases,[47] the *Marshall* case[48] and the *Kutz-Bauer* case.[49] In these cases – which were decided prior to the prohibition of age discrimination by the Employment Framework Directive[50] – the ECJ did, however, only deal with one ground of discrimination, namely gender. In the coming years, the ECJ is likely to be confronted explicitly with multiple and intersectional cases of discrimination and will have to deliver rulings on the interpretation of the existing rules – where multiple grounds of discrimination are prohibited – in such cases.

2.5.2 Equality and discrimination concepts

The principle of equal treatment of women and men is explicitly referred to in the United Nations Convention on the Elimination of All Forms of Discrimination against Women (CEDAW), in EU legislation and ECJ case law and in (many) national constitutions and national equality acts. Sex discrimination is prohibited with regard to practically all aspects of employment and occupation both at national, international and EU-level. For the purposes of the Gender Equality Directives, the principle of equal treatment between men and women shall, according to Art 2 in the Equal Treatment Directive,[51] mean that:

1. (a) there shall be no direct discrimination based on sex, including less favourable treatment of women for reasons of pregnancy and maternity;
    (b) there shall be no indirect discrimination based on sex.

2. Harassment and sexual harassment within the meaning of this Directive shall be deemed to be discrimination on the grounds of sex and therefore prohibited. A person's rejection of, or submission to, such conduct may not be used as a basis for a decision affecting that person.

One of the important consequences of increased EU involvement in gender equality law is that the basic concepts have become Community concepts. Those concepts have evolved over a period of approximately 30 years – first through ECJ case law on employment sex discrimination and free movement of workers – later through legislation on a number of discrimination issues.

2.5.2.1 Is there conceptual unity across the different discrimination grounds?

In 2002, the Equal Treatment between Men and Women in Employment and Occupation Directive[52] was amended to consolidate the practice of the ECJ and to align it with the definitions of basic concepts used in the Ethnic Equality Directive and the Framework Employment Directive. The Directive on Equal Treatment between Women and Men in the Provision of Goods and Services[53] took over the basic concepts as defined in the Equal Treatment in Employment and Occupation Directive in almost identical terms. In the following I discuss these concepts and their consequences when applied to multiple and intersectional discrimination cases.

2.5.2.2 Direct sex discrimination

Direct discrimination occurs where one person is treated less favourably, on grounds of sex, than another is, has been or would be treated in a comparable situation. According to the Gender Equality Directives, the principle of equal treatment between men and women shall mean that there shall be no direct discrimination based on sex, including less favourable treatment of women for reasons of pregnancy and maternity.

Many cases of discrimination consist of unfavourable treatment of sub-groups of women or sub-groups of men. The targeted persons are not selected exclusively on grounds of sex but on grounds of sex plus something more.

Among women, pregnant women, single mothers and mothers of small children are probably those who are most exposed to discrimination. In the Staff Working Paper[54] on the proposal for the Directive on Equal Treatment in the Access to and Supply of Goods and Services, refusal to provide a mortgage to pregnant women is mentioned as an example of discrimination that has been reported to the Commission. One of the respondents in an analysis by the Danish Agency for Trade and Industry stated[55] that single mothers do not have much chance of obtaining a loan for their enterprises. The Gender Equality Directives explicitly classify less favourable treatment of women for reasons of pregnancy and maternity as discrimination. In *Dekker,*[56] the ECJ held that unfavourable treatment on grounds of pregnancy is direct discrimination.

For men, sex discrimination often occurs in combination with age, for example, discrimination against young men looking for car insurance[57] or – mainly in countries where state social security is based on different pension ages for men and women – discrimination against older men who have passed the pension age for women but not reached the pension age for their own sex. In the UK – where the state pension age at the material time was 60 for women and 65 for men – the House of Lords has decided a case where a married man who was 61 wanted to visit a swimming pool together with his wife who was also 61. She was admitted free of charge because she had passed the pension age while he was required to pay an admission fee because he had not passed the pension age. This was held to be unlawful under the UK Sex Discrimination Act 1975.[58]

Multiple and intersectional discrimination cases may be seen as examples of such sex plus discrimination and will be unlawful. If an employer, for example, openly states that he will not accept applications from ethnic minority women, that would be direct sex discrimination in contravention of the existing gender equality legislation. In countries – like Denmark – where there is better enforcement machinery for sex discrimination than for ethnic discrimination claims, the case could be brought before the Complaints Board for Gender Equality.[59] The combination of discrimination grounds may, however, make the situation less transparent than it would be in a single-ground discrimination case and enable the employer to more easily conceal the discrimination which could create evidential end enforcement problems.

2.5.2.3 Indirect sex discrimination

The current definition of indirect discrimination is inspired by the case law of the ECJ in cases involving the free movement of workers.[60] Indirect sex discrimination occurs where an apparently neutral provision, criterion or practice *would put* persons of one sex *at a particular disadvantage* compared with persons of the other sex, unless that provision, criterion or practice is objectively justified by a legitimate aim, and the means of achieving that aim are appropriate and necessary.

According to this definition, an apparently neutral provision, criterion or practice will be regarded as indirectly discriminatory if it is intrinsically liable to adversely affect a person or persons on the grounds referred to in the Directive. This 'liability test' may be proven on the basis of statistical evidence or by any other means that demonstrate that a provision would be intrinsically disadvantageous for the person or persons concerned. This definition is modelled over the jurisprudence of the ECJ in the *O'Flynn* case.

As the definition of indirect discrimination is worded[61] it is not necessary for there to be indirect discrimination that a formally neutral criterion actually operates to the disadvantage of one sex. It is sufficient that there is a possibility that the criterion would put one sex at a disadvantage.

Indirect discrimination may be justified by objective reasons. The starting point is that differential treatment is an expression of discrimination unless it can be shown that such treatment is justified in objective terms. The leading case is still *Bilka*[62] where the ECJ ruled that Art 141 EC is infringed by an undertaking which excludes part-time employees from its occupational pension scheme, where that exclusion affects a far greater number of women than men, unless the undertaking shows that the exclusion is based on *objectively justified factors unrelated to any discrimination* on grounds of sex. Such factors may lie in the fact that the undertaking seeks to employ as few part-time workers as possible, where it is shown that that objective corresponds to a *real need* on the part of the undertaking and the means chosen for achieving it are *appropriate* and *necessary*. The ECJ thus requires three conditions to be met:

(1) There must be a real need for the employer to apply the 'suspect' criteria;
(2) The means chosen by the employer must be necessary to achieve this goal; and
(3) The means must be appropriate: that is, there must be a reasonable proportion between end and means.

The *Bilka* test is based on application of the *principle of proportionality*. Prohibitions of wearing political or religious symbols, including the Islamic headscarf, are examples of using an apparently neutral provision, criterion or practice which could put women at a particular disadvantage compared to men and therefore will be unlawful unless the prohibition is objectively justified by a legitimate aim, and the prohibition is an appropriate and necessary means of achieving that aim.

2.5.2.4 Positive action

Positive action is an option for the Member States. There is never a duty under EU law for the Member States to take positive action or to allow or impose a duty upon their businesses/citizens to take positive action.

The general principle underlying ECJ case law on positive action[63] is that the principle of proportionality shall be observed. This means that any special measures that favour one sex shall serve a lawful purpose, they shall be appropriate and necessary for the attainment of this goal, and they must not go beyond what is necessary to attain it. Article 141(4) EC and all the existing Equality Directives contain provisions allowing positive action in respect of each specific protected criterion (gender, age, ethnicity, etc). This probably means that it will be in accordance with EU law to take positive action to support sub-groups suffering from multiple or intersectional discrimination.[64]

To some extent EU law prohibits positive action, namely proclaimed positive action measures that do not pursue a genuine equality purpose or apply excessive means to achieve its (lawful) purpose. If measures are within the sphere of lawful positive action under EU law it is for the Member States, in accordance with their political choices, to decide whether or not to allow or prohibit positive action in the individual country.

2.5.2.5   Formal and substantive equality

Substantive equality recognises that for individuals to receive equal treatment in practice they must often receive different or unequal treatment, see for example the wording of Art 141(4) EC on positive action which provides 'With a view to ensuring full equality in practice . . . .'. Formal equality, on the other hand, forbids any form of discrimination in order to achieve equal treatment.

EU law on gender equality covers both substantive and formal equality. The ban on direct sex discrimination contributes mainly to securing formal equality while the ban on indirect sex discrimination, the mainstreaming strategy and positive action are mainly directed at achieving substantive equality. In *Kalanke*, Advocate General Tesauro explained the concepts of substantive and formal equality in the following terms:[65]

16. The principle of substantive equality necessitates taking account of the existing inequalities which arise because a person belongs to a particular class of persons or to a particular social group; it enables and requires the unequal, detrimental effects which those inequalities have on the members of the group in question to be eliminated or, in any event, neutralized by means of specific measures.

Unlike the principle of formal equality, which precludes basing unequal treatment of individuals on certain differentiating factors, such as sex, the principle of substantive equality refers to a positive concept by basing itself precisely on the relevance of those different factors themselves in order to legitimize an unequal right, which is to be used in order to achieve equality as between persons who are regarded not as neutral but having regard to their differences. In the final analysis, the principle of substantive equality complements the principle of formal equality and authorizes only such deviations from that principle as are justified by the end which they seek to achieve, that of securing actual equality. The ultimate objective is therefore the same: securing equality as between persons.

The approach of the EC Treaty to the gender factor is not only an anti-discrimination approach, but also increasingly – and particularly after the coming into force of the Amsterdam Treaty as at 1 May 1999 which placed the mainstreaming duty at Treaty level – a proactive, substantive equality approach. The appropriate action required by Art 13 EC – which is the legal basis of the proposed Directive on Equal Treatment in the Provision of Goods and Services – is to combat sex discrimination. Other provisions like the mainstreaming provision in Art 3(2) and the positive action provision in Art 141(4) more directly pursue substantive gender equality. Article 3(2) EC provides that in all the activities referred to in this Article – that includes everything the EU has competence to do in matters of contract law – the Community shall aim to eliminate inequalities (not just combat discrimination), and to promote equality, between men and women. Article 141(4) EC refers to the aim of ensuring full equality in practice between men and women in working life and allows for some forms of specific positive action measures.

2.5.3 Equality or non-discrimination as an underlying general principle

In *Mangold*,[66] the ECJ held that the principle of non-discrimination on grounds of age must be regarded as a general principle of Community law. Similarly, non-discrimination on the other prohibited grounds can probably be interpreted as a general underlying principle of Community law that ranks higher than secondary legislation and, in accordance with the principle of supremacy of Community law, prevails over conflicting national law.

2.5.4 Enforcement

According to settled case law, in the absence of EU rules governing the matter, it is for the domestic legal system of each Member State to designate the courts and tribunals having jurisdiction, to lay down the detailed procedural rules governing actions for safeguarding rights which individuals derive from Community law, and to choose the relevant remedies. The choice of procedural arrangements and penalties thus remains within the discretion of the Member States but their choice must be exercised with respect for the general EU law principles of equivalence, effectiveness and proportionality.

In addition to the general principles, which apply in all matters governed by Community law, Member States are required to comply with the specific requirements provided for in the Equality Directives on judicial and administrative procedures, compensation or reparation, legal standing, dialogue with organisations, time limits, burden of proof and specific equality bodies to control that the principle of equal treatment is observed.[67]

It is up to the Member States to decide whether they will set up single-ground or multi-ground equality bodies. In countries that have chosen to set up single-ground enforcement machinery persons experiencing multiple or intersectional discrimination may encounter problems when seeking to obtain redress.

2.6 Conclusion

The substantive content of the existing bans on sex discrimination covers multiple and intersectional discrimination. The combination of discrimination grounds may, however, reduce transparency and create evidential and enforcement problems.

At the conceptual level EU law has not yet produced any definition of multiple and intersectional discrimination. The term 'multiple discrimination' is used both in binding and non-binding sources of EU law whereas the term 'intersectional discrimination' is absent from EU legal texts.

Multiple discrimination in EU equality law has mainly been addressed explicitly with a view to gender-mainstreaming the fight against other kinds of discrimination (discrimination on grounds of ethnic origin, age, etc).

Notes

1 See generally R Nielsen (2006) 'EU law and multiple discrimination', *CBS Law Studies* WP 2006–01, available at http://cbs.dk/content/view/pub/38578 (accessed 13 September 2007).

2 Cf S Fredman (2005) 'Double trouble: Multiple discrimination and EU law', *European Anti-Discrimination Law Review*, 2: 13–21, available at http://ec.europa.eu/employment_social/fundamental_rights/pdf/legnet/05lawrev2_en.pdf (accessed 13 September 2007) and M-T Lanquetin (2002) *La double discrimination à raison du sexe et de la race ou de l'origine ethnique: Approche juridique, synthèse du rapport final*, available at www.lacse.fr/ressources/files/etudeset-documentation/syntheses/Lanquetin_02.pdf (accessed 13 September 2007).

3 Application no 44774/98.

4 See on the concept of intersectionality where gender, ethnicity, class, religion and other identities meet K Crenshaw (1991) 'Mapping the margins: Intersectionality, identity politics, and violence against women of Color', *Stanford Law Review*, 43: 1241–99.

5 Ontario Human Rights Commission (2001) *An Intersectional Approach to Discrimination. Addressing Multiple Grounds in Human Rights Claims. Discussion Paper*, available at www.ohrc.on.ca/en/resources/discussion_consultation/DissIntersectionalityFtnts/view (accessed 13 September 2007).

6 See for a discussion of the multidimensionality of EU equality law D Schiek (2005) 'Broadening the scope and the norms of EU gender equality law: towards a multidimensional conception of equality law', *Maastricht Journal of European and Comparative Law*, 12: 427–66.

7 Decision 771/2006/EC establishing the European Year of Equal Opportunities for All (2007) – towards a just society [2006] OJ L146/1.

8 Recital 14.

9 Council Directive 2000/43/EC implementing the principle of equal treatment between persons irrespective of racial or ethnic origin [2000] OJ L180/22.

10 Council Directive 2000/78/EC establishing a general framework for equal treatment in employment and occupation [2000] OJ L303/16.

11 Council Directive 2004/113/EC implementing the principle of equal treatment between men and women in the access to and supply of goods and services [2004] OJ L 373/37.

12 Council Directive 2000/78/EC, Recital 3 in the Preamble.

13 Directive 2002/73/EC amending Council Directive 76/207/EEC on the implementation of the principle of equal treatment for men and women as regards access to employment, vocational training and promotion, and working conditions [2002] OJ L269/15; Council Directive 98/52/EC on the extension of Council Directive 97/80/EC on the burden of proof in cases of discrimination based on sex to the United Kingdom of Great Britain and Northern Ireland [1998] OJ L205/66; Council Directive 97/80/EC on the burden of proof in cases of discrimination based on sex [1998] L14/6; Council Directive 96/97/EC amending Council

Directive 86/378/EEC on the implementation of the principle of equal treatment for men and women in occupational social security schemes [1997] OJ L46/20; Council Directive 86/378/EEC on the implementation of the principle of equal treatment for men and women in occupational social security schemes [1986] OJ L225/40; Council Directive 76/207/EEC on the implementation of the principle of equal treatment for men and women as regards access to employment, vocational training and promotion, and working conditions [1976] OL L39/40; Council Directive 75/117/EEC on the approximation of the laws of the Member States relating to the application of the principle of equal pay for men and women [1975] OJ L45/19.

14 Directive 2006/54/EC on the implementation of the principle of equal opportunities and equal treatment of men and women in matters of employment and occupation (recast) [2006] OJ L204/23.

15 Directive 2002/73/EC, Recital 3 in the Preamble.

16 Decision 1554/2005/EC amending Council Decision 2001/51/EC establishing a programme relating to the Community framework strategy on gender equality [2005] OJ L255/9 and Council Decision 848/2004/EC establishing a Community action programme to promote organisations active at European level in the field of equality between men and women [2004] OJ L159/18.

17 COM(2006) 92, A Roadmap for equality between women and men 2006–2010.

18 Council Decision 2000/750/EC establishing a Community action programme to combat discrimination (2001 to 2006) [2000] OJ L303/23.

19 COM(2005)33.

20 Decision 1672/20006/EC establishing a Community programme for employment and social solidarity – PROGRESS adopted by the European Parliament and the Council on 24 October [2006] OJ L315/1.

21 Decision 771/2006/EC of the European Parliament and of the Council of 17 May 2006 establishing the European Year of Equal Opportunities for All (2007) – towards a just society [2006] OJ L146/1.

22 Recital 14.

23 See further R Nielsen (2004) *Gender Equality in European Contract Law*, Copenhagen: DJØF Publishing, Ch 1.

24 See further OM Arnardóttir (2003) *Equality and Non-Discrimination under the European Convention on Human Rights*, The Hague: Martinus Nijhoff Publishers.

25 See case C-260/89 *ERT v DEP* [1991] ECR I-2925.

26 Case 130–75 *Prais v Council of the European Communities* [1976] ECR 1589.

27 Council Directive 2004/113/EC, proposal in COM(2003) 657, p 2.

28 Case 149/77 *Gabrielle Defrenne v Société anonyme belge de navigation aérienne Sabena ('Defrenne III')* [1978] ECR 1365.

29 Case 43/75 *Gabrielle Defrenne v Société anonyme belge de navigation aérienne Sabena ('Defrenne II')* [1976] ECR 455, paras 8–11.

30 Case C-50/96 *Deutsche Telekom AG v Lilli Schröder* [2000] ECR I-743, para 57.

31 L Roseberry (1999) *The Limits of Employment Discrimination Law in the United States and the European Community*, Copenhagen: DJØF Publishing.

32 See in particular Art 141 EC and the recast Directive 2006/54/EC.

33 See Council Directive 2004/113/EC.

34 See Council Directive 2000/43/EC Art 3.

35 A Andersen and R Nielsen (2007) *Mainstreaming i juridisk perspektiv*, Copenhagen: Jurist- og økonomforbundets Forlag.

36 Council of Europe (1998) *Gender Mainstreaming. Conceptual Framework, Methodology and Presentation of Good Practices*, Strasbourg, available at www.coe.int/t/e/human_rights/equality/02._gender_mainstreaming/099_EG(1999)03.asp (accessed 13 September 2007).

37 See Council Resolution of 20 May 1999 on women and science [1999] OJ C 201/1.

38   Council Regulation 2836/98/EC of 22 December 1998 on integrating of gender issues in development cooperation [1998] OJ L354/5. This Regulation expired in December 2003. In the Commission's work programme for 2003, COM (2002)590, it is announced that it will be revised taking into account the main elements of the Programme of Action for the mainstreaming of gender equality in Community Development Co-operation COM(2001)29–5.
39   Directive 2002/73/EC.
40   Case C-186/01 *Alexander Dory v Deutschland* [2003] ECR I-2479, point 102–3.
41   In *Dory* the Equal Treatment Directive 76/207/EEC.
42   Directives 2000/43/EC (Ethnic Equality Directive), 2000/78/EC (Employment Framework Directive), 2002/73/EC (amended Gender Equal Treatment Direct-ive), 2004/113/EC (Goods and Services Gender Equality Directive), 2006/54/EC (Recast Gender Equality in Employment Directive).
43   Case 14/83 *Von Colson and Kamann v Land Nordrhein-Westfalen* [1984] ECR 1891.
44   Case 79/83 *Dorit Harz v Deutsche Tradax GmbH* [1984] ECR 1921.
45   Case 237/82 *Jongeneel Kaas and others v State of the Netherlands and Stichting Centraal Orgaan Zuivelcontrole* [1984] ECR 483.
46   Case C-224/01 *Gerhard Köbler v Republik Österreich* [2003] ECR I-10239.
47   Case 80/70 *Gabrielle Defrenne v Belgian State* [1971] ECR 445; *Gabrielle Defrenne v Société anonyme belge de navigation aérienne Sabena ('Defrenne II')* [1976] ECR 455 Case 43/75; and Case 149/77. *Gabrielle Defrenne v Société anonyme belge de navigation aérienne Sabena ('Defrenne III')* [1978] ECR 1365.
48   Case 152/84 *MH Marshall v Southampton and South-West Hampshire Area Health Authority (Teaching)* [1986] ECR 723.
49   Case C-187/00 *Helga Kutz-Bauer v Freie und Hansestadt Hamburg* [2003] ECR 2741.
50   Council Directive 2000/78/EC.
51   Council Directive 76/207/EEC as amended by 2002/73/EC.
52   Directive 2002/73/EC amending Council Directive 76/207/EEC.
53   Council Directive 2004/113/EC.
54   SEC(2003)1213, p 7.
55   Danish Agency for Trade and Industry (2000) *The Relations of Banks to Women Entrepreneurs* 2000, available at http://videnskabsministeriet.dk/site/forside/pub-likationer/2000/the-relations-of-banks-to-women-entrepreneurs/ren.html (accessed 13 September 2007). The quotation on single mothers is from part 2.2. The respondents in the analysis were staff in the banks and independent advisors to the banks, e.g. chartered accountants.
56   Case C-177/88 *Elisabeth Johanna Pacifica Dekker v Stichting Vormingscentrum voor Jong Volwassenen (VJV-Centrum)* [1990] ECR I-3941.
57   See for example a Norwegian case *Vedtak* 1/2004, where the majority of the Nor-wegian Complaints Board for Equality held that sex and age-based pricing of car insurance was a violation of the Norwegian Equality Act.
58   C McCrudden (1994) *Equality in Law between Men and Women in the European Community*, United Kingdom, Luxembourg, OOPEC, p 42.
59   See e.g. Case 6/2007 where the Complaints Board dealt with a case about the Islamic headscarf.
60   See in particular Case C-237/94 *John O'Flynn v Adjudication Officer* [1996] ECR 2417.
61   The English version reads: 'would put at a disadvantage', the French version: *'est susceptible d'entraîner un désavantage'* and the German version: *'können benachteiligen'*.
62   Case 170/84 *Bilka-Kaufhaus GmbH v Karin Weber von Hartz* [1986] ECR 1607.
63   See Case 312/86 *Commission v France* [1988] ECR 6315, Case C-450/93 *Eckhard Kalanke v Freie Hansestadt Bremen* [1995] ECR I-3051, Case C-409/95 *Hellmut*

Marschall v Land Nordrhein-Westfalen [1997] ECR I-6363, Case C-158/97 *Georg Badeck and Others* [2000] ECR I-1875, Case C-407/98 *Katarina Abrahamsson and Leif Anderson v Elisabet Fogelqvist* [2000] ECR I-5539, Case C-79/99 *Schnorbus v Land Hessen* [2000] ECR I-10997, and Case C-476/99 *Lommers v Minister van Landbouw, Natuurbeheer en Visserij* [2002] ECR I-2891.

64 See for the same view S Fredman (2005b) 'Double trouble: Multiple discrimination and EU law', *European Anti-Discrimination Law Review*, 2: 13–21, available at http://ec.europa.eu/employment_social/fundamental_rights/pdf/legnet/05lawrev2_en.pdf (accessed 13 September 2007)

65 Case C-450/93 *Eckhard Kalanke v Freie Hansestadt Bremen* [1995] ECR I-3051, point 16.

66 Case C-144/04 *Werner Mangold v Rüdiger Helm* [2005] ECR I-9981.

67 See for details R Nielsen (2004) *Gender Equality in European Contract Law*, Copenhagen: DJØF Publishing, Ch 5 on Remedies and enforcement.

3 Multidimensional equality from within

Themes from the European Convention on Human Rights

Oddný Mjöll Arnardóttir

3.1 Introduction

In international human rights law legal prescriptions establishing individual justiciable rights are typically formulated in generally phrased principles. Article 14 of the European Convention on Human Rights (the Convention)[1] stipulates that: 'The enjoyment of the rights and freedoms set forth in this Convention shall be secured without discrimination on any ground ...' and provides a non-exhaustive list of examples of possible discrimination grounds. Matters such as the circumstances constituting discrimination, the possibilities for justifying a difference in treatment and the allocation of the burden of proof, to name a few, are not addressed. Content and meaning of the legal norm are therefore derived almost entirely from its interpretation and application in individual cases. A further important characteristic of international human rights law is the highly complicated political and legal process necessary to amend the legal instruments. The Convention cannot be amended easily to reflect developments in society or new theoretical insights. For example, discussions on a specific protocol on non-discrimination began in the 1960s, but only in 2000 was Protocol 12[2] finally adopted. Subsequently, a further five years elapsed before the Protocol had been ratified by the required 10 states for it to take effect, and as of early September 2007 only 15 of the 47 Member States had ratified.

As a result, the development of the law is highly dependent on the European Court of Human Rights' (the Court's) interpretation of the Convention in light of present day social conditions and on the translation of theoretical insights into the interpretation and modes of analysis applied by the Court. This is the key both to the understanding and the development of the Convention's discrimination law.

This chapter will address the interaction between theoretical insights on substantive and multidimensional equality and legal practice under the European Convention on Human Rights. The intriguing questions arising out of that interaction are as follows:

1. Is it possible to bridge the gaps between theoretical insights on

multidimensionality and the practical application of Art 14/Protocol 12 and if so, how?

2. Are there any lessons to be learned from the unique situation under the Convention which may be of relevance to the new multidimensional future of EU equality law?

I suggest that both of these questions can be answered with a cautious 'yes'. Several characteristics appear to exist in the existing Convention case law which, if developed correctly, may enable the Court to deal with multidimensionality and intersectionality. Likewise, it may hold some interesting lessons for other legal regimes such as EU law and domestic systems which traditionally have a more compartmentalised approach to non-discrimination. For example, Sandra Fredman has argued that multiple discrimination calls for a reconstruction of the notion of difference as not being about absolute difference ('otherness') from a single norm but about defining group membership by fluid boundaries where groups may intersect. Flowing from that, her argument continues: 'Such an approach can only be captured legally by a single harmonised statute which includes all the relevant grounds of discrimination, and does not necessitate harsh distinctions between different grounds'.[3] Perhaps the Convention regime may function as a test site for the notion of a single harmonised multidimensional statute currently under discussion in European circles as a response to the situation under the new EU Equality Directives.[4]

The title of this chapter refers to multidimensional equality and I refer throughout to multidimensional equality and intersectionality. It is necessary at the outset to clarify these concepts as applied in this chapter. I adopt the term 'multidimensional equality' as encompassing both different conceptions of equality and a multitude of discrimination grounds.[5] As such, it is an umbrella concept which has the potential to encompass both compound discrimination, sometimes also referred to as double, triple or multiple discrimination, and intersectionality. Analysis according to the concept of compound/multiple discrimination makes use of existing identity categories, with the difference, however, that it is capable of simultaneously addressing more than one discrimination ground. The most obvious consequence of that approach is the possibility to treat the existence of multiple discrimination grounds as aggravating factors. Compound/multiple discrimination may also be part and parcel of the second concept mentioned, intersectionality. However, more specifically, the concept of intersectionality refers to the situations which occur when two or more discrimination grounds or identities combine to create a unique situation that is more complex and represents more than just the sum of its parts.[6] For example, Kimberlé Crenshaw lists the following forms of discrimination as a typology of how the intersectionality of race and gender might play out in real life experiences: (a) targeted discrimination (intentional) towards ethnic women; (b) compound discrimination where ethnic and gender identities each command separate types of exclusion;

(c) structural-dynamic discrimination where policies specifically directed at ethnic or gendered groups intersect with structural disadvantage to create unique burdens; (d) structural subordination where facially neutral policies intersect with structural disadvantage to create uniquely disproportionate burdens; and (e) political intersectionality where individual claims of discrimination are construed as a threat to the collective identity of the group the particular individual belongs to and, thus, constitute a unique and difficult space to negotiate for the individual in question.[7] While the concept of intersectionality can embrace the simpler forms of targeted and compound discrimination, conceptually it requires us to look beneath the surface and beyond the prevailing norm paradigm that leaves various synergetic vulnerabilities unnoticed in the margins. It also conceptually informs our understanding of how individual and group identities creating vulnerabilities are fluid, intersectional and, particularly, dependent on the context or positioning of the individual who experiences discrimination.

3.2 Non-discrimination under the European Convention on Human Rights

3.2.1 Article 14 and Protocol 12

As regards the European Convention on Human Rights a few preliminary observations are necessary concerning the main characteristics of Art 14 and the dynamics of the case law.

First, a few words on the relationship between Arts 14 and 1 of Protocol 12 are required. Both provisions prohibit discrimination on any ground and list the same examples of discrimination grounds. The conceptual frameworks employed by the provisions also converge, as is clear from the explanatory report to Protocol 12.[8] Hence, the only significant difference between Art 14 and Art 1 of Protocol 12 relates to scope. Whereas Art 14 only applies in conjunction with the other substantive rights of the Convention, Protocol 12 establishes an independent right to non-discrimination. For reasons of simplicity the remainder of this chapter will refer only to Art 14. However, the arguments and conclusions presented apply to Art 14 and Protocol 12 alike.

Second, it must be observed that Art 14 is an open model non-discrimination clause which is not bound by a limited list of discrimination grounds. It establishes the general principle that no one may be subject to discrimination on any ground and lists the following discrimination grounds as examples: sex, race, colour, language, religion, political or other opinion, national or social origin, association with a national minority, property, birth or other status. To that extent, the provision may be seen as aspiring to ensure multidimensional equality in the sense that a claimant wishing to bring a discrimination claim may do so based on a multitude of identities.

As already indicated, the indeterminate and open-ended language of Art 14 leaves almost everything to be decided in its application. The actual content and impact of the provision derives from the context, interpretation and methods of analysis applied in individual cases. In doctrinal terms, the Court adopts its express analytical approach according to which it must first find that a difference in treatment has occurred and then it will test whether an objective and reasonable justification for that difference in treatment exists. This will be the case if the treatment in question pursues a legitimate aim and satisfies the Court's proportionality test.[9] Upon closer inspection, however, we may observe that the analytical approach under Art 14 is not really capable of explaining the case law and instead only functions to mask the true normative reasoning and impact of individual judgments. Rather, we can come much closer to the content of Art 14 by focusing on the strictness of review and on the factors that influence it.

3.2.2 *A three-tiered model of factors that influence the strictness of review*

The case law on discrimination can be explained by a three-tiered model of interacting factors which influence the strictness of review in cases under Art 14. Moreover, these factors do not only influence the strictness of review with regard to objective justification but also the Court's approach to the establishment of prima facie discrimination and the issue of whether the Court reviews a case under Art 14 or finds it 'not necessary' to address the discrimination claim raised.[10]

The first and most important influencing factor is the discrimination ground. The Court has established more or less clearly that the 'suspect' discrimination grounds calling for strict scrutiny include sex, ethnic origin/ race, birth in or outside marriage, nationality, religion and sexual orientation. There is an intermediate category of discrimination grounds where the relevant discrimination ground is based on more or less clearly defined personal identities but has not been elevated to the 'suspect' category which indicates strict scrutiny. Examples of that category include transsexualism, disability, age, language, political or other opinion, social origin and birth. A final category of cases consists of instances where the relevant comparisons have no reference to real personal identities and in those cases the scrutiny becomes very lenient.

The second influencing factor is the type of claim being made. Under this influencing factor, claims based on negative state obligations and claims based on express or overt discrimination indicate strict scrutiny, whereas claims based on positive obligations and the disproportionate effect of facially neutral measures indicate more lenient scrutiny.

The first aspect of this influencing factor relates to the general distinction drawn between positive and negative state obligations. The positive obligation to accommodate for differences was acknowledged in *Thlimmenos* which established that discrimination within the scope of Art 14 may also include a failure to make reasonable accommodations.[11] However, claims based on reasonable accommodation meet lenient scrutiny as is evidenced by the fact that since *Thlimmenos* no other applicant has been successful in bringing such a claim. Moreover, positive action programmes are acknowledged and permitted under the Convention, but their use is not prescribed.[12] Accordingly, the position on positive obligations under Art 14 may be summarised as including failures to prevent and remedy instances of discrimination, even on the *Thlimmenos* construction of discrimination as a failure to accommodate differences, but not reaching so far as to prescribe the promotion of equality through positive action programmes.[13] In conceptual terms, however, the line distinguishing between an obligation to prevent discrimination and an obligation to promote equality is both thin and unclear. Nonetheless, there can be no doubt that the Convention's primary focus is on negative state obligations and, accordingly, that claims which concern only negative obligations will meet stricter scrutiny. While the need for positive state obligations and appropriate accommodation for differences is recognised under Art 14, these are conceptualised as exceptions which in turn leads to them indicating more lenient scrutiny.

The second aspect of this influencing factor concerns the concept of indirect discrimination and the distinction between individualised and group-oriented models of equality. The concepts of indirect discrimination and disproportionate effect analysis are only beginning to evolve in the Convention jurisprudence. This underdeveloped state of the law may, in part, be explained by the fact that in jurisdictions which operate on open models with non-exhaustive lists of discrimination grounds the need for formulation in terms of indirect discrimination does not arise as acutely as in systems operating under closed models. The particular injustice perceived can be addressed simply in terms of the expressly identifiable discrimination ground.[14] Developing a concept of indirect discrimination would, nevertheless, raise the level of protection under the Convention. First, it would enable links to be identified between the situation challenged and the relevant history of disadvantage. In light of the influencing factor of the interest at stake (set out below), such links should produce direct consequences in terms of the strictness of review. Second, disproportionate effect analysis would shift the focus from an individualised model of equality to a more group-oriented model. This development is already underway as the Court has acknowledged the concept of disproportionate effect analysis.[15] Claims based on disproportionate effect have, however, generally met lenient scrutiny. Before *DH and Others* this occured through the Court's imposition of a strict requirement on the applicant to prove either an underlying systematic practice or pattern of discrimination or a subjective intent to discriminate.[16] In *DH and Others* the Court relaxed this requirement, but at the time of writing it remains the only judgement where a successful disproportionate effect claim has been brought under the Convention.[17]

The third influencing factor is one that I have labelled 'the interest at stake'. This influencing factor is the least developed in the case law and the literature. A generally acknowledged example of this factor at play is to be found in the typically lenient scrutiny applied in cases concerning property rights. On a closer inspection of the case law we can discern an increasingly contextual approach under this heading. This point will be elaborated in more detail in 'Themes from within' (below) in an attempt to develop and address this type of factor in a manner which consciously accommodates multidimensionality.

The above three-tiered model of factors that influence the strictness of review under Art 14 relates to three basic variables that exist in any discrimination claim. These variables are: (a) a claim of a particular type of discrimination; (b) based on a particular discrimination ground; and (c) relating to a particular type of interest. It is important to notice that the model is not symmetrical as it would be if each influencing factor identified always resulted in the same type of scrutiny. Instead, the model is asymmetrical as the influencing factors exist in interplay with each other and may function to support or negate the influence of each other. Thus, while a claim of indirect discrimination indicates lenient scrutiny, this may be offset by the indication towards strict scrutiny inherent in the 'suspect' discrimination grounds.

3.2.3 Democratic legitimacy?

As strictness of review is the key both to the understanding and the development of the Convention's discrimination law, a deeper understanding of how the Court adjusts strictness of review is necessary. The Court's main tool for adjusting the strictness of review is the doctrine of the margin of appreciation. It is not a complete and elaborate theory but its contours have been developed most clearly by Paul Mahoney.[18] He argues that it has its basis in the principle of subsidiarity, that is to say, the Convention system is a subsidiary machinery of protection with the initial responsibility and assessment in each case situated with sovereign member states at the domestic level. The margin of appreciation also seeks legitimation in one of the basic values of the Convention system, democracy and adherence to democratic rule. This entails that the Court must act with due deference to the democratic processes at work in the member states. Further, as pluralism is one of the hallmarks of democratic society, a margin of appreciation should be left allowing room for cultural diversity and different solutions depending on the context in each of the member states.[19]

The factors that influence the margin of appreciation are not always easily identifiable. The Court has spelled out what they are in some of its judgments. In the context of Art 14, the Court has stated: 'The scope of the margin of appreciation will vary according to the *circumstances*, the *subject matter and its background*; in this respect, one of the relevant factors may be the existence or non-existence of *common ground* between the laws of the Contracting States'.[20] In determining whether to allow a narrow or a wide margin of appreciation, whether to be strict or lenient in the review of discrimination cases, the Court generally places a great emphasis on the 'consensus' or 'common ground' in the legislation of the member states. In other words, the

Court firmly locates the Convention within the mainstream of the dominant culture and core values of the Member States. Here lies the perpetual site of contestation as the case law under Art 14 evolves through addressing individual claims from the margins.

In support of the legitimacy of the margin of appreciation doctrine Paul Mahoney argues that: 'Recognition of legitimate cultural variety is not the same as cultural relativism'.[21] On the other side of the coin we can also discern that the margin of appreciation can easily function in the opposite manner, not as potentially resulting in cultural relativism but in crude majority rule where there is no room for legitimate cultural variety. There is a balance to be struck. The point needs elaboration: cultural variety and pluralism are hallmarks of the Convention core value of democracy. They are referred to in support of the margin of appreciation doctrine. However, the margin of appreciation is predominantly adjusted according to the existence (or indeed lack) of 'common ground' in the legislation of the majority of member states. Drawing on the insights derived from substantive approaches to equality we can discern that, in practice, the margin of appreciation may function to exclude or restrict pluralism as soon as individuals leave the cultural mainstream and find themselves located in the margins. Where state action that has its basis in a marginalised culture is contested, the margin of appreciation is likely to narrow and exclude cultural variety. Whereas, if an individual in a marginalised situation claims to be the victim of state action that has its basis in mainstream 'common ground' culture, the margin of appreciation is likely to widen and exclude recognition of cultural variety. Thus, in a sense, the margin of appreciation doctrine may – and I am not arguing that it always does – function in opposition to one of its underlying and justifying rationales. The dividing line does not lie within the margin of appreciation doctrine itself, but rather in the factors that influence it and in its adjustment by the Court in individual judgments.

To illustrate the point let us take gender equality as an example. As the case law stands today, the Court considers equality of the 'sexes' to be a primary goal in all Council of Europe member states and, accordingly, a state wishing to justify a difference in treatment based on sex must advance very weighty arguments in support.[22] The scrutiny of discrimination based on sex is strict with a considerably narrowed margin of appreciation. Correspondingly, positive measures intended to alleviate the structural disadvantages experienced by women are permitted and do not necessarily face particularly strict objective justification scrutiny.[23] Seemingly, the struggle for sex equality, accompanied by decades of feminist scholarship and critique, has in a sense left the margins and entered the mainstream. Thus, the margin of appreciation approach and methodology of the Court now appear to empower applicants who claim discrimination on the basis of their biological sex. The question of equality in terms of socially constructed gender is, however, only beginning to evolve as a non-discrimination issue under the Convention. As evidenced in *Christine Goodwin* the right of 'men' and 'women' to marry under Art 12 has already been interpreted as encompassing socially constructed gender identities and transgender issues are easily conceptualised as protection of private life issues.[24] This development is likely to have a bearing on future case law under Art 14 as has already occurred with regard to sexual orientation discrimination.[25] As yet, however, issues relevant to transgender people are not conceptualised by the Court as discrimination and the Court finds it unnecessary to review such cases under Art 14. In terms of equal rights claims, the issues of transgender people remain confined to the margins. Also, the concern for 'sex' equality represented in the mainstream is constructed around the position of non-minority women. Thus, while many feminists may look on the Court's approach with approval, *Leyla Sahin* who was, so to speak, de-veiled by the Court in 2004 probably deplores that approach since it represents the marginalisation of her choice and her identity and culture by way of contrast with mainstream Western culture.[26] Thus, whilst a non-minority biological woman might interpret the case law of the Court as being substantive and effective, many others may well conclude that it signifies a formal approach that does not take relevant cultural context and individual experience into account.

With those realisations in mind, we can identify the central issue: Is it possible to deliver a more complex and multidimensional justice on the basis of Art 14? What factors do we need to consider to ensure that the margin of appreciation doctrine does not function to keep the marginalised in the margins?

3.3 Themes from within

This section seeks to explore certain themes from the Court's case law in order to identify how the Court could, from within its own tradition, begin to develop its modes of analysis with a view to recognising and accommodating intersectionality.

3.3.1 Defining groups and identities

The study of intersectionality focuses attention on how analysis in terms of the sameness or difference from a single comparator does not capture the complexity of human identity and human experiences and how traditional one-dimensional and compartmentalised non-discrimination law can be an unsuitable tool to combat such discrimination.[27] On this issue, the open model structure of Art 14 contains a few lessons.

First, it is well established in the case law that the Court has not generally subjected applicants to a strict formal requirement to demonstrate comparability (sameness/difference) with a comparator in order to establish a prima facie case of discrimination. This is particularly true when the identity claimed by the applicant is connected to the 'suspect' discrimination grounds.[28] Second, the non-exhaustive list of discrimination grounds means that the Court has reviewed many discrimination claims where there are in fact no obvious links with any of the usual 'suspect' discrimination grounds such as gender, ethnic origin, religion, etc. Examples of such cases include victims of child sexual abuse,[29] lawyers[30] or particular categories of tenants or landowners.[31] In certain cases the discrimination ground alleged is not even identifiable as such and simply consists in the contested treatment, but the court has reviewed the situation under Art 14 all the same.[32] Third, the case law exhibits a very fluid approach to the construction of the discrimination grounds themselves. By means of this approach, the traditional focus on natural or immutable differences is complemented by an awareness of the complexity of the social construction of identities.[33] Admittedly, the label 'awareness' may not be a wholly accurate description of the Court's approach. This fluid approach to the precise construction of the discrimination grounds may equally be the result of an indifference which arises easily when operating an open model like Art 14. A good example of this approach can be seen in *Thlimmenos*. Mr Thlimmenos was a conscientious objector to military service and had been denied appointment as a chartered accountant due to a conviction for insubordination. He claimed that the group of persons he belonged to was: '. . . male Jehovah's Witnesses whose religion involved compelling reasons for refusing to serve in the armed forces . . .' a group which for the purposes of comparison was: '. . . different from the class of most other criminal offenders'.[34] These characteristics were sufficient for the Court to review the discrimination claim. The question of defining and comparing identities or deciding whether they constituted a particular fixed 'analogous ground' to the ones expressly listed in Art 14 was simply not an issue.[35] Nor did the legal analysis result in dead ends, such as findings of no sex discrimination because the applicant compared himself with other men; no religious discrimination because the practice contested did not affect all religions or even a disproportionately large section of religious people, or no evidence of a difference in treatment since the group of 'other offenders' did not constitute a legitimate comparator. Further, it may come as a surprise to many readers to discover that this judgment, one based on such a loosely construed discrimination ground, constituted the first recognition of reasonable accommodation equality under Art 14. In contrast, in many other legal regimes reasonable accommodation is reserved for the most narrowly construed groups of persons, for example in EU law for persons with disabilities.[36]

Thus, it is clear that when faced with the complexities of individual and collective identities and histories of social marginalisation, the Court does not have to hit a dead end in its legal analysis. It has already exhibited that it can deal with multidimensional situations. From within its own tradition it has the potential to develop a multidimensional outlook.

3.3.2 *Differences between and within discrimination grounds*

It is important to stress that the last point on a fluid approach to individual and collective identities should not be construed as an argument in support of an approach that applies the same type of scrutiny to all different identities. Different identities do, in fact, receive different levels of scrutiny as already explained. Indeed, that approach should be maintained in order to reflect the different underlying rationales.[37] This differentiated framework in fact represents a substantive approach to equality since the different identities claimed command different types of situational privilege or disadvantage.

According to the approach taken by the Court, the discrimination ground (identity) constitutes the only explicit factor influencing the strictness of review and certainly must be regarded as the most important factor. The discrimination grounds commanding strict scrutiny all refer to personal characteristics that might be construed as 'natural' or 'immutable' in classical terms. Closer inspection reveals, however, that these personal characteristics also relate to group identities which may equally be characterised by reference to a history of social marginalisation and structural disadvantage and this is also reflected in the Court's approach. The claims of applicants in situations of social privilege who claim to be victims of discrimination meet very lenient scrutiny, as can be seen in the claims of companies, lawyers and landlords, whereas a position of historical structural disadvantage will indicate stricter scrutiny as evidenced within the 'suspect' discrimination grounds.

Of particular interest in this respect is the fact that some otherwise unexplained variations in strictness of review can be explained by reference to histories of social disadvantage and marginalisation, even where the same discrimination ground is at issue. For example, the claims of landlords meet more lenient scrutiny than the claims of tenants,[38] the claims of majority churches meet much more lenient scrutiny than the claims of persons belonging to disadvantaged religious groups,[39] and interestingly enough we can also discern that, depending on context, the discrimination claims of men may in fact meet more lenient scrutiny than the claims of women.[40] Indeed, in recent years, the Court appears to have become increasingly aware of the social context of cases. This is evidenced clearly in the 2006 case *Stec and Others*, where the Court reasoned:

> In conclusion, the Court finds that the difference in State pensionable age between men and women in the United Kingdom was originally intended to correct the disadvantaged economic position of women. It continued to be reasonably and objectively justified on this ground until such time that social and economic changes removed the need for special treatment for women.[41]

To be sure, many categories of cases still exist where a distinction is based on a clearly defined identity associated with a history of social marginalisation, but where the Court has not expressly elevated the relevant discrimination ground to the 'suspect' category indicating strict scrutiny. In those cases, the Court struggles with the appropriateness of judicial intervention on the basis of the discrimination claim. The values behind conceptualising such issues as equality claims are not as developed as in respect of the usual suspects. Hence, such discrimination grounds can be said to be under development and to command intermediate scrutiny. In many such cases the Court deals with the issues under other Convention Articles, such as the protection of private life under Art 8, and hence finds it unnecessary to review the discrimination claim. Examples belonging to this category include transsexualism, disability, age, language, political or other opinion, social origin and similar identities.[42]

In conclusion, it is an express part of the Court's repertoire to differentiate between the different discrimination grounds. In more subtle ways it also differentiates within single discrimination grounds by reference to the different contexts and social positioning implied. The established and valid rationale for differentiating between discrimination grounds can and should be brought to bear on differences within single discrimination grounds and also between different combinations of discrimination grounds liable to create synergetic vulnerabilities. Again, the ingredients already exist within the Court's own tradition to facilitate a multidimensional approach.

3.3.3 Purposeful and contextual review

Notwithstanding this open and fluid model for dealing with multiple identities and intersectionality, one very difficult issue remains. As already explained the margin of appreciation methodology as applied by the Court has a certain potential to keep the marginalised in the margins. The danger is particularly acute when the Court emphasises the 'common ground' across the legislation of the Member States. The resulting picture risks constituting a hegemony of mainstream majoritarian approaches, that is to say, if the injustice or marginalisation in question is not generally recognised by national legislators, the Court considers it unnecessary to acknowledge or act upon that injustice. Accordingly, the compelling questions relevant to multidimensional equality appear to be as follows: When should particular identities or particular combinations of identities be raised to the level of indicating strict scrutiny and when and how should particular contexts figure in adjusting the strictness of review? Again, it seems possible to seek some guidance from the dynamics of the case law on Art 14.

The basic values permeating the whole of the Convention system are adherence to democratic rule, a western liberal conception of the state and a certain focus on individualism. The emphasis is on civil and political rights and negative obligations. At the same time, however, under Art 14, the Court exhibits sensitivity to the situation of disadvantaged and marginalised groups and has moved towards a substantive approach to equality. The state of the case law on Art 14 now represents a moderate form of a substantive equality paradigm consisting of the following key ingredients: a normative import into the equality maxim that reflects a concern for equal outcomes and social justice; the conceptualisation of equality and non-discrimination in terms of social groups as well in terms of individuals; and a contextual analysis of equality, difference and structural patterns of disadvantage. This approach can be summarised in the keyword of *inclusion* that has become an intrinsic normative factor in the concepts of equality and non-discrimination under the Convention. Although departures from formal and symmetrical equality are conceptualised as exceptions, in the future this normative value of inclusion will have to be accorded increasing weight in striking a balance with the foundational formal approach.[43]

The type of review of individual discrimination claims which accompanies such a substantive paradigm may be characterised as both purposeful and contextual. The review is *purposeful* in that it is premised on the end result of equal outcomes as between groups, thus one can speak of the Court as having a particular aim or purpose in mind when applying Art 14. In addition, the review is *contextual* in that it focuses attention on structural patterns of privilege/disadvantage and inclusion/exclusion in the analysis of individual cases. The ingredients of such an approach already exist in the case law of the Court. Their existence can be discerned from the characteristics of the case law already discussed in this chapter, that is to say, a fluid approach to the construction of the relevant individual and collective identities and a variable approach to the strictness of review which is sensitive to the context and unique situation of each applicant. Notwithstanding the presence of those ingredients, the approach has not been expressly thought out or consciously developed by the Court. Rather, the approach may only be discerned when analysing the trends and patterns that appear in the Art 14 case law. At the same time, however, it is clear that the case law exhibits other strong trends and patterns which spring from a foundational formal and individualised approach to equality.[44] These function as limits on the extent to which a purposeful and contextual approach can be developed. Indeed, the internal tension between the formal and substantive models of equality represented in the Convention and the case law on Art 14 will continue to exist. The search for a balance is a gradual and cyclical process. However, the value of inclusion and the attendant contextual and purposeful scrutiny has decisively entered into the balancing act. This is the situation referred to above as the perpetual site of contestation as the case law on Art 14 evolves, that is to say, where the traditional 'common ground' mainstream approaches which reflect either the formal, individualised paradigm or the classical one-dimensional approach to equality are challenged with arguments and claims from the margins which reflect the more substantive and multidimensional schools of thought.[45]

The way to avoid the potential hegemony of the mainstream 'common ground' approach is to develop further a workable concept of *purposeful and contextual* review based on existing trends within the Convention case law.

Such review critically addresses asymmetrical structures of power and dominance and is conscious of the need to examine carefully how our conceptions of rights, our tools and approaches may in unsaid and covert ways function to maintain or aggravate situations of marginalisation and exclusion. Some situations, such as intersectional situations, may need specific accommodation and acknowledgement in order to achieve true equality and inclusion of the marginalised. A first important step towards developing such a tool is to ensure that the majoritarian 'common ground' analysis is tempered by way of balancing it against the other factors that the Court has identified as relevant to the width of the margin of appreciation, namely, the factors relating to the background and context of the case. If these contextual factors focus on the particular positioning of the individual victim of discrimination in terms of histories of social disadvantage and exclusion, this permits a deeper understanding of equality and multidimensionality to be developed. Another very important factor in fashioning an effective tool of purposeful and contextual review would be to adopt a bottom-up and not top-down approach to the analysis.[46] Such a bottom-up approach entails that the Court endeavours to adopt the internal standpoint of the aggrieved person and to analyse the case not from within the prevailing norm, which may only function to perpetuate the situation contested, but from the situation of the aggrieved persons themselves. Drawing on the Convention's existing understanding of substantive equality, it follows that the emphasis in the analysis must be placed on inclusion on the terms of the marginalised (the other) and not on the terms of the privileged (the prevailing standard).[47] From within the Court's interpretative tradition, the well-established purposive method of interpretation and the principle of effectiveness of protection strongly support this approach.[48]

3.3.4 Balancing acts

A compartmentalised ('additive') approach to equality law refers to the situation when new discrimination grounds are added to existing ones, but each ground has its own domain and legal framework. It has been pointed out that such an approach is likely to result in the development of hierarchies as a technique for the resolution of conflicts between discrimination grounds.[49] The argument reflects Kimberlé Crenshaw's critique that the top-down approach of compartmentalised equality law misses intersectional vulnerabilities.[50] As an example of this weakness we might consider the Islamic headscarf issue where gender may be prioritised over ethnicity. As an alternative, an integrated approach to all the different discrimination grounds has been proposed by which such hierarchies could be avoided.[51]

Once again, the dynamics in the Convention case law and a human rights approach may have something to offer on this point. The Convention entails very few absolutes or hierarchies.[52] Instead, the Convention and its case law are permeated with balancing acts between opposing interests and colliding rights. As examples, it suffices to mention Paragraph 2 in each of Arts 8 to 11 which allow limitations to rights if they are 'necessary in a democratic society', and the margin of appreciation doctrine which applies generally across the Convention subject only to a few exceptions related to Convention absolutes.[53] Under Art 14, the tradition of performing balancing acts in relation to opposing interests and colliding rights may be brought to bear on situations where different identities and equalities have the potential to collide. Under a human rights approach, resolving the conflicts will rest on a balancing act and not hierarchies. Guidance on how to perform the balancing act can be provided by a developed concept of purposeful and contextual review as set out above.

3.4 Conclusions

The title of this chapter, 'Multidimensional equality from within', refers to two interconnected themes. First, it refers to the seeds that lie within the Convention itself and the Court's own tradition and which may permit a successful analysis of multidimensional situations. Second, it refers to the standpoint of analysis from within the context and situation of the aggrieved person, where this standpoint constitutes a key ingredient in such analysis.

Seemingly the seeds exist for an approach which has the potential to answer the calls for multidimensional equality developed at a theoretical level and which demand better informed attention to the situations of those who are disadvantaged the most. Such an approach would truly embrace the real task of human rights law, to ensure the fair and proper treatment of the marginalised and to prevent the abuse of dominant positions. It would correspond to the deeper and more developed human rights law of the twenty-first century that seeks to move beyond the dualities, hierarchies and dichotomies of the past.[54] The indifference of the single open-model discrimination clause to the precise construction of discrimination grounds and the unique sensitivities of the human rights model to context, pluralisms and balancing acts have much to offer to equality law and equality discourse in the national or European setting. Arguably, the model of Art 14 may serve as a good test site for the application of a single harmonised non-discrimination clause enabling the multidimensionality of human identities and experiences to be addressed.

The development of a purposeful and contextual approach under the Convention is, however, no easy task. Moreover, such an approach will not be able to provide any easy answers to the hard cases. In *Leyla Sahin* the Court reiterated the principle that: 'Democracy does not simply mean that the views of the majority must always prevail: a balance must be achieved which ensures the fair and proper treatment of people from minorities and avoids any abuse of dominant position'.[55] The judgment itself is difficult to assess in light of this principle. It can be argued that Leyla Sahin's religious and ethnic identity was subjugated to the mainstream western construction of her headscarf as a sign of female oppression.[56] Arguably, therefore, the Court got the balancing act wrong in its judgment. The Court's review, however, placed great weight on the unique Turkish context of the case.[57] Thus, we may query whether there is perhaps a difference between the contexts in this case and many other cases. Within the scope of a contextual review we also need to ask questions such as: Is Leyla Sahin's situation a disadvantaged one in its local Turkish context? Is the requirement not to wear the headscarf at her university oppressive in that context? Would it be different in a different context? It is not the aim of this chapter to answer these questions; rather the point is to demonstrate that purposeful and contextual review takes them into account.

The model of Art 14 does not constitute a magical solution to all the issues raised, and by no means does this chapter argue that any magical solution can be achieved through the adoption of any type of legislation.[58] Rather, the point is that although legal solutions are not magical ones we should avoid discounting or disregarding their potential altogether. The development of appropriate solutions to the many different situations that need to be addressed will be an extremely cumbersome project under the open and general principle prescribed in Art 14. For example, in *Stec and Others* and *Christine Goodwin*, developments under the more ground-specific approach of EU gender-equality law clearly had an effect on the Court's interpretation. The lesson to be learned is that although a single harmonised statute for all the different discrimination grounds and a human rights approach open up some of the issues relevant to multidimensional equality, they will be unable to do all of the work. For effective protection, there will also be a need for the more tailor-made approaches. In my view, whether contained in one statute or in multiple interconnected statutes, both types of approaches need to coexist in order to complement one another.

Notes

1 Convention for the Protection of Human Rights and Fundamental Freedoms, 4 November 1950, CETS 5 (effective 3 September 1953).
2 Protocol No 12 to the Convention for the Protection of Human Rights and Fundamental Freedoms, 4 November 2000, CETS 177 (effective 1 April 2005), *Explanatory report*, para 2.
3 S Fredman (2001) 'Equality: A new generation?', *Industrial Law Journal*, 30: 145–68.
4 Ibid, see also, for example, D Schiek (2005) 'Broadening the scope and the norms of EU gender equality law: Towards a multidimensional conception of equality law', *Maastricht Journal of European and Comparative Law*, 12: 427–66, at p 460 and B Hepple, M Choussey and T Choudhoury (2000) *Equality: A New Framework: Report of the Independent Review of the Enforcement of UK Anti-Discrimination Legislation*, Oxford: Hart Publishing.
5 I use the term in the same sense as developed by Schiek, ibid, p 461.
6 K Crenshaw (1989) 'Demarginalizing the intersection of race and sex: A black feminist critique of antidiscrimination doctrine, feminist theory and antiracial politics', *The University of Chicago Legal Forum*: 139–67, at p 140. She refers to intersectionality as addressing 'the complexities of compoundedness', ibid, p 166.

Thlimmenos v Greece [GC], Reports 2000-IV, provides an example of an inter-sectional situation where the combination of the sex, religion and profession of the applicant created his unique situation, discussed further in 'Themes from within' (below).

7 K Crenshaw (2000) 'The intersectionality of race and gender discrimination', draft paper on file with author, pp 12–17. An earlier version of this paper was originally presented as the background paper for the Expert Group Meeting on Gender and Race Discrimination, Zagreb, Croatia, 21–24 November, available at www.wicej.addr.com/wcar_docs/crenshaw.html (accessed 4 January 2008).

8 *Explanatory report*, paras 18–20.

9 *Belgian Linguistics Case* (1968) 1 EHRR 252, Series A, No 280, para 10.

10 OM Arnardóttir (2003) *Equality and Non-Discrimination under the European Convention on Human Rights*, The Hague: Martinus Nijhoff Publishers, Chs 4–6.

11 *Thlimmenos v Greece* [GC], Reports 2000–IV

12 Recent developments appear to indicate that the Court only applies a fairly loose proportionality test (lenient scrutiny) to the justification of such programmes that states choose to adopt. See, for example, *Stec and Others v United Kingdom* [GC], 12 April 2006, unpublished, available at http://cmiskp.echr.coe.int/tkp197/view.asp?item=1&portal=hbkm&action=html&highlight=Stec&sessionid=2174260&skin=hudoc-en (accessed 15 September 2007).

13 *Explanatory report*, paras 16 and 24–8.

14 I Sjerps (1999) 'Effects and justifications – Or how to establish a prima facie case of indirect sex discrimination' in T Loenen and PR Rodrigues (eds), *Non-Discrimination Law: Comparative Perspectives*, The Hague: Kluwer Law International, pp 237–47, at p 247.

15 *DH and Others v Czech Republic* [GC] 13 November 2007, available at http://cmiskp.eckr.coe.int/tkp/97/view.asp?item=4&portral=hbkm&action=html&highlight=D%20%7C%20H%20%7C%other&sessionid=7362694&skin=hudoc=en (accessed 3 May 2008) see also *McKerr v United Kingdom*, Reports 2001-III, para 165; and *Hugh Jordan v United Kingdom*, 4 May 2001, unpublished, available at http://cmiskp.echr.coe.int/tkp197/view.asp?item=1&portal=hbkm&action=html&highlight=Hugh%20%7C%20Jordan&sessionid=3995895&skin=hudoc-en (accessed 15 September 2007).

16 For a fuller discussion and analysis of the case law before *DH and Others*, see OM Arnardóttir (2007) 'Non-discrimination under Article 14 ECHR – the burden of proof', *Scandinavian Studies in Law*, 51: 13–39. See also J Kokott (1998) *The Burden of Proof in Comparative and International Human Rights Law*, The Hague: Kluwer Law International, p 215. Kokott argues that the allocation of the burden of proof fulfils a similar function to that of the margin of appreciation.

17 See, *DH and Others v Czech Republic* [GC], 13 November 20007, unpublished (see n 15 above for web reference), paras 193–4.

18 P Mahoney (1990) 'Judicial activism and judicial restraint in the European Court of Human Rights: two sides of the same coin', *Human Rights Law Journal*, 11: 57–88 and P Mahoney (1998) 'Marvellous richness of diversity or invidious cultural relativism?', *Human Rights Law Journal*, 19: 1–6.

19 Mahoney, 'Marvellous richness', ibid, pp 2–3.

20 *Rasmussen v Denmark*, Series A, No 87 (1985) 7 EHRR 371, para 40. Emphasis added.

21 P Mahoney (1998) 'Marvellous richness of diversity or invidious cultural relativism?', *Human Rights Law Journal*, 19: 1–6, at p 2.

22 See, for example, *Abdulaziz, Cabales and Balkandali v United Kingdom*, Series A, No 94 (1985) 7 EHRR 471, para 78.

23 *Stec and Others v United Kingdom* [GC], 12 April 2006, unpublished (see n 12 above for web reference).

24 *Christine Goodwin v United Kingdom* [GC], Reports 2002-VI. See for example para 100, where the Court argued: 'It is true that the first sentence refers in express terms to the right of a man and woman to marry. The Court is not persuaded that at the date of this case it can still be assumed that these terms must refer to a determination of gender by purely biological criteria'.

25 See the development which occured between cases such as *Dudgeon v United Kingdom*, Series A, No 45 (1983) 5 EHRR 573, para 70 and *Smith and Grady v United Kingdom*, Reports 1999-VI, para 116, in which the Court found it unnecessary to review Art 14 and the discrimination issue was left untouched to cases such as *Salgueiro da Silva Mouta v Portugal*, Reports 1999-IX, para 36 and *L and V v Austria*, Reports 2003-I, para 35, in which the discrimination aspect took precedence over the protection of private life issue.

26 *Leyla Sahin v Turkey* [GC], 10 November 2005, unpublished, available at http://cmiskp.echr.coe.int/tkp197/view.asp?item=4&portal=hbkm&action=html&highlight=Sahin&sessionid=2175563&skin=hudoc-en (accessed 15 September 2007).

27 K Crenshaw(1989) 'Demarginalizing the intersection of race and sex: A black feminist critique of antidiscrimination doctrine, feminist theory and antiracial politics', *The University of Chicago Legal Forum*: 139–67, at pp 166–7 and S Hannett (2003) 'Equality at the intersections: The legislative and judicial failure to tackle multiple discrimination', *Oxford Journal of Legal Studies*, 23: 65–86, at p 86.

28 See OM Arnardóttir (2007) 'Non-discrimination under Article 14 ECHR – the burden of proof', *Scandinavian Studies in Law*, 51: 13–39, at pp 32–5 and OM Arnardóttir (2003) *Equality and Non-Discrimination under the European Convention on Human Rights*, The Hague: Martinus Nijhoff Publishers, pp 84–91.

29 *Stubbings and Others v United Kingdom*, Reports 1996-IV. The claim concerned the lack of accommodation for the unique situation of victims of child sexual abuse as compared with victims of other intentionally caused harm. No discrimination was held to exist.

30 *Van Der Mussele v Belgium*, Series A, No 70 (1984) 6 EHRR 163. No discrimination was held to exist in the fact that trainee advocates had to do pro bono work whereas no such duty prevailed with regard to other professions.

31 *Larkos v Cyprus*, Reports 1999-I. A violation of Art 14 was held to exist in that tenants of the state were not accorded the same social protection as tenants of private property owners. *Chassagnou and Others v France*, Reports 1999-III. A violation of Art 14 was held to exist in that small landowners had to bear greater burdens than large landowners.

32 *Building Societies v United Kingdom*, Reports 1997-VII. The discrimination ground alleged consisted simply in the fact that two successive pieces of legislation did not reach all the implicated building societies in the same manner.

33 *Christine Goodwin v United Kingldom* [GC], Reports 2002–VI, is an example in the context of Art 12.

34 *Thlimmenos v Greece* [GC], Reports 2000–IV para 34.

35 For example, D Schiek (2005) 'Broadening the scope and the norms of EU gender equality law: Towards a multidimensional conception of equality law', *Maastricht Journal of European and Comparative Law*, 12: 427–66, at p 459, has pointed out how the approach of defining particular combinations of discrimination grounds (e.g. black women) as analogous to the list of prohibited discrimination grounds still forces people to categorise themselves along fixed identities.

36 Council Directive 2000/78/EC establishing a general framework for equal treatment in employment and occupation [2000] OJ L303/16, Art 2(2)(a)(ii).

37 For a good overview of the different rationales and relevant literature see D Schiek (2005) 'Broadening the scope and the norms of EU gender equality law: Towards a

multidimensional conception of equality law', *Maastricht Journal of European and Comparative Law*, 12: 427–66, at pp 443–8.

38 Compare, for example, the treatment of landlords' claims in *James and Others v United Kingdom*, Series A, No 98 (1986) 8 EHRR 123 and *Spadea and Scalabrino v Italy*, Series A, No 315-B, with the treatment of a tenant's claim in *Larkos v Cyprus*, Reports 1999–I.

39 Compare, for example, *Holy Monasteries v Greece*, Series A, No 301-A (1995) 20 EHRR 1 and *Thlimmenos v Greece* [GC], Reports 2000–IV.

40 Compare for example *Schuler-Zgraggen v Switzerland*, Series A, No 263 (1993) 16 EHRR 405 with *Rasmussen v Denmark*, Series A, No 87 (1985) 7 EHRR 371, where the same presumption on the primary role of women in childcare functioned to the detriment of a woman and a man respectively, and met different levels of scrutiny.

41 *Stec and Others v United Kingdom* [GC], 12 April 2006, unpublished (see n 12 above for web reference), para 66.

42 The discrimination ground of sexual orientation is an example of how discrimination grounds can move between the intermediate and 'suspect' categories, see above n 25. As regards disability in particular, the Court's case law on reasonable accommodation is only beginning to evolve. See *Botta v Italy*, Reports 1998-I, *Pretty v United Kingdom*, Reports 2002-III and *Tysiac v Poland*, 20 March 2007, unpublished, available at http://cmiskp.echr.coe.int/tkp197/view.asp?item= 1&portal=hbkm&action=html&highlight=Tysiac%20%7C%2014&sessionid= 2179321&skin=hudoc-en (accessed 15 September 2007).

43 OM Arnardóttir (2007) 'Non-discrimination in international and European law: Towards substantive models', *Nordisk Tidsskrift for Menneskerettigheter*, 25: 140–57, at pp 156–7.

44 In particular, as discussed earlier, the Court's approach to disproportionate effect discrimination bears witness to its prevailing individualised approach. Similarly, D Ashiagbor (1999) 'The intersections between gender and "race" in the labour market: Lessons for anti-discrimination law', in A Morris and T O'Donell (eds), *Feminist Perspectives on Employment Law*, London: Cavendish, pp 139–60, at pp 151–3, argues that an individualised equality model restricts the scope to consider the social reality of underlying structural disadvantage when establishing a prima facie case of discrimination.

45 This site of contestation in the case law occupies the same space as do critical race theory and other critical approaches which develop in the tension between the dominant mainstream (the Standard) and the margins (the Other), see generally: D Otto (1997) 'Rethinking the "universality" of human rights law', *Columbia Human Rights Law Review*, 29: 1–46, at pp 19–24. The purpose and result is not to create new dichotomies but: '. . . to continually rebuild modernisms in the light of postmodernist critique'. see AP Harris (1994) 'Foreword: The jurisprudence of reconstruction', *California Law Review*, 82: 741–85, at p 744 (also cited by Otto, ibid).

46 Kimberlé Crenshaw discusses how traditional non-discrimination law is based on the premise that the discrimination ground in question is a factor that interferes with an otherwise fair or neutral decision. This, she argues, is facilitated by a top-down approach to the analysis of discrimination claims that has the effect that: '. . . sex and race discrimination have come to be defined in terms of the experiences of those who are privileged *but for* their racial or sexual characteristics'. See K Crenshaw (1989) 'Demarginalizing the intersection of race and sex: A black feminist critique of antidiscrimination doctrine, feminist theory and antiracial politics', *The University of Chicago Legal Forum*: 139–67, at p 151.

47 This argument develops in the context of the European Convention on Human Rights, Kimberlé Crenshaw's emphasis that contextual analysis is necessary in

order to uncover intersectional vulnerabilities, see K. Crenshaw (2000) 'The intersectionality of race and gender discrimination', draft paper on file with author (originally presented as the background paper for the Expert Group Meeting on Gender and Race Discrimination, Zagreb, Croatia, 21–24 November, available at www.wicej.addr.com/wcar_docs/crenshaw.html (accessed 4 January 2008)) p 19: 'Recognizing and accommodating this problem requires that intersectional protocols place primary focus on contextual analysis. Attention to intersectional discrimination thus calls for an analytical strategy that values a bottom-up analysis. Beginning with the questions about how women live their lives, the analysis can build upward, accounting for the various influences that shape the lives and life changes of marginalized women. Particularly important is uncovering how policies and practices may shape their lives differently from those who are not exposed to similar obstacles'.

48 On these methods of interpretation see, for example, *Christine Goodwin v United Kingdom* [GC], Reports 2002–VI, para 74 and J Merrills (1988) *The Development of International Law by The European Court of Human Rights*, Manchester: Manchester University Press.

49 D Schiek (2005) 'Broadening the scope and the norms of EU gender equality law: Towards a multidimensional conception of equality law', *Maastricht Journal of European and Comparative Law*, 12: 427–66, at pp 440 and 452.

50 J Crenshaw (1989) 'Demarginalizing the intersection of race and sex: A black feminist critique of antidiscrimination doctrine, feminist theory and antiracial politics', *The University of Chicago Legal Forum*: 139–67, at pp 166–7.

51 D Schiek (2005) 'Broadening the scope and the norms of EU gender equality law: Towards a multidimensional conception of equality law', *Maastricht Journal of European and Comparative Law*, 12: 427–66, at p 454 and the references cited therein. Schiek notes, however, that a downside to such an integrated approach consists in its potential dilution of the issues and resulting loss of focus (ibid).

52 Some exceptions do nevertheless exist. Article 15(2) establishes the non-derogable nature of the rights under Arts 2, 3, 4(1) and 7. The *forum internum* under Art 9 also constitutes an absolute right. Democracy, of course, is the overarching 'super value' of the Convention system to the extent that upholding democratic rule appears to be an absolute under the Convention. In *United Communist Party of Turkey and Others v Turkey*, Reports 1998–I, para 45, the Court stated: 'The Convention was designed to maintain the ideals and values of a democratic society . . . Democracy thus appears to be the only political model contemplated by the Convention and, accordingly, the only one compatible with it'.

53 Some commentators, however, criticise the case law for its lack of coherence and argue for a more formal and legalistic (hierarchical) approach to dispensing constitutional justice. See, for example, S Greer (2003) 'Constitutionalising adjudication under the European Convention On Human Rights', *Oxford Journal of Legal Studies*, 23: 405–33.

54 Otto (1997) 'Rethinking the "universality" of Human Rights Law', *Columbia Human Rights Law Review*, 29: 1–46, at pp 36–7 argues that: 'Transformative strategies in human rights must move beyond the dualistic and hierarchical Standards of modernity . . . We must resist the duality of modernity and poststructuralism and find ways to draw on both reservoirs of knowledge in order to work towards a world without domination'. Sandra Fredman also points out how the social rights model under the EU regime has developed to represent a 'third way' beyond the traditional dichotomies between neo-liberalism and social democracy, economic policy and social policy, the market and the state, see S Fredman (2006) 'Transformation or dilution: Fundamental rights in the EU social space', *European Law Journal*, 12: 41–60, at pp 43–4. In terms of human rights law, the move beyond dichotomies is reflected in the move from the traditional emphasis on civil

and political rights and the negative obligations of states towards an increased emphasis on their combination with economic, social and cultural rights and the positive obligations of states, see generally IE Koch (2006) 'Economic, social and cultural rights as components in civil and political rights: A hermeneutic perspective', *International Journal of Human Rights*, 10: 405–30. The adoption and development of purposeful and contextual review in the form introduced in this chapter would represent yet another move beyond the dualities of the past.

55 *Leyla Sahin v Turkey* [GC], 10 November 2005, unpublished (web reference see n 26 above), para 108.

56 Ibid, para 115.

57 Ibid, paras 118–21.

58 I share the doubts of many authors as to the question of whether a legal solution, with its tendency to simplify and compartmentalise, and an individual rights claims model can ever really deal with all the complexities raised in the discourse on substantive and intersectional equality, see, for example, S Hannett (2003) 'Equality at the intersections: The legislative and judicial failure to tackle multiple discrimination', *Oxford Journal of Legal Studies*, 23: 65–86, at pp 85–6 and D Ashiagbor (1999) 'The intersections between gender and "race" in the labour market: Lessons for anti-discrimination law', in A Morris and T O'Donell (eds) *Feminist Perspectives on Employment Law*, London: Cavendish, pp 139–60, at pp 157–8.

4 Positive rights and positive duties

Addressing intersectionality

Sandra Fredman

4.1 Introduction

The expansion of EU discrimination law over a wider range of grounds opens up the possibility of addressing multiple and intersectional sources of discrimination. But the extent to which intersectionality can be addressed is hampered by established models of anti-discrimination enforcement, which depend on individual complaints to courts or tribunals. At the same time, it is increasingly recognised that the complaints-led approach to equality needs to be supplemented by proactive duties if real change is to be achieved. This chapter examines the extent to which proactive duties to promote equality can be harnessed to address the challenges of intersectionality.

Intersectionality disrupts established group demarcations used in anti-discrimination law. To assume that groups are rigidly delineated by race, gender, disability, sexual orientation or other status, is to render invisible those that are found in the intersection between those groups. Intersectionality becomes more visible through positive duties to promote equality than under a complaints-led approach, since those responsible for instituting change are required to identify group inequalities and to craft solutions, rather than reacting to self identified complainants. But by making it possible to address intersectionality, a proactive approach also exposes the limits of our current understanding of how and why we identify groups in the context of equality law. This chapter explores these challenges by examining the relationship between the definition of group identities and the conceptualisation of the goals and meanings of equality. It is not just the gender, race or other status of a group which is at issue, but the ways in which these status markers create or perpetuate disadvantage or power imbalances, obstruct participation, and undermine dignity and mutual respect. This suggests that in designing proactive measures, groups should be defined not merely in terms of their status markers, but with reference to the particular aims of equality. A closer relationship between aims of equality and group demarcation makes it possible to identify those groups who should be the focus of attention and how their claims should rank in the order of priorities.

This chapter begins by examining the challenges raised by intersectionality on the one hand and positive duties on the other. I then consider the ways in which positive duties can be used to address intersectionality. In particular, it is necessary to define the aims of equality more closely in order to derive criteria according to which groups can be demarcated. In the final section, I briefly examine the role of these concepts within EU law.

4.2 Intersectionality in a context of positive duties

The traditional model of anti-discrimination law generally proscribes detrimental treatment or impact when that detriment is on the grounds of an irrelevant characteristic or is due to membership of a group. This is based on an understanding of group-based discrimination which generally assumes a single identity ascription. EU law for over two decades focused only on gender; it was not until 2000 that other grounds of discrimination were included into EU law. Even then, different provision was made for different aspects of identity, with race and ethnic origin privileged over gender, which was in turn privileged over age, disability, sexual orientation and religion or belief. This potentially entrenches a unitary notion of discrimination: an individual faced with discrimination in respect of education or housing might have a claim under EU law if she can prove it was on grounds of her ethnic origin but not if it was due to her religion.[1]

However, an analysis based on a single source of identity is flawed in several ways. First, it ignores the fact that most people have multiple identities. We all have an age, a gender, a sexual orientation and an ethnicity; many have or acquire a religion or a disability as well. Second, it assumes that identity groups are internally homogenous. Such essentialism obscures the very real differences within identity groups. This issue has been confronted within feminism from the early days when white middle class feminists were rightly criticised by black women for assuming that their own experience was a universal characteristic of gender oppression. Still more fractured are the categories of religion and belief, disability and age. The third flaw of viewing discrimination as if based on a single source of identity is that it ignores the role of power in structuring group relations. Discrimination is not symmetrical; it operates to create or entrench domination by some over others. But such power relations can operate both vertically and diagonally. Thus black men are in a position of power in relation to their gender, but not in relation to their colour. White women conversely are in a position of power in relation to their colour, but not their gender. Power operates at an even more fundamental level, to construct identity categories themselves. Race itself is a social construct, a marker for oppression rather than a biological reality, as the Race Directive itself recognises. Ethnicity is also framed by power relations, with minorities in some countries being majorities in others. This demonstrates that structures of domination work in complex ways which cannot easily captured through a single-identity model.

It is to overcome these limitations that the concept of intersectionality has been developed. The pioneering work was done in the US by African American women, who have powerfully demonstrated the ways in which sex discrimination law focuses on white women, while race discrimination law is targeted at black men. The result is not just that discrimination overlooks the cumulative effect of multiple discrimination. It actually obscures those who fall within the intersection between two groups, negating their experience and failing to provide them with a remedy. As Kimberlé Crenshaw, a well-known thinker on this subject, has argued:

> The paradigm of sex discrimination tends to be based on the experiences of white women; the model of race discrimination tends to be based on the experiences of the most privileged blacks. Notions of what constitutes race and sex discrimination are, as a result, narrowly tailored to embrace only a small set of circumstances, none of which include discrimination against black women.'[2]

For example, in an American case, black women claimed that they had been discriminated against in the application of their employer's seniority system.[3] Because black women were recent entries to the company, they were made redundant first; thereby being worse off than both white women and black men. Thus they could not claim that they had been less favourably treated on grounds of either gender alone or race alone. It was only the cumulative situation, of being both female and black, which was the source of the discrimination.

This demonstrates that intersectional discrimination does not simply consist in the addition of two sources of discrimination; the result is qualitatively different, or synergistic. The disadvantage experienced by black women is not the same as that experienced by white women or black men. Instead, black women form a separate and unique group for the purposes of discrimination law. Within the EU, there are many illustrations of this issue. A particularly salient example is the position of migrant women.[4] Migrants of both genders tend to be concentrated in particular segments of the market, but women with a migrant background are particularly restricted, largely in low paying, low status and insecure jobs such as cleaning, catering, personal and domestic services, health and care.[5] A recent study in Spain showed that all foreign migrants are exposed to discrimination in the labour market, but that migrant women have to accept jobs below their level of qualification much more frequently than migrant men, in most cases as home helps.[6] Women immigrants to the EU from Muslim countries have particularly low activity rates and are largely excluded from the labour market.[7] Women in such communities could be facing discrimination from their own communities on grounds of gender as well as discrimination from the broader society on grounds of ethnicity or religion. In addition, women generally bear the brunt of cuts in public services and welfare, but this burden is disproportionately born by immigrant, minority, disabled and indigenous women.[8]

The resulting difficulty in bringing multiple sources of discrimination into the frame means that policy is often directed at only one aspect of an individual's identity. Thus trafficking in women and girls is usually viewed as a gender discrimination issue.[9] Recognition of an ethnic dimension is, however, crucial to appropriate policy making, since women who are racially marginalised are more at risk of becoming victims of human trafficking; while ethnic discrimination may create a particular demand in the country of destination.[10] Similarly, domestic violence could be seen in terms of the synergistic impact of gender combined with racial or religious discrimination. Many black and minority women find it difficult to speak out against domestic violence, through fear of direct racism by police, or because they are concerned in case reporting violence will reinforce negative stereotypes and expose their own communities to racist treatment, including deportation or injury. Migrant women whose status depends on marriage are particularly vulnerable, since they face deportation if they leave an abusive relationship, a vulnerability compounded by language difficulties, lack of knowledge of sources of protection, and difficulties in finding work or other sources of income to support themselves and their children.[11] This is true too of sexual harassment.[12]

Possibly most at risk of multiple discrimination are women from the Roma, Sinti and traveller communities, as a recent report on the position of Roma and Sinti in Germany[13] demonstrates. While all members of these communities are seriously disadvantaged both at school and in the labour market, women are worse off still. Roma and Sinti girls have even higher rates of abandonment of school than boys, often because they marry early, and find further advancement impossible once they have children. Lack of educational achievement leads directly to rates of employment which are even lower than Roma men, compounded by their child-care obligations and the fact that they often live in remote areas. Training projects for women from majority groups and men from Sinti or Roma groups do not service Sinti or Roma women. Sinti and Roma women are also more likely to be harassed by the police, and multiple discrimination is compounded for those who do not have the country's citizenship. It is estimated that during the 1990s, up to 100,000 of the Roma in Germany were not German citizens. Many who are in fact long-term residents in Germany have no real residence status, only a temporary stay on expulsion ('*duldung*'), which must be renewed very frequently. As a result they live under extreme stress.

Particularly sensitive is the potential conflict between minority rights and gender equality, for example, where gender equality is portrayed as a Western imposition, not appropriate for women in the minority community in question. In such circumstances, uni-dimensional approaches based on gender discrimination, race discrimination, or religious discrimination all fail to capture the complex confluence of discriminatory currents. A key question concerns whose portrayal of the religious, or community view of gender is taken as authoritative. Gender discrimination may be legitimated within ethnic or minority groups by the internal leadership structures, and defended on grounds of multiculturalism or minority rights. Yet it must be asked whether the leadership structures are representative. Where unelected male community leaders mediate relations between the state and minority communities, they may be predominantly concerned with preserving family and religious and cultural values.[14] Only when minority women are given the opportunity to frame their own position, from the perspective of both gender discrimination and discrimination based on ethnicity, race or religion, will it be possible to address this issue.

4.3 Intersectionality and the law: a blunt instrument

The synergistic nature of discrimination means that it has proved difficult to frame policy and law in ways which can address multiple discrimination. Experience of other jurisdictions, particularly in the US, demonstrates the risk that such discrimination may not be captured within the structure of discrimination law, because of an assumption that discrimination falls neatly into one of the named categories. As mentioned above, in the *DeGraffenreid* case in the US, black women's claim that they had been discriminated against in the application of their employer's seniority system failed because they could not show less favourable treatment either as women or as black people, even though they were clearly discriminated against as black women.[15] The US Federal Court of Appeals categorically refused to accept that black women formed a separate category, arguing that this gave them a 'super remedy' or 'greater standing' than black men or white women.[16] Other US cases have been more promising, with the explicit recognition by a US Federal Court of Appeal that discrimination against black women can exist even in the absence of discrimination against black men or white women.[17] However, courts remained wary of opening a 'Pandora's box' to claims by multiple subgroups. This led courts to hold that multiple discrimination should be restricted to a combination of only two of the grounds. On this analysis, only race and gender can be addressed; the impact of sexual orientation, religion, disability or age are ignored. The result is both artificial and paradoxical. The more a person differs from the norm, the more likely she is to experience multiple discrimination, the less likely she is to gain protection.

Intersectionality and multiple discrimination have been particularly difficult to address in UK anti-discrimination law because statutory protection has been developed on a strand-by-strand basis. Thus race and gender discrimination are separately protected through the Race Relations Act 1976 and the Sex Discrimination Act 1975, while disability discrimination was first prohibited in the Disability Discrimination Act 1995. After the Employment Directive came into force, further sets of regulations were separately enacted for religion and belief, sexual orientation and finally age. This separation has been reinforced by separate Commissions for race, gender and disability respectively. It is only now that a single commission has been established, and proposals for single equality legislation are being formulated. In a parallel development, however, the incorporation of the European Convention on Human Rights (ECHR) included the equality in Art 14, which does provide for a single equality guarantee covering a long and non-exclusive list of grounds.

Given this structure, it is not surprising that few cases of multiple discrimination have come before the UK courts. Legal practitioners, with the best interests of their clients at heart, encourage complainants to choose the aspect of their identity which was most likely to succeed.[18] It is possible to bring a complaint under two statutes. But in the only prominent case fully to explore this issue, the UK court insisted that each ground had to be proved separately. For gender, the applicant must find a male comparator who has or would have been treated more favourably; and for race, she must find a white comparator. Thus in *Bahl v Law Society*, the applicant, an Asian woman, complained that she had suffered discrimination both because she was a woman and because she was black. The first instance tribunal held that she had been treated less favourably than a white man would have been, thus upholding her complaint not just on grounds of race and gender, but on grounds of the combination of the two. However, both the Employment Appeal Tribunal and the Court of Appeal rejected this approach.[19]

The synergistic nature of multiple discrimination also makes it difficult to monitor. Many national statistics do not include data disaggregated by both sex and race, still less by other sources of multiple discrimination, such as ethnicity and disability. Thus a recent Irish study demonstrates the invisibility of ethnic minority people with disabilities, an invisibility underlined by the total absence of this group in national statistics.[20] Yet this group suffers in complex and often subtle ways from both race and disability discrimination. Service and healthcare providers tend to ignore their ethnicity in framing structures for accommodating disability, with the result that their culture and identity is devalued and they face greater difficulty accessing appropriate services. At the same time, they might face discrimination from their own ethnic community on grounds of disability.

However, there is now growing recognition of the process and manifestation of multiple and intersectional discrimination. In particular, gender discrimination is experienced very differently by women in different situations. Factors such as class, caste, race, colour, ethnicity, religion, national origin and disability are 'differences that make a difference'.[21] Most important was the contribution of the World Conference for Women held in Beijing in 1995, which drew attention to the fact that age, disability, socio-economic position and membership of a particular ethnic or racial group could create particular barriers for women. A framework for recognition of multiple and co-existing forms of discrimination became a key part of the resulting Beijing Platform for Action. Similarly, the Preamble to the United Nations Convention on the Elimination of All Forms of Discrimination Against Women (CEDAW) emphasises that the eradication of racism is essential to the full enjoyment of the rights of women. Correspondingly, in 2000, the Committee on the Elimination of Racial Discrimination adopted a general recommendation on gender-related dimensions of racial discrimination, which calls upon state parties to report on gendered aspects of race discrimination. As a consequence, Germany was specifically asked to undertake a comprehensive assessment of the position of foreign women and girls as part of its fifth report to the committee.

4.4 Positive duties in anti-discrimination law

The current structure of anti-discrimination law makes it particularly difficult to address intersectionality. Anti-discrimination law has traditionally depended on the complaints-led approach, relying on an individual to bring a claim to a court or tribunal for breach of her right. An individual must therefore choose which category to place herself in. Remedies are retrospective, individual and based on proof of breach, or 'fault'. This is problematic in at least four different ways.[22] First, reliance on an individual complainant to bring an action in court puts excessive strain on the victim both in terms of resources and personal energy. Litigation is lengthy and costly, and many complainants have retired or even died before their claims are resolved. Second, victim-initiated litigation means that the court's intervention is random and ad hoc. Many individuals, particularly non-unionised ones, are unable to pursue their claim. The result is that a large number of cases of discrimination go unremedied. Even if a case is pursued successfully, the result is limited to compensation for the individual or group of complainants, with no ongoing obligations to correct the institutional structure which gave rise to the discrimination. This is problematic, not just for aggrieved individuals, but for those employers who have complied with the law because of a successful complaint and are required to compete with other employers who have not had to adjust because no one has had the courage or resources to bring a complaint. Thus the model cannot produce significant or systematic progress towards the goals of gender equality. Third, the basis in individual fault means that there must be a proved perpetrator. Yet it is now recognised that much inequality is institutional and not the fault of any one person. Finally, individual claims are not only time consuming and costly, but also adversarial. Because they are based on proof of fault, such claims are resisted by employers or the state. Instead of viewing equality as a common goal, to be achieved co-operatively, it becomes a site of conflict and resistance.[23]

Proactive models aim to remedy each of the deficiencies of the complaints-led model above. First, and most importantly, instead of consisting in reactions to ad hoc claims brought by individuals, the initiative lies with policy makers and implementers, service providers or employers. This relieves individual victims of the burden and expense of litigation, achieving results within an acceptable time-frame. Second, change is systematic rather than random or ad hoc, ensuring that all those with a right to equality are covered. The institutional and structural causes of inequality can be diagnosed and addressed collectively and institutionally. Third, in recognition of the institutional basis of discrimination, there is no need to prove fault or find a named perpetrator. Instead, the duty to bring about change lies with those with the power and capacity to do so. Instead of determining fault and punishing conduct, the focus is on systemic discrimination and the creation of institutional mechanisms for their elimination.[24] This means that the right to equality is available to all, not just those who complain. Fourth, proactive duties are prospective as well as retrospective. This means that remedies are not simply retrospective, compensatory and individualised. Instead, they require steps to be taken which are also forward-looking, structural and group based.

Positive duties are an effective means of eliminating unlawful discrimination. They can also be used to go beyond the existing framework of discrimination law, and to promote equality. Positive duties in this sense are a radically new development. They are proactive in that they can be used to assess new policies and practices for their impact on affected groups. They can go further still, and require the creation and implementation of new policies to promote equality. But this in turn creates a series of new challenges. First, given that the aims go beyond existing determinations of unlawful discrimination, it becomes imperative to give some account of the understanding of equality which they are intended to promote. This is particularly so in that proactive models are able to link up different sorts of equality concerns, addressing recognition aspects of discrimination, such as prejudice, stigma and humiliation; distributive aspects, such as social exclusion and unemployment; and participative aspects. Most importantly, for our purposes, they are able to span more than one source of discrimination.

Second, by placing the initiative on those responsible for bringing about change rather than the victim herself, the model is inherently a top-down approach. While this is one of the strengths of the new model, it also creates a potential participatory vacuum. This focuses on the need to build proper participation into the new model. It also requires greater thought to be given to the role of the participant. Participation could be individual, group or representative. Its function could be simply to give or obtain information, or go further and include consultation and even co-decision-making. At their strongest, proactive models broaden the participatory role of civil society, both in norm setting and in norm enforcing. In this sense, the citizen is characterised not as a passive recipient but an active participant. This participatory dimension fundamentally influences the nature of the norms themselves. Instead of fixed and predetermined legal rights or obligations, the proactive model produces norms which are dynamic and renegotiable.

The third challenge posed by proactive duties in this sense is to create an appropriate compliance regime. To work properly, positive duties need to be championed by those at the top of the institutional hierarchy, to be an integral part of decision-making strategy rather than an add-on once major decisions have been made.[25] The recognition of the weakness of the complaints -led model requires further thought to be given to how to ensure this happens. A range of levers, particularly through procurement policies, should be available in addition to the role of stakeholders, Commissions and a long-stop judicially enforceable sanction. This, in turn, requires transparency and mechanisms for monitoring and ongoing review. Finally, the relationship between fundamental rights and positive duties needs further interrogation. Given that equality norms are delivered through policy rather than through individual litigation, there is a risk that they come to be regarded as discretionary rather than an essential mode of delivery of the fundamental right to equality.

4.5 Intersectionality and positive action

Positive duties open up many more possibilities to deal with intersectionality than a complaints-led model. This is true both in respect of the function of eliminating unlawful discrimination and the proactive function of promoting equality. Rather than relying on a self-identified complainant to show that she has been treated less favourably on a particular ground than a comparator, positive duties require public or private bodies to identify sources of inequality and take action to bring about change. There is no need to prove specifically that a person was treated less favourably than a comparator is or would be, and therefore many problems in finding an appropriate comparator are avoided. This means that cumulative, intersectional and multiple discrimination can be dealt with more effectively. A subgroup, such as ethnic minority women, or disabled older people, or gay youths can be separately identified as suffering from discrimination and measures taken to redress that.

At the same time, positive action raises its own challenges. To address intersectionality requires an understanding of how to delineate groups and subgroups. But this can only be done if we are clear about what we are trying to achieve. The traditional aim of equality legislation was to treat everyone on merit regardless of their race, gender or other prohibited ground. However, it is now acknowledged that treating people the same may have a disproportionate detrimental effect on one group, because it has or continues to suffer disadvantage. In addition, as feminist writers have long argued, 'merit' itself is not an objective concept. Instead 'merit' reflects the values of the dominant group, and is biased against the very groups who, due to discrimination, have been unable to achieve in the same way as the dominant group. This has important ramifications for the way in which we demarcate the target groups of positive action. It is not necessarily a person's race, gender, age or sexual orientation that needs to be addressed, but the detrimental consequences attached to membership of particular groups. Thus gender refers to men as well as women, race to whites as well as blacks, ethnicity to the dominant and the minority group, and sexual orientation to both heterosexuals and homosexuals. But it is not this which is at issue. Instead, it is the fact that being a woman, black or a member of an ethnic minority, being gay, old, young or disabled carries with it or is associated with detriment that equality aims to challenge. Thus, at least as a preliminary point, groups cannot be delineated simply by their gender, race, etc. Instead, an asymmetric approach is needed, which targets the disadvantaged group, women, blacks, ethnic minorities and others. Moreover, as the above discussion suggests, a further step is needed. Within each category, there are subgroups which are more disadvantaged than others, and these subgroups more often than not are those which intersect with other groups. This, in turn, requires a more sophisticated notion of the aims of positive action to promote equality.

An elaboration of the aims of equality can usefully be divided into issues relating to recognition, to redistribution and to participation and power.[26] The concept of 'recognition' in this context derives from Hegel's foundational view that individual identity derives from inter-subjective recognition within the context of social relations. An individual on this view only becomes an individual by virtue of recognising others and being recognised by them.[27] Fraser argues that recognition is about social status, the relative standing of social actors within cultural value patterns.[28] Status subordination or misrecognition arises when cultural value patterns constitute some as inferior, excluded or invisible.[29] Status groups are consequently defined not by relations of production, but of esteem, respect and prestige enjoyed relative to other groups in society.[30] Fraser points to two possible responses to status subordination. The first is to eliminate the status itself. The second is to retain the status, but to eliminate the hierarchy. The first approach is based on the underlying premise that group differences are constructed in order to establish and reinforce hierarchical relationships. This requires a deconstruction of difference. The second asserts that differences are 'benign, pre-existing cultural variations which have been maliciously transformed into a value hierarchy by an unjust interpretative schema'. This requires not elimination of group difference, but its celebration through revaluing devalued traits.[31]

Drawing on these insights, one of the primary aims of equality can be seen to remove status subordination, or mis-recognition. Fraser's first option, which entails ignoring status difference, has proved problematic because it assumes that there is a neutral position, from which all can be valued. In practice, however, the 'neutral' position turns out to be clothed in the values of the dominant group, whether it be male, white, able-bodied, heterosexual or ethnic majority. Instead, it is argued here, removing status subordination has two aspects: removing the stigmatic consequences of group identity while simultaneously respecting and supporting diverse identities. Thus a central aim of equality laws should be to prohibit the stigma, hatred, humiliation and violence which are directed at a person because of her group membership. Sexual harassment, racist abuse, prejudicial treatment, and lack of respect for one's dignity are all detriments in this sense. Simultaneously, equality requires that individuals be recognised for what they are. To demand that an individual conform to the dominant norm as a price for inclusion would undermine the principle of equality. Thus the second main aim of equality is that different identities be accommodated and respected.

The third aim of equality relates to redistributive justice rather than to recognition. This entails an acknowledgement that it is not colour, gender or some other group characteristic per se which is in issue, but the attendant disadvantage, both social and economic. It is by now more than familiar to acknowledge that economic disadvantage is disproportionately concentrated among groups experiencing status-based discrimination. Women, ethnic groups, the disabled, the young and the old, are unduly represented amongst the poorest in society. These structures of inequality are left intact by understandings of equality which focus only on individual prejudice or misrecognition. This is not to say that recognition and redistributive aspects of equality can be kept separate. Status inequalities both cause and are reinforced by socio-economic disadvantage. For example, women's unequal pay in the market is due to a misrecognition and therefore undervaluation of their work. This creates distributive disadvantage which itself contributes to women's lower status in the labour market. Thus positive duties must address both recognition and redistribution.

The fourth major goal of equality is to address power imbalances through facilitating participation. Participation itself is a multi-faceted concept. It includes participation in decision-making, giving a voice to the voiceless so that they can be part-authors of the policies and practices which affect them. It also includes participation in society, incorporating the excluded and marginalised. For example, one of the major sources of inequality for older people is the fact that they are excluded both from decision-making on issues which affect them, and from social citizenship, since they are retired from the world of work and may be unable to access other social forms. Participation is also sometimes registered in terms of outcome measures, such as the extent to which a group is under-represented in a workforce, or in Parliament or other decision-making body.

Bringing these insights together yields four goals of equality: removing recognition-based harms of harassment, prejudice, stigma and violence; affirming and accommodating identity; redressing distributive disadvantage; and enhancing participation. Each of these can be mapped on to a way of identifying groups and sub-groups which are the targets of action. This is particularly sensitive to intersectionality, since it highlights not so much the additive nature of the two sources of discrimination, but the qualitative or synergistic quality of intersectional discrimination. It also counters the fear by judges and law-makers that addressing multiple discrimination would open a 'Pandora's box' to claims by multiple sub-groups. A closer relationship between aims and group demarcation makes it possible to identify those groups who should be the focus of attention in positive duties and how their claims should rank in the order of priorities. Only if those groups or sub-groups which experience one or all of the detriments set out above, namely, stigma and prejudice, negation of identity, distributive disadvantage or marginalisation that it should be a target for positive action. For example, migrant women experience detriment under all four heads, whereas migrant men may do so only under some, and the same is true for non-migrant women; and in both cases, the intensity of detriment is of a different order. The result is to require positive measures specifically aimed at migrant women. Language teaching is a good example. Migrant women with child-care obligations have particular difficulty in accessing ways of learning the dominant language, compared to migrant men, and non-migrant women. Therefore, positive action should include providing language-teaching which facilitates participation by women with child-care obligations. Other key examples concern disabled black or ethnic minority people and Roma women.

Using positive action to address intersectionality also assists in two further arenas. The first is concerned with monitoring. Many national statistics do not include data disaggregated to reflect intersectionality. This means that policy is often directed at only one aspect of an individual's identity. However, in order to reflect intersectionality in statistics, it is necessary to have a clear understanding of which groups and subgroups should be monitored. Otherwise the statistics themselves will continue to render intersectional groups invisible. The diversity of EU Member States means that there cannot be a uniform set of groups across different states: a minority could suffer discrimination in one state and not in another. Using the above criteria, however, it would be possible to produce guidance based on national statistics as to which intersectional groups should be the appropriate target for positive action. Such guidance would permit employers to identify and monitor the appropriate subgroups. It should also be stressed that statistics and their availability should not be the only driving force behind such measures. Qualitative surveys, interviews with individuals, and common sense should all be used to supply the initial impression or suggestion that such discrimination might be occurring.

A second advantage of this understanding of intersectionality and positive action relates to the so-called 'creamy layer' problem. It is well known that the most advantaged of a disadvantaged group may make best use or even capture the benefits of positive action measures. This problem could be mitigated by targeting positive action on groups defined on the basis of multiple discrimination, which by definition comprise the least advantaged in each of the relevant groups. To continue the above example, in the provision of language learning for migrants, it would be possible to make sure that it was not only men who had use of them. In situations of actual reservation or quotas, proper attention would need to be paid to the group for whom the reservation was intended. Unless an intersectionality approach is used, as outlined here, women non-migrants might fill the quotas. Thus special attention would be needed to ensure that intersectional groups were able to benefit.

Possibly the most challenging aspect of intersectionality in the context of positive action concerns representation and involvement. It has been argued above that involvement of those affected is essential to prevent positive action from simply becoming a top-down exercise. However, unless intersectionality was taken into account, those involved might simply not speak for an intersectional group. White women might speak for women and migrant men for migrants. Thus specific attention needs to be paid to ensuring that the intersectional group has a voice. Again, the above criteria assist in both identifying the group and ensuring that it has an appropriate set of spokespeople.

4.6 Role of European Union law

At EU level, the expansion of the grounds of discrimination opens up new possibilities for the recognition of multiple discrimination. However, the structure of the Directives creates several potential obstacles. The first concerns the segmentation into three different sets of Directives: one concerning race and ethnic origin,[32] one concerning religion or belief, disability, age or sexual orientation,[33] and a set of Directives on gender discrimination.[34] The list is an exhaustive list, leaving no scope to the ECJ to expand it. This contrasts with Art 14 of the European Convention on Human Rights, which prohibits discrimination on grounds '*such as* sex, race, colour, language . . . *or other status*' (emphasis added). The non-exhaustive or open nature of this list has enabled the European Court of Human Rights to expand the list, to include, for example, disability and sexual orientation.[35]

On one argument, recognition of multiple discrimination entails the creation of a new sub-category, such as minority women, precluded by the exhaustive nature of the list, as well as the difficulty of straddling two Directives. However, a better argument would be that it is open to the court to combine two or more grounds of discrimination. This approach is supported by the fact that the Preamble of the Racial Equality Directive expressly declares that women are often the victims of multiple discrimination and therefore, that in implementing the principle of equal treatment on grounds of racial or ethnic origin, the community should aim to eliminate inequalities and to promote equality between men and women.[36] A similar provision appears in the Preamble to the Employment Equality Directive.[37]

Possibly an easier route to recognition of multiple discrimination is the use of a non-exhaustive list. In fact, several Member States have chosen to implement the Directives by using a non-exhaustive list, adding a phrase such as 'or any other circumstance'.[38] This will permit courts to recognise additional grounds of prohibited discrimination. According to the Network's study of implementation of the Directives, non-exhaustive lists are found in Finland, Hungary, Latvia, Poland and Slovenia. In Belgium, the exhaustive nature of the list of grounds included in the legislation was subsequently held to be unlawful by the Court of Arbitration.[39]

More difficult is the fact that the Directives have differing material scopes, with the Racial Equality Directive outlawing discrimination over a wider scope than the Employment Equality Directive. Thus whereas EC law prohibits race discrimination in housing and other services, it does not forbid discrimination outside employment and vocational training on grounds of religion, disability, sexual orientation or age. This makes it difficult, for example, for older members of ethnic minorities to bring a claim of multiple discrimination in respect of healthcare or housing. Such claimants would only have a claim under the Directives on grounds of ethnic origin. But such a claim might be precluded if younger members of their ethnic group do not suffer detriment. With the expansion of the coverage of the Gender Directive into a similar area as that of the Racial Equality Directive, this difficulty is unlikely to arise with respect to women suffering multiple discrimination on grounds of gender and, say, ethnic origin, but it will arise in respect of older women.

One way forward is for domestic legislation to go beyond the Directives, and provide for comprehensive coverage for all grounds covered by both Directives. This question was addressed by the recent study carried out by the Network into implementation of the two Directives in the 25 Member States.[40] The study found that many Member States have maintained the diverging scope of the two Directives, outlawing discrimination in social protection, social benefits, education, goods and services available to the public in relation only in respect of racial and ethnic origin discrimination. In such cases, the difficulty of addressing multiple discrimination remains acute. On the other hand, an important group of Member States provide for comprehensive coverage for all the named grounds. Thus, in Belgium all grounds of discrimination are legislated equally; the Czech Republic's draft law provides the same protection for all of the grounds specified in both Directives; and in France, the general principle of equality in public service guarantees equal treatment for all grounds in social protection, goods and services, and housing. Hungarian law has practically unlimited material scope, treating all grounds of discrimination equally. Irish law has equal material scope for nine grounds of discrimination; in Slovenia, all of the grounds in both Directives enjoy protection against discrimination in the field of social protection, social advantages, education and goods and services; and Spanish law prohibits discrimination in social advantages not just on grounds of race but also on the grounds of religion or belief, disability and sexual orientation. In these Member States, recognition of multiple discrimination is likely to be less problematic.

It is arguable that there is more scope for addressing intersectionality through the provision for positive duties. Article 7 of the Employment Equality Directive permits Member States to maintain or adopt specific measures in order to compensate for disadvantage 'linked to any of the grounds referred to' and Art 5 of the Racial Equality Directive similarly refers to compensation for disadvantages 'linked to racial or ethnic origin'. Measures directed at subgroups defined according to multiple discrimination would be 'linked' to one or more of these grounds and therefore would, provided they fulfilled the other requisite criteria, be potentially legitimate.

4.7 Conclusion

This chapter has argued that proactive duties to promote equality provide an opportunity to address the challenges of intersectionality, in ways which are debarred by the rigid categorisation of a complaints-led approach. But this in turn necessitates a closer understanding of the relationship between the goals of equality and the demarcation of groups to be protected or advanced by equality. I have argued that in designing proactive measures, groups should be defined not merely in terms of their status markers, but with reference to the particular aims of equality, namely, the need to eliminate stigma, harassment and violence based on a group characteristic; the need to respect, promote and accommodate different identities; the need to compensate for disadvantage; and the need to facilitate participation. A closer relationship between the aims of equality and group demarcation makes it possible to identify those groups who should be the focus of attention and how their claims should rank in the order of priorities. In this way, subgroups previously rendered invisible come into focus and a start can be made on addressing intersectionality.

Notes

1 Contrast Council Directive 2000/43/EC which covers social protection, social advantages, education and access to goods and services which are available to the public, including housing as well as employment and vocational training [2000] OJ L180/22 with Council Directive 2000/78/EC which applies only to employment and vocational training [2000] OJ L303/16.
2 K Crenshaw (1989) 'Demarginalizing the intersection of race and sex: A black feminist critique of antidiscrimination doctrine, feminist theory and antiracial politics', *The University of Chicago Legal Forum*: 139–67.
3 *DeGraffenreid v General Motors Assembly Division* 413 F Supp 142 (US Federal Court of Appeals).
4 United Nations Division for the Advancement of Women: Gender and Racial Discrimination (2000) *Report of the Expert Meeting*.
5 European Monitoring Centre on Racism and Xenophobia (2003) *Migrants, Minorities and Employment: Exclusion, Discrimination and Anti-discrimination in 15 Member States of the European Union*.
6 European Monitoring Centre on Racism and Xenophobia (2004) *Annual Report, 2003–4*.
7 European Monitoring Centre on Racism and Xenophobia (2003) *Migrants, Minorities and Employment: Exclusion, Discrimination and Anti-discrimination in 15 Member States of the European Union*.
8 F Williams (2003) 'Contesting "race" and gender in the European Union', in B Hobson (ed) *Recognition Struggles and Social Movements: Contested Identities, Agency and Social Movements*, Cambridge: Cambridge University Press, Ch 5.
9 US Department of State (2003) *Victims of Trafficking and Violence Protection Act of 2000: Trafficking in Persons Report*, Annual Report 2003, available at www.state.gov/g/tip/rls/tiprpt/2003/ (accessed 26 June 2003).
10 United Nations Division for the Advancement of Women: Gender and Racial Discrimination (2000) *Report of the Expert Meeting*.
11 S Fredman (2002) *The Future of Equality in Great Britain*, Manchester: Equal Opportunities Commission, pp 25–6.

12 K Crenshaw (1991) 'Race, gender and sexual harassment', *Southern California Law Review*, 65: 1467.

13 EU Joint Monitoring and Advocacy Program/European Roma Rights Center (2004) *Shadow Report Commenting on the fifth periodic report of the Federal Republic of Germany submitted under Article 18 of the United Nations Convention on the Elimination of All Forms of Discrimination against Women*, European Roma Rights Center and Open Society Institute, 9 January 2004, available at http://lists.errc.org/publications/legal/CEDAW-Germany_Jan_2004.doc (accessed 5 March 2008).

14 P Patel (2001) 'United Nations: An urgent need to integrate an intersectional perspective to the examination and development of policies, strategies and remedies for gender and racial equality', address by Pragna Patel to the 45th session of the UN Commission on the Status of Women (CSW), available at www.un.org/womenwatch/daw/csw/patel45.htm (accessed 7 January 2008).

15 *DeGraffenreid v General Motors Assembly Division* 413 F Supp 142 (US Federal Court of Appeals).

16 Ibid.

17 *Jefferies v Harris County Community Action Assn* 615 F 2d 1025 (5th Cir 1980) (USA Federal Court of Appeals).

18 G Moon (2006) 'Multiple discrimination: Problems compounded or solutions found', *Justice Journal* 3: 86–102.

19 *Kamlesh Bahl v The Law Society* [2004] EWCA Civ 1070 (Court of Appeal).

20 M Pierce (2003) *Minority Ethnic People with Disabilities in Northern Ireland*, Dublin: Equality Authority.

21 United Nations Division for the Advancement of Women: Gender and Racial Discrimination (2000) *Report of the Expert Meeting*.

22 See further S Fredman (2005) 'Changing the norm: Positive duties in equal treatment legislation', *Maastricht Journal of European and Comparative Law*, 12: 369–98.

23 Pay Equity Taskforce and Departments of Justice and Human Resources Development Canada (2004) *Pay Equity: A New Approach to a Fundamental Right*, Ottawa: Federal Pay Equity Task Force, available at www.justice.gc.ca/en/payeqsal/docs/PETF_final_report.pdf (accessed 4 March 2008).

24 Ibid, p 147.

25 B Hepple, M Coussey and T Choudhury (2000) *Equality: A New Framework: Report of the Independent Review of the Enforcement of UK Anti-Discrimination Legislation*, Oxford: Hart Publishing; S Sturm (2001) 'Second generation employment discrimination: A structural approach', *Columbia Law Review*, 101: 458–568.

26 See further S Fredman (2007) 'Redistribution and recognition: reconciling inequalities', *South African Journal on Human Rights*, 23: 214–34.

27 GWF Hegel (1977) *Phenomenology of Spirit*, Oxford: Oxford University Press, pp 104–9.

28 N Fraser and A Honneth (2003) *Redistribution or Recognition*, London, New York: Verso, p 13.

29 N Fraser, in *Redistribution or Recognition*, ibid, p 29.

30 Ibid, p 14.

31 Ibid, p 15.

32 Race Directive (2000/43/EC).

33 Employment Directive (2000/78/EC).

34 Equal Treatment Directive (76/207 EEC).

35 *Salgueiro Da Silva Mouta v Portugal* (Application no 33290/96) 21 March 2000; *Botta v Italy* (1998) 26 EHRR 241, 1998-I 412 (European Court of Human Rights).

36 Race Directive (2000/43/EC), Preamble, para 14.
37 Employment Directive (2000/78/EC), para 3.
38 J Cormack and M Bell (2005) *Comparative Analysis of Anti-discrimination Law in the 25 Member States*, Brussels: European Commission, paras 8–9.
39 Judgment no 157/2004 of the Court of Arbitration, delivered on 6 October 2004, available at www.arbitrage.be/public//f/2004/2004-157f.pdf (accessed 7 January 2008).
40 Available at http://europa.eu.int/comm/employment_social/fundamental_rights/public/pubst_en.htm#legnet (accessed 7 January 2008).

Part II

Theorising intersectionality from different disciplinary angles

5 Intersectionality scope and multidimensional equality within the European Union

Traversing national boundaries of inequality?

Ulrike M Vieten

5.1 Introduction

Directives 2000/43/EC,[1] 2000/78/EC,[2] 2002/73/EC and 2004/113/EC[3] signify a policy strategy willing to create more cohesive and integrating working conditions and to combat discriminations of citizens within the EU.[4] While initiating a broader implementation process of multidimensional equality law the EU framework aims to deepen national regulations and anti-discrimination practices in all EU Member States. This ambitious goal confronts solicitors and law scholars,[5] but even more so feminist sociologists[6] with theoretical and pragmatic concerns on how to evaluate, balance and generally relate different discriminatory grounds, individual claims and social systems of oppression to each other. It is proclaimed that 'EC non-discrimination law needs to maintain an adequate balance between group-related and individualistic aims'.[7] Hence, as we seek to enrich our understanding of multidimensional discrimination effects unfolding between and among different dimensions of social divisions it is necessary to go back to methodological questions: indeed, we are confronted with epistemological problems as the notion of individual differences as a matter of intersecting identities does not capture adequately the systematic impact of historically constructed group hierarchies. Besides, intersectional identities could be linked to 'hybridity'[8] and, therefore, new configurations of discriminatory grounds might occur that diffuse even more the meaning of group clusters of, for example, class, 'race' and gender, as the most prominent categories of social inequality. As the phenomenon of intersecting identities will lead our interest in how to grasp research approaches to intersectionality, we have to ask: what does intersectionality mean and why did feminists start to focus on it? And further, in what ways can we make the most of an analytical understanding of overlapping social categories that keeps a political eye on the balance between individual subjectivity and social groupings?

In the following, I am going to sketch some characteristic conceptual aspects of the term 'intersectionality' confronting theoretical considerations[9] with the distinctive logic of empirical demands that take into account the overall scope of the EU Directives. Generally, there is a tension between an analytical approach to intersectionality which argues for anti-essentialism on the one hand, and a more pragmatic purpose defining discriminatory grounds according to certain group characteristics, on the other. In order to advance an interdisciplinary discussion on methodology, that is, to discuss the need to answer the question how to study intersectionality, I turn to the arguments of the US American sociologist, Leslie McCall, who put this question at the core of her concerns.[10] McCall's systematic overview of different research approaches to intersectionality underlines that we have to understand the purpose of specific (academic) knowledge before deciding what kind of inter-sectionality approach might be appropriate to use. Not by chance, we come across a more principled dilemma between research that challenges any fixity of classifications and more strategic approaches relying on defined categories. The latter, as McCall argues, does focus on existing hierarchical relationships, that is, the salient importance of social class, in order to map the impact of group subordination and individual discrimination.

In contrast to the rather marginalised attention that is given to social class, sometimes 'invisibly' encapsulated[11] in other social categories, I argue in a further section that classed economic hierarchies underscore current political debates on cultural integration, equity and civic participation of individuals and minority communities in the EU and beyond. My neo-socialist-feminist insistence on the meaning of social class opposes those public and academic views that approach clusters such as ethnicity, religion and sexuality while neglecting the central impact of class on individual chances to secure those differences. Also, I argue that we have to take into account specific scopes of (European) policy that interfere in the regulating role of national societies while not handling fully the emergence of new social complexities. This con-tention brings me to a discussion of Sylvia Walby's timely proposal[12] in my final section who urges us to re-conceptualise social categories with reference to more flexible and less nested social systems. The notion of system has a central role to play in the way we interpret social categories and, finally, how we might understand the complex overlap (intersectionality) of social divi-sions. Hence, her intervention is particularly relevant as the transformation of national societies in and beyond single nation states pushes ahead new transgressive formations of what sociologists regard as *social systems*. My chapter will conclude while arguing that EU multidimensional equality law should privilege the intersections of particular discriminatory grounds due to its intentional policy character and its prospective wish to come to terms with historical totalitarianism and National Socialism: all in all, multidimensional anti-discrimination policy aims to strengthen the institutionalisation of the EU as a transnational (trans-nation state) community in its own right, but while constructing transnational equality parameters (*de jure*) more complex social layers and demands for social justice are generated that are stretching beyond the borders and boundaries of the EU.

5.2 Recognising differences: doing feminist research on intersectionality and social complexity

The term intersectionality indicates a commitment to analyse whether and to what extend certain socio-cultural hierarchies such as class, gender, ethnicity, nationality, 'race' and sexuality might intersect. Also, it includes in-depth studies of how social categories are constructed and in what ways these categories support one another while producing inclusion or exclusion. Therefore, the overall analytical scope reaches out for an understanding of multiple dimensions of oppressions in terms of socio-economic structures, but also its impact on the social positioning of individuals.[13] But what kind of social consequences occur when 'particular identities are lived in the modalities of other categories'?[14] Do multiple identities erase social clusters nesting within nationally framed social systems of power or might they create new social groupings?

The phenomenon of intermingling systems of social oppression was recognised before the term '*intersectionality*' appeared: back in 1990, the historian Gerda Lerner argued that sex, class and 'race' dominance are interrelated and inseparable from the very beginning. According to Lerner '[t]he form which class first took historically was genderic and racist. The form that racism first took was genderic and classist. The form the state first took was patriarchal'.[15] Without even using the term 'intersectionality', Lerner relates to 'race', gender and class, but also to patriarchy as reinforcing and backing each other. More recently, Irene Browne and Joya Misra[16] argue:

> Feminist sociologists call for an alternative theorizing that captures the combination of gender and race. Race is 'gendered' and gender is 'racialized', so that race and gender fuse to create unique experiences and opportunities for all groups – not just [for] women of color.

These different statements address the theme of overlapping gendered and racialised oppression, that is, gender and 'race' and therefore give us insights on how US feminists have approached intersecting social categories. Baukje Prins[17] claims that the 'US approach foregrounds the impact of system or structure upon the formation of identities, whereas British scholars focus on the dynamics and relational aspect of social identity'.[18] In this regard a more *systemic* and a more *constructionist* interpretation[19] of intersectionality could be identified, both of which are, nonetheless, as will be discussed later, significant to an Anglo-American research and broader public discourse context. What is of major interest here, is to find out which epistemic directions encompassing intersectionality might be more suitable to an EU framework as the impact of social divisions (systemic elements) and subjective and performative acts (constructivist elements) have developed in EU Member States unevenly and quite differently. In addition, these dissimilar legal and cultural contexts are now undergoing mutual transformations that eventually might lead to a *novel social space* in Europe and beyond.

In principle, research agendas and for that reason, applied sociological empirical studies regarding individual discriminations and their linkages to group structures are embedded in 'national'[20] (nation state) academic institutions. Methodological frameworks and socio-political conditions on how to explore and explain social hierarchies regarding gender, 'race' and ethnicity are for example connected to broader configurations of notions of citizenship, patterns of trans-border migration and racialised boundaries.[21]

Diverse national histories indicate that the national community ('the people') addressed in a definition of the democratic body is a fluid rather than a fixed sovereign. Therefore, discourses on citizenship rights and participation in democracy relate directly to nationally framed membership which gives selective and exclusive entry to a community. As John Rundell argues:

> [c]itizenship is the formal and trans-communal mechanism that draws an anonymous and even polymorphous population who inhabit the territory of a nation-state into its regulatory system. Or to put it another way, territorial-national citizenship . . . is a mechanism for the administrative control of the movement of a nation's inhabitants within and across its borders.[22]

Apart from the multiplicity of individual biographical experiences and subjective positions within state borders, 'national borders become a specific form, spatially bounded, of collectivity boundaries'.[23] Currently, perceptions of legal citizenship, community boundaries and territorial borders are modified to more complex layers of national, nation-state and EU 'imagined communities'[24] transforming the meaning of collective belonging, citizen rights and its reach in terms of territorial borders and socio-cultural boundaries. Thus, these social and ideological transformations are affecting notions of social divisions and, accordingly, academic approaches to intersectionality and multidimensional equality.

In the following, I am going to sketch some aspects of the tension between shifting academic research agendas and (feminist) political movements in their call for acknowledging different stages in understanding social complexity.

As far as the German feminist discourse on diversity is concerned Gudrun Axeli-Knapp,[25] for instance, admits that either researchers with minority background[26] or researchers working in the field of migration studies[27] pushed forward a more critical perspective on gender studies in Germany. While rightly reflecting the importance of academic status regarding the public recognition of intellectual arguments her observation disregards feminist dialogues that took place in radical feminist journals back in the early 1990s.[28] A controversial debate about naming differences among women developed after the critical interventions of Jessica Jacoby and Gotlinde Magiriba Lwanga in 1990.[29] Jacoby and Magiriba Lwanga confronted the dominant Christian and 'white' outlook of German feminists as a taken for granted hegemonic cultural lens; their publication was a reflection of controversial debates that shook the 'feminist consensus' at 'women weeks' (*Frauenwochen*) at the end of the 1980s. Knapp's perception makes clear that the academic recognition of marginalised voices, that is, their relevance for the public discourse often unfolds in a delayed (academic) institutional frame and further, that the public articulation of social movements (that is, feminist movements) does not automatically match with the academic findings of its contemporaneous (feminist) research. In contrast to a rather late academic adaptation of ideological contestations about *difference* among feminists in Germany, British feminist and post-colonial scholars of transnational, bi-national and/or ethnic minority backgrounds challenged mainstream academia in Britain much earlier. Since the early 1980s, British feminist social theory analysed intersecting complexity[30] and in the 1990s, translocational[31] social positioning of women – though as Nira Yuval-Davis remarks, '[a]pparently, without noticeable effect on policy makers'.[32]

In fact, a broader European recognition of the theme of social complexity emerged only recently while acknowledging the research on intersectionality undertaken by US black feminists, most prominently Patricia Hill Collins[33] and Kimberlé Williams Crenshaw.[34] Black feminist scholars had challenged white middle-class feminism and male-centred anti-racism for ignoring the specific and different situation of black women. Crenshaw introduced the term 'intersectionality' stressing that single-axis discrimination (that is, gender) left black women outside the focus group 'woman'. The 'no responsibility' in concrete situations of *claims* made it necessary to think about the combination of discriminatory grounds potentially overlapping in different social categories. Having said 'claims', this term signals an individual rights/interests nexus looking at, for example, the actual living conditions of women regarding employment, wage, violence or access to housing, social services and so forth. Susanne V Knudson argues that 'approaches to intersectionality have mostly been used in qualitative field studies. The theoretical inspiration has developed the complexity of analysis from observations, interviews and questionnaires'.[35] For example, Crenshaw based her critical argument on research focusing on violence against women of colour; that is, the non-reasonable accommodation they got in shelters for battered women.[36] Accordingly, we have to bear in mind two decisive angles of the concept of intersectionality: first, its more prominent rooting in an US American context focusing on skin colour and its intersections with gender and class as the most important signifier of its racialising and discriminating systems.[37] Second, and this is important to an overall inclusive political discourse, we have to understand the philosophical element of the concept of intersectionality. Naomi Zack[38] proposes that intersectionality means that we cannot impose:

[l]imits on the numbers or kinds of possible intersected identities ... there is no reason to stop at one dimension of oppression. To race can be

added class, age, physical ability, sexual preference, for starters. The only way to limit possible intersected identities is by counting only those whose proponents have managed to give recognized voice to what they are.[39]

The last remark about the 'recognized voice' brings in the explicit political dimension of public dispute and collective struggle, mentioned above. It stresses that legal, social and cultural spaces in which group representations can be articulated are contingent and open to contestation. Hence, the flux of categories as introduced above and connected to this, the historical embedding of group struggles, are at the core of feminist debates on how the concept of intersectionality engenders meaning. What I am proposing here is an ethically sensitive and reflexive understanding of the term 'intersectionality' that, in principle, offers various ways to generate emancipatory knowledge. Conceptualising and theorising social divisions evolves in a different academic sub-field than does the remedy of concrete cases of injustice or discriminations. Accordingly, there is no right or wrong in doing intersectional analysis; it rather matters to understand the range of methodological concerns on the one hand, and differing needs to find adequate research methods to solve the tension between structural (group) exclusions and concrete (individual) emanations of discriminations. Without any doubt the preference for specific approaches to intersectionality goes hand in hand with *particular* political or strategic objectives.

5.3 The meaning of social categories and subjective dimensions: looking for research strategies that improve emancipation

Leslie McCall's[40] approach to intersectionality research brings back socio-economic aspects to the theory field of researching equality and justice while differentiating *discriminatory dimensions* of individual positioning within a constellation of group hierarchies. The central question to be answered when thinking of complex social reality and multiple discriminations might be: how can complexity be managed in concrete cases of discrimination? According to McCall:

> Individuals usually share the characteristics of only one group or dimension of each category defining their social position. The intersection of identities in individuals takes place through the articulation with a single dimension of each category. Thus the 'multiple' in these intersectional analysis refers not to dimensions within categories but to dimensions across categories.[41]

Hence, McCall's differentiation between 'dimensions' and 'categories' could help to clarify the limits of subjective identity aspects of individuals (*dimension* as the personal interpretation of an overlapping belonging to certain groups) and social categories echoing systematic power relationships of historically constructed group hierarchies.

To make more explicit the difference between: (a) dimension; and (b) category we might construct a person at the intersections of various social axes,[42] for example a Protestant, middle class, gay British woman living in Yorkshire is placed at the intersections of multiple categories, that is, religion, class, sexuality, nationality, and gender. Only one single dimension of different categories is relevant in her unique social location as the multiplying of discriminatory grounds also requires that we have to clarify in what ways the relationship, that is, the tension between majority and minority categories might unfold. In this case, we could assume that in particular her (homo-)sexuality might be an objective of structural vulnerability (asymmetry) as far as dominant patterns of heterosexuality are concerned. Does it make a difference when the concrete person we are talking about would be working class instead of middle class, or Jewish instead of Protestant, or Mexican instead of British? We might agree that her individual experience of homophobic discrimination in a hetero-normative environment probably might be the same independent of other layers of minoritised status, but intersecting dimensions of specific categories will increase her vulnerability to being targeted, perhaps, by anti-Semitism and homophobia; racism, classism and homophobia or xenophobia, homophobia and sexism. According to Gill Valentine, a spatial understanding of intersecting social identities refers to 'varying levels of emotional investment in different subject positions at different temporal and spatial moments, as well as continuities and discontinuities'.[43] Thus, from the individual's perspective the 'undoing of one identity by another',[44] is part and parcel of dealing with different power situations where 'dominant spatial orderings'[45] exist. Therefore, intersecting subjective identities are embedded in a web of intersecting or overlapping social hierarchies. To come back to McCall's approach, its purpose is to differentiate 'dimensions' and 'categories' following a research logic that is interested to measure *relationships* between discriminating factors. As McCall emphasises, 'The concern is with the nature of the relationships among social groups and, importantly, how they are changing, rather than with the definition or representation of such groups per se'.[46]

In Scheme 5.1, I have clustered the three main intersectionality approaches unearthed by McCall to make clear in what ways research methods and methodology are embedded in specific intellectual projects. The classified investigating strategies to intersectionality have to be regarded as *models*[47] catching specifically designed scopes of (feminist) knowledge. Whereas the *anti-categorial (I)* and the *inter-categorial complexity (III)* approach express opposing views on the notion and accordingly, use of social categories, the *intra-categorial complexity approach (II)* attempts to mediate the deconstruction of classic holistic groups such as class, gender and 'race' while insisting on political strategies. The latter is based on the assertion that group identities could be mobilised against oppression. Nonetheless, this middle way

Table 5.1

Scope/ intersectionality	*I Anti-categorial complexity*	*II Intra-categorial complexity*	*III Inter-categorial complexity*
Characteristics	Deconstruction of 'master categories'; argues against fixed ascriptions; this approach is often linked to (white) postmodern feminism.	Analysis of 'narratives' or 'single case studies'; focuses on particularly neglected intersections, i.e. 'race, gender and class; supported by (black) feminism; feminists of colour.	Focus on 'relationality'; McCall favours this approach looking at the relationships and tensions of existing social categories.
Problematic aspects	This approach creates and multiplies categories: for example 'trans-gender', 'bisexual', 'multiracial' identities though rejecting 'stable' categories.	This approach works on and accepts 'relatively stable relationships of social categories' while interrogating boundary marking and condemning explicit definitions.	This approach requires provisional definitions of analytical categories in order to denounce group relationships; it contains the danger of re-essentialising group belonging.
Scope of knowledge	Its anti-essentialism fosters a permanent re-drafting of group categories and boundaries.	Its middle way approach announces a political challenge to specific hegemonic group hierarchies.	Its insistence on the hierarchical meaning of social categories asks for an evaluation of concrete dimensions across categories; this approach could be applied to comparative, multi-group studies.

approach accentuates conflicting social dimensions that unfold as identity elements across group categories. What becomes very clear from the different approaches is that McCall's own research, namely that of inter-categorial complexity, does focus on structural relationships that reflect social positions as an outcome of group hierarchies across different categories.

Accordingly, McCall's own epistemic project is quite distinct from other approaches to intersectionality as she clearly stresses an 'evaluating' perspective regarding equality and difference. In her own phrasing, 'meaningful inequalities'[48] matter and should be measured quantitatively. Thus, she focuses on the question of how to gather data with respect to multidimensional layers of social locations supporting distributive justice that prioritise, for example, group compensation strategies.

Further, McCall asserts that the earning gap between poor and rich populations in the US rose in the late 1970s[49] confronting feminist research with an urgent need to understand more closely wage differences between men and women, but also between women of various classed, ethnic and 'race' backgrounds. Her overall criticism that feminist research tended to focus on qualitative research neglecting methodological innovations of quantitative methods hits an ideological nail. Also, she complains that research using highly complex statistical material is difficult to publish in leading peer-journals.[50] These allegations and concerns are serious and thus, we should ask ourselves, what kind of complexity are we able to measure and what are the limits to digest complexity? Given that global poverty is on the rise, although post-industrial economic transformations are diminishing the gap in wealth between the classic North and South of the Globe (First and Third World economies),[51] McCall's plea to focus on the meaning of *social class* is reinforced. But as the remedy of individual cases of discriminations depends on comparative data and therefore methodological parameters to measure inequalities, we also have to reflect on the normative directions of inquiries (scope of knowledge).

5.4 The disappearance and re-emergence of social class: the intersecting dimensions of gender, ethnicity, class and faith

Academic approaches on ethnicity and gender,[52] and, as far as a general crisis in faith systems[53] is concerned, gendered intersections with religion (Muslim faith, in particular) have had more attention in recent years.[54] This is due to alarmed nation state governments in and beyond Europe trying to cope with 'ethnically' framed social conflicts, fundamentalist threats and organised terrorist violence in the aftermath of 11 September 2001 and 7 July 2005, as well as efforts to combat an increase of anti-Muslim racism.[55] With reference to increasing global risk and security discourses, however, we should bear in mind that beneath the surface of these regional and local debates, economically and socially excluding cultural practices[56] exist in all EU states, although perhaps varying in their scale of violent expressions and political consequences.

The Parisian Banlieu riots in 2005 and the latest of 2007, give very good examples of spontaneous eruptions of anger and frustration due to social and economic segregation. The 'criminal' face of youth violence appears in a 'cultural' or 'ethnic' make up caused by long-lasting experiences of institutionalised racism. As Alana Lentin argues, the Banlieu riots, not unlike the riots in urban black ghettos of the US in the 1960s–1970s, or the London-Brixton riots in 1981, articulate a protest against 'heavy handed policing of the poor, non-white people in neighbourhood that have become no-man's lands, severed from the centres of political, cultural and economic life'.[57]

European nation states often only 'tolerate' non-Christian populations either as foreigners, as cheap labour, as temporary working cohorts or as second-class citizens, while not standing up to the social consequences of failed integration politics and *classed* cultural exclusions. As John Rex[58] (1996) puts it:

> Although it protests loudly about being against 'Racism' and 'xeno-phobia', the European Union has devised an institution in the Migrants Forum which classifies racial and cultural minorities who are citizens together with the *gastarbeiders* who are not. The problems of minorities are, in fact, to be marginalized and dealt with outside the normal democratic process.

When we look at national reports on racist violence for example, we are confronted with information deficits of EU Member States regarding criminal records and coherent data collections. The RAXEN NFP Reports of 2005[59] for example made clear that Greece, Italy and Portugal have no public official criminal justice data on racist crimes and violence.[60] Other countries hold good or excellent data collection mechanisms, but the focus swings between 'general discrimination' and 'activities of extreme right-wing groups/ hate speech'.[61] Thus, the overall EU report concludes that 'Member States have different official systems in place for collecting data on racist crimes and violence';[62] this appears as significant and fairly typical[63] for federal policy structures undermining more coherent attempts to combat racism, that is, discrimination of religious or ethnic minorities in the EU.

Consequently, looking at the incongruence of national reports on racist violence we should act with reservations against research agendas that focus on the collection of sensitive data regarding gendered religious membership. Moreover, the current policy agenda in different European countries seems to concentrate on axes of 'gender, religion and ethnicity' while widely neglecting the central impact of (deprived) social class status and complex notions of transnational belonging. It seems that prejudiced perceptions of collective cultural competence have become central to an ideological discourse about minority ethnic group rights against female individual right claims.[64] Symptomatically, a British mainstream public discourse, for example, shifted its attention from 'race' and gender intersections to signifiers of culturalised regimes of 'female oppression': policy discourses on minority ethnic communities, for example, connected the theme of immigration and citizenship with bogus and forced marriages.[65] Hence, national state authorities which prioritise information on the potential of minorities to engage with political extremism and violent culture rather than encouraging co-ordinated EU studies on how to change patterns of prejudices and structural social exclusions underscore they do not traverse boundaries of inequality.

Hence, we should keep a critical distance from any formalised application of social categories as they only work as *approximations of constructed relationships*; they have to be read, after all, in concordance with shifting ideological implications of intersecting social categories.

Avtar Brah and Anne Phoenix[66] argue that the social category 'class' nearly passed away in sociological research over the last 20 years, but also in 'governance policy tackling, for example, child poverty, obesity or scandalising poor achievements in education'.[67] The disappearance of class as the dominant social category of subordination addressed by critical (Marxist) research, however, has to be read in concordance with advancing research on class and its other intersecting social divisions. According to Floya Anthias[68] social stratification theory focused on class only while talking about economic inequalities without reconsidering in what ways ethnicity and gender might shape concrete class positions. It seems that this trend of neglected 'class analysis' is slightly reversed in British sociology more recently, as a series of publications with the journal *Sociology* makes clear.[69] Now, we could intervene and argue that 'race', nationality, religion, citizenship, sexuality and physical ability shape concrete class positions similar to ethnicity and gender, insisting that notions of working or working-poor class appear as multidimensional when embedded in continuosly problematic and precarious living conditions. Emphasising this link means arguing that intersecting identity layers nurture notions of *class* while pinpointing individual departures in distinctive ways. All in all, social class frames individual access to economic wealth, cultural goods influencing political and public participations; and this classism is wrapped in intersected layers of different cultural, ethnic, religious and gendered economic performances.

More fracturing categories such as 'ethnicity' or 'sexuality', for example, have complicated the original scope of anti-discrimination and sex equality law. Nonetheless the contestation about income, working conditions and equal payment for women and minoritised groups underscores the policy framework of all EU Directives.

Hence, as argued here, we have to break down complex power regimes into active political perspectives in Europe: following Crenshaw, Mieke Verloo[70] underlines that the analytical model 'intersectionality' has to be approached from a structural and a political angle. Whereas the structural dimension refers to complex experiences of individual discriminations shaped by intersecting social divisions, the political realm hints at a broader collective frame embedded in policy and ideological strategies. This differentiation echoes to a certain degree McCall's advocacy for an inter-categorial approach to intersectionality that focuses on the implications of *relationships* as an outcome of asymmetrically organised social categories. However, *social categories* as unfolding in particular hierarchies have to be regarded as inflected by historical configurations of the social realm. Gudrun Axeli-Knapp's discussion of travelling theories,[71] that is, the problematic meaning of the Anglo-American triad 'gender, race, class' in a German academic context, for example, highlights some of the theoretical shortcomings of a non-reflexive adoption of historically laden social categories. Thus, the 'specific constellation of interdependent structures'[72] on the background of European integration and global transformation requires tools for a complex social analysis that takes into account different historiographies of individual oppression and group exclusions. Accordingly, we have to discuss to what extent specific social categories such as class, gender, religion and ethnicity have similar or varying grounds in discussions on intersecting social locations in European societies. Therefore, aiming to traverse national boundaries of inequality among and between 27 EU Member States requires a more fundamental revision of the ontological base of social divisions such as class, gender, ethnicity or sexuality as these social categories were analysed and understood sociologically in national (nation state) frames.[73] In this regard, the transformation of different European, but also non-European nation states is going to restructure the classic division of the public and private sphere that encircled the boundaries of economic, political and intimate relationships between men and women, between national citizens and non-citizens, between ethnic majorities and minorities. Only to remind us, feminists challenged the binary construction of a public and private sphere[74] in its gendered and restrictive function. As Rebecca Johnson asserts, this '[d]ivide is an important part of the background scenery against which intersectional theory has unfolded'.[75] Consequently, a critical debate on the chances of multidimensional equality and intersectionality in the EU also has to look at the *becoming* of social categories as well as at the *becoming* of social identities.[76]

5.5 European socialisation and intersecting social categories

Walby suggests a new concept of 'societalization' that might be more adequate to capture the 'different temporal and spatial reach'[77] of social systems (that is, gender, class, ethnicity, UM V). According to her:

> This is a process in which there is a tendency for these systems to be brought into alignment ... For example, the societalization project of the European Union introduces new principles of organizations of class, gender, ethnicity, and nation that interrupt previous projects to societalize around would-be nation states.[78]

But what would be different about the construction of social categories, that is, social systems and what does 'alignment' mean in this regard?

Nira Yuval Davis[79] argues that 'gender', ethnicity' or 'class' operate and are constructed in distinctive realms. According to Yuval-Davis:

> [t]he ontological basis of each of these divisions is autonomous, and each prioritises different spheres of social relations (Anthias and Yuval-Davis 1983; 1992). For example class divisions are grounded in relation to the economic processes of production and consumption; gender should be understood not as a 'real' social difference between men and women, but as a mode of discourse that relates to groups of subjects whose social roles are defined by their sexual/biological difference while sexuality is yet another related discourse, relating to constructions of the body,

sexual pleasures and sexual intercourse. Ethnic and racial divisions relate to discourses of collectivities are constructed around exclusionary/inclusionary boundaries.[80]

Walby criticises this approach of specifying separate ontological bases as 'segregationary reductionist'[81] as 'each strand is identified with and reduced to a single and separate base'.[82] However, Yuval-Davis's (and Anthias's) definition of class, for example, crosses the classic notion of economy[83] while stressing that it refers to 'production and consumption' taking place in different social spheres. Nonetheless, what is interesting about Walby's take is that she likes to advance the overall idea of intersecting social realms that are engendering new notions of social categories. Thus gender, for example, is constructed in economic interactions as well as in the process of symbolic boundary constructions of specific national or cultural groups. In this advanced complexity model[84] each system is approached as having the other as an environment thinking of a 'more fluid conception of the mutual impact of systems'.[85] In contrast to the single base model, she proposes 'institutionalized domains of economy, polity, violence, and civil society'[86] and 'multiple sets of social relations such as class, gender and ethnicity'.[87] Hence, each domain and each set of social relations has to be understood as interrelated, but not saturated in terms of spatially and temporally fixed meanings. While arguing against nested constellations her approach could analyse more complex overlaps between social categories that transgress the public versus private divide.[88] As a conceptual approach of theorising multiple intersecting social inequalities, Walby's model favours flexible combinations of institutionalised systems (that is, economy) and sets of social relations (that is, ethnicity). It pays attention to the current transformation of social, economic and political space in Europe affecting the way we have to understand social categories. While saying that 'polity includes not only states, but also the European Union, organized religions that govern areas of life (such as personal life) and some nations (those with developed institutions, such as Scotland)', Walby stresses the yet interwoven *institutional* layers that shape perspectives on multidimensional equality law and intersecting social divisions in all 27 EU Member States. But what tends to be lost in this proposal of complex and simultaneously operating social systems refers to the meaning of distinctive historiographies underlying any interpretation of 'domains' as institutionalised systems and also as sets of social systems.[89] But this contextualising is most important when reflecting various regimes and different regional histories of group oppressions or even genocides.

While analysing Canadian and South African jurisdiction, Jewel Amoah discusses in what ways the purpose of a legally framed equality analysis could *remedy* a situation where discrimination or unequal treatment is experienced.[90] The US American approach (explained above), the British colonial legacy as well as the Canadian and the South African contexts are all very different in terms of how issues of equality rights claims are conveyed.

Despite these differences, all these cultures actually share the prominence of 'colour' as a signifier of gendered and classed differences. 'Colour' signifies legacies of the white trade of black people as slaves, of organised exploitation of indigenous populations and as far as South Africa is concerned the persistence of post-Apartheid-racism. As Amoah emphasises, 'Consideration of context is not restricted to the current state of events, but also relates to instances of historical disadvantage (versus historical privilege)'.[91]

Agreeing with this perspective, we could argue that taking lessons from history means to advance the contemporary debate on intersectionality and multiple equality law while re-politicising the historically specific embeddings of *group recognitions* and *group exclusions*. This could mean to privilege certain categories on the background of specific historical configurations, but also to ask for a re-contextualising of social categories according to transformed social realities. Clearly, this would require contextualised evaluations that take both group divisions, but also individual positioning within and across social categories into account.

On this background looking at Europe, or to be more precise at Continental Europe, post-Holocaust societies struggle with the legacies of the genocide directed by state racism (that is, institutionalised anti-Semitism) unfolding as legal (that is, criminalising) exclusion first, and second, as the systematic mass murder of Jews, Sinti and Roma, communists, disabled people and homosexuals, Jewish and non-Jewish, men and women, children and old people likewise. It is important to acknowledge this specific historical context as it *situates* the debate on intersecting social divisions with reference to continental Europe where minority faith and ethnic groups were outlawed before they were exterminated, collectively. In the beginning of the new millennium, the EU[92] adopted the memory of the Holocaust as the 'founding moment of European civilisation'.[93] On the background of this statement, gendered dimensions of *minoritised* ethnicity, religious, health, sexual and political belonging have to be regarded as central to legal endeavours to balance intersecting group categories and individual identities.

According to the law scholar Elisabeth Holzleithner,[94] looking for the marginalised position within a category implies the quest for those who are most excluded. And here, we are clearly confronted with political evaluations that underly the different approaches to intersectionality as argued above. Although the different nation states in Europe are transforming rapidly into states that have joined the EU and those who, either willingly keep their distance or are held ideologically in distance, the real challenge to EU multidimensional equality law has to be seen in the eventual crossing of its legal borders. Hence, the logic of intersectional social categories and intersecting individual identities means actual transgressions and what Walby only takes on board with respect to the European *societalisation*, it will happen not by being 'congruent in the same territory'.[95]

5.6 Conclusion

While assessing critically various streams of intersectionality research, I intended to make clear that intersectionality, indeed, helps to identify analytically complex layers of individual subordination. However, systematic positions constructed in classed, gendered, ethnic, hetero-normative and 'racialised' terms[96] monitor individual access to privileges, cultural power and social economic inclusion in each of the, by now, 27 EU Member States differently. Despite an overarching anti-discriminatory scope of multidimensional equality law, differently situated[97] nation state legacies confront us with specific forms of prejudices, varying standards of equity and, consequently, uneven terms of (minority) *recognition* and *rights*. Although the Anglo-Dutch influence on the EU non-discrimination law packages[98] is acknowledged widely, the 'kingmaking' significance of previous political protests on the basis of political citizenship rights as a salient, but less elaborated, precondition is less acknowledged. But as underlined here, the political protest of Black Britons was essential to the legal and administrative response of what passed later as the first Race Relations Act in 1965. In this regard an ongoing complexity of social reality is inherent in the idea of intersectionality. This complexity might fabricate counter-ideological tensions in and between different EU Member States engendering new transnational political actions. Hence, the overall idea of the EU framework to harmonise different legal standards also gives way to new intersecting social and political identities that are going to boost equality efforts transcending the yet achieved EU framework. As made clear above, we should demand that our lesson from history means to advance the contemporary debate on intersectionality and multiple equality law while re-politicising the historically specific embeddings of *group recognition* and support those who are disadvantaged to air their voices, collectively.

Alain Touraine[99] argues that what is most characteristic of Europe or rather European societies at large is its *political form* of social organisation. He writes:

Europe is the part of the world where the problem of the social distribution of costs and advantages among social categories which are defined in hierarchical terms play a central role and acts as a link between mass consumption and cultural identities which, on the contrary, are separated in the USA or merged in Japan. Europe is the political continent; it is defined by the central role of social political processes.[100]

We will see what the people of Europe make out of the ideological project of EU societalisation.

Notes

1 This Directive aims at equality irrespective of race and ethnic origin in employment and occupation, social advantages, education and provision of goods and services.

2 This Directive intends to establish a framework for equal treatment in employment and occupation, covering discrimination on grounds of religion and belief, age, disability and sexual orientation.

3 These Directives deal with gender equality in employment and occupation and provision of goods and services respectively.

4 According to the European Commission's *Equality and Discrimination – Annual Report* 2006, 'The Directives protect everyone in the European Union, including persons who are not EU citizens', (p 7). See for further details European Commission – Directorate-General for Employment, Social Affairs and Equal Opportunities, Unit G4, Report published in September 2006; despite 2007 being the year of 'Equal Opportunities for All' there is no new Annual Report available in December 2007.

5 See for example J Gerrads's section on multiple discrimination (1.5): (2007) 'Chapter One: Discrimination grounds', in D Schiek, L Waddington and M Bell (eds) *Cases, Materials and Texts on National, Supranational and International Non-Discrimination Law*, Oxford: Hart Publishing, pp 170–84.

6 Unlike most of the other contributors to this book I concentrate on sociological and political considerations regarding multidimensional discriminations, equality and intersectional dimensions of social categories (i.e. class, gender, ethnicity, 'race', nationality, sexuality, etc).

7 D Schiek, L Waddington and M Bell (eds) (2007b) 'Introductory Chapter: A comparative perspective on non-discrimination law', in D Schiek, L Waddington and M Bell (eds) *Cases, Materials and Text on National, Supranational and International Non-Discrimination Law*, Oxford: Hart Publishing, p 31.

8 Emily Grabham uses Homi K Bhabha's (1996) term of hybridity to underscore the scope of intersecting dimensions as creating 'fluid movements between and across categories challenging definitional and temporal boundaries'. E Grabham (2006) 'Taxonomies of inequality: Lawyers, maps and the challenge of hybridity', *Social Legal Studies*, 15: 5–23, at p 17.

9 I am referring predominantly to an Anglo-American sociological discourse context.

10 L McCall (2005) 'Managing the complexity of intersectionality', *Signs: Journal of Women in Culture and Society*, 30: 1771–800.

11 SV Knudsen (2006) 'Intersectionality – a theoretical inspiration in the analysis of minority cultures and identities in textbooks', in E Bruillard, M Horsley, SV Knudsen and B Aamotsbakken (eds) *Caught in the Web or Lost in the Textbook?*, STEF, IARTEM, IUFM de Basse-Normandie, Paris: Jouve.

12 S Walby (2007) 'Complexity theory, systems theory, and multiple intersecting social inequalities', *Philosophy of the Social Sciences*, 37: 449–70.

13 In a background paper to a ENAR Policy Seminar in Brussels, 6–7 October 2006, intersectional discrimination is defined as implying 'a specific cumulative form of discrimination as a unique, specific synergistic situation' (p 11). Besides, multiple discrimination is regarded as covering additive and intersectional dimensions, ibid, available at www.enar-eu.org/en/events/directives/background-paper_EN.pdf (accessed 9 January 2008).

14 B Prins (2006) 'Narrative accounts of origins: A blind spot in the intersectional approach', *European Journal of Women's Studies*, 13: 277–90, at p 278.

15 Cited in P Rothenberg (2003) 'Learning to see the interrelation of race, class and

gender discrimination and privilege: implications for policy and practice', in *E-Quality-experts in gender en etniciteit*, Den Haag, pp 17–28, at p 20.

16 I Browne and J Misra (2003) 'The intersection of gender and race in the labor market', *Annual Review of Sociology*, 29: 487–513, at p 488.

17 B Prins (2006) 'Narrative accounts of origins: A blind spot in the intersectional approach', *European Journal of Women's Studies*, 13: 277–90

18 Ibid, p 279.

19 Ibid.

20 The ideological fusion of nation and state has been analysed as historically constructed; see for example AM Smith (2006) 'Narrative accounts of origins: A blind spot in the intersectional approach', *European Journal of Women's Studies*, 13: 277–90; J Breuilly (2000) 'Nationalism and the history of ideas', *Proceedings of the British Academy*, 105: 187–223; J Breuilly (2001) 'The state and nationalism', in M Gubernau and J Hutchinson (eds) *Understanding Nationalism*, Cambridge: Polity Press, pp 32–52.

21 See for further details F Anthias and N Yuval-Davis (1992) *Racialized Boundaries – Race, Nation, Gender, Colour and Class and the Anti-Racist Struggle*, London: Routledge; N Yuval-Davis (1997) *Gender & Nation*, London: Sage.

22 J Rundell (1998) 'Tensions of citizenship in an age of diversity: Reflections on territoriality, cosmopolitanism and symmetrical reciprocity', in R Bauböck and J Rundell (eds) *Blurred Boundaries: Migration, Ethnicity, Citizenship*, European Centre Vienna, Ashgate: Aldershot, pp 321–40, at p 326.

23 N Yuval-Davis and M Stoetzler (2002) 'Imagined boundaries and borders – a gendered gaze', *The European Journal of Women's Studies*, 9: 329–44, at p 334.

24 B Anderson (1991 [1983]) *Imagined Communities – Reflections on the Origin and Spread of Nationalism*, 2nd reprinted edn, New York: Verso.

25 See G Axeli-Knapp (2005) 'Race, class, gender: Reclaiming baggage in fast travelling theories', *European Journal of Women's Studies*, 12: 249–65.

26 '[d]aughters of migrants', ibid, p 256.

27 Ibid.

28 See for example the radical feminist lesbian journal *Ihrsinn*, in particular issue 3, 1991 ('*Das Verlorene Wir*') and issue, 5 1992 ('*Die Qual der Moral*'). The journal was founded in 1989 as an initiative of intellectual political lesbians in Bochum intending to establish a forum for debate outside established circles of German universities. It was published until 2004; edited by G Büchner and U Janz (Ihrsinn eV), Bochum. For further information see also www.ihrsinn.auszeiten-frauenarchiv.de/englisch/self.html.

29 J Jacoby and ML Gotlinde (1990) 'Was "sie" schon immer über Antisemitismus wissen wollte, aber nie zu denken wagte', in *Beiträge zur feministischen Theorie und Praxis*, 13: 27–95.

30 See for example F Anthias, and N Yuval-Davis (1983) 'Contextualizing feminism – ethnic, gender and class divisions', *Feminist Review*, 15: 62–75; A Brah (1996) *Cartographies of the Diaspora*, London: Routledge; N Yuval-Davis and P Werbner (eds) (1999) *Women, Citizenship and Difference*, London: Zed Books.

31 F Anthias (1998) 'Rethinking social divisions: Some notes towards a theoretical framework', *Sociological Review*, 46: 506–35; F Anthias (2001) 'The concept of "social divisions" and theorising social stratification: Looking at ethnicity and class', *Sociology*, 35: 835–54; also F Anthias (2006) 'Belongings in a globalising and unequal world: Rethinking translocations', in N Yuval-Davis, K Kannabiran and UM Vieten (eds) *The Situated Politics of Belonging*, London: Sage, pp 17–31.

32 N Yuval-Davis (2006) 'Intersectionality and feminist politics', *European Journal of Women's Studies*, 13: 193–209, at p 194.

33 PH Collins (2000) *Black Feminist Thought: Knowledge, Consciousness and the Politics of Empowerment*, New York: Routledge (first: Boston, MA: Univ Hyman, 1990).

34 K Crenshaw (1991) 'Mapping the margins: Intersectionality, identity politics, and violence against women of color', *Stanford Law Review*, 43: 1241–99.

35 SV Knudsen (2006) 'Intersectionality – a theoretical inspiration in the analysis of minority cultures and identities in textbooks', in E Bruillard, M Horsley, SV Knudsen and B Aamotsbakken (eds) *Caught in the Web or Lost in the Textbook?*, STEF, IARTEM, IUFM de Basse-Normandie, Paris: Jouve.

36 K Crenshaw (1991) 'Mapping the margins: Intersectionality, identity politics, and violence against women of color', *Stanford Law Review*, 43: 1241–99.

37 As far as the debate in Europe is concerned we have to acknowledge that there are significant similarities as far as Britain is concerned in terms of the cultural, social and civic legacy of the exposed meaning of skin colour as a marker of difference. It is beyond the scope of this chapter to discuss the complexity of differently situated nation-state histories that shape the notion of the other, racist discourses and approaches to differences.

38 N Zack (2007) 'Can third wave feminism be inclusive? Intersectionality, its problems, and new directions', in LM Alcoff and EF Kittay (eds) *The Blackwell Guide to Feminist Philosophy*, Malden, Oxford, Carlton: Blackwell Publishers, pp 193–207.

39 Ibid, p 199.

40 L McCall (2005) 'Managing the complexity of intersectionality', *Signs: Journal of Women in Culture and Society*, 30: 1771–800.

41 Ibid, p 1781.

42 McCall speaks of the model of an Arab-American, middle class and heterosexual woman, ibid.

43 G Valentine (2007) 'Theorizing and researching intersectionality: A challenge for feminist geography', *The Professional Geographer*, 59: 10–21, at p 18.

44 Ibid, p 18.

45 Ibid, p 19.

46 L McCall (2005) 'Managing the complexity of intersectionality', *Signs: Journal of Women in Culture and Society*, 30: 1771–800, at p 1785.

47 This is not to say that in praxis different approaches could merge; McCall makes clear that feminist research in this field tends to be a mixture of different approaches.

48 Ibid.

49 L McCall (2005) 'Managing the complexity of intersectionality', *Signs: Journal of Women in Culture and Society*, 30: 1771–800, at p 1788.

50 Ibid, p 1787; in a recent publication addressing intersectionality as a theme for feminist geography Gill Valentine raises this concern, too; see for details G Valentine (2007) 'Theorizing and researching intersectionality: A challenge for feminist geography', *The Professional Geographer*, 59: 10–21, at p 14.

51 See for details see D Held and A Kaya (2007) 'Introduction', in D Held and A Kaya (eds) *Global Inequality – Patterns and Explanations*, Cambridge: Polity Press, pp 1–25.

52 L Blackwell (2003) 'Gender and ethnicity at work: Occupational segregation and disadvantage in the 1991 British census', *Sociology*, 37: 713–31. Blackwell's research stresses that gender and ethnicity do not combine to create double disadvantage for minority women in the labour force' (p 713). Women of various ethnic groups, for example Indian, Sikh, white English women and Muslim Bangladeshi women obtain occupations that do not match with a general ascription of gendered and ethnic discrimination. Thus occupational performance is very distinctive.

53 I use the term 'faith' as a symbolic container for themes of national belonging, religious believe and otherwise emotional identifications with particular communities.

54 D Voas and A Crockett (2005) 'Religion in Britain: Neither believing nor belonging', *Sociology*, 39: 11–28; Y Hussain and P Bagguley (2005) 'Citizenship, ethnicity and identity: British Pakistanis after the 2001 "riots" '; *Sociology*, 39: 407–25.

55 More detailed information is available at http://eumc.europa.eu/eumc/index.php?fuseaction=content.dsp_cat_content&catid=3e4fcb8oce245 (accessed 10 January 2008).

56 P Bourdieu's (1993, 1999) research on the social deprivation of some of the immigrant Parisian suburbs sheds some light on the deep and long-lasting state of cultural and symbolic exclusions in the French society. See for details P Bourdieu (1999) *The Weight of the World: Social Suffering in Contemporary Society*, Cambridge: Polity Press.

57 A Lentin (2005) 'The intifada of the banlieus', *OpenDemocracy*, 17 November, available at www.opendemocracy.net/node/3037 (accessed 9 January 2008).

58 J Rex (1996) 'Contemporary nationalism, its causes and consequences for Europe – A reply to Delanty', *Sociological Research Online*, available at www.socresonline.org.uk/socresonline/1/4/rex.html (accessed 9 January 2008).

59 European Monitoring Centre for Racism and Xenophobia (2005) *Racist Violence in 15 EU Member States – A Comparative Overview of Findings from the RAXEN NFP Reports 2001–2004*, April, available at http://fra.europa.eu/fra/material/pub/comparativestudy/CS-RV-main.pdf (accessed 9 January 2008).

60 Ibid, p 10.

61 Ibid, p 11.

62 Ibid.

63 I found similar problems in gaining reliable comparative data regarding effectiveness and implementation of equality norms as far as Sex Equality-Plans and Reports in the 16 German Lands are concerned; see UM Vieten (2002) 'Frauenförderpläne' in D Schiek, H Dieball, I Horstkötter, L Seidel, UM Vieten and S Wankel, *Frauengleichstellungsgesetze des Bundes und der Länder – Kommentar für die Praxis*, 2nd edn, Frankfurt a M: Bund Verlag, pp 126–138.

64 O Reitman looks at the controversial debates on the relationship between multiculturalism and feminism. Frequently, single axes of inequality, for example 'sex equality' or 'sexuality' are defended against 'ethnic and religious minority rights' and thus introduced as competing layers of discrimination. Reitman differentiates minority and majority patriarchy while talking about the conflicts of cultural group rights and individual (gendered) rights. What is important to the broader theme of intersectionality is her criticism of arguments that try to *balance* dissimilar struggles against oppression. In contrast, she reminds us that a group-differentiated-rights discourse should be sensitive to a range of differences taking into account the situation of minorities within minorities, but also the asymmetric tension between hegemonic and marginal patriarchy. For details see O Reitman (2005) 'Multiculturalism and feminism – incompatibility or synonymity?', *Ethnicities*, 5: 216–47, at pp 230 and 236.

65 N Yuval-Davis, F Anthias and E Kofman (2005) 'Secure borders and safe haven and the gendered politics of belonging: Beyond social cohesion', *Ethnic and Racial Studies*, 28: 513–35.

66 A Brah and A Phoenix (2004) 'Ain't I a woman? Revisiting intersectionality', *Journal of International Women's Studies*, 5: 75–86.

67 Ibid, p 81; otherwise see B Skeggs (1997) *Formations of Class and Gender: Becoming Respectable*, London: Sage; B Skeggs, (2004) *Class, Self, Culture*, London: Routledge.

68 F Anthias (2001) 'The concept of "social divisions" and theorising social stratification: Looking at ethnicity and class', *Sociology*, 35: 835–54.

69 W Bottero (2004) 'Class identities and the identity of class', *Sociology*, 38, 985–1003; TJE Walker (2002) *Illusive Identity: The Blurring of Working-Class Consciousness in Modern Western Culture*, Lanham, MD: Lexington Books; M Maguire (2005) 'Textures of class in the context of schooling: The perceptions of a "class-crossing" teacher', *Sociology*, 39: 427–43; D Byrne (2005) 'Class, culture and identity. A reflection on absences against preferences', special issue of *Sociology*, 39: 807–16.

70 M Verloo (2006) 'Multiple inequalities, intersectionality and the European Union', *European Journal of Women's Studies*, 13: 211–28.

71 G Axeli-Knapp (2005) 'Race, class, gender: Reclaiming baggage in fast travelling theories', *European Journal of Women's Studies*, 12: 249–65.

72 Ibid, p 263.

73 Recently, Ulrich Beck became renown for his alternative vision of a *cosmopolitan methodology*. Although I agree with his argument concerning the limited perspectives of national methodologies, I do hold strong reservations towards his and other mainstream sociologists more recent attempts to reserve this proclaimed non-national methodology as decent research to strengthen Europeanisation. For details on Beck's proposal, see U Beck (2000) 'The cosmopolitan perspective: sociology of the second age of modernity', *British Journal of Sociology*, 51: 79–105.

74 C Pateman (1986) *Feminist Challenge: Social And Political Theory*, Sydney, London: Allen and Unwin; C Pateman (1989) *The Disorder of Women: Democracy, Feminism and Political Theory*, Cambridge: Polity Press.

75 R Johnson (2005) 'Gender, race, class and sexual orientation: Theorizing the intersections', in G MacDonald, RL Osborne and CC Smith (eds) *Feminism, Law, Inclusion: Intersectionality in Action*, Toronto: Sumach Press, pp 21–37, at p 22.

76 The notion of 'becoming' has been explicated in the context of intersected subjectivities more recently by Valentine in 2007, but also explicitly in a sociological reading of feminist resistance by Kalpana Kannabiran (2006) 'A cartography of resistance: the National Federation of Dalit Women', in N Yuval-Davis, K Kannabiran and UM Vieten (eds) *The Situated Politics of Belonging*, London: Sage, pp 54–71.

77 S Walby (2007) 'Complexity theory, systems theory, and multiple intersecting social inequalities', *Philosophy of the Social Sciences*, 37: 449–70, at p 462.

78 Ibid, p 462.

79 F Anthias (2006) 'Belongings in a globalising and unequal world: Rethinking translocations', in N Yuval-Davis, K Kannabiran and UM Vieten (eds), *The Situated Politics of Belonging*, London: Sage

80 N Yuval-Davis (2006) 'Intersectionality and feminist politics', *European Journal of Women's Studies*, 13: 193–209, at pp 200–1.

81 S Walby (2007) 'Complexity theory, systems theory, and multiple intersecting social inequalities', *Philosophy of the Social Sciences*, 37: 449–70, at p 452.

82 Ibid.

83 Ibid, p 453.

84 It is beyond the scope of my chapter to review the theoretical discussion that advanced around complexity theory. See for example, P Cilliers (1998) *Complexity and Postmodernism: Understanding Complex Systems*, London: Routledge; E Cudworth (2005) *Developing Ecofeminist Theory: The Complexity of Difference*, London: Palgrave.

85 S Walby (2007) 'Complexity theory, systems theory, and multiple intersecting social inequalities', *Philosophy of the Social Sciences*, 37: 449–70, at p 459.

86 Ibid.

87 Ibid.

88 This indicates that gender is not confined to the sphere of family and culture, for example, and class not determined only by economic locations and achievements.

89 This aspect is also emphasised by N Yuval-Davis (2006) 'Intersectionality and feminist politics', *European Journal of Women's Studies*, 13: 193–209, at p 203.

90 A Jewe (2004) *Constructing Equality: Identity and Intersectionality in Canadian and South African Jurisprudence*, MA dissertation, Cape Town.

91 Ibid, p 26.

92 In 2002, Daniel Levy and Nathan Sznaider analysed the cosmopolitanisation of the Holocaust memory and argue that '[t]ransnational memory cultures . . . have the potential to become the cultural formation for global rights politics'. D Levy and N Sznaider (2002) 'Memory unbound – The holocaust and the formation of cosmopolitan memory', *European Journal of Social Theory*, 5: 87–106, citation at p 88. In this text, they also critically discuss the Stockholm Forum while stating that ' "culture" offered "politics" a template for how a unified Europe, the site of the historical Holocaust, could imagine itself as a community of shared values' (p 100). During this forum the Holocaust was officially declared as a European memory.

93 Levy and Sznaider, ibid, p 102.

94 E Holzleithner (2006) 'Mainstreaming equality: Dis/Entangling grounds of Discrimination', *Transnational Law and Contemporary Problems*, 14: 927–57.

95 S Walby (2007) 'Complexity theory, systems theory, and multiple intersecting social inequalities', *Philosophy of the Social Sciences*, 37: 449–70, at p 461.

96 Bell Hooks used in her analysis the term 'white supremacy', B Hooks (1981) *Ain't I a Woman: Black Women and Feminism*, Boston, MA: South End Press (London: Pluto Press, 1982).

97 *Situating* means that a generalised pattern or a supposedly taken for granted discourse has to be approached more concretely while detecting complex and contradictory positioning(s) within particular historical, nationally specific and biographical locations. See for details on this methodological term U Vieten (2007) '*Situated Cosmopolitanisms: Notions of the Other in Discourses on Cosmopolitanism in Britain and Germany*, PhD thesis, University of East London (unpublished).

98 D Schiek, L Waddington and M Bell (eds) (2007) 'Introductory Chapter: A comparative perspective on non-discrimination law', in D Schiek, L Waddington and M Bell (eds) *Cases, Materials and Text on National, Supranational and International Non-Discrimination Law*, Oxford: Hart Publishing, pp 1–23.

99 A Tourain (1999) 'Conclusion – European sociologists between economic globalisation and cultural fragmentation', in TP Boje, B van Steenbergen and S Walby (eds) *European Societies – Fusion or Fission?*, London, New York: Routledge, pp 249–62.

100 A Tourain, ibid, pp 255–6.

6 Stigma

A limiting principle allowing multiple-consciousness in anti-discrimination law?

Iyiola Solanke

6.1 Introduction

In 2004, a complaint was brought by Kamlesh Bahl[1] against her employer, the Law Society. Bahl claimed that she had been the victim of discrimination on the grounds of her race and gender. According to Peter Gibson LJ, it was not possible for her to claim race *and* gender as a single combined ground of discrimination: these two aspects had to be treated separately and independent evidence in support of each brought forward. In other words, the law did not accommodate the notion that Bahl may have been the victim of discrimination because she was a black woman *per se* – she could be recognised as a victim of discrimination due to race *or* gender, but not both together.

Since the 1980s, African American female legal scholars have argued that the atomised approach towards anti-discrimination law, which is common in both European and American legal systems, limits the protection offered by equality law. They have promoted the idea of multiple consciousness and the concept of 'intersectionality' to enable anti-discrimination law to address cases of complex discrimination, such as *Bahl*, where the complaint rests upon more than one ground.

Whilst intersectionality loosens the constraints of the atomised approach, I suggest in this chapter that in order to move anti-discrimination law from single- to multiple-consciousness, it is necessary to go beyond intersectionality. Intersectionality, I argue, is limited because the language of 'grounds' which it employs is determined by the logic of immutability. Immutability has long served as a limiting principle[2] to determine when legal protection from discrimination should be provided. I question this use of immutability and suggest the idea of stigma as an alternative limiting principle. Whilst immutability creates limited categories, stigma draws a spectrum of characteristics, of which immutability is just one.

As Crenshaw notes, a legal prohibition by itself does not remove stigma or undermine the underlying assumptions. Stigma sticks in spite of anti-discrimination law because it rests upon 'assumptions so entrenched and so necessary to the maintenance of interlocking, interdependent structures of domination that their mythological bases and political functions have become invisible'.[3] Should stigma be given pride of place over racial discrimination as the concept which best reflects the causes of disadvantage?.[4] Are there any advantages to this? Would stigma make discrimination law more receptive to complex discrimination yet maintain its robustness and sense of purpose? I discuss how stigma could 'liberate' anti-discrimination law yet maintain limits to its use.

Focusing on a recent case in the UK concerning school exclusions, I offer an example of how the concept of stigma could provide both a limiting principle and an analytical point of departure for incorporating multiple consciousness into anti-discrimination law. The case concerns two young black men, a specific social group to whom a set of negative stigmas are attached. I show that this stigma is historical, social and political; it is negative and has long-term economic impact. It also operates at an international level: African American men face the same problems.[5] I demonstrate that it is not just their race, but the combination of their race, age and gender which makes young black men subject to unique treatment. Discrimination was based on this combination of characteristics rather than any single one. I demonstrate how the court may have reached a different conclusion had it focused its deliberations on the question of stigma.

The chapter begins with a discussion on the development of 'grounds' in anti-discrimination law and the centrality of the idea of permanence, or immutability, to this. In both British and American law, immutability acts as a principle to limit access to a legal remedy for discrimination. I then discuss the emergence of arguments in favour of a multiple-consciousness approach, and sketch the limited success of these arguments in American courts. By challenging the single-dimension approach, legal feminists hoped to go beyond the 'sex-plus' analysis of the courts. I suggest that this can be done by changing the way in which immutability is used in anti-discrimination law and using the concept of stigma as an alternative limiting principle. Finally, using the case of *Appiah and Wabwire* on school exclusions, I demonstrate how a stigma-based approach could facilitate multiple-consciousness in anti-discrimination law.

6.2 Grounds and immutability in anti-discrimination law

Anti-discrimination law operates by placing a spotlight on one attribute or the other: race *or* gender, disability *or* religion. Effectively combating disability discrimination requires different measures to ameliorating racial discrimination. Disability discrimination is not analogous to racial discrimination and neither of these may be analogous to age discrimination. In order for law to be able to provide a specific remedy for persons who suffer a detriment due to a particular characteristic – race, disability, national origin, gender – that characteristic has to be isolated. It is not only isolated, but also magnified, to tower like a totem pole so that before the law all other aspects of the individual fade into the background. This has been an effective way of highlighting the way in which these characteristics, which for so long operated in the dark, formed the invisible backdrop to many employment and other decisions. Their magnification made them visible and remediable in law. These totems are the entrenched 'grounds' upon which discrimination is unlawful.

It is fair to ask why legal protection was provided against racial and gender discrimination in the 1970s, but not for religion or sexual orientation until the twenty-first century? Or why is there no legal protection for people who may suffer discrimination as a result of their weight? For whom should law provide protection against discrimination and when should it not? How is this decided? A key value in determining the reach of anti-discrimination law has been the idea of immutability – the permanent and involuntary character of the trait which causes an individual to suffer discrimination. The idea of immutability has influenced the development and scope of both British and American anti-discrimination law.

During the political discussions in the UK on the development of the first Race Relations Act of 1965, the Society for Labour Lawyers stressed that the law should 'protect those attacked for what they are, not for what they may believe or do'.[6] For this reason, religious groups per se were not included among those it proposed should be protected, except where religion was a pointer to ethnicity. This distinction between immutable and mutable characteristics was less relevant for other groups, such as the Campaign Against Racial Discrimination (CARD), which proposed a prohibition which included religion.[7] The Labour government of the day settled the content of the legislation based upon two main considerations: first, what would be practical in application and thus effective, and second, what would be seen as in line with the emerging international instrument, the International Convention on the Elimination of All Forms of Racial Discrimination (ICERD). The ICERD focused on race and consciously excluded religion because it was seen as a chosen rather than inherent attribute. This pattern was followed by the British government.

The principle of immutability has also left a strong imprint on American constitutional law. The US Supreme Court has made it clear that immutability determines when a classification is 'suspect' and therefore subject to a strict rather than standard level of scrutiny.[8] Of the discrimination law statutes, this test applies only to the level of scrutiny applied under the Equal Protection Clause of the Fourteenth Amendment of the US Constitution. Under Title VII,[9] which only covers employment discrimination, there is only one level of protection. The determination of whether a classification is 'suspect' depends upon a number of factors: the court asks whether the group so defined has suffered a history of purposeful discrimination; whether it lacks political power to obtain redress, and whether the discrimination constitutes a level of unfairness invidious to the ideal of equal protection. When seeking to answer this final question, the court considers, amongst other aspects, whether the trait defining the group is immutable.[10]

Since the landmark case of *Brown v Board of Education*, discrimination against African Americans has been the litmus test for the question of whether a group satisfies this immutability test. In *Frontero*, the Supreme Court clarified that this meant that the group had to be defined by a permanent and unchanging feature 'determined solely by accident of birth'.[11] Accordingly, gender and national origin are also treated as immutable characteristics. This definition has, however, been criticised as vague. As it has blocked a number of claims for protection, in particular from gay men and lesbian women, the Supreme Court has been criticised for not providing a clear rationale to explain its approach to immutability.[12] Its reasoning has at times been confusing: in *Rogers v American Airlines* the court argued that a braided hairstyle could easily be changed and was therefore mutable, whilst an afro was natural and thus immutable.[13]

It is necessary to limit the scope of anti-discrimination law, and immutability provides a principle to ensure that a remedy exists for the most invidious forms of discrimination, suffered as a result of characteristics – such as skin colour, gender, or national origin – over which an individual has no, or little, control. However, if the test of immutability excludes vulnerable groups from access to legal protection against discrimination, how helpful is it in the goal of ameliorating discrimination? For example, few legal remedies[14] exist for 'fattism' described as the 'last great acceptable prejudice'.[15] The overweight and obese may have control over their size, but does this mean society can discriminate against larger persons with impunity? Whilst some argue for the adoption of a 'soft' immutability[16] others argue that immutability should be discarded completely.[17] Black legal feminists are likely to agree with the latter: the permanent/produced dichotomy of immutability also limits the potential of a multiple consciousness approach to discrimination or 'intersectionality.'

6.3 Intersectionality

The earliest articles on a 'multiple consciousness perspective'[18] or intersectionality date from the 1980s, and are linked to the emergence of black feminist legal academics. Black female legal scholars used black feminist thought[19] to create intellectual space and a language with which to analyse law from their own specific social and political perspective. Their intention was to develop and apply a black feminist legal scholarship which considered 'the interactive relationship between racism and sexism from the experiential standpoint and knowledge base of black women' and would give rise to legal theories grounded in their reality[20] and sensitise law to the specific myths surrounding the lives of this group.[21]

The early work dealt exclusively with black women. However, many recognised the broader applicability of intersectionality. For Caldwell, black women were the immediate, but not exclusive, 'physical and material representation of the intersection of race and gender'.[22] As Lacy shows, black men are also subject to stereotypes based on race and gender.[23] Scales-Trent argued that any group which demonstrates that it is discrete, insular and powerless should be able to claim similar protection.[24] Wei has articulated the way in which Asian women experience discrimination on the grounds of gender and national origin.[25] However, the first cohort of black legal feminists took the treatment of black women under US anti-discrimination law as their starting point. Their attention focused primarily on employment claims under Title VII.[26]

Black women had unsuccessfully brought discrimination claims under Title VII in the 1970s.[27] Judges rejected that black women formed a specific group, seeing them as a subset of all (mainly white) women or all blacks (mainly men). In *Degraffenreid v General Motors*,[28] a District Court rejected this idea as an attempt to create a 'super-remedy'. The plaintiffs were told to bring an action for race discrimination *or* sex discrimination, 'but not a combination of both'. In *Munford v James T Barnes & Co*,[29] where the plaintiff alleged both sexual and racial discrimination, the District Court allowed only the sexual discrimination claim to continue and granted a motion for summary judgment for the race discrimination claim.[30] In *Rogers v American Airlines*,[31] Rogers, a black woman, argued that the policy of American Airlines prohibiting braided hairstyles discriminated specifically against her as a black woman. The court denied any interactive relationship between race and gender.

However, in 1980, a federal court did accept that black women were a specific class under Title VII. In *Jefferies v Harris City Commission*,[32] the Fifth Circuit Court held that black women could be discriminated against, even in the absence of discrimination against black men or white women. In this case, a race claim or gender claim alone would have failed as the company had hired both a white female and an African American male in the position which was at the centre of the claim brought by Jeffries, an African American woman. The Circuit Court found that the District Court had erred in failing to address Jefferies intersectional claim of race and sex discrimination. It said that absent a clear statement that Congress 'did not intend to provide protection against discrimination directed especially toward black women as a class separate and distinct from the class of women and the class of blacks, we cannot condone a result which leaves black women without a viable Title VII remedy'.[33]

In *Lam v University of Hawaii*,[34] the Federal Court of Appeal (Ninth Circuit Court) overruled what it called the 'mathematical' approach taken by a District Court which looked for evidence of racism and then sexism. Lam, a female of Vietnamese descent, alleged discrimination on the basis of race, sex, and national origin following her unsuccessful application for the post of Director of the Law School's Pacific Asian Legal Studies Program. The District Court viewed the racism and sexism claims as distinct but the Ninth Circuit Court found this approach to be incorrect and stated that 'where two bases for discrimination exist, they cannot be neatly reduced to distinct components' because 'attempt[ing] to bisect a person's identity at the inter-section of race and gender often distorts or ignores the particular nature of their experiences'.[35] The court recognised that refusing the claim would leave many women without a remedy in the face of discrimination.

The multiple consciousness approach had therefore found some acceptance by the mid-1990s. However, there was concern that the 'sex-plus' approach, adopted by the court in *Jeffries*, treated black women as a departure from a white norm, as if '. . . being a woman or being black were like icing on a cake' rather than an 'integrated, undifferentiated, complete whole' consciousness.[36] In contrast, Scales-Trent described black women as being a 'synergistic' com-bination of two 'degraded statuses' – 'the disabilities of blacks and the dis-abilities which inhere in their status as women' – which resulted in a condition 'more terrible than the sum of their two constituent parts'.[37] Sociological data demonstrated the consequences of being a black women in American society, a situation overlooked because black women stand at the 'interstice' of not only two major social problems – race and gender – but also two major legal issues – the rights of blacks and the rights of women. As the title of a sociological anthology so aptly said, in legal and social discourse all the women were white and all the men black.[38] Crenshaw argued that the single-dimension logic of equality law erased the experiences of black women from anti-discrimination law. Black women 'are regarded either as too much like women or Blacks': their experience is either absorbed into the collective experiences of one of these groups, or left at the margins because it differs from both feminist and civil rights agendas.[39] As noted by Scales-Trent, employers, landlords, and institutions do not discriminate in neat categories.[40] If perpetrators do not pick grounds but simply act upon their prejudices, why must victims? The law forces complainants to make a choice – which may ultimately affect the outcome of the case[41] – where none may exist. The concept of intersectionality was intended to remove this burden upon victims by instituting a multiple-consciousness perspective.

By insisting that discrimination is not a zero-sum game intersectionality challenged this single dimension logic. However, intersectionality remains grounded in the logic of immutability. Although the aim of intersectionality is to merge 'grounds' back together in line with empirical reality, the language of 'intersectionality' continues to keep them apart – the concept of intersec-tionality continues to rely upon the language of grounds informed by the logic of immutability. This logic constrains the potential of intersectionality. In order to achieve a truly multiple consciousness in discrimination law, it is necessary to change this logic. To truly be non-additive, anti-discrimination law needs to reconsider immutability as a limiting principle. There are two ways in which the use of immutability as a limiting principle can be changed. First, a softer form of immutability, which recognises that some traits are immutable for reasons other than biology, can be used. The introduction of legal protection from discrimination on the grounds of sexual orientation and religion suggests a softer use of immutability.

Second, the use of immutability can be de-emphasised. A way to de-emphasise immutability is to take a step back, to think about discrimination prior to specification, when there were only myths, stereotypes and a complex spectrum of stigma. If we start from stigma, we end up with a spectrum of characteristics which include immutability, rather than a list of grounds determined by immutability. Stigma brings into focus the complex forms of discrimination which blight individual lives and social cohesion. It can travel alone but also in packs: black women are burdened by the stigma of race and sex; black women can also be disabled; the disabled may also suffer from the stigma attached to sexual orientation and/or age[42] It is this interaction between various forms of stigma to which multiple consciousness points.

6.4 Stigma

What is 'stigma'? Stigma does not refer to individual attitudes but focuses on negative meanings which are 'socially inscribed'[43] on arbitrary attributes, such as skin colour, sexual orientation, gender, pregnancy, disability or age. Goffman defines stigma as 'a special kind of relationship between attribute and stereotype'.[44] Stigmas have different characteristics and consequences. Some are more established than others. Some are permanent (immutable), whilst others are temporary. Some, such as obesity, are visible and conveyed involuntarily. Others, such as religious affiliation, are invisible and it is the discretion of the bearer to volunteer this information.

Stigmas can be racial, physical, behavioural or biographical,[45] acquired or inherited, or in-born. They change from place to place, and can operate at local, national, regional and international levels: the stigma attached to being a Dalit may be poignant only on the continent of Asia whilst the stigma attached to black skin operates at a global level.

Stigma goes beyond name-calling. Being stigmatised means being locked out of the norm. Stigma is never neutral – it is 'used for a reason – for social structure and for social control. It tells you what your place is, and it tells you to stay in your place'.[46] Stigmas develop over time: most are crystallised taboos and myths 'long in the making, and difficult to acknowledge or confront'.[47] These 'myths and stereotypes do much of their damage subconsciously. They seep into the inner psyche and take up residence ... they're insidious. They're sneaky. They have had centuries to sink in'.[48] The dehumanisation of an individual is key to the operation of stigma.[49] Discrimination works together with stigma – stigma provides a reason to withhold 'the presumption of equal humanity'[50] which underpins discrimination: stigma provides the social context and justification for 'doubting the person's worthiness'.[51]

Whilst stigma always excludes, it does not always result in political powerlessness, social and economic degradation. Thus not all stigma, or combination of stigmas will warrant a legal remedy. Consequently, stigma can be used to create a limiting principle whilst at the same time enabling legal recognition of the compounded ways in which discrimination is experienced in society. In order to ascertain the merits of a complaint, a legal analysis would proceed by a general examination of the social, political and economic consequences of the stigmas involved. Questions similar to those posed by the US Supreme Court in relation to the Fourteenth Amendment could be asked: has the group so defined suffered a history of purposeful discrimination? Does it lack political power to obtain redress? Does the discrimination constitute a level of unfairness invidious to the ideal of equal protection? Such an approach would make discrimination law flexible but not flaccid.

A stigma-led analysis of the issue could be framed around more specific questions. It would be necessary to ascertain the stigmas attached to the group – what do they target and what are their characteristics? Can the group created by these stigmas be described as 'discrete, insular and powerless'? Second, the consequences of these stigmas would need to be clarified: does any one, or any combination of them, result in social, political or economic degradation? Third, a causal relationship would need to be identified: is there any indication that these stigmas have contributed to the treatment complained of?

There are many advantages to this emphasis on stigma. First, a focus on stigma opens up the possibility for an incisive yet non-rigid approach to tackling discrimination. Discrimination law develops a potential to challenge a broad spectrum of entrenched stigma rather than be limited to the neat categorical logic of immutability. It not only facilitates a broader and deeper identification of discrimination but provides for a more thorough examination of the stigma and stereotype at play in society. This is important because society is complicit in discrimination – social mores are a repository of stigma providing justifications for everyday discriminatory actions and decision-making. Second, by drawing attention to the social context within which discrimination occurs, consideration of stigma will move courts to take note of the experiential world of claimants in a systematic way. An examination of complaints in context will become increasingly important as direct discrimination becomes less easily identifiable: this is not necessarily a sign that discrimination is decreasing but that it is more subtle and indirect.

Third, a focus on stigma therefore restores the connection between discrimination law and society. This connection is crucial because in the absence of this link, positive and affirmative measures to tackle discrimination are vulnerable to criticism as 'reverse discrimination'. As the recent successful attacks on affirmative action in the US show,[52] measures to ameliorate the effects of discrimination that are separated from social reality can easily be reduced to a battle between economic or political 'interests'. Discrimination law rooted in society deals with fairness: the demand for non-discrimination is not fuelled by interest group resentment but by a broader belief in social equality. It is a tool for social renewal and cohesion rather than a facilitator of individual or group progress.

6.5 A stigma-led approach as the basis for multiple consciousness: Appiah and Wabwire – race, gender, age discrimination

Reinhart Appiah and Frank Wabwire, two black teenagers, were due to complete their vocational courses in the summer of 2002. On 27 February 2002 they were involved in a fight in the sixth form common room of their school with John Benitez and Adam Daghorn, two white boys. In the course of the fight, John Benitez sustained a head injury which required a hospital visit

The incident was initially investigated by the head of the sixth form at the School, Mr Wilkins. He sent only the two black boys home whilst he investigated the event. Despite speaking to those involved and some who had been nearby, he was unable to gather consistent and conclusive information. He passed the results of his investigation to the head teacher, Mr Meadows. Meadows concluded from this inconclusive information that 'Reinhart and Frank had started the incident and had increased the level of violence' with the consequence that 'John sustained injuries which required an attendance at hospital'. He redefined the fight as an 'attack', with the two black boys being the initiators and aggressors and the two white boys their victims. This justified his decision to exclude the black boys, but not punish the white boys: 'John I regarded as a victim, nor was there anything to suggest that Adam had used violence'.

On 8 March 2002, Meadows informed the parents of Reinhart and Frank by letter of his decision to exclude permanently the two black boys. Meadows based his decision upon 'extensive investigation' but admitted that there was 'no absolute view on what took place during the confrontation'. Neither Reinhart nor Frank were allowed to return onto the school premises, but were able to complete their coursework in order to gain their qualifications. Their last day at school, therefore, became the day of the fight in the common room, when they were informally sent home. When Meadows was informed by the local education authority that the terms of the exclusion were contrary to statutory requirements, this was changed to a fixed term exclusion of 45 school days, beginning 28 February until 15 May. The end result was the same because this period ended at a point when students were on study leave to prepare for their exams. Meadow's decision was confirmed by the school governors, who described his action as 'reasonable' and the exclusion as 'appropriate'.

The parents brought a case in the County Court against the school governors claiming racial discrimination for less favourable treatment on the grounds of race, ethnicity and/or colour. They claimed that Reinhart and Frank were subjected to the unlawful sanction of an informal permanent exclusion by Meadows and subsequently victimised by the governors on two fronts: first, by the failure to investigate properly or at all complaints made by them and on their behalf of racial discrimination; and second, in upholding Meadow's decision to impose a 45-day fixed-term exclusion. They used as comparators John and Adam, stating: 'These boys had been involved in the same incident . . . but received no sanction for their misconduct'. Both white students involved in the same incident faced no sanction.

The County Court found against the black boys and upon appeal, Crawford Lindsay J dismissed the case.[53] Despite finding (in contrast to Meadows' assertion) that Benitez had provoked the fight and was the 'initial aggressor' and accepting that Reinhart and Frank had been treated differently to John and Adam, he concluded there was no proof that racism played any part in the decision to expel only Reinhart and Frank.[54] He could not believe the teachers had 'racist intent'. On the contrary, Crawford Lindsay J was impressed by Meadows, Wilkins and the chair of governors. He found that Meadows was under a lot of pressure running the school and was doing the best he could. Meadows' decision to exclude the black students was 'reasonable . . . on the evidence available'. He accepted the evidence of Meadows and Wilkins that they treated all pupils equally, and Meadows was commended for recognising that exclusions for black students were running at a very high level and for starting a Saturday school to raise black achievement rates. He concluded: 'We are satisfied the failings were not racially motivated'.

What could the findings have been had a stigma-based multiple consciousness analysis applied? Such an analysis could have given rise to reasons why Crawford Lindsay J should have been dissatisfied, at least to the extent to shift the burden of proof onto the school governors. It can be argued that the social stigmas attached to race, age and gender affected the way in which the situation at Bishop Douglas School was handled and the decision to exclude the boys. This approach highlights that young black boys as a group need the protection of discrimination law because they are stigmatised in society in general, and the school education system in particular.

6.5.1 Stigmas attached to young black men in British society

During his last year as Prime Minister, Tony Blair caused an outcry of protest when he appeared to imply that the knife and gun crime causing the deaths of many young black men in Britain was part of a distinctive black culture. His characterisation of teenage shootings presented the issue as a 'black' problem, rather than a general problem of youth culture in Britain today.[55]

The criminalisation of young black men is not a recent phenomenon. In the UK, as in the US there are very few positive images of black men outside the fields of entertainment and athletics, which 'confine young black boys to achievements of the body and not of the mind'.[56] The media presents black men as uneducated, violent, hyper-heterosexual criminals and drug runners – failures in need of discipline who make no positive contribution to their families or society. During the period of the stop-and-search (SUS) laws,[57] statistics indicate that black males were often stopped simply because they were young black males;[58] British society is wary of black males of any age, even small black children.[59] The stigma attached to this combination of race, gender and age causes society to 'assume the worst and over-react'.[60]

The potency of this stigmatisation has facilitated at least one fortune: rapper Ice Cube, renowned for his rebellious black masculinity and tough ghetto persona was raised in a well-to-do area of Los Angeles by two middle class parents and graduated from the wealthiest high school in that city.[61] He has never lived in the ghetto, nor been imprisoned but has become wealthy by exploiting the stigma attached to young black men. Whilst Ice Cube has been able to use the stigma creatively, most young black men are locked into this mythical identity. Unlike young white male malcontents, who are allowed to grow out of youthful rebelliousness, the stigma attached to young black men begins when they are young and sticks, affecting every stage of their life, including their education.

Black male youths are a hidden casualty in the British education system. When at the age of five they enter the school system, 'their test performance is as good as white and Asian children. By 11 their achievement levels are dropping. By 16 there has been a collapse'.[62] In 2003, roughly 70 per cent of them left school with less than five higher grade examination results. This represents the lowest level of achievement for any ethnic group of school children.[63] Unsurprisingly, black men are the least likely of any group to have a degree.[64]

The under-achievement of black boys in school has been a concern for their parents and communities for more than four decades. In the 1960s and 1970s, many black boys were placed in Special Needs Units (a situation similar to that endured by Roma children in Eastern Europe today) or in classes where they could not study for university entrance exams. As long ago as 1977 a House of Commons Select Committee on Race Relations and Immigration urged the government to undertake a high-level and independent inquiry into the causes of the under-achievement of West Indian children. In 1999, Ofsted reported that the gap between African-Caribbean pupils and the rest of the school population continued to widen.[65] It was only in 2002 that the government appointed a black British academic, Dr Richard Majors, to review this issue. Majors concluded that the UK 'faced a 'national emergency' if it failed to tackle the problem of these marginalised pupils.

In his observations, Majors noted that the majority of teachers, being white, were unlikely to be free from the racial stereotypes that permeate society about black men. Unfamiliarity with black culture turns any physical contact into an act of violence and gives rise to accusations of aggression and hostility. According to Abbott 'a black boy doesn't have to be long out of disposal nappies for some teachers to see him as a miniature gangster rapper'.[66] The lack of genuine cultural exposure and close contact with black children meant that teachers could not tell when a black boy is messing about or seriously angry.[67] Conduct by black students which would not be hostile in a black environment becomes 'disruptive' or suspendable conduct in the predominantly white environment of the school.[68] Surreptitiously, the stigma imbibed via the media produces discriminatory practices in schools: black children are discouraged to participate and less praised in the classroom, expectations for attainment and behaviour are lowered, punishment is disproportionate and discipline more frequent, harsher and for less serious misbehaviour than other pupils, and – as in the case of Appiah and Wabwire – disciplinary measures are differentially applied, in particular exclusions. Exclusion can be seen as the culmination of a continuum of discriminatory treatment.

Exclusion is an iconic issue within black communities.[69] Black pupils are three times more likely to be excluded than white pupils. Every year, 1,000 black pupils are permanently excluded and nearly 30,000 receive a fixed-period exclusion. In the London Borough of Croydon, one out of every 10 black schoolchildren is expelled before reaching the age of 17.[70] Since 2000, the proportion of black pupils excluded has increased, and more rapidly than for any other group. In addition to this official data, there is a large body of qualitative and anecdotal evidence on 'unofficial exclusions' – instances where schools avoid official exclusion by, for example, persuading the parents to remove the student from school, or not reporting exclusions. It has been argued that official exclusions data mask a wider unofficial exclusions gap, and perhaps that decreases in exclusions mask increases in unofficial exclusions.[71]

6.5.2 The consequences of these stigmas

Exclusions matter because racial inequalities in the education system mirror and entrench inequalities in society. Exclusion from school is an absolute denial of education and the improved life chances that go with it. It is widely recognised as a driver for wider social disaffection, being highly correlated with unemployment and involvement in crime. According to Martin Narey, Director General of HM Prison Service (2001), the '13,000 young people excluded from school each year might as well be given a date by which to join the prison service some time later down the line'. Statistics corroborate this. The UK prison population is disproportionately male and black. In 2003, over 12 per cent of prisoners were black compared to 2 per cent of the British population.[72] Half of the 400 young people in a Young Offender Institution had been excluded from school.[73] There are twice as many black men in prison as at university.[74] Few attend university or reach higher paying jobs and professional occupations that go with higher educational qualifications.

On average, excluded pupils will do less well educationally, are more likely to be unemployed after school and more likely to drift into a life of petty crime. Lack of achievement becomes a self-fulfilling prophecy once young black men enter the spiral set in play by exclusions: impoverished life chances, deeper social exclusion, repeated unemployment, lower wages, and increased chances of incarceration at some point in life.[75] School exclusion has a cumulative effect: it diminishes the pool of older black men who possess and are able to pass on useful skills, institutional and personal contacts to help younger black men gain employment opportunities.[76] Indeed, this is critical because generations overlap and '. . . much of social life takes place outside the reach of public regulation, and extant social affiliations condition the development of personal and intellectual skills in the young'.[77] The consequences of present prejudice will therefore be inherited by future generations of black families and ultimately British society. Present exclusions promise future growth of a permanent disenfranchised black underclass.

The British government has finally acknowledged the problem of racial discrimination in the education system. In November 2006, the Department for Education and Skills (DfES) High Level Group on Race Equality identified exclusions of black pupils as a priority area for action. Their Report[78] supported what academic commentators, researchers and black families had been saying for over 20 years: that the education system treats black pupils differently from others. It is now officially recognised that racial stigma negatively affects the educational experience of black children in school.

Amongst other factors, the Report argued that this racism stems from long-standing social conditioning involving negative images of black men in particular, which stereotype them as threatening. Such conditioning is reinforced by the media portrayal of black 'street culture'. It encourages school staff to expect black pupils to be worse behaved and to perceive a greater level of threat and challenge in their interactions with individual black pupils. The Report compared white methods of sub-cultural expression, such as 'Goths', who are seen as strange and different but not met with the same hostility by teachers. Although white children who are 'Goth' are equally hostile to the academic environment, they are less stigmatised in society and so benefit in school from a more tolerant approach. The clear message of the Report is that, to a significant extent, the exclusions gap is caused by systematic racial discrimination in the application of disciplinary and exclusions policies. The stereotype of black boys being aggressive and unruly is unconsciously communicated in the interaction between black students and school teachers.

In response to these findings, the government determined that local authorities should lead a policy response. This would form part of their existing duty under the Race Relations (Amendment) Act and their new role, set out in the Education and Inspections Bill, of ensuring that every child fulfils his or her potential. It also noted that a much more robust response from Ofsted (in terms of both policy and on the ground practice) was needed. Some commentators have recommended the creation of a Race Relations Act Compliance Unit with the combined statutory powers of DfES, Ofsted and the Commission for Racial Equality (CRE). One arena for this change which the Report omitted to mention was the judiciary.

6.5.3 Identification of a causal connection between these stigmas and the treatment complained of

Young black men form a discrete group which has suffered a history of discrimination. They also overwhelmingly lack political power. Had the court kept the reality outlined above in mind, it could have considered whether this had influenced decision-making by the headmaster and the governors. In order to answer this, it could have looked at objective factors such as the pattern of exclusions at the school and the exclusions procedure: in particular, the quality of the school investigation, contact with the parents, consideration of other options and whether best practice was followed. As will be seen below, consideration of these questions makes it apparent that there were worrying irregularities in the exclusions practice and procedure.

6.5.3.1 Exclusion practice: pattern of exclusions at the school

The rate of exclusions of black pupils from Bishop Douglas Roman Catholic High School, in East Finchley, north London is disproportionately high: black students made up 74 per cent of all exclusions between 1998 and 2002 even though only 40 per cent of the total school population is black. In 2002, the year Reinhart and Frank were expelled, 86 black students were given fixed term exclusions compared to 27 white students.

6.5.3.2 Exclusion procedure

The quality of the investigations is questionable. Wilkins spoke with those involved and some who had been 'nearby': one can only wonder what this means – were they in an adjacent room, outside the common room, or down the hall? In his letter to the parents, Meadows provides no explanation of how he carried the investigation forward in order to reach his conclusions. He asserted 'a history of on-going and low-level antagonism between a small number of students', but gave no details as to what these were, when they occurred or the level of involvement of Reinhart and Frank. Admitting that there was no 'absolute view on what took place during the confrontation' he, nonetheless, decided to assume the worst of the black boys and permanently exclude them both. His witness statement contained the erroneous assertion that Reinhart and Frank had started the incident; however, John Benitez was found by the court to be the initial aggressor.

There is no indication of the former conduct of the boys. It is unlikely that either had a record of violence or troublesome behaviour in school – had this been the case, it would have been mentioned. It is likely that this was their first serious offence. As the DfES Report noted, black children tend to be subjected to the harshest punishment immediately. There is no indication that an alternative discipline was considered or discussed – Meadows reached for the harshest punishment immediately despite the fact that it was a crucial time in their academic life.[79] Questions surround the lack of contact with the parents. There was an unexplained delay of 10 days between the incident and communication informing both parents of the exclusion. Meadows was unavailable to speak to them during this period. The parents were not told why expulsion had been chosen as the suitable sanction and the absence of words such as 'permanent exclusion' in the letter did not made it clear what action was actually taken. Furthermore, Meadows discouraged the parents from any further action with his statement that the matter was now considered closed.

Perhaps the most objective indication is whether best practice was followed. There is now substantial legislative authority to help schools tackle the high level of exclusions amongst black children. Since the Race Relations (Amendment) Act 2000 came into force, the Race Relations Act 1976, s 71(1) has required schools and local authorities amongst others to 'have due regard to the need' to: eliminate unlawful racial discrimination; promote equality of opportunity between different racial groups; and promote good race relations between different ethnic groups. The CRE has published a Statutory Code of Practice to advise schools on how they might meet this general duty and the specific duties imposed on them by the Race Relations Act 1976 (Statutory Duties) Order 2001. The Code in particular mentions the need to assess the impact of behaviour, discipline and exclusion policies on different ethnic groups. It suggests that, to meet their duties under the Act, schools should make effective use of data and involve minority ethnic pupils, parents and communities in policy making, consulting them about their needs and opinions.

In addition, since 1999 Circular 10/99 has stated that 'every avenue of prevention has to have been exhausted beforehand, and the decision to fixed-term or permanently exclude should be taken only in response to serious breaches of a school's discipline policy after other strategies have failed; and continuing presence of the pupil may be harmful to themselves or others. Finally, the School Standards and Framework Act 1998, s 68 binds local education authorities, headteachers and governors to prevent exclusions and follow the exclusion procedures.

Many of the facts demonstrate that Meadows, supported by the governors, did not actively seek to change the exclusions practice at the school by adopting best practice as laid out in these documents and the Race Relations Act. It is surprising that Crawford Lindsay J was satisfied despite evidence of both the disproportionate exclusion practice and flawed exclusion procedures: the boys were told to 'go home' and were not told that they had been excluded; Meadows simply wrote that the pair were not to return and would be sent work to complete at home – this had to be rectified when the local authority advised Meadows that a permanent exclusion was contrary to statutory requirements; the parents had to wait two and a half months for the governors exclusions appeal hearing on 9 May which confirmed the decision;

Meadows failed to advise the parents that they had a right to appeal to the school governors. However, perhaps most importantly of all, no alternative to exclusion was considered.

Were the court to have proceeded from a stigma-based analysis enabling multiple-consciousness of discrimination rather than grounds-based analysis, it may have been sensitive to the way stigma attached to race, gender and age affected the decision to exclude the two black boys. The school's decision-making, necessarily subjective given the lack of reliable objective information, was influenced by the stereotypes attached to young black men. The decision to exclude was a reaction to these stereotypes rather than an objective response to the events in the sixth form common room. In reacting, it failed to follow exclusion procedure or best practice. Whilst it may not have been its deliberate intent to discriminate, its actions appear to have, nonetheless, been influenced by race, gender and age: it assumed the worst because it was dealing with young black boys, and overreacted.

6.6 Conclusion

It is no longer adequate for anti-discrimination law to focus on single-dimensions of unlawful treatment. The language of grounds has kept forms of discrimination apart from each other, and in so doing has made groups such as young black men and black women invisible in anti-discrimination law. The logic of immutability which underlies anti-discrimination law does not accommodate the complex reality of discrimination as it is often experienced. Specification has resulted in a rigid legal framework which has difficulty dealing with discrimination on more than one ground. The assumption that the experience of discrimination falls neatly within one ground or the other no longer fits reality – if it ever did. Whilst law imagines a focused and rational perpetrator who carefully targets bits of identity, it is unlikely that discriminators are ever as thoughtful this. In addition, as discriminators become more sophisticated, new ways are needed to tackle indirect discrimination.

I argued that intersectionality does not go far enough to achieve a multiple-consciousness: it still rests upon the logic of immutability. I argued for a need to loosen with the link with immutability and grounds in order to reach the full promise of intersectionality and multiple-consciousness. I suggested therefore that immutability be de-emphasised, in particular by its reincorporation into a spectrum of stigmatised characteristics. This, I argued, had many advantages. Not only would such a starting point give rise to more holistic and flexible protection from discrimination, but it would re-identify anti-discrimination law as a tool for social justice. Discrimination may occur between individuals, but social stigmas provide the background justification for this.

I used the recent case of Appiah and Wabwire to demonstrate how the idea of stigma in anti-discrimination law could facilitate a multiple-conciousness approach. As Caldwell points out, black men also stand at the interstice of race and gender. As I have shown above, they are also a discrete, insular and powerless group. The case illustrated the limits of a single category approach in anti-discrimination law. At present, this confluence of race, gender and age discrimination cannot be recognised by anti-discrimination law in the UK. A claim covering these three aspects could not be brought: the two men concerned would have to choose between a gender claim under the Sex Discrimination Act 1975 or a race claim under the Race Relations Act 1976. An age claim under the new Age Regulations of 2006[80] would be impossible as the Regulations cover employment only.

The decision in this case is a missed opportunity to challenge the social stigmas which blight the future of this group. Not only did the court dismiss the empirical data on the rates of exclusion of black boys at the school as not being 'indicative of racism', it left unchallenged the school's evasive responses to the questionnaire. Together, these would have sufficed to shift the burden of proof under the new Race Relations Act.[81] In the case of *Adebayo*[82] it was stated that evasive or delayed response to the questionnaire could be used to effect this shift.

Had the school been required to present evidence that it did not conduct unlawful discrimination, this case could have been used to support, rather than undermine current government efforts in this area. The DfES faces an uphill battle in trying to address the exclusion of young black boys: according to a CRE study of 2003, schools are hostile to the concept of race relations – it found that 33 per cent of schools believed that race equality laws produced no positive benefits. In America, where the courts have been more attentive to racial discrimination in education in general,[83] more progress has been made on this issue.

Genuine multiple consciousness in discrimination law can be achieved by taking the many dimensions of stigma into account. The concept of stigma could be the starting point for a new jurisprudence, 'one founded not on an ideal of neutrality, but on the reality of oppression'[84] both historical and contemporary. This fresh perspective could be useful nationally, for example in the UK where the historical atomised approach to discrimination legislation is being replaced by a single equality framework. In addition, a stigma-based approach to discrimination law could facilitate a robust interpretation of European anti-discrimination law whilst recognising that the empirical reality of discrimination varies between Member States. Furthermore, this perspective would also keep the law in this area grounded in the reality of those requiring its protection[85] rather than limiting claims to a single departure from the white male Christian heterosexual norm,[86] itself no more than a fictional construct.[87]

Notes

1 *Bahl v Law Society* [2004] IRLR 799.
2 *McClesky v Kemp* 481 US 279, 283 (1987).

3 PM Caldwell (1991) 'A hair piece: Perspectives on the intersection of race and gender', *Duke Law Journal*: 365–96, at p 371.

4 GC Loury (2002) *The Anatomy of Racial Inequality*, Cambridge, MA: Harvard University Press, at p 10.

5 DA Lacy (2007) 'The most endangered Title VII plaintiff? African-American males and intersectional claims', available at http://works.bepress.com/d_aaron-_lacy/ (accessed 14 January 2008).

6 Public Records Office, London: 'LAB 8/3070, Memorandum on Draft Bill'.

7 Public Records Office, London: 'LAB 8/3070, CARD Proposals for Legislation'.

8 A classification subject to 'strict scrutiny' must demonstrate that it 'serves a compelling state interest' and is 'necessary . . . to the accomplishment' of its objective.

9 Title VII 42 USC 2000e-2(a) (2004).

10 MR Shapiro (2002) 'Treading the Supreme Court's murky immutability waters', *Gonzaga Law Review*, 38: 409–44.

11 *Frontiero v Richardson* 411 US 677 (1973). See also *Garcia v Gloor* 618 F2d 264 (5 Cir 1980), cert denied, 499 US 1113 (1981); *Caban v Mohammad*, 441 US 380 (1979); *Holland v Illinois* 493 US 474 (1990). Balog asks whether the trait has to be visible. See K Balog (2005) 'Equal protection for homosexuals: Why the immutability argument is necessary and how it is met', *Cleveland State Law Review*, 53: 545.

12 MR Shapiro (2002) 'Treading the Supreme Court's murky immutability waters', *Gonzaga Law Review*, 38: 409–44.

13 ML Turner (2001) 'The Braided uproar: A defense of my sisters hair and an indictment of Rogers v American Airlines', *Cardozo Women's Law Journal*, 7: 115–62.

14 K Horner (2005) 'A growing problem: Why the federal government needs to shoulder the burden in protecting workers from weight discrimination', *Catholic University Law Review*, 54: 589–613. Michigan is the only American state with laws that include height and weight as protected categories under anti-discrimination law: the Elliot Larsen Civil Rights Act 453 of 1976, Sec 209 (Mich Comp Laws Ann § 37.2102 (1985 and Supp 1993) bans discrimination in employment based on race, color, religion, national origin, age, sex, height, weight or marital status. Some municipalities have enacted ordinances barring weight and personal appearance discrimination: Washington, DC prohibits discrimination based on personal appearance (DC CODE ANN, § 1–2501 (1987 and Supp 1993); San Francisco bars weight and personal appearance discrimination (SAN FRAN ADMIN. CODE, CHAPTERS 12A, 12B and 12C; SAN FRAN MUNICIPAL/POLICE CODE, ART 33); Santa Cruz, CA (July 1992), defines unlawful discrimination as 'differential treatment as a result of that person's race, color, creed, religion, national origin, ancestry, disability, marital status, sex gender, sexual orientation, height, weight, or physical characteristic'; District of Columbia, Human Rights Law (Subchapter II, Sec 1–2512) outlaws discrimination in employment based upon 'race, color, religion, national origin, sex, age, marital status, personal appearance, sexual orientation, family responsibilities, physical handicap, matriculation, or political affiliation'.

15 R Pelling (2005) 'Of course it's ok to call another woman a hobnob-guzzling, lazy lard-arse', *Independent on Sunday*, 18 September.

16 J Landau (2005) "Soft immutabilty" and "imputed gay identity": Recent developments in transgender and sexual orientation based asylum law', *Fordham Urban Law Review*, 32: 237–64.

17 DL Hutchinson (2003) 'Unexplainable on grounds other than race: The inversion of privilege and subordination in equal protection jurisprudence', *University of Illinois Law Review*: 615–700.

18 M Matsuda (1989) 'When the first quail calls', *Women's Rights Law Reporter*, 11: 7–10.

19 b hooks (1981) *Ain't I a Woman: Black Women and Feminism*, Boston, MA: South End Press (London: Pluto Press, 1982); P Hill Collins (1986) 'The emerging theory and pedagogy of black women's studies', *Feminist Issues*, 6: 3–17.

20 PM Caldwell (1991) 'A hair piece: Perspectives on the intersection of race and gender', *Duke Law Journal*: 365–96.

21 C Jones and K Shorter-Gooden (2003) *Shifting: The Double Lives of Black Women in America*, New York: Harper Collins.

22 PM Caldwell (1991) 'A hair piece: Perspectives on the intersection of race and gender', *Duke Law Journal*: 365–96, at p 372.

23 DA Lacy (2007) 'The most endangered Title VII plaintiff?' African-American males and intersectional claims', available at http://works.bepress.com/d_aaron-_lacy/ (accessed 14 January 2008).

24 J Scales-Trent (1989) 'Black women in the Constitution: Finding our place and asserting our rights', *Harvard Civil Rights-Civil Liberties Law Review*, 24: 10–44.

25 V Wei (1996) 'Asian women and employment discrimination: Using intersectionality theory to address Title VII claims based on combining factors of race, gender and national origin', *Boston College Law Review*, 37: 771–845.

26 JA Winston (1991) 'Mirror, mirror on the wall: Title VII, section 1981 and the intersection of race and gender in the Civil Rights Act of 1990', *California Law Review*, 79: 775–805.

27 R Castro and L Corral (1993) 'Women of colour and employment discrimination: Race and gender combined', *La Raza Law Journal*, 6: 159–173.

28 *Degraffenreid v General Motors* 413 F Supp 142 (E D Mo 1976).

29 *Munford v James T Barnes & Co* 441 F. Supp 459 (ED Mich 1977).

30 J Ellis (1981) 'Sexual harassment and race: A legal analysis of discrimination', *North Dakota Journal of Legislation*, 8: 30–45.

31 *Rogers v American Airlines* 527 F Supp 229 (SDNY 1981).

32 *Jefferies v Harris Cty Community Action Association* 615 F 2d 1025 (5 Cir 1980).

33 *Jeffries*, ibid, para 1032.

34 *Lam v University of Hawaii* 40 F 3d 1551, 1561 (9 Cir 1994). See also *Hicks v Gates Rubber Co* 833 F2d 1406 (10 Cir 1987) and *Lewis v Bloomsburg Mills Inc* 773 F2d 561 (4 Cir 1985).

35 *Lam*, ibid, para 1562.

36 R Austin, (1989) 'Sapphire bound!', *Wisconsin Law Review*, 3: 539–78, at p 540.

37 J Scales-Trent (1989) 'Black women in the Constitution: Finding our place and asserting our rights', *Harvard Civil Rights-Civil Liberties Law Review*, 24: 10–44, at p 9.

38 G Hull, P Scott and B Smith (1982) *All the Women are White, all the Blacks are Men, But Some of Us are Brave*, New York: Feminist Press at CUNY.

39 K Crenshaw (1989) 'Demarginalizing the intersection of race and sex: A black feminist critique of antidiscrimination doctrine, feminist theory and antiracial politics', *The University of Chicago Legal Forum*: 139–67, at p 150.

40 J Scales-Trent (1989) 'Black women in the Constitution: Finding our place and asserting our rights', *Harvard Civil Rights-Civil Liberties Law Review*, 24: 10–44, at p 16.

41 PK Chew (2007) 'Freeing racial harassment from the sexual harassment model', *University of Pittsburgh School of Law Working Paper Series*, No 54.

42 J Scales-Trent (1989) 'Black women in the Constitution: Finding our place and asserting our rights', *Harvard Civil Rights-Civil Liberties Law Review*, 24: 10–44, at p 34.

43 GC Loury (2002) *The Anatomy of Racial Inequality*, Cambridge, MA: Harvard University Press, at p 59.

44 E Goffman (1990) *Stigma: Notes on the Management of Spoiled Identity*, London: Penguin, at p 14.

45 For example, being the child of an alcoholic.

46 J Scales-Trent (1995) *Notes of a White Black Woman: Race, Colour, Community*, University Park, PA: Pennsylvania University Press, at p 123.

47 GC Loury (2002) *The Anatomy of Racial Inequality*, Cambridge, MA: Harvard University Press, at p 59.

48 C Jones and K Shorter-Gooden (2003) *Shifting: The Double Lives of Black Women in America*, New York: Harper Collins, at p 11.

49 MC Nussbaum (2004) *Hiding from Humanity*, Princeton, NJ: Princeton University Press, at p 220.

50 GC Loury (2002) *The Anatomy of Racial Inequality*, Cambridge, MA: Harvard University Press, at p 81.

51 Ibid, p 61.

52 For example, Proposal 209 in California, or more recently, Proposal 2 in Michigan, where voters decided in 2006 to amend the state constitution to prohibit the use of criteria such as race or gender in admissions to public institutions.

53 *Appiah & anr v Governing Body of Bishop Douglass Roman Catholic High School* [2007] EWCA Civ 10, Case No A2/2005/2495.

54 L Holloway (2005) 'Carry on excluding', *Black Information Link*, 23 October, available at www.blink.org.uk/pdescription.asp?grp=7&cat=28&key=9798 (accessed 11 January 2008).

55 K Barling (2007) 'Dying for an answer', *BBC London*, available at www.bbc.co.uk/london/content/articles/2007/04/17/kurt_bill_guns_feature.shtml (accessed 25 April 2007).

56 PH Collins (2005) *Black Sexual Politics: African Americans, Gender and the New Racism*, New York: Routledge, at p 157.

57 The SUS laws gave the police power to arrest people not just for crimes that had been committed, but also for crimes that they suspected might be committed.

58 B Leapman (2006) 'Three in four young black men on the DNA database', *The Sunday Telegraph*, available at www.telegraph.co.uk/news/main.jhtml?xml=/news/2006/11/05/nrace05.xml (accessed 17 December 2007).

59 Tony Sewell tells the story of how, after teaching bicycle road safety to his seven-year-old son where he emphasised the importance of wearing his helmet, he heard him talking to someone at the front door: 'It was a white motorcyclist who thought his son had threatened to cut his throat. As this man had approached his house, his son had noticed that the motorcyclist's helmet had not been secured under his chin and had pointed this out by drawing his finger across his throat. The motorcyclist had interpreted this piece of public safety advice as a threat.'

60 T Sewell and L Jasper (2003) 'Look beyond the street', *Guardian Unlimited*, 19 July, available at www.guardian.co.uk/comment/story/0,3604,1001151,00.html (accessed 11 January 2008).

61 P Hill Collins (2005) *Black Sexual Politics: African Americans, Gender and the New Racism*, New York: Routledge, at p 160.

62 D Abbott (2002) 'Teachers are failing black boys', *Guardian Unlimited*, 6 January, available at http://observer.guardian.co.uk/comment/story/0,,628287,00.html (accessed 14 January 2008).

63 Greater London Authority (2004) *Increase black teacher numbers to improve education outcomes for black children*, available at www.london.gov.uk/view_press_release.jsp?releaseid=4304 (accessed 25 April 2007).

64 H Muir and R Smithers (2004) 'Black boys betrayed by racist school system, says report', available at http://education.guardian.co.uk/racism/story/0,,1298791,00.html (accessed 25 April 2007).

65 Ofsted (1999) *Raising the Attainment of Minority Ethnic Pupils*, available at www.ofsted.gov.uk/publications/index.cfm?fuseaction=pubs.displayfile&id=771&type=pdf (accessed 25 April 2007).

66 D Abbott (2002) 'Teachers are failing black boys', *Guardian Unlimited*, 6 January, available at http://observer.guardian.co.uk/comment/story/0,,628287,00.html (accessed 14 January 2008)

67 M Bright and G Hinsliff (2002) 'Bad teachers betraying black boys, says expert. National emergency feared if nothing is done', available at http://observer.guardian.co.uk/race/story/0,,632074,00.html (accessed 25 April 2007).

68 FD Weatherspoon (1998) *African American Males and the Law*, Maryland, Boston, MA: University Press of America, at p 70.

69 A survey of attendees at the 2002 the London conference, *Towards a Vision of Excellence: London Schools and the Black Child*, which was attended by over 1000 Black parents and other stakeholders, demonstrated that exclusions were a key issue.

70 L Holloway (2007) 'One in ten', available at www.blink.org.uk/pdescription.asp-?key=14284&grp=7&cat=28 (accessed 25 April 2007).

71 Department for Education and Skills (2006) 'Priority review: Exclusion of black pupils "Getting it. Getting it right" ', available at www.standards.dfes.gov.uk/ethnicminorities/ (accessed 1 May 2007).

72 Economic and Social Research Council (2005) 'Society today: Inequality in the UK', available at www.esrcsocietytoday.ac.uk/ESRCInfoCentre/facts/UK/index51.aspx?ComponentId=12699&SourcePageId=18134 (accessed 1 May 2007).

73 G John (2006) *Memorandum submitted by Gus John to the Home Affairs Committee*, available at www.publications.parliament.uk/pa/cm200607/cmselect/cmhaff/181/181we37.htm (accessed 20 July 2007).

74 T Phillips (2005) 'Running faster into the same brick wall', *Guardian Unlimited*, 31 May, available at http://education.guardian.co.uk/egweekly/story/0,,1495513,00.html (accessed 14 January 2008).

75 Department for Education and Skills (2006) 'Priority review: Exclusion of black pupils "Getting it. Getting it right" ', available at www.standards.dfes.gov.uk/ethnicminorities/ (accessed 1 May 2007).

76 DA Lacy (2007) 'The most endangered Title VII plaintiff?' African-American males and intersectional claims', available at http://works.bepress.com/d_aaron_lacy/ (accessed 14 January 2008)

77 GC Loury (2002) *The Anatomy of Racial Inequality*, Cambridge, MA: Harvard University Press, at p 103.

78 Department for Education and Skills (2006) 'Priority review: Exclusion of black pupils "Getting it. Getting it right" ', available at www.standards.dfes.gov.uk/ethnicminorities/ (accessed 1 May 2007).

79 L Holloway (2005) 'Fighting the powers that be', *Black Information Link*, 7 October, available at www.blink.org.uk/pdescription.asp?key=9758&grp=7 (accessed 14 January 2008).

80 Employment Equality (Age) Regulations 2006.

81 Race Relations Act 1976, s 54a states: 'where the complainant proves facts from which the tribunal could conclude in the absence of an adequate explanation that the respondent (a) has committed an act of discrimination or harassment against the complainant, or (b) is to be treated as having committed an act of discrimination or harassment against the complainant, the tribunal shall uphold the complaint unless the respondent proves that he did not commit or, as the case may be, is not to be treated as having committed, that act'.

82 *DKW Ltd v Adebayo* [2005] IRLR 514, para 515.

83 *Hawkins et al v Coleman et al* 376 F Supp 1330 (N D Texas 1974); *Ross v Sittmarsh* 500 F Supp 935 (1980). FD Weatherspoon (1998) *African American Males and the Law*, Maryland, Boston, MA: University Press of America, pp 65–78.

84 Matsuda (1989) 'When the first quail calls', *Women's Rights Law Reporter*, 11: 7–10, at p 10.

85 PR Smith (1991) 'Separate identities: Black women, work and Title VII', *Harvard Women's Law Journal*, 14: 21–75, at p 74.
86 C Scarborough (1989) 'Conceptualising black women's employment experiences', *Yale Law Journal*, 98: 1457–78, at p 1474.
87 MC Nussbaum (2004) *Hiding from Humanity*, Princeton, NJ: Princeton University Press, at p 218.

7 Multidimensional exclusion

Viewing Romani marginalisation through the nexus of race and poverty

Morag Goodwin

7.1 Introduction

It is widely accepted that Roma are the most impoverished, marginalised and discriminated group in Europe.[1] It is an assumption backed up by data. A United Nations Development Programme (UNDP) report from 2003 noted of Roma in Bulgaria, the Czech Republic, Hungary, Romania and Slovakia, 'by such measures as literacy, infant mortality and basic nutrition, most of these country's four to five million Roma endure conditions closer to sub-Saharan Africa than Europe'.[2] It is a damning conclusion; particularly coming nearly 20 years after Roma first became the focus of intense efforts by international organisations and civil society actors to mitigate their plight.

The main focus of these efforts in this period has been on achieving social change by rectifying the widespread discriminatory attitudes towards Roma that are prevalent in Central and Eastern Europe (CEE). However, non-discrimination law has undergone a number of important theoretical developments. The doubts that have been raised about the problematic nature of non-discrimination law in addressing issues of substantive equality, exclusion and identity have led to calls for a more nuanced approach to equality, both practically and normatively.[3] This chapter will take the deeply entrenched and multi-faceted problems that many Roma in CEE face on a daily basis and consider the extent to which a specific litigation strategy based on non-discrimination can address these complex problems.[4] It will focus on multi-dimensional inequality and, in doing so, hope to stress the necessity of a more nuanced line of attack to tackling the long history of Romani marginalisation and discrimination. The argument does not focus on the intersection of two recognised 'grounds', such as race and gender, but on the intersection of race and poverty.

This chapter will begin by sketching the extent of Romani socio-economic marginalisation in CEE in order to be able to assess the breadth and depth of the problems faced by Romani and those that wish to assist them. The third section will illustrate possible uses of non-discrimination law by drawing on a recent case brought by the most prominent Romani rights organisation, the European Roma Rights Centre (ERRC). This will suggest a failure of the strategy to address effectively the complex problem of, in this case, accessing an equal standard of education. The fourth section will discuss the alleged failings of this strategy in more detail, before recommending an alternative approach better able to take account of the interrelation of poverty and race that may well achieve more in addressing extreme marginalisation where racial discrimination and poverty appear to create, exacerbate and reinforce one another.

7.2 The breadth and depth of Romani socio-economic marginalisation

The Decade of Roma Inclusion that began in 2005 has seen an increasing focus on quantifying Romani deprivation and marginalisation;[5] in this, the World Bank (WB) has been particularly active. In a 2005 report entitled, *Roma in an Expanding Europe: Breaking the Poverty Cycle*, WB researchers attempted to quantify Romani poverty in comparison with the non-Romani population across CEE and a number of Western European countries. The most uncontroversial aspect of their report is the conclusion that Roma constitute the most prominent poverty risk group in the region of CEE: 'they are poorer than other groups, more likely to fall into poverty, and more likely to remain poor'.[6]

An analysis of poverty levels across Bulgaria, Romania and Hungary from the 2000 data revealed a striking pattern in which poverty rates for Roma ran at a level several times higher than that of non-Roma. The analysed data shows, for example, that 80.1 per cent of Roma in Bulgaria live on $4.30 a day as opposed to 36.8 per cent of non-Roma; of the much lower absolute poverty line of $2.15 a day, 10 times as many Roma as non-Roma are affected. Similar patterns are reported in Romania and Hungary. Although Hungary is a much wealthier country than the more recent accession countries, for example, 13 times more Roma live at the absolute poverty line and 40.3 per cent of the Hungarian Romani population live on the relative poverty line of $4.30 a day as compared to just 6.9 per cent of the non-Romani Hungarian population.

A second WB 2005 report on Roma, focusing on Serbia and Montenegro,[7] had similar although perhaps even more dramatic findings. Household data from 2003 suggested that, in contrast to a continuing rise in living standards in these countries, a 'staggering' 60.5 per cent of Roma residing in settlements (taken apart from integrated Roma in cities) fall below the 'very poor' threshold of 3,997 Dinars a month (excluding housing costs) in comparison to 6 per cent of the general population;[8] of the extremely poor, 9.8 per cent of Romani households fall within this band as compared to 0.2 per cent of the non-Romani population. However, Romani deprivation is not confined to income poverty. Both WB reports draw the conclusion that Romani poverty is multi-faceted. By examining these 'multiple non-income dimensions of deprivation'[9] from the perspective of social exclusion, the researchers are able to build a layered understanding of Romani deprivation as incorporating not just income deprivation, but poverty in relation to education, employment, health, housing, and in relation to access to and under-utilisation of public services. The picture they build is a complex one.

7.2.1 Educational deprivation

In addition to being poorer, Roma are also significantly more likely to be educationally poor than non-Roma, refugees or internally displaced persons. Of Romani children aged 7 to 20 in Serbia, 35 per cent are not enrolled in school at all, compared to just 2 per cent for the general population. In Bulgaria, only 35 per cent of Romani children completed primary school, with only 10 per cent going on to secondary education.[10] In general, the majority of Romani children do not complete any meaningful level of education. There are a number of possible explanations for the failure of Romani parents either to enrol their children or to ensure their attendance. As the researchers noted in relation to Serbia and Montenegro, while schooling is free of charge, it is associated with not insignificant costs in terms of school equipment such as schoolbooks, notebooks and clothes. It is also expensive in terms of lost revenue from those children. Similarly, data from Serbia noted that pre-school institutions and primary schools are not often built in the vicinity of Romani settlements and young children therefore have far to travel if they are to attend, incurring travel costs. It is thus predictable that the surveys from both Serbia and Montenegro found that the main reason for Romani families not to send their children to school is a lack of financial means.

However, there are also other obstacles to overcome in getting Romani children to school. One is perhaps low levels of expectation – itself a consequence of social exclusion – although such attitudes are difficult to measure. Geographical boundaries present obstacles separate from the mere financial cost of travelling to school, such as the working time lost to parents in taking their children to school or the psychological barrier to travelling far. The failure of Romani children to attend pre-school institutions is also an important factor in undermining subsequent primary school enrolment and completion; only 7 per cent of Romani children attend school aged 3 to 7 in Serbia. As these institutions are fee-charging this is not surprising. Another significant factor in the failure to attend school concerns the high levels of non-registration of Romani households which can prevent Romani children from being enrolled and certainly prevents enforcement of the requirement that children attend school.

However, even where Romani children attend school, they are likely to fare worse than their non-Romani peers. Data from Serbia, for example, shows that Romani children lag behind across all subjects but experience particular difficulty with the Serbian language, which for the majority of Romani children is not their native tongue. This poor performance is due, according to the WB researchers, to the failure of Roma children to receive the same standard of education, either in special schools or in regular schools, because of irregular attendance and insufficient classroom support; it could also be added that adaptation to schooling in Serbia is hampered by non-attendance of pre-school institutions.

7.2.2 Labour market poverty

Romani poverty is, however, more directly related to employment, or lack of it. While Roma appear to be significantly more likely to be unemployed,[11] even where the difference in the overall figure of unemployment between Roma and non-Roma is not so stark, as in Serbia and Montenegro (62.2 per cent as opposed to 51 per cent), crucial differences nonetheless exist behind the figures. What the numbers hide is the significantly worse labour-market status suffered by Roma, particularly for Romani women. Romani work is, generally speaking, informal, part-time or short-term and low-skilled; it is thus lower paid and thus Roma are more likely to belong to the 'working poor' than non-Roma. Further, while appreciably less Roma in the age groups 45–54 and 55–64 participate in the labour market, 70 per cent of Roma aged 15–24 are in some form of paid work, as opposed to 32 per cent of non-Roma. Thus, in contrast to work done by those in the older categories, which tends to be more secure employment and better paid, Roma are over-represented instead in the category of young workers, which is, in general, less secure, poorly paid in comparison and implies that a significant proportion of Roma have failed to continue their education beyond the age of 15. However, the latter implication is perhaps less important than it might seem as WB analysis demonstrates that educational attainment makes less difference for Roma in terms of employment; unlike the statistics for non-Roma, Romani unemployment is relatively unaffected by factors such as primary, secondary or vocational schooling and only higher education impacts upon their unemployment figures. Thus, as stated by the WB researchers in relation to Bulgaria, Hungary and Romania, 'the probability of being poor is higher than that for non-Roma, irrespective of educational achievement and employment status'.[12] This phenomenon is even more significant for Romani women, who are least likely to benefit in terms of poverty alleviation from employment or educational achievement.

A further point worth noting is that the types of employment in which Roma engage can be a source of vulnerability in itself. In Montenegro, for example, 50 per cent of respondents described their work as physically demanding, and Romani 'occupations' are disproportionately of the trash and scrap metal collecting type, and are thus more likely to lead to health problems. On a final note, Roma are far less likely to be involved than non-Roma in subsistence farming, which can provide a vital safety net for those in the countryside, making Romani families even more vulnerable to a lack of employment, whether formal or informal.

7.2.3 Housing deprivation and geographical location

A multi-layered approach also highlights a link between poverty, geographic location and housing quality. Roma face unique problems in access to decent standards of accommodation. In addition to the fact that Romani settlements are usually located far outside the boundaries of towns and villages, as noted in relation to accessing education, Romani accommodation is frequently below the standard of non-Roma. For example, only 63.2 per cent of Romani households enjoyed a water supply in Serbia in comparison to 91.5 per cent of non-Romani dwellings; similarly 29 per cent of Romani households had an inside toilet as opposed to 82 per cent of non-Romani accommodation. In terms of social exclusion, it is also interesting to note that only 17.6 per cent of Romani households possess a telephone in Serbia as against 78.2 per cent of non-Romani households. In Bulgaria, 52.3 per cent of Romani dwellings are connected to the sewage system as opposed to 90.3 per cent for non-Romani households. In addition to a lack of amenities, Romani areas suffer from chronic over-crowding. Romani households are nearly twice the size of non-Romani households, despite the size of Roma dwellings being on average 20 per cent smaller in Romania, for example, than is the case for non-Romani Romanians.

A further aspect that has affected Romani communities and families across the region of CEE is the legal status of their housing. The lack of clarity of property rights under Communism saw considerable upheaval in the transition process. As housing subsidies were withdrawn, significant numbers of Roma were evicted from state-owned apartments; properties were then privatised or returned to prior owners. As a consequence, many Roma live illegally. This in itself has a drastic impact on the ability to access social services, as proof of residence and identity papers are generally required in order to access social security benefits, health-care services and education. It also means that such families must either tap illegally in to water or electricity services, with all the personal risk that attempting to do the latter entails, or go without.

7.2.4 Health-care poverty

While reliable data on the health of Romani communities is fragmented and limited, a picture nonetheless emerges of a life expectancy on average 10 years lower than their non-Romani compatriots; in Hungary the discrepancy is 10–15 years.[13] This pattern is reflected in significantly higher levels of infant mortality. In the Czech and Slovak Republics, infant mortality is twice that of non-Roma, for example. In general, Romani women have much lower levels of reproductive health. As a consequence of poor living conditions and inadequate nutrition during pregnancy, as well as high birth and abortion rates, Romani women are disproportionately at risk of complications during pregnancy. A lack of access to health information also means that at the end of the 1990s in Hungary, for example, 63 per cent of Romani women smoked throughout their pregnancy.[14] Across the region, Romani women are significantly more likely to give birth to premature or low-weight babies, a factor increasingly recognised as being significant in predicting health problems throughout life.[15] Moreover, the low nutritional intake of Romani children in their formative years has a negative impact on their growth and the development of their immune system. A study in the Slovak Republic, for example, has documented the stunting of Romani children in comparison to non-Romani children of the same age.[16]

The pattern of low life expectancies is, further, made up of a particular susceptibility to communicable diseases such as tuberculosis and hepatitis.[17] Unsanitary living conditions and overcrowding also saw outbreaks of polio and diphtheria in the early 1990s in Romani communities in Bulgaria; polio continues to occur among children in Romani communities in Bulgaria, Romania and the FYR Macedonia. Poor vaccination records are also leaving Romani children susceptible to measles outbreaks, a number of which have been reported in communities in Hungary and Slovakia in recent years.

Very limited information is available on the non-communicable, general health of Romani communities. Evidence suggests, however, that they are more at risk from disease relating to smoking, poor nutrition and alcoholism; levels of drug-taking and prostitution also seen to be significantly higher than among the non-Romani population.[18] Further, as noted above in relation to employment, Roma are more likely to be employed in hazardous, unregulated occupations, such as scrap-metal collecting, unofficial recycling, or heavy physical labour, which increase the risk of exposure to toxic materials or work-related injuries. Similarly, their living conditions not only expose Roma to the risk of communicable disease but the settlements are frequently located near or on top of environmentally degraded sites, risking exposure to hazardous materials.[19]

The conclusion of the WB researchers, faced with all these interrelated and mutually aggravating elements has been that Romani poverty is pervasive, inter-generational and multi-faceted. It is hugely complex. The sheer extent and internal interaction of the problems that Roma face suggest that any attempt to achieve equality must first begin by addressing them. The WB has, in response to its findings, focused on funding small-scale, locally based poverty alleviation projects, such as those run by the Hungarian-based Autonómia Foundation.[20] However, the Roma Rights movement has focused primarily on racial discrimination as a framework within which to understand Romani exclusion, in which strategic litigation has taken centre stage.

7.3 Focusing on discrimination in access to socio-economic rights: Roma rights[21] and the *Ostrava* case

The most prominent pro-Romani organisation in Europe is the Budapest-based ERRC. It has been operating as a public interest law organisation since

1996 and, despite some diversification into human rights education and training of Romani activists, the law remains the prime focus in tackling economic injustice against Romani communities. According to the legal department's mission statement, ERRC's core work is 'to initiate impact human rights litigation on behalf of Roma before domestic and international courts to achieve the following: (a) encourage more interest among local lawyers for Roma rights litigation; (b) generate judicial opinions which expand human rights jurisprudence; and (c) ultimately, bring about social change on a scale which would benefit Roma throughout Europe'.[22] To these ends, the legal department trains a network of local lawyers throughout the region in the techniques of high impact strategic litigation. Moreover, the ERRC cooperates with other non-governmental organisation (NGO) actors at the European level, developing common litigation strategies to push back the limits of race discrimination instruments.[23] As such, the ERRC has a clear organisational purpose 'to combat anti-Romani racism'.[24] While its work is not entirely focused on questions of socio-economic exclusion, the mission to bring about social change beneficial to Roma means that it is reasonable to assess its strategy by reference to its success in tackling deprivation.

A recent case challenging the placement of disproportionate numbers of Romani children in 'special schools' before the Strasbourg Court illustrates the ERRC's approach.[25] The *Ostrava* case formed in fact the centrepiece of the ERRC's strategy and thus it is considered in some detail here. This case was arguably seen by those in or intimately connected to the movement to be the Romani equivalent of *Brown v Board of Education*.[26] While a chamber of the European Court of Human Rights rejected the applicants' claims by a 6:1 majority in early 2006, on 13 November 2007, the Grand Chamber overturned the earlier ruling by a 13:4 majority.[27]

7.3.1 The facts of the case and the court's findings

The facts in *Ostrava*, so named after the Czech town at the centre of the case, were that between 1996 and 1999, the 18 applicants, all Romani children born between 1985 and 1991, were placed in 'special schools' for the learning impaired. 'Special schools' are designed, according to Czech law, for children suffering from learning impairments and are thus outside the ordinary schooling system.[28] The most immediate consequence of placement in a special school for these children was the vastly inferior quality of education to that offered in normal schools but also entailed that they were no longer eligible to continue their education at a secondary level, that is, beyond the age of 11.[29] The decision to place a child in a special school was taken by the head teacher on the basis of tests designed to measure the intellectual abilities of that child, which were carried out by independent educational psychologists. The parents were then notified and given the opportunity to contest the categorisation of their child in this way.

The data that the ERRC, representing the applicants, had collected concerning the placement of children, both Romani and non-Romani, in Ostrava in 1999 demonstrated that whereas only 1.8 per cent of non-Romani children attended special schools, 50.3 per cent of all Romani children did so, despite only constituting 5 per cent of the school population in the town. A Romani child was therefore 27 times more likely than a non-Romani child to be placed in a school for the learning impaired. Accordingly, the applicants lodged an application alleging a breach of Art 14 (non-discrimination provision) in conjunction with Art 2 of Protocol No 1 (the right to education) of the European Convention on Human Rights. Their claim was that the statistical data established clearly that the operation of the special schooling system in Ostrava indirectly discriminated against Romani children to an overwhelming degree.

The applicants argued, in line with the need for a 'reasonable and objective' justification for differential treatment as laid down in the *Belgian Linguistics* case,[30] that as an insufficient command of the Czech language,[31] socio-economic disadvantage,[32] or parental consent could not constitute reasonable and objective justification for the gross disparity demonstrated, the Czech government had thus failed to provide a sufficient explanation of their prima facie evidence of racial segregation.

Where the second Chamber section rejected both the statistical data and the applicants' argument, the Grand Chamber was much more amenable to taking the wider circumstances of the claim into account.

7.3.2 The wider picture

Leaving aside a considered analysis of the reasoning of either judgment,[33] it is necessary to reflect upon the background to the case to understand why it carried such a burden of hope, as well as of resources in the ERRC strategy. Not covered by the WB's analysis of disproportionate educational poverty was the fact that Roma are subject to segregation in education right across the region of CEE on the grounds of race. According to ERRC research published in May 2004 and in February 2007,[34] Romani children form 80–90 per cent of the special school population in Bulgaria; in Hungary they constitute 50 per cent, despite forming only 2 per cent of the overall population.[35] In Slovakia, Roma are estimated to occupy 80–100 per cent of places in the special school system; and in the Czech Republic, the situation in Ostrava is better than the national average. In a report to the Committee on the Elimination of Racial Discrimination (CERD) that was presented to the Court, the Czech government itself determined that 75 per cent of all Romani children in the Czech Republic were being educated in special schools, 25 per cent more than in Ostrava.[36]

That efforts were focused on this case was not only related to the sheer pervasiveness of the practice across the region but also to its deep and lasting effects. At stake was both the future of individual children as well as the means for achieving greater economic and political power for Roma as a section of society. Although the practice of special school segregation may not be a conscious means of maintaining the exclusion of Roma as a political or social force from mainstream society, the effect is the same.[37] However, the immediate focus is the impact on the children themselves. Unlike the applicant's claim in *Brown*, the main element of the determination to fight racial segregation of Romani children is less the psychological harm of being labelled learning impaired – although that is clear – but that placement in such schools, in denying access to a decent education, has an enormous implication for the life chances of any child. The segregation of Romani children into special schools could never be mistaken for being 'separate but equal'.[38]

7.4 Analysing the Roma rights strategy: the relationship of discrimination to socio-economic injustice

The focus of the Roma Rights movement on education is thus not questioned here; nor is the need to consider discrimination on the grounds of race as a vital element in overcoming socio-economic injustice. Rather, the remainder of this chapter will question the strategy of litigation and the *overwhelming* focus on racial discrimination to the exclusion of other factors as capable of breaking the cycle of deprivation the WB reports highlight so well. Before considering the Roma Rights strategy in more detail, it is worth first examining in brief the theoretical relationship between socio-economic subordination and discrimination.

7.4.1 Achieving substantive equality: the relationship between discrimination and socio-economic injustice, or between race and poverty

This chapter does not seek to add to the massive bibliography on concepts of equality law, characterised by the move from understanding equality as requiring equal treatment, that is, a formal equality, to one focused on the societal changes necessary to achieving substantial equality. This has been well charted elsewhere.[39] This section only highlights some elements in order to provide a framework for the ensuing analysis.

In Europe, it is no longer seriously doubted that substantive equality is a fundamental element of a just society.[40] While diverse concepts of the notion prevail, substantive equality entails a focus on realities on the ground that is necessarily relational in viewing equality by comparison with the dominant group in society, depending on the ground under consideration.

In the US, however, the notion of substantive equality, and the ideal of justice underpinning it, has led to a dichotomy between recognition and redistribution as the best means of achieving the illusive goal of equality. The shift in political theory away from a libertarian understanding of freedom as the absence of interference to a social theory of justice, in which a just society is one which ensures the basic minimum of goods necessary to enable individuals to live out their idea of the good life,[41] puts the (re-) distribution of goods back at centre stage.[42] It is in part for this reason that there is a growing focus in the US on class rather than race as the great divide in American society.[43] However, the gulf that appears to open up between the requirements of non-discrimination law – governing distribution of valuable opportunities – and the demands of justice – of a basic minimum of goods for all – is of course a false one, and on two levels.

On one level, an egalitarian model prohibits discrimination precisely because it imposes disadvantage on the basis of a ground that is morally irrelevant, that is, race, gender, religion, etc. and by doing so removes choice from individuals in a morally arbitrary way. However, the relationship also runs deeper. Discrimination and socio-economic injustice have a systemic relationship, in that each reflects and perpetuates past and present patterns of the other. It is for this reason that non-discrimination laws are understood to play a vital role in structuring a society that aims at a just distribution of the benefits and burdens of a common life together.[44] Indeed, what the distributive paradigm of an egalitarian approach therefore entails, as one US-based author notes, is that social groups play a central role in both 'justifying and specifying anti-discrimination laws'.[45] Thus, even where one rejects the basis of recognition theories such as Taylor's 'politics of difference',[46] the identification and protection of social groups is necessary to remedy a socio-economic inequality that runs along identity lines. Such normative justification sees non-discrimination law as an integral part of tackling socio-economic exclusion.

A recent contribution to the debate has taken the link between race and socio-economic marginalisation a step further. Powell has traced the profound interaction between and mutual definition of the categories of race and class throughout US history, suggesting that the particular categorisation of race and class visible in the US today are a result of mutual constitution, that is, that they develop through what he terms 'cumulative mutual causation'.[47] His analysis provides a salient warning to those in the US who would focus redistribution efforts on class alone. Instead, Powell argues that creating a socially-inclusive society requires an agenda that addresses the intersectional nexus of race and class. The strength of Powell's argument lies in his detailed analysis of American history; thus any attempt to apply his conclusions without a similar analysis must acknowledge the danger of doing so; moreover, there is a similar danger in assuming an equivalence between the category of class and socio-economic marginalisation. Thus, much more research into the social categorisation of poverty in CEE and in particular the possibility of a relationship between marginalisation and Romani slavery is needed.[48] Yet the examination of the situation of many Romani communities as painted in the foregoing sections suggests that viewing discrimination as both the cause and the effect of socio-economic exclusion is not unreasonable; if this is the case, a focus on the past and present of racially discriminatory attitudes towards Roma as an explanation for the gross socio-economic injustice they continue to endure is insufficient. While an awareness of the interactive relationship between race and poverty is acknowledged in the call for substantive equality, what is less acknowledged, at least explicitly, is the corresponding need for a genuinely intersectional approach that addresses both the problems of racial discrimination and socio-economic marginalisation simultaneously.

7.4.2 The uses and misuses of discrimination law: focus on the Roma

What shall be suggested in the remainder of this chapter is that despite the mutually reinforcing nature of socio-economic exclusion and discrimination, making discrimination the sole focus is not the best way in which to tackle exclusion. The argument thus made is a practical one.

As the studies presented in Section 7.2 (above) illustrate, Roma face a scope and depth of problems unprecedented in Europe. Moreover, the question is not one of whether Romani socio-economic exclusion is racially discriminatory; nor is the question purely one of systemic, unconscious discrimination. Instead, Roma face both systemic disadvantage and the deeply ingrained prejudice of the majority. Taking *Ostrava* as an example, Romani children and their parents must overcome both the culturally insensitive nature of the psychological testing that sees Romani children fail at a shockingly disproportionate rate, but also the prejudice that expects this and harasses those Romani children that gain access to the mainstream sector. The suggestion that will be made here is that for equality to prevail not only must a focus on litigation be re-thought but that any approach that makes the discriminatory nature of socio-economic exclusion the central focus risks exacerbating the situation rather than overcoming it. Instead, it will be suggested that the place best to begin addressing both the systemic nature of discrimination against Roma and the widely held prejudicial attitude of the majority is nonetheless where the abuses are felt: at the local level.

7.4.2.1 The blind spot of racism as explanation

One of the most important arguments that can be levelled against focusing on the discrimination aspect of socio-economic deprivation is that, in the case of the Roma, it is ineffective. There are two elements to this. The first – that of an overly narrow focus or blind spot – will be considered here, and the second – that of failing to take seriously the importance of inter-community relations in overcoming Romani deprivation – in the section that follows. A good place to begin is perhaps by considering what difference the recent victory in *Ostrava* is likely to make.[49] Will the victory in *Ostrava* ensure Romani children an equal education?

Unlike the infamous system of Jim Crow laws in the US, the type of segregation Romani children face is that of indirect effect or disparate impact. It is through a whole combination of circumstances that Romani children 'end up' in special schools. When Romani children are enrolled in schools, either special or normal, they are significantly more likely to drop-out than their non-Romani peers. They also under-perform at every level when placed in the mainstream.[50] There are serious reasons to doubt that this would change were the psychological testing that *Ostrava* aims to stop actually ended, and the reason for this lies both in the interacting layers of socio-economic problems that Romani families face and in the interrelation between discrimination and inequality.

To begin with, victory in *Ostrava* would not begin to tackle the main reason that Romani children fail to attend school according to the studies conducted by the WB, that of lack of financial resources. Parents will still rely upon their children's income to enable the family to survive, in part because of their own lack of education, in part because of the nature of Romani employment, because they have been debilitated through work, or because they are incapacitated as a result of the higher levels of sickness and alcohol and substance abuse among Romani populations in comparison to non-Roma.

Further, as in the US, one of the reasons for the de facto segregation of Romani children in the public school system is segregation in the housing sector.[51] Challenging the psychological testing children undergo will not address the fact that Romani settlements are usually located far away from the last non-Romani house; or that public transport either does not go there or does so infrequently, and the sheer poverty in such communities is likely to mean that children lack the kind of clothing and footwear necessary to walk such distances in the type of winter normal for the region.

Additional reasons why victory in *Ostrava* would fail to overcome inequality in education include the lack of access to basic health-care services, such as childhood inoculations, which, in conjunction with the type of living conditions common for Romani families, is likely to mean that Romani children are sick more often than their non-Romani peers. As a consequence, they will miss more school through illness and are likely to fall behind – a fact that may reinforce feelings of low self-worth and further demotivate a child in what is often the hostile environment of a mainstream school. The poor nutritional intake and high stress levels of mothers during pregnancy that often result in low birth weights also impact upon their children's ability to do well at school, being manifested in such ways as lower levels of concentration.

Moreover, housing conditions effect not only the health of parent and child but are also likely to mean that there is no electrical light by which to do homework in the evening. The lack of financial means that too often prevents Romani children from attending school at all also ensures that there is no spare money for textbooks or exercise books. Romani children in settlements do not grow up surrounded by books and other educational materials such as television or the internet; and the inter-generational aspect of poverty and exclusion observed by the WB entails that their illiterate parents cannot assist them with homework. This fact is, as was important in the *Ostrava* case, also likely to mean that their parents will not fully understand the implications of agreeing to their child being placed in a special school.

One of the main reasons for the *Ostrava* case failing at the Chamber stage was that the court looked very unfavourably upon the fact that Romani parents had consented to the placement of their children in special schools as required by Czech law, and that even when informed of their right to insist upon transferral to a normal school, few of the parents chose to do so.[52] That the court originally tried to frame this choice as bad parenting also missed the point, as the Grand Chamber made clear; but the fact that special schools can be attractive to Romani parents for the hot meals and, for residential institutions, the accommodation that they provide, cannot easily be factored into the framing of the situation in narrow legal rights. Nor can the reasonable fear that their child will suffer abuse and harassment in a normal classroom, where Romani children form only a tiny percentage of pupils, in comparison to being safe in a vastly inferior classroom alongside all Romani faces, be captured by a case that revolves purely on the numbers of pupils placed where. What the *Ostrava* case attempted to do was to bring the whole system of deprivation and discrimination before the Strasbourg Court; that the Grand Chamber was willing to accept this where the Chamber did not may mean that the court is now charting a path down a fuller, more context-based concept of rights – a move that can only be welcomed. Yet the split that this fairly dramatic shift appears to have caused within the court, as evidenced by the four bitter dissenting opinions, suggests perhaps that progress along these lines should not be taken for granted.[53] Moreover, indeed a context-based approach in the court will not address the other reasons that see Romani children failing to access a decent education.

All the factors described above are at play without even entering the uncomfortable territory of perhaps suggesting that there is a traditional cultural element that has not valued formal education as highly as other sections of society have traditionally done. As the research into the underperformance of black boys in US schools suggests, the question of underperformance of children of such groups is considerably more complex than outright racism.[54]

Thus, while the predominance of Romani children in special schools is nothing short of outrageous, the web of circumstances that combine to see Romani children placed there is more complex than simply the prejudice of assessors, teachers and non-Romani parents, or even systemic prejudices. The narrow way in which a complaint must be framed in order to bring a complaint before a court necessarily fails to take into account the thick web of circumstances which see Romani children disproportionately 'educated' in special schools. The broader point is of course that segregation is one, very visible, reason why Romani children do not receive the education that they are entitled to, but it is not the only one, and perhaps it is not even the most important one.

Litigation on the basis of racial discrimination undoubtedly works well in a range of areas, for example in gaining individual justice for individual acts of conscious discrimination, and it also has a place in the arsenal of measures to tackle systemic discrimination where wider society is unaware of the disproportionate impact of a given measure and can be shamed into forcing change; but what a litigation approach arguably cannot do is take into consideration the overlapping problems that Roma face. What it does, instead, is exclude all the other factors that interact to create the desperate situation that the majority of Roma are in; that is, it denies the complexities of the situation and attempts to reduce to it a one-factor issue: race. The focus on racial discrimination – particularly so where the problem must be framed in legal terms – encounters a blind spot in which no other explanation for Romani marginalisation is acceptable or relevant. Thus other relevant or partial explanations, or the way in which individual aspects of exclusion are magnified by combination with others, are ignored.

Roma have, for example, conventionally focused on traditional occupations that do not lend themselves to a market economy, a choice for which the market severely punished them in the transition period.[55] That this was compounded by blatant prejudice does not dilute this factor. These traditional occupations did not require formal education and hence Roma are left playing 'educational catch-up' with other groups in society without all the other difficulties attached to full mainstream school attendance. Indeed, the focus on traditional occupations is perhaps more important a factor in explaining Romani income poverty than discrimination in access to the workplace – an observation that does not make discrimination any less pernicious but it does perhaps make it the wrong place to begin addressing Romani unemployment or 'segregation' into the unskilled areas of the employment field. The blind spot effect is demonstrated by a recent ERRC report into the exclusion of Roma from employment across Bulgaria, the Czech Republic, Hungary, Romania and Slovakia. The sole conclusion of the report, that 'employment discrimination against Roma is endemic and blatant' does not take into account any of the interacting factors drawn out by the WB researchers, such as lack of education, lack of work experience, inability to get to where work is because of the location of Romani settlements and so on, but is ascribed instead almost entirely to 'pervasive racism'.[56]

Framing this complex set of problems as a single legal wrong inevitably attracts attention away from the complexity of the issues in favour of a seemingly simple solution – the prejudice of the majority. Although discrimination is undeniable, it fails to take into account the interaction between prejudice and socio-economic disadvantage in creating and reinforcing each other. For this reason, it is unlikely to be successful as a strategy.

If the complexity of Romani marginalisation is not well dealt with by a strategic litigation approach focused on racism, how does it fare with the deep-seated prejudices of the majority populations that this approach so clearly identifies?

7.4.2.2 The polarising effect of focusing on race

While the foregoing focuses primarily on the dangers of using litigation as a tool for tackling socio-economic exclusion, and thus does not really address the issue of a non-discrimination focus per se, this section deals primarily with the latter. Thus, although non-discrimination law would appear to be most effective at addressing the negative stereotypes that cause, underpin and justify the injustice of Romani socio-economic exclusion, it will be argued that, instead, insisting on discrimination as being at the root of the problem has a polarising effect, distancing Roma from the majority community in which they live, and where their problems ultimately have to be solved. The frame within which the critique below is set is that of the unavoidability of good inter-community relations as a factor in overcoming the socio-economic injustice of the Romani situation. While the aim is ostensibly a redistributive one, it will be suggested that it is only likely to occur by taking seriously the role that a positive recognition dialectic plays in overcoming relationships of sub-ordination.[57]

There are two ways in which the development of a positive recognition dialectic between the two communities – Romani and non-Romani – is undermined. The first is that focusing on discrimination necessarily attributes blame, either to individuals, individual communities or to society as a whole. Where it is difficult to identify individual or community instances of discrimination, a focus on systemic discrimination on a national level as a sort of 'wake-up call' can of course be very effective in highlighting problems and motivating change;[58] however, this is, it is suggested, rarely the case with the types of problems that Romani communities suffer. In situations of deeply embedded socio-economic exclusion rooted in centuries of discrimination and persecution, one of the great difficulties in effecting change is persuading those discriminating that what they are doing is unjust. So far back does the socio-economic exclusion of Roma go, that one could argue that mainstream society has little awareness of the cause and effect relationship between discrimination and disadvantage. In situations such as these, the charge of discrimination finds no hook on which to hang. Labelling a problem as racial discrimination only works in affecting change where it strikes a chord with those accused, and this happens only where there is widespread acknowledgment that discriminating against the group in question is wrong.[59] The difficulty of addressing Romani exclusion in CEE is the lack of societal acceptance that discriminating against Roma is wrong. Instead of needing a wake-up call, what the situation arguably requires is a full-scale battle for hearts and minds. Yet where antipathy to Roma both runs so deep and is so socially acceptable, it will not be enough to highlight the discriminatory nature of non-Romani behaviour, but instead the fears and prejudices that underpin it will need to be addressed in a different manner.

The counter-example to the strategy of the *Ostrava* case is the approach taken by a Romani community organisation in the town of Vidin, Bulgaria.

While 80–90 per cent of Romani children in Bulgaria attend either special schools or are segregated within the mainstream into all-Romani schools, the children of the Novi Pat settlement were fully integrated into the normal education system in 2000 following an initiative by a local community-based organisation, Organisation Drom. Instead of focusing on the legal rights of the children or on the discriminatory aspect of the situation, the NGO began their efforts, in the words of the Chairwoman of the organisation, by 'creat-[ing] a positive environment in both the Romani community and community at large'.[60] This involved regular meetings with the Romani parents, the non-Romani parents and the teachers and directors of the mainstream schools to lay out the desegregation plans. Organisation Drom worked hard within the Romani community to overcome parents' fears that their children would not be able to cope in normal schools and to persuade them of the educational benefits of attending normal school. From the outset, the project also focused attention on the practical problems that prevent Romani children from achieving a decent education by providing school buses from the settlements to the schools, as well as free school materials, such as bags, textbooks and exercise books, to the poorest families, some 80 per cent of those involved. Further, to allay parental fear that their children would suffer abuse in a strange system and to reassure non-Romani parents that educational stand-ards would not drop by having Romani children in their child's classroom, the project also included anti-bias teacher training and a close system of monitoring the progress not only of each Romani child but also the class as a whole. Additional classes were provided for Romani children to enable them to catch up on the education they had missed out on in the years that they had attended a Romani school and a winter camp in the holidays was organ-ised for those children that struggled in their first term. Romani classroom assistants were taken on by the schools and parents were asked to volunteer as bus monitors, thus simultaneously involving them in their children's education whilst providing further reassurance.

Regular meetings with parents from both communities and with teachers continued throughout the first year of the project so that problems could be addressed as they arose and not be allowed to fester. By March of the first academic year of desegregation, it was clear that this method of desegrega-tion saw Romani children attending school on a regular basis and the previ-ous problems of chronic absenteeism had drastically reduced. Moreover, although the Romani children were far behind their non-Romani classmates when the year began, they had made strong progress in catching up and were clearly motivated to do well. A further and unexpected success of the project was that the grades of non-Romani children markedly improved following desegregation, adding additional impetus to the breaking down of barriers.

The success of the Vidin project in desegregating schools in the town and in raising educational standards for all – integrating Romani children and their parents into the normal social life of the town whilst respecting their difference[61] – suggests that not only is dialogue and co-operation across the community divide more likely to be successful in overcoming socio-economic injustice than a court-based litigation strategy, but that focusing on what the two communities share is more effective than stressing the divisions between them. By doing this, the project was able to avoid the simple problem that the hostile majority simply thwart the enforcement of rights, even where court-ordered.[62] Thus unlike the prediction of the Vidin municipal authorities that initially opposed the desegregation project, desegregation did not raise ethnic tensions but in fact brought the two communities together by focusing on what they had in common: the desire for a good education for their children.

The second reason why focusing so heavily on the issue of racial discrimination is likely to have a negative effect in addition to worsening inter-community relations is the risk that Roma themselves internalise their role as victim. An interesting posting on the Council of Europe-hosted site, Dosta!, in an area of the site entitled 'Meet your Romani neighbours', by Carmen Santiago Reyes, a Spanish national delegate to the European Roma and Travellers' Forum, states, 'When I was a child, the main problems Roma were facing in Spain were the access to education, housing, and employment. Now it is clear that the main problem we have to deal with is discrimination'.[63] There are two ways of reading such a statement. The first is to suggest that the situation in Spain has improved to the point that equal access to basic services such as education and housing can now be taken for granted; this seems overly optimistic.[64] The second is that whereas 10–15 years ago Romani marginalisation was understood in terms of socio-economic problems, it is now seen instead as an issue of non-discrimination. If it is the latter, it may reflect a shift in self-understanding whereby a practical attitude to problems – we need housing – is replaced with a narrative of victimhood: we are victims of discrimination. Like the danger of further polarising communities, this shift risks denying the dialogical nature of interaction between Roma and non-Roma, portraying the relationship instead as one in which the non-Roma act and the Roma suffer. Such a narrative is disempowering, despite the seemingly uplifting rhetoric of Roma Rights, and it also relieves Roma of the burden of any responsibility for the good functioning of inter-community relations. In the end, even Hegel's slave bears some responsibility for his subjugated role.

One should, arguably, not be tempted to draw too much from just two case-studies. However, it is possible to suggest that there is a paradoxical element to approaching Romani socio-economic injustice from a non-discrimination perspective; that is, while at the same time that the strategy is trying to achieve equality by overcoming the prejudice that divides communities into 'we' and 'they',[65] it is polarising the same groups into an 'us' and 'them' approach which undermines the likelihood of achieving meaningful equality. Such an approach fails to take seriously the role of each in constituting the other. Instead, the fears and misunderstanding that drive prejudice *on both sides* are best addressed by dialogue and attempts to gain mutual sympathy and a shared social feeling. An ongoing dialogue establishes and maintains the

Romani community as citizens of equal concern in a mutually constituted shared social space;[66] it is from here that questions of discrimination begin to have meaning.

7.5 Taking a different approach

The foregoing has attempted to suggest that focusing on racial discrimination, particularly where the strategy for affecting change is that of litigation, will not only fail to move towards meaningful equality for Romani communities but will in fact decrease the likelihood of overcoming gross socio-economic disadvantage by further polarising the two communities. Similarly, demands for positive action on the part of the government towards tackling the extreme marginalisation of Romani communities, although vital, without acknowledging both the importance of the intersection between race and poverty as well as the realities of life at the local level will also fail. Instead, the suggestion is that a focus at all levels of community on ensuring the socio-economic rights that all citizens share and doing so via negotiation between communities themselves in the local arena is more likely, in taking the importance of the recognition dialectic seriously, to break the cycle of overwhelming disadvantage.[67]

There are two obvious objections to this approach. The first is that focusing on Roma Rights is empowering. Racial discrimination is so vicious and undermining of one's sense of self that it is necessary to make combating racism explicit in order to restore dignity to those affected, as well as to have any chance of combating such a many-headed monster.[68] There are two possible responses. The first is to concede that an explicit approach has certain advantages but to note that there is no dignity in destitution; the challenge is thus for advocates of such an approach to show how they would overcome the practical problems attached to this strategy. The second response would concede less ground, and highlight instead that a focus on recognition as crucial in addressing Romani exclusion insists upon a focus on Roma as a group. This entails therefore that the problem of both prejudice and systemic discrimination as factors in economic injustice continue to be implicitly addressed. The suggestion is not that the focus should shift, for example, to an individually based formal equality or one based on re-distribution as a social minimum; or that racial discrimination be ignored in a misguided attempt to move beyond race.[69] Instead, the focus stays on the particular disadvantage that Roma as a group face; what is different is that the approach taken to tackle it is in stressing what is in common rather than highlighting difference by placing the emphasis on racial discrimination.

This, however, leads into what is likely to be a second objection; namely that of the essentialising dangers of recognition in general as have been outlined both by recognition theorists,[70] as well as feminists in relation to gender discrimination.[71] However, as Choudhry has suggested in his analysis of the role of groups in tackling economic injustice, there seems to be no way out of this dilemma where one accepts that cycles of deprivation affect different groups unequally, that is, certain social groups suffer more. Thus, while the focus on groups is in one sense highly problematic, it is also indispensable. Moreover, by focusing on the local level, the suggested approach avoids some of the worst elements of essentialisation, such as court-determined ascriptions of identity[72] or of the broad characterisation of parents from one ethnic group being unaware of what is in their child's best interests,[73] and allows individual communities to determine, in negotiation with the non-Roma around them, what being Romani means for them. Further, by stressing the socio-economic rights that all share, the obvious freezing effect of legal rights attached to a single group can also be by and large avoided.[74] By placing the emphasis on mutual constitution in a dialogue at the local level, it is more likely that the nature of recognition as a perpetual becoming can be realised.[75]

Yet a further objection may well be that the emphasis on the role of inter-community dialogue in affecting change makes huge demands of leadership. What if a leader of the quality of Donka Panayotova does not come forward to initiate a project such as the Vidin school plan? Or what if dialogue is refused by the non-Romani community who are only interested in maintaining their dominance? These questions are not easily answered. It may well be that an incentive structure needs to be put in place so that both groups are persuaded of the benefits of negotiation, and one could imagine that the positive obligations of the state may include a state funding structure that rewards projects that are genuinely inter-community in nature, for example.[76] But the difficulties in this should not be underplayed. However, attempting to impose social change from outside is also not an option and the alternatives to integration into a jointly determined common community life remain unpersuasive in the face of the breadth and depth of Romani exclusion.[77] Where co-operation is unforthcoming, Romani communities should insist upon the human rights that they share with all, in which the charge of racial discrimination in access to those rights remains a last resort. It is not that allegations of racial discrimination should never be considered as an option, but rather that they should be used with real caution and never as a trump card to avoid the difficult process of communication.

7.6 Concluding remarks

In attempting to determine which strategy is most likely to achieve success in creating social change, it needs to be clear how success is defined. Here, success has not been defined as convincing a court to label an institution or policy as racist. Rather, success is defined as enhancing dignity and realising the freedom to choose one's own conception of the good life in relation to others with which one shares social space. This requires an end to the cycle of deprivation and destitution that marks so many Romani communities. But what this chapter has attempted to demonstrate as well is that for socio-economic exclusion to be overcome, the importance of changing social relations at the local level should not be underestimated. To achieve dignity in freedom, ultimately one has to claim it and make it real oneself; it cannot be provided by courts or external bodies or actors. While the meaningful realisation of human rights is necessary to achieve equality, freedom and dignity come not from rights themselves but from the equal participation in the life of the community that rights help to ensure.

The argument put forward here has intended to demonstrate that the Roma Rights strategy of racial discrimination-based litigation is unlikely to overcome Romani socio-economic exclusion because it fails to address the interaction between prejudice and disadvantage in maintaining and reinforcing each other. However, it is not suggested that one should do away with a legal approach, or more specifically, the legal structure of rights.[78] As Douzinas has argued, legal recognition must supplement the Hegelian inter-personal process of reciprocal recognition, but it cannot replace it. While he made his point in a general sense of special group-targeted rights, it is especially pertinent for the Roma, where the deeply ingrained hostility of the majority that finds expression in both systemic and conscious acts of discrimination is so socially acceptable. This coupled with the sheer scale of socio-economic disadvantage suggests that it is particularly necessary, in attempting to effect social change beneficial to Roma, that redistribution and recognition, that poverty and race, be addressed simultaneously. Thus it is a question of how those rights are to be best realised and not one of whether the law is useful.

Fredman has suggested that racism occurs along three axes and that correspondingly equality concerns need to address three issues: redressing racial stereotyping and humiliation; breaking the cycle of deprivation; and addressing the positive affirmation and accommodation of difference that is a part of equal concern.[79] It is suggested that focusing on a narrative of socio-economic rights shared by all citizens at the local level, in which the emphasis is upon achieving these rights through a dialogue of reciprocal recognition, is most likely to overcome the current relationship of domination, address the prejudice of the majority and gain acceptance of Romani difference whilst addressing the practical matters of the complexity of socio-economic exclusion. In the end, however, and at the risk of a lame conclusion, much more research is needed on the interaction between poverty and race in the specific situation of Roma in the various countries of CEE before a viable strategy for tackling the problems that sit at that intersection can be developed.

Notes

1 E.g. (2004) *'Zigeuners meest gediscrimineerd'*, *de Volkskrant*, 11 October.
2 United Nations Development Programme (2003) *Avoiding the Dependency Trap. The Roma Human Development Report 2003*, available at http://roma.undp.sk/ (accessed 23 September 2007).
3 See, *inter alia*, K Crenshaw (1989) 'Demarginalizing the intersection of race and sex: A black feminist critique of antidiscrimination doctrine, feminist theory and

antiracial politics', *The University of Chicago Legal Forum*: 139–67; D Schiek (2005) 'Broadening the scope and the norms of EU gender equality law: Towards a multidimensional conception of equality law', *Maastricht Journal of European and Comparative Law*, 12: 427–66, at pp 453–60.

4 Roma in CEE form the focus of this article, notwithstanding that Roma in the rest of Europe face prejudice and marginalisation as well (as demonstrated, e.g. by recent eviction actions in Italy). For the CEE region, most data is available on Roma socio-economic marginalisation. The analysis presented applies to many Romani communities, but not to all, thus summarising diverse groups under 'Roma' for ease of communication.

5 For details on the Decade, see the official website at www.romadecade.org/itentcms/www/roma/index.php.

6 D Ringold, MA Orenstein and E Wilkens (2005) *Roma in an Expanding Europe. Breaking the Poverty Cycle*, Washington DC, available at http://web.worldbank.org/ (accessed 9 January 2008). Unless otherwise stated, all facts in this section are taken from this report.

7 C Bodewig and A Sethi (2005) *Poverty, Social Exclusion and Ethnicity in Serbia and Montenegro: The Case of the Roma*, Washington DC, available at http://web.worldbank.org/ (accessed 9 January 2008). Unless otherwise stated, all facts on Serbia or Montenegro are taken from this report.

8 Equivalent to approximately €50 (checked 14 September 2007).

9 C Bodewig and A Sethi (2005) *Poverty, Social Exclusion and Ethnicity in Serbia and Montenegro: The Case of the Roma*, Washington DC, available at http://web.worldbank.org/ (accessed 9 January 2008), p 3.

10 D Ringold, MA Orenstein and E Wilkens (2005) *Roma in an Expanding Europe. Breaking the Poverty Cycle*, Washington DC, available at http://web. worldbank.org/ (accessed 9 January 2008), p 42.

11 While some countries register rates of unemployment for Roma as high as 90 per cent, WB researchers were sceptical because of the exclusion of the informal sector. For example, Ringold et al, ibid, pp 39–41.

12 Ibid, p 32.

13 Ibid, p 48.

14 L Purporka and Z Zádori (1999) *The Health Status of Roma in Hungary*, Budapest: World Bank Regional Office Hungary, NGO Studies, No 2; cited in ibid, p 50.

15 Low-birth weight has been linked to an increased risk of death and disability, as well as to a range of long-term health problems, such as heart disease, diabetes, Attention Deficit Hyperactivity Disorder (ADHD), infertility in women and depression. See, for example from among the many articles, C Thompson, H Syddall, I Rodin, C Osmond and DJP Barker (2001) 'Birth weight and the risk of depressive disorder in late life', *British Journal of Psychiatry*, 179: 450–55. Also, (2005) 'Lasting legacy of low birthweight', *New Scientist*, 2 July: 2506.

16 ECOHOST (2000) *Health needs of the Roma population in the Czech and the Slovak Republics. A Literature Review*, Final Report 2000, available at www.lshtm.ac.uk/ecohost/roma.pdf (accessed 5 March 2008).

17 Further, studies from Hungary suggest that Romani women have a heightened susceptibility to tuberculosis in comparison to Romani men. L Purporka and Z Zádori (1999) *The Health Status of Roma in Hungary*, Budapest: World Bank Regional Office Hungary, NGO Studies, No 2; D Ringold, MA Orenstein and E Wilkens (2005) *Roma in an Expanding Europe. Breaking the Poverty Cycle*, Washington DC, available at http://web.worldbank.org/ (accessed 9 January 2008), p 51.

18 Ringold et al, ibid, p 53.

19 See, for details of the settlement of Romani communities in environmentally hazardous areas in Kosovo, for example, C Cahn (2007) 'Birth of a nation: Kosovo

and the persecution of Pariah minorities', *German Law Journal*, 8: 81–94, at pp 89–90.

20 For details, see the Roma page of the World Bank, with links to all of its grantees, at www.worldbank.org/eca/roma/about.htm#cial (accessed 8 January 2008).

21 The strategy of the ERRC and related organisations, following the title of their quarterly journal, can be labelled 'Roma Rights'.

22 See the website at www.errc.org/Litigation_index.php (accessed 8 January 2008).

23 For example, the ERRC co-operated with Interrights and Minority Rights Group to develop a common strategic litigation plan to test implementation of the EU Race Directive (2000/43/EC) and Protocol 12 of the European Convention on Human Rights. The project was entitled 'Implementing European Anti-discrimination Law' and ran from 2001 to 2004 covering 26 countries. A list of and access to publications that came out of the project are available at www.migpolgroup.com/topics/2111.html (accessed 8 January 2008).

24 See the website at http://errc.org/ (accessed 9 January 2009).

25 *DH and Others v the Czech Republic*, Application no 57325/00, judgment of 7 February 2006, available at www.echr.coe.int/echr (accessed 9 January 2008).

26 *Brown et al v Board of Education of Topeka et al* 347 US 493 (1954). This assertion is supported by a variety of documents from and about the Ostrava case at the New York-based Open Society's Justice Initiative, the ERRC's partner organisation in this case, directed by James Goldston (former ERRC Legal Director). See, e.g. J Goldston (2005) 'European Court to address racism in landmark cases', *Open Society Justice Iniative*, 28 February, available at www.justiceinitiative.org/db/resource2?res_id=102627 (accessed 9 January 2008), drawing the parallel explicitly.

27 *DH and Others v the Czech Republic*, Application no 57325/00, judgment of the Grand Chamber of 13 November 2007, available at www.echr.coe.int/echr (accessed 9 January 2008).

28 Article 2(4) of Decree No 127/1997 on specialised schools; this decree was repealed by Decree No 73/2005, which came into force on 17 February 2005.

29 This legislation has been replaced in 2000, although research by the ERRC suggests that impact on improving the education of Romani children is minimal. See ERRC (2007) *The Impact of Legislation and Policies on School Segregation of Romani Children. A Study of Anti-Discrimination Law and Government Measures to Eliminate Segregation in Education in Bulgaria, Czech Republic, Hungary, Romania and Slovakia*, Budapest, available at www.ceeol.com/aspx/publicationdetails.aspx?publicationId=a46f1076-f8a4-45d0-8ef4-cf113f5a65d0 (accessed 5 March 2008), pp 42–6.

30 *Belgian Linguistics Case* (1968) 1 EHRR 252, Series A, No 280, para 10.

31 No other language groups (e.g. Vietnamese, Polish, etc.) suffered from the same disparity. Moreover, it was argued that it would be wholly disproportionate to condemn children with poor knowledge of the Czech language to schools for the mentally impaired.

32 According to the case presented, poor children of non-Romani origin are able to excel in the Czech school system.

33 For analysis of the Chamber ruling, see M Goodwin (2006) 'DH and Others v Czech Republic: A major set-back for the development of non-discrimination norms in Europe', *German Law Journal*, 7: 421–32.

34 ERRC (2004) *Stigmata: Segregated Schooling of Roma in Central and Eastern Europe*, Budapest, available at www.errc.org/cikk.php?cikk=1892 (accessed 8 January 2008); ERRC (2007) *The Impact of Legislation and Policies on School Segregation of Romani Children. A Study of Anti-Discrimination Law and Government Measures to Eliminate Segregation in Education in Bulgaria, Czech Republic, Hungary, Romania and Slovakia*, Budapest, available at www.ceeol.com/aspx/

publicationdetails.aspx?publicationId=a46f1076-f8a4-45d0-8ef4-cf113f5a65d0 (accessed 5 March 2008).

35 The percentage of Roma in Hungary comes from the official Hungarian 2001 census. See the website at www.nepszamlalas.hu/eng/volumes/volumes.html (accessed 8 January 2008).

36 Fourth periodic report of state parties, Addendum Czech Republic, 26 November 1999, CERD/C/372/Add.1, para 134.

37 This was the conclusion of a study by the European Monitoring Centre on Racism and Xenophobia into Romani education in public schools in the European Union. EUMC (2006) *Roma and Travellers in Public Education*, May, available at http://fra.europa.eu/fra/index.php?fuseaction=content.dsp_cat_content&cat id=43d8bc25bc89d&contentid=448ee6612aa4c (accessed 9 January 2008).

38 'Separate but equal' was the test that the US Supreme Court applied to test the constitutionality of the segregation of African Americans into separate facilities throughout the education system. Developed in *Plessy v Ferguson* (163 US 537 (1896), it was overturned in *Brown et al v Board of Education of Topeka et al* 347 US 493 (1954).

39 See C Barnard and B Hepple (2000) 'Substantive equality', *Cambridge Law Journal*, 59: 562–85; also, S Fredman (2002) *Discrimination Law*, Oxford: Oxford University Press, especially 'Introduction'.

40 See, for example, S Fredman (2001) 'Combating racism with human rights: The right to equality', in S Fredman (ed) *Discrimination and Human Rights: The Case of Racism*, Oxford: Oxford University Press; B Hepple (1990) 'Discrimination and equality of opportunity – Northern Irish lessons', *Oxford Journal of Legal Studies*, 10: 408–21; B Hepple, M Coussey and T Choudhury (2000) *Equality: A New Framework: Report of the Independent Review of the Enforcement of UK Anti-Discrimination Legislation*, Oxford: Hart Publishing; H Collins (2003) 'Discrimination, equality and social inclusion', *Modern Law Review*, 66: 16–43.

41 See, primarily, J Rawls (1971) *A Theory of Justice*, Oxford: Oxford University Press (2nd revised edn, 1999).

42 See, for example, N Fraser (2000) 'Rethinking recognition', *New Left Review*, 3: 107–20.

43 For a characterisation of the disastrous response to Hurricane Katrina as class-based rather than due to race, see AL Reed, 'The real divide', *The Progressive*, November, 69(11), available at http://progressive.org/?q=node/2660 (accessed 4 March 2008).

44 See S Choudhry (2000) 'Distribution vs recognition: The case of anti-discrimination laws', *George Mason Law Review*, 9: 145–78, following Rawls. Also S Fredman (2001) 'Combating racism with human rights: The right to equality', in S Fredman (ed) *Discrimination and Human Rights: The Case of Racism*, Oxford: Oxford University Press; B Hepple (1990) 'Discrimination and equality of opportunity – Northern Irish lessons', *Oxford Journal of Legal Studies*, 10: 408–21 and B Hepple, M Choussey and T Choudhoury (2000) *Equality: A New Framework: Report of the Independent Review of the Enforcement of UK Anti-Discrimination Legislation*, Oxford: Hart Publishing. But, E Holmes (2005) 'Anti-discrimination rights without equality', *Modern Law Review*, 68: 75–194.

45 Choudhry, ibid, 158.

46 C Taylor (1992) 'The politics of recognition', in A Gutmann (ed) *Multiculturalism and the Politics of Recognition*, Princeton, NJ: Princeton University Press.

47 JA Powell (2007) 'The race and class nexus: An intersectional perspective', *Law and Inequality*, 25: 355–428.

48 For accounts of Romani slavery in the region, which continued in places until 1856, A Fraser (1992) *The Gypsies*, Oxford: Blackstone, pp 57–9; also, I Hancock (2002) *We are the Romani people*, Hatfield: University of Hertfordshire Press, p 29.

49 The case was appealed to the Grand Chamber, and the verdict reversed the Chamber's decision. Oral arguments before the Grand Chamber were heard on 17 January 2007; the verdict was rendered on 13 November 2007 (above for 27). For submissions, see website at www.justiceinitiative.org/db/resource2?res_id= 102627 (accessed 9 January 2008).

50 D Ringold, MA Orenstein and E Wilkens (2005) *Roma in an Expanding Europe. Breaking the Poverty Cycle*, Washington DC, available at http://web.world bank.org/ (accessed 9 January 2008). The assumption that Romani children 'drop-out' because of the worthlessness of a special school education is undone by the data on Romani truancy levels at normal schools.

51 For a detailed comment on the failure of *Brown v Board* to impact on racial segregation in US schools, in part because of residential divisions, see J Kozol (2005) 'Still separate, still unequal. America's educational apartheid', *Harper's Magazine*, 311(1864): 41–54.

52 *DH and Others v The Czech Republic*, Application no 57325/00, judgment of the Grand Chamber of 13 November 2007 (web reference see n 27 above), paras 50–1.

53 See the dissenting opinions of Judges Zupančič, Jungwiert, Borrego Borrego and Šikuta. *DH and Others v The Czech Republic*, Application no 57325/00, judgment of the Grand Chamber of 13 November 2007 (web reference see n 27 above).

54 DS Strickland and C Ascher (1992) 'Low-income African-American children and public schooling', in Philip W Jackson (ed) *Handbook of Research on Curriculum*, New York: Macmillan, found that poor academic achievement among black children was the consequence of a combination of any number of factors, including low wages and high unemployment among black men, inappropriate academic evaluation and placement, poverty and poor schools, poor physical health, high rates of teenage pregnancy, instability in home life, social isolation of the black poor, the physical deterioration of black neighbourhoods, etc.

55 D Ringold, MA Orenstein and E Wilkens (2005) *Roma in an Expanding Europe. Breaking the Poverty Cycle*, Washington DC, available at http://web.world bank.org/ (accessed 9 January 2008), p 38.

56 ERRC (2007) *The Glass Box. Exclusion of Roma from Employment*, Budapest, available at www.ceeol.com/aspx/publicationdetails.aspx?publicationId= a46f1076-f8a4-45d0-8ef4-cf113f5a65d0 (accessed 5 March 2008), pp 9–10.

57 RR Williams (1997) *Hegel's Ethics of Recognition*, Berkeley, CA: University of California Press; N Fraser (2000) 'Rethinking recognition', *New Left Review*, 3: 107–20; also S Fredman (2001) 'Combating racism with human rights: The right to equality', in S Fredman (ed) *Discrimination and Human Rights: The Case of Racism*, Oxford: Oxford University Press, p 10.

58 One thinks in this regard of the MacPherson report in the UK that investigated racial bias in the Metropolitan Police Service, and made a finding that the force was 'institutionally racist', *The Stephen Lawrence Inquiry*, February 1999, available at www.archive.official-documents.co.uk/document/cm42/4262/4262.htm. See also discussion in Fredman, ibid.

59 Using again the example of the MacPherson report, the finding against the Metropolitan Police Service was so powerful because both within the police force and society at large there is broad acceptance that discriminating against a group on grounds of race is wrong.

60 D Panayotova (2002) 'Successful Romani school desegregation: The Vidin Case', *Roma Rights*, 3–4: 44–51.

61 Romani folktales and history have been incorporated into the curriculum in a number of the schools, for example.

62 See, for example, *LR et al v Slovakia*, Communication No 31/2003, CERD/C/66/ D/31/2003 – a housing case from the town of Dobsina. More than two years following victory before CERD in 2005, this Romani community are yet to see any

improvement in their desperate living conditions, which comprise shacks made from cardboard and no connection to either the sewage system or running water, because the local council under the influence of a hostile majority non-Romani community refuse to act upon it.

63 See website at http://dosta.org/?q=node/192 (accessed 11 April 2007). Dosta! (Enough!) is a forum for Roma to present themselves, their families, their lifestyle and their culture.

64 See the Spain section of the ERRC website for regular reports on the negative situation of Roma in Spain, available at www.errc.org (accessed 9 January 2008).

65 S Fredman (2001) 'Combating racism with human rights: The right to equality', in S Fredman (ed) *Discrimination and Human Rights: The Case of Racism*, Oxford: Oxford University Press, p 11.

66 See R Dworkin (2000) *Sovereign Virtue. The Theory and Practice of Equality*, Cambridge, MA: Harvard University Press.

67 This approach takes inspiration from Fredman's call for pregnancy rights located in shared social responsibility. S Fredman (1994) 'A difference with distinction: Pregnancy and parenthood reassessed', *Law Quarterly Review*, 110: 106–23.

68 See, e.g. the approach of the former Executive Director of the ERRC, Dimitrina Petrova; D Petrova (2001) 'Racial discrimination and the rights of minority cultures', in S Fredman (ed) *Discrimination and Human Rights: the Case of Racism*, Oxford: Oxford University Press, pp 45–76.

69 See JA Powell (2007) 'The race and class nexus: An intersectional perspective', *Law and Inequality*, 25: 355–428.

70 For example, P Markell (2003) *Bound by Recognition*, Princeton NJ: Princeton University Press.

71 For example, W Brown (2000) 'Suffering rights as paradoxes', *Constellations*, 7: 230–41.

72 Choudhry provides an excellent example from Canada to illustrate this danger. Choudhry (2000) 'Distribution vs recognition: The case of anti-discrimination laws', *George Mason Law Review*, 9: 145–78, at pp 176–7.

73 For example, the understandable but problematic statement of the Grand Chamber in explaining the failure of the majority of the parents in the Ostrava case to challenge their child's placement; *DH and Others v The Czech Republic*, Application no 57325/00, judgment of the Grand Chamber of 13 November 2007 (web reference see n 27 above), para 203.

74 C Douzinas (2002) 'Identity, recognition, rights or what Hegel can teach us about human rights?', *Journal of Law and Society*, 29: 379–405.

75 H Arendt (1959) *The Human Condition*, New York: Doubleday Anchor; J Tully (1995) *Strange Multiplicity*, Cambridge: Cambridge University Press.

76 For the role of the state in achieving social change towards equality by means of purchasing power, C McCrudden (2007) *Buying Social Justice. Equality, Government Procurement and Legal Change*, Oxford: Oxford University Press.

77 This is not to suggest that outside support is either unwelcome or unnecessary – Organisation Drom received vital support and financial assistance from international civil society such as the Romani Participation Project. Rather, the process and their own needs must be determined by the communities themselves.

78 Woodiwiss's point that politics grounded in an optimistic view of nature is unlikely to be sufficient to see an ethical path maintained is well taken. See A Woodiwiss (2006) 'The law cannot be enough: Human rights and the limits of legalism', in S Meckled-García and B Çali (eds) *The Legalization of Human Rights*, London: Routledge, pp 33–4.

79 S Fredman (2001) 'Combating racism with human rights: The right to equality', in S Fredman (ed) *Discrimination and Human Rights: The Case of Racism*, Oxford: Oxford University Press, p 15.

8 From single to multidimensional policy approaches to equalities

The example of contract compliance

Michael Orton and Peter Ratcliffe

8.1 Introduction

The aim of this chapter is to examine multidimensional approaches to equality from a variety of perspectives: theoretical, policy, and practice. In particular, it examines the efficacy of a certain mode of interventionism. First, however, we need to clarify what we mean by multidimensionality. Schiek rightly points out that the term is open to some confusion in that it may, for example, refer to different conceptions of equality or to different sets of grounds specified in order 'to achieve equality for multi-faceted human beings in social reality'.[1]

It is multidimensionality in this latter sense that we address in the current chapter. It explores the challenges presented by both 'complementarity' (or 'additivity') and intersectionality in the UK context. To be more precise, it involves looking at both aspects of multidimensionality through the lens of a form of policy initiative that has, for a variety of reasons, been underutilised in the UK: contract compliance. For reasons to be clarified shortly it focuses on how an initiative targeted at addressing a single 'ground', 'race', might be developed into a much more powerful policy tool by simultaneously addressing a number of strands, or dimensions, of the equalities agenda. These strands may be addressed separately, in an 'additive' or complementary form, or as interrelated sources of identity and affect, that is, as intersecting elements.

Moves towards a multidimensional approach, in the sense adopted in this chapter, are exemplified in the UK by the creation (under the Equality Act 2006) of the Equality and Human Rights Commission which came into being on 1 October 2007. The Equality and Human Rights Commission brings together the work of three existing Commissions: the Commission for Racial Equality, the Disability Rights Commission, and the Equal Opportunities Commission (which dealt with gender issues). Importantly, in accordance with the new generic approach, its remit will extend beyond that of the former Commissions to deal with other forms of proscribed act and have a statutory duty to promote a positive human rights culture. The key benefits are perceived as twofold:[2] one, this is the first governmental body responsible for promoting and protecting human rights since the UK government enacted the Human Rights Act 1998 which provided UK citizens with the right directly to enforce in UK courts human rights protected under the European Convention on Human Rights. Second, this new approach to dealing with discriminatory behaviour of an individual or collective, institutional nature should provide a more effective means of addressing intersectionality (discriminatory acts that cut across conventional strands of equality policy and practice). The previous Commissions were frequently berated for failing to deal adequately with cases that raised issues of both 'race'/ethnicity and gender. The interaction between the latter in many cases revealed quite specific forms of discriminatory behaviour.[3]

Under New Labour governments since 1997, equalities have been a significant focus of policy development, and we have witnessed a raft of new legislation, for example, the Race Relations (Amendment) Act 2000; the Employment Equality (Age) Regulations 2006; and the Disability Discrimination Act 2005. Following the recently published report of the Equalities Review and the deliberations of the Discrimination Law Review (currently at consultation stage), work is underway on a Single Equality Act (destined to enter the Statute Book in 2009).[4] The latter is designed both to simplify and to strengthen the current legislative framework. What makes this particularly significant for the current chapter is the fact that the Equalities Review came down heavily in favour of using contract compliance to further the equalities agenda, and this will be taken into account in the outcome of the Discrimination Law Review. The Equality and Human Rights Commission, as the policing body of the proposed Single Equality Act, is therefore keen to see evidence of the effectiveness in practice of approaches such as the use of contract compliance. This is to be expected as the Commission for Racial Equality, following the initiative outlined in this chapter, produced detailed, if not entirely unambiguous, guidance for public authorities on these issues.[5]

However, it has long been argued that in tackling inequality and discrimination there is a need for a variety of political, administrative, policy and legislative responses.[6] This is clearly illustrated by the fact that, although racial discrimination in employment was made unlawful in the UK over 30 years ago (under the Race Relations Act 1976), it is still evident in the contemporary labour market, as will be demonstrated below.

In adopting a policy perspective on multidimensional approaches to equalities the chapter therefore assesses, as an exemplar, the use of contract compliance to promote equal opportunities in employment.[7] In particular, it draws on the authors' evaluation of an innovative policy introduced by a group of local authorities in the West Midlands region of England, specifically aimed at redressing racial inequality in employment (known as the 'West Midlands Common Standard' (WMCS)).[8] It is important to point out here that, in the UK, equality initiatives driven by legislation are historically far more developed in the area of 'race' than in any other policy area (including gender). This being the case, our selected exemplar was always likely to high-light best the possibilities of wider application.

The chapter examines whether this single-dimension policy approach (that is, based on redressing racial inequality) can be adapted to a multidimensional framework.[9] These debates are linked to the theory and practice of intersectionality and explore the limits of efficacy in relation to public policy. The analysis is divided into four parts. First, it discusses the use of contract compliance to promote equality issues. Second, it examines the specific example of the WMCS, which seeks to tackle racial inequality in employment. Third, the meaning and significance (in the labour market context) of intersectionality and complementarity/additivity are explored so as to facilitate an assessment of the potential for this unidimensional approach to be adapted to a multidimensional framework. Fourth, the chapter considers the broader question of the 'space' available for equalities (whether from a single or multidimensional perspective) within current UK economic and social policy. We conclude with some comments on the possible future trajectory of contract compliance as a tool for promoting equal opportunities within a multidimensional framework.

We begin by discussing contract compliance as a means of redressing inequality.

8.2 Contract compliance and equal opportunities[10]

The term 'contract compliance' originated in the US and is commonly used to describe procedures adopted by public sector organisations to ensure that companies to which they give contracts operate an equal opportunities policy.[11] In the US, contract compliance has been the subject of extensive debate from its introduction in the 1940s within an equal opportunities approach, through to affirmative action, calls for a new 'economic empowerment model'[12] and questions as to the effectiveness of contract compliance.[13] Erridge and Fee characterise the debate on contract compliance as being about balancing labour costs and benefits and the impact on competitiveness against ethical and moral arguments.[14] Certainly the concern with cost is an important one as is the concern that affirmative action priorities may have led to failings in public procurement. These partially explain why, although contract compliance in the US is generally considered to have been an effective policy instrument,[15] certain reservations remain – hence some retreat from its use.[16]

In the UK, its use has been more limited (than in the US), but there is still considerable debate about its role.[17] One particular concern is uncertainty as to what is permitted under both national and EU legislation. Indeed, the complexity of the available legal framework has been characterised as a 'double jeopardy', meaning that if action is not prevented by UK law then it may well be prohibited by EU regulations.[18] In short, there is a series of EU Directives on procurement based on an economic rationale which aims to create competitive conditions in which public contracts can be awarded without discrimination between companies from different member states, and within which the use of social criteria as part of the procurement process, while not precluded, is limited.[19] However, it has been argued that it is not the detail of what the regulations say, but the *perception* that they hinder the use of contract compliance, that is the more important point.[20] This will be seen later as being critical to prospects of achieving positive change via public sector procurement.

Before doing so, however, it is worth considering the range of powers vested in public sector bodies. Prior to the coming into effect of the Race Relations (Amendment) Act 2000, the statutory duty to combat discrimination and promote good relations between communities covered by the legislation was confined to local authorities (under s 71 of the Act). The Amendment Act, however, widened the coverage of the duty to encompass public authorities more generally. It also defined the latter in such a way as to include all bodies that fulfil a public function. In other words, a private company contracted to undertake work for a public authority would thereby assume the mantle of a public authority. Crucially, however, the responsibility for ensuring compliance with the legislation rests with the body awarding the contract. Despite this, it nevertheless means that public authorities can justify to potential contractors a policy seeking to ensure such compliance.

In this chapter, we are limiting ourselves to the local authority sector, but it is important to realise the wider significance of our case study. The move towards a legal and policy framework based on a generic equalities strategy also provides much wider scope for transferability of best practice approaches. We shall deal with these matters in later sections.

In terms of available compliance models, the US affirmative action approach is not permitted under UK law.[21] This means that an alternative such as the equal opportunities framework needs to be pursued.[22] There is also a specific legal framework relating to UK local authorities,[23] to which we turn now.

8.2.1   Contract compliance at the local level in the United Kingdom: a single-dimension approach to equalities

A recent central government review of local authority procurement adopted a broad definition encompassing the whole process of acquisitions including the purchase of goods, the commissioning of services (often used in the context of social services) and the procurement of works such as building projects.[24] Procurement therefore includes local authority contracts awarded, primarily to private-sector companies, for anything ranging from basic items of stationery to multi-million pound contracts for the provision of social care and construction work. The extent and significance to the wider labour market of local government procurement should not be under-estimated. Total non-pay revenue expenditure by local authorities in England stands at

£42.2 billion, including £6.6 billion capital expenditure.[25] Over half of local government spending is now on contracts.[26]

We will discuss below the changing legislative and policy context, but the starting point for this chapter is legislation from the 1980s. In the late-1980s the use of contract compliance by local authorities was severely restricted by the Local Government Act 1988. This on the one hand introduced Compulsory Competitive Tendering (CCT), imposing a legal obligation on local authorities to put certain services out to competitive tender, and on the other made it illegal for councils to entertain any 'non-commercial considerations', including equal opportunities, in awarding contracts. The key exception was that the Secretary of State approved six questions which councils could ask potential contractors regarding racial equality in employment. While the six questions were ostensibly rather limited in scope, councils were allowed to ask firms to supply documents in support of their responses, thereby providing the opportunity to request a copy of a company's racial equality policy and supporting documentation. Despite a rapidly changing policy context, the six questions remain in place today.[27]

To iterate an earlier point, the legislative framework from the 1980s allowed only for the consideration of racial inequality – pointing to a single rather than multidimensional approach. Hence, the legislation permitted the consideration of racial equality in local government procurement but not other strands of the equalities agenda, such as gender or disability. Despite this, it will be seen shortly that when we examine the specific example of the WMCS, on which this chapter draws, at a policy level there is considerable blurring of references to a racial equality policy and a more generic equal opportunities policy. This is significant in a number of ways, but before considering the point further we shall briefly discuss the need for measures to redress racial inequality in employment in the UK.

8.2.2 Racial inequality in employment in the United Kingdom

In empirical terms, racial inequality is a well-documented feature of the UK labour market.[28] For some time there has been evidence of divergence in the circumstances of the principal minority ethnic groups, and between men and women within those groups,[29] but in overall terms the unemployment rate for people from minority ethnic groups is often at least twice the rate for white people and can be three times higher.[30] Economic activity rates also tend to be lower; much lower in the case of certain groups (for example, Muslim women of Pakistani and Bangladeshi origin). All of these points are confirmed in a recent government report.[31] In terms of work, there is also a discernible tendency for different minority ethnic groups to be concentrated in distinct economic sectors, and the range of occupations is more restricted than for white people.[32]

In explaining these patterns, studies have considered a wide range of contributory factors – such as lack of English language skills, qualification deficits and geographical location – but discrimination remains a key explanatory factor. For example, when such variables are controlled for:

> there remains a residue of disadvantage and exclusion that cannot be so easily explained. As a result, it is difficult to avoid the conclusion that, despite 35 years of 'race relations' legislation, discrimination continues to play a significant part in the labour market placement of minority ethnic groups.[33]

There has been considerable debate in the UK over the recent past about the need to develop the level of social capital in migrant/minority communities.[34] The underlying concern is not simply that of squandering human resources, but that exclusion from the labour market fosters or exacerbates a lack of 'community cohesion'.[35] Tackling racial inequality in employment is therefore not just about increasing the human capital of ethnic minorities but about confronting discrimination lest it contributes to increasing social instability.

Contract compliance offers one possible way forward. The sheer size of the public purse, and hence power and significance in the labour market, underlines the point. To explore this theme in more detail we now turn to our exemplar: the WMCS.

8.2.3   Contract compliance in practice: the West Midlands Common Standard (WMCS)

The WMCS has already been discussed in detail elsewhere,[36] so here we confine ourselves to a summary of key points. The WMCS was developed by six councils in the West Midlands working together as the 'West Midlands Forum', and in conjunction with the UK Commission for Racial Equality (CRE). All six councils had since the introduction of the Local Government Act 1988 used the six questions, but the CRE wanted to explore whether their use could be developed further and therefore suggested that the councils work together to implement a 'Common Standard' for their contractors (regarding racial equality).

Contract compliance can be implemented at different points in the procurement process,[37] and the WMCS is based on what is described as the 'pre-qualification' stage. This relies on the councils having 'standing lists' of approved contractors. A standing list is a database of firms who have expressed interest in tendering for work from the council, and have been assessed by the council as being suitable to do so. Typically, a firm that contacts a council will be asked to complete a pre-qualification questionnaire probing such matters as the company's technical competence and financial soundness. Each of the councils involved in the West Midlands initiative has a standing list of several hundred companies. While the *raison d'être* for such a list may be the desire to minimise the possibility of contracting unsuitably qualified or financially dubious firms, it also provides the scope for other criteria to be considered, including racial equality.

The focus on the pre-qualification stage has a number of advantages. It means that the councils ensure that all potential contractors, not just those awarded contracts, have a racial equality policy, thereby widening the impact on the available pool of companies. It also means that having a racial equality policy is not the determining factor at contract award stage (although there could be examples, such as the provision of care for Asian elders, where equalities' issues would be central to the specific tender),[38] thereby addressing concerns (noted earlier) about contract compliance leading to failings in procurement decisions.

We have already noted that at a policy level there is considerable blurring of references to a racial equality policy and a more generic equal opportunities policy. From the outset, the aim of the WMCS was seen as being 'To raise contractors' performance in race equality in employment and equal opportunities in general'. Thus, despite the legislative framework of the 1980s allowing only for a single-dimension approach, the WMCS sought to promote a broader equalities agenda. In practice, this meant that policymakers responsible for the WMCS talked in terms not of companies having a racial equality policy, but an equal opportunities policy (EOP).[39] In discussing the WMCS we will therefore tend to use the term 'EOP' rather than 'racial equality policy'.[40]

As far as the actual requirements of the WMCS are concerned, these set various criteria that companies must meet, with having an EOP of central importance. There is a separate debate about the use and effectiveness of EOPs in general.[41] For our purposes, what is important is not discussion of the philosophical issues involved, but the recognition of EOPs as a tangible means of addressing inequality. As early as 1984 the CRE produced a Code of Practice for the Elimination of Racial Discrimination and the Promotion of Equality of Opportunity in Employment (which became known as the CRE Code of Practice in Employment).[42] This Code, which was approved by Parliament, set out practical steps which employers should take (in order to avoid the risk of falling foul of the legislation). These include: having a written policy; communicating the policy to employees and job applicants; adopting disciplinary procedures for dealing with discrimination in the company; training managers and supervisors in ensuring equality; reviewing the company's recruitment, promotion and training practices regularly; taking positive action to encourage greater representation of under-represented ethnic groups in the workforce; recording the ethnic origin of job applicants and members of the workforce; and using such records to monitor the effectiveness of the company's equal opportunities policy. It is these points that the WMCS requires companies to adopt.

A key factor is that a detailed assessment of a company's EOP is undertaken to ensure that it meets the set criteria. The WMCS also includes initiatives aimed at addressing the issue of moving beyond simple procedural requirements to monitoring impact on the employment of minority ethnic groups. Thus, it provides for a three-yearly review of companies' EOPs. In addition, there is a system of contract monitoring. This involves meeting with contracted companies to investigate whether formal, written policies are actually being implemented.

The Common Standard was launched in 1998 and by 2001 over 2,500 companies had been assessed. It was at this stage that the evaluation took place.

8.2.4   The evaluation

The evaluation included analysis of the WMCS database but was principally based on in-depth interviews with 33 people drawn from 24 different contractors.[43] The aim was to provide case studies of how contractors have responded to the introduction of the WMCS. Sampling was guided by the need to generate a range of companies of different sizes and in different sectors, reflecting in broad terms the variety of companies on the WMCS database. There was an even split between companies that essentially did work only in the West Midlands and those that covered a larger part of the country, or worked nationwide. The companies ranged from one with just 11 employees to another which forms part of one of the top 20 largest companies in the US.

8.2.5   The impact of the West Midlands Common Standard on companies

The WMCS was found to have had a significant impact by encouraging firms to adopt EOPs. Some companies had never before had an EOP and the introduction of the WMCS meant that for the first time these companies were engaging with equalities issues and addressing how to ensure their employment practices promoted equality of opportunity. In such cases, the impact of the WMCS was dramatic. Other companies had formerly relied on an equal opportunities statement expressing their commitment to the principle of equality. There is, of course, a significant difference between a statement of commitment to racial equality and the introduction of a formal policy and procedures to achieve that end. Implementation of the WMCS meant companies had to develop such a strategy. Once again, the impact of the WMCS initiative was immediate. A third group of companies already had an EOP in place. But, even here, the WMCS had an impact in that it encouraged firms to review, update and revise policies, for example, addressing areas of weakness such as the failure to monitor workforce composition.

With regard to policy implementation, the evaluation also found a broad range of generally positive responses. The research provided examples of companies making great progress on equal opportunities: for example, through the provision of training on equalities issues, the development of more formalised recruitment practices and even the adoption of positive action strategies.[44]

There were also, however, companies which claimed to be taking no steps at all to implement their policy. But closer examination invariably revealed that this was not quite true: they had, for example, circulated the new policy to staff and stated in job advertisements that the company was an equal opportunities employer. For firms that had not previously engaged with equalities' issues at all, even such small steps represented clear progress.

The evaluation considered the question of whether the introduction of the WMCS had already had a discernible impact on minority ethnic employment. In order to assess this, ethnic monitoring by companies would need to be widespread. Unfortunately, however, the research found this not to be the case. Only one company could provide evidence of an annual monitoring exercise being undertaken. In small companies, managers were able during the course of the research interview to list their employees from memory, and cite the number from minority ethnic groups. But the absence of systematic monitoring meant there was no real sense of how the composition of a company's workforce was changing over time and whether under-representation of minorities was being redressed.

In order to address this, there is a need to be more explicit about the aims of the WMCS. We therefore recommended that it should be made clear to companies that redressing the under-representation of ethnic minorities (applying this to our example) was the principal objective of the WMCS. Doing so would encourage councils to prioritise the need for companies to undertake formal workforce monitoring. As we have seen, the councils already have the 'tools' to do this, in the form of the three-yearly review of companies' EOPs and contract monitoring. The WMCS database could then be used to measure change over time in the make-up of the overall workforce and provide the evidence on which ameliorative action could be taken. Without such active monitoring gains may be limited. Nevertheless, it is worth pointing out that the pilot scheme was in its relative infancy, so our conclusion, as previously argued,[45] was cautiously optimistic. It argued that this example of using contract compliance at the local level to address racial inequality in employment is working in a number of clearly identifiable ways, and with further development offers a potential means of redressing racial inequality in employment.

The success of the initiative has led to considerable interest from those active in national policy circles as well as in local government. Indeed, the approach has been adopted, at least partially, by a number of other councils and especially amongst Inner London boroughs. Interest has also widened to include a number of other public bodies such as the police and fire service. Crucially also, it has been endorsed as a good practice model by the Office of Government Commerce (OGC), and has influenced thinking about contracting and service delivery for the London Olympics of 2012. The big question is how it might be adapted so as to meet the challenges of a multidimensional approach to equalities. In particular, how might it deal with the complex issue of intersectionality?

8.3 Intersectionality, additivity and the potential for developing an effective multidimensional approach

Theoretical questions about intersectionality and 'additivity', for example in the context of the 'race'–gender nexus, have sparked a voluminous body of literature, arguably given renewed impetus in the UK by the work of Anthias and Yuval-Davis.[46] Philosophical debates about the relationship between these and wider strands of the equalities agenda were then the subject of an important book by Phillips.[47] Whilst it is beyond the scope of this chapter to review these works, we do need to explore precisely what contract compliance can and cannot hope to achieve in a multidimensional equalities context.

First, however, there is a need to return to a theme to which we alluded earlier in the chapter. This relates to the wide disparities in the labour market position of those from different minority groups and, within them, of men and women. Not only have we long witnessed a highly gendered labour market in the UK, there has also been evidence of different approaches towards, and experiences of, engagement with the market on the part of (say) women from different groups (viewed not just in terms of culture, but also of faith, not to say age, and so on). To explore these fully would require a major treatise in itself. We shall therefore confine ourselves to a single example: Muslim women (largely of Pakistani and Bangladeshi origin) of working age.

We know from many data sources that economic activity levels amongst this 'group' tend to be considerably lower than amongst other groups of women.[48] This has normally been explained by discrimination on grounds of faith (for example, Islamophobia), a differentialist racism or neo-racism[49] and/or cultural factors, most notably social conventions imposed by *purdah* and the attendant domestic responsibilities. A combination of these factors, exacerbated by low expectations (and commitment) on the part of teachers therefore contributes towards constrained career options.[50] This has been seen as explaining the 'popularity' of (or perhaps more accurately resort to) homeworking and a reliance on 'sweatshops'.[51] A very different story is however emerging. As Dale *et al.* argue,[52] these groups are now making significant progress in the labour market; and Bradby has pointed to new means by which they, along with other South Asian women, are beginning to prolong their period of education and thereby achieve 'success' in career terms (as normatively represented).[53] This clearly points to the need to assess workforces in complex intersectional terms rather than see issues of ethnicity, gender and faith (say) as merely representing independent sets of concerns which operate additively, or even as alternative sources of discrimination. We need to bear this in mind when considering the following comments.

The main thrust of a contract-compliance policy is to generate a balanced workforce by creating an 'equal opportunity' environment. Contractors are required to instigate policies that ensure this balance is achieved over the short to medium term, by mainstreaming monitoring systems within management decision-making processes. In our case study, the ultimate aim was to increase the representation of minority ethnic staff at all levels of companies contracted to undertake work (for the six local authorities). The pre-qualification assessment questionnaire focused on eliciting as much information as was feasible (and permissible under current legislation) about policies and monitoring systems. It would be a relatively straightforward task to extend this formally to cover gender, disability, age, and so on. Insofar as all but the smallest companies are likely to have computerised human resource systems, it would also not represent an unacceptable imposition on contracted companies (that is, those that have already passed the equalities audit at pre-qualification stage) to request data, for example, on the ethnicity/age/gender breakdown of employees by payroll grade. This would clearly permit an analysis of where the gaps are (in terms of producing a workforce that more closely mirrors the local labour force – in an intersectional, as well as additive, sense).[54] It should also promote a debate within the company as to the source and nature of intersectional concerns in the workplace (that is, not simply in the realm of recruitment). As implied by our discussion of Muslim women above this would also raise more general policy issues, many of them inevitably outwith the remit, or sphere of influence, of individual companies.

We should remind the reader at this point that, although both in the West Midlands and elsewhere in the UK where the model has been adopted, it has thus far been limited to issues of 'race', this is destined to change. With the proposed Single Equality Act on the horizon, policymakers are starting to look to the West Midlands model as a basis for more complex and effective procurement tools. The national Equalities and Service Provision Group, which brings together representatives of the old Commissions, the Local Government Association and senior figures from the public sector, is acting as the spearhead for policy development in this area (principally by lobbying, and entering into discussions with, central government).

The question remains as to how far all of this takes us in terms of dealing with the implications of intersectionality. It is clear, for example, that the mere fact of having the 'appropriate' numerical representation of men and women from different minority groups (say) does not necessarily mean that a company respects the interests of those groups equally. There has, indeed, been much (justifiable) criticism in the past of 'tick-box' practice in the UK more generally, that is, an overly bureaucratic (but substantively weak) adherence to the principles and practices of 'multiculturalism'. Nor is it necessarily the case that members of putative groups influence company policy and practice in line with their interests and concerns. This should not, however, be used as an excuse for a retreat from the policy initiatives we have suggested. Although, as Schiek rightly argues, 'experience from the UK, US and Canada suggest that intersectional discrimination is not easy to address', the time is right to press forward with rather more ambitious policies and practices, and put pressure on the private sector to take their social responsibilities more seriously.[55]

The quality of human resource management has thus far tended to be inferred from the statistical data and from accompanying equalities documentation. To perform a thorough equalities audit, even of small and medium-size enterprises, would be a complex and time-consuming exercise, with severe resource implications for the public authorities involved. This explains why the councils in our case study have adopted a rather more modest system of post-contract monitoring that relies on questionnaire and site-visit data at specified intervals. The solution, as suggested in our concluding remarks below, is to press for a greater sense of commitment (including funding) from central government to provide some 'real teeth' to policy reforms in the realm of equalities.

The key point is that contract compliance does not, in itself, constitute an immediate panacea to the complex ramifications of intersectionality or even additivity. In theory, however, it should provide a useful tool within a wider strategy. Returning to our case study, there are two points to consider both of which concern the efficacy of the approach. First, there is the question of implementation of the WMCS at policy level; and second, the thorny issue of the changing legislative context.

8.3.1   The policy level

At the level of policy implementation of the WMCS what is of interest is that despite the formal emphasis on a single equality dimension (that is, redressing racial inequality in employment), which reflected the restrictions of 1980s' legislation, the evaluation found that the impact of the policy was multi-dimensional. We have already seen that there was a blurring at the policy level of the distinction between a racial equality policy and an EOP. When asked to comply with the requirements of the WMCS, the evaluation found that companies took a more multidimensional approach to equalities than the councils were allowed by 1980s legislation to require, in that they did not only incorporate racial equality policy, but also considered other grounds too (at least at the level of nomenclature and discursive rhetoric).

None of the contractors interviewed in our research described their approach as involving a 'racial equality policy': all had generic equalities policies and in many cases had taken steps that went beyond the requirements of current anti-discrimination legislation. For example, at the time of the evaluation it was not illegal to discriminate on the basis of age (this only became illegal from October 2006) but several companies included age as a category in their equal opportunities policies, stating that job applicants and current employees would not be discriminated against on this basis. Gender and disability were categories in the policies of all the companies who were interviewed, and many included other issues such as sexuality and responsibility for dependants. This immediately suggests that the WMCS had an impact beyond simply promoting racial equality and, reflecting the reality of companies' stated policies rather than the constraints of legislation, a multidimensional approach was evident.[56] It was, of course, beyond the remit of the evaluation research to examine the real impact of this multidimensionality in practice.

Nevertheless we can conclude that, whilst in a formal sense the WMCS reflects a single-dimension approach concerned solely with racial inequality, in practice it already offers a promising model for the development of a multidimensional approach to the use of contract compliance which other public sector organisations could adopt. This is reinforced by the changing legislative context.

8.3.2 The changing legislative context: the 'Best Value' regime

As we have seen, the WMCS was based on the use of the six questions provided for in the Local Government Act 1988, which legislated for CCT. The Local Government Act 1999 replaced CCT with Best Value, which ostensibly aimed to provide greater scope for consideration of local service delivery and a broader definition of 'value for money'. Confusingly, the 1999 Act repealed sections of the 1988 Act relating to CCT but did not repeal the section prohibiting the use of non-commercial considerations. Because Best Value aimed at a broader approach than CCT, this caused confusion within local government as to what exactly was permissible. To address this confusion, in 2001 the government made an order in the form of a statutory instrument (the Local Government Best Value (Exclusion of Non-commercial Considerations) Order 2001, SI 2001/909), which was subsequently included in a Circular containing statutory guidance.[57]

The guidance makes clear that equal opportunities can be given much greater consideration under Best Value than was the case with CCT. The guidance states that 'Best value authorities may take account of the practices of potential service providers in respect of equal opportunities (for example, race, gender, disability, religion, age, and sexual orientation)', extending considerably the areas of discrimination that can be taken into account.[58] Also, while authorities 'will continue to be able to ask the six questions . . . they are no longer restricted to these six questions as the sole means of taking account of racial equality. In addition, and *where relevant to the contract*, and for the purposes of achieving best value, the authority will be able to ask some further questions in relation to racial equality' (our emphasis).[59] There is now clearly scope for authorities to transcend the limitations of the 1988 Act and do a great deal more. This is evidenced by the Equal Opportunities Commission (which was concerned with sex discrimination) in April 2007 producing its own draft advice on contract compliance and gender.

The impact of these developments is, however, immediately limited by a number of further factors because the statutory guidance places riders on the potential use of contract compliance. First, unlike the 1988 Act which specified questions that local authorities could ask, this is not the case with Best Value. This creates a strong sense of uncertainty among local authorities as to exactly what is permissible. Second, while it is stated that equal opportunities can be considered in pre-qualification questionnaires, the main thrust of the guidance is in stressing that equal opportunities must be 'relevant' to a specific contract (as indicated by the above quotation). The phrase 'where relevant to the contract' appears repeatedly, giving a strong suggestion that the consideration of equal opportunities is about service delivery and not about ensuring that contractors have an EOP encompassing human-resource matters. Third, while the importance of equal opportunities considerations is acknowledged, a further recurring theme is that a balance needs to be struck with other considerations, and authorities must 'avoid making requests for information that are disproportionate . . . and not strictly relevant to the contract'.[60]

For authorities committed to using procurement to promote equal opportunities, there is undoubtedly greater scope to do so. However, it is far from clear how best to proceed, and individual authorities are left to form their own view as to what the law allows them to do and where the right 'balance' is to be struck. Moreover, as noted earlier, authorities are cautioned to ensure that their policies do not fall foul of European legislation. Given this background, even those authorities most committed to advancing the equalities agenda are likely to hesitate before adopting new policies.[61] And critically, there is no direct requirement that authorities consider the use of contract compliance: the impact is therefore likely to be limited. There remains considerable ambiguity regarding the use of procurement to pursue equalities. In contrast, as noted earlier, the Equalities Review states explicitly that this is an area where government leadership is absolutely essential.[62] However, as there has been little evidence of such political will to date, the omens are not good. This is where the new expanded Commission could, and arguably should, play a vital role.

What is evident is that debates reflect closely Erridge and Fee's characterisation of discussion of contract compliance as being about costs and competitiveness versus ethical and moral arguments.[63] Evidence demonstrating that contract compliance works as an effective means of prompting private sector companies to adopt EOPs therefore stands in tension with concern about potentially 'negative' impacts, of which the issue of cost appears most significant. To take just two examples, a major review of racial inequality in the labour market by the UK government included evidence of the effective use of contract compliance to promote racial inequality in employment, but then cited a series of reasons why using procurement to pursue racial equality may be considered problematic:

- there may be regulatory burdens and costs;
- there is a risk of discouraging potential bidders;

- UK and EU law are so complex on this issue that there is a danger of authorities adopting an approach that is unlawful; and
- contract compliance might confuse judgments about value for money.[64]

A comprehensive review of local government procurement reached very similar conclusions. It stated that councils can use procurement to achieve their wider 'social objectives', but immediately undermined this argument by adding a number of riders including:

- where a policy involves additional expenditure, specific costings should be included so local citizens can understand what is being done on their behalf;
- distorting the procurement process to favour specific suppliers will often have a cost to the community as a whole which is disproportionate to the benefits derived by a small number of people.[65]

This apparent conflict between using contract compliance for pursuing equalities issues versus concerns about costs, raises the issue of the space available for the pursuit of equalities within the broader context of economic policy.[66]

8.4 Contract compliance, economic policy and the space available for equalities [67]

Here, we reflect on factors that might undermine the widespread adoption of contract compliance as a means of pushing forward the equalities agenda. There are two key points to consider: (i) the tension between the use of contract compliance to promote social objectives and a concern with fiscal restraint and control of public spending; and (ii) the importance of the UK's commitment to labour market flexibility.

First, Fee argues that the use of contract compliance raises basic political and ideological questions about the pursuit of social objectives 'versus the central value for money principle of New Public Management'.[68] We have now presented quotations illustrating that increased cost and a threat to efficiency are seen as reasons to be wary of the use of contract compliance. Best Value certainly does not mean that cost is no longer an issue and control of public expenditure has continued to be a major priority, not least in relation to local government.[69] Thus, contract compliance may be acknowledged as a means of pursuing equal opportunities in employment but this is subordinate to the control of public expenditure. The room for policy development on equalities is immediately restrained by this overriding priority.

Second, the UK government currently remains committed to maintaining the most lightly regulated labour market of any leading economy.[70] The importance of this commitment can be seen in a number of policy arenas. Dean argues, for example, that in relation to policy development on work–life balance, making it possible for parents to combine paid employment and family life means adopting an approach to labour-market policy that places unequivocal social obligations on business.[71] But the government's position is that to legislate for flexible working practices might undermine best practice and stifle innovation. The outcome is a legal right to request, but not necessarily achieve, flexible working and it 'is hard to avoid the conclusion that the government is inclined to put the interests of business above the needs of low-income families'.[72] Similarly, there has been considerable government policy development on gender inequality in the labour market, especially in relation to the gender pay gap.[73] Government departments are required to undertake pay reviews, but with the private sector the emphasis remains heavily on encouraging and persuading, not requiring, employers to adopt equality practices. Progress has been slow, and data show the pay gap widened slightly in 2002.[74]

We noted at the start of this chapter that under New Labour governments since 1997 equalities have been a significant focus of policy development and new legislation; certainly compared with Conservative governments of the 1980s and early 1990s. But at the same time, New Labour has not abandoned neo-liberal economic policies pursued in the UK since the late-1970s. Thus, the scope for discussion of equalities issues is certainly greater than in the 1980s and this, in turn, gives rise to greater consideration of contract compliance. Our argument is that there appears to be a hierarchy of policy development under New Labour. Policy development on equalities must take place within the context of a primary commitment to labour-market flexibility and control of public spending, and the room for developing action to confront inequality is constrained. When policy development threatens (say) to encroach upon labour-market flexibility then the restricted scope becomes apparent. The tensions and ambiguities we have identified regarding contract compliance do not necessarily reflect a contradiction on the part of the UK government. Rather, when looking at other policy areas such as work–life balance and the gender pay gap, what is apparent is a consistent professed aspiration for social change, but subject to the constraints imposed by a dominant commitment to the maintenance of neo-liberal economic policies.

8.5 Conclusion

In this chapter we have examined multidimensional approaches to equality from policy, practice and empirical, perspectives. In particular, we have examined, as an exemplar, the use of contract compliance to promote equal opportunities in employment. In considering the specific example of the WMCS, we have seen that the changing legislative context means that this single-dimension policy approach (with its focus on racial inequality) could certainly be adapted to a multidimensional one. More than this, the practical implementation of the WMCS, to a point, blurred distinctions between racial inequality and a more generic approach. However, despite the WMCS appearing to offer a promising model which other public-sector organisations could adopt, we have identified broader ambiguities surrounding the use of contract compliance. There is a particular tension between evidence demonstrating that contract compliance is an effective means of promoting equal opportunities in employment, and concern about potentially 'negative' impacts, with cost appearing to be the key issue. In making sense of this ambiguity, it is an overriding commitment to neo-liberal economic policy that appears to provide the answer. The promotion of equalities is seen as taking place within the framework of neo-liberal economic policy.

Under the Race Relations (Amendment) Act 2000, public authorities are required to undertake Race Equality Impact Assessments of both new and proposed policies: these being incorporated within Best Value Performance Indicators (evaluated by the Audit Commission Inspection regime). Parallel assessment procedures are likely to apply to all other equalities under the forthcoming Single Equality Act. As we have demonstrated, contract compliance would permit impact to be measured in a key area of social policy. However, as we have also seen, although the government supports the approach in theory, authorities are, in practice, being discouraged from adopting it.

Widespread discrimination in employment remains stubbornly common in the absence of strong political will from central government. There is no evidence from any major Western economy that merely encouraging employers not to discriminate has succeeded. As a consequence, discrimination remains the prime factor in explaining inequality in employment. Contract compliance offers a way forward by actually requiring (rather than simply encouraging) employers to incorporate equal opportunities as a core element of their human resource strategy. Whether a single- or multidimensional approach to equalities is taken, if the government maintains a profound reluctance to intervene in what are assumed to be the sovereign rights of private-sector employers, then only limited progress can be expected. This being the case, it has to be pressure from without, most notably from pressure groups, equalities professionals, politicians, academe and human rights lawyers acting both independently and collectively via the Equality and Human Rights Commission, that holds the key to any real change. The mechanisms are there; they simply need to be activated.

Notes

1 D Schiek (2005) 'Broadening the scope and the norms of EU gender equality law: Towards a multidimensional conception of equality law', *Maastricht Journal of European and Comparative Law*, 12: 427–66, at p 462.

2 There are also debates, however, about whether the generic approach might lead to a lack of focus on certain equality strands, for example, 'race' (see P Ratcliffe (2004) *'Race', Ethnicity and Difference: Imagining the Inclusive Society*, Maidenhead: Open University Press). In the UK, equality professionals working in this area have consistently warned that their concerns would be likely to 'slip down the

policy agenda'. More recently, in the run-up to the launch of the new Commission, parallel concerns were voiced by EOC policymakers (concerning the profile of gender issues).

3 Ratcliffe, ibid. It remains to be seen, of course, whether the Equality and Human Rights Commission will succeed in addressing such issues, especially in the context of a merging of three bodies with their own well-established organisational cultures. Footnote 2 above illustrates at least one source of tension.

4 HMSO (2007) *The Equalities Review, Fairness and Freedom: The Final Report of the Equalities Review*, London: Cabinet Office.

5 Commission for Racial Equality (2003) *Race Equality and Public Procurement: A Guide for Public Authorities and Contractors*, London: CRE.

6 For example see L Lustgarten (1989) 'Racial inequality and the limits of law', in R Jenkins and J Solomos (eds) *Racism and Equal Opportunities Policies in the 1980s*, 2nd edn, Cambridge: Cambridge University Press; J Wrench (2007) *Breakthroughs and Blind Spots: Trade Union Responses to Immigrants and Ethnic Minorities in Denmark and the UK*, Oslo: Fafo.

7 While the effects of discrimination are multifaceted, affecting issues ranging from health to housing, discrimination with regard to work is of particular significance. This is because 'Employment is perhaps the single most important measure of life-chances. It is at the centre of most discussions not just of racial equality but of social justice generally': T Modood, R Berthould, R Lakey, J Nazroo, P Smith, S Virdee and S Beishon (1997) *Ethnic Minorities in Britain: Diversity and Disadvantage*, London: Policy Studies Institute, p 5.

8 M Orton and P Ratcliffe (2003) *Working for an Inclusive Britain: an Evaluation of the West Midlands Pilot Project*, Sandwell: West Midlands Forum.

9 However, in examining the particular example of the 'West Midlands Common Standard' it emerges that in effect a (weak) form of multidimensional policy approach may already be in place.

10 We have discussed the general points in this introductory section in M Orton and P Ratcliffe (2004) 'Race, employment and contract compliance: A way forward for local authorities?', *Local Economy*, 19: 150–8; and M Orton and P Ratcliffe (2005) 'New labour ambiguity or neo-liberal consistency? Racial inequality in employment and the debate about contract compliance' *Journal of Social Policy*, 34: 255–77.

11 R Fee (2002) 'Contract compliance: Subnational and European influences in Northern Ireland', *Journal of European Social Policy*, 12: 107–21.

12 SL Wallace (1999) 'Minority procurement: Beyond affirmative action to economic empowerment', *The Review of Black Political Economy*, 27: 73–98.

13 See A Pinkney (1984) *The Myth of Black Progress*, Cambridge: Cambridge University Press; BR Taylor (1991) *Affirmative Action at Work: Law, Politics and Ethics*, Pittsburgh: University of Pittsburgh Press; C Herring and SM Collins (1995) 'Retreat from equal opportunity? The case of affirmative action', in MP Smith and JR Feagin (eds) *The Bubbling Cauldron: Race, Ethnicity and the Urban Crisis*, Minneapolis, MN: University of Minnesota Press; JJ Jackson (1995) 'Race-based affirmative action: Mend it or end it?', *The Black Scholar*, 25: 30–42; Ratcliffe (2004) *'Race', Ethnicity and Difference: Imagining the Inclusive Society*, Maidenhead: Open University Press

14 A Erridge and R Fee (1999) 'Contract compliance: National, regional and global regimes', *Policy and Politics*, 27: 199–216.

15 R Fee (2002) 'Contract compliance: Subnational and European influences in Northern Ireland', *Journal of European Social Policy*, 12: 107–21.

16 P Ratcliffe (2004) *'Race', Ethnicity and Difference: Imagining the Inclusive Society*, Maidenhead: Open University Press.

17 For example see R Fee (2002) 'Contract compliance: Subnational and European

influences in Northern Ireland', *Journal of European Social Policy*, 12: 107–21; A Erridge and J McIlroy (2002) 'Public procurement and supply management strategies', *Public Policy and Administration*, 17: 52–71; A Erridge and R Fee (1999) 'Contract compliance: National, regional and global regimes', *Policy and Politics*, 27: 199–216; R Fee, P Maxwell and A Erridge (1998) 'Contracting for services – A double jeopardy? An analysis of contract compliance in the context of European and UK social and public procurement policy', *Public Policy and Administration*, 13: 79–84; A Erridge and J Gordon Murray (1998) 'Lean supply: A strategy for best value in local government procurement?', *Public Policy and Administration*, 13: 70–85.

18 Fee *et al.*, ibid. EU regulations have been discussed in detail by J Cormack and J Niessen (2002) 'Public procurement and anti-discrimination legislation', in I Chopin and J Niessen (eds) *Combating Racial and Ethnic Discrimination: Taking the European Legislative Agenda Further*, Brussels: Migration Policy Group; Fee, ibid; S Martin, K Hartley and A Cox (1999) 'Public procurement directives in the European Union: A study of local authority purchasing', *Public Administration*, 77: 387–406.

19 Fee, ibid.

20 Department for Transport, Local Government and the Regions (2001) *Delivering Better Services for Citizens – A Review of Local Government Procurement in England*, London: DTLR.

21 P Ratcliffe (2004) '*Race', Ethnicity and Difference: Imagining the Inclusive Society*, Maidenhead: Open University Press.

22 An alternative approach is that based on 'managing diversity', though there are serious questions as to whether the desire to avoid ethnic essentialisms undermines attempts to monitor on the basis of ethnicity. See D Mason (2000) *Race and Ethnicity in Modern Britain*, Oxford: Oxford University Press; P Ratcliffe (2004) '*Race; Ethnicity and Difference: Imagining the Inclusive Society*, Maidenhead: Open University Press; Department for Communities and Local Government (2006) *Managing for Diversity: A Case Study of Four Local Authorities*, London: DCLG.

23 The contemporary system of local government consists of two tiers. In simple terms (and there are some exceptions) urban areas have a city or municipal borough council responsible for all local authority functions. In rural, or 'shire', areas responsibilities are divided between district (or non-metropolitan) councils and a county council. The terms 'council' and 'local authority' tend to be used interchangeably.

24 Department for Transport, Local Government and the Regions (2001) *Delivering Better Services for Citizens – A Review of Local Government Procurement in England*, London: DTLR.

25 Department for Transport, Local Government and the Regions (2001) *Local Authority Procurement. A Research Report*, London: DTLR.

26 Cabinet Office (2003) *Ethnic Minorities and the Labour Market: Final Report*, London: Cabinet Office.

27 There is one small, but nonetheless significant, caveat to this. In recent government guidance to local authorities the latter have been instructed that they may, if they so wish, go beyond the six questions to delve more deeply into the policies and practices of contractors. Crucially, however, they have not been informed as to how they might do this. It is therefore left to councils to decide how to proceed, and so many will be dissuaded from acting decisively in case they inadvertently transcend the bounds of what is permitted under their statutory duty.

28 See Cabinet Office (2002) *Ethnic Minorities and the Labour Market: Interim Analytical Report*, London: Cabinet Office; Cabinet Office (2003) *Ethnic Minorities and the Labour Market: Final Report*, London: Cabinet Office; B Twomey (2001)

'Labour market participation of ethnic groups', *National Statistics: Labour Market Trends*, 109: 29–42; R Berthoud (2002) 'Poverty and prosperity amongst Britain's ethnic minorities', *Benefits*, 10: 3–8; D Mason (2003) 'Changing patterns of ethnic disadvantage in employment', in D Mason (ed) *Explaining Ethnic Difference: Changing Patterns of Disadvantage in Britain*, Bristol: The Policy Press; P Ratcliffe (2004) *'Race', Ethnicity and Difference: Imagining the Inclusive Society*, Maidenhead: Open University Press; L Platt (2005) *Migration and Social Mobility: The Life Chances of Britain's Minority Ethnic Communities*, York: Joseph Rowntree Foundation.

29　For example see T Modood, R Berthould, R Lakey, J Nazroo, P Smith, S Virdee and S Beishon (1997) *Ethnic Minorities in Britain: Diversity and Disadvantage*, London: Policy Studies Institute.

30　D Mason (2003) 'Changing patterns of ethnic disadvantage in employment', in D Mason (ed) *Explaining Ethnic Difference: Changing Patterns of Disadvantage in Britain*, Bristol: The Policy Press

31　Department for Communities and Local Government (2007) *Improving Opportunity, Strengthening Society: Two Years On*, London: DCLG.

32　T Modood, R Berthould, R Lakey, J Nazroo, P Smith, S Virdee and S Beishon (1997) *Ethnic Minorities in Britain: Diversity and Disadvantage*, London: Policy Studies Institute; D Mason (2003) 'Changing patterns of ethnic disadvantage in employment', in D Mason (ed) *Explaining Ethnic Difference: Changing Patterns of Disadvantage in Britain*, Bristol: The Policy Press; Platt (2005) *Migration and Social Mobility* York: Rowntree Foundation.

33　Mason, ibid, p 80.

34　D Halpern (2005) *Social Capital*, Cambridge: Polity Press; Department for Communities and Local Government (2006) *Managing for Diversity: A Case Study of Four Local Authorities*, London: DCLG.

35　Commission on Integration and Cohesion (2007) *Our Shared Future*, London: DCLG.

36　M Orton and P Ratcliffe (2003) *Working for an Inclusive Britain: an Evaluation of the West Midlands Pilot Project*, Sandwell: West Midlands Forum; M Orton and P Ratcliffe (2004) 'Race, employment and contract compliance: A way forward for local authorities?', *Local Economy*, 19: 150–8; M Orton and P Ratcliffe (2005) 'New labour ambiguity or neo-liberal consistency? Racial inequality in employment and the debate about contract compliance' *Journal of Social Policy*, 34: 255–77

37　A Erridge and J McIlroy (2002) 'Public procurement and supply management strategies', *Public Policy and Administration*, 17: 52–71

38　Under the criterion of 'relevance to the contract'.

39　As the demands for a more generic approach to equalities grew through the 1990s, policy discourse tended to mirror these trends.

40　It should be stressed at this point, however, the use of the term 'EOP' does not imply that either policymakers or contractors necessarily interpreted this as going beyond the 'weak' sense, i.e. that they had a general commitment to the idea of equal opportunity. As far as individual companies are concerned this might not go much further than stating on job advertisements and publicity material that they are an 'equal opportunity employer'. This, of course, is precisely why both the initiative and the evaluation research reported in this chapter are so important.

41　For example see RD Osborne (2003) 'Progressing the equality agenda in Northern Ireland', *Journal of Social Policy*, 32: 339–60; L Harris (2000) 'Issues of fairness in recruitment processes: A case study of local government practice', *Local Government Studies*, 26: 31–46; A Phillips (1999) *Which Equalities Matter?*, Cambridge: Polity Press.

42 A Code recently strengthened. See 'Race' publications, available at www.equalityhumanrights.com/en/Pages/default.aspx (accessed 8 January 2008).

43 For a more detailed discussion of the evaluation and findings see M Orton and P Ratcliffe (2003) *Working for an Inclusive Britain: an Evaluation of the West Midlands Pilot Project*, Sandwell: West Midlands Forum; M Orton and P Ratcliffe (2004) 'Race, employment and contract compliance: A way forward for local authorities?', *Local Economy*, 19: 150–8

44 As noted earlier, affirmative action is not permitted under current UK law. Positive action, on the contrary, is: moreover, it is quite properly seen as an example of best practice. In the recruitment sphere, for example, a company might begin to advertise vacancies in the minority press, or on local minority-run radio stations.

45 M Orton and P Ratcliffe (2003) *Working for an Inclusive Britain: an Evaluation of the West Midlands Pilot Project*, Sandwell: West Midlands Forum; M Orton and P Ratcliffe (2004) 'Race, employment and contract compliance: A way forward for local authorities?', *Local Economy*, 19: 150–8

46 F Anthias and N Yuval-Davis (1992) *Racialized Boundaries – Race, Nation, Gender, Colour and Class and the Anti-Racist Struggle*, London: Routledge.

47 A Phillips (1999) *Which Equalities Matter?*, Cambridge: Polity Press

48 L Platt (2007) *Poverty and Ethnicity in the UK*, Bristol: The Policy Press; Department for Communities and Local Government (2007) *Improving Opportunity, Strengthening Society: Two Years On*, London: DCLG.

49 E Balibar (1991) 'Is there a neo-racism?', in E Balibar and I Wallerstein (eds) *Race, Nation, Class: Ambiguous Identities*, London: Verso.

50 Y Alibhai-Brown (2001) *Who Do We Think We Are? Imagining a New Britain*, Harmondsworth: Penguin.

51 A Phizacklea and C Wolkowitz (1995) *Homeworking Women*, London: Routledge.

52 A Dale, N Shaheen, E Fieldhouse and V Kalra (2002) 'Routes into education and employment for young Pakistani and Bangladeshi women in the UK', *Ethnic and Racial Studies*, 25: 942–68.

53 H Bradby (1999) 'Negotiating marriage: Young Punjabi women's assessment of their individual and family interests', in R Barot, H Bradley and S Fenton (eds) *Ethnicity, Gender and Social Change*, Basingstoke: Macmillan.

54 Even working with a single equalities issue, this raises highly complex and technical questions. It therefore featured prominently in training sessions for contractors run by the West Midlands Forum. The question is essentially: how does a contractor set fair targets for the numbers of employees from different ethnic groups? The obvious option would be local population census figures (better, numbers economically active) for different ethnic groups. An alternative would be to use 'travel-to-work area' data. The problem is that the distance people are willing to travel depends on the level of the post. Ultimately, heuristic solutions need to be sought. In a multi-way equalities scenario, target-setting is clearly even more challenging. (We also have to recognise that certain occupations have different levels of appeal to different communities – meaning that numerical imbalance may not necessarily imply policy failure.)

55 D Schiek (2005) 'Broadening the scope and the norms of EU gender equality law: Towards a multidimensional conception of equality law', *Maastricht Journal of European and Comparative Law*, 12: 427–66, p 464.

56 A word of caution should perhaps be sounded here, however. As with our earlier comments concerning (overly) bureaucratic, formalistic adherence to policy guidelines, in order to ensure that a contract compliance policy was truly effective we would need to interrogate the reality of decision-making processes 'on the ground' and at all levels of a company. In practice, this is simply not going to happen. But it should be recognised that any pragmatic solution inevitably involves compromise.

57 Office of the Deputy Prime Minister (2003) *Local Government Act 1999: Part 1 Best Value and Performance Improvement*, ODPM Circular 03/2003 (March), London: ODPM.

58 Ibid, p 44.

59 Ibid, p 45.

60 Ibid.

61 Certainly, in-house lawyers are likely to take a conservative line when asked their views as to the legality of such key policy decisions. Even more crucially in some ways, local authorities who are not firmly committed to the equalities agenda have a ready-made excuse for not giving proper consideration to the use of contract compliance. This tendency flies in the face of the existing equalities legislation (see 'Conclusion' below) and is likely to render future legislation equally impotent.

62 HMSO (2007) *The Equalities Review, Fairness and Freedom: The Final Report of the Equalities Review*, London: Cabinet Office.

63 A Erridge and R Fee (1999) 'Contract compliance: National, regional and global regimes', *Policy and Politics*, 27: 199–216

64 Cabinet Office (2003) *Ethnic Minorities and the Labour Market: Final Report*, London: Cabinet Office, p 137.

65 Department for Transport, Local Government and the Regions (2001) *Delivering Better Services for Citizens – A Review of Local Government Procurement in England*, London: DTLR p 35.

66 See also Commission for Racial Equality (2003) *Race Equality and Public Procurement: A guide for Public Authorities and Contractors*, London: CRE, pp 14–16.

67 For a more detailed discussion see M Orton and P Ratcliffe (2005) 'New labour ambiguity or neo-liberal consistency? Racial inequality in employment and the debate about contract compliance' *Journal of Social Policy*, 34: 255–77

68 R Fee (2002) 'Contract compliance: Subnational and European influences in Northern Ireland', *Journal of European Social Policy*, 12: 107–21, at p 111.

69 N Rao (2000) *Reviving Local Democracy*, Bristol: The Policy Press.

70 H Dean (2002) *Welfare Rights and Social Policy*, Harlow: Prentice Hall.

71 H Dean (2002) 'Business versus families: Whose side is New Labour on?', *Social Policy and Society*, 1: 3–10.

72 Ibid, p 9.

73 D Kingsmill (2001) *The Kingsmill Review of Women's Pay and Employment*, London: Cabinet Office, Department of Trade and Industry, and Department for Education and Skills; S Dench, J Aston, C Evans, N Meager, M Williams and R Willison (2002) *Key Indicators of Women's Position in Britain*, London: DTI; Equal Opportunities Commission (2003) *Facts About Men and Women in Great Britain 2003*, Manchester: EOC.

74 Equal Opportunities Commission, ibid.

Part III

Comparative approaches to multidimensional equality law in Europe

9 Utility-based equality and disparate diversities: from a Finnish perspective

Kevät Nousiainen

9.1 Gender equality as an issue of resource management

9.1.1 Finnish equality politics

National ethnic unity and social inclusiveness were essential features of Finnish political ideology until the 1990s. At the time when Finnish nation state building and citizenship of the nineteenth and early twentieth centuries in general were projected in terms of homogeneous ethnicity and a blurring of boundaries between the state and civil society,[1] the emancipation of women was encouraged as a part of the nation-building process.[2] A new ideology of socially grounded citizenship was typical of the Nordic welfare states, and became a mainstay of Finnish political ideology in the 1960s. A major reorientation of Finnish politics occurred then, while Finland was progressing from a traditional agrarian society with limited social welfare state institutions into a late-modern economy and welfare state. Social policy was intended to support economic growth.[3] A sense of community and social cohesion was seen as part of the ideology of the comprehensive type of welfare state as developed by Marshall. State action was to be aimed at removing class difference in a normative process that would promote a sense of community.[4]

The practical framework to carry out the societal programme needed in Finland was a political regime based on a so-called *incomes policy*, which became a feature of politics in most Organisation for Economic Co-operation and Development (OECD) countries at that time. In Finland, it became a part of economic planning in 1964; the aim was to achieve a centralized settlement under which wages would rise in line with growth of gross national income. This regime was institutionalised by establishing negotiation authorities and statistics production. The state became thus a key actor in the labour market, and so-called incomes policy agreements (*tulopoliittinen sopimus* or TUPO in Finnish) a core issue of national politics.[5] The Ministry of Finance, the Bank of Finland and the tripartite negotiators, all of whom were involved in the incomes policy agreements, became leading actors in politics.[6] Indexes, measurements and statistics became standard tools; politics became quantitative and couched in objective-sounding socio-economic aims. Politics was in a sense reduced to effective resource management. Finnish equality politics and anti-discrimination law still reflect this setting.

Second wave feminism appeared in Finland in the 1960s coincidental with the new orientation of social and economic politics; and the two agendas became intrinsically entwined. The Nordic concept of equality in the 1960s and 1970s was, in Raija Julkunen's words, a super-ideology, to which also women's issues were delegated. Until then, the 'position of women' had been discussed as 'emancipation', but now 'equality' became the conceptual framework. In contrast to the liberal individualist framework, equality was understood as a social concept connected to social justice. The reforms carried out were only partly due to the feminist movement(s); rather, several motivations coexisted. Social welfare and welfare services were extended. Statistics and research became involved in equality politics from the 1980s onwards.[7]

A good example of the intertwined agendas of social and gender equality is the committee set up by the government in 1966 to consider the position of women.[8] The committee's vision of society was gender neutral and gender equal. Women were needed in the labour market, and the obstacles to women's full participation were to be removed by making public day care for children available. In order to encourage dual-breadwinner families, a tax system based on individual instead of family income should be adopted. Whilst Finnish women's labour-market participation already exceeded the average of Western Europe, that fact was now approved and encouraged. One of the very rare references to discrimination in the committee's report is connected to the discussion of factors that are detrimental to women's professional status and refers to the UN Declaration on the Elimination of Discrimination against Women of 1967.[9] Women's labour-market participation and their ensuing economic independence were seen as the key to gender equality.[10]

The Council for Equality between Men and Women was established in 1972 as an advisory body for equality politics.[11] During the first years of its existence, it aimed at an integration of gender equality into all public-sector activities. Labour market participation, social welfare, care and education were the main focus of activities. Finnish gender equality politics in the 1980s and 1990s were proactive. The first Finnish government equality programme was adopted for the period 1980–5, and gender equality politics became integrated into government equality planning.[12] Many municipalities established equality boards in the 1980s. The Act on Equality between Women and Men of 1986 (1986/609) is strong in programmatic norms on equality planning. The most disputed and also most effective norm of the Act is the quota rule contained in s 4a, under which state and municipal committees and similar organs must have a minimum of 40 per cent of men and women respectively.[13] The arguments in favour of the quota stressed the utility to national resources if more women were drawn into decision-making processes.[14] Economic and social utility were thus offered as the main justification for proactive equality politics.

Gender mainstreaming was incorporated into the agendas of several ministries in the 1990s,[15] although the outcome of the various projects was not institutionalised. Nonetheless, these older practices could be turned into gender mainstreaming in the sense promoted by the UN Beijing conference. For example, in Finland's periodic country report for 1992–6 to the Convention on the Elimination of All Forms of Discrimination against Women (CEDAW) committee,[16] the Finnish government emphasised that 'mainstreaming a gender perspective in all policies and programmes' is vital for gender equality. According to a recent Finnish study, the use of different indicators in the EU and the UN has had an important impact on gender equality policies in Finland.[17] Finnish public agendas often claim a high level of sensitivity to equality, but explicit mainstreaming measures remain rare.[18] Mainstreaming 'from above' best describes the type of measures that have been undertaken.[19]

With short interruptions, a political regime based on coalition governments and incomes-policy agreements has continued in Finland up until the present, and gender equality has been an aspect of Finnish incomes policy agreements in various forms until recently. For example, in 2005, the government committed itself to pursue an Equal Pay Programme together with labour-market organisations, establishing a tripartite working group for that purpose. The resulting programme contains a wide set of measures for closing the pay gender gap.[20] The former Prime Minister and Speaker of Parliament Paavo Lipponen was appointed as chairman of the high-level monitoring group.

As a socio-economic agenda, Finnish gender equality policy has been a success. The Finnish labour force consists of roughly an even number of women and men, and the number of women in employment has long exceeded the EU's Lisbon Targets.[21] Women's strong presence in the labour market has entailed a relatively high level of female economic independence. In terms of non-discrimination, the outcome is less satisfactory. The pay gender gap has remained consistently at 20 per cent for more than two decades, and Finnish women report the highest bullying and harassment figures in the EU, to mention but a few persistent inequalities.[22]

9.1.2 Gender equality rather than non-discrimination

Through the tradition of tripartite gender equality policies, gender equality is firmly established as a labour market and social welfare issue, rather than as an inalienable right to non-discrimination. Within this tradition, it has been difficult to extend the scope of equality politics into the private area, to such issues as bodily integrity. At times, the tripartite agreements aimed at promoting equality have clearly conflicted with the principle of non-discrimination.[23] The motivation for anti-discrimination law in Finland has consequently come from 'outside', mainly from international human rights conventions and from the early 1990s onwards, from EC law.[24]

Whilst during the Cold War Finland remained outside the Council of

Europe, the Finnish state actively participated in UN human rights activities, also ratifying the International Convention on the Elimination of All Forms of Racial Discrimination (CERD)[25] in 1966. Explicit anti-discrimination law with regard to discrimination on grounds of race remained, however, modest. The first anti-discrimination provisions appear to have been introduced in the 1970s. Ratification of ILO Convention No 111 resulted in a prohibition on the discrimination of employees on various grounds, including sex, in the Finnish Employment Contracts Act of 1970 (Law 1970/320).[26] The prohibition had little effect.

The Act on Equality between Women and Men was drafted in the early 1980s mainly in order to permit Finland to ratify the CEDAW convention.[27] Labour market organisations, in particular the employers', were set against introducing an equality law.[28] These reservations are certainly one reason behind the relatively weak, mostly consultative competences of the bodies established to monitor the Act on Equality, the Equality Ombudsman and Equality Board. Anti-discrimination law was necessarily involved in and often in conflict with the incomes-policy mainstays, including collective agreements. According to the first Equality Ombudsman during the period prior to Finnish EU membership, Paavo Nikula, the issue of equal pay for work of equal value was controversial from the outset, as pay was considered a matter for regulation by collective agreement. For example, whilst differential retirement ages for men and women under some collective agreements were discussed, no litigation ensued. Gender-specific retirement ages for military personnel existed also under the State Employees' Pension Act (Law 1966/280), s 8, until the relevant provision was amended in 2004.[29]

Nor has the Supreme Court decided many gender discrimination cases, and, in any event, it has tended to interpret discrimination in a restrictive manner. For example, the Supreme Court held in 1992 that a dismissal on the grounds of pregnancy was a violation of the Employment Contracts Act, but not of the Act on Equality, because the dismissal did not take place directly on grounds of sex.[30] The decision was criticised heavily, and the government presented a bill to amend the Act on Equality. Legislative zeal was probably enhanced by the fact that the European Court of Justice (ECJ) had established discrimination on the basis of pregnancy as sex discrimination in *Dekker*;[31] Finland had signed the EEA Agreement in 1992, and the requirements of EC law were already well in sight.[32]

9.1.3 Gender equality in the economic agenda of the European Union

In some important respects, the EU's policies – described by its critics as neo-liberal – are similar to the Finnish policies implemented by welfare-state-oriented coalition governments. For both, the context of equality politics has been social policy, with an overall aim of economic growth. In the early days of Common Market, achieving equal pay was left to co-operation between the 'social partners' at a Community level. During the first decades of the

European Community, there was no anti-discrimination law or policy. Article 119 of the Treaty of Rome did not explicitly prohibit discrimination – rather, it was worded as a statement that equal pay was to be the norm for the Community. After a long period of national reporting, statistics and critique from the Commission, it became clear that Member States considered equal pay too expensive. In 1969, the European Commission's Directorate General responsible for equal pay[33] commissioned a sociological study on obstacles to women's work by the sociologist Evelyne Sullerot. Her report analysed the issue on the basis of various data sources.[34] When as a result of the economic stagnation following the oil price crisis of the 1970s a more active interest in EC level social policies was developed and the use of directives was widened into the field of social policy, the first directive adopted in this field was the Equal Pay Directive.[35]

EU decision-making in social policy matters often proceeds through the form of 'social dialogue', that is, negotiations and hearings held between the EU level 'social partners'. Social dialogue developed as part of the drive for more effective governance.[36] The dialogue can lead to agreements that are later adopted as directives, or to agreements of a rather obscure legal nature, which the social partners themselves have to implement. Until now, the legislative input of the social partners has often been in areas which are highly relevant for gender equality: parental leave, part-time work and fixed-term work.

Although gender mainstreaming was originally launched in the Platform for Action of the UN Beijing conference in 1995, it was also supported by many international and regional organisations, such as the World Bank, the International Labour Organization (ILO), the OECD, and the Nordic Council,[37] and was rapidly adopted by the European Commission's various Directorates General. In the late 1990s, the Commission established a multi-tiered network of centralised co-ordination of mainstreaming for the EU.[38] Some forms of gender mainstreaming are clearly related to evidence-based policies or 'indicator policies'. Judith Squires[39] claims that this is typical for the type of mainstreaming attempting to integrate gender into existing policies. Anna van der Vleuten and Mieke Verloo suggest a change has occurred from equality policies based on legal standards that are interpreted by courts, towards politics based on relative comparison and assessment of Member States.[40] This makes the choice of indicators politically highly relevant. Instead of fearing a shaming before the ECJ, Member States now try to select and fulfil equality indicators which enable them to retain their reputation as equality-conscious societies.

The Community framework strategy on gender equality for 2001–5 contained economic tools for promoting gender equality in the EU. 'Indicator policy' was high on the agenda. Statistics, studies, gender impact assessment, indicators and benchmarks were to become an important part of EU equality politics.[41] The Lisbon meeting of the European Council clearly presented gender equality or 'equal opportunities in employment policies' in terms of

quantitative objectives, such as increasing the number of women in employment from an average of 51 per cent in 2000 to 60 per cent in 2010. Gender
equality was seen as an issue highly relevant to the target of transforming
Europe into an economic superpower.

The proposal for the Community Programme for Employment and Social
Solidarity (PROGRESS) for the years 2007–13[42] tied issues of EU gender
equality and anti-discrimination policy to the aims established by the Lisbon
European Council 'to build a competitive and dynamic knowledge-based
economy capable of sustaining economic growth with more and better jobs
and greater social cohesion'. Non-discrimination, described as a fundamental
principle in the EU, is separated from the principle of equal treatment for
women and men, which is also described as a fundamental principle of EC
law in the programme as adopted.[43] Article 7 on anti-discrimination and
diversity and Art 8 on gender equality are formulated very similarly: in both
cases, the effective implementation of the EC law principles is to be supported
and mainstreamed in EU policies by 'indicator policies', implementation of
legislation, awareness-raising and 'developing the capacity of key EU net-
works to pursue EU policy goals'.

9.1.4   The role of anti-discrimination in equality politics: European and national

Since the 1990s, the focus of European gender equality politics has shifted to
gender mainstreaming. Feminist evaluations of equality politics often assume
an evolution from individualistic non-discrimination to positive action and
further to gender mainstreaming,[44] or 'from a narrow focus on equal treatment
in the workplace, to a gradual acceptance of specific, positive actions, and,
since 1996, an institutional commitment to mainstreaming gender across
the policy process'.[45] Whilst mainstreaming is criticised on various grounds,
many feminist scholars view it as a political strategy more comprehensive
than anti-discrimination policy.[46]

Although EC equality law has been largely motivated by market-related
considerations, the ECJ has recognised gender equality law as based on
human rights and European fundamental rights.[47] Anna van der Vleuten
claims that the EC has pursued relatively 'strong' equality politics entailing
costly consequences even against unwilling 'large' Member States. According
to her, Member States involved in the multi-legal governance process can be
caught between the 'pincers' consisting of Commission efforts and the ECJ
judgments on the one hand, and national democratic forces on the other.[48]

It seems, moreover, that the formula according to which equality politics
mutates from anti-discrimination to positive measures and further to gender
mainstreaming[49] is a simplification that does not describe EC equality politics
correctly. Proactive measures and methods typical for gender mainstreaming
were already in use in connection with social resource management when the
first provisions on discrimination were adopted as described above. As Mary

Daly points out, the evolution of gender equality policy in Europe involves ongoing significant changes not only in gender mainstreaming, but also regarding positive action and equal treatment; thus the three approaches are evolving simultaneously.[50] The initially limited concept of non-discrimination based on Art 119 of the EEC Treaty has expanded from 'something that looked like nothing' into a 'fundamental principle of constitutional aspirations', involving an important substantive development of the concepts of equality and non-discrimination, or a shift from a formal to a substantive understanding of equality. Sacha Prechal claims that the limited tools of EC law have achieved more than national and international human rights instruments.[51] Considering the Finnish experience, EC law can certainly be said to have motivated national anti-discrimination law.

Today's European perspective is complicated. There is a recognised need for more active immigration policies and, thus, a need to facilitate multicultural integration. There is more emphasis on the fundamental right to non-discrimination. Some features of so-called 'new governance' are anchored in the tradition of resource management, which is not very sensitive to a discourse of rights. Providing for equality and diversity, as well as combating discrimination, requires a mélange of political and legal strategies, and it is often difficult to see where politics ends and law begins. Political scientists and feminist lawyers have repeatedly pointed out that anti-discrimination law is not well suited to change structural social inequalities. From a legal perspective, however, reducing law to politics is not unproblematic. The role of anti-discrimination law needs to be considered carefully while, following a boost of interest for human and fundamental rights and a heightened interest in accommodating diversity, new grounds for prohibited discrimination have been introduced, and unification of anti-discrimination law is on the agenda in many countries, including Finland.[52]

9.2 Post-Cold War rise of rights discourse resulting in a disparity of gender and ethnic disadvantage?

9.2.1 Boost to rights in Europe and expansion of prohibited grounds of discrimination

The end of the Cold War boosted human and fundamental rights in Europe. Intense globalisation in the past decade has encouraged economic migration to and within Europe. European politics finds itself caught between the fear of unwanted illegal immigration and apprehension about the shortage of labour on the ageing continent. All these developments have an impact on anti-discrimination policy. The demand for political attention to be paid to various forms and grounds of disadvantage is concomitant with a weakening political ambition to provide universal welfare measures. During the 1990s, neither EC nor Finnish law provided rules against racial or ethnic discrimination. In the following analysis, only ethnic diversity and its relation to gender are discussed. Any other prohibited ground of discrimination in combination with gender would, however, merit a similar consideration.

At an EU level, when the Treaty of Amsterdam introduced a legal basis for combating a number of grounds of discrimination in the form of Art 13 EC the 'new' grounds of prohibited discrimination were incorporated in a political and legal setting that was more attuned to developing an EU citizen-ship vested with fundamental rights.[53] The Charter of Fundamental Rights, the Treaty of Amsterdam and the drafting of the Constitutional Treaty all imply an emphasis on individual rights not merely concomitant of the 'social' in the sense of effective resource management. Established EC equality law contains a wider spectrum of measures to be used against gender disadvan-tage than the rest of EC anti-discrimination law allows. While gender equality as an aim of the EU is to be mainstreamed into all EU policies (Arts 2 and 3 EC), the Union is committed only to combating discrimination on the other prohibited grounds under Art 13 EC – although there is nonetheless an inter-est in mainstreaming race equality.[54] Secondary legislation in the form of the Race Equality Directive[55] and the Framework Directive on Employment Equality[56] soon followed.

The motivations behind the new anti-discrimination law were mixed. As Evelyn Ellis points out, these comprise both social and economic concerns.[57] Recitals 2 and 3 of the Preamble to the Race Equality Directive refer to respect for human rights and fundamental freedoms, as well as equality before the law and protection against discrimination as universal rights. Recitals 8 and 9, on the other hand, stress that policies aimed at combating discrimination against ethnic minorities foster conditions for a socially inclu-sive labour market, and that racial or ethnic discrimination may undermine the attainment of a high level of employment and of social protection. Anti-discrimination is in this sense related to European-level economic and social resource management.[58] It is characteristic of European social policy that it is not formulated in the language of rights.[59] The 'new' grounds of discrimin-ation even under the post-Amsterdam sensitivity to non-discrimination as a fundamental right still show the tendency to consider equality as a strategy to achieve economic competitiveness.[60]

The Charter of Fundamental Rights was due to be given legal effect as a part of the Constitutional Treaty, following whose collapse the treaty reform process was completed by the Brussels European Council in June 2007 and the subsequent signature of the Treaty of Lisbon in December 2007. Once this Treaty enters into force, the EU will recognise the treaty value of the Charter (Art 6(1)), and shall also accede to the European Convention on Human Rights (Art 6(2)).[61]

9.2.2 Boost to rights in Finland

The boost to fundamental rights experienced in EC law had an even stronger counterpart in Finnish national law. Finland joined the Council of Europe and ratified the European Convention on Human Rights in 1990, and subsequently in 2005 it also ratified the protocol on discrimination adopted in 2000.[62] The Finnish Constitution of 1999 (Law 1999/731) is greatly influenced by an integration of human rights into the constitutional text. Community law, and especially its primacy over national law, effectively enhanced independence of Finnish courts. Section 106 of the new Constitution introduced judicial review of decisions by ordinary courts; and constitutional doctrine adopted essential elements from the German Constitutional Court's doctrine. This resulted in an enhanced constitutionalism and rights discourse.[63]

The principle of equality in the new Constitution (s 6) contains a prohibition on discrimination with an open-ended list of grounds (s 6(2)), and it also refers to the proactive promotion of gender equality (s 6(4)).[64] EU membership and the obligations arising earlier from the predecessor EEA agreement required Finland to amend the Act on Equality several times, for example, introducing an explicit definition of discrimination and widening the sanctions for prohibited discrimination. New provisions against discrimination were introduced into the Penal Code of Finland in 1995.[65]

More extensive anti-discrimination legislation was needed to implement the Race Equality Directive and Framework Directive on Employment Equality. Both Directives were implemented by a single piece of legislation, the Non-Discrimination Act (Law 21/2004). In this context, the tasks of the former Ombudsman for Foreigners (renamed Ombudsman for Minorities) were widened to include monitoring anti-discrimination policies with regard to ethnic origin, and a Discrimination Board was established. These authorities supervise the prohibition on discrimination based on ethnic origin in areas other than employment (Non-Discrimination Act, s 11). The Discrimination Board has the competence to prohibit the continuation or repetition of a discriminatory act, to conciliate and confirm a conciliation settlement between the parties and to give opinions in cases of ethnic discrimination where requested by other authorities and associations (Non-Discrimination Act, ss 13 and 14). The Ombudsman for Minorities and the Discrimination Board thus monitor only certain issues falling within the scope of the Race Equality Directive. Other forms of prohibited discrimination fall to be considered by the occupational safety and health authorities under the Act on Occupational Safety and Health Enforcement and Cooperation on Safety and Health at Workplaces (Law 44/2006). The safety and health authorities, unlike the anti-discrimination bodies, have a network of local officials, as well as the assistance of the workplace safety ombudsmen. In that sense, supervision by the occupational health authorities has the potential to be effective, but as the task of combating discrimination is not a part of the traditional activities of those authorities, it appears to remain subsidiary to other tasks.

9.2.3 *Disparities between gender equality and ethnic discrimination*

Since the adoption of the Non-Discrimination Act a widely shared popular and official tendency to make a distinction between gender equality and equality in terms of diversity as required by the Non-Discrimination Act has become apparent in Finland. The distinction is accentuated by the fact that gender equality today is usually referred to by the term '*tasa-arvo*', which is commonly used also of substantive social equality. The Non-Discrimination Act uses the Finnish term '*yhdenvertaisuus*', which has of old been used in the context of (formal) 'equality before the law'. Very often, the prohibition on discrimination is located at a complete distance from national discourses on gender equality.

The disparities in public opinion with regard to gender equality and non-discrimination on ethnic grounds are apparent in a recent Eurobarometer survey on discrimination in the EU,[66] both as regards the Europe of the 25 Member States, but especially with regard to Finland. The survey was motivated by the adoption of the Race Equality and Framework Directives addressing 'new' grounds of prohibited discrimination, and monitors public opinion in that regard. Unsurprisingly, the survey does not attempt to cover intersectional discrimination, as the Directives contain no provisions on such matters. On average, EU citizens were quite critical of the treatment experienced by 'vulnerable groups'. A broad majority believed that being disabled, belonging to the Roma community or an ethnic minority, being older or being homosexual tends to be a disadvantage in their country. Only one-third believed that being a woman is a disadvantage, although half of them saw being a man to be an advantage.[67] Two-thirds of the interviewees believed that discrimination on the basis of ethnic origin was widespread, but only a minority of 40 per cent believed that to be true of sex discrimination.

Of the Finnish interviewees, only 24 per cent considered sex discrimination to be widespread in Finland, while 70 per cent believed ethnic discrimination to be common. The survey also included a question on the position of the Roma ethnic minority, the largest ethnic minority in the enlarged EU. Eighty-five per cent of the Finnish interviewees thought that it was a disadvantage to belong to the Roma community. Finns were the most likely in Europe to answer in the affirmative when asked whether enough has been done to eradicate discrimination. Also, more than in any other Member State, interviewees in Finland believed they knew of their rights as a victim of harassment.

The majority belief that gender discrimination does not exist reflects the Finnish tradition of not considering gender equality in terms of discrimination. That the belief may be based on an unrealistic appreciation of the situation can be suspected from the fact that there was a considerable discrepancy between Finnish and Swedish views on the prevalence of gender discrimination: 50 per cent of Swedes (against 24 per cent of Finns) believed that sex discrimination was widespread in their country. Both Finland and

Sweden have prospered well in 'beauty contests' measuring, for example, women's level of education and participation in political and working life. There is little reason to assume a profound difference in the de facto prevalence of discrimination between these neighbouring countries, let alone that discrimination would be less common in Finland than in Sweden.

How does the unwillingness to consider gender disadvantage in terms of discrimination, a much stronger willingness to believe in hardship connected to minority ethnicity, and a tradition of equality politics connected to economic and social utility as features of a national tradition influence the recognition of intersectional discrimination? It seems obvious that in these circumstances discrimination of minority women is easily subsumed under ethnic discrimination. It can also be assumed that the economic context of gender equality can make it difficult for minority women to voice gender discrimination. Moreover, ethnic minorities amongst themselves are far from similar, and intersectional discrimination accordingly takes different forms. In the following section, Finnish ethnic minorities are considered from this point of view.

9.3 Diversities within diversity: diverse outcomes for intersectional discrimination

Intersectional discrimination was named as such by African American feminists, who pointed out that their experience did not correspond to that of white feminists, and does not simply consist of ethnic discrimination added to gender discrimination.[68] Other intersections, such as gender and class have since been considered.[69] Intersectional discrimination denotes discrimination where different grounds of prohibited discrimination coincide. The situation has been described also as multiple discrimination, gender-plus discrimination or cumulative discrimination, but intersectional discrimination should be reserved to denote situations where separate prohibitions on the 'old' grounds of discrimination do not cover the specific problems, vulnerability and marginalisation that arise in a situation where several types of discrimination are at work.[70] The situation differs from the one in which a person in the course of his/her life is met with discrimination on several grounds, for example, where a person is discriminated against as a gay person at one point in life and later as an elderly person seeking a job. Gender is, of course, very specific as a ground for discrimination in the sense that it is always potentially present in connection with any other discrimination ground (a disabled member of any religious community, an old person or a person of any sexual orientation are also defined through their sex), and it is very often a contributory ingredient in the gendered manner that discrimination takes in most, if not all, of its forms. Nor is it the case that able-bodied, heterosexual men belonging to the majority *ethnos* and a well-established religious community have to pay much attention to their ability, ethnicity, sexual orientation or religion as a potential basis for disadvantage.

The problems that arise when several grounds of discrimination can be applied to a situation and yet do not seem to cover the issue properly has been noted both in national and international law, and the term 'intersectional discrimination' has been widely adopted to denote many types of situations where this applies. In international human rights law[71] the Human Rights Committee in its General Comment No 28 on the International Covenant of Civil and Political Rights (ICCPR) observes that:

(d)iscrimination against women is often intertwined with discrimination on other grounds such as race, colour, language, religion, political or other opinion, national or social origin, property, birth or other status. States parties should address the ways in which any instances of discrimination on other grounds affect women in a particular way, and include information on the measures to counter these effects.[72]

The Committee on the Elimination of Racial Discrimination has also recognised the problem of racial discrimination coexisting with other types of discrimination.[73] The Committee on the Elimination of Discrimination against Women has in a general recommendation on health issues also taken up intersectional issues.[74] The general recommendation on disabled women[75] and the recommendations on violence against women[76] and on political and public life[77] also involve intersectionality. Immigrant, refugee and minority women have been singled out as vulnerable groups whose position ought to be improved.

European discrimination law until now has not addressed intersectional discrimination, nor does Finnish law contain any provisions on it. In each European state there are many ethnic minorities, and these differ from one another. Sandra Fredman[78] and Christopher McCrudden[79] have drawn attention to the inconsistent and hierarchical manner in which different inequalities are regulated at different levels in Europe. Yet policies such as the European Commission's 'Stop Discrimination' campaign are based on the questionable assumption that diverse inequalities are similar.[80] In contrast, the following analysis of the intersectional discrimination experienced by various groups of ethnic minority women in Finland takes as its starting point Mieke Verloo's claim that the mechanisms and processes constituting inequalities are not equivalent.[81] Immigration is often discussed as a relatively recent phenomenon, but groups of people have migrated within Europe and even globally during all known historical periods. However, on account of differences in their legal treatment, 'new' and 'old' minority groups are discussed here separately, and among the latter, indigenous people are given specific attention.

9.3.1 Immigrants or 'new' ethnic minorities in Finland

Traditionally, Finland is a land of emigration; the flow turned, however, in the 1980s. During the Cold War, Finnish immigration politics were restrictive. There was no shortage of labour, and accepting refugees and asylum seekers was complicated by the political problems connected with accepting Soviet citizens. Even today, Finland neither lies on the well-trodden path of refugees nor on the path of economic or environmental migrants. Nonetheless, Finland's foreign population has increased sixfold since 1980. Few immigrants come to Finland in order to work, and only very recently have immigrants been considered as an economic resource. The present government's programme promises to promote work-related immigration giving 'due regard to the demographic trends in Finland and Europe'.[82] Both in relative and in absolute terms, Finland remains the European country with the least foreigners, around 2 per cent of the population are foreign citizens, and around 3 per cent were born abroad. Many immigrants live in the Helsinki metropolitan area where foreigners account for over 5 per cent of the population.[83]

Immigrants in general have worse living conditions and higher unemployment figures than the rest of the population. Yet, there is often a hierarchy amongst the immigrant groups. For example, Finnish unemployment figures are at their highest for non-European immigrants. The Finnish media of today presents increasing immigration as a necessity, but also depicts immigrants as people who run a greater risk of discrimination and marginalisation than the majority. The labour market and the political system are not seen to be in need of change in order to accommodate multiculturalism.[84]

An element of immigration into Finland consists of people repatriated especially from Sweden and from Russia. The Nordic states have formed a common labour market since the 1950s which makes migration and repatriation easy. Immigration from Sweden has consisted of ethnic Finns who are culturally little different from the majority population. The same does not apply to the former Soviet Union citizens having Finnish nationality, who after the end of the Cold War were given the right to repatriation.[85] The peak of repatriation in the first half of the 1990s coincided with a deep economic recession, which made it difficult for the newcomers to find employment and hardened negative attitudes towards them. In principle, repatriation is based on an assumption of Finnish ethnicity. Repatriates from Russia and Estonia, in spite of their Finnish origins, often did not speak Finnish and differ also culturally from the majority population. With the arrival of these repatriates, therefore, Russian became the most common foreign language in the first decade of the twenty-first century (Finnish and Swedish are considered national languages).[86] In the immigration process, Finnish officials based their selection on an assumption of Finnish ethnicity, based on language (Finnish compared with Russian or Estonian), religion (Lutheran compared with Orthodox Christianity or secularism), and moral features such as honesty, diligence, cleanliness, order and sobriety. Not surprisingly, having regard to the difficulties that religious and ethnic communities faced during the Soviet era, not all repatriates were able to live up to such ethnic expectations.[87]

Russian-speaking repatriates in Finland feel that they have been negatively labelled in the same way as any Russians would be, and are associated with criminal behaviour. The Russian speakers consider that society discriminates against them and accuse the media of stereotyping. Repatriates with Finnish language skills, on the other hand, accuse Russian-speaking ones of being impostors who spoil the image of all repatriates from Russia. Estonian repatriates do not attribute their negative experiences to discrimination and racism as much as Russian speakers do.[88] According to a recent study, Finns are even more reluctant to have a Russian next-door neighbour than a neighbour of non-majority race.

Russian and to some extent Estonian women in Finland bear a stigma of prostitution, as sex work is referred to today: with the increase in foreign sex workers, public opinion turned against the phenomenon, and re-criminalisation followed in 2003 through the Act on Public Order.[89] A few years ago, it was estimated that 90 per cent of the sex workers in Finland were foreigners, mostly from Estonia and Russia. Some 2,000–3,000 professional sex workers living in each of those countries were estimated to work as prostitutes in Finland.[90] Another estimate suggests that of the approximately 8,000 sex workers currently working in Finland 50 per cent are Finns and foreigners respectively. Prostitution is functionally divided along ethnic lines: Finns offer services as call girls, Thais erotic massage, while Russians and Estonians visit Finland to offer traditional sex services. Even though crime, poverty, social marginalisation and drug abuse are not associated with all forms of prostitution, they are present in some parts of it, especially as regards illegal immigrants.[91] Some of the prostitution associated with crime may fall within the scope of trafficking in human beings.[92] The 2003 Act, sanctioning both offering sex for money and buying it 'in a public place', in practice targets 'other' sex workers, as Finnish sex workers rarely operate in a public place. In this context, gender and ethnicity combined result in severe discrimination against all Russian and Estonian speaking women and women from Thailand.

Since 1985, Finland has received refugees under the UN Third Country Refugee Resettlement programme. Finland has received small numbers of refugees from Vietnam, Iran, Iraq, Somalia, the Former Yugoslavia, Myanmar and Afghanistan; the number is restricted by a yearly quota. Immigration to Finland often takes place for family-related reasons. Immigrant women are vulnerable to violence from their (Finnish or immigrant) partners and husbands. Becoming a victim of violence seems to follow specific ethnic patterns. Somali women, for example, appear often to fall victim to battery, but not sexual violence, whereas Russian and Estonian women are more often victims of sexual violence.[93] The number of immigrant women in Finnish asylums for battered women is high, especially in the larger cities.[94] Immigrant women do not have a safety net of relatives and friends, which partly explains their over-representation. Immigrant girls may seek asylum on being prevented from participating in education or having a job.[95]

The country reports of the Finnish government to the CEDAW committee give an indication of the manner in which the issue is considered at a national level. In the periodic country report for 1992–6[96] to the CEDAW, and in the session itself,[97] the Finnish government emphasised that 'mainstreaming a gender perspective in all policies and programmes' was now considered vital for gender equality. Comparative statistics, indicators and benchmarking were held to be critical in selecting the right policy and commitments.[98] Some pages of the country report referred to 'minority groups', including both the indigenous group Sámi, the Roma, immigrants and some other disadvantaged groups. The Committee urged the Finnish government to increase its international co-operation with regard to trafficking, and expressed concern at the continuing discrimination against immigrant and minority women, particularly Roma and Sámi women, who 'suffer from double discrimination, based on both their sex and ethnic background'. The Committee also urged the government to undertake studies on the participation of minority women and take effective measures to eliminate discrimination against them and strengthen efforts to combat racism and xenophobia in Finland.[99]

In the next periodic country report submitted in 2003 the Finnish government paid more attention to minority groups. The government referred now to its Action Plan against Racism and Discrimination, which resembled the Community Action Programme of the European Commission. The government was also able to refer to new legislation, the anti-discrimination measures largely based on the need to implement the Race Equality and Framework Directives. The government emphasised that identification of multiple discrimination was a priority. Non-discrimination projects had trained contact persons, tested procedures and networked, published booklets and used the media. Those projects had been implemented in co-operation with several Ministries, organisations and equality bodies.

Unfortunately, the Non-Discrimination Act that the government referred to contains no provision on intersectional discrimination. Neither the Ombudsman for Minorities, nor the Discrimination Board has taken specific action in cases involving both gender and ethnic discrimination. Rather, the burden of dealing with discrimination against immigrant women has been shouldered by non-governmental organisations, with some organisational and/or economic help from the government. An Advisory Board for Ethnic Relations (ETNO) was set up by the government in 2001, and the Board set up a division for women's issues and families. The Ministry of Health and Social Welfare established a project for the prevention of violence against immigrant women for 1998–2002,[100] but subsequently the task of providing assistance has fallen on non-governmental organisations. An association for immigrant women (*Monika-Naiset-Liitto ry*) has set up a centre for women who have experienced violence.

9.3.2   Minorities in the setting of multiculturalism

Nations and ethnic minorities have been created by the same historical process: national borders exclude aliens, and some residents within the borders are excluded from rights based on citizenship. National minorities are an old, yet continuously potent cause of international disagreements, and therefore their position is often addressed in instruments of international law and national constitutions. There has been an extensive discussion on the legitimacy of claims by national minorities against nation states, and between nation states themselves among philosophers, historians and political scientists. International law gives indigenous groups a position which differs from that enjoyed by other minority groups.[101] Because Europe was the originator and hub of colonialism, merely the margins of the continent are *loci* of contested indigenous rights. Although the number of ethnic minority groups and minority languages recognised within the EU is high, the only indigenous minority is the Sámi population in the Nordic states.

Will Kymlicka, who favours the proposition that indigenous groups differ from immigrants, considers that immigrants are entitled to respect on the basis of liberal principles, but that indigenous groups have a legitimate claim to self-determination. According to this reasoning, anti-discrimination law is an adequate legal measure to regulate relations between majority and minority citizenry within a nation state. Indigenous minorities need to be accommodated to a greater degree than ethnic immigrants who have willingly migrated to a pre-existing state.[102] Recognition of a diversity of cultural identities within a state may require a redistribution of decision-making competences, rights, duties and burdens. In strong versions of multiculturalism, identity groups are to be granted extensive self-government in a society, and state sovereignty has to accommodate such an arrangement. In weak versions of multiculturalism, identity groups have different sets of minority rights limited by universal, individual rights. Conflicts within the identity group and internal power hierarchies are not addressed. Many affiliations create group members' identities, and some members belong to subordinated categories in their culture. No multicultural solution can escape the condition of the modern state and its intervention which shapes groups and their cultures. Accordingly, should the state interfere on behalf of a vulnerable individual in a minority group, even at the cost of alienating her from her group?[103] Strong multicultural requirements go against what Seyla Benhabib[104] calls the 'politics of recognition', which would make room for dialogue, change and exchange between groups, and foster 'identity politics' based on a conservative collective identity construction and separatism. All international instruments on minority rights define minorities as having a genuine culture and language to protect. In fact most minorities are neither monolingual nor mono-cultural, but in order to establish itself in accordance with the requirements of international and EU minority protection, the minority in question has to adapt to a 'dress code' for minorities.[105]

The instruments that protect indigenous people are very clear on this point.[106]

The requirement of establishing a monolithic collective identity is less pronounced in international law on other minorities than indigenous people. The Council of Europe's European Charter for Regional or Minority Languages of 1992 and the Framework Convention for the Protection of National Minorities of 1995 both stress cultural diversity within national sovereignty and the protection against assimilation. Persons belonging to national minorities are to be permitted to preserve 'the essential elements of their identity, namely their religion, language, traditions and cultural heritage' (Framework Convention, Art 5(1)), whilst at the same time they are guaranteed the right of equality before the law free from discrimination (Art 4(1)). Proactive measures are not considered discrimination (Art 4(3)). Legal treatment of established regional or national minority languages and protection of national minorities combines a measure of cultural and social self-determination with anti-discrimination provisions.

9.3.3 The Sámi and the Roma: 'old' minority groups in Finland

The Sámi population altogether numbers in excess of 50,000 people, and is settled in the northernmost parts of Norway, Sweden, Finland, and the Kola peninsula of Russia. Between 5,000 and 7,000 of them are Finnish citizens.[107] Indigenous people have a historical relationship to the region they live in, and certainly the Sámi have lived in the Arctic area since time immemorial, at least since the last ice age. Baltic Finns also lived in the northern area, but the latter group adopted agriculture, and from the Middle Ages onwards, the Sámi were gradually pushed northwards and developed a way of life organised around reindeer herding. Sámi customary law and land use became contested issues within the nation state framework. The rise of the welfare state as such did not improve the economic and social position of the Sámi due to their specific living conditions.[108] Assimilation policies through governance and education practically eradicated the Sámi dialects. Since the 1980s, the school system has allowed more choice and municipal decision-making. The northernmost municipalities were then in a position to introduce teaching in the Sámi dialects (three Sámi dialects are spoken in Finland), and the status of the Sámi language also benefited from Finnish accession to the EC and the Finnish constitutional reform.[109]

The human-rights-oriented Finnish Constitution of 1999 pays attention to old minorities. Section 17(4) names the Sámi as an indigenous people and as a group with the right to 'maintain and develop their own language and culture'. Provisions on the right to use the Sámi language before authorities are to be specified in legislation.[110] Section 121 of the Constitution concerns municipal and other regional self-government with s 121(5) establishing that the Sámi 'have linguistic and cultural self-government, as provided by an Act', in their 'native region'. In practice, self-government is limited to a consultative representative organ, elected by the Sámi population (*Sámediggi*, or *saamelaiskäräjät* in Finnish).[111] The *Sámediggi* stated in 2006, that the Sámi are treated as a regional linguistic minority without any real autonomy. As an indigenous people who have a historical relationship to the land and natural resources of the region, the Sámi consider that they should also have land ownership rights on the basis of which their traditional livelihoods are practised.[112] In addition, there are political aspirations to more extensive Sámi nation-building in a supra-state context.[113]

Politics that serve the minority interest of gaining greater authority over their affairs sets specific demands on Sámi women. Identity groups that maintain a normative culture, or *nomos*, often celebrate women's responsibilities as the bearers of legitimate children and as primary socialisers of the young. The task of transmitting collective identity in the reproduction of future members of the collective is allocated to women, and their function as 'cultural conduits of the group's unique history and identity' often makes them a target of monitoring by the group.[114] The Sámi women are also seen as wardens of the cultural identity of the minority, and declarations that 'Sámi women are bearers of fundamental values and know-how that must be specially emphasised', and have 'equal opportunities to participate in all areas of Sámi society' are motivated by this factor.[115] The children and the young must learn Sámi languages and culture, and the burden of education falls mainly on women. The Nordic Sámi gender-equality prize in 2007 was given to Risten Rauna Mugga for her exemplary contribution in promoting health and other services in Sámi. According to the Finnish *Sámediggi*, if day care is not available, a Sámi woman may have no other choice than to care for children herself. Gender-related grievances that are publicly voiced deal with matters that are in the interest of the group as a whole. Whatever the nature of gender discrimination which appears within the Sámi group, it is not likely to emerge within the Finnish institutions.

Another 'old' minority in Finland are the Roma people. Groups of Roma arrived in Finland from the sixteenth century onwards. Despite an official policy of prohibition, the Roma made a living through barter and diverse petty activities. Their assimilation through education became an official goal following Finnish independence. In the 1920s and 1930s, the Finnish Roma were not targeted by racial theories as they were in many European countries,[116] and under the post-war welfare regime positive measures concerning economic and educational matters increased. Special housing legislation was enacted in order to settle the Roma in decent housing conditions.[117] According to Camilla Nordberg, the emphasis until the 1990s was on the social rather than cultural dimension of citizenship, and with very little Romani agency.[118]

The right to maintain and promote the Romani language and culture is also mentioned under s 17(4) of the Finnish Constitution of 1999, but the right is couched to an even lesser extent in legal terms than that of the Sámi. The Advisory Board on Romani Affairs is an old organ of cooperation between the government and the Roma.[119] The Roma themselves claim that they are part of the Finnish nation and set themselves apart from the 'new' immigrant minority groups. Unlike the Sámi, the Finnish Roma distance themselves from the European-level attempts to promote a transnational identity or 'nation'. Rather, the Finnish Romani activists justify their position as part of the Finnish identity. In the 1990s, activists emphasised the promotion of Romani culture and language instead of social welfare, but equality in housing, work and education were stressed as facilitating Romani contributions to the nation building. Equality and non-discrimination were voiced as concerns more often, but everyday life was seen as the source of discrimination, whereas the state was considered a benevolent presence.[120] For the Roma, as well as for some other 'old minorities', the shibboleth of belonging to the nation even today is that the male members of the group fought in the Finnish army in the Second World War (paradoxically for groups such as Jews and Roma, since Finland was allied to Nazi Germany's operation Barbarossa).[121] For example, Finnish Romani activists justify their position as part of the Finnish identity by referring to Finnish Romani men as 'fighting like any other Finn' during the war, or doing military service, working and paying taxes. Military service is a significant factor in the construction of Finnish masculinity, and an explanation offered for the high level of male violence in the Finnish society.[122] In contrast to many other European states involved in the Second World War, the Finnish war experience was 'old-fashioned'. War took place at the frontier, and civilian casualties remained relatively few. Consequently, the war was a highly gendered experience. Finnish military defence still relies on a conscription army, and the obligatory male military service has remained popular.

In any case, the 'old' Finnish minorities, save the Sámi, stress their position as part of the nation, and in doing so distinguish themselves from the newcomers. In the case of the Roma, the welfare state type of equality politics have brought some improvements in housing and other circumstances which are subject to 'indicator politics'. However, bringing up gender controversies within the group is difficult. First, the Finnish gender equality tradition downplays such controversies, and inclusion within the Finnish nation involves assimilation in terms of considering gender relations in terms of economic utility. Second, an emphasis on cultural identity – which has become stronger with the boost accorded to minority rights – also makes it difficult to voice controversy and diversity within the minority group. Gendered patterns within the groups are thus seldom discussed in terms of discrimination.

It is perhaps symptomatic that the gendered problems voiced by both Sámi and the Roma women are those easily accommodated within the dual constraints of Finnish equality politics and the demands of minority identity. A perfect example of a 'suitable' problem is the lack of day care for children. Both Sámi and Roma have made demands for specific day care, imbedded in their minority language and culture. Such day care would help children to maintain their cultural identity, while allowing women to opt for working life – a most suitable claim in the Finnish context.

9.4 Conclusion

Plans to unify equality and anti-discrimination laws and institutions are underway in Finland, as in many other EU Member States. When the Racial Equality Directive and the Framework Directive on Employment Equality were implemented in Finland by Non-Discrimination Act, the Parliament required the government to amend equality law. Equality law was to be based on the Finnish Constitution and its system of fundamental rights. The Parliament requested that equal treatment of and similar remedies and sanctions for all prohibited grounds of discrimination be taken as the basis of amended anti-discrimination law. A committee was set up to do preparatory work for equality law in January 2007, and is expected to present guidelines for amendment in January 2008. Gender equality institutions have expressed a fear that legal unification could lead to a loss of resources for gender equality. Because of the failure of the Finnish society to recognise various forms of harm and disadvantage caused to women as discrimination, such fear may be well-founded.

Gender equality has been mainstreamed into hard-core national and EC politics since the 1970s, because of the economic importance of drawing women into the labour force. Paying attention to outcomes through indicators has been helpful for attaining some socio-economic goals. Currently, labour-related immigration is of great interest in decision-making circles, and interest in mainstreaming equality on ethnic and racial grounds is also increasing. The corporatist machinery, which has a long history of involvement in matters related to gender equality, is today deeply involved with diversity in the labour market. In Finland, gender relations were never really considered in terms of discrimination, whereas ethnic discrimination has recently received some attention. Unification of equality law and machinery could in principle help recognition of intersectional discrimination. On the other hand, unification could also further diminish sensitivity to gender-based discrimination, also in its capacity as an ingredient of intersectional discrimination.

Ethnic minorities differ from each other even in Finland, which is arguably the least multicultural of all European states. Different legal provisions are applied to 'old' and 'new' minorities. Disadvantages suffered by women belonging to various ethnic minorities are often different both from those experienced by majority women, and also different from one group to another. Therefore, equality law and policies should address harm and systemic disadvantage in a manner that is sensitive to these differences. Standard measures used for promoting gender equality in Finland are geared to labour market considerations. Such measures can be useful for minority women, who wish to gain more economic independence and an easier integration into the Finnish society. It is crucial, however, that the amended legislation pays attention to discrimination against women in general, and the various discriminatory practices, attitudes and expectations that minority women face both within the minority and elsewhere in society.

Diverse grounds of discrimination are not born equal; human beings are. Women in diverse ethnic groups suffer from different types of discrimination, which require differentiated measures rather than equal treatment in the sense of similar measures for all.

Notes

1 H Stenius (2003) 'Kansalainen', in M Hyvärinen, J Kurunmäki, K Palonen, T Pulkkinen and H Stenius (eds) *Käsitteet liikkeessä. Suomen poliittisten käsitteiden historia*, Tampere: Vastapaino, pp 309–62, and A Anttonen (1998) 'Vocabularies of citizenship and gender: Finland', *Critical Social Policy*, 18: 355–73.

2 A Pylkkänen (2001) 'The responsible self: Relational gender construction in the history of Finnish law', in K Nousiainen, Å Gunnarsson, K Lundström and J Niemi-Kiesiläinen (eds) *Responsible Selves: Women in the Nordic legal culture*, Aldershot: Ashgate, pp 105–28.

3 Pekka Kuusi's book on a social policy for the 1960s, published in 1961, is considered both presaging and a token of the Finnish economic and social reorientation from a traditional agrarian society and a state with very limited social welfare institutions into a modern economy and welfare state, P Kuusi (1961) *60-luvun sosiaalipolitikka*, Porvoo: WSOY. Kuusi's book presented a political programme which was widely approved and influential, R Julkunen (1979) *Sosiaalipoliittinen uudistustoiminta 1960-luvulla Suomessa*, Jyväskylä: Jyväskylän yliopiston yhteiskuntapolitiikan laitos, pp 10–11. Kuusi argued for a social policy that would support economic growth, demanding that consumers, entrepreneurs and the state must co-operate in order to achieve economic growth in the common interest: Kuusi, ibid, p 101.

4 G Brochmann and A Hagelund (2005) *Innvandringens velferdspolitiske konsekvenser: nordisk kunnskapsstatus*, Oslo: Nordisk ministerråd (Nordic Council of Ministers).

5 The first Finnish national incomes-policy agreement was made in 1968. The collective agreement between the main national-level labour market organisations was linked to promises by the government to maintain stability in price developments and taxation and to improve employment and social policy.

6 J Gronow, P Klemola and J Partanen (1977) *Demokratian rajat ja rakenteet. Tutkimus suomalaisesta hallitsemistavasta ja sen taloudellisesta perustasta*, Porvoo: WSOY, pp 419–44.

7 R Julkunen (2007) 'Tasa-arvolaki kaksikymmentä vuotta', *Tasa-arvolaki 20 vuotta*, 1: 85–107.

8 The Committee published its report in 1970, Komiteanmietintö (1970) A 8 *Naisten asemaa tutkivan komitean mietintö*, Helsinki.

9 Ibid, pp 65–70.

10 Of its total of 144 pages, the committee discusses women in working life on 59 pages, education and teaching on 21 and family politics on 40 pages. Of these, four pages each are used for reform of marriage law and the position of single parenting, and six for birth control, three of which are dedicated to abortion. Day care of children is discussed on 13 pages, division of family costs in society, division of labour in families and family taxation on five pages each, and participation of women in society on seven pages. Personal integrity of women is hardly mentioned – even the discussion of abortion argues for a more equal access to birth control and for de facto access to abortion.

11 The Council for Equality (TANE) is an advisory body nominated by political parties and appointed by the government.

12 AM Holli (1992) *Miehisestä tasa-arvosta kohti naisten käsitteellistä tilaa: Tasa-arvoasiain neuvottelukunnan tasa-arvopoliittinen diskurssi*, Helsinki: Helsingin yliopisto, pp 59–62.

13 In its original form, the norm did not set a numeric quota. Because authorities often took the formulation to mean that only one woman was enough, the formulation was amended in 1995, following combined lobbying of women in Parliament.

14 E Raevaara (2005) *Tasa-arvo ja muutoksen rajat. Sukupuolten tasa-arvo poliittisena ongelmana Ranskan paritè- ja Suomen kiintiökeskusteluissa*, Helsinki: TANE Publications, Ministry for Social Affairs and Health, Council for Gender Equality.

15 L Horelli and M Saari (2002) *Tasa-arvoa valtavirtaan: Tasa-arvon valtavirtaistamisen menetelmiä ja käytäntöjä*, Helsinki: Ministry of Social Affairs and Health.

16 Finland's third periodic report to the Committee on the Elimination of Discrimination against Women. See the Report of the Committee on the Elimination of Discrimination against Women, 24th and 25th sessions, 2001, para 288.

17 AM Holli and J Kantola (2007) 'State feminism Finnish style: Strong policies clash with implementation problems', in J Outshoorn and J Kantola (eds) *Changing State Feminism*, Chippenham: Palgrave Macmillan, pp 62–81.

18 An evaluation of government so-called policy programmes in 2004 showed that gender equality was seldom explicitly mentioned. When asked, the persons involved in the programmes often claimed that gender equality was somehow 'naturally' implicitly included 'at the back of one's head', K Nousiainen *et al.* (2004) *Kansalaisvaikuttamisen politiikkaohjelman sukupuolinäkökulman valtavirtaistamisselvitys*, Ministry of Justice, available at www.om.fi/uploads/9aad82q10c.pdf (accessed 11 December 2007).

19 Whilst states have introduced many different models of mainstreaming, they can generally be divided into a 'participative-democratic' model which engages the agency of the groups whose interests are at stake, and an 'expert-bureaucratic' one, where mainstreaming is undertaken by a small group of specialists, F Beveridge, S Nott and K Stephen (eds) (2000) *Making Women Count: Integrating Gender into Law and Policy-Making*, Aldershot: Ashgate. The Finnish understanding is of the latter type, although the explicit exercises of mainstreaming so far are mainly limited to the ones undertaken by the Ministry of Health and Social Affairs, which is the ministry responsible for gender equality issues. The explicit exercises include, for example, gender mainstreaming of the government bills on pensions legislation and gender budgeting.

20 Measures include dismantling gender segregation, introducing career planning for women, decreasing the use of fixed-term work, introducing better means for combining work and family, monitoring pay systems, increasing the use of statistics and increasing corporate social responsibility in general.

21 The Lisbon European Council of 2000 subscribed to the goal of raising the average European employment rate of women from 54 to 60 per cent by 2010. In 2005, Finland was among the eight Member States where female employment rates exceeded 60 per cent (A Parent-Thirion, E Fernández Macías and G Vermeylen (2007) *Fourth European Working Conditions Survey*, Dublin: European Foundation for the Improvement of Living and Working Conditions, p 4). In October 2007, the male and female employment rates in Finland had further risen to 70.7 and 68.8 per cent respectively (Statistics Finland, available at www.stat.fi/ajk/tiedotteet/v2007/tiedote_026_11_20en.html (accessed 11 December 2007)).

22 More than 20 per cent of Finnish women reported having been subjected to bullying and harassment in the workplace in 2005, when the EU average was 6 per cent. The figures for Finnish men were also high, A Parent-Thirion,

E Fernández Macías and G Vermeylen (2007) *Fourth European Working Conditions Survey*, Dublin: European Foundation for the Improvement of Living and Working Conditions, p 37.

23 One example is a 2006 Government proposal of higher parental leave benefits for fathers than mothers. The parental leave system, as originally introduced through tripartite agreement, made leave fully transferable. Thus, it was predominantly used by mothers. As a consequence of profound labour market segregation, employers in sectors mainly employing women bear a disproportionate burden of leaves. The motive of the proposal, developed in tripartite negotiations, was to encourage fathers to take leave more often by higher benefits, which should ultimately promote gender equality. The Parliament's Constitutional Committee considered the Bill unconstitutional.

24 K Nousiainen (2005) 'Tasa-arvon monet kasvot: kansainvälisistä vaikutuksista Suomen tasa-arvo-oikeudessa', *Lakimies*, 7–8: 1188–209.

25 International Convention on the Elimination of All Forms of Racial Discrimination of 26 December 1965.

26 Section 17(3) of the Act provided, 'The employer must treat employees equally, so that no one is without due cause put in a different position from others on the grounds of birth, religion, sex, age, political and labour union activity or any other comparable ground'. 'Birth' in the legislative text referred to race, colour, ethnicity and social origin, T Kahri and J Vihma (1971) *Vuoden 1970 työsopimuslaki*, Helsinki: Weilin & Göös, pp 89–92.

27 The Act was drafted by the Consumer Ombudsman Gerhard af Schultén and administrative lawyer Ulla Lång from the Ministry of Education. The preparatory work was done in co-operation with the administrative Equality Unit which already existed in the Prime Minister's Office. The draft was overseen by a group of bureaucrats, a Bill presented to Parliament in 1985 and the Act entered into force in 1987.

28 P Nikula 'Samapalkkaperiaate vaikea pala alusta saakka', *Tasa-arvolaki 20 vuotta*, 1: 15–24.

29 The provision was considered discriminatory by the ECJ on a preliminary reference in Case C-351/00 *Niemi* [2002] ECR I-7007, and subsequently held to be discriminatory and therefore void by the Finnish Insurance Court, Insurance Court decision 2003/2276:96.

30 Supreme Court decision KKO: 1 992:7. The word 'directly' in the decision was '*välittömästi*' in Finnish. The court did not discuss the difference between direct and indirect discrimination, however.

31 Case C-177/88 *Elisabeth Johanna Pacifica Dekker v Stichting Vormingscentrum voor Jong Volwassenen (VJV-Centrum) Plus* [1990] ECR I-3941.

32 The Agreement creating the European Economic Area between the EFTA member states and EC was signed in May 1992. The Agreement required the Member States to accept the Community *acquis* in the field of the four freedoms. The Agreement entered into force in 1994, and Finland became an EC Member State in 1995.

33 DG V, today's Directorate General for Employment, Social Affairs and Equal Opportunities was responsible for equal pay in the EC.

34 Here, strikingly similar to the Finnish committee report on the position on women of 1970, the emphasis was on facts rather than norms. Only 16 pages of Sullerot's report of 200 pages discussed legal obstacles.

35 Council Directive 75/117/EEC on the approximation of the laws of the Member States relating to the application of the principle of equal pay for men and women [1975] OJ L45/19. See A van der Vleuten (2007) *The Price of Gender Equality: Member States and Governance in the European Union*, Aldershot, Burlington, VT: Ashgate.

36 The Single European Act created an institutional basis for the social partners inserting Art 118b of the EEC Treaty (now, after amendment, Art 139 EC). The Treaty of Amsterdam gave an even stronger position to the EU-level social partners. Under Art 138(1) EC the Commission's task is to facilitate 'social dialogue'. Under Art 138(2) and (3) EC it has to consult the social partners on any proposals on social policy. Under Art 138(4) EC, the social partners may inform the Commission that they wish to negotiate on the issue at hand, following which the Commission must postpone its proposals and wait for the outcome of the social dialogue.

37 S Razavi and C Miller (1994) 'Gender mainstreaming: A study of efforts by the UNDP, the World Bank and the ILO to institutionalize gender issues', Occasional Paper No 4, UN Fourth World Conference on Women, Geneva.

38 MA Pollack and E Hafner-Burton (2000) 'Mainstreaming gender in the European Union', *Journal of European Public Policy*, 7: 432–56.

39 J Squires (2005) 'Is mainstreaming transformative? Theorizing mainstreaming in the context of diversity and deliberation', *Social Politics: International Studies in Gender, State and Society*, 12: 366–88.

40 A van der Vleuten and M Verloo (2006) 'Disappointing pioneers and surprising laggards: Understanding disparities between reputation and performance', paper presented at the Third Pan-European Conference of the European Consortium for Political Research Standing Group on the European Union, Istanbul.

41 Council Decision No 2001/51/EC establishing a Programme relating to the Community framework strategy on gender equality (2001–2005) [2001] OJ L17/22.

42 Proposal for a Decision of the European Parliament and of the Council establishing a Community Programme for Employment and Social Solidarity, COM(2004) 488 final.

43 Council Decision No 1672/2006/EC establishing a Community Programme for Employment and Social Solidarity – PROGRESS [2006] OJ L315/1.

44 T Rees (1998) *Mainstreaming Equality in the European Union: Education, Training and Labour Market Policies*, London: Routledge.

45 MA Pollack and E Hafner-Burton (2000) 'Mainstreaming gender in the European Union', *Journal of European Public Policy*, 7: 432–56, at p 450.

46 F Beveridge and S Nott (2002) 'Mainstreaming: A case for optimism and cynicism', *Feminist Legal Studies*, 10: 299–311.

47 S Fredman (2001) *Discrimination and Human Rights. Essays in European Law*, Oxford: Oxford University Press.

48 A van der Vleuten (2007) *The Price of Gender Equality: Member States and Governance in the European Union*, Aldershot, Burlington, VT: Ashgate, pp 1–29.

49 The formula first appeared in the influential article of MA Pollack and E Hafner-Burton (2000) 'Mainstreaming gender in the European Union', *Journal of European Public Policy*, 7: 432–56

50 M Daly (2005) 'Gender mainstreaming in theory and practice', *Social Politics: International Studies in Gender, State and Society*, 12: 433–50.

51 S Prechal (2004) 'Equality of treatment, non-discrimination and social policy: Achievements in three themes', *Common Market Law Review*, 41: 533–51.

52 In Finland, a committee was set to consider the need to unify anti-discrimination law in 2007, and it is expected to outline its proposals by January 2008.

53 G More (1999) 'The principle of equal treatment: From market unifier to fundamental rights?' in P Craig and G de Búrca (eds) *The Evolution of EU Law*, Oxford: Oxford University Press.

54 J Shaw (2004) *Mainstreaming Equality in European Union Law and Policymaking*, Düsseldorf: ENAR, pp 22–3.

55 Council Directive 2000/43/EC implementing the principle of equal treatment between persons irrespective of racial or ethnic origin [2000] OJ L180/22.

56 Council Directive 2000/78/EC establishing a general framework for equal treatment in employment and occupation [2000] OJ L303/16.

57 E Ellis (2005) *EU Anti-Discrimination Law*, Oxford: Oxford University Press, p 29.

58 The relevant decisions were made at Tampere during the Finnish presidency of the European Council in 1999. The Preamble also refers to the Employment Guidelines 2000, agreed by the European Council in Helsinki in 1999. The legal instruments resonate very much with the Nordic tradition of considering equality from a point of view of social and economic utility.

59 G de Búrca and B de Witte (eds) (2005) *Social Rights in Europe*, Oxford: Oxford University Press.

60 S Fredman (2001) *Discrimination and Human Rights. Essays in European Law*, Oxford: Oxford University Press, pp 24–6.

61 A Protocol on the application of the Charter of Fundamental Rights of the EU to Poland and to the UK provides that the Charter does not extend the ability of the ECJ or a Polish or UK court to find that the national law of Poland or UK is inconsistent with the rights under the Charter, Art 1 of the Protocol. The protocol somewhat constrains the effect of the Charter in EU law.

62 Many EU Member States have not yet ratified Protocol No 12 to the Convention for the Protection of Human Rights and Fundamental Freedoms of 2000.

63 Kaarlo Tuori has shown the influence of the German doctrinal ideology of '*Verfassungsgerichtlicher Jurisdiktionsstaat*' (a state based on constitutional decisionism) upon Finnish law (K Tuori (2007) *Oikeuden ratio ja voluntas*, Helsinki: WSOY, pp 256–65.)

64 Constitution (Law 731/1999). Chapter 2 of the Constitution on basic rights and liberties was amended in 1995, but comprehensive reform of the constitution was not undertaken until 1999.

65 Discrimination in public and private services was prohibited under Chapter 11, s 9, and ethnic agitation under Chapter 11, s 8 of the Code. Employment discrimination was made punishable under Chapter 47, s 3 of the Penal Code of Finland (as amended by Law 578/1995).

66 European Commission (2007) *Special Eurobarometer 263: Discrimination in the European Union*, Brussels: European Commission. The fieldwork for the survey was conducted in summer 2006, and the survey was published in January 2007.

67 Ibid, pp 13–14.

68 K Crenshaw (1991a) 'Mapping the margins: Intersectionality, identity politics, and violence against women of color', *Stanford Law Review*, 43: 1241–99 (reprinted in MA Fineman and R Mykitiuk (eds) (1992) *The Public Nature of Private Violence*, New York: Routledge).

69 M Verloo (2006) 'Multiple inequalities, intersectionality and the European Union', *European Journal of Women's Studies*, 13: 211–28.

70 T Makkonen, (2002) *Multiple, Compound and Intersectional Discrimination: Bringing the Experience of the Most Marginalized to the Fore*, Institute For Human Rights Åbo Akademi University, available at http://web.abo.fi/instut/imr/norfa/timo.pdf (accessed 4 January 2008), p 11.

71 For an overview of international law provisions and politics on intersectional discrimination, see Makkonen, ibid.

72 Human Rights Committee, General Comment No 28 on equality of rights between men and women of 29 March 2000, para 30.

73 Committee on the Elimination of Racial Discrimination (ICERD), General Recommendation 19 on racial segregation and apartheid of 18 August 1995, General Recommendation 25 on gender related dimensions of racial discrimination of 20 March 2000 and General Recommendation 27 on discrimination against Roma of 16 August 2000.

74 Committee on the Elimination of Discrimination against Women (CEDAW), General Recommendation on women and health of 2 February 1999. Also General Recommendation 14 on the issue of female circumcision of 2 February 1990 can be considered to take a position on intersectional discrimination.

75 CEDAW General Recommendation 18 on disabled women of 4 January 1991.

76 CEDAW, General Recommendation 19 on violence against women of 29 January 1992.

77 CEDAW, General Recommendation 23 on political and public life of 13 January 1997.

78 S Fredman (2005b) 'Double trouble: Multiple discrimination and EU law', *European Anti-Discrimination Law Review*, 2: 13–21, available at http://ec. europa.eu/employment_social/fundamental_rights/pdf/legnet/05lawrev2_en.pdf (accessed 13 September 2007).

79 C McCrudden (2005) 'Thinking about the discrimination directives', *European Anti-Discrimination Law Review*, 1: 17–23.

80 M Verloo (2006) 'Multiple inequalities, intersectionality and the European Union', *European Journal of Women's Studies*, 13: 211–28.

81 Ibid, pp 222–4.

82 Government statement to Parliament on the programme of Prime Minister Matti Vanhanens' second cabinet appointed on 19 April 2007, p 22.

83 M Jaakkola (2005) *Suomalaisten suhtautuminen maahanmuuttajiin vuosina 1987–2003*, Työvoimapoliittinen tutkimus, Työministeriö, pp 5–6.

84 H Blomberg-Kroll (2004) 'Integration through work in a multicultural society? A study on elite groups debate on immigrants and the labour market in two Nordic welfare states', in V Puuronen, A Häkkinen, A Pylkkänen, T Sandlund and R Toivanen (eds) *New Challenges for the Welfare Society*, Joensuu: Yliopistopaino, pp 237–56.

85 In 1990, the president of Finland declared that citizens of the USSR who have Finnish origin or 'nationality' in Soviet terms were to be considered repatriates.

86 O Davydova and K Heikkinen (2004) 'Produced Finnishness in the context of remigration', in V Puuronen, A Häkkinen, A Pylkkänen, T Sandlund and R Toivanen (eds) *New Challenges for the Welfare Society*, Joensuu: Yliopistopaino, pp 176–92. In the 1990s, some 25,000 repatriates with their family members were received from Russia, while theoretically some 100,000 would have qualified. In the Soviet Union, Finns as well as other nationalities were subjected to assimilation, rendering it difficult to preserve Finnish traditions. Preserving religious and linguistic traditions does not as such necessarily correlate with ethnic consciousness: see Davydova and Heikkinen, ibid, pp 177–9.

87 The handbook *Inkerinsuomalaiset* (Ingrian Finns), written by two Finns of Ingrian origin, published by the Ministry of Social Affairs and Health in 1995 to be used as a source of information for officials, media and public.

88 E Kyntäjä (2004) 'The meaning of stigma for self-identication and psychological well-being amongst Estonian- and Russian-speaking immmigrants in Finland: A qualitative interview study', in V Puuronen, A Häkkinen, A Pylkkänen, T Sandlund and R Toivanen (eds) *New Challenges for the Welfare Society*, Joensuu: Yliopistopaino, pp 193–207.

89 Act on Public Order (Law 612/2003). Finnish Penal Code (Law 37/1889) sanctions pandering, ss 20:9 and 20:9a, buying sexual services from a young person (i.e. a person under 18), s 20:8, and abuse of a person who is a victim of trafficking, s 20:8a.

90 M Lehti and K Aromaa (2002) *Trafficking in Human Beings and Illegal Immigration in Finland*, Helsinki: HEUNI Report Series No 38.

91 A Kontula (2005) *Prostituutio Suomessa*, Tampere: SEXPO Säätiö.

92 Trafficking was criminalised in Finnish law in 2004, but as yet only one conviction

for trafficking has been handed down by the Helsinki Appellate Court, Helsingin HO R 06/2317.

93 K Pohjanpää, S Paananen and M Nieminen (2003) 'Maahanmuuttajien elinolot. Venäläisten, virolaisten, somalialaisten ja vietnamilaisten elämää Suomessa vuonna 2002 Elinolot 2003:1', *Tilastokeskus* (Statistics Finland).

94 T Haarakangas, N Ollus and S Toikka (2000) *Väkivaltaa kokeneet maahanmuuttajanaiset – haaste turvakotipalveluille Suomessa*, Ministry of Social Affairs and Health, Publications on Equality 3, and N Ollus and T Haarakangas (2002) 'Väkivaltaa kokeneiden maahanmuuttajanaisten auttaminen – turvakotien kokemuksista palvelujen kehittämiseen', in R Nurmi and R Helander (eds) *Väkivalta ei tunne kulttuurisia rajoja. Maahanmuuttajanaisiin kohdistuva väkivalta Suomessa*. Naisiin kohdistuvan väkivallan ja prostituution ehkäisyhanke (1998–2002), Helsinki: Yliopistopaino, pp 55–69.

95 S Aaltio (2002) 'Maahanmuuttajanaiset turvakotien asiakkaina', in Nurmi, R and Helander, R (eds) *Väkivalta ei tunne kulttuurisia rajoja. Maahanmuuttajanaisiin kohdistuva väkivalta Suomessa*, Naisiin kohdistuvan väkivallan ja prostituution ehkäisyhanke (1998–2002), Helsinki: Yliopistopaino, pp 49–54.

96 Third periodic report to the Committee on the Elimination of Discrimination against Women.

97 Report of the Committee on the Elimination of Discrimination against Women, 24th and 25th sessions, 2001.

98 Ibid, para 288.

99 Ibid, paras 304–6.

100 Nurmi and Helander (eds) (2002) *Väkivalta ei tunne kulttuurisia rajoja. Maahanmuuttajanaisiin kohdistuva väkivalta Suomessa*, Naisiin kohdistuvan väkivallan ja prostituution ehkäisyhanke (1998–2002), Helsinki: Yliopistopaino.

101 ILO Convention (No 169) concerning Indigenous and Tribal Peoples in Independent Countries of 27 June 1989. Finland has not ratified the Convention, mainly due to problems connected with contested rights to land ownership.

102 W Kymlicka (1995) *Multicultural Citizenship: A Liberal Theory of Minority Rights*, Oxford: Oxford University Press, pp 20 and 63.

103 A Shachar (2001) *Multicultural Jurisdictions: Cultural Differences and Women's Rights*, Cambridge: Cambridge University Press, pp 28–32 and 64.

104 S Benhabib (2002) *The Claims of Culture: Equality and Diversity in the Global Era*, Princeton, NJ: Princeton University Press.

105 R Toivanen (2004) 'Anthropology and the paradox of rights in a multicultural context', in V Puuronen, A Häkkinen, A Pylkkänen, T Sandlund and R Toivanen (eds) *New Challenges for the Welfare Society*, Joensuu: Yliopistopaino, pp 107–23.

106 Article 1(2) of ILO Convention 169 on indigenous peoples imposes self-identification as indigenous or tribal as the fundamental criterion for determining the groups to which the provisions of the Convention apply.

107 R Toivanen (2001) 'Saami in the European Union', in A Foellesdal (ed) Special Issue on Sámi Rights in Finland, Norway, Russia and Sweden, *International Journal on Minority and Group Rights*, 8: 303–23.

108 A Häkkinen and M Tervonen (2004) 'Ethnicity, marginalization and poverty in the 20th century Finland', in V Puuronen, A Häkkinen, A Pylkkänen, T Sandlund and R Toivanen (eds) *New Challenges for the Welfare Society*, Joensuu: Yliopistopaino, pp 22–39.

109 U Aikio-Puoskari and M Pentikäinen (2001) *The Language Rights of the Indigenous Saami in Finland – under Domestic and International Law*, Juridica lapponica 26, Rovaniemi: University of Lapland/Northern Institute for Environmental and Minority Law.

110 The law in question (Law 1086/2003) specifies the right to use the Sámi language

when dealing with the authorities. In the northernmost municipalities of Finland, which is defined as the Sámi native region, the authorities have to be able to serve clients in the Sámi language.

111 *Sámediggi* translates as Sámi Parliament, an expression which gives an exaggerated view of the competences bestowed on the organ; see the Act on the Sámi Parliament (Law 974/1995).

112 Sámi Parliament, Memorandum of 15 December 2006.

113 All Nordic Sámi parliaments and representatives of Russian Sámi held a conference in Jokkmokk in 2005 and joined in a declaration which demanded that Finland, Norway, Russia and Sweden recognise Sámi indigenous rights to land and natural resources on which the traditional Sámi industries depend. The Sámi are described as 'one people who have the right to develop their society . . . and their culture across and without regard to national borders, and the national states are therefore requested to fully coordinate the . . . conditions for the Sámi in the various countries', Jokkmokk Declaration. The Sámi have a flag and a national day to celebrate the co-operation between the Nordic Sámi that traces back to a meeting held in 1917.

114 A Shachar (2001) *Multicultural Jurisdictions: Cultural Differences and Women's Rights*, Cambridge: Cambridge University Press, pp 56–7.

115 Jokkmokk Declaration, p 8.

116 P Pulma (2006) *Suljetut ovet: Pohjoismaiden romanipolitiikka 1500-luvulta EU-aikaan*, Helsinki: Suomalaisen kirjallisuuden seura.

117 K Suonoja and V Lindberg (2000) *Strategies of the Policy on Roma*, Helsinki: Ministry of Social Affairs and Health.

118 C Nordberg (2007) *Boundaries of Citizenship: The Case of the Roma and the Finnish Nation-State*, Helsinki: University Press.

119 General information on the board can be found on the website of the Ministry of Social Affairs and Health, available at www.stm.fi/Resource.phx/publishing/documents/1183/index.htx (accessed 11 December 2007).

120 C Nordberg (2007) *Boundaries of Citizenship: The Case of the Roma and the Finnish Nation-State*, Helsinki: University Press, p 96.

121 Mainly the Sámi and the Roma are discussed here as 'old' minorities, the Sámi as an indigenous group and the Roma because recognised as 'old' minority in many EU Member States. The Tatars are a small minority group with an actively used Turkish-related language and Islamic religion that arrived in Finland in the nineteenth century. In 1900, all 'old' ethnic minorities in Finland taken together constituted less than 2 per cent of the total population, see A Häkkinen and M Tervonen (2004) 'Ethnicity, marginalization and poverty in the 20th century Finland', in V Puuronen, A Häkkinen, A Pylkkänen, T Sandlund and R Toivanen (eds), *New Challenges for the Welfare Society*, Joensuu: Yliopistopaino, p 31. The Swedish-speaking minority may also be considered as an 'old' minority, but due to its strong social, economic, cultural and legal position, it is not discussed here.

122 A Jokinen (2000) *Panssaroitu maskuliinisuus. Mies, väkivalta ja kulttuuri*. Tampere: Tampere University Press.

10 Comparative approaches to gender equality and non-discrimination within Europe

Susanne Burri and Sacha Prechal[*]

10.1 Introduction

The focus of the present chapter is the conceptualisation of gender equality and non-discrimination in EU law.[1] The central subject is how this 'European conceptualisation' influences the law of some of the Member States. The choice of the countries deliberately deviates from mainstream Anglo-American research. We concentrate on the Netherlands, France and the Czech Republic. This choice can, in part, be explained by the language knowledge of the authors. In addition, it arises as a matter of curiosity, since France and the Czech Republic are not well known for a strong stance or firm tradition in combating gender discrimination. Finally, the Netherlands can be situated somewhere between the rather developed non-discrimination discourse and practice of the UK/US tradition and the countries which are only just starting out.

Our starting point and approach is above all a practical one and builds upon well-known notions of equality and non-discrimination law. Since equality and non-discrimination play an important role in EU law,[2] the question as to their meaning and scope is vital.[3] First, in our view, one of the prime rationales of equality and non-discrimination law is to improve the lot of a disadvantaged group of individuals, both in actual and structural terms, the latter requiring a change of the dominant standards. Like non-discrimination, the principle of equality is an instrument that should enable individuals to develop their personality, talents, abilities, etc. Both notions belong to one's fundamental feelings of 'justice'.

Second, although not universally accepted, there is a broad agreement that the standard definition of the principle of equality, that is, that like cases should be treated alike, is the absolute minimum.[4] This concept of 'formal' equality is a rather thin notion, referring above all to consistency in treatment. It is based on the idea that people should be treated according to their own merit and characteristics. Its apparent neutrality is deceptive in that it operates on the basis of assumptions about the 'alikeness' of individuals while not taking into account the social, economic, cultural contexts in which many of these persons find themselves. Similarly, this 'thin notion' says, as such, nothing about outcomes, as under this definition of equality, treatment which is equally as poor, is also acceptable. The same is to a certain extent true for discrimination. Non-discrimination provisions can be considered a step forward compared to the above definition of equality since they make explicit the grounds (characteristics) which may in principle not be used to justify different – less favourable – treatment. However, even a prohibition of discrimination remains often a blunt tool for the promotion of equality, unless it is stretched beyond a formal reading.

The proponents of a much richer understanding of equality that should help the disadvantaged groups to improve their position, have convincingly argued that social, cultural, economic or other de facto realities must be taken into account when giving substance to equality.[5] According to some, instead of turning a blind eye to differences, one should focus on them, especially on those which cause the disadvantages a group is experiencing. In terms of the Aristotelian definition of equality (like cases should be treated alike and different cases should be treated differently, in proportion to their unlikeness) this means that both strands of the postulate are included.[6] The notions which go hand in glove with this richer understanding of equality are substantive equality, equality of results or equality of opportunity, with the latter often situated somewhere on the scale between the formal and the more substantive understanding of equality.

Central to our chapter is a 'double layered' question: first, whether EU gender discrimination law is evolving towards such a richer understanding of equality and, second, whether, under the influence of EU law, the more substantive notion of equality has penetrated the discrimination law of three EU Member States. The rich or, what we like to call 'thick' concept of equality, is characterised by various features which are more or less clearly present in any particular legal system and which may be translated into a number of parameters. For the purposes of our exploration we limit ourselves to the identification of three parameters.

The first parameter is the use of the notion of substantive equality, alongside the notion of formal equality. The former notion is broader as it does not relate only to similar situations being treated differently, but also covers instances where different situations are treated the same. At least one caveat should be made here: in judicial rhetoric courts (and *mutatis mutandis* legislators) may easily endorse the claim of equality in substance, without, however, giving effect to that concept.

The second parameter is the familiarity with the concept of indirect discrimination. Under commonly accepted definitions direct discrimination occurs where a difference in treatment can be explained by the implicit or explicit use of a forbidden criterion, such as nationality or sex. Indirect discrimination occurs where the effects of certain requirements or practices, which do not themselves apply a forbidden criterion, are discriminatory. A measure may apply a neutral criterion (that is, one that is not prohibited) or neutral conditions or requirements, which nonetheless have the same effect as if a forbidden criterion had been applied. As indirect discrimination focuses on the effects of the rules applied or the effect of a certain behaviour, it takes into account socio-economic or other realities and includes the fact that people are often differently situated due to individual and societal differences. For that reason indirect discrimination is linked to a substantive understanding of equality and is one of the pointers that the particular legal system accepts a certain degree of 'thick' equality. Another important parameter is the existence and use of preferential treatment. However, in order to keep the present contribution within reasonable proportions we are not exploring this aspect.

Third, since equality and non-discrimination law is about improving the position of a disadvantaged group of human beings and where necessary requiring a change of the dominant standards, we also pay attention to gender stereotypes and their often implicit presence in legal constructions and/or in case law, in particular in relation to parenthood. Such may be observed in the application of the 'comparability test', that is to say, in determining whether two situations are comparable and which differences are relevant in a particular case, and which are not. This is a notoriously difficult matter with a considerable risk that subjective factors slip into the test.

10.2 European Union gender equality law

10.2.1 EC Treaty and secondary legislation

In the EC Treaty and in Community secondary legislation there are some indications as to a richer understanding of equality. Arts 2 and 3(2) of the EC Treaty, following the additions inserted by the Treaty of Amsterdam, impose the objective of promoting equality between men and women in the Community and as such they reflect to a certain degree the adoption of a proactive approach.

Whilst Art 13 EC refers to measures 'to combat discrimination', it does not make clear what concept of equality underlies that legislative competence. Does it simply concern the fight against discrimination or does it seek also to enhance equality? Since the Directives based on this Article all contain a provision on positive action,[7] its scope is seemingly not limited to an austere prohibition on discrimination but also includes certain aspects of achieving equality in practice.

The definitions of indirect discrimination in the Sex Equality Directives 2002/73/EC,[8] 2004/113/EC[9] and 2006/54/EC[10] correspond with the definition of indirect discrimination on grounds of nationality and those laid down in Council Directives 2000/43/EC (Race Directive)[11] and 2000/78/EC (Framework Directive).[12] Unlike their predecessor in Council Directive 97/80/EC (Burden of Proof),[13] they reflect better the definition of indirect discrimination developed by the European Court of Justice (ECJ). Accordingly, indirect discrimination is said to occur 'where an apparently neutral provision, criterion or practice would put persons of one sex at a particular disadvantage compared with persons of the other sex, unless that provision, criterion or practice is objectively justified by a legitimate aim, and the means of achieving that aim are appropriate and necessary'.

Protection of women, 'particularly as regards pregnancy and maternity'[14] is still framed as an exception to the main rule, that is, the principle of equality. On the one hand, this type of protection may be understood as an expression of an equality principle that takes into account the differences between men and women and that accommodates the specific needs of the latter. Such a reading is confirmed by guarantees for women when they return from maternity leave.[15] On the other hand, it is well known that protective and in particular overprotective provisions of this type entail a risk of perpetuating, legitimising and even reinforcing discrimination rather than helping to achieve equality. Much depends on the fleshing out of these well-meant yet Janus-faced provisions and on their interpretation by the courts. In this respect, even more doubtful are existing provisions allowing for differences in retirement age[16] or which exclude from the application of the principle of equal treatment 'advantages in respect of old-age pension schemes granted to persons who have brought up children' and 'the acquisition of benefit entitlements following periods of interruption of employment due to the bringing up of children'.[17] Whilst probably inspired by the wish to take into account the different position of men and women with respect to the combination of professional work and family responsibilities, these provisions relate to the ability to be a parent, which women and men possess equally, and in respect of which they should be treated equally in order to remove stereotypes.

Finally, there is the 'trap of comparability'. The legislator has, on the one hand, acted rather successfully to avoid one paradigmatic comparability problem by making clear that less-favourable treatment of a woman on grounds related to pregnancy or maternity leave is included within the prohibition on discrimination.[18] On the other hand, there is a certain immanent danger present in the definition of direct discrimination, namely that 'one person is treated less favourably on grounds of sex than another is, has been or would be treated in a *comparable situation*'.[19] The reference to 'a comparable situation' may open the door to various escape routes.[20]

10.2.2 *The case law of the European Court of Justice*

In the case law of the European Court of Justice (ECJ) in the field of gender equality there are some instances of a clear recognition of substantive equality. In *Thibault*,[21] for instance, the ECJ observed that the aim pursued by Council Directive 76/207/EEC[22] was substantive and not formal equality. Other cases also bear witness to a substantive approach. In *Sass* the ECJ held that the exercise of rights granted to a woman on account of pregnancy and maternity may not permit unfavourable treatment in terms of promotion and the attendant higher rates of pay.[23]

Another major achievement of the ECJ jurisprudence is its recognition of grounds which are inextricably linked with sex, such as pregnancy, as constituting direct discrimination.[24] A good example of a more substantive approach to equality can also be seen in *Meyers*, concerning the right to deduct child-care costs from a person's – in this case a single parent's – gross income in order to obtain family credit.[25]

A crucial achievement was the introduction into gender equality law of the notion of indirect discrimination, introduced for the first time in the not entirely satisfactorily decided *Jenkins* case.[26] The basic test was firmly laid down some years later in *Bilka*[27] and was subsequently elaborated in a whole string of cases,[28] causing every now and again some confusion. This was, in particular, the case in *Schnorbus*[29] where the criterion of having fulfilled military service was treated as a matter of indirect discrimination despite the fact that only men could qualify as having fulfilled this service.[30]

Yet, not all the case law points in the direction of substantive equality. In *Cadman*,[31] for example, the ECJ accepted that an employer does not have to provide special justification for recourse to the criterion of length of service for pay purposes. In the view of the ECJ, rewarding acquired experience, which enables the worker to perform his/her duties better, constitutes a legitimate objective of pay policy. However, the ECJ did recognise that there may be situations in which recourse to the criterion of length of service must be justified by the employer in detail, in particular where there are serious doubts about the criterion of length of service as an appropriate means to reward experience. In other words, the ECJ left the door ajar for challenges to the length-of-service criteria, which are widely used and operate to the detriment of women.

In *Grau-Hupka* the ECJ considered it not incompatible with the principle of equal pay that receipt of a retirement pension be assimilated to the pursuit of a main occupation affording social security, even where that pension had been reduced by loss of earnings as a result of bringing up children.[32]

In some cases the ECJ may also engage in wrong comparisons which, moreover, seem to foster the traditional public-private divide, subordinating the latter to the former. The most well-known example of this is *Helmig*, a case concerning alleged indirect discrimination of female employees.[33] The problem was that part-time employees (with a weekly contractual working time of 18 hours) did not receive a supplement for overtime (the nineteenth and subsequent hours). According to the ECJ no problem arose, since the worker received the same overall pay as a full-time employee for the same number of hours. Consequently, it held that there was no difference in treatment and, therefore, correspondingly, no indirect discrimination of female workers. However, the nineteenth hour worked is not the same for a part-time employee whose contractual hours are only 18 and for a full-time employee.

The nineteenth hour of a part-timer should be compared with the first over-time hour of a full-timer. Adoption of that comparison would demonstrate that there was equal treatment of unequal situations.[34] Another example of an unfortunate comparison which blurred a situation of indirect discrimination may be seen in *Österreichischer Gewerkschaftsbund* where the court refused to treat periods spent in military service and periods of parental leave as comparable for the purposes of calculation of a termination payment.[35] Parental leave was said to be taken voluntarily and in the individual interest of the worker, whereas military service was considered a civic obligation imposed in the public interest.

Another area in which the case law is somewhat ambiguous concerns preferential treatment. The ECJ began by treating Art 2(4) of Council Directive 76/207/EEC as constituting an exception to the prohibition on discrimination rather than as a justified form of differentiated treatment, as a means to achieve real equality.[36] To an extent that approach was not so surprising if we keep in mind that Art 2(4) was framed as an exception and that only gradually the concept of 'positive action' began to develop in legislation. In part, the new provisions were a reaction to the severe judgment of the ECJ in *Kalanke*. In addition, the shift in perception concerning preferential treatment was also mirrored in the ECJ case law itself. In the cases which followed *Kalanke*, the ECJ has softened its position on preferential treatment and, arguably, moved – somewhat timidly – in the direction of a 'thicker' understanding of equality.[37]

Nor is the case law of the ECJ without its ambiguities as regards the 'special protection' of women. On the one hand, there are cases in which the ECJ construed Art 2(3) of Council Directive 76/207/EEC and the Pregnant Workers Directive[38] in a less than satisfactory manner. In *Hofmann* the ECJ accepted that under Art 2(3), maternity leave was not limited to the mere period necessary for physical recovery after childbirth.[39] The provision also aims at the protection of the special relationship between a woman and her child. In this way, periods of childcare were brought under the scope of Art 2(3), which allows special protection of women, while excluding male would-be child-carers. The same assumption is reflected in the Pregnant Workers Directive and in the case law on that Directive.[40] The latter fleshes out the exception provided for in Art 2(3) of Council Directive 76/207/EEC. However, instead of giving a narrow interpretation both to this article and the Pregnant Workers Directive and of adhering to the biological differences between men and women, the ECJ has reinforced the stereotype of women as care-givers.

On the other hand, there are cases in which the ECJ has made an effort to delineate the protection on grounds of maternity in the narrow sense[41] from the capacity of men and women as parents, which does not fall within the scope of derogatory provisions aiming at 'special protection'.[42] Another – somewhat timid – move towards recognition of everyday life problems that should be accommodated in an unstereotypical manner can be seen in *Hill and Stapleton* where the ECJ held that Community policy in the area of equal treatment aims at the reconciliation of work and family life.[43] It considered that the protection of women and men at the workplace and in family life is a principle that, in the legal orders of the Member States, is commonly considered as a 'natural corollary' of the equality between men and women.

In brief, it would seem that in taking into account the everyday realities, including not only biological but also social differences between men and women, the ECJ also demonstrates a substantive understanding of equality. The question arises, however, to what extent this probably well-intentioned attempt does, in fact, maintain stereotypes or even reinforce gender discrimination.

10.2.3 Summary of findings

Within the EU, both at legislative and case law level there is an evolution in the direction of substantive equality. Notwithstanding the political call for a proactive approach to equal opportunities, in terms of specific legal rules and obligations, developments remain rather discrete. For instance, whilst legislation frames positive action in permissive terms, the ECJ places close limits on such action. The incorporation into the Directives of the element of comparability may also be considered a drawback.

However, there are also positive aspects to report concerning the introduction and streamlining of indirect discrimination and the shift to understanding positive action as an element of equality instead of as an exception. The recognition of pregnancy and maternity discrimination as a form of direct discrimination may also help to avoid a well-known comparability trap in national case law. In the area of the protection of women on grounds of maternity there is a visible effort to find an equilibrium between adequate protection and the detrimental effects this may have on women's careers. In brief, there are elements in EU gender discrimination law which, on correct implementation and application – thus provided effective 'transfer mechanisms' exist – ought to contribute to a more substantive understanding of equality within the Member States.

10.3 France

10.3.1 The context

Combating discrimination is a central theme in France at present.[44] The launch of the HALDE (*Haute Autorité de Lutte contre les Discriminations et pour l'Égalité*) in 2004 constituted an important step in dealing with different forms of discrimination in practice.[45] The HALDE is an independent public authority attributed extensive powers in many fields with far-reaching investigatory competences.[46] Its general aims are to provide information to all kinds of groups (employers, private persons, associations), to assist victims of discrimination and to investigate and publish examples of good practice. The number of complaints regarding diverse forms of discrimination is swiftly rising and amounted to 4,058 in 2006.[47] However, the annual reports published so far (2005 and 2006) indicate that until now relatively few complaints concern gender discrimination.[48]

Litigation on gender equality in general and indirect sex discrimination in particular has been rather scarce up until now in France. It is worth noting that little attention is paid in legal literature to the development of EU gender equality law and the case law of the ECJ, except where specific focus is directed to the case law of the ECJ as such. The majority of the literature on equality/non-discrimination refers only to national legislation and case law. There is a rather limited amount of legal writing on formal and substantive equality and the conceptualisation and application of the concepts of direct and indirect discrimination.[49] Only few writings reflect a gender approach and point to the structural roots of gender discrimination.[50]

10.3.2 Legislation

Equality has been deeply entrenched in French constitutional law ever since the Declaration of Human Rights of 1789. The first article reads: '*Les hommes naissent et demeurent libres et égaux en droits. Les distinctions sociales ne peuvent être fondées que sur l'utilité commune*'. After the Second World War, respect for the fundamental principles of the 1789 Declaration and those recognised by the laws of the French Republic were confirmed and extended in the Preamble of the French Constitution of 1946. This Preamble not only establishes the inalienable and sacred rights of human beings without distinction in terms of race, religion or belief, but also guarantees women equal rights to men in all fields. The Constitution of 1958 reaffirms once again the principle of equality of all citizens before the law without any distinction based on origin, race or religion.[51]

The Criminal Code contains a definition of discrimination. Discrimination comprises any distinction applied between persons by reason of their origin, sex, family situation, pregnancy, physical appearance, family name, state of health, disability, genetic characteristics, morals, sexual orientation, age, political opinions, union activities, or their membership or non-membership, real or supposed, of a given ethnic group, a nation, a race or religion.[52] Legal exceptions from that principle concern discrimination based on health and disability in specific cases and where sex is a determining factor in access to employment or occupational activities.[53]

The application of the principle of equality in labour law is rather recent, except in the field of equal pay and equal treatment between men and women.[54] The Labour Code contains many provisions prohibiting discrimination. A prohibition on discrimination in the field of employment is defined in Art L 122-45 in similar terms to the definition contained in the Criminal Code.[55] This provision forbids both direct and indirect discriminatory measures. However, legal definitions of those concepts are lacking. A chapter of the Labour Code is devoted to equal treatment between women and men in employment.[56]

In 2006, a specific law was adopted regarding equal pay between men and women.[57] The relevant provisions concern access to vocational training, equal pay between men and women, protection of women in relation to maternity and the reconciliation of professional and family life. This Act also enhances the role of social partners in this area. For example, the law requires negotiations to be held on an annual basis aiming to define and identify measures in order to abolish the gender pay gap by 2010.[58] In 2006, however, in most undertakings no such negotiations had taken place and a comparative report on equal pay between men and women was lacking.[59]

French legislation still contains some rather outdated provisions granting special rights to women, who have taken care of children, which potentially reinforce stereotypes regarding the caring role of women. The ECJ has held some provisions to be contrary to EU gender equality law.[60] However, provisions similar to those at stake still exist: for example the rule granting a longer period of old age pension to women who have raised children, at issue in *Griesmar*.[61]

Whether a broad range of new gender-neutral policies will be developed regarding, for example, the reconciliation of work, private and family life, reflecting a more substantive approach to equality in employment cannot yet be predicted. Levelling down is an option which the French legislature has sometimes also adopted.[62]

10.3.3 Case law

Despite the extensive anti-discrimination legislation litigation concerning discriminatory provisions or measures in which anti-discrimination provisions were invoked was poorly developed until the 1990s both in civil and criminal law.[63] Interestingly, the French legal conception of discrimination was developed primarily in the field of criminal law, with a particular emphasis on intentional discrimination. Most cases concerning indirect discrimination relate to trade union membership.[64] However, our analysis is limited to indirect sex discrimination and maternity-related rights. Such cases are scarce and the complaints have been often rejected.

In the first series of cases decided by the *Cour de Cassation, Chambre criminelle* with an explicit reference to indirect sex discrimination, a prohibition on Sunday work was at stake.[65] The plaintiffs argued that since predominantly women are employed in retail undertakings such prohibition disproportionately affects more women than men both in terms of remuneration and access to work. Such forms of indirect sex discrimination were said to be contrary to Art 119 of the EEC Treaty and Council Directive 76/207/EEC. The plaintiffs argued:

> *qu' il y a discrimination lorsqu'une législation nationale a pour effet*

> *de défavoriser les travailleurs de sexe féminin à raison du simple fait qu'elles représentent un pourcentage plus faible d'une catégorie bénéficiant d'avantages ou plus élevé d'une catégorie subissant un traitement moins favourable.*

However, the *Cour de Cassation* rejected that approach considering that the regulation on weekly rest was adopted in the interest of workers, both male and female, and that it constitutes a social advantage. Accordingly, it amounted neither to direct nor indirect discrimination of either group. Martin comments that this decision fails to take into account the fact that the ban on Sunday working might disadvantage some individuals who have no other choice than to pursue part-time work at the weekend and that women could be over-represented in these categories.[66] It should be noted that in these cases employers, and not employees, sought to invoke the concept of indirect sex discrimination. However, the cases demonstrate clearly the *Cour de Cassation*'s failure to apply the principle of indirect sex discrimination even when raised by the applicants in argument.

A case on (indirect sex) discrimination in relation to part-time work decided by the *Cour de Cassation, Chambre sociale* in 1996 concerned the determination of seniority for the purposes of promotion and greater remuneration.[67] The applicant had been refused promotion on the grounds that her period of professional practice was insufficient. In argument before the court she made reference to the relevant provisions and case law of Community law. The *Cour de Cassation, Chambre sociale* merely observed that the lower court had investigated whether the measure was discriminatory, even in indirect terms, and had decided that this was not the case. It is striking that the *Chambre sociale* did not review this aspect of the lower court's judgment and that references to relevant ECJ case law, in particular *Danfoss* and *Nimz*[68] are lacking. However, such references were also omitted in the applicant's plea insofar as it is reported in the judgment. Nor in a more recent equal value case did the *Cour de Cassation, Chambre criminelle* make reference to ECJ case law in deciding which criteria could justify a pay difference between a woman and her male colleagues. According to the lower court differences in the sectors which sales staff had to visit and disparities in sales volumes justified the pay differences. Furthermore, the female worker had a lower workload and bore fewer responsibilities. The *Cour de Cassation, Chambre criminelle* considered that the lower court's decision was substantiated, and again failed to review the reasoning of the lower court in the light of relevant ECJ case law.[69]

The concepts of direct and indirect discrimination were misunderstood in a case of pregnancy discrimination.[70] At stake was a rule of the CNAVTS (*Caisse Nationale d'Assurance Vieillesse des Travailleurs Salariés*), which required six months of effective presence at work to be entitled to an assessment (*notation*) prior to possible promotion to a higher level. During 1987, Ms Duchemin was on sick leave followed by maternity leave and in total absent from work for 124 days. Assessment was therefore denied. According to the court, such requirement applied indistinctly both to women and men and, therefore, could not amount to sex discrimination. It is striking that two commentators considered this rule to constitute indirect, not direct sex discrimination and that they criticised the *Cour de Cassation, Chambre sociale* for not applying the concept of indirect discrimination.[71] In a latter case with similar facts, *Thibault*, the *Cour de Cassation* requested a preliminary ruling.[72] The ECJ made clear that the case concerned direct discrimination contrary to Arts 2(3) and 5(1) of Council Directive 76/207/EEC. A French commentator expected that this judgment would oblige the French judges to apply the concept of indirect discrimination.[73] These comments indicate that even in legal writings the concept of indirect discrimination has been sometimes misunderstood.[74]

Up until now, French law tends in general to favour a formal approach to equality. Therefore a substantial number of discriminatory practices, in particular indirectly discriminating ones, remain unaddressed. The French approach to equality is less substantive than the approach adopted by the ECJ.[75] Certain authors consider that the French concept of equality, which is historically closely linked to the republican principle of one nation, impairs an approach that distinguishes between groups and allows specific measures.[76] Berthou also argues that, as a definition of indirect discrimination is lacking, the courts have taken it very rarely into account.[77] It would seem that French legal culture also plays a role. Wallace, for example, explores some systemic features of the French legal system in order to explain why the concept of indirect sex discrimination is absent in French case law. She suggests that the requirement of legal certainty has contributed to emphasise a formal approach to equality in law and has hampered the development of the concept of indirect sex discrimination. This is partly due to the fact that the concept of indirect discrimination allows very different situations to be brought under the scope of anti-discrimination provisions, with unpredictable outcomes. Furthermore, the limited interpretative role of judges could also be a reason why the concept of indirect sex discrimination is absent in French case law.[78] A final reason may consist in the limited number of court actions concerning indirect sex discrimination.

The restrictive approach might, however, be relaxed in the future. Recently the *Cour de Cassation* applied the concept of indirect discrimination in relation to the health of a female worker,[79] albeit without any reference to EC law. In addition, the HALDE has applied the concept of indirect discrimination in its decisions.[80]

The continuing legislative existence of outdated responses to maternity, which reinforce gender stereotypes, has also been addressed before courts. Such a provision (Art L 351-4 of the Social Security Code) was not considered unconstitutional by the *Conseil Constitutionnel* in 2003. The *Conseil* categorised the case under Council Directive 79/7/EEC rather than under Art 141 EC. It held that the exception of Art 7(1) of the Directive applied. This judgment met considerable criticism arguing that the *Conseil's* approach violated EC law in the light of the ECJ judgment in *Griesmar*.[81]

The problem of levelling down can be demonstrated by the legislative response to *Griesmar*.[82] In this case, the ECJ considered that a national provision attributing a service credit to female civil servants for bringing up their (adopted) children in the calculation of their retirement pension was contrary to Art 119 EEC. An important argument of the ECJ was that such provision excluded from entitlement to this credit male civil servants who were able to prove that they had assumed the task of raising their children. This service credit has been abolished for children born or adopted after 1 January 2004 and has not been replaced by a new gender-neutral service credit for (adoptive) parents raising children.[83]

10.4 The Netherlands

10.4.1 The context

Compared to France, the Netherlands has no such established tradition of a constitutional principle of equality.[84] However, in the Netherlands Constitution adopted in 1983, Art 1 provides: 'All persons in the Netherlands shall be treated equally in equal circumstances. Discrimination on the grounds of religion, belief, political opinion, race or sex or on any other grounds whatsoever shall not be permitted'. This Article has, in practice, a rather limited role as the Dutch courts are not permitted to review most laws in the light of this Article.[85]

According to Art 93 of the Constitution, the Dutch courts have the possibility to apply self-executing provisions of international treaties. National laws have been reviewed, for example, in the light of the prohibition on discrimination in Art 26 of the International Covenant on Civil and Political Rights (ICCPR). According to Art 94 of the Dutch Constitution, in case of a conflict between national and international law, the latter prevails. Therefore Dutch courts, especially the higher ones, are rather familiar with some provisions on equal treatment in international treaties and their application in national case law.

Rich legal literature is available in Dutch on the conceptualisation of equality, equal treatment and discrimination and the potentials and limits of these concepts with a view to realising substantive equality between men and women and to combat systemic forms of discrimination against women. The dominant male standards in law are challenged in legal writings. In these debates not only national and EU law are addressed, but also international treaties against discrimination, such as the Convention on the Elimination of All Forms of Discrimination against Women (CEDAW). A significant section of research adopts a comparative perspective, including, for example, British and American approaches to equality.[86] Holtmaat in particular critically assesses ECJ case law acknowledging the danger of reinforcing gender stereotypes by using sex equality law in view to improve the position of women.[87]

10.4.2 Legislation

The main legal instrument to combat discrimination is the Equal Treatment Act (ETA) adopted in 1994, which elaborates the constitutional principle of equality.[88] As far as sex discrimination is concerned the ETA covers employment and occupation and (access to the) supply of goods and services. In order to implement EC Equal Treatment Directives specific provisions were inserted in the Civil Code and other legislation.

The Dutch equal treatment legislation is drafted along the lines of the EC Directives. Often a structure and wording similar to the Directives is used. This is true for provisions in the Civil Code (Arts 7:646–7:647), the ETA and specific Acts, such as the Act on Equal Treatment of Men and Women, the Equal Treatment (Working Hours) Act, Equal Treatment (Permanent and Temporary Employees) Act, the Equal Treatment (Disability or Chronic Illness) Act or the Equal Treatment in Employment (Age Discrimination) Act.[89]

The concepts of direct and indirect discrimination are defined in legislation as are the prohibitions on harassment and sexual harassment. Discrimination[90] includes both direct and indirect discrimination (ETA, Art 1). Direct discrimination is regarded as discrimination between persons on the grounds of religion, belief, political opinion, race, sex, nationality, heterosexual or homosexual orientation or civil status. Indirect discrimination is regarded as discrimination on the grounds of characteristics or behaviour other than those referred to above resulting in direct discrimination. The prohibition on discrimination in the ETA does not apply to indirect discrimination which is objectively justified by a legitimate aim and where the means to achieve that aim are appropriate and necessary (ETA, Art 2(1)). This formula is derived from the case law of the ECJ on indirect sex discrimination, in particular *Bilka*. Other Acts on equal treatment contain similar provisions.

A few provisions in the Criminal Code define discrimination and prohibit various forms of discrimination on different grounds, such as sex and race.[91] These provisions supplement those introduced in civil law and, in contrast to France, have had a rather limited impact in practice up until now.

Women are not attributed specific rights in relation child-rearing responsibilities in Dutch law.

10.4.3 Case law

In many cases brought before the ECJ, Dutch statutory rules, provisions of collective agreements or regulations of undertakings were at stake. Many cases concern indirect sex discrimination in relation to part-time work, which is very common in the Netherlands, especially amongst women. ECJ judgments have sometimes led to subsequent legislative amendments. The General

Act on Incapacity for Work (*Algemene Arbeidsongeschiktheidswet, AAW*) was amended after the *Ruzius-Wilbrink*[92] judgment. The Reparation General Disability Act (*Reparatiewet AAW*) adopted after this judgment has also been subject to preliminary rulings (*Roks* and *Posthumma-Van Damme*[93]). The ECJ considered the indirectly discriminatory income requirement of the Reparation Disability Act as being objectively justified and therefore not to infringe Council Directive 79/7/EEC. Ultimately, the number of persons eligible to benefit from the new scheme was further reduced compared to the situation under the former General Disability Act. These developments are clear examples of levelling down by the legislator; and both the national and ECJ judgments reflect a formal approach to equality.

However, there are also examples of ECJ case law and subsequent amendments to legislation and collective agreements which have contributed to improving the employment position of large groups of women (and some men). Exclusions from access to pension schemes in respect of married women (*Fisscher*[94]) or certain groups of part-time workers (*Vroege*[95]) were successfully challenged and led to amendments. The Pension Act, for example, since 1994 has explicitly prohibited the exclusion of part-time workers from pension schemes.[96] No objective justification can be provided. In 1996, a specific law on equal treatment in employment as regards working hours entered into force.[97] The law closely follows the case law of the ECJ as regards indirect sex discrimination in relation to part-time work. Unfortunately, this includes the ECJ's approach in *Helmig*,[98] a judgment which has been widely and strongly criticised.[99]

Since the Act on equal pay between men and women entered into force in 1975, a specialised equality body has been in existence capable of delivering non-binding opinions when requested to do so by individuals (or organisations). In the ETA a specific section is devoted to the Equal Treatment Commission (ETC) which plays a very active role in the enforcement of the equal treatment legislation. In its opinions (in the last few years more than 200 each year, some 50 or so concerning discrimination on the grounds of sex) the ETC often applies case law of the ECJ in its opinions.[100] In numerous cases decided by the national courts an opinion of the ETC plays a role. Increasingly, judges refer to the relevant opinions and often address the considerations and final decision of the ETC in the case. It is generally considered appropriate to provide specific justification in a judgment when the outcome of the case differs from the non-binding opinion of the ETC. Although there is no legal obligation in this regard, this practice demonstrates that the opinions of the ETC are taken seriously and, thus, their references to EC law. In sex discrimination cases national courts often refer to relevant ECJ case law. In the past, many ECJ judgments on equal pay and equal treatment between men and women in employment and social security were delivered as a result of preliminary references submitted by Dutch courts. However, more recently, courts seem more reluctant to seek a preliminary ruling. The length of the preliminary rulings procedure may play a role in this respect.

Not only does the ETC enjoy the competence in response to a request to investigate whether unlawful discrimination has occurred, it may also conduct an investigation of its own initiative to determine whether such discrimination is occurring on a systematic basis (ETA, Art 12). Up until now the ETC has conducted only a few such investigations; however, sometimes an opinion also addresses more structural forms of discrimination. An example is to be found in an opinion on job classification schemes in the health sector.[101] The ETC carried out an in-depth analysis of pay differences between men and women in some job classification schemes applied in this sector. The analysis made clear that some aspects and tasks in functions predominantly performed by women were rewarded less than other aspects and tasks in functions with a higher representation of men. It should be noted that an expert in this field has been working with the Commission for many years. Such opinions clearly reflect a more substantive approach to equality, analysing whether gender-biased criteria might influence certain aspects of job classification schemes. It addresses the roots of potential indirect sex discrimination and reflects a more structural approach to combating gender pay gaps.

Despite the lack of specific legislation granting preferential treatment to women on grounds of parenthood, Dutch courts have had ample opportunity to consider the child-bearing capacity of women in relation to gender equality law. In many cases, direct discrimination in relation to pregnancy has been at stake. It is striking that in the light of the numerous judgments of the ECJ on this issue, in several cases the findings of national courts differed. For example, in two cases concerning access to private insurance covering the risk of pregnancy and disability of self-employed workers, a Dutch Tribunal[102] did not consider it contrary to the ETA to impose a qualifying period of two years to cover the risk of loss of income due to pregnancy. The reasoning of the court was that insurance covering income replacement in the event of pregnancy and disability insurance constituted two separate insurance contracts. As only women run the risk of income loss in the event of pregnancy and therefore only women could insure against this risk, the two year requirement applies only to women. According to this court, only women can suffer such disadvantage and in so far as such a requirement discriminates between persons, it does so as between two groups of women. Therefore no discrimination between men and women occurs. In our view, the reasoning of this Tribunal is clearly contrary to ECJ case law in relation to pregnancy in the field of pay and employment.[103] An appeal in this case is still pending. Similar provisions were at stake in other cases and the issue has also been addressed on appeal by a higher court.[104] According to the appellate court, as the definition of incapacity to work was framed in sex-neutral terms the provision gave rise to indirect sex discrimination. However, it considered that the considerable financial consequences for insured persons would probably constitute objective justification. It is striking that the national court did not refer to any relevant ECJ case law. The case is pending before the Dutch Supreme Court.

In a few other cases concerning the conjunction of school holidays and pregnancy with maternity leave, the Dutch Supreme Court and the Central Board of Appeal ought arguably to have referred the matter to the ECJ which perhaps ultimately would have resulted in a more substantive approach. The regulations applying to teachers did not include a specific provision dealing with the situation where a woman's pregnancy and maternity leave fall within the school holidays. According to the ETC and a few District Courts,[105] the lack of compensation applies only to female teachers who are on pregnancy and maternity leave during (a part of) school holidays and, accordingly, they enjoy fewer school holidays, which thus constitutes direct sex discrimination contrary to EC law, in particular, Art 11 of the Pregnant Workers Directive and the judgments in *Thibault, Brown* and *Boyle*.[106] The Central Board of Appeal has also decided a few appeals on this matter.[107] A similar regulation was also at stake in three cases decided by the Dutch Supreme Court.[108] Both the Central Board of Appeal and the Dutch Supreme Court considered that the provision regarding school holidays does not give a right to a certain amount of holidays, but defines the period during which holidays can be enjoyed. Both courts considered that in most cases, the conjunction of pregnancy and maternity leave will not result in a worker enjoying less than the statutory minimum holiday entitlement. The possibility cannot be excluded that in some cases female workers on pregnancy and maternity leave will suffer a disadvantage when they are not able to fulfil additional tasks or follow a course for example. Ultimately, the court which had to take the final decision in the light of the Supreme Court judgment concluded that the principle of equal treatment between men and women had not been infringed in the case at hand because the female worker enjoyed the statutory minimum of holidays.[109] *Merino Gómez*,[110] however, offers a more substantive approach. In that case the ECJ decided that a worker must be able to take her annual leave during a period other than the period of her maternity leave, even when the period of maternity leave coincides with the general period of annual leave fixed by collective agreement for the entire workforce. Whether this approach is also applicable to school holidays has not yet been the subject of an ECJ ruling.

10.5 Czech Republic

10.5.1 The context

Equality and, in particular, gender equality has never been the subject of much debate in the Czech Republic. This fact is reflected clearly in current opinion on the matter, both in societal terms and in terms of law and legal culture. Various historical reasons can be given in this context. First, no strong tradition of protection against discrimination existed during the Habsburg monarchy and later in the Czechoslovak Republic before the Second World War. Equality was considered a programmatic principle and a guideline for the legislature. It was not seen as justiciable and could certainly not give rise to an enforceable right.[111] Another historic-sociological explanation advanced by Šiklová points to the fact that over many years men and women in Czech lands enjoyed common enemies – Habsburgs, Germans, Russian – which prevented men and women from perceiving their different roles in society and for women to acknowledge their suppression by men.[112]

During the Communist era equality was a matter of state-imposed egalitarianism in which the notion of equality was basically empty and at any rate highly formal.[113] In relation to gender equality a clear paradox existed. On the one hand, equality between men and women was a part of state ideology, with women's economic independence playing a spearhead role.[114] Access to work, training and education for women all became self-evident matters. Their political participation was ensured through a quota system.[115] On the other hand, certain stereotypes about women's roles remained deeply entrenched both in law and society.

The legacy of the totalitarian era results in a strong societal bias concerning the equality of men and women and their respective roles and in minimal debate on gender equality issues. Obviously, these circumstances do not constitute a very promising context for an active promotion of gender equality as a fundamental value of European civilisation. In addition, equality law derived from EC provisions is perceived by some as another set of 'imposed' rules not attracting much sympathy.[116]

The crucial question is how far the perception of equality issues in general and gender equality in particular is going to change under influence of EU membership and as a result of social and economic developments. As certain authors have observed, the introduction of a market economy brings about or at least makes more visible certain inequalities, which may, in turn, translate into legal arguments.[117] To deal adequately with these issues, an appropriate conceptual apparatus is indispensable. However, there appears to be very little debate on the conceptualisation of equality and discrimination in Czech legal writing and accordingly also on the questions of formal and substantive equality. Only in a very recent publication – *Rovnost a discriminace* (Equality and Discrimination)[118] – is an extensive legal[119] treatise given to the questions at issue in the present chapter. It is striking, however, that that book builds strongly on UK, US and German sources and on the European Convention on Human Rights (ECHR) and EC law. There are hardly any references to a debate amongst legal scholars in the Czech Republic itself, probably because such debate is non-existent.

10.5.2 Legislation

Constitutional guarantees of equality are laid down in Arts 1 and 3 of the Czech Charter of Fundamental Rights and Basic Freedoms. Article 1 states that 'All people are free, have equal dignity, and enjoy equality of rights. [. . .]'. According to Art 3(1), 'Everyone is guaranteed the enjoyment of her fundamental rights and basic freedoms without regard to gender, race, color of skin, language, faith and religion, political or other conviction, national or social origin, membership in a national or ethnic minority, property, birth, or other status'.

At the level of legislation,[120] the most important legislative instruments for our purposes are the Labour Code and the relatively recent 2004 Employment Act.[121] The Labour Code from 1965[122] has been amended various times, in particular after EU accession. These changes were vital since under the 'socialist' legislation the role of women as child bearers and carers was firmly supported by long periods of paid leave, almost exclusively for women, and (over)protection in the workplace.[123] Those provisions were not situated within an equality discourse but were considered a matter of helping accomplish women's 'maternity mission', explicitly protected in the Labour Code, Sickness Insurance Act and a number of other laws.[124] The result of that approach is not difficult to imagine: a fostering of stereotypes, while the protective rules worked in many respects to the disadvantage of women when considered in terms of labour-market equality and related issues, such as pensions, since the rules were rather protective towards women, for instance, in terms of pensionable age and with periods of caring being automatically regarded as insured periods.

Recently, the 1965 Labour Code has been replaced by a new 2006 Labour Code.[125] The most important changes to the Labour Code in relation to gender discrimination took place in 2000 (implementation of Council Directives 76/207/EEC and 97/80/EC) and in 2004 (implementation of Directive 2002/73/EC). One of the initial problems was that the 2000 amendments introduced the notions of direct and indirect discrimination, but did not define these. As this distinction and, in particular, the concept of indirect discrimination was new in Czech law, legal practice was somewhat at loss how to apply it.[126] Full and EU-compliant definitions of direct and indirect discrimination were introduced in 2004 in both the Employment Act and the Labour Code. Direct discrimination is also defined as including discrimination on grounds of pregnancy and maternity.

Enabling provisions in both the Employment Act and the Labour Code permit positive action measures. According to Art 4 of the Employment Act measures that are designed to prevent or correct disadvantages, stemming from a individual's membership of a discriminated group and which aim to ensure equal treatment in practice, are not considered to constitute discrimination.

Article 16(3) of the new Labour Code permits employers to take temporary measures which aim to achieve equal representation of men and women in relation to recruitment, training and the opportunity to obtain a specific position. The basis for such measures must be the unequal representation of men and women with that employer and the procedure may not disadvantage an employee of the opposite sex who is better qualified than the employee benefiting from 'preferential treatment.'

The entry into force of the 2006 Labour Code on 1 January 2007 created a significant gap. The definitions of discrimination and other concepts, as well as other detailed rules on equal treatment were deferred to the new Anti-discrimination Act which even at the time of editing this chapter (December 2007) had still not been adopted by the Czech Parliament.

The first draft of the Anti-Discrimination Act, aiming at protection against discrimination in all spheres of life and on a long, non-exhaustive list of grounds, was presented to the Chamber of Deputies on 21 January 2005, which approved it with a number of amendments and several close votes. However, the Senate did not accept the draft and returned it to the Chamber of Deputies on 26 January 2006. At the second reading in the Chamber of Deputies, the required absolute majority of 101 votes failed to be reached. An amended proposal adopted by the government on 11 June 2007 was sent in mid-July to the Chamber of Deputies for debate.[127]

Two important aspects in the rejection of the first proposal were fears of too broad a scope and the far-reaching impact of anti-discrimination rules and little sympathy for positive action or positive discrimination.[128] However, on reading the debates, one gets the impression that above all the very concept of positive action was wholly unclear to the persons concerned. This is also closely linked to the second problem raised, namely what was described as 'the slavish translation from foreign languages'. Although the main argument was that the text was badly drafted, one gets the impression that what was actually at stake was the unfamiliarity of the *concepts* as such.[129]

The latest 2007 draft of the Anti-discrimination Act incorporates all the EU Anti-discrimination Directives, including the latest Sex Equality Directives 2004/113/EC and 2006/54/EC. The definitions of discrimination, both direct and indirect, are drafted very closely along the lines of the relevant Directives.[130] Discrimination on grounds of pregnancy and maternity is equated to discrimination on grounds of sex. According to sec 5(5) of the draft law, measures aiming at the protection of women, particularly as regards pregnancy and maternity, are excluded from the prohibition on discrimination provided that they are necessary and proportionate to that objective. These provisions mean that issues of pregnancy and maternity are brought *within* the framework of equal treatment and non-discrimination.[131]

A striking feature, however, is that the provision on positive action, included in the 2005 draft, has initially been deleted. A new, less generously worded text has been reinserted into the draft only at the very last moment.[132]

The entry into force of the Anti-Discrimination Act is badly needed. Apart from the legal gap, mentioned above, that exists now in relation to the 'new' Labour Code, another crucial issue is earmarked for regulation by the Anti-Discrimination Act, namely the establishment of an equality body, as required by the EU Directives. Under the current draft, the ombudsman's office – officially the office of the Public Protector of Rights – is designated to perform the tasks. In addition to fulfilling Community law obligations, such bodies – as was set out earlier with reference to the Dutch Equal Treatment

Commission – can play an important role in the development and application of gender equality law.

Finally, as has been observed in the legal literature, as long as the Anti-Discrimination Act remains unadopted and does not enter into force, protection against gender discrimination still consists of a patchwork of provisions,[133] with no uniform definition of discrimination and, in some cases, the need to fall back on the very open provisions of the Charter of Fundamental Rights and Basic Freedoms. This obviously complicates the application of the law in specific cases[134] and, in our opinion, is by no means conducive to a coherent conceptualisation of equality.

10.5.3 Case law

At first sight, the Czech legislation appears to be in line with EU requirements and in this respect it also mirrors to an extent the elements for a substantive understanding of equality as they exist in EU law. This holds true, in particular, for the notion of indirect discrimination and to a much lesser extent for positive action. Yet, even in cases of adequate transposition of the relevant EU rules, as is well known, much depends on the actual application and interpretation of the legal provisions both by the courts and more generally. In this respect, a number of difficulties should be highlighted.[135]

Various key concepts transposed from Community instruments into Czech law are new for that legal system, foreign bodies (*Fremdkörper*) so to speak, which – even if defined – do not connect properly to existing national law and legal tradition; accordingly, nor are they entirely comprehensible. This holds particularly true for indirect discrimination, but also for notions such as harassment and sexual harassment. In order to give substance to these 'foreign' notions, one has to take into account the interpretation of these notions at EU level, in particular by the ECJ. The problem here is the very limited availability of Czech translations of the relevant cases and other EU documents which still continues to cause problems.[136] Although cases decided after accession in 2004 are translated, the accessibility and sometimes also the quality of translation of older case law is limited. To this one may add the unfamiliarity of Czech lawyers and judges with the teleological interpretation method of EU law, which in the meantime has also penetrated the national level through the obligation of consistent interpretation. The latter obligation requires, in fact, a double effort: first, to ascertain the meaning at EU level and, second, to construe national law in conformity with that meaning. Moreover, the obligation of consistent interpretation is not a self-evident matter for a Czech lawyer. It requires them to consider sources of law which were until recently unknown to the legal system. Arguably, this may and will change over time as was the case in other EU Member States. An example of such a change can be seen in a judgment of the Constitutional Court (*Ustavní Soud*, abbreviated as US) from 2006 concerning a shift of the burden of proof in a race discrimination case.[137]

However, in seeking to assess the courts' application of gender discrimination provisions, we run into one major problem: there is hardly any relevant case law.[138] According to a report of the Ministry of Justice, between 2000 and 2005 there were only two cases concerning gender discrimination. In the first half of 2006, nine cases were decided.[139] Various reasons can be given for this lack of case law: little awareness of equality rights, lengthy judicial procedures, difficulties with evidence, the costs of litigation, little trust in courts, the low level of damages awarded and insufficiently developed non-governmental organisations or equality bodies to support individual litigants. Moreover, all the cases seem to concern direct discrimination only. In legal writing it was observed that in the event of alleged indirect discrimination quite some effort would be necessary in order to convince courts that any discrimination at all exists. This may explain why as yet no cases in ordinary courts on indirect discrimination have been decided as such.[140] The only indirect discrimination case brought to the Constitutional Court until now was on the placing of Roma children in special educational institutions. However, the case was dismissed since the statistical evidence was deemed insufficient to raise a suspicion of indirect discrimination.[141]

This brings us to the jurisprudence of the Constitutional Court. A striking feature here is that very little litigation is centred around suspect classifications, such as minority, sex, race, and, accordingly, these are hardly applied. Much more common are cases concerning 'non-qualified grounds', that is to say, cases brought on the basis of any other ground. Sometimes, even in a specific case, it is not clear what this other ground is.[142]

One of the rare exceptions is the decision of the Constitutional Court in case US 42/04.[143] The case concerned – at least on a superficial reading – 'special rights' for women in the sense that caring fathers are treated less favourably than mothers. While the conditions of the Czech social security systems are in principle gender neutral, a problem exists in relation to pensionable age. The pensionable age of women is reduced in relation to that of men (or other women) according to the number of children they have raised. In the case of a woman, the period of care is taken into account automatically as an insured period, without any necessity to apply for such. A man who has raised children may also qualify to have his period of care taken into account for old-age pension purposes, but only if he applies for that concession within a period of two years following the end of the caring period.[144] In other words, there was a presumption that women care for their children whereas men had to notify the fact to the relevant authorities.

The Constitutional Court declared the relevant provisions unconstitutional since caring men and caring women are in the same situation and the distinction at issue could not be justified since the means adopted were disproportionate, in particular, they could not be regarded as necessary.[145] In examining the justification, the Constitutional Court found that the objective, namely the efficient use of public finances, was a legitimate one. However, that aim could have been secured by other non-discriminatory means. The underlying reason why men had to notify and women were exempted was one of practicability and administrative convenience, which was in turn based on the traditional division of roles between men and women in Czech society. However, according to the Constitutional Court, practicability and administrative convenience cannot serve to justify a limitation on a fundamental right, such as non-discrimination.

In addition to this strict test applied by the Constitutional Court which undoubtedly also helps to strike down gender stereotypes, the decision is interesting for a number of other reasons.

First, in developing the legal framework for analysis, the Constitutional Court refers not only to the relevant provisions of the Charter of Fundamental Rights and Basic Freedoms, but also to Art 14 of the ECHR and Art 26 of the ICCPR. What might seem surprising in this context is that no reference is made to EU Gender Equality Directives. This may be explained in part by the fact that Art 7(1)(b) of Council Directive 79/7/EEC permits the Member States to exclude from the equal treatment principle 'advantages in respect of old-age pension schemes granted to persons who have brought up children; . . .'. This is a point that would have at least merited mention. Moreover, discussion of ECJ case law on similar issues[146] might have been helpful as a source of inspiration for the Constitutional Court. A more probable reason for ignoring Community law, however, is the fact that the Czech Constitutional Court is rather ambiguous on the question whether to apply EU Directives.[147]

Second, the Constitutional Court also touches briefly upon the notions of formal and substantive equality. Formal equality is defined as equal treatment of formally equal subjects in formally equal situations. Substantive equality is described as formally unequal treatment of de facto unequal subjects which aims to compensate the de facto inequality and helps to achieve real equality between the subjects. The court points out that the latter situation is also referred to as positive discrimination insofar as it introduces preferential treatment of subjects who are disadvantaged in comparison with other subjects. The Constitutional Court deduces from this that preferential treatment as such is not necessarily in conflict with equality and non-discrimination, as long as it aims to redress existing de facto discrimination. The legislator enjoys a certain degree of discretion whether or not to introduce preferential treatment, provided that objective and reasonable grounds exist for such treatment and that the requirement of proportionality is met.[148]

Next, the court turns to the case at hand in order to establish whether the rules at issue are a form of justified preferential treatment. However, without addressing this question explicitly, the court continues with the reasoning set out above. That reasoning reveals implicitly that the rules at issue were in no way inspired by a wish to compensate inequality and had certainly nothing to do with preferential treatment aiming to redress a situation of de facto inequality. Interestingly, in a minority opinion one of the judges expressed the view that there was an objective and reasonable ground for treating men and women differently, namely the very fact that women still form the majority of those who care for young children. Obviously, such an argument based on traditional stereotypes can hardly be considered as justification for preferential treatment since it does not reduce actual instances of inequality, but instead fosters traditional roles.

Although the fact should be applauded that the Constitutional Court is willing to reason in terms of substantive equality, its discussion of the relationship between substantive equality, preferential treatment and positive action or discrimination is not very clear. Arguably, the court brackets together too easily the different manifestations of substantive equality, ignoring the differences that exist between them and the particular conditions for their application. In addition, it is not clear in the court's reasoning, when different – preferential – treatment may be justified by considerations of establishing 'real' equality and on other objective and reasonable grounds.

10.6 A comparative summary

In the first section we indicated that sufficient elements in EU law exist to induce the Member States to introduce a more substantive notion of gender equality in their own legal orders. What then is the situation in the three Member States under review in this chapter? The historical development of equal treatment legislation is rather different in these Member States. This, indeed, influences the impact of EC law on national legislation or case law.

France has a longer tradition of equality protection than the two other states. However, gender equality law has developed there in a rather autonomous manner. The Netherlands and, more recently the Czech Republic, would seem to be much more under the influence of EC gender equality law, in the latter state especially as regards its legislation. References to European law and ECJ case law are rather common in the Netherlands, although more recently it is striking that fewer preliminary questions are referred to the ECJ, even in cases where the interpretation of gender equality law is far from clear. In France, references to EC law and ECJ judgments are considerably less widespread. For the Czech Republic nothing can be reported since no case law of the ordinary courts exists. The Constitutional Court seems hesitant in this respect since gender equality law is very much grounded in Directives and the review of national law in the light of EC law Directives is a disputed matter.

In France, existing legal texts tend to favour a non-discrimination approach and a formal approach to equality. It is striking that neither the Criminal Code, nor the Labour Code contains any definition of direct and indirect discrimination. This is different in the two other Member States, where both notions are defined. However, our exploration also made clear that such definitions do not of themselves guarantee correct application. In the Netherlands some courts have caused considerable confusion by making the wrong comparisons. This was the case in relation to pregnancy discrimination, labelled by the ECJ as a form of direct discrimination. Fortunately, overall, the concept of indirect discrimination is well known and, in general, it would seem to be applied correctly. In relation to the Czech Republic it was argued that in particular indirect discrimination, as a completely new notion, poses a problem. No reported court cases exist which have made use of this notion.

The need for protection of 'maternity' seems still to be a deeply entrenched idea in the French and Czech legal systems. In France, special rights for women have still not been abolished. Gender-neutral approaches which challenge stereotypes regarding the respective roles of men and women and dominant standards still have to be developed. The Czech Republic still has to face some leftovers from this former ideology. While the legal system has been made more gender-neutral in this respect, not least under influence of EC law, the fact remains that stereotypes are still flourishing within Czech society. The same holds true for the Netherlands, which is characterised by the high proportion of female part-time work.

A issue worthy of note in France is that in many legislative provisions specific competences are attributed to the social partners. It seems, however, that up until now, only scarce use has been made of the possibilities offered.

The Dutch example illustrates vividly the important role played by gender – or more general – equality bodies. In the Netherlands it is above all the ETC which follows closely EC law developments, contributes to a more substantive understanding of equality and enhances the effectiveness of non-discrimination law. The HALDE in France may develop in the same direction and thus contribute to a broader and deeper debate on the conceptualisation of equality. In the Czech Republic such a body is still sorely missing.

In all three countries a thick notion of substantive equality has still to be developed. The application of the concept of indirect discrimination is rather hesitant in France and problematic in the Czech Republic, although more firmly embodied in legislation and case law in the Netherlands. Nevertheless, there still remains a long way to go until in law, politics and, above all, society, a more substantive notion of gender equality in particular becomes the everyday standard.

Notes

* The authors wish to thank Kristina Koldinská, Hélène Masse-Dessen, Sylvaine Laulom, Eric Millard, Isabelle Guerlais and Frédérique Ast for their help, comments and suggestions. The responsibility for eventual errors rests of course with the authors.
1 Although we use the term 'EU law', we refer, in principle, to Community law, i.e. the law of the First Pillar of the EU.
2 In particular non-discrimination on grounds of nationality and on grounds of sex constitutes a fundamental principle in EU law.
3 See, for example, S Fredman (2002) *Discrimination Law*, Oxford: Oxford University Press; E Ellis (2005) *EU Anti-Discrimination Law*, Oxford University Press, at pp 2–7.
4 See S Fredman (1992) 'European community discrimination law: A critique',

Industrial Law Journal, 21: 119–34; T Hervey and J Shaw (1998) 'Women, work and care: Women's dual role and double burden in EC sex equality law', *Journal of European Social Policy*, 8: 43–63; D Schiek (2002) 'A new framework on equal treatment of persons in EC law? Directives 2000/43/EC, 2000/78/EC and 2002/73/EC changing directive 76/207/EEC in context', *European Law Journal*, 8: 290–314; S Prechal (2004) 'Equality of treatment, non-discrimination and social policy: Achievements in three themes', *Common Market Law Review*, 41: 533–51; Ellis, ibid, p 3.

5 See, for example, the references mentioned in n 3 above.

6 Considerable discussion exists whether the Aristotelian model as such can accommodate substantive understanding of equality. For critique see, in particular, C MacKinnon (1988) *Feminism Unmodified. Discourses on Life and Law*, Cambridge, MA: Harvard University Press.

7 Article 5 of Council Directive 2000/43/EC implementing the principle of equal treatment between persons irrespective of racial or ethnic origin [2000] OJ L180/22; Art 7 of Council Directive 2000/78/EC establishing a general framework for equal treatment in employment and occupation [2000] OJ L303/16; and Art 6 of Council Directive 2004/113/EC implementing the principle of equal treatment between men and women in the access to and supply of goods and services [2004] OJ L373/37.

8 Directive 2002/73/EC amending Council Directive 76/207/EEC on the implementation of the principle of equal treatment for men and women as regards access to employment, vocational training and promotion, and working conditions [2002] OJ L269/15.

9 Council Directive 2004/113/EC.

10 Directive 2006/54/EC on the implementation of the principle of equal opportunities and equal treatment of men and women in matters of employment and occupation (recast) [2006] OJ L204/23.

11 Council Directive 2000/43/EC.

12 Council Directive 2000/78/EC.

13 Council Directive 97/80/EC on the burden of proof in cases of discrimination based on sex [1998] OJ L14/6.

14 For instance, Directive 2006/54/EC, Art 8.

15 Directive 2006/54/EC, Art 15.

16 Article 7(1)(a) of Council Directive 79/7/EEC on the progressive implementation of the principle of equal treatment for men and women in matters of social security [1979] OJ L 6/24.

17 Council Directive 79/7/EEC, Art 7(1)(b).

18 Directive 2006/54/EC, Art 2(2)(c).

19 Directive 2002/73/EC, Art 2, Council Directive 2004/113/EC, Art 2 and Directive 2006/54/EC, Art 2.

20 See above, p 271 and also below, p 219.

21 Case C-136/95 *Caisse nationale d'assurance vieillesse des travailleurs salariés (CNAVTS) v Thibault* [1998] ECR I-2011.

22 Council Directive 76/207/EEC on the implementation of the principle of equal treatment for men and women as regards access to employment, vocational training and promotion, and working conditions [1976] OJ L39/40.

23 Case C-284/02 *Land Brandenburg v Sass* [2004] ECR I-11143.

24 For example, Case C-177/88 *Dekker v Stichting Vormingscentrum voor Jong Volwassenen (VJV-Centrum) Plus* [1990] ECR I-3941 and Case C-394/96 *Brown v Rentokil Ltd* [1998] ECR I-4185.

25 Case C-116/94 *Meyers v Adjudication Officer* [1995] ECR I-2131.

26 Case 96/80 *Jenkins v Kingsgate* [1981] ECR 911.

27 Case 170/84 *Bilka v Weber* [1986] ECR 1607.

28 See, for instance, Case C-196/02 *Nikoloudi v Organismos Tilepikoinonion Ellados AE* [2005] ECR I-1789 and Case C-187/00 *Kutz-Bauer v Freie und Hansestadt Hamburg* [2003] ECR I-2741.

29 Case C-79/99 *Schnorbus v Land Hessen* [2000] ECR I-10997.

30 And indeed, there are also very unsatisfactory cases such as Joined Cases C-399/ 92, C-409/92, C-425/92, C-34/93, C-50/93 and C-78/93 *Stadt Lengerich v Helmig et al* [1994] ECR I-5727 and Case C-220/02 *Österreichischer Gewerkschaftsbund v Wirtschaftskammer Österreich* [2004] ECR I-5907, see below.

31 Case C-17/05 *Cadman v Health & Safety Executive* [2006] ECR I-9583.

32 Case C-297/93 *Grau-Hupka v Stadtgemeinde Bremen* [1994] ECR I-5535.

33 *Helmig* (see n 30 above).

34 This case was at the core of some of the debates in academic literature in the Netherlands. See R Holtmaat (1996) 'Deeltijdwerk, gelijkheid en gender. Een beschouwing naar aanleiding van de zaak Helmig inzake overwerktoeslagen voor deeltijdwerkers', *Nemesis*, 1: 4–17; T Loenen (1996) 'Holtmaat en *Helmig*, of: het trekken van verkeerde conclusies uit een verkeerd arrest', *Nemesis*, 4: 123–5; A Veldman (1996) 'De bescheiden functie van het juridisch gelijkheids-beginsel. Het fundamentele verschil tussen juridische leerstukken en weten-schappelijke concepten binnen vrouw en recht', *Nemesis*, 2: 31–8 and R Holtmaat (1996) 'Alle dingen die opwaarts gaan komen ergens samen', *Nemesis*, 4: 125–31.

35 ECJ Case C-220/02 op cit. fn. 30.

36 Case C-450/93 *Kalanke v Freie Hansestadt Bremen* [1995] ECR I-3069.

37 See Case C-409/95 *Marschall v Land Nordrhein-Westfalen* [1997] ECR I-6363; Case C-158/97 *Badeck* [2000] ECR I-1875; Case C-407/98 *Abrahamson* v *Elisabet Fogelqvist* [2000] ECR I-5539; Case C-476/99 *Lommers v Minister van Landbouw, Natuurbeheer en Visserij* [2002] ECR I-2891 and Case C-319/03 *Brihêche v Ministre de l'Intérieur, Ministre de l'Éducation nationale and Ministre de la Justice* [2004] ECR I-8807.

38 Council Directive 92/85/EEC on the introduction of measures to encourage improvements in the safety and health at work of pregnant workers and workers who have recently given birth or are breastfeeding (tenth individual Directive within the meaning of Art 16 (1) of Council Directive 89/391/EEC) [1992] OJ L 348/1.

39 Case 184/83 *Hofmann v Barmer Ersatzkasse* [1984] ECR 3047.

40 See Case C-342/93 *Gillespieand others v Northern Health and Social Services Boards* [1996] ECR I-475 and Case C-411/96 *Boyle and Others v Equal Opportunities Commission* [1998] ECR I-6401.

41 Case C-218/98 *Abdoulaye Others v Régie nationale des usines Renault SA* [1999] ECR I-5723.

42 For instance, Case 222/84 *Johnston v Chief Constable of the Royal Ulster Constabulary* [1986] ECR 1651; Case C-285/98 *Kreil v Bundersrepublik Deutschland* [2000] ECR I-69; Case 312/86 *Commission v France* [1988] ECR 6315; Case C-366/99 *Griesmar v Ministre de l'Economie, des Finances et de l'Industrie et al* [2001] ECR I-9383 and Case C-206/00 *Mouflin v Recteur de l'académie de Reims* [2001] ECR I-10201.

43 Case C-243/95 *Hill and Stapleton v The Revenue Commissioners and Department of Finance* [1998] ECR I-3739. Note, however, critique of *Hill and Stapelton* in C McGlynn (2000) 'Ideologies of motherhood in European Community sex equality Law', *European Law Journal*, 6: 29–44.

44 See for a picture beyond gender equality and focused on multi-dimensionality Laulom, Chapter 12, in this book. See also F Favennec-Héry (2007) 'Non-discrimination, égalité, diversité, la France au milieu du gué', *Droit social*, 1: 3–7, at p 3.

45 See its website at www.halde.fr/ (accessed 12 January 2008). The HALDE was established by the Law of 30 December 2004 (*Loi n° 2004-1486 du 30 décembre 2004 portant création de la haute autorité de lutte contre les discriminations et pour l'égalité*), subsequently amended by the Law of 31 March 2006 (*Loi n° 2006-396 du 31 mars 2006 pour l'égalité des chances*). The legislation is available at www.legifrance.gouv.fr/ (accessed 12 January 2008); See also L Bonnard-Planke and P-Y Verkindt (2006) 'Égalité et diversité: quelles solutions?', *Droit social*, 11: 968–80, at pp 973–4.

46 However, the far-reaching competences of HALDE have been also criticised for interfering with the judicial enforcement of anti-discrimination law by the national courts: F Favennec-Héry (2007) 'Non-discrimination, égalité, diversité, la France au milieu du gué', *Droit social*, 1: 3–7, at p 7.

47 HALDE, *Rapport annuel 2006*, available at http://halde.fr/rapport-annuel/2006/rapport_annuel_2006.html (accessed 10 January 2008).

48 In 2005: 86 complaints, 6.10 per cent of all complaints; in 2006: 203 complaints, 5 per cent of all complaints. However, family situation is invoked in 5.5 per cent of all complaints in 2005 and 2 per cent of all complaints in 2006. There might be a link with gender discrimination in most of those cases.

49 See, for example, M-Th Lanquetin (2001) 'Le principe de non-discrimination', *Droit Ouvrier*, Mai: 186–93; D Loschak (1987) 'Réflexions sur la notion de discrimination', *Droit social*, 11: 778–90; P Rongere (1990) 'A la recherche de la discrimination introuvable: l'extension de l'exigence d'égalité entre les salariés', *Droit social*, 1: 99–106; E Dockès (2002) 'Equality in labour law: An economically efficient human right? Reflections from a French law perspective', *IJCLLIR*, 18: 187–96; K Berthou (2003) 'New hopes for French anti-discrimination law', *IJCLLIR*, 19: 109–37; A Jeammaud (2004) 'Du principe d'égalité de traitement des salariés', *Droit social*, 7/8: 694–705; F Héas 'Discrimination et admission de différences de traitement entre salariés', *La semaine juridique-Édition sociale*, 20 March: 11–14; F Favennec-Héry (2007) 'Non-discrimination, égalité, diversité, la France au milieu du gué', *Droit social*, 1: 3–7.

50 See, for example, L Bonnard-Planke and P-Y Verkindt (2006) 'Égalité et diversité: quelles solutions?', *Droit social*, 11: 968–80.

51 Available at www.legifrance.gouv.fr/html/constitution/constitution.htm (last accessed 12 January January 2008). The legal texts mentioned in this paragraph can all be found at www.legifrance.gouv.fr (last accessed 12 January 2005).

52 Translation by the authors. Original text available at www.legifrance.gouv.fr/WAspad/RechercheSimpleArticleCode (accessed 12 January 2008).

53 Article 225-3 of the Criminal Code.

54 Relevant legislation was introduced in the 1980s, see further: E Dockès (2002) 'Equality in labour law: An economically efficient human right? Reflections from a French law perspective', *IJCLLIR*, 18: 187–96, and L Bonnard-Planke and P-Y Verkindt (2006) 'Égalité et diversité: quelles solutions?', *Droit social*, 11: 968–80, at p 972.

55 This and the following articles will be replaced by Arts L. 1131-1 *et seq.* by 1 March 2008.

56 Articles L. 123-1–L. 123-7 of the Labour Code. This Chapter will be replaced by Arts L. 1141-1 *et seq.* by 1 March 2008.

57 *Loi n°2006-340 du 23 mars 2006 relative à l'égalité salariale entre les femmes et les hommes*. See on this: M-Th Lanquetin (2006) 'L'égalité des rémunérations entre les femmes et les hommes, réalisée en cinq ans?', *Droit social*, 6: 624–35. In a recent decision the *Conseil Constitutionnel* held some provisions of this law on positive action to be unconstitutional: Judgment of 16 March 2006, decision 2006-533 DC.

58 See, in particular, Art L. 132-27-2 of the Labour Code.

59 In 72 per cent of the undertakings no negotiations were held and 60 per cent of the undertakings had not published a report on equal pay: S Canada-Blanc (2006) 'L'égalité salariale et professionnelle: les femmes y parviendront-elles? A propos de la loi no 2006-340 du 23 mars 2006', *JCP G*: 870, cited in L Bonnard-Planke and P-Y Verkindt (2006) 'Égalité et diversité: quelles solutions?', *Droit social*, 11: 968–80, at p 976.

60 See Case 312/86 *Commission v France* [1988] ECR 6315 and Case C-366/99 *Griesmar* [2001] ECR I-9383.

61 For example Art L. 351-4 of the Social Security Code which reads: *'Les femmes assurées sociales bénéficient d'une majoration de leur durée d'assurance d'un trimestre pour toute année durant laquelle elles ont élevé un enfant, dans des conditions fixées par décret, dans la limite de huit trimestres par enfant'*. It is striking that the Law of 21 August 2003 amended this Article without abolishing the direct discrimination between men and women.

62 See text accompanying n 82 below.

63 M-Th Lanquetin (2001) 'Le principe de non-discrimination', *Droit Ouvrier*, Mai: 186–93, at p 186. This section is further mainly limited to case law of the *Cour de Cassation* and the *Conseil Consitutionnel* and does not include case law of the *Conseil d'État* which has issued quite a number of judgments on equal pay and equal treatment between men and women.

64 On the relevance of these see Laulom, Chapter 12, in this book, text accompanying nn 30–33.

65 The first of these cases accessible through the website www.legifrance.fr is: *Cour de Cassation, Chambre criminelle*, 10 January 1995, case no 94-82725. Most subsequent cases decided by the *Cour de Cassation, Chambre criminelle* were similar and the court took the same or a similar approach. For a short overview see D Schiek (2007) 'Indirect discrimination', in D Schiek, L Waddington and M Bell (eds) *Non-Discrimination Law*, Oxford: Hart Publishing, pp 360–5, with a translation of the French excerpt below at p 362.

66 Ph Martin (1996) 'Droit social et discriminations sexuelles: à propos des discriminations générées par la loi', *Droit social*, 6: 562–8, p 565.

67 *Cour de Cassation, Chambre sociale*, 9 April 1996, case no 92-41103, the first case of the *Cour de Cassation, Chambre sociale* which explicitly mentions indirect sex discrimination. See also: *Cour de Cassation Chambre sociale*, 24 January 2007, case no 05-42054; *Cour de Cassation, Chambre sociale*, 6 March 2007, case no 04-42080.

68 Case 109/88 *Handels- og Kontorfunktionærernes Forbund I Danmark Danfoss* [1989] ECR 3199 and Case C-184/89 *Nimz v Freie und Hansestadt Hamburg* [1991] ECR I-297.

69 *Cour de Cassation, Chambre criminelle*, 5 March 2002, case no 01-82285.

70 *Cour de Cassation, Chambre sociale*, 30 March 1994, case no 90-43645.

71 M-A Moreau (1994) 'Congé de maternité. Obstacle à la notation. Absence de discrimination, Cour de Cassation (Chambre sociale 30 mars 1994 CNAVTS c/ Duchemin)', *Droit social*, 6: 561–2 and Ph Martin (1996) 'Droit social et discriminations sexuelles: à propos des discriminations générées par la loi', *Droit social*, 6: 562–8, at p 564.

72 Case C-136/95 *Caisse nationale d'assurance vieillesse des travailleurs salariés (CNAVTS) v Thibault* [1998] ECR I-2011.

73 M-A Moreau (1995) 'Egalité de traitement hommes/femmes. Congé de maternité. Absence de notation. Renvoi en interprétation de la directive du 9 février 1976. Cour de Cassation (Chambre sociale) 28 mars 1995 CNAV c. Thibault', *Droit social*: 1036–7, at p 1037.

74 See also CJ Wallace (1999) 'European integration and legal culture: Indirect sex discrimination in the French legal system', *Legal studies*, 19: 397–414, at p 403.

75 K Berthou (2003) 'New hopes for French anti-discrimination law', *IJCLLIR*, 19: 109–37, and E Dockès (2002) 'Equality in labour law: An economically efficient human right? Reflections from a French law perspective', *IJCLLIR*, 18: 187–96, at p 189.

76 See, for example, Berthou, who also points to the reluctance to collect the statistical data needed to establish a prima facie case of indirect discrimination: K Berthou (2003) 'New hopes for French anti-discrimination law', *IJCLLIR*, 19: 109–37, at p 118.

77 Ibid, p 117.

78 CJ Wallace (1999) 'European integration and legal culture: Indirect sex discrimination in the French legal system', *Legal studies*, 19: 397–414, and Ph Martin (1996) 'Droit social et discriminations sexuelles: à propos des discriminations générées par la loi', *Droit social*, 6: 562–8, at pp 564–5.

79 *Cour de Cassation, Chambre sociale*, 9 January 2007, case no 05-43962.

80 See, for example, decision 2005-32 on seniority and the annual reports of Halde, available at www.halde.fr/ (accessed 12 January 2008).

81 Decision 2003-483 of 14 August 2003. See X Prétot (2003) 'La conformité à la Constitution de la loi portant sur la réforme des retraites. Un décision bien peu convaincante', *Droit social*: 917 and J-Ph Lhernould and D Martin (2007) 'Majoration d'assurance de l'article L. 351-4 du Code de la Sécurité sociale: fin programmée de la discrimination à l'égard des pères en matière de pension de vieillesse', *Droit social*, 3: 319–22, at p 321. See also *Cour de Cassation, Chambre civile*, decision 02-30978 of 15 June 2004.

82 Case C-366/99 *Griesmar* [2001] ECR I-9383.

83 See Art L. 12 of the *Code des Pensions civiles et militaires de retraite*.

84 For an overview of Dutch equal treatment law in employment see, for example, IP Asscher-Vonk and AC Hendriks (2005) *Gelijke behandeling en onderscheid bij de arbeid*, Deventer: Kluwer; SM Koelman (2005) *Algemene wet gelijke behandeling; Wet gelijke behandeling van mannen en vrouwen, Wet gelijke behandeling op grond van handicap en chronische ziekte, Wet gelijke behandeling op grond van leeftijd bij de arbeid*, Deventer: Kluwer; E Cremers-Hartman (2004) *Gelijke behandeling bij de arbeid in zes wetten. Een actueel overzicht van hoofdlijnen, overeenkomsten en verschillen*, Deventer: Kluwer; JH Gerards and AW Heringa (2003) *Wetgeving gelijke behandeling*, Deventer: Kluwer.

85 Article 120 of the Constitution. However, a proposal is pending before the First Chamber of Parliament which would amend this Article to permit a review of laws in the light of Art 1 (and certain other Articles of the Constitution): *Kamerstukken II* 2001/02-2004/05 and *Kamerstukken I*, 2004/05-2006-2007, 28 331.

86 See, for example, JE Goldschmidt (1993) *We need different stories. Een ander verhaal in het recht. Verhalen van verschil*, Zwolle: WEJ Tjeenk Willink; T Loenen (1992) *Verschil in gelijkheid. De conceptualisering van het juridische gelijkheidsbeginsel met betrekking tot vrouwen en mannen in Nederland en in de Verenigde Staten*, Zwolle: WEJ Tjeenk Willink; R Holtmaat (1992) *Met zorg een recht? Een analyse van het politiek-juridisch betoog over het bijstandsrecht*, Zwolle: WEJ Tjeenk Willink; K Wentholt (1990) *Arbeid en zorg. Een verkenning vanuit het gelijkheidsbeginsel van de rechtspositie van werknemers met zorgverantwoordelijkheden*, Amsterdam: Universiteit van Amsterdam; A Veldman (1995) *Effectuering van sociaal-economisch recht volgens de chaostheorie*, dissertation, Utrecht; S Burri (2000) *Tijd delen. Deeltijd, gelijkheid en gender in Europees- en nationaal-rechtelijk perspectief*, Deventer: Kluwer; JH Gerards (2002) *Rechterlijke toetsing aan het gelijkheidsbeginsel: een rechtsvergelijkend onderzoek naar een algemeen toetsingsmodel*, Maastricht: Universiteit Maastricht.

87 R Holtmaat (1999) 'The issue of overtime payments for part-time workers in the *Helmig* case: Some thoughts on equality and gender', in Y Kravaritou (ed) *The*

Regulation of Working Time in the European Union; Gender Approach, Brussels: Peter Lang, pp 411–44.

88 Legislation is available at http://wetten.overheid.nl/cgi-bin/sessioned/browser-check/continuation=05495-002/session=026424107520009/action=javascript-result/javascript=yes (accessed 12 January 2008).

89 An English translation of most of these provisions can be found on the website of the ETC (www.cgb.nl). available at www.cgb.nl/legislation.php.

90 In the Dutch text, the term '*onderscheid*' is used, which means distinction or differentiation. But it is generally accepted that this term should be read as discrimination in the sense of the EC Directives.

91 Articles 90quater, 137d–f and 429quater.

92 Case C-102/88 *Ruzius-Wilbrink v Bestuur van de Bedrijfsvereniging voor Over-heidsdiensten* [1989] ECR 4311.

93 Case C-343/92 *Roks and others v Bestuur van de Bedrijfsvereniging voor de Gezondheid, Geestelijke en Maatschappelijke Belangen and others* [1994] ECR I-571 and Case C-280/94 *Posthuma-Van Damme* [1996] ECR I-179.

94 Case C-128/93 *Fisscher v Voorhuis Hengelo BV and Stichting Bedrijfspensioen-fonds voor de Detailhandel* [1994] ECR I-4583.

95 Case C-57/93 *Vroege v NCIV Instituut voor Volkshuisvesting BV and Stichting Pensioenfonds NCIV* [1994] ECR I-4541.

96 Article 2a of the *Pensioen- en spaarfondsenwet*, now Art 8 of the *Pensioenwet*.

97 *Wet verbod van onderscheid naar arbeidsduur*, *Stb*, 1996, 391.

98 C-78/93 *Helmig* [1994] ECR I-5727. See also above, p 219.

99 See R Holtmaat (1999) 'The issue of overtime payments for part-time workers in the *Helmig* case; Some thoughts on equality and gender', in Y Kravaritou (ed) *The Regulation of Working Time in the European Union; Gender Approach*, Brussels: Peter Lang, pp 411–44.

100 These non-binding opinions are published once a year, with comments of various experts regarding each ground of discrimination: See, for example, S Burri (ed) (2006) *Gelijke behandeling: oordelen en commentaar 2005*, Nijmegen: Wolf Legal Publishers; and JH Gerards, BP Vermeulen and PJJ Zoontjes (2007) *Gelijke behandeling: oordelen en commentaar 2006*, Nijmegen: Wolf Legal Publishers.

101 Opinion 1998-55.

102 Rb. Utrecht, 3 May 2006, *LJN* AW7505, Rb. Utrecht, 3 May 2006, *LJN* AX1926.

103 However, the ETC and some district courts adopted a different approach: ETC opinion 2004-44, Vrz. RB. Utrecht, 27 May 2004, *LJN* AP0146 and Vrz. Rb. Utrecht, 15 November 2005, *LJN* AU6168.

104 Hof Den Haag, 19 October 2006, *LJN* AZo509.

105 ETC opinion 98-134, Ktr. Middelburg, 6 September 1999, *JAR* 1999/201 and Ktr. Middelburg, 10 January 2000, *JAR* 2000/93, Rb. Zwolle, 31 March 2000, *TAR* 2000/84, Ktr. Apeldoorn, 7 June 2000, *JAR* 2000/157; Ktr. Lelystad, 10 January 2001, *JAR* 2001/89, Rb. Middelburg, 4 April 2001, *NJ* 2001/545.

106 Case C-136/95 *Caisse nationale d'assurance vieillesse des travailleurs salariés (CNAVTS) v Thibault* [1998] ECR I-2011; Case C-394/96 *Brown v Rentokil Ltd* [1998] ECR I-4185; and Case C-411/96 *Boyle and others v Equal Opportunities Commission* [1998] ECR I-6401.

107 CRvB 17 May 2001, *LJN* AB1704; CRvB 17 May 2001 *LJN* AE8632; CRvB 17 July 2001, *LJN* AB2690.

108 HR 2 August 2002, *JAR* 2002/206, HR 9 August 2002, *LJN* AF2180 and HR 9 August 2002, *JAR* 2002/207.

109 Hof Den Haag, 15 July 2005, *LJN* AU1871.

110 Case C-342/01 *Merino Gómez v Continental Industrias del Caucho SA* [2004] ECR I-2605.

111 See M Bobek, P Boučková and Z Kühn (eds) (2007) *Rovnost a discriminace*, Prague: Beck, p 5. This was at least the situation from a legal point of view.

112 L Rovná, referring to J Šiklová (Professor of sociology at the Charles University and a leading figure in gender studies in the Czech Republic), unpublished paper, presented at the Jean Monnet Conference on 'Gender Equality and the New European Union', Brussels, 4 March 2003.

113 M Bobek, P Boučková and Z Kühn (eds) (2007) *Rovnost a discriminace*, Prague: Beck, p 104.

114 For a discussion in English on the situation in the Czech Republic see, *inter alia*, the now somewhat outdated report by B Havelková (2005) 'Equal opportunities for women and men, monitoring law and practice in Czech Republic 2005', Open Society Institute Network Women's Program, available at www.soros.org/initiatives/women/articles_publications (accessed 5 December 2007), B. Havelková (2008) 'Challenges to the effective implementation of EC gender equality law in the Czech Republic – an early analysis', in K Arioli, M Cottier, P Farahmand and Z Küng (eds) *Wandel der Geschlechterverhältnisse durch Recht?*, Zürich: DIKE (forthcoming) and the regular contributions by K Koldinská to the reports of the Commission's Network of legal experts in the fields of employment, social affairs and equality between men and women and the Network's Bulletin 'Legal Issues in Gender Equality', available at http://ec.europa.eu/employment_social/gender_equality/legislation/bulletin_en.html (accessed 5 December 2007).

115 M Bobek, P Boučková and Z Kühn (eds) (2007) *Rovnost a discriminace*, Prague: Beck, p 225.

116 Ibid, p 105. Symptomatic in this respect is the way in which the draft for the Anti-discrimination Act was rejected by the Parliament. See on this B Havelková (2008) 'Challenges to the effective implementation of EC gender equality law in the Czech Republic – an early analysis', in K Arioli, M Cottier, P Farahmand and Z Küng (eds) *Wandel der Geschlechterverhältnisse durch Recht?*, Zürich: DIKE (forthcoming).

117 Bobek *et al*, ibid, p 105.

118 Edited by Bobek *et al*, ibid, which was indeed of great help when writing this section on the Czech Republic.

119 In the area of gender equality, there are some more sociological or sociology of law publications.

120 A detailed overview of implementing the EU non-discrimination directives into Czech law is given by Kristina Koldinská, Chapter 11, in this book.

121 Act no 435/2004. Other acts we mention only in passing are the Act on State Service (employment of civil servants) from 2002, the Act on Civil Servants in the Regions and Municipalities (2002) and the Act on Service in the Security Forces (2003).

122 Act no 65/1965.

123 See, A Sloat (2004) *Legislating for Equality: The Implementation of the EU Equality Acquis in Central and Eastern Europe*, Jean Monnet Working Paper 08/04, New York, p 14.

124 No doubt, pro-natalist policies played a part here too. See, however, also the special protection of women and mothers in France. This, too, was never defined in terms of equal treatment.

125 Act no 262/2006.

126 K Koldinská (2005) 'Contribution on the Czech Republic', in *Bulletin*, 1: 22, available at http://ec.europa.eu/employment_social/gender_equality/legislation/bulletin_en.html (accessed 5 December 2007). See also B Havelková (2006) 'Law and equality for men and women', in P Pavlik (ed) *Shadow Report on Equal Treatment and Equal Opportunities for Women and Men, 2006*, Open Society

Fund Prague, available at www.osf.cz/en/ (accessed 8 October 2007), p 50. It should be noted that the concept of indirect (sex) discrimination appeared for the very first time in the Czech legal system in 1997, when the Czech Republic proceeded with a harmonisation of its laws under the Association Agreement with the EU. However, here again, it was not defined any further.

127 Sněmovní tisk 253 Vlnz o rovném zacházení a ochraně před diskriminací – EU.

128 See also M Bobek, P Boučková and Z Kühn (eds) (2007) *Rovnost a discriminace*, Prague: Beck, p 89.

129 It must also be pointed out that there was a 'political' reason behind the failure of the draft, namely a coalition of right wing and Euro-sceptical liberals and the Communist party who were opposed to the legislation.

130 As are also other aspects defined in the EU Directives, such as harassment, sexual harassment and instructions to discriminate.

131 Details of the protective measures are worked out in other pieces of legislation, such as the Labour Code, Arts 238 *et seq.*

132 Article 7(2) allows for measures which aim to prevent or equalise disadvantages which are the consequence of belonging to a 'discriminated' group, and which safeguard equal treatment and equal opportunities; Art 7(3) prohibits, as far as access to employment is concerned, preferential treatment of persons who are less qualified for the job than other applicants.

133 Obviously, there are more relevant laws which we do not discuss here.

134 See M Bobek, P Boučková and Z Kühn (eds) (2007) *Rovnost a discriminace*, Prague: Beck, pp 206–7.

135 Ibid, pp 103–8 and 207–9 and B Havelková (2005) 'Equal Opportunities for Women and Men, Monitoring law and practice in Czech Republic 2005', Open Society Institute Network Women's Program, available at www.soros.org/initiatives/women/articles_publications (accessed 5 December 2007).

136 Clearly illustrated by Case C-161/06 *Skoma-Lux v Celní ředitelství Olomouc* [2007] ECR I-0000 (not yet reported).

137 Case US 37/04 (case of a Roma individual who was not served in a restaurant), Jurisprudence 2006, pp 51–7 (comment by Z Kühn). See also B Havelková (2007) 'Burden of proof and positive action in the Czech and Slovak Constitutional Courts', *European Law Review*: 686–704.

138 At least insofar as it is available, which is another problem. See B Havelková (2006) 'Law and equality for men and women' in Pavlik (ed) *Shadow Report on Equal Treatment and Equal Opportunities for Women and Men, 2006*, Open Society Fund Prague, available at www.osf.cz/en/ (accessed 8 October 2007), p 51 and the regular contributions by Koldinská to the Bulletin 'Legal issues in gender equality', referred to in n 112 above.

139 See M Bobek, P Boučková and Z Kühn (eds) (2007) *Rovnost a discriminace*, Prague: Beck, p 252.

140 Ibid, p 209.

141 Case US 297/99, mentioned in Bobek *et al*, ibid, p 210. Meanwhile, the Grand Chamber of the ECtHR found that the same practices, which were at issue in US 297/89, constitute a breach of Art 14 of the ECHR, read in conjunction with Art 2 of Protocol No 1 (Case *DH and others v Czech Republic*, judgment of 13 November 2007). On the latter, more extensive comments are made in the contributions by Morag Goodwin, Chapter 7, and Kristina Koldinská, Chapter 11, in this book.

142 This seems to be common practice of many Central and East European Constitutional Courts. See Bobek *et al*, ibid, pp 106 and 178. A quick scan of the Constitutional Court discrimination cases available at the website www.judikatura.cz confirms this.

143 Available at www.judikatura.cz. Also published under no 405/2006.

144 The rules concern care for children up to four years. It should be noted that this possibility was introduced in 1996. Before that year, men could not benefit from these provisions in any circumstances.

145 The Constitutional Court understands the test of proportionality as relating to the question whether the measures are adequate and necessary to reach the stated aim.

146 For example, Case C-366/99 *Griesmar* [2001] ECR I-9383.

147 See US 36/05. A case in which the Constitutional Court was prepared to take into account an EU anti-Discrimination Directive is US 37/04, see n 137 above. Regardless of the broader debate on the application of EU law by constitutional courts in general and the Czech Constitutional Court, in particular, taking no account of EU anti-discrimination law, inextricably linked to the protection of human rights, would in our view be highly regrettable.

148 The Constitutional Court builds here on an earlier case, US 15/02, where it accepted preferential treatment for former miners since such treatment compensated for the extremely difficult, risky and demanding work in physical and psychological terms previously performed.

11 Multidimensional equality in the Czech and Slovak Republics

The case of Roma women

Kristina Koldinská

11.1 Introduction

Czechs and Slovaks shared a common history for more than 70 years. They underwent together the whole period of communism, which began in Czechoslovakia in February 1948; they lived together in hope, followed by the disillusion of the 1968 spring, and they peacefully gained common liberty in the Velvet Revolution of 1989. Due to political disagreement, both countries separated in 1993 establishing two new states – the Czech Republic and the Slovak Republic. Nevertheless, both states maintain very good relationships and have a very similar legal system. On 1 May 2004, both states joined the EU together with eight other states.

Within the process of approximating Czech and Slovak law to EC law, probably the most difficult challenge in the area of social law was the implementation of Directives on equal opportunities and anti-discrimination measures. In fact, implementing EC legislation on equal opportunities addressed an entirely new theme that had not been covered by Czech or Slovak legislation until preparations started to be made for entry into the EU.[1] The lack of legislation is very closely connected to the lack of public awareness on equal opportunities. It is very difficult to assess whether lack of legislation resulted in little public awareness, or the minor importance of this issue for the public led to the lack of legislation. This chapter attempts to approach the matter from both perspectives. The chapter will therefore focus first on legal issues and demonstrate some of the difficulties faced when implementing European equal opportunities legislation.

As the theme of this book is multidimensional equality law, the second part of this chapter will try to move the argument a step forward by focusing on this issue in both states. We understand multidimensional equality law to be a body of law that aims at equality in relation to a multiplicity of grounds on which discrimination is prohibited. On the other hand, we consider multidimensional discrimination to occur when a person is treated differently on more than one ground.[2] The situation of Roma women will be discussed as an example of a field in which multidimensional equality law is urgently needed in both states. This issue will be discussed from the legal point of view, as well as from the socio-economic point of view. Recent experience in ensuring equal opportunities for Roma women will be examined before proposing certain measures to protect them against discrimination.

These experiences of both states and their different approaches to the problem may contribute to answering the question of how far and in what way the experience of some new Member States may contribute to further reflections on multidimensional equality in Europe.

11.2   Equality: a new concept for the Czech and Slovak societies

As I have already mentioned, implementing European legislation on equal treatment was quite a demanding exercise for the Czech and Slovak Republics.

The concept of equality was, of course, not entirely unknown to both societies. Some Czechoslovak philosophers and politicians strongly supported the idea of equality between men and women and of equal treatment for ethnic and national minorities.[3] The Czechoslovak Constitution from 1920 guaranteed to women and national minorities the right to vote and the concept of equality as a basic democratic principle was mentioned. This concept remained merely a constitutionally guaranteed right, however, without further elaboration in specific legislation. Amongst other matters, the Second World War demonstrated the non-acceptance of the concept of national and ethnic equality within Czechoslovak society, whereas the period of Communist rule saw a hardening of the inequality between men and women (and also among ethnic and national minorities) in society. Inequality was a factual element of socialist society, even if rhetoric declared the opposite to be true.

Therefore, it is possible to argue that the concept of equality never had a real chance to take root in Czech and Slovak societies. That is why for both states, the requirement to implement EC legislation on equal opportunities appeared to offer new chances not only for national legislation, but also for society as a whole – a chance to change the legislative corpus by incorporating an important concept, a chance to start a serious discussion which would engage the whole society and thus to change some inequality stereotypes which prevailed within society.

As new EU Member States, the Czech and Slovak Republics were in an easier position than the old Member States. They inherited a well-developed complex of equal opportunities legislation, interpreted by a broad apparatus of European Court of Justice (ECJ) case law which could be used to good effect in implementing the relevant Directives. On the other hand, the new Member States had to accept and implement an existing legislative package, the *acquis communautaire*, without having the opportunity (as the old Member States had had) to follow the maturing of the equal opportunities concept and to implement the EC legislation step by step. For this reason, it is obvious, that there was (and still is) a high probability, that the new Member States will need some years to 'digest' the whole concept of equal opportunities, as defined by the EU. In the second part of this chapter, a symptomatic example of this need for digestion time will be presented from the socio-economic point of view.

Both states – the Czech Republic and Slovakia – made a good start by transposing the Equal Opportunities Directives into national legislation. In the following part of this chapter, the transposition process will be examined in more detail.

11.3 Anti-discrimination measures in Czech and Slovak labour law: transposition of relevant EC Directives

When the accession process began, both states modified their labour legislation and implemented the relevant Community Directives regarding equal opportunities, amending, in particular, their labour codes, employment acts and other regulations. At the same time, both states attempted to adopt a universal anti-discrimination act. In this regard Slovakia was more successful. As the manner, form and style of implementation of EC legislation on equal opportunities is quite interesting, it would seem instructive to present a small overview on the implementation in both states. From the following overview it may become more apparent that both states adopted a simple (and not incorrect) manner of implementing EC legislation by (in some cases) incorporating word for word whole parts of relevant Directives. Further reflection on ensuring equality and multidimensional equality in new Member States may be easier as a result of these changes.

11.3.1 Implementation of anti-discrimination measures in the Czech Republic

In the Czech Republic, equal opportunities in labour relations are currently addressed, in particular, by the Labour Code, the Employment Act, the Act on Labour Inspectorates and some other Acts. As from 2000, the labour legislation was amended in order to harmonise it with EC equal opportunities legislation. The aim of that task was, of course, the same as that pursued by the Directives, which is to ensure equality and equal treatment especially in labour relations.

11.3.1.1 Law at present

At present, the most extensive legislation on equal treatment can be found in the Employment Act. Article 4 of the Act No 435/2004 on employment contains a legal definition of direct and indirect discrimination and discrimination grounds, and sets out circumstances in which ostensibly discriminatory conduct is deemed not to be discrimination.[4]

Understandably, however, the Act on employment only concerns legal relations relating to employment policy. Section 4(1) of the Act on employment provides that[5] 'the participants in legal relations of employment shall be obliged to ensure the equal treatment of all natural persons exercising the right to work'.[6] The Act on employment applies only to legal relations arising in connection with recruitment. Therefore, it applies, for example, to discrimination arising during the selection process for a particular position.

The Act, which is expected to provide protection against discrimination within employment relationships, is the new Act No 262/2006, the Labour Code. As it was expected that the legislature would adopt the anti-discrimination Act,[7] the new Labour Code contains merely a general definition of equal opportunities and employer obligations in that regard.[8] The previous Labour Code regulated equal opportunities and the prohibition on discrimination much more extensively. It included all the legal definitions relating to direct and indirect discrimination, harassment and sexual harassment. These matters were removed since the whole issue of discrimination was expected to appear within the anti-discrimination Act.

As regards the monitoring of employer behaviour in the area of equal opportunities, the Act No 251/2005 on labour inspection transferred powers relating to equal treatment from labour offices, the Czech public employment service (which previously supervised activities of employers in this area), to the newly established labour inspectorates.[9] The Act on labour inspection defines, *inter alia*, misdemeanours by natural persons and administrative offences which may be committed by legal persons in the area of equal treatment.[10]

There are some other special laws and Acts guaranteeing equal rights, in particular equality between men and women – for example, in the area of social security and regarding parental leave.

Equal access to education is guaranteed by the Act No 561/2004 on education in primary, secondary and specialist schools (s 2 defines equal access to education free from any discrimination as a fundamental principle of the education system) and also by the Act No 111/1998 on high schools and universities.

Equal access to goods and services is guaranteed, for example, by the Act No 634/1992 on consumer protection, s 6 prohibits discrimination in access to public services and goods), the Act No 257/2001 on libraries and conduct of public library and information services (s 2 sets out that all library and information services must be provided ensuring equal access to those services free from any distinction), the Act No 42/1994 on private pension insurance (s 2a prohibits any type of discrimination against any insured person, ignoring for those purposes any discrimination on grounds of sex arising through the use of sex-based tables on life expectancy in the calculation of pension entitlement'), the Act No 64/1986 on the Czech market supervision authority (s 2 allocates the competence to the Czech market supervision authority to determine whether fair conditions – including a prohibition on discrimination – are observed in the provision of goods and services).[11]

11.3.1.2 Anti-discrimination Act proposal

As indicated, a new anti-discrimination Act has been in preparation for several years. However, the first Bill of 2006 was unsuccessful. The new draft of 2007 aims to be a universal measure governing all aspects of equal treatment and is intended to implement all the relevant Directives relating to this issue. The draft has been passed by Parliament and the President's signature is expected in 2008. The Act is expected to set out definitions of direct and indirect discrimination, define discriminatory grounds, and to regulate certain aspects of the fight against discrimination. There are, however, no special provisions on multidimensional equality. If multidimensional discrimination occurs, the only means of legal recourse is to claim a multidimensional breach of the Act.

As in the previous draft, it is envisaged that the authority which will oversee equal treatment and equal opportunities compliance will be the Czech ombudsman.[12] Its office shall play the role of an independent body overseeing the application of the equal treatment principle in accordance with the requirements of the relevant Directives. When this aspect of the equal opportunities legislation was being discussed, proposals for the establishment of a new specialist independent authority failed to be accepted, mainly out of concern for public administration costs. Broadening the powers of the ombudsman's office was seen as the most economical solution.[13]

Despite some shortcomings in the Czech legislation which may still be found in the area of equality, it may be assumed nonetheless that Czech law has implemented the Directives governing equal treatment and equal opportunities. However, it will take several years for equal treatment to become a matter of course for society itself. As regards the concept of multidimensional equality, no special measure is to be found in the Czech legal system. Nevertheless, it is possible to claim protection for individual rights in cases of multidimensional discrimination, by basing such a claim on more than one ground of discrimination.

11.3.2 Implementation of anti-discrimination measures in the Slovak Republic

The situation with regard to discrimination law is much clearer in Slovakia. That is because Slovakia was able to adopt an anti-discrimination Act in 2004, that is to say, a general regulation governing all aspects of equal treatment and the prohibition on discrimination.

The Act No 365/2004 on equal treatment and on protection against discrimination applies to the following areas:

- social security and healthcare;
- the provision of goods and services;
- education;
- labour and equivalent relations.

The most extensive part of the Act is devoted to compliance with the principle of equal treatment in labour relations. In that area, discrimination is prohibited on grounds of gender, religious persuasion or faith, racial origin, national or ethnic origin, disability, age, and sexual orientation. In this context, the principle of equal treatment is applied in conjunction with existing labour law rights.

The Act provides a more detailed definition of gender-based discrimination where discrimination is based on pregnancy or motherhood,[14] and of disability-based discrimination in access to employment or career advancement.[15]

As is the case with the Czech legislation, no provision exists on multidimensional equality and thus, if any multidimensional discrimination occurs, legal recourse is possible only by invoking several provisions of the Antidiscrimination Act or other special acts.

In procedural terms, the Act lays down the right for all persons, not just Slovak citizens, to seek the cessation of discriminatory conduct before a court, more specifically a civil court. The burden of proof is on the person who is alleged to have violated the principle of equal treatment. The Act does not introduce a special independent body or authority to oversee equal opportunities. However, it amends the Act No 308/1993 on the Establishment of the Slovak National Centre for Human Rights, extending the competences of that body to include equal opportunities issues. Overall, the Act is somewhat chaotic and unsystematic, which in turn diminishes legal certainty in this area. On the other hand, it undoubtedly constitutes a positive step in the sense that it gives Slovak law a single comprehensive piece of legislation, chiefly aimed at implementing EC law in this area.

The Act No 311/2001, the Labour Code, contains general provisions concerning equal treatment and related obligations on employers. In doing so, the Labour Code refers to the Anti-discrimination Act. Section 13 of the Labour Code thus contains merely a general provision to the effect that in labour relations employers are obliged to treat employees in accordance with the principle of equal treatment. Additionally, it affords employees the right to complain to their employer in connection with a violation of the principle of equal treatment and the employer's obligation to respond to the complaint without undue delay, to redress the situation, to refrain from such conduct, and to eliminate any consequences arising there from.[16]

The Act No 5/2004 on employment services does not deal with equal treatment at any great length. Section 13 merely regulates the obligation on the Labour Office (public employment service) to inform jobseekers of their right to equal treatment in access to employment.

The Slovak legislation on equal treatment appears to be a little simpler than its Czech counterpart, in particular, on account of the fact that the Slovak legislation already contains a single piece of legislation on equal treatment – the Anti-discrimination Act. Slovakia implements the main requirements of the EC Equal Treatment Directives chiefly through this Act, although other legislation also exists, containing special provisions on equality.

As is the case with the Czech legal system, the Slovak legislation does not contain any provision on multidimensional equality, thus not even in the Slovak legal system is this concept well known.

11.3.3 Legal guarantees: are they adequate to introduce equal opportunities?

Whereas in the Czech Republic special acts constitute the primary legal source in the area of equal treatment, in Slovakia these regulations merely complement the general Anti-discrimination Act, and this may be seen as an advantage. Both countries' experiences demonstrate, however, that the form taken by anti-discrimination rules is not the most important aspect in protection against discrimination. EC anti-discrimination rules are de facto implemented in both countries.

As both states have transposed practically all the requirements of the Directives into their legal orders, the anti-discrimination dimension is stressed very much in both states. It may be considered a major success that within a few years both states are on the verge of applying their own specialised anti-discrimination Acts (indeed, Slovakia already applies such legislation).

To date, a legal framework has been established, equal treatment has been legally defined and instruments for individuals seeking to enforce their equal treatment rights have been developed. The adoption of anti-discrimination measures in both countries may be understood as a very important step on the way towards equality for all, setting as it does a commonly accepted standard for society as whole. It is a significant achievement that the journey has already been commenced and the legislation provides good opportunities to continue along that route.

However, both societies now face a far tougher challenge, that of putting the legal rules into practice and establishing the principle of equal treatment and equal opportunities in the life of society as a whole. In order to overcome the historical 'handicap' of the Member States with regard to equal treatment, it is necessary to encourage a change of mentality within society and to 'download' the concept of equal opportunities into normal ways of thinking. The present legal framework, implemented in accordance with the Directives' requirements, may not be sufficiently robust to achieve that ambitious aim.

From the text above, it may be concluded that the legislation in both states predominantly (and in some areas exclusively) comprises anti-discrimination measures. In both legal systems, the possibility to react or respond in a defensive manner against discrimination has been enacted, but there is little (or sometimes even no) space for a proactive approach to equality as such. A question arises here: are anti-discrimination measures framed around an individual litigation approach adequate to promote the principle of equality within society? In this respect, some authors[17] have already suggested that there are limits to the anti-discrimination approach. According to McCrudden:

> this approach is not primarily concerned with the general effect of decisions on groups. It is markedly individualistic: concentrating on securing fairness for the individual . . . The individual justice model is said to misconceive the deep structure of discrimination in some contexts, such as discrimination against women.

The Czech and Slovak experiences may well confirm this view (as will be explained below in more detail).

In order actively to promote equality, the possibility exists to adopt additional instruments aimed at reinforcing the anti-discrimination measures which may be used in individual legal relations, complemented by some further measures focused on certain aspects of society as a whole. Such so-called 'proactive measures' have recently been discussed together with positive duties and are seen by some as constituting a new approach to equality law. Positive duties are presented as offering an alternative to an individual complaints-led model with its known limitations. The idea is to go beyond the so-called 'anti-discrimination model' and to 'develop effective mechanisms designed to bring about substantial equality and recognition of the needs of disadvantaged groups'.[18] In another work, Fredman distinguishes between an individual complaints led-model based on a traditional view of human rights and a proactive model, aiming at institutional changes, pointing to the proactive model's dependency on policy as one of its weaknesses.[19] Each type of legal subject – public institution, employer, non-governmental organisation (NGO) or individual – may be engaged within proactive measures. McCrudden understands the proactive promotion of equality of opportunity as a situation, where 'certain public authorities are placed under a duty actively to take steps to promote greater equality of opportunity and good relations for particular groups'.[20]

Today, in both countries under examination, it seems to be very important to develop a really effective proactive strategy in favour of equality.

Naturally, some concrete measures in favour of ensuring equal opportunities would have to start at the point where legal measures and their attendant impact ends. In pursuit of that approach perhaps one should start by examining a concrete and obvious case of discrimination, identifying its grounds and main causes and subsequently propose some methods better to ensure equal opportunities for that discriminated group. The second part of this chapter aims to provide some assistance in this regard.

Following our clarification of the implementation of EC equal opportunities legislation (which can be generally assessed as thorough and successful) and certain reflections on the efficiency of purely legal measures in the area of equality, it may be useful to examine also non-legal strategies, as a second step towards the achievement of substantive equality. In order to illustrate my reflections below in context, the concrete situation of Roma women has been selected as an example.

11.4 Multidimensional discrimination in the Czech and Slovak Republics: the situation of Roma women

In the second part of this chapter, I aim to focus on the second step towards equality in practice. Whereas the first step appears to be achieved through law, the second one presupposes reflection on some proactive strategies. In order to set our reflections within a specific context, the situation of Czech and Slovak Roma women may be examined.

Having regard to their relatively long period of common history both countries have a similar ethnic structure and, therefore, both countries have a significant population of Roma, a nation which has traditionally suffered discrimination. The situation of Roma women would appear, therefore, to be worthy of closer examination. Moreover, it constitutes a 'classical' example of a complex situation, which can be understood and solved better, if the concept of multidimensional equality is effectively applied.

The example of Roma women and their socio-economic situation is used in this chapter also to show that multidimensional equality is not only a legal concept and that in some situations legal instruments (described in the first part of this chapter) may not be robust and effective enough to ensure equality or multidimensional equality within society. Let us propose a hypothesis in this regard, to the effect that at least in some new Member States; legislation which is not complemented by proactive strategies may fail to ensure multidimensional equality within society.

As has been shown in the first part of this chapter, legal instruments already exist which may be invoked in order to achieve protection against discrimination and to claim equal treatment. The situation of Roma women, described below in more detail, proves, however, that the possibility to invoke legal protection does not of itself automatically change social stereotypes and negative attitudes. In order to achieve real change, it may be necessary to use not only legal, but also other instruments.

11.4.1 A short overview on the situation of Roma in the Czech and Slovak Republics: some basic facts

Both states, the Czech and Slovak Republics, are strongly criticised because of the situation of their Roma population. In both countries the Roma people constitute a significant minority of the whole population – in Slovakia they represent some 7 per cent (some 380,000) and in the Czech Republic some 3 per cent (some 300,000). In both countries, Roma live in very poor conditions; especially in Slovakia there are segregated suburbs, districts or whole villages, often without electricity and water, despite the fact that these areas house an estimated population of 124,000 inhabitants.

A recently published study on the living conditions of Roma households in Slovakia shows that the general situation of Roma is currently quite poor.[21] The study states that within Roma communities a high level of dependency on social benefits exists, whilst 73 per cent of households live in material poverty.

In the Czech Republic, a larger part of the Roma population is to a greater extent integrated in housing terms and is resident in houses or apartment blocks. This fact does not mean, however, that the situation of the Roma in the Czech Republic is much better than in Slovakia. In 2006 a quite shocking study[22] was published, according to which some 80,000 people in the Czech Republic live in some 300 localities, which may be described as ghettos. Most of those people are Roma. The following map shows the localities which were defined as ghettos (see Figure 11.1).[23]

Another two maps show the interaction between ghettoised locality and relatively high levels of unemployment and dependency on social benefits. The second map clearly shows that especially in northern Bohemia, where the level of unemployment has long been very high, there is also a heavy concentration of Roma-segregated localities. This would appear to imply a connection between poor social situation (unemployment) and social exclusion (segregation) (see Figure 11.2)

The last map simply confirms the previous observation. The more difficult the social situation and the greater the dependency on social benefits is, the greater the probability that social exclusion and segregation will be found to exist (see Figure 11.3).

It should be stressed already at this point, that all the maps above express another fact, which is important for the further development of this chapter. According to the study cited, all the segregated localities are almost exclusively inhabited by Roma. It is obvious, however, that areas with a high unemployment rate and thus with a high dependency on social benefits are populated not only by Roma. This leads to the conclusion that Roma-segregated localities exist not only because of social problems, but probably also because of inequality and unequal treatment, which in turn results in segregation and practical exclusion from the majority society.

Living in a segregated area impacts strongly also on the life of women. Roma women are subject to multidimensional discrimination in both countries – they share the difficult situation of the Roma population in general, but the situation of Roma women is even worse, as will be explained in the following text.

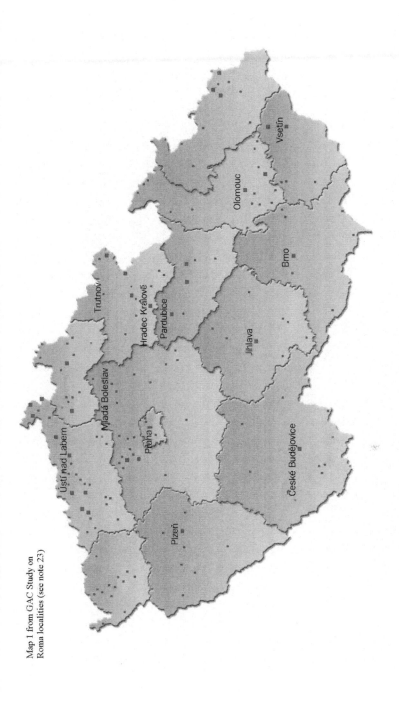

Map 1 from GAC Study on
Roma localities (see note 23)

Figure 11.1 Socially excluded Roma localities.

Source: Gabal Analysis and Consulting, analysis of social excluded Roma localities, 2006: Map 1

Note: On the map, a bigger square indicates city with more than three localities of social exclusion, a smaller square indicates a city with one or two excluded localities.

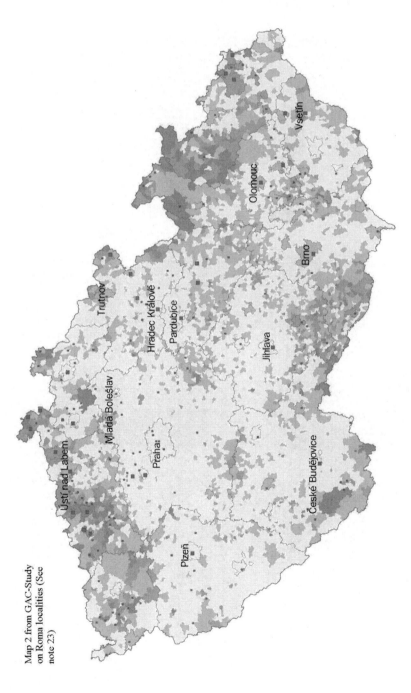

Figure 11.2 Unemployment in socially excluded Roma localities.

Source: Gabal Analysis and Consulting, analysis of social excluded Roma localities, 2006: Map 2

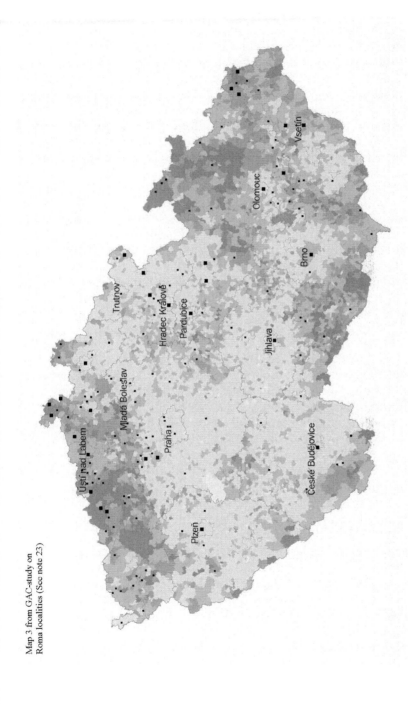

Figure 11.3 Dependency on social benefits in socially excluded Roma localities.

Source: Gabal Analysis and Consulting, analysis of social excluded Roma localities, 2006: Map 3

11.4.2 Roma women in the Czech and Slovak Republics

According to a report of the European Parliament on the situation of Roma women in the EU:[24]

> Roma women face prejudice in hiring, promotion and salary. Moreover, many Roma women remain entirely excluded from the formal economy, constrained by limited educational opportunities, inadequate housing and poor healthcare, traditional gender rules and general marginalization from the majority communities. The unemployment rate among adult Roma women is in some places many times higher than that of the majority population . . . on the topic of multiple discrimination, which affects Roma women, the language used in EU legislation is ambiguous. It also does not address discrimination based on nationality, which is used as an excuse for continued discrimination of Roma.

In the following text, attention will be paid to the position of Roma women in education and in the labour market, which can be understood as examples of additive discrimination. Finally, the problem of involuntarily sterilisations of Roma women will be mentioned as an example of intersectional discrimination of Roma women.[25] In all of the above situations, Roma women are facing inequality and discrimination, on grounds of race and ethnic origin and of sex.

11.4.2.1 Poor access to education

Roma people in general face many problems already at a very early age – during their first years in the education system. A majority of Roma pupils in the Czech Republic and in the Slovak Republic go to 'special' schools which primarily exist for the education of children with learning difficulties.

In Slovakia, there is no statistical data on this topic. A recent report by Amnesty International, however, indicates that there appears to be a segregated school system in Slovakia, especially in eastern parts of the country. According to the report, in that region, in almost all localities the school system is 100 per cent segregated and parents do not have the possibility to choose a school for their child.[26]

The Czech government estimates that some 75 per cent of Roma children go to a 'special' school.[27] It is obvious that this fact does not result from lower levels of intelligence amongst Roma children. In the majority of cases, the reason why a Roma child is sent to a 'special' school is that the child has difficulties in following lessons and in behaving in an appropriate manner. Understandably, those difficulties experienced by many Roma children have their roots in substandard housing and in the extremely poor social situation of Roma families in general.

The practice by which Roma children are often sent to special schools has repercussions for the level of education of the Roma population in general. In Slovakia in 2004 there were more than 7,000 Roma children in such schools.

Table 11.1 Ethnic origin of secondary and university education students

	Roma	*Non-Roma*
Secondary school education	6.5%	25.7%
University education	0.6%	8.4%

Some interesting statistical data from 2004 exists[28] on the ethnic origin of students who completed secondary and university education (see Table 11.1).

Both countries have attempted alleviate this situation, in particular by introducing 'Roma pedagogical assistants' into primary schools. A Roma pedagogical assistant works individually with a Roma child in the class and helps him/her to follow the lessons and if necessary, clarifies the parts of the lesson, which were not clear to the child. Roma pedagogical assistants usually work with children during their first year at school and often constitute a great help to them in getting used to the school regime and in learning how to follow lessons. This method has reduced somewhat the percentage of Roma children sent to special schools. However, there are still not enough of these assistants in order to resolve the problem systematically.

Recently, the Grand Chamber of the European Court of Human Rights, overruling the Chamber decision of May 2006[29] decided a very important case in this regard. The judgment confirmed that Roma children had suffered discrimination through the authorities' decision to place them in a 'special' school.[30] In its decision, the court states that:

the applicants were placed in schools for children with mental disabilities where a more basic curriculum was followed than in ordinary schools and where they were isolated from pupils from the wider population. As a result, they received an education which compounded their difficulties and compromised their subsequent personal development instead of tackling their real problems or helping them to integrate into the ordinary schools and develop the skills that would facilitate life among the majority population. Since it has been established that the relevant legislation as applied in practice at the material time had a disproportionately prejudicial effect on the Roma community, the Court considers that the applicants as members of that community necessarily suffered the same discriminatory treatment. Consequently, there has been a violation in the instant case of Article 14 of the Convention, read in conjunction with Article 2 of Protocol No. 1, as regards each of the applicants.[31]

The court admitted that the applicants have sustained non-pecuniary damage as a result of the humiliation and frustration caused by the indirect discrimination of which they were victims and assessed this damage sustained by each of the applicants at €4,000.

Roma women in general have even less access to education than Roma men. Within the Roma community, gender stereotypes tend to be rather strict, and many Roma (including women) believe that the primary task of women is to marry early and give birth to many children.[32] Low levels of educational achievement are a major contributory factor to the low level of employability of Roma, especially women.

11.4.2.2 Poor access to the labour market

Perhaps one of the most significant aspects of multidimensional inequality faced by Roma women can be observed in the area of employment. The labour market is barely accessible to Roma women.

Figures presented in Figure 11.4 clearly demonstrate that there is a strong inequality faced by Roma women in the labour market. In the Czech Republic, the unemployment rate is currently quite low. However, Roma women face an average unemployment rate of around 45 per cent, while women in the majority population in close proximity to Roma are in general unemployed at a rate of only 4.5 per cent. Interestingly, the situation of Roma men is a little better. They still face a higher unemployment rate (some 26.3 per cent), but when contrasted with the unemployment rate of men from the majority population in close proximity to Roma (8.3 per cent) the difference between both groups is not as significant as it is in the case of women.[33]

In Slovakia, the Report on the Situation of the Roma Population[34] argues that the Roma population is more commonly than normal subject to long-term unemployment, which results in a reduction in the qualification attained and thus also in the employability of Roma. Among the Roma population, Roma women experience more difficulties in finding employment than men. Whilst 10.5 per cent of Roma men are employed (51.7 per cent of men in the majority population), only 4.6 per cent of Roma women are employed (41.2 per cent of women in the majority population).

Another much smaller study[35] argues that the risk of unemployment is 4.2 times higher for Roma than for the average population, whereas the risk of long-term unemployment is 5.2 times higher. Even worse is the situation of Roma women, who are less educated and often have to fulfil the social role of wife and mother starting at a very early age. If in those circumstances they ever find work, this is generally unqualified and low-paid. As a result, in many cases Roma women are totally dependent on social benefits.[36]

The above-mentioned disparities between Roma women and Roma men and also between Roma women and women from the majority population cannot be fully explained merely by the lower levels of educational attainment of Roma women. It is obvious that a good part of this inequality is caused by discrimination on grounds of ethnic origin and of sex. Here, without a doubt, multidimensional inequality is at play.

Roma women suffer discrimination at the hands of employers. In the 1990s, however, they were unequally treated – as Roma – also by the labour

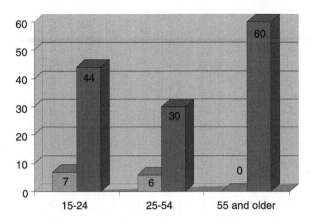

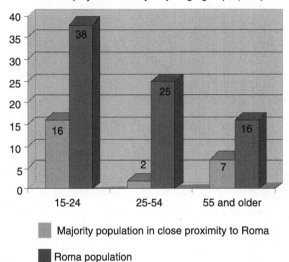

Figure 11.4 Czech Republic unemployment rate.

Source: Faces of Poverty, Faces of Hope, UNDP 2005

offices (public employment service) in the Czech Republic. Many of those offices permitted employers with job vacancies to state whether or not they accepted Roma. This information supplied by employers appeared on the list of vacancies available at the desk in the labour office. The vacancy was marked with 'R' (Roma accepted) or 'N' (no Roma accepted).

The Czech NGO 'Gender Studies' argues that there is profound discrimination against Roma women in the labour market, but notwithstanding the availability of legal instruments to fight this discrimination, they are in general not used, not even by Roma women who experience discrimination. Most activities in this area are undertaken by NGOs; government activities to combat gender stereotyping are inadequate.[37]

This evidence together with the statistics mentioned above would appear to confirm the argument already advanced that in some cases, especially in cases of multidimensional discrimination such as that faced by Roma women; legal instruments are insufficiently accessible to groups facing (multidimensional) inequality. Unfortunately, there are no statistics in this regard, since no data has been collected on litigation pursued by Roma or by Roma women.[38] There has also been no research whatsoever focusing on this issue. Nevertheless, at this point, some possible reasons may be advanced which seek to explain why Roma women do not use their right to claim a remedy when experiencing discrimination.

As a first problem the lack of information available to Roma women may be mentioned. Often, the women concerned are inadequately informed about their rights and about the possibility of taking legal action. Roma women generally also have little access to legal assistance, even though some NGOs are already active in this field providing pro bono legal assistance. Moreover, Roma women are part of Czech society which in general does not love litigation very much. Czech courts are overloaded and a case could also last for many years, with increasing procedural costs and an uncertain outcome.

These reflections may confirm my earlier suggestion that legal instruments should be accompanied by some other measures, which would aim at the better enforcement of individual rights and at implementing the equality principle into the life of society.

To sum up, there is no doubt that discrimination against Roma women does exist. There is also evidence that the discrimination occurs because people who are discriminated against are Roma and are women. In general, Roma are discriminated against on the ground of their ethnicity and there is discrimination in education as well as in the labour market. Women are also discriminated against on the ground of their sex and there is discrimination especially in the labour market.[39] The fact of being a woman and being Roma seem to add to each other. The intensity and frequency of discriminatory behaviour is enhanced, while both grounds are reinforcing each other. Discrimination in education and employment faced by Roma women may be called 'additive' discrimination, as there are more grounds of discrimination, which reinforce each other. In the specific case of Roma women, ethnic origin seems to have more bearing on their societal position than their gender. The ethnic discrimination seems to be more intense. In both countries, there are quite strong anti-Roma feelings (sometimes even expressed by violence against them). Gender discrimination against women compared with ethnic discrimination against Roma does not lead to violent episodes. Even if there is domestic violence against women in both countries, it is an excess within family life. Some violent episodes against Roma have their roots in general anti-Roma feelings in the society. However, being a woman reinforces the ethnic discrimination deriving from being ascribed a Roma ethnicity.

11.4.2.3 Specific example of discrimination against Roma women: involuntary sterilisation

To conclude this part of the chapter, it would seem important to mention one alarming example illustrating the consequences of the multidimensional discrimination which Roma women are facing, the practice of involuntary sterilisation. The following appears to take this chapter beyond the discourse on the implementation of the legal principles of equality and anti-discrimination in the labour market and in other areas; nevertheless it reveals close connections to the discrimination against Roma in general.

Involuntary sterilisation can be labelled as a consequence of multidimensional discrimination although not so widespread, but which exists in both countries. It occurred during the Communist era and even continued into the 1990s.

During the Communist era the sterilisation of Roma women was used as an instrument to regulate the demographic increase in the Roma population. Although after 1989 this practice was no longer widely used, regrettably in the Czech Republic there is one last case noted as late as 2001. This matter has been examined by the Czech ombudsman particularly in relation to the behaviour of the Ministry of Health as regards the hospitals which may perform involuntary sterilisations. In his report, he stated that protective legislation already exists, prohibiting involuntary sterilisations not justified by the health condition of a patient. He recommended changes to the current legislation in order to improve its application and enforcement. Furthermore, he strongly recommended the adoption of political and other measures and the payment of compensation to the victims.[40]

However, until now only a few women have received compensation. In the Czech Republic, two cases have recently been decided in this area. In the first case the hospital was ordered to apologise officially to the Roma women who had been involuntarily sterilised, and in the second case, the women concerned received financial compensation.[41] This was the first time ever in the Czech and Slovak Republic that financial compensation was paid as a result of involuntary sterilisation.

In both cases, the circumstances of the sterilisation of two very young Roma women (19 and 21 years old) were almost identical. This was their second pregnancy. The first time they gave birth by Caesarean section. Only a few minutes before the start of the second confinement, they were made to sign a request to be sterilised, without receiving appropriate information about the consequences of the sterilisation. Both women wanted to have other children, one of them even tried four times to get pregnant by *in vitro* fertilisation, but without success.

Both women applied for damages and in both cases the defendant argued that the claims were time-barred. In the first case, the Regional Court (*krajský soud*) and then the High Court found the right for damages was already time-barred as the applicant applied in 2005 for damages suffered in 2001 (the time limit is three years). In the second case, the Regional Court argued, however, that the right to non-pecuniary damages cannot be time-barred, as it is a personal right. The court assessed the damage at CZK 500,000 (some €17,500). The defendant's appeal against this decision is still pending.

It is worth mentioning that, among the courts which decided the cases, no one has discussed the discrimination in its reasoning. All the courts questioned only the correct application of the legislation on sterilisation relating to the human right to health (including the ability to get pregnant and to give birth) and to private life (including the possibility of raising one's own children). In addition to these, the UN Committee on the Elimination of Racial Discrimination (CERD) has called on the Czech Republic to accept responsibility and to facilitate access to justice for involuntarily sterilised women. The Committee also called for an information campaign among doctors in order to avoid such cases in the future.[42] In the same tone were recommendations directed to the Czech Republic, issued by the UN Committee on the Elimination of Discrimination Against Women (CEDAW). In this regard, the Committee urges the Czech Republic:

> to take urgent action to implement the recommendations of the Ombudsman with regard to involuntary or coercive sterilization, and adopt without delay legislative changes with regard to sterilization, including a clear definition of informed, free and qualified consent in cases of sterilization . . . and to provide ongoing and mandatory training of medical professionals and social workers on patients' rights; and elaborate measures of compensation to victims of involuntary or coercive sterilization.[43]

It should be noted that involuntary sterilisation is not only a case of discrimination against women (sterilising men would bring about the same result: infertility), but most certainly also a case of discrimination against Roma since there are no cases of involuntary sterilisation of non-Roma women. Gender issues are at stake here, as the stereotype of a 'good' Roma woman being a multiple mother plays a significant role in the consequences faced by sterilised women within their community.[44]

This type of discrimination is of a slightly different nature than the above-mentioned discrimination in the education and labour market. As this discrimination occurs in a specific part of healthcare and has consequences on the position of a sterilised woman within her community, the involuntary sterilisation of Roma women may be called 'intersectional discrimination'.

11.4.3 Insufficient answers at an EU-law level?

It seems appropriate to examine whether there are sufficient instruments provided by international law and European law in order to fight efficiently additive as well as intersectional discrimination.

International standards prohibiting racial discrimination have been defined in the Convention on the Elimination of all Forms of Racial Discrimination, adopted by the UN in 1965. Article 5 of this Convention obliges state parties to:

> prohibit and to eliminate racial discrimination in all its forms and to guarantee the right of everyone, without distinction as to race, colour, or national or ethnic origin, to equality before the law, notably in the enjoyment of the . . . economic, social and cultural rights, in particular . . . the rights to work, to free choice of employment, to just and favourable conditions of work, to protection against unemployment, to equal pay for equal work, to just and favourable remuneration; . . . the right to public health, medical care, social security and social services; the right to education and training.

Discrimination based on sex has been prohibited by the UN Convention on Elimination of All Forms of Discrimination against Women, adopted by the UN in 1979. Articles 10 and 11 state that states parties shall take all appropriate measures to eliminate discrimination against women in the fields of education and employment in order to ensure, on the basis of equality of men and women, the same rights. According to Art 12, 'States shall take all appropriate measures to eliminate discrimination against women in the field of healthcare in order to ensure, on a basis of equality of men and women, access to healthcare services, including those related to family planning'. From the provisions cited above it is clear that there are international instruments present in both conventions guaranteeing equality and equal treatment in education, labour market as well as in the field of healthcare. This means that the multiply and intersectional discrimination are covered by the international law. Application of the conventions is monitored by the respective committees and can be enforced to a certain extent.[45]

As regards enforcement, however, it would have been more efficient to provide protection against the above mentioned types of discrimination through the EU law. Its enforcement mechanism is much more efficient than the one of the Conventions. Moreover, European law plays a continuously more and more important role in defining European anti-discrimination standards. It is for two reasons: first, because of the increasing number of Directives adopted in the field of equal opportunities (it is one of the most dynamic fields of the European law); second, because of increasing number of Member States upon whom the Directives are binding.

There are also Directives covering discrimination on grounds of race and on grounds of sex. Let us shortly examine whether those Directives sufficiently cover the additive and intersectional discrimination of Roma women.

Council Directive 2000/43/EC[46] on racial discrimination within its scope applies to all persons, as regards both the public and private sectors, including public bodies, in relation to conditions for access to employment, to self-employment and to occupation, including selection criteria and recruitment conditions, whatever the branch of activity and at all levels of the professional hierarchy, including promotion, social protection, social security and healthcare and education.[47] This Directive covers discrimination in education, labour market and in healthcare, on grounds of race and ethnic origin.

A question remains whether there are similar instruments also in the Directive on discrimination on grounds of sex in order to protect against multiple and intersectional discrimination. Council Directive 76/2007/EEC as amended by Directive 2002/73/EC[48] forbids discrimination on grounds of sex in employment, vocational training and promotion, and working conditions, but there is no ban on discrimination in education. In this area, the EU law seems to fail in defending individuals against multiple discrimination in the area of education.

In order to examine the ban on discrimination on grounds of sex in the area of healthcare,[49] Council Directive 2004/113/EC[50] on equal treatment between men and women in the access to and supply of goods and services shall be examined. Paragraph 12 of the Preamble states that differences between men and women in the provision of healthcare services, which result from the physical differences between men and women, do not relate to comparable situations and therefore, do not constitute discrimination. As regards education (which could be defined as a special kind of service), Art 3, para 3 of the Directive excludes education from the scope of the Directive. This means that education is not covered by this Directive, whereas the healthcare may be covered in situations where differences between men and women do not result from the physical differences between them. The Directive thus provides a wide exception in regard to healthcare.[51]

To sum up, the EC law still fails in covering multiply and intersectional discrimination, whereas international law already provides instruments to protect people against these types of discrimination. Bearing in mind the fact that there may be other examples of additive and intersectional discrimination in European societies, not only against Roma women, one may suggest that a further development of EC law in this regard could be a positive step forward in ensuring equality in Europe.

As already mentioned many times in this chapter, better legal instruments should be compounded by some proactive measures. In the next section, one strategy already followed in Central and Eastern Europe will be shortly described.

11.4.4 Solutions currently proposed in the Czech and Slovak Republics

Whereas the situation of Roma is in both countries quite alarming (they are probably the largest group threatened by social exclusion, or, rather, the largest group already excluded), public action plans and other activities are mostly oriented towards the solution of problems of a general nature. Moreover, activities are limited, thus there remains little space or capacity for the promotion of multidimensional equality.

In both countries there are some governmental activities, and governmental subsidies and donations to NGOs which focus on some of the problems of Roma communities. The activities of local government are mainly restricted to issuing strategic documents and to the inclusion of both countries in the international initiative, the 'Decade of Roma Inclusion 2005–2015'.

Within the Decade project, eight central European countries are gathering forces in order to exchange best practices, consult on common problems and define some common steps. Included in this project, financed by the World Bank and the Open Society, are the following countries: Bulgaria, Croatia, Serbia, Montenegro, the Czech Republic, the Slovak Republic, Hungary, Macedonia and Romania. It is, however, more of a political platform which has formulated certain objectives, but is lacking in concrete tools to reach those objectives.

In 2007 a first report on applying the Decade in the European states has been published. Roma activists assessing the progress of the Decade rate it as a positive and useful tool; however, they mention also some weaknesses of the Decade – despite some progress, the Decade has not reached the critical point that would guarantee success. They call attention to the fact that most governments think about Roma inclusion in terms of projects and sporadic measures but not in terms of programmes or integrated policies. While Decade Action Plans have been adopted in most countries, they do not appear to inform government decision-making and policy planning as much as they could.[52]

In the Czech Republic, the government defined a strategy for the integration of Roma in 2005 and has also adopted a long-term strategy/concept for the integration of Roma for the period to 2025. Moreover, every year the Czech government provides a number of NGOs with subsidies in order to finance their projects focused on improving the situation of Roma.

In Slovakia, a National Action Plan of the Slovak Republic for the Decade of Roma Inclusion has been published, and the Slovak government, like the Czech government, finances the activities of NGOs with projects focused on the Roma population.

Accordingly, it follows that the major work concerning Roma in general and therefore also towards Roma women falls on the shoulders of NGOs, which could be interpreted as a sign of positive development within civic society. On the other hand, it must be investigated whether the activities of

NGOs respond adequately to the situation of the Roma population, including Roma women. In neither country is there a concept or document focused on multidimensional equality for Roma women.

To sum up, in the Czech Republic and in Slovakia, little or no attention is paid to multidimensional equality, even though it would appear to be a very important concept to both countries, at least having regard to the situation of Roma women.

It is very important, therefore, to find other ways in order to start resolving the problems and to act in favour of multidimensional equality.

11.5 Some recommendations in place of a conclusion

Instead of a conclusion, which is hard to draw as the discourse on multidimensional equality is in both countries at its very inception, some reflections and recommendations will be offered as an alternative.

First, in the second part of this chapter, the situation of Roma and Roma women in the Czech Republic and Slovakia has been described in some detail. Stress has been put on the social situation of Roma women, their position in the labour market, with regard to education and highlighting some consequences of their situation. It is very difficult to identify the concrete causes of their situation. However, it may be suggested that the social conditions in which they live are in good part a reflection of long-lasting discriminatory practices towards Roma women – on grounds of ethnic origin and of sex. Naturally, one can identify some other causes of their situation including their own traditional behaviour and historical errors towards the whole Roma people during the Communist era, the consequences of which are still felt today. However, without a doubt, the situation experienced by Roma women can be defined as a consequence of multidimensional discrimination, which in the cases mentioned in this chapter, may be called additive and intersectional discrimination.

Second, it would appear that the whole concept relating to the application and enforcement of rights to equality and equal treatment is a difficult one for the new Member States to digest. In this respect, multidimensional equality may seem to be something extra, something that is not yet for the new Member States. One might imagine that the important task at present is to try actually to implement the concept of equality as such into society and that when this is done we can start to think about multidimensional equality.

On the other hand, introducing and stressing this concept not only in law but through other instruments could help some new Member States to implement the concept of equality into the practical life of society within a short period, and possibly in a more effective manner. In this respect, new Member States could develop the concept of multidimensional equality more rapidly than old Member States, which have to develop it as an 'add-on' to structures and instruments established already. This may be regarded as a possible contribution of new Member States to the discussion on multidimensional equality in Europe, thus broadening and enriching European thinking on multidimensional equality in this respect.

As regards Roma women, some recommendations could be made for ensuring multidimensional equality.

• Governments should be the primary platform for promoting multi-dimensional equality regarding Roma women.

Multidimensional equality in general is quite a complicated issue with several aspects. Where it has to be applied, the activities and measures adopted ought to be co-ordinated and preferably follow a common concept. Therefore, it would improve effectiveness if national governments were the primary and unifying platform for promoting multidimensional equality.

• Governments should continue and, if necessary, insist on collaboration with NGOs in order to launch an information campaign on multidimensional equality, with the main part of this campaign focusing on Roma women. NGOs should continue monitoring and reporting on the situation of the Roma population, preferably with special attention to Roma women.

Governments ought only to represent a platform, co-ordinate activities and adopt certain framework measures. The specific activities, projects and studies ought to remain the responsibility of NGOs. The latter are more effective and flexible and, at least in some respects, are able to develop their activities in a more visible, and for society also more acceptable, manner.

• Continued collaboration between states with similar problems should be pursued. An appropriate platform for this collaboration is provided by the EU, possibly through the use of the open method of co-ordination (OMC).

International collaboration could effectively compound national activities and measures which seem to be necessary in the practical implementation of equality and multidimensional equality. The OMC might prove to be a good conduit for such collaboration, for example, by extending existing OMC related to gender and social exclusion (the European Employment Strategy and social inclusion policy).

The positive aspects of that approach are to be found in two features: first, it is not legislation, but nonetheless based on common agreement to which all Member States may contribute. Second, it is not overly binding, but is structured and regularly monitored such that Member States must become involved and report on their activities.

In general, legal measures and any anti-discrimination law need to be compounded by proactive strategies which are well designed, thus increasing their effectiveness.

Both types of measure, anti-discrimination strategies and proactive strategies, could regarded as 'two sides of the same coin' in that they both protect and promote equality in a broad sense. Both types of strategy need to be effective and interact with one another, in order to ensure that individual rights are protected and enforceable and that the principle of equality becomes firmly rooted as a human right within society. At least in two new Member States, the Czech Republic and the Slovak Republic, that approach appears to represent a good strategy for implementing multidimensional equality.

Notes

1 Both states introduced the principle of equality into their constitutions but did not adopt any special legislation in this regard.

2 For a wider discussion of the notions of multidimensional equality and multidimensional discrimination see the contribution of D Schiek (with V Chege), Chapter 1, in this book.

3 E.g. Tomáš Garique Masaryk, Františka Plamínková, Karel Čapek, etc. writing in the 1920s and 1930s.

4 For example, s 4(1) provides that 'Different treatment stipulated by this act or a special legal regulation shall not be considered as unequal treatment'. Similarly, s 4(3) provides that 'Different treatment shall be deemed not to constitute discrimination if it follows from the nature of the work activities or context that the reason constitutes a fundamental and decisive requirement for the performance of the work to be done by the employee and which is essential for the performance of such work; the objective of such an exemption must be legitimate and the requirement commensurate'.

5 All translations of the Czech and Slovak legislative materials are by the author herself.

6 In line with its socialist traditions, but also with the ICESCR, the Czech Republic guarantees a right to work in its constitution and refers to it in legislation.

7 This Act has not been adopted yet, as the anti-discrimination Bill was rejected by the Senate (Upper Chamber of Parliament) and the Chamber of Deputies declined to adopt the act in May 2006. This resulted in a fairly paradoxical situation, as the new labour code regulates the implementation of equal opportunities to a far lesser extent than the old code. Moreover, the Labour Code's reference to non-existent legislation creates something of a legal vacuum, which is not desirable. The Czech government issued newly-drafted proposal in July 2007, the adoption of which is expected in 2008.

8 Section 16 of the Code provides that: '(1) Employers shall be obliged to ensure the equal treatment of all employees as regards their working conditions, remuneration and the provision of other monetary consideration and consideration of monetary value, professional training, and opportunities for promotion or other advancement in employment. (2) Any kind of discrimination shall be forbidden in labour relations. The concepts of direct discrimination, indirect discrimination, harassment, sexual harassment, instructions to discriminate and incitement to discriminate, and cases where different treatment is admissible, shall be governed by a special legal regulation'.

9 The establishment of labour inspectorates is sometimes perceived in the Czech Republic as fulfilling the Community law requirement to set up an independent body overseeing compliance with equality legislation. This view is questionable in

so far as labour inspectorates do not satisfy the condition of independence. They are established by law, fall under the authority of the Ministry of Labour and Social Affairs and are financed out of the state budget.

10 See ss 11 and 24 of Act No 251/2006 on labour inspection.

11 Additional legislation on equality governs matters such as the civil service and employment in specific areas.

12 The official Czech title of the ombudsman is 'public defender of rights' *veřejný ochránce práv* – see Act No 349/1999, on the public defender of rights. His primary function is to defend citizens against mistreatment or inadequate hearing by the public administration. Sometimes, the public defender of rights can initiate an administrative procedure against the public administration.

13 This does not seem an ideal solution, as the public defender will find it difficult to accomodate the broadening of competences. Until now, this office defended citizens against maltreatment by the public administration. Under the Anti-discrimination Act, it will have to interfere in cases of private rights, mainly in the role of mediator and legal consultant.

14 Section 6 of Act No 365/2004, the Anti-discrimination Act.

15 Ibid, s 7.

16 Section 13(4) of Act No 311/2001, the Labour Code.

17 C McCrudden (2003) 'The new concept of equality,' *ERA Forum*, 4: 9–23; C O'Cinneide (2003) 'Taking equal opportunities seriously: The extension of positive duties to promote equality', London: Equality and Diversity Forum/Equal Opportunities Commission, available at www.edf.org.uk/news/Cinneide%2026%20Nov.doc (accessed 5 December 2007).

18 S Fredman and S Spencer (2006) 'Delivering equality: Towards an outcome-focused positive duty', submission to the Cabinet Office Equality Review and to the Discrimination Law Review; O'Cinneide, ibid.

19 S Fredman (2005) 'Changing the norm: Positive duties in equal treatment legislation', *Maastricht Journal of European and Comparative Law*, 12: 369–98; see also the same author's contribution to this book: Chapter 4.

20 C McCrudden (2003) 'The new concept of equality,' *ERA Forum*, 4: 9–23.

21 J Filadelfiová, D Gerbery and D Škobla (2007) *Report on the Living Conditions of Roma in Slovakia*, UNDP, Friedrich Ebert Stiftung.

22 Analysis of socially excluded Roma localities, prepared by GAC (Gabal Analysis and Consulting), available at www.gac.cz/documents/brozura_4.pdf (accessed 30 November 2007).

23 The maps are available at www.esfcr.cz/mapa/stav_mapy_obce.html (accessed 30 November 2007).

24 European Parliament document A6–0148/2006: *Report on the situation of Roma Women in the European Union (2005/2164(INI))*, Committee on Women's Rights and Gender Equality, Rapporteur: L Járóka.

25 For the theoretical disctinction between additive and intersectional discrimination, we refer to the contribution of D Schiek Chapter 1, in this book (see text accompanying nn 88–91 in that contribution).

26 Amnesty International (2007) *Slovensko – Stále segregovaní, stále v nerovnom postavení, Porušovanie práva na vzdělanie romských dětí na Slovensku*, November, available at www.amnesty.cz/zpravy/Romske-deti-na-Slovensku-nemaji-rovny-pristup-ke-vzdelani (accessed 30 November 2007).

27 V Kristková (2006) 'Právo na vzdělání – segregace romských dětí v základním školství', in: *Zpráva o vývoji práv dětí v ČR v letech 2003–2005*, Liga lidských práv, Brno, available at www.llp.cz/_files/file/Zprava_deti.pdf (accessed 30 November 2007).

28 J Nátherová and A Bučková (2006) 'Position of Roma women in Slovakia' (speech delivered to the European Parliament, February, available in the Slovak

language at www.rnl.sk/modules.php?name=News&file=article&sid=4498 (accessed 30 November 2007).

29 On this and the factual circumstances of the case see in more detail Morag Goodwin, Chapter 7, in this book.

30 Case No 57325/00 *DH and Others v Czech Republic*.

31 Ibid, paras 207–210 of the judgment.

32 M Hibschannova (ed) (2007) 'Romové v České republice (1945–1998)', *Socioklub, Prague*: 102–4.

33 Whereas the unemployment rate of Roma women is 10 times higher than that of the majority population, the unemployment rate of Roma men is 'merely' three and a half times higher.

34 J Filadelfiová, D Gerbery and D Škobla (2007) *Report on the Living Conditions of Roma in Slovakia*, UNDP, Friedrich Ebert Stiftung.

35 J Nátherová and A Bučková (2006) *Postavenie rómskych žien na Slovensku – minulost, súčasnost', budúcnost'*, a study prepared for European Parliament, 19 May.

36 K Magdolenová (2006) *Postaveni rómskych žien na trhu práce na Slovensku*, Roma Press Agency, Košice.

37 A Králíková (2006) *Porušování lidských práv*, Praha: Gender Studies.

38 A recommendation made by the League for Human Rights (*Liga lidských práv*) notes that it may be dangerous in the long-run for states to gather statistics without ethnic differentiation. Accordingly, it recommends ethnic differentiation within statistics. See: Liga lidských práv (2007) *Sběr dat určujících etnickou příslušnost jako nástroj pro zjištění rozměru diskriminace romských dětí*, Brno.

39 In almost all European countries, fewer women than men are employed and the pay gap is another everlasting problem.

40 Ombudsman's report, (2005) *Závěrečné stanovisko veřejného ochránce práv ve věci sterilizací prováděných v rozporu s právem a návrhy opatření k nápravě*, December, available at www.ochrance.cz/documents/doc1135861291.pdf (accessed 30 November 2007).

41 Case No 1 Co 43/2006 (done in Olomouc, 17 January 2007, final) and Case No 23C 187/2005–55 (done in Ostrava, 12 October 2007, not final).

42 CERD (2007) Concluding observations of the Committee on the Elimination of Racial Discrimination, Czech Republic, CERD/C/CZE/CO/7, 11 April, available at www2.ohchr.org/english/bodies/cerd/docs/CERD.C.CZE.CO.7.doc (accessed 5 December 2007).

43 CEDAW observations issued to the Czech Republic in August 2006: CEDAW/C/CZE/CO/3.

44 M Hibschannova (ed) (2007) 'Romové v České republice (1945–1998)', *Socioklub, Prague*: 44–6.

45 K Henrard (2007) 'The protection of minorities through the equality provisions in the UN Human Rights Treaties: the UN Treaty Bodies', *International Journal on Minority and Group Rights*, 14: 141–80.

46 Council Directive 2000/43/EC implementing the principle of equal treatment between persons irrespective of racial or ethnic origin [2000] OJ L180/22.

47 Article 3 of Council Directive 2000/43/EC.

48 Council Directive 76/207/EEC on the implementation of the principle of equal treatment for men and women as regards access to employment, vocational training and promotion, and working conditions [1976] OJ L 39/40 as amended by Directive of the European Parliament and of the Council, Directive 2002/73/EC [2002] OJ L269/15.

49 There is, however, a question as to whether this Directive should be discussed at all. It is not clear whether the involuntary sterilisation of Roma women shall be understood as discrimination on grounds of sex. Let us say it certainly constitutes

discrimination on grounds of ethnicity, and most probably discrimination on grounds of sex, because only women are sterilised, not men.

50 Council Directive 2004/113/EC implementing the principle of equal treatment between men and women in the access to and supply of goods and services [2004] OJ L 373/37.

51 E Ellis highlights the ambigious wording of Council Directive 2000/43/EC in her recent work: (2005) *EU Anti-Discrimination Law*, Oxford: Oxford University Press, pp 255–6.

52 A Haupert and M Nicoara (2007) 'Roma activists assess the progress of the Decade on Roma inclusion', available at http://demo.itent.hu/roma/portal/downloads/DecadeWatch/DecadeWatch%20-%20Complete%20(English;%20Final).pdf (accessed 5 December 2007).

12 French legal approaches to equality and discrimination for intersecting grounds in employment relations

Sylvaine Laulom

12.1 Introduction

Although some principles of non-discrimination in employment relations have long been enshrined in French law, it is only recently that discrimination issues have become a main concern for employment policies and labour law. The main provision prohibiting discrimination at work is Art L122-45 of the Labour Code first introduced by a Law of 1982.[1] Prior to that development, specific provisions existed prohibiting discrimination on the ground of trade union membership and pay discrimination between men and women. Since 1982 the list of prohibited discrimination grounds has been extended repeatedly,[2] in part to comply with Community law requirements. In 2001, the Anti-Discrimination Act of 16 November significantly reshaped the legal framework for combating discrimination. It sought to implement the EU Framework Directive on Equal Treatment[3] and, in addition, to give effect to a government programme of anti-discrimination measures. To that extent, the Act in part goes beyond the Directive's requirements. It supplements the existing provisions of the Labour Code, adding a new Article L122-45 which broadens the field of prohibited forms of discrimination. Moreover, the notion of indirect discrimination is inserted into the Labour Code; and the rules on the burden of proof in discrimination cases are amended.[4]

One of the main characteristics of the French legislative framework concerning anti-discrimination matters is that it does not distinguish between different discrimination grounds. Despite that lack of compartmentalisation, at least among lawyers, however, the issues of multiple discrimination have been scarcely discussed and French law has up to now not addressed multiple discrimination.

In this chapter I will first present the main features of French anti-discrimination legislation and analyse its capacity to address the issue of multiple discrimination. Second, I will examine the case law of the *Cour de cassation* (Court of Cassation) and the complaints brought before the equality body HALDE (*Haute Autorité de Lutte contre les Discriminations et pour l'Egalité* or 'High Authority to fight against discrimination and for equality')[5] to evaluate whether multiple discrimination is at all raised. My conclusion notes that even though the French legal framework does not preclude claims of multiple discrimination, up until now very few cases of multiple discrimination have been brought. On a final point, I will suggest reasons explaining the apparent lack of concern in French law for multiple discrimination.

12.2   A French legal framework seemingly favourable to a multiple discrimination approach

French anti-discrimination legislation is characterised by a certain neutrality towards the various prohibited grounds of discrimination. The approach taken cannot be considered as ground specific. Despite the existence of specific provisions relating to certain grounds of discrimination (B), the general legal framework applicable is the same (A).

12.2.1   *A general legal framework for combating discrimination in employment*

The same principles apply for every form of discrimination: direct and indirect discrimination are prohibited, specific sanctions apply with regard to discriminatory acts and the new equality body created at the end of 2004, the HALDE, has the responsibility to cover all grounds of discrimination.

Today, the prohibited grounds for discrimination listed in Art L122-45 of the Labour Code comprise: origin, sex, sexual orientation, lifestyle, age, family status, pregnancy, genetic features — actual or assumed — belonging to an ethnic group, a nation or a race, political opinion, trade union activities, religious belief, physical appearance, name, state of health and disability.

According to Art L122-45 of the Labour Code, the protection of employees from discrimination covers every aspect of working life. Employees are protected against discrimination in the areas of recruitment, disciplinary action, redundancy, pay, training, redeployment opportunities, posting, qualifications, promotion, geographical re-assignment and contract renewal. In addition, advertisements of job vacancies may not contain any discriminatory statements. Both direct and indirect discrimination are prohibited. The burden of proof is the same for every ground of discrimination listed in Art L122-45. Since the adoption of the 2001 Act,[6] the burden of proving a discriminatory act no longer lies solely with the employee but it now falls equally upon the employer. Employees or job applicants who consider that they have been subject to discrimination must present the court with evidence 'that leads one to believe that direct or indirect discrimination has taken place'. In the light of this evidence, it is up to the defendant to 'prove that the decision taken was justifiable according to objective facts that had no connection with any form of discrimination'.[7]

The issue of sanctions is also very important in discrimination cases. Under Art L122-45 of the Labour Code all discriminatory acts by employers are regarded as a matter of course as null and void and, accordingly, the employee retains all previously held rights. In the context of dismissal, this means that any dismissal on discriminatory grounds may be annulled as of right and a worker dismissed on a discriminatory ground can claim reinstatement with the result that he/she is regarded as never having left the job. This is a specific sanction applying to discrimination cases. By way of contrast, if a dismissal is merely 'unfair', that is to say, there is no serious and genuine cause for the dismissal, but not discriminatory, the sanction provided by law is compensation (a minimum of six months' wages for workers with at least two years' length of service and working in an enterprise employing at least 11 employees) but there is no right to reinstatement. In discrimination cases labour courts ('*Conseil de prud'hommes*') are required to order reinstatement if a worker requests it. Where workers do not seek reinstatement, they are eligible for a compensatory payment equal to at least the previous six months' wages in addition to the compensation granted for unlawful dismissal. Penal sanctions are also possible even if they are rarely used. The employer additionally risks a maximum of three years' imprisonment and a fine of €45,000.[8]

The legislation also contains additional flanking measures which aim to provide a more effective level of protection against discrimination and, in addition, the 2001 Act introduces new provisions to facilitate the bringing of discrimination claims and the referral of such cases to the courts. Accordingly, no employee may be disciplined, dismissed or subject to a discriminatory act as a result of testifying to have witnessed discrimination or having reported it.[9] The right to bring legal proceedings concerning discrimination has been extended to representative trade unions.[10] They can act for an employee who claims to be the victim of discrimination without having to have a mandate to that effect. This trade union right of action is subject only to the condition that the employee is given written notification of the action and does not oppose the union action within a 15-day period. Furthermore, associations legally established for at least five years, and whose purpose is combating discrimination, may bring legal proceedings on behalf of an employee. In such cases, unlike those brought by trade unions, the employee concerned must give his written consent.

At the end of 2004,[11] a new institution was created: the HALDE, a body which has already demonstrated its willingness to play a new and active role in the fight against discrimination. The HALDE is an independent administrative body and legislation has already extended its powers.[12] The mandate of the HALDE covers all forms of direct and indirect discrimination prohibited by French legislation or in international agreements ratified by France. Its main decision-making body consists of 11 members who are designated jointly by leading political and judicial authorities.[13] The HALDE has two principal tasks: first, to address cases of discrimination and, second, to promote equality. Victims of discrimination may present their case directly to the HALDE. Alternatively, cases of discrimination may be brought to the attention of the HALDE by intermediaries such as MPs. In addition, victims may bring their cases jointly with an association. Finally, the High Authority may also take up cases ex officio with the consent of the victim.

Without replacing the traditional channels of redress for discrimination within the legal system, the HALDE is capable of identifying discriminatory practices. It may also assist victims in formulating a case against agents of discrimination and, by way of its special powers, it may carry out investigations and demand explanations from defendants by conducting hearings and collecting other evidence, including on-site gathering of information. It may issue recommendations and publish them, thus encouraging the defendant to comply. The HALDE may equally engage in mediation between the victims and the defendant. It is also entitled to refer the case to the public prosecutor who is competent to initiate a prosecution. The HALDE may also propose to the perpetrators of discrimination a compromise settlement including a fine (to a maximum of €3,000 for an individual and €15,000 for a legal person) and, where necessary, compensation for the victim. The compromise agreement needs to be ratified by the public prosecutor, since it brings the public prosecution to a close.

The second objective of the HALDE is to promote equality, by carrying out and commissioning studies and research, by promoting and supporting initiatives of both public and private bodies aiming at the promotion of equality, and by identifying best practices. Finally, the HALDE may recommend amendments to existing law or the adoption of new legislation. Similarly, the HALDE will be consulted by the government on all questions concerning anti-discrimination and the promotion of equality. Notwithstanding its recent creation, as is evidenced by its first two annual reports, the HALDE has quickly established itself as an important actor in the fight against discrimination.

12.2.2 *Specific provisions for specific grounds of discrimination*

This general framework against discrimination is complemented by some specific provisions concerning certain grounds of discrimination. For example, whilst the Anti-Discrimination Act of 2001 recognises age as a ground of discrimination, the specific features of that ground have been taken into account with the Act reproducing the exception authorised by the Framework Directive.[14] Disabled persons enjoy special protection in the field of employment.[15] For example, in any undertaking with over 20 employees disabled persons must constitute at least 6 per cent of the workforce.[16] Specific penal sanctions apply to sex discrimination[17] and trade union discrimination.[18] The specific provisions applying with regard to sex discrimination are of particular importance arguably because legislation on this issue existed long before 1982,[19] the year in which a prohibition on other grounds of discrimination was introduced. This is particularly important for pay discrimination on grounds of gender. Article L140-2 of the Labour Code provides for equal pay for men and women performing 'the same job or a job of equal value'.

According to Art L140-3, pay must be established according to the same rules; job categories and classification must be established using the same criteria, etc. At a sectoral level and in enterprises where collective bargaining has to take place annually, collective bargaining must also concern remuneration. In order to ensure the effectiveness of the mandatory bargaining, specific information must be provided on the situation of male and female workers including a comparison between both groups. Detailed requirements relating to that information are set out in Art D. 432-1 of the Labour Code. A very important cross-industry national agreement was concluded on 1 March 2004 between national organisations of employers and trade unions, in order to promote occupational equality between men and women. It contains commitments to make information available and to reduce wage differentials. More recently, the Law of 23 March 2006 on Equal Pay between Men and Women[20] has introduced new provisions profoundly modernising the relevant rules. The new law aims at reducing the wage disparities between men and women. Indeed, it goes so far as to specify that the gap must disappear by 31 December 2010 and entrusts the parties to collective bargaining to achieve that aim. The new law does not impose obligations as such but aims to induce the social partners to find the means to reduce wage disparities. In fact, this constitutes an extension and reinforcement of existing provisions, introduced by the Law of 9 May 2001, requiring each industry to take measures to ensure equality at work between men and women.[21] The new provisions specify in detail that the actions taken must be founded on precise, pertinent measures and on a precise analysis of the gap between the remuneration of men and women. However, no incentive or sanction is laid down. In addition, there are provisions on maternity and the remuneration to which employees are entitled after that period. According to the legislation, wages must be increased after maternity leave, in order to reflect general pay increases as well as the average individual increase enjoyed during that period by employees of the same category.

Nonetheless, the existence of these special provisions for some prohibited grounds of discrimination does not preclude a transversal approach to discrimination, that is to say, a common approach applying to all types of discrimination. Since the law is framed in transversal terms for all grounds of discrimination, the same principles apply to each and every ground. This can be seen in the fact that cases are referred to as precedents whether or not they discuss issues related to the same ground of discrimination. What has been decided for one ground of discrimination could apply to others. This transversal approach which is one of the main characteristics of the French legal framework seems to allow for a multiple discrimination approach since it would appear to be perfectly possible to apply these general principles to multiple discrimination cases.

Moreover, the list of the prohibited grounds of discrimination may be considered non-exhaustive.[22] While some of the prohibited grounds of discrimination relate to an activity linked to fundamental freedoms, others relate to the characteristics of the person and it seems perfectly possible to imagine that other characteristics could also be taken into account. However, even if we consider that the list is not an open one, it is certainly long enough to cover a large spectrum of discrimination. For example, the HALDE considers that discrimination against a smoker can be classified as discrimination on the grounds of lifestyle as prohibited by Art L122-45.[23] The reference to physical appearance and name in the list of prohibited grounds also functions to cover assumed characteristics. Some grounds are also overlapping. For example, in a case where an employee was dismissed for refusing to take off her Islamic scarf, the claim seems to have been based on discrimination on grounds of religious belief and physical appearance.[24] It seems perfectly possible to combine different grounds of discrimination. In any case, as the list has been extended several times, should it prove necessary, it will be possible without any great difficulty to add other grounds.[25] In that respect, the French legal framework differs from the Community law framework. The Community law approach to discrimination is segmented into three different sets of Directives (one concerning race and ethnic origin, one concerning religion or belief, disability, age or sexual orientation and finally a set of Directives on gender discrimination) which could create difficulties at a Community level for the recognition of multiple discrimination.[26]

In summary, the French anti-discrimination legislation appears to be capable of dealing with claims of multiple discrimination and to take their specificities into account. However, in practice, multiple discrimination issues are not raised and complaints brought before the tribunals and the HALDE tend to focus on one ground of discrimination.

12.3   The scarcity of multiple discrimination claims

An analysis of both the decisions of the French *Cour de cassation*[27] and the claims brought before the HALDE[28] clearly shows that there are very few claims brought on grounds of multiple discrimination and a possible explanation of this phenomenon will be offered. However, certain recent proposals contain the first indications that an evolution in anti-discrimination policy is underway.

12.3.1 The facts

A review of the judgments of the *Cour de cassation* reveals that the most common approach to discrimination claims is one that tends to focus on a single ground. Between 2001 and 2007 of some 450 judgments relating to discrimination claims only four such judgments refer to more than one ground of discrimination.[29] Those judgments were not considered 'important' judgments of the *Cour de cassation* since they were neither published nor the subject of legal comment.

One of the cases concerns trade union activities and the worker's state of health.[30] The decision is not very clear. It seems that the claim in essence concerned trade union discrimination and in its judgment the *Cour de cassation* held that the employer had failed to justify the difference in the worker's career progression by objective facts which had no connection with trade union activity or the applicant's state of health.

Two cases concern gender and trade union activity.[31] In one case, the female applicant was a trade unionist who claimed that she was paid less than another worker. Thus, in fact the case concerned equal pay (discussed further below), and accordingly it was sufficient merely to establish a difference in pay. However, in all the circumstances of the case, the court considered that the specific experience of the workers concerned justified the pay difference.[32] The other case is not very clear. From the judgment it appears that only the issue of sex discrimination was analysed and that the workers were unable to establish any difference in treatment. In the final case[33] the claim concerned disability and trade union activities and it appears that the worker considered that he had suffered discrimination but did not know whether it was on grounds of his disability or his trade union activities. In this case the *Cour de cassation* annulled the Court of Appeal's decision. The Court of Appeal had considered the difference in treatment to be justified by virtue of differences in qualification, whereas, according to the Court of Cassation, it should have analysed how the worker ought to have been promoted in accordance with the relevant collective agreement.

With so few decisions existing, however, it is not possible to make any general conclusions concerning the judicial approach to multiple discrimination, in particular, because those decisions are unpublished and hence very short. They indicate merely that it is possible to bring a case based on more than one ground of discrimination and that judges are capable of dealing with such claims and possibly even taking the specificities of multiple discrimination into account. Of the four judgments it should be noted that three are very recent, a fact which of itself can be interpreted as a sign of change.

Evidence concerning litigation in cases of multiple discrimination can also be found in recent research commissioned by the Ministry of Labour.[34] The research published in 2006 relates to the implementation of the Law of 16 November 2001. The study offers a quantitative and qualitative appraisal of judicial decisions taken in discrimination cases in France. One of the main aspects of the research is its selection and analysis of judgments issued by industrial tribunals. The research reports some claims of multiple discrimination (concerning age and origin, disability and trade union activities and sex and trade union activities) although in quantitative terms those claims remain relatively unimportant. In the multiple discrimination cases very often gender is one of the discrimination grounds alleged. Of a total of 432 decisions analysed, only 47 concern gender discrimination, and among those 47, a further 14 alleged another ground of discrimination. Only one judgment concerns three grounds of discrimination, namely, those of health, family status and trade union activity.

One case stands out in this analysis.[35] It concerns a black woman employed by the Parisian public transport authority (RATP) who claimed that she had suffered discrimination on the grounds of sex and race both in terms of career progression and access to vocational training. A comparison with the situation of others workers clearly revealed that her career progression had come to a halt at a particular point. The group used for the purposes of comparison included a woman. Thus, seemingly, she was entitled to compare herself to a group composed mainly of men (white men) and a woman. On the facts, the employer was unable to provide objective grounds justifying the difference in treatment. Of particular interest is the analysis of the Court of Appeal. It appears to treat the discrimination as a specific form of discrimination using an intersectional approach. It does not approach the matter asking first if there was discrimination based on gender and second if there was discrimination based on race. A further point worth noting in this case emerges from the judgment of the *Cour de cassation* to which the matter was brought following the judgment of the Court of Appeal. The *Cour de cassation* confirms the judgment of the Court of Appeal, in a very short judgment of its own.[36] The *Cour de cassation* simply states that the inequality has been proven. When we read the judgment of the *Cour de cassation* it is impossible to know on which grounds the claim was originally based. Two conclusions can be drawn from this judgment. First, it confirms that the French legal framework as interpreted by the courts is capable of dealing with cases of multiple discrimination, for example, by comparing the situation of a black woman to that of other workers. Second, it reveals that the manner in which judicial decisions are written sometimes hides the fact that multiple discrimination was initially alleged.

Turning to the activities of the HALDE, we note that claims are classified according to the ground of the alleged discrimination and that the HALDE does not report claims based on multiple discrimination. The analyses of the HALDE are also grounds based with separate sections for different grounds. In its most recent annual report, there is only one reference to multiple discrimination which demonstrates that there is nonetheless space for these types of claim even if in practice their position up to now has been wholly marginal.

12.3.2 The reasons

Several hypotheses could be advanced to explain this absence of multiple discrimination litigation.

For simply pragmatic reasons, claimants and their lawyers may prefer to choose one ground of discrimination because it is the easiest to prove or it is the one that the tribunals are more familiar with. The process of selecting the discrimination ground may also be made by the court itself.

Another, and I think more important, reason is that until now in France, most discrimination claims were based on the ground of trade union activities.

Anti-union discrimination constitutes the largest share of the litigation. In the report on the implementation of the Law of 16 November 2001, of a total of 478 cases analysed, 301 concerned trade union discrimination, followed by only 49 cases on sex discrimination, 46 on the worker's state of health and merely 15 on race. Most of the *Cour de cassation* judgments on discrimination in employment relations also relate to trade union discrimination. In France, the rules on the burden of proof in discrimination cases, developed through the influence of European Court of Justice (ECJ) case-law, were first applied by the *Cour de cassation* in anti-union discrimination cases. Judges, lawyers and trade unionists are now familiar with this type of discrimination and case law on this issue has grown rapidly. Thus, the HALDE has received few claims of anti-union discrimination, most likely because the well-recognised judicial pathway was preferred by claimants who are generally supported by trade unions. Further, it is possible to argue that multiple discrimination claims are so few because certain types of discrimination are lacking in the legal debate. Certain tools used in anti-union discrimination – like indirect discrimination or the comparative method – are not used by the different actors, including workers, lawyers, trade unions, and judges. One explanation for this could be that some situations or certain manifestations of indirect discrimination are not always seen as discriminatory. This helps explain the importance of the HALDE and the significance of the contribution it has already made to raising the visibility of certain grounds of discrimination. For example, until very recently, age was not really considered as a possible ground of prohibited discrimination. This was because for a long time, there had been a strong consensus among employers, workers, social partners and governments to use age as an adjustment variable in the labour market and early retirement along with other similar measures which had been widely used in employment policies to accompany company restructuring.

Another reason, similar to the second one, is perhaps to be found in the equal treatment principle applied by the courts in equal pay cases. Most discrimination cases relate to wages, in particular, since 1996, when the *Cour de cassation* held that there is an equal treatment principle under which workers have a right to 'equal pay for equal work'.[37] The *Cour de cassation* 'discovered' this principle in a specific rule, considering that equal pay between male and female workers[38] constitutes merely the application of the more general principle of equal pay between all employees, provided that such employees share the same circumstances.[39] The consequences of this principle are very important and litigation has significantly increased since that judgment also because the *Cour de cassation* allocates the burden of proof in equal pay cases in the same manner as it does in discrimination cases.[40] In equal pay cases the claimant has to demonstrate that he/she is subject to a difference in pay whatever the ground of that difference may be. Thus the ground of the difference established becomes irrelevant. The comparators are simply people doing the same work and, accordingly, there is no focus on the personal characteristics of claimants. It is merely enough that the claimant establishes facts from which it may be presumed that there has been a difference in treatment. Once that has been done, the burden shifts to the employer to prove that this difference in treatment is justified by objective grounds. Judgments in these equal pay cases do not provide any information on the source of the difference of treatment and the characteristics of the claimants are ignored. Instead, commentators have concentrated on the reasons considered by the *Cour de cassation* as sufficient to justify unequal pay. Here, too, the techniques of indirect discrimination and statistical comparison are rarely used perhaps because the judicial approach is more of an equal treatment approach (where the claimant just has to prove the difference in treatment) than a discriminatory approach (where the claimant has to establish that the difference of treatment is based on a prohibited ground). One of the reasons for this may lie with the fact that French lawyers are more familiar with the principle of equality within a universalistic framework than with the principle of discrimination.[41]

Thus, in summary, we may note that case law has concentrated on anti-union discrimination and on equal pay issues. It has contributed to concealing the specific causes of discrimination and there is no evidence that anti-discrimination law has been used to fight systemic discrimination. However, it is possible to see the first indications of an evolution in anti-discrimination policy.

12.3.3 An evolution?

Arguably, case law on anti-union discrimination could be fruitfully applied to other types of discrimination. Lawyers, judges and the legal literature are becoming more familiar with the instruments of anti-discrimination regulation. It is obvious that there is an increasing volume of litigation on discrimination issues, and not simply with regard to anti-union discrimination.

Until recently, the different types of discrimination were not clearly distinguished but some recent initiatives show that there is an increasing emphasis on issues concerning gender discrimination, age discrimination and with regard to diversity.[42] The Law of 23 March 2006 on equal pay between men and women aims at reducing the wage disparities between men and women through the process of collective bargaining. Whilst the objectives of the Law are evidently unfeasible since the pay gap is not going to disappear by 2010, nonetheless the Law obliges the relevant actors at least to begin to analyse the reasons underlying wage disparities and the means of their reduction. An equality label has also been created which is to be awarded to undertakings for a period of three years if they satisfy 18 quality criteria such as taking action to promote equality stressing the importance of management and human resources and which pays attention to the situation of parents and to the reconciliation of professional and family life. As regards diversity, the Charter for Diversity adopted in October 2004 encourages signatory undertakings to 'try to reflect the diversity of French society in their staff by paying particular attention to ethnic diversity among their workforce'. Over a three-year period, three national cross-industry agreements were concluded, one concerning gender discrimination,[43] one on the employment of older workers[44] and the last one on diversity.[45]

Clearly, these initiatives have developed a ground-specific approach. However, in starting to analyse better the features of certain grounds of discrimination, it may also lead to account being taken of multiple discrimination. For example, in March 2006, a law was adopted which makes it mandatory for all undertakings with 50 or more employees to preserve the anonymity of job candidates.[46] The Law refers to the practice of the 'anonymous CV' which some companies have started to apply. This is a practice by which all the references which can produce discrimination must be deleted (age, gender, family situation, name, nationality, origins and photo are deleted from the CV). However, a decree was needed in order to implement the Law and the government subsequently decided not to adopt the decree leaving it to collective bargaining to decide whether or not to adopt this measure. Clearly, the anonymous CV cannot constitute the only response in the fight against labour market discrimination. However, its aim to 'neutralise' the main characteristics of a person at one stage of the recruitment procedure could also be of use in multiple discrimination cases.

Testing is also under development in France and a 2006 Act allows for officials from the HALDE to use 'discrimination testers' to discover discrimination. Testing has also been recognised as a way to prove discrimination in penal cases. Until now, the tests performed were based on one possible ground of discrimination (origin, age or disability), but it is perfectly possible to imagine tests which combine grounds of discrimination.

Finally, the HALDE is a very new institution which only began work in 2005. Until now it has analysed discrimination on the basis of single grounds. However, in its second annual report, two decisions on multiple discrimination were reported. Both dealt with discrimination in job adverts where several indications were discriminatory.[47] Some other decisions are also on multiple discrimination: sex and physical appearance,[48] sex and family situation (the discrimination was because the woman was a mother),[49] origin and trade union activity.[50] In the last situation, it appears that the claimant did not know whether she suffered discrimination because of a trade union activity or because of her origins.[51] Thus, it is likely that in the future the HALDE will have to address multiple discrimination claims.

12.4 Concluding remarks

While Community law has contributed to framing the legal instruments to combat discrimination, it has not contributed to raising the question of multiple discrimination. Until now very little information has been available on multiple discrimination cases and further investigation is needed on how claimants select the ground or grounds of discrimination alleged and whether the courts prefer to analyse claims in terms of one ground of discrimination or another. Despite this lack of empirical evidence, it is likely that the interest which multiple discrimination raises at European level will also have repercussions in France. One of the questions to be raised will be whether the current legal framework is consistent with a fight against that form of discrimination. It can be argued that because French law has not, until now, distinguished between different types of discrimination, the courts are in a position to deal with multiple discrimination claims and to take into account their specificities.

Notes

1 Article 1 of Law No 82-689 of 4 August 1982 inserted in the Labour Code a new Article L.122-45 which prohibits the disciplining or dismissal of an employee on the grounds of 'origin, sex, family status, ethnic, national or racial belonging, political opinion, trade union activities or religious belief'.

2 In 1990 (by way of Law No 90-602 of 12 July 1990), lifestyle, state of health and disability were added to the prohibited grounds of discrimination. The Anti-Discrimination Act of 16 November 2001 (*Loi No 2001-1066 relative à la lutte contre les discriminations*) adds sexual orientation, age, physical appearance and name to the list. Since 2001 further new grounds of discrimination have been included in the legal protection against discrimination: in 2005 genetic features were added (Law No 2005-102 of 11 February 2005) and finally pregnancy in 2006 (Law No 2006-340 of 23 March 2006 on equal pay between men and women).

3 Council Directive 2000/78/EC establishing a general framework for equal treatment in employment and occupation [2000] OJ L303/16 (Framework Directive).

4 On the Anti-Discrimination Act see M-A Moreau (2002) 'Les justifications des discriminations', *Droit Social*: 1112–24; M Miné (2001) 'Les apports de la nouvelle loi à la lumière du droit communautaire', *Semaine Sociale Lamy*, numéro spécial 'Les discriminations dans l'emploi', 1055, 17 December: 5 and M Keller (2002) 'La loi du 16 novembre 2001 relative à la lutte contre les discriminations', *Recueil Dalloz*: 1355.

5 As required by Council Directive 2000/43/EC implementing the principle of equal treatment between persons irrespective of racial or ethnic origin [2000] OJ L180/22 (Race Directive) and by Council Directive 76/207/EEC on the implementation of the principle of equal treatment for men and women as regards access to employment, vocational training and promotion, and working conditions [1976] OJ L39/40 as amended by Directive 2002/73/EC [2002] OJ L269/15 (the Equal Treatment Directive), a Law was adopted at the end of 2004 to establish an equality body (the HALDE) to promote equality, particularly in providing assistance to victims of discrimination and producing independent reports (Law No 2004-1486 of 30 December 2004 and Decree No 2005-215; Law No 2006-396 of 31 March 2006 and Decree No 2006-641 of 1 June 2006).

6 More precisely, amendment to the burden of proof resulted first from caselaw influenced by EC Directives and judgments of the ECJ and second from the 2001 Act. See Cass. Soc. judgment of 23 November 1999, Bull. V No 447 and Cass. Soc., judgment of 28 March 2000, (2000) *Droit Social*: 589.

7 Article I.122-45, final paragraph.

8 Articles 225-1 and 225-2 of the Penal Code. The same list of prohibited grounds is to be found both in the Penal Code and in the Labour Code.

9 Article L.122-45-2 of the Labour Code.

10 Article L.122-45-1 of the Labour Code.

11 Law No 2004-1486 of 30 December 2004.

12 Law No 2006-396 of 31 March 2006.

13 The members are designated by the President, the Prime Minister, the Presidents of the Assemblies and the Social and Economic Council as well as the vice-president of the Council of State and the First President of the Court of Cassation.

14 According to the Act of 2001, 'differences of treatment on grounds of age shall not constitute discrimination if they are objectively and reasonably justified by a legitimate aim, such as employment policy, and if the means of achieving that aim are appropriate and necessary. Such differences of treatment may include among others: the prohibition on access to employment or the setting of special working conditions in order to ensure the protection of young and older workers, or the fixing of a maximum age for recruitment which is based on training requirements if the post in question or the need for a reasonable period of employment before retirement'.

15 See Arts L.323-1–L.323-35 and R.323-1–R.323-119 of the Labour Code.

16 However, at present the employer can satisfy this obligation by other indirect means, including payment of a contribution to a specific fund. See also the new Law No 2005-102 on equal rights and opportunities and social protection for disabled persons.

17 Article L.152-1-1 of the Labour Code.

18 See Art L.481-3 of the Labour Code.

19 Thus the principle of equal pay for men and women was recognised by the Law of 11 February 1950 and the law included this principle in the mandatory provisions to be inserted in collective agreements.

20 Law No 2006-340.

21 See Direction des relations du travail (2006) *La négociation collective en 2005*, Ministère de l'Emploi, Editions Législatives, in particular, the chapter on collective bargaining on equality between men and women, pp 180 *et seq*. See also R Silvera (2006) 'Les accords sur l'égalité de rémunération à la loupe', *Semaine Sociale Lamy*, 1264: 2.

22 This point is discussed in E Dockès (2005) *Droit du Travail, relations individuelles*, Paris: Dalloz, coll. HyperCours, see in particular the chapter on equality, p 142. See also by the same author, (2005) *Valeurs de la Démocratie, 8 notions fondamentales*, Paris: Dalloz, coll. Méthodes du droit, the chapter headed 'L'Egalité', pp 31–62.

23 Decision No 2007-32 of 12 February 2007.

24 *Dallila Tahri*, Paris Court of Appeal, judgment of 19 June 2003. The court annulled the applicant's dismissal on the basis of Article L.122-45.

25 For example, the HALDE has recently recommended modifying the Labour Code, in particular Article L.122-45, to include a new prohibited ground, that of 'association', that is to say the ground of association with a person who exhibits a characteristic protected by Article L.122-45. In the case in point the woman was living with a trade unionist. I have my doubts as to the necessity of this amendment (see Decision No 2007/75 of 26 March 2007).

26 See S Fredman (2005) 'Double trouble: multiple discrimination and EU law', *Anti-discrimination Law Review*, October, 2: 13–21.

27 We concentrate on the *Cour de cassation* judgments for two main reasons. First, its interpretation will be followed by other tribunals and the judgments of the *Cour de cassation* have a legal authority that the other judgments do not have. Second, all the judgments of the *Cour de cassation* are now published on the Legifrance website (www.legifrance.gouv.fr) which makes it possible to perform an exhaustive survey of the litigation on a particular issue. Nonetheless, a selection must be

made since the *Cour de cassation* issues around 25,000 judgments per year (see Ministère de la Justice, *Les chiffres clefs de la Justice*, October 2006). The decisions of the other tribunals (Courts of Appeal and in labour law industrial tribunals) are rarely published and other types of research are therefore necessary to analyse litigation on a particular issue.

28 The HALDE issues decisions (known in French as *délibérations*) which are published. The HALDE is not a judicial body thus its decisions are not legally binding but where discrimination is found to exist the HALDE can encourage the defendant to follow the recommendations set out in its decision. The annual report gives information on the claims lodged and decisions adopted by the HALDE and, in addition, the HALDE publishes its decisions and recommendations.

29 On a keyword search it is possible to select all the judgments of the *Cour de Cassation* referring to 'discrimination', or 'Article L.122-45 of the Labour Code' or which use the term 'discriminatory'. I chose 2001 as my starting point because litigation on discrimination matters started to develop with the Anti-discrimination Act of 2001. I excluded claims where both discrimination on the grounds of the applicant's state of health and disability are mentioned since these grounds are invariably linked in the judgments.

30 Cass. Soc., judgment of 29 November 2006, No 05-43855.

31 Cass. Soc., judgment of 4 July 2001, No 99-45598; Cass. Soc., judgment of 24 January 2007, No 05-42054.

32 Cass. Soc., judgment of 24 January 2007, No 05-42054.

33 Cass. Soc., judgment of 20 March 2007, No 05-42487.

34 M-T Lanquetin and M Grevy, *Premier bilan de la mise en œuvre de la loi du 16 novembre 2001 relative à la lutte contre les discriminations*, final report, December 2005, available at www.social.gouv.fr/IMG/pdf/etude_afem_122005.pdf (accessed 21 December 2007).

35 Judgment of the Paris Court of Appeal, 29 January 2002, No 2001/32582.

36 Cass. Soc., judgment of 29 September 2004, No 02-42427.

37 It is one of the most famous cases of the Court of Cassation, *Ponsolle*, Cass. Soc., judgment of 29 October 1996. See A Lyon-Caen (1996) 'De l'égalité de traitement en matière salariale', *Droit Social*: 1013–15; J Pélissier, A Lyon-Caen, A Jeammaud, E Dockès (2004) *Les grands arrêts de droit du travail*, Dalloz, p 253; T Aubert-Monpeyssen (2005) 'Principe "à salaire égal, salaire égal" et politiques de gestion des rémunérations', *Droit Social*: 18–30 and G Auzero (2006) 'L'application du principe d'égalité de traitement dans l'entreprise', *Droit Social*: 822–5.

38 The principle is enshrined in Article L.140-2 of the Labour Code.

39 In the 1996 case, it was a woman complaining that she was less paid that another woman.

40 This is true even though the legal bases for the claims are different. See Cass. Soc., judgment of 10 October 2000, Bull. V No 317.

41 On the difference between the principle of equality and the principle of non-discrimination see A Jeammaud (2004) 'Du principe d'égalité de traitement des salariés', *Droit Social*: 694–705.

42 L Bonnard-Plancke and P-Y Verkindt (2006) 'Egalité et diversité: quelles solutions?', *Droit Social*: 968–80.

43 National cross-industry agreement on gender equality and gender balance in workforce composition concluded in March 2004.

44 National cross-industry agreement concluded in October 2005 on promoting the employment of older workers. See P-Y Verkindt (2005) 'Changer le regard sur le travail des seniors après l'ANI du 13 octobre 2005', *Semaine Sociale Lamy*, 1234: 6–11; C Willmann (2006) 'Promouvoir le vieillissement actif: les modestes propositions des partenaires sociaux', *Droit Social*: 144–55, and F Favennec-Héry (2005)

'L'ANI relatif à l'emploi des seniors: un premier pas', *La Semaine Juridique Social*, 21: 1329.

45 Cross-industry agreement on diversity in undertakings, signed in February 2007. See F Favennec-Héry (2006) 'Vers un ANI sur la diversité dans l'entreprise', *La Semaine Juridique Social*, 47: 1914.

46 B Bottois (2006) 'Le CV anonyme, un outil parmi d'autres au service d'une politique de la diversité', *Semaine Sociale Lamy*, 1287: 3.

47 Decision No 2006-83 of 9 May 2006 and Decision No 2006-211 of 9 October 2006.

48 Decision No 2006-81 of 10 April 2006 and Decision No 2006-78 of 10 April 2006.

49 Decision No 2007-72 of 12 March 2007.

50 Decision No 2007-45 of 5 March 2007.

51 In this case, mediation was proposed and accepted.

13 Multiple equality claims in the practice of the Norwegian anti-discrimination agencies

Hege Skjeie

13.1 Introduction

The reorganisation of anti-discrimination legislation and the institutions enforcing such legislation is today a trend which cuts across Europe. The present developments encompass at least three interconnected trends. First, new grounds of discrimination are included in the legal protection against discrimination. Second, the various laws protecting against discrimination on different grounds are increasingly becoming harmonised. Third, there is a tendency towards co-ordinating and merging the different bodies responsible for the enforcement and monitoring of anti-discrimination laws and equality policies. An 'integrated approach' to discrimination is emphasised by the European Commission as a necessary step towards providing a more coherent and effective strategy for combating discrimination, allowing for common legal and policy approaches to different grounds and addressing cases of multiple discrimination more effectively.[1]

Not all integration efforts are, however, EU driven. Norway – not a member of the EU – has recently introduced significant changes to its anti-discrimination and equality machinery. Until 2006, the Gender Equality Act of 1978 was the only comprehensive anti-discrimination law in force in Norway. However, as of January 2006 those provisions have been supplemented by the Act on Prohibition of Discrimination on the basis of ethnicity, national origin, ancestry, skin colour, language, and religion. Both laws are upheld by a reorganised equality and anti-discrimination institution, which now monitors the Gender Equality Act and the Discrimination Act as well as the anti-discrimination regulations in the Labour Environment Act and in the housing legislation. Thus, the new institution is responsible for combating discrimination and promoting equality on a range of grounds which have been expanded rapidly. The institution is the first of its kind among the Nordic countries, all of which, however, now find themselves initiating processes of reorganisation and re-legislation.

An integrated approach to discrimination is often considered advantageous on account of its potential, first, to provide coherence, consistency, clarity and simplicity concerning individual rights to non-discrimination and, second, in terms of a projected increase in the effectiveness and influence of the monitoring and enforcement authorities. Also, it is regularly claimed that perceived 'hierarchies of grounds' may be diminished through such integration, and that an integrated approach is necessary to take account of intersecting grounds of discrimination.[2]

Critics, however, point to potential dangers and shortcomings of the integrated approach to discrimination. For instance, there have been examples of anti-discrimination/equality bodies, especially the older, well-established ones, worrying that integration would result in a weakening of their ability to protect specific strands, in the sense of weakened political influence, reduced public attention and resources or a neglect of the specific circumstances and characteristics relating to their field of responsibility. Both gender equality agencies in Norway and Sweden, as well as the Commission for Racial Equality in the UK, are known to have opposed institutional mergers on that basis.

In this chapter I discuss some lessons to be learned from efforts towards institutional integration, based on the experiences of the new Norwegian enforcement agencies' in their (admittedly) brief period of existence. I do this from the vantage point of being a member of the new Equality Tribunal, which rules on individual cases of discrimination following an initial investigation by the Ombud agency. After close to two years in office, the Tribunal has attempted to engage in critical self-evaluation, and I will address some of the considerations in this respect.

13.2 A revised institutional framework

An Ombud institution was first created in Norway in 1978/1979 to secure compliance with the new Gender Equality Act, which provided protection against gender-based discrimination in 'all areas of society' – notably, however, with a general exemption clause covering the 'internal affairs of religious communities'.[3] The Ombud's task was both to handle individual complaints and to work in furtherance of gender equality. Her evaluations of complaints could be appealed to an independent appeals board, with the possibility of further appeal through the regular court system. Generally, the Ombud agency was intended to offer a low-threshold agency, free of cost, with both proactive, advisory and complaints-handling tasks. This low threshold function is clearly stated also in the presentation of the new agency's website:

> The Ombud provides guidance and advice on legal rights. You can contact the Ombud for an opinion on whether you have been subjected to illegal discrimination. The Ombud also provides advice on how you can proceed with your case.
>
> The Ombud handles complaints and decides whether illegal discrimination has taken place. Anyone who believes they have been discriminated against may submit the case to the Ombud. The Ombud will investigate

the matter and assess whether illegal discrimination has occurred. The services of the Ombud are free of charge.[4]

The new Equality and Anti-discrimination Ombud was set up in January 2006, and now monitors two comprehensive laws, three anti-discrimination chapters in other laws and two UN conventions, the Convention on the Elimination of All Forms of Discrimination against Women (CEDAW) and the International Convention on the Elimination of All Forms of Racial Discrimination (ICERD), which are incorporated, respectively, into the Gender Equality Act and the Discrimination Act. Proactive tasks are extended also within the scope of the Ombud's general mandate. She is expected to engage in advisory activities, public debate, and 'awareness-raising campaigns'. Her staff numbers have been increased, and her organisation is now divided into specific departments focusing, on the one hand, on legal issues, and, on the other hand, on analytic, investigative and proactive work. The Ombud's task is, generally speaking, to promote equality irrespective of gender, ethnicity, national origin, descent, colour, language, religion or belief in all areas of society. In the area of employment, the Ombud promotes equal treatment irrespective of political views, membership of employee organisation, sexual orientation, disability or age. She is also under a duty to promote equal treatment irrespective of sexual orientation in the housing sector. Thus, the degree of protection enjoyed by individuals is not uniform across all strands. It is clearly more comprehensive for gender-based discrimination than, for instance, discrimination on grounds of disability, or sexual orientation.

Furthermore, the Ombud's competences are limited within the new institution in the sense that she cannot – as a general rule – adjudicate complaints, but only offer her evaluation as to whether laws have been violated.[5] Her task is to attempt to reconcile opposing parties, and, if possible, to construct compromises and improved arrangements to avoid discrimination in future. But binding rulings in individual discrimination cases are made by the new government-appointed Equality Tribunal.[6]

The decisions of the Tribunal may be appealed through the regular courts, as was the case with the rulings of the old Appeals Board. In addition, only the regular courts may rule on compensation to victims of discrimination. On any appeal, the office of the Attorney General will represent the Tribunal. The mandate for the Tribunal particularly stresses the need to secure legal expertise on the board – if not to the exclusion of, at least to the marginalisation of, other kinds of expertise. In the governmental white paper on the mandate for the new integrated institution, it is stressed that the composition of the Tribunal should 'not exclude' other expertises. Other expertises are expected to have in-depth knowledge about the different discrimination strands, but are not supposed to act as protagonists, or 'representatives', in this respect.[7] The narrow space which is provided for expertise from backgrounds other than law was originally considered to be a productive asset ensuring a broad(ened) approach to discrimination. But the Tribunal's task is strictly limited to the legal interpretation of the package of anti-discrimination legislation, and to the handling of cases which has been investigated and evaluated by the Ombud. In reality, the Tribunal's 'non-lawyers' regularly have to confront a legal framing of the issues, which, in the absence of a legal background, is often difficult to deconstruct. My own assessment of the matter, based on two years of meetings, is simply that the 'non-lawyers' contributions clearly are modest with respect to broadening the perspectives in anti-discrimination law. Increasingly, such work is being professionalised as a field of specific legal competence.

The institutional mandates envisage a division of roles where the Ombud is the 'protagonist' whilst the Tribunal secures and legitimises the 'neutrality' of the joint institution. The governmental outline of the mandate for the Tribunal thus uses the concepts of 'independence' and 'neutrality' in constructing a set of founding premises. The independent/neutral role of the Tribunal, particularly in relation to the Ombud, is further highlighted through the establishment of a board secretariat to prepare the cases for hearings, whereas previously in the days of the Gender Equality Ombud and Appeals Board that task was performed by the Ombud's own lawyers.

As a result, having regard to the new mandates for the integrated bodies, one important consequence of integration may be observed: an enlargement of the Ombud's tasks and a concurrent questioning of the agency's status as an impartial actor is accompanied by an expansion of the decision-making powers of the Tribunal which rest on strongly articulated norms about (judicial) impartiality.

The new Tribunal is – as a matter of principle – not bound by any legal interpretations made by the Ombud. Naturally, however, her evaluations are taken into account by the Tribunal, and in approximately only 20 per cent of the cases has it reached a different conclusion. Nonetheless, the respective roles of the two agencies may still be somewhat confused, as may be observed, for instance, when the Ombud reports a pregnancy discrimination case on the institution's website as follows:

> The woman did not take a postponed exam because she was giving birth, and was denied continuation of her studies. She claimed that she was discriminated against because of her pregnancy, but did not receive support for this claim by the Ombud. Such support was, on the other hand, provided by the Equality Tribunal which heard the appeal.[8]

On the other hand, although the new Tribunal develops 'case law' on the basis of older decisions, including those of the former Gender Equality Ombud and Appeals Board, this fact is not easily discerned on its decisions. In this sense, the message from the politicians, enshrined in the mandate for the Tribunal, is repeated by the Tribunal's own decision making practice: it is the Tribunal (and not the Ombud), which now constructs the Norwegian case law on discrimination.

The current 'separation of powers' between the Ombud and the Tribunal might be considered as containing the potential to provide clarity and 'user-friendliness' and – as a result – increased legitimacy, as its proponents would argue. Currently, however, the possible downsides to the new arrangements are just as easy to outline. The politically determined need for a 'neutral' body creates, in and of itself, a rather large question mark with regard to the Ombud's objectivity. Accordingly, her role becomes more one of a spokes-person for disadvantaged groups, and less one of a guardian of individual rights to non discrimination. Thus a new separation is politically con-strued, between activist work for 'equality' and impartial work for 'anti-discrimination'. This is, in my view, a too severely drawn distinction. In a 'worst case scenario', it might contribute to question also the Ombud's law assessment practices.

Also, it is the office of the Ombud – and not the Equality Tribunal – which traditionally, in public opinion, has held the reputation of a guardian of rights. In this capacity, the Ombud is fairly well known. With regard to 'user-friendliness', matters are clearly complicated by the strict division of the roles of the two agencies, where one is publicly well known and one hardly known at all. To be overly specific: at the earlier stages of a case, the parties are in close contact with the office of the Ombud; however, at a later stage, they are confronted with a brand new agency – the Tribunal. In both written cor-respondence and in hearings before the Tribunal, they have to answer new questions. But what kind of creature is the Tribunal? Very few people know. The room where the parties meet the Tribunal for hearings of the case is clearly not a courtroom. There are no judges present. But neither is this a negotiation table. There are no negotiators present. Decisions have to be reached – but who exactly are those holding the decision-making power? And on what basis do they have this authority? Such specific forms of new 'unclarities' were, in my view, severely understated as the political ambitions for reorganisation unfolded and the new mandates were created. For 'low threshold' agencies, however, these 'unclarities' remain problematic.

The Tribunal tries to compensate for the unclarities, which the strict 'separ-ation' regime produces, through its website presentation. However, comparing this presentation to the Ombud's, we still glimpse the more formalistic frame of the Equality Tribunal:

• The Norwegian Equality Tribunal was established on 1 January 2006.
• The Tribunal enforces the various Norwegian equality and anti-discrimination acts:

the Gender Equality Act, the Act on Prohibition of Discrimination on the basis of ethnicity, national origin, ancestry, skin colour, language, religious and ethical orientation (the Discrimination Act), the anti-discrimination regulations in the Labour Environment Act (these regulations protect against labour-market-related discrimination on the grounds of disability, sexual orientation, age, political views and membership of a trade union), the anti-discrimination regulations in the housing legislation.

- The tribunal receives governmental funding, but carries out its functions in an independent manner, free from governmental instruction.
- The tribunal is accessible to the general public and its services are free of charge.
- Only the Equality and Anti-discrimination Ombud has the competence to investigate alleged non-compliance with the law. The Ombud can make a recommendation which can be appealed before the Tribunal. A case can only be handled by the Tribunal after the Ombud has made a recommendation.
- The rulings of the Tribunal are administratively binding. Such rulings, however, may be overruled by a court of law. The Tribunal may order the payment of a daily fine until compliance with such rulings.
- When it comes to administrative decisions made by municipal and state institutions, the powers of the tribunal are more limited. In such cases the tribunal can only give recommendations.[9]

13.3 A new approach to discrimination? Not yet . . .

The regulations for the Equality and Anti-discrimination Ombud explicitly state that the agency shall develop interdisciplinary competence and ability to handle multiple discrimination and discrimination in the intersection of gender and other discrimination grounds.[10] More generally, a major argument in favour of integrating anti-discrimination legislation and enforcement is that such an approach is necessary to take account of intersecting grounds and situations of discrimination. What is meant by this?

The new EC report on multiple discrimination, practices, policies and laws, tries to clarify the concepts in the following way: multiple discrimination describes a situation where discrimination takes place on the basis of several grounds operating separately. Intersectional discrimination refers to a situation where several grounds operate and interact with each other at the same time in such a way that they are inseparable.[11]

The concept of intersectionality has gained significant theoretical and political relevance in recent years. Kimberlé Crenshaw coined the term 'intersectionality' as a means to articulate the ways in which women of colour were subjected to both sexism and racism in society in general (structural intersectionality), and as a critique of the feminist as well as the anti-racist movements for not acknowledging that the identities and situation of black women were shaped by their gender *and* their colour at the same time (political intersectionality).[12] The common ground in intersectional approaches is to be found in a focus on the ways in which social categories such as gender, ethnicity, colour, age and sexual orientation, interact and constitute power hierarchies in different contexts and situations.[13] An intersectional approach thus recognises that identities as well as structural patterns of inclusion and exclusion in most cases are shaped and affected by more than one factor.

In Norwegian public-policymaking there has traditionally been little awareness of this fact. The general tendency in policymaking has rather been privileging a compartmentalisation of equality strands. It has been extensively documented, for instance, how a long tradition of parliamentary and governmental gender-equality policies hardly ever make a conscious effort to integrate ethnic minorities' concerns. Similarly, affirmative governmental policies on religious pluralism hardly ever pay attention to gender equality. Finally, separate policies have been established for what we could call 'ethnic minority specific' gender-equality concerns. These policies largely develop within a 'crisis' frame of measures which aim to combat forced marriages, genital mutilation or honour-based violence. This crisis frame, in turn, creates a paradoxical situation of limited hyper-visibility.[14]

'Intersectionality' may in this context merely constitute a catchphrase or a label. If, for instance, we go back to the Norwegian Parliament's decision in 2005 to create a joint equality and anti-discrimination institution, we observe that the arguments in favour of this innovation were mainly constructed in efficiency terms. That is to say, as was discussed above, arguments were advanced on the increased 'influence' for the institution concerned, the potential for 'learning' across the different discrimination grounds, and as regards 'user-friendliness'. Nonetheless, in the latter stages of the institutionalisation debate, 'intersectionality' became a catchphrase in favour of reorganisation. It constituted merely a catchphrase because, in reality, no substance was provided to the term.[15]

More important, however, is the question as to how intersectionality is addressed in specific discrimination cases. From the cases which the Equality Tribunal has addressed, the answer is simple: not at all, as yet. As I write this (November 2007), the Tribunal has considered a total of 48 cases. Admittedly, all in all, not that many cases, but taken together they permit the compilation of some simple statistics. In the Tribunal's own reports the cases are strictly compartmentalised. Two-thirds of the cases concern gender discrimination. Of the gender cases, around half concern discrimination on grounds of maternity leave. Five cases concerned the right to equal pay for men and women. The rest of the cases relate to discrimination on account of age, language and ethnic or national background. In autumn 2007, the Tribunal handled its first case on the equal treatment of people with disabilities.

In its first year of operation, the Tribunal's caseload was dominated by gender cases (90 per cent). In 2007 the picture is different, with more than half the cases related to other discrimination grounds, ethnicity, age, language, disability and non-membership of a trade union.

Table 13.1 shows the statistics as presented by the Equality Tribunal, as of November 2007.[16]

Table 13.1 Equity Tribunal caseload breakdown, November 2007

Issue	Number of cases
Maternity leave	15
Equal pay for men and women	6
Other gender-related grounds	13
Age	4
Ethnicity	7
Language	1
Disability	1
Non-membership of trade union	1

No tendency can be observed whereby the legal framing of discrimination has expanded to include intersectionality. No categories are presented to cover such cases. But neither have cases been presented to the Tribunal as cases of intersectional problematic.[17] Admittedly, Norwegian legal approaches might be particularly backward. However, in the recent report from the European Commission on multiple discrimination, such 'backwardness' actually appears as the dominant trend in legal approaches to discrimination across Member States. Based on interviews with equality agencies in 10 Member States, this report shows that in cases where multiple discrimination is claimed, each grounds are often handled separately. If, for example, a case involves the grounds of race and gender, the allegation of race discrimination is usually considered separately from the allegation of gender discrimination and not as inextricably linked with the gender discrimination. Furthermore, round-table discussions with equality agencies have shown that it is common practice for legal advisors handling cases involving more than one ground to apply a tactical approach, where a strategic decision is made to 'choose the strongest ground' and to leave out other grounds of discrimination because they are difficult to prove, either vertically ground by ground, or in combination.[18]

In rulings on intersectional discrimination there is thus a general 'no cases' problem. The 'no cases' problem arises from the simple fact that discrimination cases are generally handled one discrimination ground at time. The statistics provided by the Norwegian Equality and Anti-discrimination Ombud show the same pattern. Here as well, the complaints are compartmentalised similarly to the statistics presented by the Equality Tribunal. Neither office thus appears to treat cases on a cross-cutting basis.

Table 13.2 shows the complaints statistics as presented by the Equality and Anti-discrimination Ombud, in the 2006 yearly report.[19]

The last category is not expanded upon in the report, which more generally presents important cases which can be regarded as guides to the legal practices of the agency. The cases are all addressed on single ground basis, and multiple discrimination is not a theme in the report as such. In other contexts,

Table 13.2 Equality and Anti-discrimination Ombud caseload breakdown, 2006

Ground	Number
Gender	148
Ethnicity, national origin, skin colour	61
Age	51
Disability	1
Sexual orientation	1
Religion	8
Language	10
'Other'/'several grounds'	8

the Ombud treats the 'no cases' problem as one of 'individual experiences which do not fit the legal framework'. Although individuals never can be reduced to any one single facet of complex identities, 'the lowest common denominator' emerges as the basis for the very legal protections which are meant to safeguard against discrimination. It is through the definition of vulnerable groups that legislation outlawing direct and indirect discrimination has been framed, and thus legal protection against discrimination is contingent on one's ability to prove membership of a specific, protected category. Nonetheless, according to the Ombud, it is the agency's ambition to develop cross-sectoral expertise and an ability to deal with multiple discrimination at the interface between all grounds of discrimination.[20] As yet, however, the practical examples of that approach are largely lacking.

13.4 Intersectionality in practice: the Muslim headscarf

There is, however, one particular set of decisions by the Norwegian Ombud institution which actually points in another direction. This set of decisions, and I am tempted to add 'of course', addresses the Muslim headscarf, the hijab – often depicted as the paradigm symbol of intersectionality in legal discourse. Interestingly, this set of decisions simultaneously illustrate how intersectionality may be addressed even on the basis of single-ground legislation. I will explain this in some detail. Prior to 2006, only gender equality was comprehensively addressed in Norwegian anti-discrimination law. In 2004, the Gender Equality Ombud received a series of examples of different employers' prohibition on wearing the religious headscarf in the work place. From this compilation of examples, the Ombud chose one specific case, and treated this complaint as raising issues of indirect sex discrimination.

The facts of the case are as follows: a large hotel in the Oslo area operated an employee uniform code which hotel management claimed was irreconcilable with the wearing of hijab. The Appeals Board agreed with the Ombud in her assessment that this prohibition would have negative consequences predominantly for women employees. The uniform code – although gender neutral in its wording – could thus be seen as producing gender-specific discriminatory effects. In this assessment, the Ombud also contrasted the operation of those rules with uniform regulations in the armed forces which accommodate the wearing of headgear such as turbans. Furthermore, she reasoned that for women who wear headscarves on religious grounds, the hijab constitutes an element of their personal integrity. Many would find it difficult to seek employment if they could not wear the headscarf. Thus, a prohibition would entail significant disadvantages for these women.[21]

Another hijab case assessed by the Gender Equality Ombud concerned a large furniture store where the management demanded of an employee: 'scarf off', again with reference to internal dress code regulations. In correspondence with the Ombud, the employer stated that it had established the dress code in order to ensure value neutrality. The Ombud found the promotion of a common staff profile to be a legitimate aim, but considered the attainment of such through a prohibition on wearing the hijab to be a disproportionate infringement of the rights of the woman concerned, given that the headscarf constituted an element of her personal integrity. Although the Ombud could envisage that, in certain situations, value neutrality might legitimate a prohibition on the hijab, she indicated that the facts would have to show that the specific workplace had some special need for signalising value neutrality. The Ombud found that the furniture store had no such special need. Thus, the employer had violated the prohibition on indirect gender discrimination.[22]

The new Equality and Anti-discrimination Ombud has also, in 2007, evaluated a workplace hijab ban. A woman had been fired from work as a shop assistant because she refused to remove the headscarf at work. The Ombud split the case into, first, an assessment on indirect gender discrimination, and, second, an assessment on direct discrimination on religious grounds. The employer was found to have violated both prohibitions. The Ombud agency now presents this as a case example of multiple discrimination, which happens to be only one treated by the new agency so far.[23]

In my view, this series of assessments are particularly important because they frame the hijab as an issue of complex gender equality. The assessments made by the Gender Equality Ombud explicitly refrained from considering various interpretations of the possible symbolic meanings of the scarf and, instead, treated the complex as a locus of intersecting individual rights. In this regard, the decisions also run counter to general statements made by the European Court of Human Rights, in *Dahlab*[24] and *Sahin*.[25] After viewing bans on headscarves as constituting an interference with the right to manifest one's religion, the court nevertheless accepted the states' reasons for doing so. In this, the court also took special pains to repeat notions expressed by Switzerland and Turkey that the wearing of a headscarf 'seems hard to reconcile with the principle of gender equality'.[26]

What then, is to be concluded from the headscarf decisions in terms of intersectionality? Simply, it must be noted that discussions are sometimes unnecessarily complicated. Intersectional approaches to law enforcement may exist even where only one ground of discrimination is alleged. Similarly, there may be a total absence of an intersectional approach in judgments which, as in the case of the European Court of Human Rights, interpret a generally phrased discrimination clause offering protection on a multiplicity of grounds.

Furthermore, I consider that an argument could be made for the importance of political activism in this respect. The Ombud's reasoning on the right to wear a headscarf at work, construed as a matter of intersecting gender equality rights, is also, unambiguously, in line with the reasoning and collective actions of Norwegian minority women's organisations. The first case brought before the Gender Equality Ombud in 2004 was in fact a compilation of 14 different cases gathered by two minority women's organisations – the Mira Centre and the Islamic Women's Group in Norway – in co-operation with the national government-sponsored Centre to Combat Ethnic Discrimination.[27] Generally speaking, minority organisations in Norway have worked hard to frame the hijab issue primarily as one of prohibitions which reveal discriminatory attitudes and practices in the larger society. In this, they have undoubtedly been heard by the Ombud.

Such efforts may also have benefited from the more general political approach to religious pluralism in Norway. Generally, Norwegian public authorities have pursued an active policy of accommodation with regard to religious dress, although this has been mainly exhibited in terms of non-discrimination between religions. For instance, as regards the wearing of religious headscarves in schools, public authorities regularly explain that the very existence of a Christian intention clause for public educational institutions in Norway makes it unacceptable to deny the expression of other religious beliefs. Accommodation of the hijab thus falls within a category of policies promoting religious pluralism. Important in this respect is, however, that the assessments by the Gender Equality Ombud situate gender-equality concerns at the core of pluralist policies, and, in this, demonstrate how equality may be consistently sought.

13.5 Conclusion

Developments towards an expansion of anti-discrimination legislation across Europe appear to encompass – at least – three interconnected trends. First, *new grounds of discrimination* are included in the legal protection against discrimination. The sequences of expansion may vary from state to state depending on the grounds which were first covered by national legislation. However, there appears to be an international standard of (at least) six strands in operation – gender, ethnicity/race, religion, age, sexual orientation, disability – to which national legislation will sooner or later apply. The Norwegian tradition in this respect has – as in most other Nordic countries – been the institutionalisation of strong gender equality legislation and virtually no other comprehensive protection against discrimination – until the field suddenly 'exploded' shortly before the advent of the new millennium.

This coincides with a second general tendency. As legislation proliferates, an argument is being advanced on the need for various laws offering protection against discrimination on different grounds to be *harmonised*. The strength of the individual protection against discrimination may vary across strands. Gender may, for example, enjoy a more rigorous protection against indirect discrimination than ethnicity does, as is the case in Norwegian legislation. Or, it may be the case, that the prohibition on gender discrimination may cover more areas of social life than the prohibition on discrimination on grounds of sexual orientation – which, for instance, in Norwegian law only is protected with regard to working life and housing. Such differences imply that there are different justice regimes applying to different grounds. Currently, new political initiatives are underway aiming to harmonise legislation, and in Norway, a governmental commission has recently been appointed specifically to address the issue of adopting a single unified anti-discrimination law. It is, however, an open question whether such initiatives will manage to take full consideration of the fact that there are particular, and different, structures and situations of discrimination which need also to be addressed on specific grounds.

Third, and connected to the two previous trends, new initiatives are seeking to pursue a *reorganisation of institutions* to monitor the law(s) and promote equality. In the Nordic context, reorganisation ambitions appear to be pointing towards a 'pooling of resources' in an integrated institution. In favour of a pooling of resources, a new argument has recently emerged that is, the argument of intersectionality, and the need for equality-promoting agencies to address complex structures and situations of discrimination in society. From the Norwegian experience it must be noted, however, how such an argument, while possibly expressing a genuine political concern, can also be used primarily as a tactical argument. By this I mean that intersectionality references regularly function as catchphrases, devoid, however, of substantive meaning.

As of present, there are few indications that actual law enforcement has expanded to include intersectionality and multiple discrimination grounds. The dominant trend is still to treat cases on one 'single ground' basis, or at best, as a series of 'single ground' claims. In cases where multiple discrimination is claimed, each ground is often handled separately. Strategic decisions are regularly made to 'choose the strongest ground', and to leave out other grounds of discrimination. Paradoxically, the 'best practice' example so far, in Norwegian efforts to combat intersectional discrimination, arose where intersectionality was addressed on the basis of single ground legislation. This was the situation which emerged when the prohibition to wear a Muslim headscarf in the work place was held to violate the prohibition on indirect discrimination established by the Gender Equality Act.

In the Norwegian context, we have seen how an integration of institutions in charge of combating different forms of discrimination has been accompanied by a sharp division of tasks within. The power to decide on complaints is concentrated within the Equality Tribunal, and this decision-making is the Tribunal's only task. The Equality and Anti-discrimination Ombud investigates and assesses alleged non-compliance with laws, and is also in charge of proactive equality work. It is, however, doubtful whether the division of tasks in itself manages to provide 'clarity' and 'user-friendliness' – as proponents have argued. It may contribute to strengthen perceptions of the law enforcement practices of the Tribunal as being 'neutral' and 'impartial'. But the downside to the arrangement is as easy to outline. When the Ombud's perceived role becomes more one of a spokesperson for disadvantaged groups, and less one of a guardian of individual rights to non-discrimination, the agency also risks being perceived mainly as an 'unobjective activist'.

Much of the debate circulating on the consequences of recent expansions to the anti-discrimination regime, as may be currently witnessed in Norway, also relates pragmatically to the issue of numbers. How many laws can there be? How many grounds can be protected? And how should that be done? How many enforcement agencies are necessary? Consequently, new legislation is followed by yet newer initiatives, where the primary concern for ensuring protection against discrimination on a multiplicity of grounds becomes supplanted by a concern to standardise legislation, preferably in the form of one single anti-discrimination law. Such legislation could contain a standard protection clause against discrimination on the basis of a series of strands, or potentially, protect against discrimination on the grounds of 'any status'. In the case of an 'any status' option, all previously held ambitions or traditions in support of contextually sensitive legislation and implementation will however, consequently be eliminated. This is clearly problematic in a situation where enforcement agencies still strive to grasp the complex facts and consequences of multiple and intersectional discrimination.

Notes

1 European Commission (2004) *Equality and Non-Discrimination in an Enlarged European Union*, Green Paper, Luxembourg: Office for Official Publications of the European Communities, p 10.
2 See for instance V B Strand (2007) 'Vern mot direkte og indirekte diskriminering etter norsk rett – et ensartet vern?', *Lov og rett*, 47: 131–53.
3 This general exemption clause is interesting in its own right, and is, with some variation, repeated both in the Discrimination Act and the Labour Environment Act. The exemption clause is discussed in H Skjeie (2007) 'Religious exemptions to equality', *Critical Review of International Social and Political Philosopy*, 10: 471–90.
4 Likestillings- og diskrimineringsombudet (2007) 'What does the Ombud do?', available at www.ldo.no/en-gb/TopMenu/Om-ombudet2/Information-in-english/ What-does-the-Ombud-do/ (accessed 23 November 2007).
5 Exceptions are made for urgent cases, cf § 4 in Diskrimineringsombudsloven, LOV-2005-06-10-40.

6 The commission which prepared the new anti-discrimination legislation on ethnicity, nationality, language, religion, etc, originally proposed a strict two-level system which allocated decision-making competence within the Ombud agency, with appeals channelled to a separate appeals board (NOU 2002:2).

7 Ot. prp. nr. 34 (2004–2005), Om lov om Likestillings- og diskrimineringsombudet og Likestillings- og diskrimineringsnemnda (-diskrimineringsombudsloven), 43.

8 Likestillings- og diskrimineringsombudet (2007) 'Tilrettelegging av eksamen', 21 August, available at www.ldo.no/no/TopMenu/Uttalelser/2006/Kjonn/Tilrettelegging-av-eksamen/ (accessed 23 November 2007) (author's translation from the Norwegian original).

9 Likestillings- og diskrimineringsnemnda (undated) 'The Norwegian Equality Tribunal', available at www.diskrimineringsnemnda.no/wips/1416077327/ (accessed 23 November 2007).

10 § 1, Forskrift om organisasjon og virksomhet for Likestillings- og diskrimineringsombudet og Likestillings- og diskrimineringsnemnda. FOR-2005-12-16-1524, available at www.lovdata.no/for/sf/bl/tl-20051216-1524-001.html#1 (accessed 23 November 2007).

11 European Commission (2007) *Tackling Multiple Discrimination. Practices, Policies and Laws*, Directorate-General for Employment, Social Affairs and Equal Opportunities, Unit G.4, Luxembourg: Office for Official Publications of the European Communities, pp 15–6.

12 K Crenshaw (1991) 'Mapping the margins: intersectionality, identity politics, and violence against women of color', *Stanford Law Review*, 43: 1241–99.

13 A Phoenix (2006) 'Interrogating intersectionality: Productive ways of theorising multiple positioning', *Kvinder, Køn & Forskning*, 15: 21–31.

14 H Skjeie and M Teigen (2007) 'Likestilling og minoritetspolitikk', *Tidsskrift for kjønnsforskning*, 31: 21–39; B Siim and H Skjeie (2007) *Tracks, intersections and dead ends. Multicultural challenges to state feminism in Denmark and Norway*, August (unpublished, on file with the authors); A Bredal (2007) 'Den "spesielle" volden. Vold mot minoritetsjenter på sidelinjen', in K Storberget et al. (eds) *Bjørnen sover. Om vold i familien*, Oslo: Aschehoug, pp 56–61.

15 Cf. Ot. prp. nr. 34 (2004–2005), Diskrimineringsombudsloven.

16 Likestillings-og diskrimineringsnemnda, available at www.diskriminerings nemnda.no/wips/1416077327/ (accessed 23 November 2007).

17 With one possible exception, for a complaint which at the outset raised questions about multiple discrimination on grounds protected through the Discrimination Act. The case was, however, in the legal assessments narrowed down to 'single ground' claims.

18 European Commission (2007) *Tackling Multiple Discrimination. Practices, Policies and Laws*, Directorate-General for Employment, Social Affairs and Equal Opportunities, Unit G.4, Luxembourg: Office for Official Publications of the European Communities, pp 22–3.

19 Likestillings-og diskrimineringsombudet (2006), Praksis 2006, Oslo: Likestillings-og diskrimineringsombudet: 11.

20 B Gangaas (2006) 'Intersectionality as a challenge for the Equality and Anti-discrimination Ombud', presentation at seminar at the University of Oslo, 'Multiple discrimination and equality agendas: Intersectionality in practice', 4 December (unpublished, on file with the author).

21 K Mile (2004) 'Diskriminering av kvinner', in N Høstmælingen (ed) *Hijab i Norge – Trussel eller menneskerett?*, Oslo: Abstrakt forlag, pp 220–30.

22 Safety, health and hygiene may still provide legitimate reasons for justifying a workplace prohibition on the religious headscarf. The Norwegian Labour Inspection Authority ('*Arbeidstilsynet*') has issued written guidance to employers on headscarf policies which states, for example, that an employer may require that a

hijab be fastened in a specific way for safety reasons, and that criteria regarding the hijab's colour, design and material fabric may also be adopted. Cf R Craig (2006) 'The religious headscarf (hijab) and access to employment under Norwegian anti-discrimination laws', lecture for the Dr juris degree, February (unpublished, on file with the author).

23 Likestillings- og diskrimineringsombudet (2007) 'Oppsigelse på grunn av hijab er multi-diskriminerende', available at www.ldo.no/no/TopMenu/Uttalelser/2007/Oppsigelse-pa-grunn-av-hijab-er-multi-diskriminerende/ (accessed 23 November 2007).

24 *Dahlab v Switzerland*, Application no 42393/98, ECHR 2001-V.

25 *Sahin (Leyla) v Turkey*, Application no 44774/98, 29 June 2004, (2005) 41 EHRR 8.

26 I discuss the important contrasts between the ECtHR evaluation of gender equality with the Norwegian Gender Equality Ombud and Appeals Board's decisions in H Skjeie (2007) 'Headscarves in schools: European comparisons', in T Loenen and J Goldschmidt (eds) *Religious Pluralism and Human Rights in Europe: Where to Draw the Line?*, Antwerp: Intersentia, pp 129–46.

27 This agency was in 2006 subsumed under the new Equality and Anti-Discrimination Ombud.

Part IV

A symbol of intersectionality in legal discourse: the headscarf enigma

14 The headscarf debate

Approaching the intersection of sex, religion and race under the European Convention on Human Rights and EC equality law

Titia Loenen

14.1 Introduction

European Union (EU) equality law has become much more encompassing and multidimensional since the adoption of several Directives covering discrimination on the basis of race, religion, sexual orientation, disability and age. Whereas formerly the European Equal Treatment Directives concerned sex equality only,[1] we now have a Directive on equal treatment irrespective of race or ethnic origin in employment and regarding access to and supply of goods and services (Race Directive),[2] and a Directive covering discrimination on the basis of religion or belief, sexual orientation, disability and age in employment (Framework Directive).[3] The latter Directive thus does not extend to goods and services. Regarding sex equality, on the other hand, a Directive banning discrimination on the basis of sex regarding access to and supply of goods and services has been added.[4]

The choice to have different instruments for different grounds of discrimination raises the question as to the relationship between the equality and non-discrimination standards in the Directives. This is of special interest in cases where grounds of discrimination intersect. An interesting case study in this respect, which has received much attention in Europe, is the issue of banning headscarves in public education. Here we find an intersection of (potential) discrimination on the basis of sex, race and religion.[5] How should we approach this under the Equality Directives? To complicate matters further, another type of European multidimensionality is at stake as well since this issue is subject not just to EC law, but also to the binding standards deriving from the European Convention on Human Rights (ECHR).

This chapter endeavours to explore and compare approaches to the headscarf in public education under these two legal regimes. The European Court of Human Rights has rendered several decisions concerning the question whether prohibitions to wear a headscarf in public education are compatible with the ECHR. EU equality law also covers major aspects of the headscarf issue. This chapter discusses the similarities, differences and potential conflicts between the approaches to this issue under the two legal regimes. To start with, I will briefly sketch the way in which sex, race and religion intersect in debates on the headscarf. The next paragraph will address some points concerning the relationship between the ECHR and EU equality law to keep in mind, as well as concerning the overlap between the standards set under both legal settings, all of course only as far as relevant for this chapter. After discussing the case law of the European Court of Human Rights on headscarf bans and the approach to take under the EU Directives, I will draw some conclusions on the questions posed.

14.2 Headscarves at the intersection of sex, race and religion

The Islamic headscarf has become a contested issue in Europe, especially the French legislation banning it from public schools, which attracted attention worldwide. Due to increasing tensions between 'the West' and 'Islam' as for instance manifested in the September 11 attacks, the wars in Iraq and Afghanistan, and the Danish cartoon crisis, the issue seems to have become symbolic of Western approaches to Islam.

On one level, the reasons put forward to ban wearing a headscarf in a public school, be it by schoolchildren or by teachers, concern religion as such. Being a manifestation of religion, the headscarf is deemed to jeopardise the denominationally neutral and open educational environment which the state has to guarantee to pupils of public schools, so as to give full respect to all religions and beliefs, including atheistic ones, which the pupils and their parents may nourish. Whatever its merits, in this reasoning it is not just headscarves that pose problems, but equally Sikh turbans or Jewish *kippas*. As soon as people enter the public sphere, they have to forego manifestations of their private convictions and beliefs. Thus, the French legislation, which was adopted in 2004, bans all ostentatious religious symbols in French public schools.

Yet, if one takes a closer look at the context in which the French ban was introduced, it seems pretty clear that this was not so much to curb religious manifestations per se, but to curb expressions of Islam.[6] Clearly, Islam is not an indigenous religion in France or any other European country, but only has become a considerable element in those countries with the influx of Muslim immigrants over the last decades. In France, and this could very well hold true similarly for other European countries with considerable immigrant Muslim minorities, banning religious symbols in public schools thus, in fact, is connected closely with issues of race.[7] Race here used in its broad meaning, including ethnic origin.[8] In this reading, banning religious symbols in public schools is not really just about guaranteeing the denominational neutrality of schools, but about how the majority society perceives and reacts to the position of its immigrant minority groups of non-Western descent. Is this non-Western, immigrant identity allowed to be seen and to express itself in the public sphere, or is it to remain hidden in the private sphere only? Put together in this way, the ban on religious symbols in public schools does not just raise the question whether it is a justified infringement of religious freedom in general, but also whether it would constitute (indirect) discrimination on the basis of religion and/or race.

To complicate matters further, on a third level the discussion on banning headscarves from public schools touches on gender equality. A major argument put forward to ban headscarves in public schools derives from the idea that the headscarf is symbolic of the inferior position of women in Islam and that many girls and women are pressured into wearing it.[9] If valid, this argument could work as a powerful counterclaim to claims that banning religious manifestations in public schools constitutes, in fact, discrimination on the basis of religion and/or race. On the other hand, if this argument is unfounded one might also argue that banning headscarves, or religious symbols as such – potentially – constitutes indirect discrimination on the basis of sex, as in many European countries it will probably affect and disadvantage much more women than men.[10]

14.3 Relationship between the European Convention on Human Rights and European Union equality law

Before embarking on a comparison between the applicable EU Directives and the ECHR, a few remarks concerning the relationship between the two regimes are in order. In fact, this relationship is of increasing importance due to several factors. To start with, the Treaty on European Union specifically refers in Art 6 to the ECHR by stating that '. . . The Union shall respect fundamental rights, as guaranteed by the European Convention for the Protection of Human Rights and Fundamental Freedoms . . .'. This suggests the ECHR is to be given priority whenever legal norms stemming from both legal regimes conflict.[11] Similarly the EU Charter of Fundamental Rights pays tribute to the ECHR by stipulating that insofar as the Charter contains rights which correspond to rights in the ECHR, 'the meaning and scope of those rights shall be the same as those laid down by the said Convention', be it that EU law may provide more extensive protection (Art 52, s 3).[12]

The commitment to abide by the human rights standards as guaranteed under the ECHR is reflected in the Recitals to both the Framework Directive and the Race Directive. In addition, the Framework Directive contains a general limitation clause to the principle of equal treatment notwithstanding religion or belief, disability, sexual orientation and age, which closely resembles limitation clauses in the ECHR. Article 2, s 5 of this Directive stipulates:

> This directive shall be without prejudice to measures laid down by national law which, in a democratic society, are necessary for public security, for the maintenance of public order and the prevention of

criminal offences, for the protection of health and for the protection of the rights and freedoms of others.

14.3.1 Different mandates

When exploring the relationship between EU law and the ECHR it seems very important to keep in mind the different legal role and function or mandate of the European Court of Justice (ECJ) and the European Court of Human Rights respectively. The main function of the former is to guarantee a uniform interpretation of EU law throughout the EU, whereas the latter is called upon to decide whether a state party violates the ECHR in a specific case. In this respect, in the case law of the European Court of Human Rights the 'margin of appreciation' to be left to the states parties plays an important role. Besides, the ECHR sets minimum standards only, which means EU law is free to give more human rights protection. Problems arise if EU law would give less protection than the ECHR. In that case EU law would have to be amended to conform to the ECHR minimum standards.

14.3.2 Overlapping standards concerning headscarves in public education

It is important to note that the ECHR mainly concerns vertical relationships, not horizontal ones. This means that any overlap between EU law and the ECHR in an area such as employment will be limited mainly to public employment. Adoption of the Twelfth Protocol, which adds a general non-discrimination provision to the ECHR, has not changed this.[13] The Twelfth Protocol is important, however, in a different way, as it has broadened the scope of application of non-discrimination under the ECHR considerably by giving the prohibition of discrimination an independent status instead of the accessory one provided for in Art 14 of the ECHR. This means that complaints concerning discrimination do not have to be connected to one of the other rights protected in the ECHR, but can be brought to the European Court of Human Rights in their own right. Regretfully, not many countries so far have ratified the Twelfth Protocol.[14]

As for the overlapping provisions of the EU Directives and the ECHR concerning the issue of prohibiting headscarves in public education, the applicability of the ECHR to this issue poses no problems. Under the ECHR, state regulations prohibiting teachers or pupils to wear a headscarf or religious symbols in general fall under the scope of Art 9 of the ECHR. Section 1 of Art 9 guarantees everyone's right to freedom of thought, conscience and religion, which 'includes freedom to change his religion or belief and freedom, either alone or in community with others and in public or in private, to manifest his religion or belief, in worship, teaching, practice and observance'. Under s 2, limitations are allowed only if they are 'prescribed by law and are necessary in a democratic society in the interests of public safety, for the protection of public order, health or morals, or for the protection of the rights and freedoms of others'. Article 14 may be applicable as well if discrimination on the basis of sex, race or religion is at stake, but so far it has played no significant role in the court's case law, given its accessory character.[15]

The picture under the EU Directives, however, is much more complicated. As far as teachers are concerned, if discrimination on the basis of religion is involved it would be covered by the Framework Directive, as far as sex discrimination is at stake the directive on equal treatment between men and women in employment would apply; and concerning potential discrimination on the basis of race or ethnic origin the Race Directive is applicable. All three Directives cover both public and private employment.

As far as the pupils are concerned, the Race Directive is the only one to apply fully to education, as explicitly provided for in Art 3, s 1(g). The Directive on equal treatment of men and women in the access to and supply of goods and services explicitly *ex*cludes the area of education from its scope of application (Art 3, s 3). This leaves us with the sex equality in employment Directive, which covers education as far as 'vocational training' is concerned (Art 1). Vocational training covers any form of education which prepares for a qualification or the necessary training and skills for a particular profession, trade or employment, whatever the age and level of training of the pupils or students, and even if the training programme includes an element of general education. Primary and general secondary education as such seem to be excluded.[16] In respect of discrimination on the basis of religion the Framework Directive similarly applies to vocational training only (Art 3, s 1(b)).

The above shows that the issue of the headscarf in public education is largely covered by both legal regimes, except where pupils in primary and general secondary education are concerned. Prohibitions on wearing a headscarf affecting the latter do not fall within the scope of application of the EU Equality Directives, except where race discrimination is involved.

14.4 The European Convention on Human Rights and prohibiting headscarves in public education

As far as the ECHR is concerned, two important cases dealing with the prohibition of headscarves in public education merit attention. The first case, *Dahlab v Switzerland*, concerns a public school teacher, the second, *Sahin v Turkey*, a state university student.[17]

14.4.1 Dahlab v Switzerland

The case of *Dahlab v Switzerland* concerned a female, Catholic teacher at a Swiss public school who converted to Islam and started wearing a headscarf. After three years the General Director of primary education in the *Kanton* Geneva initiated action and prohibited her from wearing the headscarf. The

Director considered that wearing a headscarf, being a religious manifest-ation, jeopardised the principle of the separation of church and state and endangered the neutrality to be upheld by the state in a public school class-room. The Swiss Federal Court that heard her case upheld the ban and gave priority to the right of the pupils to receive education in a religiously neutral context over the teacher's freedom to manifest her religion.

Bringing a complaint to the European Court of Human Rights, Dahlab claimed that her right to freedom of religion was infringed, as well as her right to non-discrimination, as a Muslim man could teach at a state school without being subject to any form of prohibition.

The European Court of Human Rights upheld the judgment of the Swiss court in 2001. The interference with Dahlab's freedom of religion as pro-tected by Art 9 of the ECHR was considered to be justified. The European Court emphasises the national court has been very careful in balancing the rights at stake. The fact that, before the General Director's actions, already three years had passed without complaints by either parents or the school board does not influence the court's judgment.

The most crucial part of the decision starts with the court's consideration that it is difficult to assess what the exact impact of wearing a clearly religious sign like a headscarf will have on the freedom of conscience and religion of the pupils, especially on pupils of such a tender age, four to eight-year-olds, who are even more vulnerable to being influenced than older children. Inter-estingly, the court then links the question of the required neutrality of the teacher to the question how wearing a headscarf relates to gender equality. This is rather surprising, as the Swiss Court time and again identified the problem a teacher wearing a headscarf poses as one of religious expression as such, and only referred to its possible meaning in terms of women's inequality in a sideline. Yet, according to the court, in the circumstances:

> it cannot be denied outright that the wearing of a headscarf might have some kind of proselytizing effect, seeing that it appears to be imposed on women by a precept which is laid down in the Koran and which, as the Federal Court noted, is hard to square with the principle of gender equality. It therefore appears difficult to reconcile the wearing of an Islamic headscarf with the message of tolerance, respect for others and, above all, equality and non-discrimination that all teachers in a democratic society must convey to their pupils.[18]

After this rather sweeping denouncement of what a headscarf represents the conclusion of the court cannot come as a surprise: the interference with Dahlab's freedom to manifest her religion is justified. As far as the claim of discrimination on the basis of sex is concerned the court is pretty brief. As the prohibition to wear a headscarf is 'not directed at her as a member of the female sex but pursued the legitimate aim of ensuring the neutrality of the state primary-education system', such a measure 'could also be applied to a man who, in similar circumstances, wore clothing that clearly identified him as a member of a different faith'. The court accordingly concluded that there was no sex discrimination at stake.[19]

14.4.2 Sahin v Turkey

The second case concerning headscarves in a public educational setting worth mentioning here is the case of *Sahin v Turkey*. It concerned a university student who objected to the dress regulations of a Turkish state university, which prohibited religious attire being worn in the university. In 2004 the European Court of Human Rights held the ban to be compatible with the rights enshrined in the ECHR. The Grand Chamber of the court confirmed this decision in 2005.[20] In its decision the court repeated its consideration, citing from *Dahlab*, that wearing a headscarf is hard to reconcile with the principle of gender equality, tolerance, respect for others and non-discrimination.[21] In its further considerations, however, it kept its distance and emphasised that 'where questions concerning the relationship between state and religions are concerned, on which opinion in a democratic society may reasonably differ widely, the role of the national decision-making body must be given special importance'.[22] Thus, it left a large margin of appreciation to the Turkish government to decide whether it is indeed 'necessary' in the Turkish context to prohibit wearing religious symbols in teaching institutions. The court accepted the arguments put forward by the Turkish government, especially those which referred to the specific Turkish history regarding *laïcité* and the strong political significance which wearing a headscarf had taken on in Turkey with the growing influence of extremist political movements in that country.

Although Sahin raises the issue of sex-discrimination in her complaint as well, she did not dwell on this in any significant way, but focused on her freedom of religion. Subsequently, the court did not feel inclined to explore this issue any further either. It just remarked that the reasons that led the court to conclude that there was no violation of Art 9 also apply to the complaint under Art 14, taken together with that Article or individually.

In the above cases the way in which the European Court of Human Rights perceives wearing a headscarf as 'difficult to reconcile' with the notions of gender equality and more generally tolerance and respect for others, stands out. In deciding the resulting conflict between the right to freedom of religion and those notions the court gives prevalence to the latter. The rather sweeping and very principled character of the court's statements in this respect raises the question whether state parties to the ECHR would not just be *allowed* to prohibit headscarves in public education, but would perhaps even be *required* to do so. Yet, the judgment in *Sahin* seems to decide that question in the negative, as it expressly leaves a large margin of appreciation to the state parties where the regulation of the relationship between state and religion is concerned. Thus it seems more likely the court will be reluctant to get in the way of the national authorities' assessment whether a ban on religious symbols in public education (or elsewhere) is 'necessary' or not. If this is a correct interpretation of the *Sahin* judgment, it will mean the decision on the limits to be put on religious manifestations is left largely at the national level. This could mean that the European Court allows freedom of religion to mean something fundamentally different between European countries.

In terms of discrimination, the court does not address the question whether Art 14 is infringed in the cases at hand, at least it does not do so in any serious way. As the complainants did not do so themselves in anything but a very superficial manner, this is hardly surprising.

14.5 The EC Directives and prohibiting headscarves in public education

As no case law by the ECJ on the subject of prohibiting headscarves in public education exists yet, we have to hypothesise about how the Directives apply to this issue. In the following I will try to do this by addressing the issue in terms of (potential) discrimination on the basis of religion, sex or race successively. I will address the applicability of the EU Directives covering these grounds of discrimination, and if so, the possible outcome of applying the standards contained in them to the case at hand.

14.5.1 Applicability of the Directives

14.5.1.1 Discrimination on the basis of religion

As far as potential discrimination on the basis of religion is at stake in headscarf bans, the Framework Directive is determining. Prohibiting a headscarf falls within its scope of application as it poses a barrier to access to employment (as far as teachers are concerned) and vocational training (as far as pupils are concerned) based on religion.

An important question seems to be whether direct or indirect discrimination is at stake. The answer depends on the form of the prohibition. Prohibiting all religious symbols as such because of their religious nature constitutes direct discrimination on the basis of religion (that is, discrimination between persons with and without a religion of whatever kind). If, however, dress codes are formulated neutrally to guarantee state neutrality in a broader way (for instance by prohibiting all symbols showing personal convictions, be they religious, political, or other) they would not constitute direct discrimination, but could still amount to indirect discrimination, if religious individuals are more affected than non-religious ones or the individuals belonging to a specific faith are much more affected than others.[23] This seems, in fact, often the case. Neutral bans like this are quite likely to pose indirect discrimination on the basis of religion, as they seem to disproportionately affect non-Christian faiths, which are more often acquainted with dress codes, such as dress codes for Muslim women and male Sikhs.[24]

Whether or not the issue of prohibiting headscarves in public education is to be constructed as direct or indirect discrimination on the basis of religion may be less important after all as the Framework Directive provides for an open system of review regarding both direct and indirect discrimination. By this, I mean to say that the legal space to refute a claim of discrimination is not limited to specific exemption clauses, but can be based on any kind of justification. As far as indirect discrimination is concerned this is provided for by the 'objective justification' clause (Art 2, s 2(b)), which is familiar to EC equality law for many years now from the area of sex discrimination. To justify a measure having a discriminatory effect, it must be shown to pursue a 'legitimate aim' and to be 'appropriate and necessary' to achieve that aim. The latter basically boils down to a (rather strict) proportionality test.[25]

But as far as both direct and indirect discrimination are concerned, Art 2, s 5 contains another general justification clause:

> This directive shall be without prejudice to measures laid down by national law which, in a democratic society, are necessary for public security, for the maintenance of public order and the prevention of criminal offences, for the protection of health and for the protection of the rights and freedoms of others.

This limitation clause is clearly inspired by the ECHR, which contains very similar provisions, including in Art 9 of the ECHR (see para 3.1). Applying these provisions, the European Court of Human Rights is concerned mostly with the requirement that limitations must be 'necessary in a democratic society'. In this respect it requires the interference to correspond to a 'pressing social need' and to be 'proportionate to the legitimate aim pursued'.[26]

As it is, this test in its turn shows several basic similarities with the 'objective justification' test by also demanding a legitimate aim (be it in this case limited to several specific ones such as the protection of the rights of others) and a relationship of proportionality between this aim and the measures taken to realise it.

14.5.1.2 Discrimination on the basis of race

The Directive on equal treatment irrespective of race or ethnic origin covers both employment and access to goods and services, including education, so both teachers and pupils could invoke the Directive against a headscarf ban or a more general ban on all religious symbols, that is if such a ban also constitutes discrimination on the basis of race or ethnic origin (race for short). It seems evident a ban like that cannot be construed as direct discrimination on the basis of race, but a claim of indirect discrimination seems quite feasible, given the fact that the majority of people affected by the ban will be of non-Western origin. If so, this is only allowed if the ban is based on a legitimate, non-discriminatory aim and is appropriate and necessary to achieve that aim (the objective justification test, see Art 2, s 2(b) of the Race Directive).

14.5.1.3 Discrimination on the basis of sex

The Directive concerning equal treatment of men and women in employment applies to teachers, and to pupils as far as vocational training is concerned. As mentioned before, two sex equality issues may be at stake in prohibiting headscarves in public education. First, it is often contended that the Islamic headscarf is a symbol of the inferior position of women in Islam and that women are often pressured into wearing it.[27] As such, allowing it in public education constitutes condoning sex inequality. This is a highly contested issue. The case of *Dahlab* shows that the European Court of Human Rights takes it on board. Yet, interestingly, in Germany the Constitutional Court, the *Bundesverfassungsgericht*, has taken a very different position on this issue. In 2003, it decided that prohibiting a teacher in a public school from wearing a headscarf must have a basis in law and that it is up to the legislatures of the states to decide whether valid reasons exist to do so. At the same time, it explicitly stated that such a decision could not be based on the presumption that wearing a headscarf is symbolic of women's oppression. The German court referred to recent research which shows young women often start wearing a headscarf to lead self-chosen lives without foregoing their culture of origin.[28] I would think this is the more convincing position to take, as research indeed suggests many Muslim women start wearing a headscarf for this or other reasons not involving a sense of their inferiority.[29] The European Court of Human Rights does not refer to any research whatsoever in its assessment of the headscarf being 'hard to reconcile' with notions of equality and non-discrimination.

But even if one concluded otherwise, it would seem very hard to bring the issue of *not prohibiting* headscarves in public education under the scope of application of the sex equality Directive. It would mean constructing this as an act of discrimination on the basis of sex by the employer (as far as the teacher is concerned) or by the school (in the case of the pupil). I wonder whether the Directive covers such 'acts of omission'.

The second sex equality issue that may be at stake in prohibiting headscarves (or religious symbols more generally) in public education goes in the opposite direction: such a prohibition entails indirect sex discrimination against the pupil or teacher, because it will affect mainly Muslim women. If so, it is only allowed if it can be objectively justified, that is if it has a non-discriminatory aim and if it is appropriate and necessary to achieve that aim. In fact, this is the approach taken by the Norwegian Ombud in a case involving a private employer who did not allow a Muslim worker to wear her headscarf at work.[30]

To conclude: teachers wearing a headscarf in public education are protected under EC law against discrimination on the basis of religion, sex and race. Pupils, however, are not always protected under EC law against all three forms of discrimination. Protection against discrimination on the basis of race is guaranteed in all types of education, but protection against religious discrimination and sex discrimination is limited to vocational training. The latter does not include primary and general secondary education. So for pupils it can make a difference which grounds of discrimination are indeed considered to be at stake.

In all instances, EC law allows for the possibility of justifying banning headscarves from public education. So far no case law exists on this specific issue, but what outcome can we expect if we apply the EC non-discrimination standards described above?

14.5.2 Application of the EC standards to headscarf bans in public education

As we have seen, the 'objective justification' test to be applied when indirect discrimination is at stake and the general limitation clause of Art 2, s 5 of the Framework Directive boil down to very similar requirements. Thus at the end of the day, and irrespective which Directive is applied, banning headscarves or other religious symbols from public education is allowed only if this pursues a legitimate aim, can reasonably be expected to achieve that aim and is proportional. Much then seems to depend on the question how strictly this test is applied, especially the proportionality test.

Applying similar criteria, the European Court of Human Rights upheld headscarf bans in public education regarding both teachers and pupils. This would seem to suggest the ECJ could very well come to the same conclusion under the Directives. Yet, several factors seem to me to point to a different conclusion. To start with, as mentioned before, the European Convention on Human Rights provides for minimum standards only, so the ECJ could provide more protection to Muslim teachers and pupils than the European Court of Human Rights is prepared to give. Second, in upholding the ban in the Turkish case of *Sahin* the European Court of Human Rights stressed the wide margin of appreciation to be left to the state parties to the ECHR in organising the relationship between state and religion. Given the role and the mandate of the court this seems understandable, yet one wonders whether it makes as much sense in the context of EU law, which is more concerned with uniform application in all member states. Last but not least, EU law traditionally requires a strict application of the objective justification test before accepting any exceptions to equal treatment irrespective of sex.[31] I would contend the same applies in cases of indirect discrimination on the basis of race, race being the classic example of a suspect category. Religion would seem to call for a pretty strict approach as well, given the similar role of race, sex and religion as core identity markers.

A strict application of the objective justification test and of the general limitation clause of Art 2, s 5 of the Framework Directive would seem to lead to the conclusion that headscarf bans in public education cannot be justified. Generally speaking, three arguments tend to be put forward to justify headscarf bans in public education: headscarves are incompatible with the notion of sex equality, with the requirement of state neutrality in public education and with public order.[32] None of these arguments is really convincing.

The first argument was dealt with above and seems to be untenable. Even if it may have validity in some cases, research indicates it is not true as a general rule in the European context.

The second major argument also seems unconvincing. Not because state neutrality is not to be protected in public education, but because wearing a headscarf as such cannot be presumed to endanger it. For this contention we can find support in a Dutch case decided by the Dutch Equal Treatment Commission under the General Equal Treatment Act.[33] This Act prohibits direct and indirect discrimination on the basis of religion, belief, political orientation, race, gender, nationality, sexual orientation and civil status. The case concerned a student teacher at a public primary school, who was not allowed by the school authorities to wear her headscarf in class. The argument turned on the required neutrality of the state. As public education must respect all religions and denominations, teachers must have an open attitude towards different convictions and beliefs. This, in turn, means teachers should be very reluctant in expressly manifesting their adherence to a particular religion or conviction. This is all the more so, the school authorities added:

> . . . in case a way of dressing identifies a person with a group which does not only live according to strict opinions themselves, but which also has shown little tolerance towards persons with different opinions within the same religion. It seems evident that an Islamic woman, who considers it her duty to wear the headscarf even in the intimacy of her classroom, bears witness to holding very stringent opinions, also in comparison with the large majority of her fellow-believers, and may thus be perceived as threatening to other women and girls of the same religion, who mostly achieved the right to a freer way of living with difficulty.[34]

In assessing whether the exclusion of the student teacher amounts to discrimination on the basis of religion, the Equal Treatment Commission is very brief. The Commission affirms the legitimacy of requiring public school teachers to have and display an open attitude towards all convictions and beliefs. Yet, to find out whether the student teacher complied with this requirement it was not legitimate for the school to just presume from her wearing a headscarf that this open attitude was missing. The school should have inquired after the actual opinions and ideas of the teacher instead.

The public order argument put forward to ban religious symbols from the classroom seems rather shaky as well. Given the controversies surrounding the headscarf, it may indeed create a lot of tension and unrest in schools. The Commission Stasi put quite some emphasis on this point.[35] Likewise, the German constitutional court, the *Bundesverfassungsgericht*, considered it could provide a legitimate reason to prohibit headscarves being worn by public school teachers.[36] Although tensions created by the headscarf issue can, indeed, sometimes lead to serious problems, one wonders whether this should ever be a sufficient argument to put a ban on religious symbols in school. It would rather seem like giving in to intolerance.

14.6 Conclusions

A comparison of the ECHR and the EU legal regimes shows up different approaches to the issue of banning headscarves from public education. Under the ECHR, the issue is mainly discussed in terms of freedom of religion, not in terms of (indirect) discrimination, as it is under the EC Directives. Yet, similar criteria are used to decide whether a prohibition to wear headscarves or other religious symbols in public education is allowed.

Does that mean the outcome of this test must be the same under both legal regimes, as the ECHR would take priority over EU law in cases of conflict? From the perspective of EC law, I would answer this question in the negative. Several reasons can be put forward. First, the ECHR intends to give a minimum standard only. EU law can give more protection, as is expressly provided for in the EU Charter of Fundamental Rights. I would say the EU should do so, given its enhanced commitment to human rights. Second, the European Court of Human Rights leaves large margin of appreciation to the state parties to regulate religious expressions, whereas the ECJ is focused much more on setting a uniform standard for all Member States. And lastly, traditionally exceptions to sex discrimination are supposed to be reviewed very strictly. I would say the same holds true for race and religion, as both are very important as identity markers; Applying a strict test, I would say that no sufficiently strong arguments exist for prohibiting headscarves in public education as such. At the same time, we have to be aware of the politically sensitive nature of the issue, so we will have to wait and see what direction the ECJ will take if ever it is confronted with it.

Notes

1 The most important of these are Council Directive 75/117/EEC on the approximation of the laws of the Member States relating to the application of the principle of equal pay for men and women [1975] OJ L45/19, incorporated by [1994] OJ L1/ 484; Council Directive 76/207/EEC on the implementation of the principle of equal treatment for men and women as regards access to employment, vocational training and promotion, and working conditions [1976] OJ L 9/40, Derogation in 194N, incorporated by [1994] OJ L1/484 and Council Directive 79/7/EEC of 19 December 1978 on the progressive implementation of the principle of equal

treatment for men and women in matters of social security 1979 OJL 6/24, incorporated by [1994] OJ L1/484.

2 Council Directive 2000/43/EC implementing the principle of equal treatment between persons irrespective of racial or ethnic origin [2000] OJ L180/22.

3 Council Directive 2000/78/EC establishing a general framework for equal treatment in employment and occupation [2000] OJ L303/16 (Framework Directive).

4 Council Directive 2004/113/EC implementing the principle of equal treatment between men and women in the access to and supply of goods and services [2004] OJ L 373/37.

5 Wherever I use the term 'race' in this chapter I mean it to cover racial and ethnic origin, as in the EC Directive.

6 The initiative to ban religious symbols in schools was largely inspired by incidents concerning the *hijab*, and the headscarf was the main issue in the subsequent debates. Many considered it a reaction to the failing integration of Muslim immigrant groups in French society. See more extensively on this issue, e.g. TJ Gunn (2004) 'Religious freedom and *laïcité*: a comparison of the United States and France', *Brigham Young University Law Review:* 419–505.

7 Cf. Germany, where the case of *Ludin*, a Muslim teacher who was refused as a public school teacher because she was wearing a headscarf, created similarly heated debates as in France. Here again it was not religion as such which can explain the agitation it created throughout Germany, since in some of the German *Länder* no such turmoil surrounds the Catholic nuns who sometimes still teach in public schools, even in full religious dress. See more extensively on the German debate, e.g. D Schiek (2004) 'Just a piece of cloth? German courts and employees with headscarves', *Industrial Law Journal*, 33: 68–73 or M Mahlmann (2003) 'Religious tolerance, pluralist society and the neutrality of the state: the Federal Constitutional Court's decision in the headscarf case', *German Law Journal*, 4: 1099–116, available at www.germanlawjournal.com/ (accessed 8 January 2008).

8 The Convention on the elimination of all discrimination on the basis of race embraces a broad definition as well. Race under this Convention includes 'colour, descent, or national or ethnic origin' (Art 1, s 1).

9 See, e.g. the report of the Stasi Commission, which advised the French Government on the headscarf ban: Commission de réflexion sur l'application du principe de laïcité dans la République (2003) *Rapport au président de la République*, 11 décembre 2003, available at http://lesrapports.ladocumentationfrancaise.fr/BRP/034000725/0000.pdf (accessed 8 January 2008).

10 In a country such as the UK a general ban on religious symbols will also affect a large number of male Sikhs who wear a turban for religious reasons.

11 In the *Bosphorus* decision the European Court of Human Rights clarified the relationship between the European Convention on Human Rights and Community law and the responsibilities of the states parties under both. The Court's general approach is rather deferential: as the protection offered by the Community can be considered to be 'equivalent' to the protection offered by the Convention, the European Court of Human Rights will presume no conflict with the Convention exists unless 'in the circumstances of a particular case, it is considered that the protection of the Convention rights was manifestly deficient', ECHR, 30 June 2005, *Bosphorus v Ireland*, Application no 45036/98, s 156.

12 Charter of Fundamental Rights of the European Union [2000] OJ C 364/1. The Reform Treaty agreed upon at the European Council meeting in June 2007 stipulates that the Charter 'shall have the same legal value as the Treaties'. This means it will become legally binding after all.

13 See Protocol No 12 to the Convention for the Protection of Human Rights and Fundamental Freedoms, 4 November 2000, CETS 177, *Explanatory Report*,

available at http://conventions.coe.int/treaty/en/Reports/html/177.htm (accessed 8 January 2008).

14 To date, only about 15 states have ratified the protocol.

15 Article 14: 'The enjoyment of the rights and freedoms set forth in this Convention shall be secured without discrimination on any ground such as sex, race, colour, language, religion, political or other opinion, national or social origin, association with a national minority, property, birth or other status'.

16 Case 293/83 *Françoise Gravier v City of Liège* [1985] ECR 593.

17 ECHR, 15 February 2001, *Dahlab v Switzerland* (decision on admissibility), Application No 42393/98, and ECHR, 10 November 2005, *Sahin v Turkey* (Grand Chamber), Application No 44774/98, available at www.echr.coe.int/ECHR/EN/Header/Case-Law/HUDOC/HUDOC+database/ (accessed 8 January 2008).

18 *Dahlab v Switzerland* (decision on admissibility), Application No 42393.

19 For a long time the ECHR has been quite reluctant to acknowledge the concept of indirect discrimination. See more extensively D Schiek (2007) 'Indirect discrimination', in D Schiek, L Waddington and M Bell (eds) *Non-Discrimination Law*, Oxford: Hart Publishing, pp 341–5.

20 ECHR, 10 November 2005 (Grand Chamber), *Sahin v Turkey*, available at http://cmiskp.echr.coe.int/tkp197/view.asp?item=4&portal=hbkm&action=html&highlight=Sahin%20%7C%20v.%20%7C%20Turkey&sessionid=4499387&skin=hudoc-en (accessed 8 January 2008).

21 Ibid, para 111.

22 Ibid, para 109.

23 Another way in which direct discrimination on the basis of religion could be at stake regards the situation of the Islamic religion being singled out. Although this may be the hidden agenda, states probably will not expressly do so. Thus French legislation is formulated neutrally by banning all ostentatious religious symbols.

24 This is, in fact, the approach taken by the Dutch Equal Treatment Commission, see e.g. oordeel 2001–53, available at www.cgb.nl/ (accessed 8 January 2008) (available in Dutch only).

25 See extensively C Tobler (2005) *Indirect Discrimination. A Case Study into the Development of the Legal Concept of Indirect Discrimination under EC Law*, Antwerpen, Oxford: Intersentia.

26 P van Dijk, F van Hoof, A van Rijn and L Zwaak (eds) (2006) *Theory and Practice of the European Convention on Human Rights*, 4th edn, Antwerpen, Oxford: Intersentia, pp 334–42.

27 In fact this was a major argument for the Commission Stasi to advise the French government to ban headscarves and other ostentatious religious symbols from public schools, see its report, op cit., fn 9.

28 BVerfGE 108, 282–340 (24 September 2003 – file no 2 BvR 1436/02): '*Die Forschungsergebnisse zeigen jedoch, dass die Deutung des Kopftuchs nicht auf ein Zeichen gesellschaftlicher Unterdrückung der Frau verkurzt werden darf. Vielmehr kann das Kopftuch für junge muslimische Frauen auch ein frei gewähltes Mittel sein, um ohne Bruch mit der Herkunftskultur ein selbstbestimmtes Leben zu führen*' (s 52). For more detail on this see U Sacksofsky, Chapter 16, in this book.

29 E.g. C Dwyer (1999) 'Veiled meanings: Young British Muslim women and the negotiation of differences', *Gender, Place and Culture*, 6: 5–26, and C Killian (2003) 'The other side of the veil. North African women in France respond to the headscarf affair', *Gender & Society*, 17: 567–90.

30 This case is mentioned in H Skjeie (2007) 'Headscarves in schools: European comparisons', in T Loenen and J Goldschmidt (eds) *Religious Pluralism and Human Rights in Europe: Where to Draw the Line?*, Antwerp: Intersentia, pp 129–46.

31 See extensively C Tobler (2005) *Indirect Discrimination. A Case Study into the Development of the Legal Concept of Indirect Discrimination under EC Law*, Antwerpen, Oxford: Intersentia; exceptions regard mainly social security cases.

32 See, e.g. the case of *Sahin v Turkey* (Grand Chamber), Application No 42393/98 and the report of the Stasi-Commission (see n 9 above).

33 Oordeel (decision) 1999–18 and 1999–103, available at www.cgb.nl/ (accessed 8 January 2008) (the decisions are available in Dutch only).

34 The translation is by the author. The original Dutch reads: '*Die noodzaak tot terughoudendheid geldt te meer als het gaat om een wijze van kleden die de betrokkene vereenzelvigt met een groepering, die niet alleen voor zichzelf zeer strenge opvattingen naleeft, maar ook weinig blijk geeft van tolerantie ten opzichte van andersdenkenden binnen dezelfde religie. Het lijkt evident dat een Islamitische vrouw die zelfs in de beslotenheid van het eigen klaslokaal meent de hoofddoek te moeten dragen, ook in vergelijking met de grote meerderheid van haar geloofsgenoten, getuigt van zeer stringente opvattingen en daarmee impliciet bedreigend kan overkomen op de vrouwen en meisjes van dezelfde godsdienst, die zich veelal met grote moeite het recht op een vrijere leefwijze hebben verworven*'.

35 See report of the Stasi-Commission (see n 9 above).

36 See BVerfGE 108, 282–340 (see n 28 above).

15 Religion, ethnicity and gender in the Danish headscarf debate

Lynn Roseberry

15.1 Introduction

In the years from 2000 to 2005 the Danish courts decided three cases concerning employer dress codes that had the effect of excluding Muslim women who practice veiling[1] from employment. In one case, a chocolate factory that had strict dress regulations for hygienic and safety reasons refused to employ a Somalian woman who wore a veil that covered her head and shoulders, leaving only her face free. In the other two cases, one Muslim woman of Turkish and one Muslim woman of Moroccan origin were not allowed to come to work wearing headscarves because their employers had adopted dress codes that were intended to project a particular public image. In all three cases, the plaintiffs claimed that only discrimination on grounds of religion had occurred. Only one of the cases resulted in a judgment in favour of the plaintiff.

The claims in these cases were based on employment discrimination legislation passed in 1996 before the adoption of Council Directive 2000/78/EC establishing a general framework for equal treatment in employment and occupation and Council Directive 2000/43/EC implementing the principle of equal treatment between persons irrespective of race or ethnic origin (hereinafter 'the Discrimination Directives'). Nevertheless, in the last case, decided in 2005, the Danish Supreme Court indicated in *dicta* that its decision in favour of the employer would not have been different had the case been brought under the legislation implementing the Discrimination Directives. The court's judgment did not include any discussion of whether and how it had interpreted the implementing legislation to be in conformity with the Discrimination Directives.

These cases raise a number of issues with regard to how national courts are to apply Community law prohibiting discrimination to claims of indirect discrimination against Muslim women arising from private employers' dress codes. Do the Discrimination Directives permit Muslim women's claims in these cases to be formulated as multiple discrimination on grounds of not only religion but also sex and ethnic origin? If so, how should the courts determine that differential treatment on the claimed prohibited grounds has occurred? Should the courts first compare women with men, then Muslims with non-Muslims, and then ethnic minorities with members of the ethnic majority? How should the courts then analyse the employers' justifications?

In this article, I hope to answer these questions by analysing the facts, arguments of the parties and reasoning of the courts in the Danish headscarf cases. I proceed by first summarising the cases and then turn to the question of whether Community law permits discrimination claims on multiple grounds, if so how differential treatment is to be determined when multiple prohibited grounds are involved and then how the multiple grounds of discrimination must be factored into the evaluation of the employers' justifications. I hope to show that the European Court of Justice's (ECJ's) case law on the general principle of non-discrimination provides the basis for an argument that claims arising from dress codes that indirectly discriminate against Muslim women who wear headscarves or other kinds of veils should be analysed as instances of multiple discrimination on grounds of ethnic origin, religion and sex. Further, that in order to ensure Muslim women the protection of the principle of equal treatment in these dress code cases courts must pay careful attention to the links between ethnic origin, religion and sex not just when determining whether differential treatment on prohibited grounds has occurred but also when evaluating employers' justifications for their directly or indirectly discriminatory policies.

Before beginning my analysis of the Danish headscarf cases I want to explain how I will be using the terms 'race' and 'ethnic origin'. First, I wish to emphasise that I adhere to the view that racial classifications based on presumed biological differences have no scientific validity. Rather, I subscribe to the modern view that race is a cultural and socio-political construct that singles out certain physical characteristics as criteria for defining a social group and legitimating domination.[2] Second, 'ethnicity' is often used in popular and political discourse in ways that imply distinctions based on physical markers, and thus makes it indistinguishable from race. Some social scientists reject the use of physical characteristics as a way of identifying ethnicity in order to avoid racialising ethnicities.[3] Instead, these social scientists consider ethnicity as something that is identifiable on the basis of an amorphous concept of cultural distinctiveness, based on such things as shared language, shared religion, shared traditions, and/or shared origins that lead to a sense of identity.[4] Others argue that the concepts 'race' and 'ethnicity' are indistinguishable. Stuart Hall, a well-known British sociologist, has written:

> Biological racism privileges markers like skin colour, but those signifiers have always been used, by discursive extension, to denote social and cultural differences. The biological referent is never wholly absent from discourses on ethnicity, though it is more indirect.[5]

When I argue that policies that disadvantage Muslim women who wear headscarves constitute indirect discrimination on the basis of, *inter alia*, race or ethnic origin in Denmark, I mean that these women are immigrants or descendants of immigrants, whom many Danes would not identify as ethnically Danish because of their appearance as well as their language and religion. Veiling is primarily practiced by immigrant women from Turkey, the Middle East, Africa and Asia or by descendants of these immigrants. Thus, the concept of ethnicity in Denmark, and popular identifications of ethnic origin includes physical appearance, and is thus difficult to separate from the concept of race. I will tend to use ethnic origin and race interchangeably in this chapter for that reason. Another aspect of the meaning I ascribe to 'ethnic origin' and 'race' is based on the Norwegian anthropologist Frederik Barth's constructivist view of ethnicity according to which people identify with groups and that groups are formed on the basis of perceptions of boundaries between groups, not on the basis of a collection of objective, measurable differences.[6] Veiling by Muslim women can be perceived by the wearers and the observers as marking various boundaries between different groups. The veil can mark the boundary between religions, social classes, cultures, and national or ethnic origin. Thus, I am not so concerned with identifying which ethnic groups are disadvantaged by the dress codes (what are contained within the boundaries), but rather with the boundary itself as a marker of differences which are covered by the prohibitions against discrimination.

15.2 Danish case law on Muslim headscarves and veils at work

In the first Muslim veiling case to reach the Danish Court of Appeals,[7] a young woman brought a religious discrimination claim when a department store, Magasin, refused to allow her to work as a trainee because she came to work wearing a headscarf. The department store justified its actions by claiming that it was contrary to its guidelines for employees' dress. The Court of Appeals held that the department store had violated the 1996 employment discrimination legislation's prohibition against discrimination on the basis of religion and required the store to pay the woman DKK 10,000. The court reasoned that the department store's guidelines regarding employees' dress were too loosely formulated to provide an objective basis for refusing to let the young woman work in the women's clothing department. In particular, the guidelines did not prohibit employees from wearing anything on their heads, nor did they require them to wear any kind of uniform or any specific type of clothing.

The second veiling case[8] was decided by the Court of Appeals for the Eastern District in 2001 and concerned a chocolate factory's, Toms, refusal to hire a Muslim woman to work in their production department because she insisted that covering her hair, neck, throat, ears and forehead were a part of her religious practice. The factory insisted that she must cover her head with a special net that all the employees in the production area were required to wear for hygienic and safety reasons. Since she could not fit her veil entirely under the net hat, the factory refused to hire her. The Court of Appeals found that although the factory's policy indirectly discriminated against Muslim women who chose to wear this kind of head covering, the hygienic and safety reasons justified the policy. Furthermore, the court emphasised that the requirement was applied uniformly to all employees and that since 20 per cent of the employees had another ethnic, cultural and/or religious background than the Danish cultural majority, the policy was not an expression of intentional ethnic, cultural or religious discrimination. The plaintiff appealed the judgment to the Supreme Court, but the parties reached a settlement while the case was still pending. The factory agreed to hire the woman after they together developed a special hat that she could pull over her head, cover everything she wanted to cover, and still fit under the employer-provided net cap.

The third and most recent case was decided on appeal at the Supreme Court, which handed down its judgment on 21 January 2005.[9] In this case a supermarket, Føtex, fired a young Muslim woman when she began to wear a headscarf to work four years after she had begun her employment at Føtex. She began wearing the headscarf after she had begun studying the Koran with four other female friends. After she was fired, she sued Føtex for indirect discrimination on grounds of religion. Føtex defended against the claim primarily by arguing that it had a strict dress code that required the employees to wear a uniform and also prohibited employees from wearing anything on their heads. Furthermore, the purpose of the dress code was to ensure that the employees had a neutral and uniform appearance. The employer's evidence on these points included statistics showing that it employed a large number of ethnic minorities, that the dress code only applied to employees who worked in areas with customer contact, and testimony that while Føtex's competitors allowed their Muslim female employees to wear headscarves, it was very important to Føtex that the business had a neutral public appearance and that it did not provide a platform for agitation. Føtex was particularly concerned that its employees' communication with customers should not be disturbed by political or religious symbols, and that some customers could be disturbed by meeting an employee wearing a Muslim headscarf while others could be disturbed by meeting an employee wearing a Rotary emblem or the Social Democrats' symbolic rose. Føtex did not present any evidence regarding the need for banning employees who wear religious and political symbols and work in areas requiring customer contact.

The Danish Supreme Court held that Føtex's dress code indirectly discriminated against Muslim women who wear headscarves for religious reasons, but that the dress code did not violate the discrimination law's prohibition against discrimination because the dress code was based on a legitimate and neutral objective. In support of this conclusion, the court quoted the explanatory remarks in the preparatory works for the 1996 employment discrimination law's provision on indirect discrimination.[10] The remarks explain that the provision on indirect discrimination does not prevent employers from requiring employees to wear uniforms or a certain kind of clothing if it is part of the undertaking's public image and if the requirement is consistently applied to all the employees in the same positions. In addition, the Supreme Court held that the case law of the European Court of Human Rights (ECtHR) did not provide any basis for finding that enforcement of the dress code is contrary to Art 9 of the European Convention on Human Rights. Finally, the Supreme Court asserted that the legislation Denmark had passed in 2004 to implement Council Directives 2000/43/EC and 2000/78/EC (hereinafter 'the Discrimination Directives') did not change anything in the way Danish courts were to analyse indirect discrimination resulting from employers' dress codes.[11] The Supreme Court supported this assertion by pointing out that the explanatory remarks for the 2004 implementing legislation contain an explicit statement to the effect that the legal status of dress codes remains the same as it was under the Employment Discrimination Act 1996.[12]

15.3 Community law and claims of indirect discrimination on multiple grounds

The plaintiffs in the Danish cases chose to focus their claim of indirect discrimination on their religion rather than on their sex or ethnic origin, even though they could have chosen any of these factors, since Muslim *women* are particularly burdened by these dress codes and most of them are members of ethnic minority groups in Denmark. The fact that only religion was chosen as the basis of the discriminatory effect of the dress code is consistent with practice in the US[13] and UK,[14] where the prevailing view of discrimination has been that it occurs primarily because of the presence of one protected factor. This view of discrimination is reflected in the way the legislation has been drafted and in the way the courts identify comparators for purposes of establishing disparate treatment or effect.[15] When this view of discrimination is applied to plaintiffs who cannot be identified with an entire group that shares one protected trait, for example all women, all Muslims, or all members of a specific ethnic minority, the courts dismiss their claims for failure to prove differential treatment on any prohibited ground. The American legal scholar Kimberlé Crenshaw, who was one of the first to call attention to this problem, explains that American minority women's lack of success in obtaining legal protection from discrimination was largely due to the limitations of the predominant conceptualisation of discrimination:

> Discrimination which is wrongful proceeds from the identification of a specific class or category, either a discriminator intentionally identifies this category, or a process is adopted which somehow disadvantages all members of this category. According to the dominant view, a discriminator treats all people within a race or sex category similarly. Any significant experiential or statistical variation within this group suggests either that the group is not being discriminated against or that conflicting

interests exist, which defeat any attempts to bring a common claim. Consequently, one generally cannot combine these categories.[16]

This conceptualisation of discrimination has denied the protection of anti-discrimination law to ethnic and racial minority women because discrimination against ethnic and racial minority women is often directed specifically against women of particular ethnic and racial minorities rather than men in those groups or against white women.[17] For example, American employers have historically discriminated against black women in pay and promotions, even though the same employers have not discriminated against Black men or white women in pay or promotions.[18]

The choice of one basis of indirect discrimination in the Danish headscarf cases suggests that the single-factor model of discrimination that prevails in the US and UK may be just as dominant in Denmark. At least one Danish legal article has applied the single-factor model to the *Føtex* case and concluded, despite the findings of the Danish courts, that Føtex's dress code did not discriminate against Muslims because a relatively large number of Føtex's employees were Muslims.[19] The question thus arises whether the ECJ is likely to follow the single-factor model. Some aspects of the current Community law on discrimination suggest that it might. Like the anti-discrimination legislation in the US and UK, the Discrimination Directives do not contain any explicit provision permitting or defining multiple-factor claims. Furthermore, like the current UK discrimination legislation, the various prohibited bases of discrimination are split up among different instruments. One might conclude on this basis alone that the ECJ may be unlikely to interpret the Discrimination Directives as permitting multiple discrimination claims – particularly if the claims involve multiple discrimination beyond the employment sphere, since only the Race Directive's scope encompasses more than employment.

One factor militating in favour of the ECJ's recognition of multiple discrimination claims is that the Preambles of the Discrimination Directives do include Recitals that mention multiple discrimination. They state, 'In implementing the principle of equal treatment, the Community should, in accordance with Article 3(2) of the EC Treaty, aim to eliminate inequalities, and to promote equality between men and women, *especially since women are often the victims of multiple discrimination*'.[20] However, no substantive provisions in the Directives address the problem of multiple discrimination. The ECJ could conclude that the Recital merely indicates that the legislator imagines that by adding more specific discrimination prohibitions, albeit in different instruments, sex equality will be advanced because women who are discriminated against on grounds other than sex can bring claims on those grounds as well.

Another factor that may persuade the ECJ to recognise claims of discrimination based on multiple grounds is its method of interpreting secondary Community legislation. When the ECJ interprets secondary EC legislation, it seeks as far as possible to interpret the legislation consistently with the purpose and provisions of the EC Treaty and general principles of Community law.[21] Thus, the ECJ is not likely to limit its interpretation of the Discrimination Directives to the Directives' texts alone. The Treaty Articles that the ECJ will refer to in interpreting the Discrimination Directives are Art 13 EC, which is the direct Treaty basis for the Directives, and Arts 2 and 3 EC, which set out the aims and activities of the Community. Article 13 EC provides:

Without prejudice to the other provisions of this Treaty and within the limits of the powers conferred by it upon the Community, the Council, acting unanimously on a proposal from the Commission and after consulting the European Parliament, may take appropriate action to combat discrimination based on sex, racial or ethnic origin, religion or belief, disability, age or sexual orientation.

To the extent that the reference to multiple discrimination in the Directives' Preambles may persuade the ECJ that multiple discrimination can and does occur, it seems unlikely that the ECJ would insist that either Directive precludes simultaneous application of several prohibited factors to one instance of discrimination simply because Art 13 EC lists the prohibited bases using the word 'or' instead of 'and'. Even American courts have recognised that the word 'or' used between the prohibited bases of discrimination can be read to suggest an intent to prohibit discrimination on any or all of the listed characteristics.[22]

Furthermore, according to Art 2 EC, one of the tasks of the Community is 'economic and social cohesion and solidarity among Member States' and for that purpose, Art 3(1)(k) EC includes among the activities of the Community, 'strengthening of economic and social cohesion'. The Preambles of the Discrimination Directives include a number of Recitals indicating that one of the main purposes of these Directives is to strengthen economic and social cohesion. Recitals in both Directives note that '[t]he Employment Guidelines for 2000 agreed by the European Council at Helsinki on 10 and 11 December 1999 stress the need to foster a labour market favourable to social integration by formulating a coherent set of policies aimed at combating discrimination against groups'.[23] Both Directives recognise in their Preambles that '[d]iscrimination [based on the protected factors] may undermine the achievement of the objectives of the EC Treaty, in particular the attainment of a high level of employment and social protection, raising the standard of living and the quality of life, economic and social cohesion and solidarity, and the free movement of persons'.[24] The Framework Directive notes that '[e]mployment and occupation are key elements in guaranteeing equal opportunities for all and contribute strongly to the full participation of citizens in economic, cultural and social life and to realizing their potential'.[25] If the ECJ accepts the premise of the Directives' Preambles, that multiple discrimination occurs and especially affects women, and that all forms of discrimination undermine the

Community's efforts to improve social and economic cohesion, then the ECJ is likely to accept the idea of combating multiple discrimination through the simultaneous application of several prohibited factors to an individual's claim of discrimination.

Furthermore, the gender mainstreaming provision contained in Art 3(2) EC requires all Community actors, including the ECJ and national courts in their capacity as Community courts, to promote equality between men and women in all the Community activities listed in Art 3(1) EC.[26] The mainstreaming obligation could be understood as requiring the ECJ and national courts to consider the gender impact of their analysis of all discrimination claims and to avoid any interpretation of Community law that is detrimental to the goal of sex equality. At the very least then, the ECJ and national courts must include sex equality in their analysis of any case of discrimination that falls within the scope of either of the Discrimination Directives.

Finally, it could be argued that the Community principle of non-discrimination obligates the ECJ and the national courts to consider all prohibited bases of discrimination that are present in a given case, even if they fall outside the scope of application of one of the Directives. As noted above, the ECJ seeks to interpret Community legislation consistently with general principles of Community law. The ECJ has recognised the principle of equal treatment and non-discrimination generally, unrelated to any specific grounds, as a fundamental right under Community law.[27] It has also recognised prohibitions against discrimination on grounds of gender[28] and, most recently and controversially, age,[29] as fundamental rights that are included in the general principle of equal treatment. Most importantly, the ECJ has asserted in *Mangold* that 'Directive 2000/78 does not itself lay down the principle of equal treatment in the field of employment and occupation'.[30] Rather, '. . . the sole purpose of the directive is "to lay down a general framework for combating discrimination on the grounds of religion or belief, disability, age or sexual orientation" '.[31] The ECJ finds 'the source of the actual principle underlying the prohibition of those forms of discrimination . . . in the constitutional traditions common to the Member States'.[32] By characterising the specific prohibitions against discrimination set out in the Framework Directive as specific expressions of a more general principle of equal treatment, the ECJ has indicated that all the specific prohibitions against discrimination in the Discrimination Directives are included in the general principle of equal treatment. The ECJ's characterisation of the individual grounds of discrimination as specific expressions of a more general Community principle of non-discrimination, supports the view that the Directives should be interpreted as allowing proof of unequal treatment based on the multiple protected factors that lead to the disadvantage from which the claim arises. Thus, in the Danish headscarf cases each of the claims of indirect discriminations were correctly evaluated as indirect discrimination against Muslim women. The courts did not compare the impact of the dress codes on all Muslims or all women, but rather recognised that Muslim women were disadvantaged as compared with Muslim men and as compared with non-Muslim women.

15.4 The general princple of non-discrimination and justification of indirect discrimination against Muslim women

If the general principle of non-discrimination requires the courts to treat Muslim women as a distinct group that is different from 'Muslims' and 'women', then the same principle must apply at all stages of the analysis, not just to the admissibility of the claim. In the following discussion, I intend to show how considering the multiple grounds of discrimination at the justification stage in the dress code cases can affect the outcome of dress code cases like those seen in Denmark.

The plaintiff in the department store case won a judgment in her favour because the dress code did not even meet the standard described in the explanatory remarks to the employment discrimination statute. The employees were not required to wear uniforms, and the vague dress requirements that the employer sought to uphold were not consistently applied to all the employees in the same positions. Consideration of the multiple grounds of discrimination at the justification stage of the analysis would not have made any difference.

In the chocolate factory (*Toms*) case, the employer's dress code was adopted to serve safety and hygienic reasons. The main disagreement between the parties was whether the employer had sufficiently demonstrated that no other alternatives to the employers' dress code were available. The burden of proof provisions in the Discrimination Directives were not implemented in Denmark until 2004. The normal rules of evidence were applied, which are arguably less strict than the Directives. Had the courts recognised the gender dimension of the discriminatory effects of the dress code, Community law on the burden of proof in sex discrimination cases could and should have been applied. Applying the stricter burden of proof required by the law on sex discrimination could have resulted in a different outcome.

Consideration of the multiple bases of discrimination could have similarly affected the outcome of the case in *Føtex*. The plaintiff in the *Føtex* case argued that the employer failed to prove that creating a uniform and neutral appearance among the employees was necessary or even important to the business or that the unconditional prohibition against head coverings was a proportionate means of achieving that goal. Both the Danish Court of Appeals and the Supreme Court in the *Føtex* case decided instead to follow the well-established Danish rule of statutory interpretation that courts must defer to the explanatory remarks attached to the legislation. Since the explanatory remarks clearly state that presenting a neutral appearance to the public is an objective and therefore legitimate aim, the courts did not require evidence of the business interest in having its employees with customer contact adopt a 'neutral' appearance. It was merely assumed that such an objective is legitimate in all cases. Furthermore, since the explanatory remarks clearly state that the dress code must be consistently enforced with regards to all employees in the same position, the question of whether the same goal could be achieved by allowing Muslim women to wearing head-scarves that matched the uniform was not addressed. Indeed, the explanatory remarks on the legislation indicate that uniform application of the dress code is necessary to be considered lawful.

Had the courts considered that the dress code also indirectly discriminated against women, the ECJ's case law on justification of indirect sex discrimination should have been considered relevant. The leading case on justification of indirect sex discrimination is still *Bilka Kaufhaus v Weber* in which the ECJ held that employers must justify indirectly discriminatory policies or practices by showing that the purpose of those policies or practices are based on 'objective factors that are unrelated to any discrimination on grounds of sex'.[33] The ECJ repeatedly refers to its original holding in *Bilka* that private employers satisfy the requirement of objective justification of indirectly discriminatory measures if the national court finds that the measures chosen by the employer correspond to a real need on the part of the undertaking, and are appropriate with a view to achieving the objective pursued and are necessary to that end.[34] The ECJ has also held that although Community law grants the Member States a broad margin of discretion in implementing Community social policy, a Member State's mere generalisations about the objective of indirectly discriminatory legislative measures are not enough to show that their aim is unrelated to any discrimination based on sex nor are they sufficient evidence to support a finding that measures chosen were suitable for achieving that aim.[35] As a matter of Community law, then, the Danish courts cannot simply rely on the explanatory remarks' generalisation that all dress codes adopted for the purpose of creating the business's public image that require a uniform or some kind of specific clothing and is consistently applied to all employees in the same position are objectively justifiable. As the plaintiff in *Føtex* argued, the employer should have offered evidence of the preferences and needs of its customer base, to the extent they did not relate to racial or religious preferences, to support the assertion that a uniform and neutral appearance was an objective business interest having nothing to do with religious or racial preferences. In the absence of such evidence, the indirectly discriminatory dress code at *Føtex* should have been found unlawful.

Now that Denmark has implemented the Discrimination Directives the same burden of proof provisions that have applied to sex discrimination cases apply to cases concerning discrimination on the other grounds as well. Furthermore, since the Discrimination Directives build on the earlier sex discrimination Directives and on the ECJ's case law on sex discrimination, the ECJ will most probably apply its case law on indirect sex discrimination to indirect discrimination involving any of the prohibited grounds. That case law has established that justification of indirect sex discrimination must be based on 'objective factors unrelated to any discrimination on grounds of sex'.[36] The ECJ is therefore likely to hold that justification of indirect racial/ethnic origin and/or religious discrimination must be justified on grounds that have nothing to do with race or ethnic origin or religion. The employer's justification in the *Føtex* case probably does not satisfy this requirement as employer representatives testified in court that the aim of the dress code was to avoid 'disturbing' customers with any indication of the employees' religious beliefs or political opinions. The Muslim headscarf was given as an example of a religious symbol that could offend some customers. This testimony suggests that the dress code is, as regards religion, primarily aimed at satisfying the preferences of customers who object to either Islam itself, Muslim veiling practices, or to religions that include rules about how one is to dress or wear one's hair.[37]

In light of the foregoing, the Danish Supreme Court's unexplained remark that the Danish legislation implementing the new Discrimination Directives would not change Danish practice on indirectly discriminatory dress codes is puzzling. Danish legal commentary on the headscarf cases sheds light on the legal arguments that might be made to support the Danish Supreme Court's interpretation of the Danish implementing legislation. The arguments proceed from one or all of the following assertions:

(a) Religious clothing and political expression should be treated the same way.
(b) All Muslim veiling practices, including headscarves, are symbols of sex inequality and an expression of the oppression of Muslim women.
(c) The case law of the ECtHR on Muslim headscarves supports the view that the Community principle of non-discrimination should be interpreted to grant the Member States a broad margin of discretion in adopting legislation that permits restrictions on women wearing headscarves in public areas in order to protect public order and the rights and freedoms of others.

I will address each of these assertions separately below. I intend to show that each of these assertions is untenable when understood in light of the links between religion, ethnic origin, and gender in Muslim veiling practices.

15.4.1 *Religion and political opinion*

A commentary on the Danish employment discrimination statute of 1996 explains that the statute treats discrimination on the basis of religion and political opinion as the same thing.[38] According to this view, the statute prohibits employers from distinguishing between political and religious 'symbols'. The commentary asserts that if an employer allows Muslim female employees to wear headscarves along with their uniforms, then the employer must allow a male employee with Nazi political opinions to shave his head and come to work with a swastika tattooed on his head.[39] Thus, according to this interpretation of indirect discrimination resulting from employer dress codes there is no objective basis for an employer to distinguish between religious 'symbols' worn as part of religious practice (for example, Muslim headscarves, Jewish skull caps and Sikh turbans) and political opinions.

Interpreting the principle of equal treatment as requiring employers to avoid distinctions between Muslim women and Nazi men is conceptually problematic for a number of reasons, not least of which is the erasure of the gender and racial dimensions of the dress code. 'Race' is implicated in the dress code because of the construction of racial categories based on the particular characteristics of different minority ethnic groups, including the different ways in which ethnic groups identify themselves through dress. Sociological studies have contributed to an increasing recognition that the concept of 'race' is a social construct that reflects 'ideological attempts to legitimate domination' of certain groups in society.[40] The 1950 UNESCO statement, 'The Race Question', which was written by a team of internationally renowned scientists, including Claude Lévi-Strauss, recommended dropping the term 'race' altogether because 'to most people, a race is any group of people whom they choose to describe as a race'.[41] The statement points out that 'many national, religious, geographic, linguistic or cultural groups have, in such loose usage, been called "race" ', when they clearly are not.[42] According to these studies, identifying a 'racial' group with a particular religion, language, customs, and dress is part of the process of constructing a 'racial' category that then serves to legitimate domination.

A useful example of how religion and race can become inextricably linked in the process of legitimating the domination of an ethnic minority is the legal construction of an enemy Japanese 'race' in the US during the Second World War. During the Second World War Japanese Americans were identified as a racial group that posed a threat to American national security and were, accordingly, confined to prison camps and subjected to legally sanctioned economic discrimination. Before the war, Japanese American Buddhists were viewed as more 'foreign' and therefore more closely tied to Japan.[43] After the onset of war the Federal Bureau of Investigation classified Buddhist priests as 'known dangerous Group A suspects' and included them in the first round of government arrests and detentions.[44] Concern over religious difference was then linked to Japanese Americans' educational choices for their children. Earl Warren, in his capacity of Attorney General of California at the time, testified before the US Congress that the US-born Japanese that were sent to Japan for education also received religious instruction, 'which ties up their religion with their Emperor, and they come back here imbued with the ideas and the politics of imperial Japan'.[45] Writing for the majority in *Hirabayashi v US*, Justice Stone then picks up this line of thought and refers to the education of Japanese children in Japanese language schools as evidence of un-assimilability[46] which is considered as a legitimate reason for imposing a curfew on Japanese Americans in certain designated areas of the country. By this time, the Western Defence Command had also issued the so-called 'Final Report', which advanced the view that the Japanese in America were 'a tightly knit racial group, bound to an enemy nation by strong ties of race, culture, custom and religion'.[47]

This historical record illustrates how a 'racial' group can be constructed for the purpose of domination by ascribing homogenous traits to the members of the group. Although Japanese Americans were adherents to several different religions, they were conceived as having either the same religious beliefs or their differences were simply dismissed as inconsequential. This understanding of the way 'racial' categories are constructed suggests that ethnic minorities must be regarded as differently situated than political minorities, who cannot be identified with an ethnic minority, and that the equal treatment principle requires differential treatment of political symbols and clothing worn as a matter of religious conviction and/or ethnic identity.

A slightly different version of the foregoing argument is that Muslim veiling practices, besides being the fulfilment of religious precepts, also symbolise an anti-democratic political programme that includes the oppression of women.[48] This contention is a categorical generalisation about the meaning of Muslim veiling practices that resembles the generalisations about Japanese Americans' religious beliefs that ignored the actual heterogeneity within that group. Anthropological studies document the heterogeneity of Muslim women's experiences with veiling and show that Muslim veiling is a complex phenomenon that 'was and is a practice that is differentiated and variable, with each variant deeply embedded in the cultural systems'.[49]

Muslim women who wear veils are not necessarily representing such political programmes. For many of them, it is simply a part of their identity. In her study of Muslim veiling, anthropologist Professor El Guindi notes that veiling is an important part of Muslim women's formation of their identity, which includes not just their religion but also their ethnicity.[50] This characterisation of the function of Muslim women's veiling practices is based on anthropological studies of the social meaning of dress. These studies show that customs regarding dress serve to define a group geographically and historically, linking the individual to that specific community.[51]

If Muslim veiling is a way of marking cultural or ethnic identity, then policies that restrict their use can have the effect of repressing Muslim women's ethnic identity. Muslim veiling cannot therefore be regarded as being primarily part of a political programme without attributing a non-existent homogeneity to Muslim women that contributes to the social construction of an illusory racial group.

Finally, if veiling practices serve as a sign that the individual belongs to a certain group, it also differentiates the same individual from all others. This property of simultaneous inclusion and exclusion makes the need to scrutinise justifications for policies that have the effect of excluding Muslim women who wear veils. The well-known German psychologist Erik Erikson has explained that the flip side of this sense of belonging that arises from ethnic identity is an image of a 'negative identity', which we all learn to repress in order to live up to the expectations of our cultural groups.[52] This phenomenon explains why people who belong to other groups with other ways of behaving make us feel uncomfortable. Not only has our own acculturation not prepared us to understand their behaviour, their differentness 'serve[s] handily as a screen on which we can project our own negative identities. Our psychic response is predictable: we want to repress the outsiders' incorrect, foreign ways'.[53] This urge to repress and exclude those whose appearance signals a different ethnic identity from our own describes the psychological mechanism driving both direct and indirect discrimination and highlights the importance of heightened scrutiny of justifications offered for employer policies that have the effect of excluding ethnic minority Muslim women. The requirements of objective justification and proportionality must be applied in a way that minimises the influence of ethnic bias. This can be achieved by interpreting the requirement that 'the provision, criterion or practice is objectively justified by a legitimate aim' as requiring the employer to show that the aim of his policy is to achieve a real business need that has nothing to do with subjective perceptions of the social meaning of the headscarf or any other religious dress.

15.4.2 The conflict between religious freedom and sex equality

The contention that all Muslim veiling practices should be considered as symbols of Muslim women's oppression similarly seeks to portray Muslim veiling practices as one phenomenon with one single meaning forecloses the possibility of recognising the heterogeneity of Muslim women's own experiences and understandings of the meaning of veiling. I have already mentioned that one of the meanings veiling can have is the marking of one's ethnic and religious identity in opposition to other ethnic and religious identities.

Muslim women have also used veiling to communicate their resistance to forced assimilation to foreign cultures. One example of the veil as a symbol of resistance is the Algerian women's use of veiling to symbolise their resistance to the French occupation. When the French arrived in Algeria in 1830 most inhabitants were Arabic-speaking Sunni Muslims.[54] One of the colonising strategies of the French occupation was to Gallicise Algeria. Accordingly, French law was imposed and Algerians, who were then called the 'Muslims', were forbidden by law to study Arabic in the public schools. Algerian women were especially targeted for Gallicisation, as the veil was such a visible cultural difference, and it was thought that unveiling women would somehow allow French culture to take root.[55] 'The effect was the opposite of that intended by the French – it strengthened the attachment to the veil as a national and cultural symbol on the part of patriotic Algerian women, giving the veil [and Algerian culture] a new vitality'.[56] El Guindi attributes the continuing strength of veiling practices in Algeria 51 years after formal independence in 1956 to the continuing struggle to establish an independent national identity – as evidenced by the fact that Arabic was established as the official language as late as 1998.[57]

Another example of how women may choose to wear a veil as a symbol of resistance was Iranian women's use of veiling as a symbol of resistance against the Shah's regime before the revolution in 1979.[58] Reza Shah banned the veil in 1936. The police arrested women who wore the veil and forcibly removed it. 'To ordinary women "appearing in public without their cover was tantamount to nakedness" ', while on the other hand the ban 'was welcomed by Westernized and upper-class men and women, who saw it in liberal terms as a first step in granting women their rights . . .'.[59] After the Shah's abdication in 1941, the policy of unveiling was abandoned, but among the Westernised and upper-class men and women, wearing the veil during the Pahlavi era continued to be regarded as a 'badge of backwardness'.[60] By the 1970s veiling began to represent resistance to the Pahlavi dictatorship. Many middle-class urban working women voluntarily began wearing a headscarf, and by 'March 1979, when the intentions of the new regime became clear, [Iranian] women once again took to the streets, this time to protest against the veil'.[61]

These examples show that rather than being a constant symbol of Muslim women's oppression by Islam, veiling has been practiced by Muslim women to mark their ethnic identity in resistance to cultural domination. 'Emancipation can be expressed by wearing the veil or by removing it. It can be secular or religious'.[62]

In addition to expressing resistance to cultural domination, Muslim women can also choose to wear the veil, as the plaintiff in the *Føtex* case testified that she did, as part of a sincere religious practice. To characterise a woman's decision to wear a headscarf as nothing more than an expression of their oppression through Islam echoes the 'false consciousness' arguments developed by various radical critiques of dominant ideology beginning with Engels and Marx.[63] 'False consciousness' arguments generally seek to explain seemingly free choices made by members of an oppressed group that seem to perpetuate the patterns of their own oppression. Such choices are generally described as 'being the product of internalization, by the oppressed group, of essential elements of the dominant ideology', a process which is supposed to occur 'beyond the conscious comprehension of the oppressed group: members of the group may perceive their actions as freely chosen, or as influenced by a range of non-ideological factors'.[64] Abrams argues that claims of ideological determination are vulnerable to the criticism that they are both reductionist and essentialist.[65] They are reductionist because they attribute entire categories of decisions to one single influence: ideology. They are essentialist because they assume that all women experience gender oppression in the same way regardless of race, class and sexual orientation. By asserting that the Muslim veil is in and of itself a symbol of women's oppression, non-Muslim female academics of white Western European ethnic origin overlook race, class and sexual orientation as powerful sources of differentiation among women, and present as universal their own perceptions of what constitutes oppression of women. The choices and experiences of Muslim women that do not conform to this portrayal are simply dismissed as evidence of false consciousness.

Levelling accusations of 'false consciousness' against Muslim women who assert that they choose to veil themselves because of their own sincere religious belief also bears a disquieting resemblance to one of the attitudes that has generated discrimination against women throughout history and across cultures: 'the belief that women are deficient in those faculties necessary to make important decisions'.[66] Muslim women in Algeria and Iran have been forced to both wear and not wear the veil because their own choices have not been respected. The belief that women are incapable of making important decisions has also fuelled the exclusion of women from the franchise, political office, and public life in general.[67] Against this historical background, justifications of dress codes that ban Muslim female employees from wearing headscarves that are based on the goal of promoting sex equality is not only an affront to the women who feel they have chosen to wear the headscarf but fails to satisfy the requirement of objective justification. Rather than promoting sex equality, this kind of justification perpetuates sexist portrayals of women as being weak-willed and unable to act in their own best interests.

Even if, as a number of feminists contend, a good number of Muslim women in Europe have been pressured to wear headscarves or other kinds of veils by Islamist groups that seek to assert their role as the deciders of what is 'appropriate' behaviour for women,[68] dress codes that preclude Muslim women from employment if they wear headscarves cannot be justified by the claim that they aim to promote sex equality. When Muslim women don a veil in response to these edicts, it can be regarded as a symbol of patriarchal oppression, but banning headscarves in the workplace would most likely only marginalise these women further. Wearing a headscarf to work may be the only way a woman in such circumstances will find it possible to obtain employment without risking her position in the ethnic/religious community into which she has been born or socialised. If the prevailing view in her community is that a 'respectable' Muslim woman must cover herself up, she can choose to wear the headscarf or veil and retain the respect and recognition of her religious and/or ethnic community but risk being excluded from employment and denounced as unwilling to conform to Western standards of sex equality. She could choose not to wear the headscarf and perhaps gain employment but suffer the loss of her honour – which can have a number of exceedingly unpleasant consequences over which she has little control, such as exclusion from the social life of the community, withdrawal of familial support, intimidation, threats, and even violence. Further constraining her choices is the knowledge that merely removing her headscarf is not a guarantee against employment discrimination if she is identified as not belonging to the majority ethnic population, nor can she count on finding any substitute for the withdrawn support of her family and community or protection from intimidation and violence. These factors constitute patriarchal oppression of which the headscarf is merely a symbol for these women. Prohibiting head-scarves at work makes women pay the price – again – for their own oppression and thus fails to address the conditions that constrain their choices and construct their sex inequality.

15.4.3 The Community principle of non-discrimination and the case law of the European Court of Human Rights

Some Danish legal scholars have argued that the decisions of the ECtHR in *Dahlab*[69] and *Sahin*[70] require the Discrimination Directives to be interpreted as allowing the Member States broad discretion with regards to bans on Muslim veils in the employment setting.[71] These cases concerned policies supporting the principle of the government's secularity in institutions of public education. It is difficult to argue on the basis of these cases, that the interest of a private employer, such as Føtex, should be protected rather than the religious freedom of an ethnic minority female employee. Furthermore, secularity is not a public value in Denmark as it is in Turkey. Denmark has a state church and Christianity is still taught in the public schools.

As for the more general argument that the Discrimination Directives must be interpreted in accordance with the ECtHR's case law on dress codes the problem here is that the ECJ's scrutiny of national derogations from the principle of equal treatment on grounds of public order or security have been far more strict than the ECtHR's scrutiny of the states' defences in the *Dahlab* and *Sahin* cases. The ECJ has consistently held that any derogation from the principle of equal treatment must be interpreted narrowly and that the Member States must prove their necessity and proportionality.[72] The ECJ has explained that the national court must satisfy itself that the necessity of derogating from the equal treatment principle was well-founded in fact on the basis of evidence presented by the state.[73] In contrast to the ECJ's approach in this case law, the ECtHR did not require Turkey to provide any evidence that the wearing of headscarves at Istanbul University actually constituted a threat to public order or democracy.[74] It merely accepted Turkey's assertion that this was so.

Finally, the Race Directive does not even permit derogations on grounds of public order or security. This is not to say that public order or security could never be legitimate grounds for *indirectly* race discriminatory measures. Nevertheless, the ECJ's case law together with current understandings of the way racism develops on the basis of generalisations about the religious beliefs and customs of ethnic minorities suggests that courts should be careful to ensure that when such a justification is sought to be applied to a private employer's dress code, that the dress code is in fact *indirectly* discriminatory and the employer carries its burden of proof. The facts of the *Føtex* case do not live up to this standard. At most, the neutral appearance sought to be achieved by the dress code was intended to avoid offending customers. Other stores allowed their female Muslim employees to wear headscarves without any apparent disturbance of the public order or security. Should a similar case come before the ECJ, the ECJ is likely to continue its prior case law and require the national court to apply a higher standard of proof to the employer's justification than that applied by the ECtHR to the Swiss and Turkish government.

15.5 Conclusion

In this chapter I have drawn on anthropological, sociological and legal scholarship documenting and analysing links between religion, gender and ethnic origin to show that all three factors determine the veiling practices of Muslim women. Only Muslim women wear veils, and the way they are worn, and the fabric chosen for them varies primarily because of differences in ethnic origin. Muslim women wear veils because they are Muslim, female, and most often because it is part of their ethnic identity – not just because they are Muslim.

Based on this understanding of the interconnections between religion, gender and ethnicity, I conclude that the differential impact of dress codes on Muslim women does not merely arise from religious differences, but also from gender and ethnic differences. Case law from the UK and the US show that failure to recognise the inextricable links between prohibited grounds of discrimination riddles the equal treatment principle with holes through which victims of unjustified disparate treatment fall. If Muslim women are to enjoy the benefits of the principle of non-discrimination, which are outlined in the Preambles to the Discrimination Directives, policies that indirectly discriminate against them must be analysed as instances of multiple discrimination.

The ECJ's case law on the general principle of non-discrimination supports the conclusion that the Discrimination Directives should be interpreted as allowing Muslim women who are excluded from employment as a result of dress codes that prohibit head coverings to claim indirect discrimination on multiple grounds. Equally important is to recognise that the general principle of non-discrimination requires more than just recognising that the differential impact that plaintiffs must prove in these cases does not arise from one single protected characteristic but from the combination of several. It also requires analysis of employer justifications for indirect discrimination in conformity with the knowledge that several prohibited grounds of discrimination are implicated. Following the ECJ's case law on justification of indirect sex discrimination indicates that Community law requires employers to prove that their indirectly discriminatory dress codes are based on objective factors that are unrelated to any discrimination based on sex, religion, ethnic origin, or any other prohibited ground.

The debate in Denmark about the dress code cases highlights the importance of analysing these cases as involving potential multiple-factor discrimination based on ethnic origin, religion and sex. Recognition of the link between religion and ethnic origin as determining factors in the headscarf cases is necessary to ensure that religious belief is not confused with political opinion and therefore treated in the same way. The approach I have argued for here would allow indirectly discriminatory dress codes that permit Muslim headscarves, Sikh turbans and/or Jewish skull caps but exclude political symbols like the Nazi swastika or the Social Democratic rose. Recognition of the gender dimension in these cases requires employers' justifications to be based on something other than the view that the headscarf is a symbol of sex discrimination. According to the ECJ's case law, indirect discrimination cannot be justified by reasons related to sex discrimination. More concretely this means that to the extent Muslim women assert that they wear the veil as a matter of personal religious belief, employers cannot justify an indirectly discriminatory dress code by claiming that the policy promotes sex equality because the headscarf is a symbol or direct expression of women's oppression. This view is merely a restatement of the traditional sex discriminatory belief that women are incapable of making important decisions. To the extent that some Muslim women may be forced to wear a veil, excluding all Muslim women who wear veils from employment is not a necessary or proportionate means of promoting sex equality among Muslim women. Rather than forcing them to unveil, such policies may force them to remain at home and ensure their continued dependence on male family members.

I do not argue that European employers must always allow Muslim female employees to wear headscarves or other kinds of veils at work. Safety and hygiene are clearly objective reasons for restricting Muslim veiling. The dress regulations must still satisfy the proportionality requirement, however. Marketing or selling Western women's fashion could also provide an objective basis for insisting that female employees dress in a way that promotes the image being marketed. In such cases the focus of analysis should be on the proportionality of the dress code. A business that is dependent on personal, face-to-face communication with customers could satisfy the requirement of an objective reason for a policy prohibiting employees from wearing veils that cover the face or obscure the employees' body language by showing that the policy is intended to ensure that customers are able to receive the service they need and understand what is communicated to them by the employees. The proportionality of dress codes that seek to meet this kind of business need must be carefully considered as a safeguard against the impulse to measure alternatives according to a subjective standard of comfort. The employer must therefore show that the various ways in which communication with customers occurs have been considered and that the least restrictive policy was chosen.

The approach outlined above conforms to the Discrimination Directives' definitions of indirect discrimination, and the requirements that the ECJ has imposed on employers' justifications in its case law on indirect sex discrimination. It is hoped that it also shows how to close the gaps between the different prohibited grounds of discrimination so that groups that experience disadvantage as the result of the simultaneous presence of several prohibited grounds of discrimination can be assured of the equal treatment principle's protection.

Notes

1 I use the word 'veil' to refer to all the various ways Muslim women cover themselves. I will use the word 'headscarf' when the kind of veil being used only covers the head.
2 See text accompanying nn 42–4 below.
3 See S Dein (2006) 'Race, culture and ethnicity in minority research: A critical discussion', *Journal of Cultural Diversity*, 13: 68–75.
4 Ibid.
5 S Hall (2000) 'Conclusion: The multicultural question', in B Hesse (ed) *Un/Settled Multiculturalisms: Diasporas, Entanglements, Transruptions*, London: Zed Books, p 223.
6 See generally, F Barth (1969) *Ethnic Groups and Boundaries: The Social Organisation of Cultural Difference*, Boston, MA: Little, Brown & Company.
7 *Ugeskrift for Retsvæsen*, 2000, 2350\.
8 *Toms Fabrikker*, 18 afdeling sag B-0877/00, judgment of 5 April 2001.
9 Ugeskrift for Retsvæsen 2005, 1265H.
10 Preparatory works to Law no 459 of 12 June 1996 regarding the prohibition against discrimination on the labour market, remarks regarding § 1(1) (Folketingstidende 1995–95, tillæg A, p 352 f). The explanatory remarks, which are attached to legislative proposals, are authoritative sources for the interpretation of Danish legislation.
11 This part of the court's analysis was not strictly necessary to the decision since the case had arisen out of circumstances that occurred in 2001 – three years before the Directives were implemented in Denmark. (See Case 80/86 *Kolpinghuis Nijmegen* [1987] ECR 3969.) In the *Føtex* case, the principles of legal certainty and non-retroactivity arguably required the Danish Supreme Court to interpret the Danish legislation in accordance with the explanatory remarks to the 1996 law.
12 The relevant explanatory remarks are published in Folketingstidende 2003–04, tillæg A, pp 1248 *et seq*, in the remarks on § 1 (2) and (3) of the legislative proposal.
13 K Crenshaw (1989) 'Demarginalizing the intersection of race and sex: A black feminist critique of anti-discrimination doctrine, feminist theory and anti-racial politics', *The University of Chicago Legal Forum*: 139–67 (reprinted in K Bartlett and R Kennedy (eds) (1991) *Feminist Legal Theory: Readings in Law and Gender*, Boulder, CO: Westview Press, pp 57–80, at p 64.
14 S Fredman (2002) *Discrimination Law*, Oxford: Oxford University Press, pp 68–9.
15 In the UK sex discrimination and race discrimination were treated by two separate Acts, which did not cover religious discrimination. Fredman, ibid, p 69. Fredman explains that the exclusion of religion from the Race Relations Act has meant that Sikhs, Muslims, Jews and Rastafarians facing discriminatory treatment need to argue that they belong to a group defined by ethnic origin and not (just) by religion. While the Sikhs were accepted as an ethnic group, Muslims and Rastafarians were not (ibid, p 72). Religious discrimination is covered today by the Human Rights Act 1998 and by Employment Equality (Religion and Belief) Regulations 2003 (in force since 2 December 2003, implementing the EU Discrimination Directives). In the US, there is one statute covering the subject of employment discrimination, Title VII of the US 1964 Civil Rights Act. It lists the prohibited grounds of discrimination (race, colour, religion, sex, national origin) as alternatives ('or') rather than as cumulative ('and'). See 42 USC. § 2000e–2(a). The most

frequently cited example of American courts' failure to recognise multiple discrimination claims is *DeGraffenreid v General Motors Assembly Division*, 413 F Supp. 142 (E D Mo 1976) (see a case summary in Fredman, Chapter 4, in this book).

16 K Crenshaw (1989) 'Demarginalizing the intersection of race and sex: A black feminist critique of anti-discrimination doctrine, feminist theory and anti-racial politics', *The University of Chicago Legal Forum*: 139–67 (reprinted in K Bartlett and R Kennedy (eds) (1991) *Feminist Legal Theory: Readings in Law and Gender*, Boulder, CO: Westview Press, pp 57–80, at p 64.

17 See generally ibid, pp 57–80, and JA Winston (1991) 'Mirror, mirror on the wall: Title VII, section 1981 and the intersection of race and gender in the Civil Rights Act of 1990', *California Law Review*, 79: 775–805.

18 C Scarborough (1989) 'Conceptualizing black women's employment experiences', *Yale Law Journal*, 98: 1457–78, at pp 1463–4. The Fifth Circuit Court of Appeal was the first to permit a multiple discrimination claim in *Jeffries v Harris Community Action Ass'n* 615 F2d 1025 (5 Cir 1980). Other appellate courts have followed. See, e.g. *Lam v University of Hawaii* 40 F3d 1551 (9 Cir 1994); *Hicks v Gates Rubber Co* 833 F2d 1406 (10 Cir 1987). Nevertheless, women of colour have continued to have difficulty at the evidentiary stage when combining several protected categories into one group: K Abrams (1994) 'Title VII and the complex female subject', *Michigan Law Review*, 92: 2479–540.

19 K Ketscher (2005) 'Etnisk ligebehandling, religionsfrihed og ligestilling mellem kvinder og mænd – set i lyset af Føtex-sagen', *Ugeskrift for Retsvæsen*, 26: 235–43, at p 239.

20 Recital 3, Council Directive 2000/78/EC establishing a general framework for equal treatment in employment and occupation [2000] OJ L303/16; Recital 14, Council Directive 2000/43/EC implementing the principle of equal treatment between persons irrespective of racial or ethnic origin [2000] OJ L180/22, (emphasis added).

21 See, e.g. Case 283/81 *CILFIT v Italian Ministry of Health* [1982] ECR 3415; Case C-98/91 *Herbrink v Minister van Landbouw, Natuurbeheer en Visserij* [1994] ECR I-223, para 9.

22 See *Jefferies v Harris Community Action Ass'n* 615 F2d 1025 (5 Cir 1980).

23 Recital 8 in both Directives.

24 Recital 11, Council Directive 2000/78/EC; Recital 9, Council Directive 2000/43/EC.

25 Recital 9, Council Directive 2000/78/EC.

26 R Nielsen (2004) *Gender Equality in European Contract Law*, Copenhagen: DJ\F Publishing, 2004, p 31.

27 Cases 103 and 145/77 *Royal Scholten-Honig (Holding) Ltd v Intervention Board for Agricultural Produce* [1978] ECR 2037. In this case, glucose producers challenged the legality of a system of production subsidies whereby sugar producers were receiving subsidies financed in part by levies on the production of glucose. The claimants argued that the regulations implementing the system were in breach of the general principle of equality, and therefore invalid, because glucose and sugar producers were in competition with each other. The English court in which the case was brought referred the question of the regulations' validity to the ECJ, which agreed with the claimants and held the regulations invalid.

28 Case 149/77 *Gabrielle Defrenne v Société anonyme belge de navigation aérienne Sabena* [1978] ECR 1365, para 27.

29 Case C-144/04 *Mangold v Helm* [2005] ECR I-9981.

30 Ibid, para 74.

31 Ibid.

32 Ibid.

33 Case 170/84 *Bilka Kaufhaus GmbH v Weber von Hartz* [1986] ECR 1607, paras 30 and 31. The ECJ continues to use the same formulation in recent decisions. See, e.g Case C-25/02 *Rinke v Arztekammer Hamburg* [2003] ECR I-8349, para 33; Case C-226/98 *Jorgensen v Foreningen af Speciallæger and Sygesikringens Forhandlingsudvalg* [2000] ECR I-2447, para 29; Case C-381/99 *Brunnhofer v Bank der österreichischen Postsparkasse AG* [2001] ECR I-4961, paras 66 and 79.

34 Case C-381/99 *Brunnhofer v Bank de Osterreichischen Postparkasse AG* [2001] ECR I-4961, para 67.

35 Case C-167/97 *Regina v Secretary of State for Employment, ex parte Nicole Seymour-Smith and Laura Perez* [1999] ECR I-623, para 76.

36 See cases cited in n 33 above.

37 For an argument that conforming to the traditional Danish understanding of religion as a private matter, rather than something for public display, is a legitimate business reason for adopting dress codes like the one in *Føtex*, see K Ketscher (2005) 'Etnisk ligebehandling, religionsfrihed og ligestilling mellem kvinder og mænd – set i lyset af Føtex-sagen', *Ugeskrift for Retsvæsen*, 26: 235–43, at p 238.

38 A Andersen, R Nielsen and K Precht (2001) *Ligestillingslovene med kommentarer*, 4th edn, Copenhagen: Jurist- og \konomforbundets Forlag, p 381.

39 Ibid.

40 S Fredman (2002) *Discrimination Law*, Oxford: Oxford University Press, p 53.

41 UNESCO (1950) 'The Race Question', para 6. The General Conference of UNESCO adopted three resolutions in 1949 which committed the Organisation 'to study and collective scientific materials concerning questions of race', 'to give wide diffusion to the scientific material collected', and 'to prepare an educational campaign based on this information', ibid, p 1. To lay the groundwork for this programme, UNESCO invited a number of anthropologists and sociologists from different countries to meet as a committee of experts in December 1949, ibid, p 2. 'The Race Question' was drafted by those scientists as a result of their meeting.

42 Ibid.

43 M Chon and D Arzt (2005) 'Walking while Muslim', *Law and Contemporary Problems*, 68: 225.

44 Ibid.

45 Ibid.

46 320 US 81, 63 SCt 1375, 1384 (1943).

47 M Chon and D Arzt (2005) 'Walking while Muslim', *Law and Contemporary Problems*, 68: 225, at p 226.

48 See K Ketscher (2005) 'Etnisk ligebehandling, religionsfrihed og ligestilling mellem kvinder og mænd – set i lyset af Føtex-sagen', *Ugeskrift for Retsvæsen*, 26: 235–43.

49 Fadwa El Guindi (1999) *Veil: Modesty, Privacy and Resistance*, Oxford: Berg Publishers, p 12.

50 Ibid, pp 58–61.

51 Ibid, p 58, citing R Barnes and J Eicher (eds) (1992) *Dress and Gender: Making and Meaning in Cultural Contexts*, Providence, RI and Oxford: Berg.

52 E Erikson (1977) *Toys and Reasons*, New York: WW Norton, p 20.

53 K Karst (1986) 'Paths to belonging: The Constitution and cultural identity', *North Carolina Law Review*, 64: 303–77, at p 309.

54 El Guindi (1999) *Veil: Modesty, Privacy and Resistance*, Oxford: Berg Publishers, p 170.

55 Ibid.

56 Ibid.

57 Ibid, p 173.

58 Ibid.

59 Ibid, p 174 quoting Z Mir-Hosseini (1996) 'Women and politics in post-Khomeini Iran: Divorce, veiling and emergent feminist voices,' in H Afshar (ed) *Women and Politics in the Third World*, London, New York: Routledge, p 153.

60 Ibid, p 175.

61 Ibid.

62 Ibid, p 172.

63 See C MacKinnon (1989) *Toward a Feminist Theory of the State*, Cambridge, MA: Harvard University Press, p 117.

64 K Abrams (1990) 'Ideology and women's choices', *Georgia Law Review*, 24: 760–800, at p 763.

65 Ibid.

66 Ibid, p 784.

67 See generally SM Evans (1989) *Born for Liberty: A History of Women in America*, New York: The Free Press.

68 B Winter (2006) 'The great hijab coverup', *Off Our Backs*, 36: 38–40, at p 39.

69 *Dahlab v Switzerland*, Application no 42393/98, ECHR 2001-V.

70 *Sahin (Leyla) v Turkey*, Application no 44774/98, 29 June 2004, (2005) 41 EHRR 8.

71 A Andersen, R Nielsen and K Precht (2001) *Ligestillingslovene med kommentarer*, 4th edn, Copenhagen: Jurist- og \konomforbundets Forlag, p 210; K Ketscher (2005) 'Etnisk ligebehandling, religionsfrihed og ligestilling mellem kvinder og mænd – set i lyset af Føtex-sagen', *Ugeskrift for Retsvæsen*, 26: 235–43, at pp 237–9.

72 Case 30–77 *Régina v Pierre Bouchereau* [1977] ECR 1999; Case C-273/97 *Angela Maria Sirdar v The Army Board and Secretary of State for Defence* [1999] ECR I-7403.

73 Case 222/84 *Johnston v RUC Constabulary* [1986] ECR 1651, paras 21 and 36.

74 K Altiparmak and O Karahanogullari (2006) 'After Sahin: The debate on head-scarves is not over', *European Constitutional Law Review*, 2: 278–83.

16 Religion and equality in Germany

The headscarf debate from a constitutional perspective

Ute Sacksofsky

16.1 Introduction

The headscarf debate is a particularly interesting example of multidimensional equality law. The 'little piece of cloth' divides not only German society as a whole but also the feminist movement. Gender equality and freedom of religion seem to require different answers. Quite a few influential feminists, such as the German feminist icon Alice Schwarzer, argue that gender equality requires banning headscarves.[1] In her view, headscarves are a symbol of gender oppression. Women covering their heads are viewed as endangering the progress (insufficient as it is) achieved by the women's movement. On the other hand, religious freedom seems to require the liberty to live according to one's faith, including the right to dress according to one's religion. Both freedom of religion and gender equality are guaranteed in the German Constitution (Arts 3 and 4).[2] This is typical for modern constitutions[3] and human rights treaties: both rights are guaranteed, for example, in the constitutions of Italy (Arts 3 and 8), the Netherlands (Arts 1 and 6), Spain (Arts 14 and 16), Greece (Arts 13 and 116, para 2), Poland (Arts 33 and 55) and Portugal (Arts 9 lit. h and 41) as well as international treaties such as the European Convention on Human Rights (Arts 9 and 14), the International Covenant on Civil and Political Rights (see in particular Arts 3 and 18) and the Charter of Fundamental Rights of the European Union (Arts 10 and 23). The headscarf issue will be used in this chapter as a prism through which to examine whether a tension really does exist between these two fundamental rights.

The article proceeds in four steps. First of all, I will give an overview of the development, focus and the current status of the headscarf debate in Germany. Second, I will analyse the role of religious freedom in the context of state neutrality. Third, I will discuss the issues of gender equality raised with respect to the headscarf. Finally, I will finish with a brief observation referring to the debate in a broader sense.

16.2 Development of the headscarf issue in Germany

For years, headscarves had not been an issue of public debate or legal action in Germany.[4] Around the turn of the millennium this changed completely; since 2000 the headscarf has become a hotly debated issue.[5] In the legal sphere the issue started with the *Ludin* case. Fereshta Ludin applied for a teaching position in a public school in the state of Baden-Wuerttemberg. She was turned down for one reason only: she refused to teach without covering her head with a headscarf. Interestingly, in the legal proceedings the school administration did not even try to argue that there was any doubt as to her qualification. Ludin had been teaching as an assistant teacher during her training period with no complaints from her supervisors or parents, her ratings were good and there was no record that she held extremist views or tried to indoctrinate her pupils. In the media, there were actually some allegations that she was an Islamic fundamentalist but the school administration never followed up on these. Thus, in the courts, the case presented a clear cut issue: can teachers be denied a position in a public school solely because they believe their religion requires them to wear a headscarf? Ludin took the case to court and lost three times, in the Administrative Court,[6] the Higher Administrative Court[7] and the Federal Administrative Court (*Bundesverwaltungsgericht*).[8] The courts held that religious neutrality of the state could justify denying the claim to teach in a public school while wearing a headscarf. The headscarf, as a highly visible symbol, was seen as endangering state neutrality. The courts also saw a violation of the (negative) religious freedom of children and parents not to be exposed to a religion. In 2003, the case reached the Federal Constitutional Court (*Bundesverfassungsgericht*). The Federal Constitutional Court handed down a split decision that was clearly a compromise.[9] Ludin won and lost at the same time. The court held that freedom of religion in the Federal Constitution does not necessarily include the right to wear religious symbols as a teacher in a public school. The court, therefore, left it up to the states to decide whether they wanted to ban the wearing of religious symbols in schools.[10] However, doing so would need to be specifically addressed by a state statute. Technically, this meant that Ludin won at this stage as no such specific statute existed at the time. The case was sent back to the Federal Administrative Court which delayed the proceedings until Baden-Wuerttemberg had passed a new statute banning the headscarf. In the end, Ludin lost; she never became a tenured teacher in Baden-Wuerttemberg. But it should be noted that she did not pursue her case to the very end. After she lost in the Federal Administrative Court for the second time,[11] she did not take the case back to the Federal Constitutional Court (for a second round, although this would have been possible), but rather left standing the judgment of the Federal Administrative Court.

As the decision of the Federal Constitutional Court in 2003 framed the issues for the following debates, it is useful to look a little more closely at the reasoning of the court. The decision was supported by a majority of five judges, while three judges delivered a dissenting opinion. The first issue of debate between the majority and the minority was the question of the role of religious freedom as regards public servants. In para 2 of Art 33, the German Constitution contains a right of every German to be equally eligible for any public office according to aptitude, qualifications and professional achievements. In addition, Art 4 guarantees religious freedom.[12] The majority construed the relationship between both guarantees to mean that the right to enter public service could not be denied if such denial constituted a violation of religious freedom. In sharp words the minority rejected this argument. They emphasised that public servants did voluntarily choose to enter public service. Therefore, public servants could be exposed to a stricter standard of personal behaviour, including special duties of 'loyalty to the state'. According to the minority's view this also meant that public servants had a more limited right to religious freedom compared to individuals outside the employment of the state.[13] The minority's argument came as a surprise. It reminded one of the times when German constitutional jurisprudence had generally excluded the public service from the realm of fundamental rights, using the category of '*besonderes Gewaltverhältnis*' (meaning a special relationship of subordination).[14] One had thought that this view, which expressed a more authoritarian view of the state, had been overcome with the modern development of a democratic state, but the headscarf issue revived this issue. For most of the remaining part, the (majority's) decision reads as if they wanted to argue that the justifications given by the state for banning headscarves would not hold. Strangely enough, the court does not bring its arguments to a full conclusion.[15] Many arguments such as the effect of a headscarf on children and the rights of parents and children are mentioned but not followed through. Instead, the court changed its perspective and proceeded to a more formal argument, requiring a specific statute addressing the issue of religious clothing in schools. It held that the general rules of eligibility for public service which referred to aptitude and qualifications did not suffice to deny a position on the sole ground that the applicant was going to wear a headscarf. According to the court, it is the privilege of Parliament to decide whether wearing a headscarf can be considered to interfere with the ability to teach. As the field of primary education falls under the regulatory competences of states rather than of federal government, the issue could only be resolved by state Parliaments. The court emphasised that this could lead to different regimes in the different states, thereby stating clearly that the federal guarantee of religious freedom did not contain a right to wear a headscarf as a teacher in a public school. Nevertheless, the Federal Constitutional Court emphasised that all religions had to be treated 'strictly' equal.[16] If a statute forbade the wearing of religious clothing in schools, this would only be constitutionally valid, if it applied equally to all religious denominations.[17]

As a result of the decision of the Federal Constitutional Court, there have been heated debates over the last four years as to what to do about headscarves in nearly all state Parliaments. So far, eight German states have passed statutes banning the wearing of religious symbols by teachers in public schools.[18] Hessen has even gone further and banned all civil servants from donning religious symbols.[19]

But most states did not want to ban all religious symbols from schools. They still wanted to have Christian nuns or monks teach in full habit in German public schools. Thus, instead of just forbidding all religious symbols, they included an exception for wearing symbols showing Christian or Judeo-Christian values.[20] This obviously led to a problem concerning the equal treatment of religions which is – undoubtedly – guaranteed in the Constitution. The states have therefore tried to disguise their goal leading to a rather strange phrasing of the statute. For example, the Hessen statute provides:

> . . . teachers are obliged to keep political, religious and ideological neu-
> trality in school and in lessons; . . . In particular, they may not don or
> apply clothes, symbols or other characteristics which are objectively
> suited to impair the trust in the neutrality of the performance of their
> duties or to endanger the political, religious or ideological peace in
> school. . . . When determining whether the requirements of sentences
> one and two are fulfilled, one has to adequately consider the western
> tradition of the State of Hessen which has been formed by Christian and
> humanistic ideas.[21]

In my position as public advocate to the Hessian State Constitutional Court (*Landesanwältin beim Staatsgerichtshof des Lands Hessen*)[22] I brought the Hessian statute before the State Constitutional Court (*Staatsgerichtshof des Landes Hessen*). The decision came down on 10 December 2007.[23] The case was decided with the narrowest margin possible: with six to five votes the court upheld the statute; the five judges in the minority handed in three different dissenting votes. The result of the decision came as quite a surprise, because the court did not formally decide on Muslim headscarves. The court explicitly left open the question of whether Muslim women are allowed to wear headscarves when employed as teachers or civil servants.[24] Instead, the court took the wording of the statute at its face value. As the statute only bans clothes, symbols or other characteristics which are objectively suited to impair the trust in the neutrality of the performance of their duties or to endanger the political, religious or ideological peace in school, it is left to the administration and the lower courts to decide whether the headscarf constitutes such a symbol. The court majority emphasises the importance of state neutrality and the right of the state to ensure such neutrality by banning clothing that could be understood to be hurtful to state neutrality. But it did not declare outright that Muslim headscarves could be banned from the civil service.

Therefore, an individual Muslim woman whose application for a teaching job is denied on account of her wearing a headscarf can challenge this denial before the Administrative Courts. If she is not successful before the Higher

Administrative Court,[25] she can then choose whether to go further to the federal level (Federal Administrative Court and Federal Constitutional Court) or whether to bring the case before the State Supreme Court of Hessen. She has to do all this at her own risk; she may be successful, but she may also lose. The refusal of the court to decide on the issue which every one knew the statute was about, was criticized in one of the dissenting opinions. Four justices argued that the majority did not comply with the decision of the Federal Constitutional Court.[26] The Federal Constitutional Court had required state Parliaments to indicate clearly the 'dangers' of wearing headscarves. As the Hessian State Supreme Court has now declared that it is left to the administration to decide whether Muslim headscarves were banned or not, Hessen lacks the clear statutory regulation which the Federal Constitutional Court had required. According to the dissenting justices, the Hessian rule to ban headscarves for all civil servants was unconstitutional as it was too broad.[27]

The Hessen State Supreme Court also declared constitutional the rule privileging symbols stemming from Christianity; this part of the decision led to a dissenting vote in which three judges joined.[28] The court states clearly that privileging the Christian religion would be unconstitutional. But it construes the statutory provision in a way as not to contain a privilege for religion but instead a privilege for traditions formed by Christianity. According to the court 'Christian' in the sense of the statute means a world of values ('*Wertewelt*') that reflects Western Christian traditions and culture but is detached from its religious origins.[29] Similar statutes have been challenged before other courts. So far at least on the higher level,[30] these other claimants have also been unsuccessful. The Federal Administrative Court[31] and the Bavarian Constitutional Court,[32] stating that Christian symbols constitute culture as opposed to religion, have both held such statutes constitutional. The Federal Constitutional Court has not yet ruled on the issue. I think these decisions are plainly wrong. It is one thing whether one can ban teachers from wearing religious symbols; it is quite another question whether it is constitutionally permissible to grant special privileges to Christian teachers. In my opinion, this 'Christian is good' clause is unconstitutional, as it clearly violates the freedom of religion which requires equal treatment of religions. And, it is hard to imagine what kind of symbol would show Christian values but not Christian religion. Most likely the Federal Constitutional Court will strike down such clauses as it emphasised in its 2003 decision the importance of strict equal treatment of religions. It held that bans on religious clothing could only be passed if they applied evenly to all religions.[33]

So far, the debate about headscarves in schools has been limited mostly to teachers. There is nearly no debate on the veiling of pupils so far. One reason may be that school uniforms very rarely exist in Germany. Only the case of students wanting to cover themselves fully (including their face) has received some attention. In 2006, two 18-year-old pupils were banned from school because they wanted to wear a burkha covering the face fully.[34] The Prime

Minister of the State of Hessen has announced recently that he wants to ban full veiling for students in public schools.[35] Headscarves for pupils or in the public that do not cover the face are generally accepted or at least have not been challenged in the courts.

Recently, the debate about headscarves has even extended to elected positions. Courts had to decide whether women with headscarves can serve as jurors; the decisions varied.[36] The denial of the right of jurors to wear headscarves is particularly difficult as jurors are elected and should represent all groups of the population.[37]

Unlike public servants, private employees' rights to wear headscarves in their workplaces are only limited by a substantiated prospect of economic loss on the part of their employers. The position has been affirmed by the Federal Labour Court in 2002.[38] This decision was criticised when it was handed down but has been widely accepted in the meantime. The difference between the decisions about headscarves in public service and headscarves in the private labour market are quite surprising, as the fundamental right of freedom of religion applies to state action more stringently than to private employers; it would therefore seem to follow that employees in the public sector have more rights to follow their religious beliefs than employees in the private sector. The difference between those two groups turns on the concept of the religious neutrality of the state.[39]

16.3 Religious neutrality

Two different concepts of religious neutrality exist: the laical model and the accommodating model. In the laical understanding there is no room for religion in the public sphere. Religions should remain private and should not be displayed in the public space. This model clearly requires that public servants or members of public institutions such as pupils in public schools do not show their religious affiliation. The other model, which I call the accommodationist model, requires the state to be neutral in a way that makes room for religions. In this understanding the state may not promote or discriminate against a particular religion, but it should make it possible for its citizens to live according to their faith.

I do not want to discuss here the question of which model is preferable in a theoretical, philosophical sense. Empirically, liberal democracies have very different approaches to dealing with religion.[40] There are not many areas where constitutions are so varied. In Europe, they range from the explicit identification of a predominant or even state religion (for example, Denmark, Greece, UK, Malta and Ireland) to the laical model (France, Turkey).[41] This explains why the European Court of Human Rights upheld the headscarf ban[42] as the European Convention on Human Rights must leave room for different constitutional regimes regarding religion.

But if we look at German federal law, it is undisputed that in Germany neutrality has never been understood in a laical way. The German Constitution forbids the establishment of a state church but it does not decree the separation of church and state. Quite to the contrary, the German constitution requires co-operation between churches and the state in many different ways. Religious communities can acquire a special status as corporations under public law (*Körperschaft des öffentlichen Rechts*). The status of such corporations under public law entails important privileges, for instance the right to levy tithes and have the state collect them. Religious education is part of the official school curriculum in most of the German states, even though it is taught by persons belonging to the religious bodies. These provisions were designed with only the two major Christian churches in mind, but are neutrally phrased and other religious communities can and have acquired this status, including Jews and Jehovah's Witnesses.[43] Under the German system, religion and religious communities are traditionally well protected by constitutional law, and the decisions of the Federal Constitutional Court have been very favorable towards churches and religious freedom. The Muslim headscarf decision is a clear departure from this tradition. Actually, religious clothing of teachers in public schools had become an issue in German courts before the headscarf. In 1988, a supporter of the Osho movement was not permitted to wear the traditional orange clothing signifying his adherence to Bhagwan any longer. The Federal Administrative Court dismissed his claim.[44] But the case never reached the Federal Constitutional Court and there is some evidence that the Federal Administrative Court is less friendly towards (minority) religions than the Federal Constitutional Court.[45] Therefore, I still hold that if the religious clothing case had concerned a nun's habit it would have been a slam-dunk case: the probability would have been very high that she would have been permitted to keep wearing her habit; considering Germany's Nazi history, it is even surer that an orthodox Jew wearing a yarmulke would have been permitted to become a teacher in Germany.

Banning the headscarf could be interpreted as a move towards modernising Germany's accommodationist model in the direction of a more secular or laical order. But such an argument, while conceivable in theory, does not grasp the specifics of the German debate about the headscarf. Certainly, there is something to be said for reworking the constitutional provisions relating to religion. The constitutional regime of the relations between religion and the state stems from nearly a century ago[46] and was designed with the two big Christian churches in mind, at a time when the vast majority of Germans belonged to one of these churches. These provisions are not well equipped for dealing with substantial religious diversity. However, the banning of teachers' headscarves in schools cannot be explained as a general overhaul of the position towards religious symbols. Instead, there is something peculiar at work, something more specifically directed against the Muslim headscarf. First of all, one has to wonder about the timing of the debate. Both factors working in favour of overhauling the constitutional regime of religion, emerging new religions and the lesser influence of Christian religion, have been present for decades. Second, the majority of the states banning religious symbols and clothing from schools have included an exemption for Christian symbols. The states passing such statutes did not want to lessen the role of the Christian religion in the public sphere or minimise the influence of religion in general as long as it was the right one. To a large extent, it seems, the headscarf debate is not about the role of religion or religious clothing in general, it is about the role of Islam in Germany. This argument may also explain the recent decision by the Düsseldorf Labour Court.[47] A teacher in North Rhine–Westphalia had been ordered not to wear a headscarf in school. She complied by wearing a pink beret. The Labour Court upheld her dismissal judging that the pink beret constituted a 'surrogate' for the headscarf and was therefore also not admissible. As explicitly stated in the decision, the court found particularly offensive the combination of pink beret and pink sweater with a roll-neck collar which the teacher wore to the proceedings.[48]

16.4 Gender equality

In the public debate as well as in parliamentary and court proceedings, gender equality plays a predominant role in justifying the banning of headscarves. It is often argued that persons who do not embrace 'our' constitutional values may not be permitted to teach in public schools. One of the most important values named is gender equality. But this does not withstand scrutiny: many of those using gender equality to justify the headscarf ban have never before been heard even to mention let alone embrace gender equality.[49] On the contrary, many of those using gender equality as an argument against the headscarf embrace the way of thinking of those parties or groups denouncing the women's movement for destroying families and leading to the general deterioration of society. It is quite obvious that these people use gender equality now only as a tactic. In truth, their objections are founded on the idea that immigrants should adopt the majority's standards of behaviour. Understanding the fight against the headscarf as part of a fight against 'foreigners changing German ways' also explains why the debate is so emotionally charged and why those standing up against a ban on headscarves receive hate mail and threats.

But the ban on headscarves is also demanded by feminists,[50] by women whose position on gender equality is to be taken seriously. Are they right?

Within the feminist movement there is great concern about the rights of women within domestic Islamic communities. And of course, it is to be abhorred how some Islamic states or groups, like for instance the Taliban in Afghanistan, treat women. It is unacceptable for women to be kept from education, to be forced to wear burkhas, for their word to be given lesser value than that of men in official proceedings, and to generally be relegated to second-class citizens.[51] It is also unacceptable if human rights violations happen in Western Europe among immigrant communities. Of course, the state has to ensure that all women enjoy fundamental rights. It is therefore quite important to apply to immigrant communities the same standard that is generally found in the law of the land. Forced marriages, murders of women who do not adhere to the norms decreed by their family patriarchs, genital mutilation and barriers to self-determination for women are to be eliminated.[52] But does a ban on headscarves for teachers in public schools help this cause? There is little evidence for that. Obviously, a ban on headscarves does not change anything abroad. It does not help women in Afghanistan and Iran in any way if Muslim women with a headscarf in Germany cannot become teachers. Thus, the question becomes whether teachers with headscarves make violations of women's rights in immigrant communities within Germany more likely than if no such teachers exist.

One argument could be that women who are forced to wear headscarves can resist the pressure from their families more easily if they would lose their jobs when complying. But are these the women who want to become teachers? Sociological studies show that most of the women students wearing headscarves in Germany do it of their own free will;[53] frequently the families have not encouraged them to wear a headscarf and some families even object. Considering that female students are among the most elite and educated groups of immigrant women it seems quite plausible that they make their own choice whether to wear a headscarf or not. But even assuming that some of the female students who want to become teachers are forced to wear headscarves, it is still not clear that a ban on headscarves would help them. It might just be that it takes away their source of economic independence.

Another argument for banning headscarves is that teachers wearing headscarves will influence children to adopt traditional views of gender hierarchy in two possible ways: by explicitly enhancing views in favour of women's subordination to the children, or tacitly by simply wearing the headscarf.

Both assumptions are unconvincing. Certainly, the headscarf is used as a political symbol by Islamist fundamentalists. But this cannot be ascribed to the women who wear headscarves. All sociological studies on students in Germany have led to the conclusion that women wearing headscarves do not necessarily have a more traditional view of gender relations than their counterparts.[54] And, how about the views on gender equality among the Christian or secular majority?[55] After all, in the western part of Germany over two-thirds of the people are still convinced that for the children's benefit the mother has to stay home at least while the children are young.[56] In the light of the fundamental right to freedom of religion, the state should not be permitted to interpret a religious symbol as a political symbol even though some people may use the symbol in a political way. As long as it cannot be established that the religious reasons are only strategically employed to cover up a political meaning, the state has to respect religious freedom. The state is not permitted to persecute people faithful to their religion by claiming that all expression of the religion shows enmity to the state. This is the meaning of a constitutional right to freedom of religion.

Of course, teachers in schools are not permitted to indoctrinate children. There is no room for missionaries in public schools. However, just wearing the headscarf does not constitute such a missionary impetus. Seeing a woman wearing a headscarf will not lead children to embrace Islamic fundamentalism. Quite the contrary, seeing some teachers with headscarves and some without will help children experience diversity, and may therefore help to teach and encourage tolerance. And after all, tolerance is an important educational goal, formulated in many state statutes or even constitutions. The dissenting opinion of Lange J particularly emphasises this point in his argument why teachers should be permitted to wear headscarves.[57]

Above all, it seems a bit suspicious that in fighting Islamic fundamentalism one of the most important demands is to keep women of Islamic faith from teaching in schools, thereby drastically reducing their opportunities for economic independence. Women who teach are, by their very being, proof that it is possible to adhere to more orthodox strands of the Islamic faith and still not be restricted to the house.

If one looks at the headscarf ban from a legal perspective, it seems clear that it constitutes indirect discrimination against women. The idea of indirect discrimination comes originally from the US[58] and for a long time, the European Court of Justice has accepted this concept.[59] Discrimination is no longer limited to actions that directly distinguish between both sexes but can also be found in apparently neutral provisions.[60] The Federal Constitutional Court only focused on direct discrimination until the late 1990s, but has since then accepted that women are also protected from indirect discrimination on constitutional grounds.[61] The new European Equal Treatment Directives[62] define indirect discrimination as follows:

(1) indirect discrimination shall be taken to occur where an apparently neutral provision, criterion or practice would put persons of a racial or ethnic origin at a particular disadvantage compared with other persons

(2) unless that provision, criterion or Practice is objectively justified by a legitimate aim and the means of achieving that aim are appropriate and necessary.

This new definition of indirect discrimination has changed the requirements somewhat.[63] The older definition of European Directives required a 'substantially higher proportion of the members of one sex'. According to the new criteria, statistical evidence of disadvantage is no longer required, though it may still be accepted.

Thus, indirect discrimination occurs where a gender-neutral practice has the unjustifiable effect of placing members of one sex at a particular disadvantage compared to the other. Only women will be hindered by a headscarf ban from becoming teachers. Fundamentalist male teachers will not be affected in the least. As there are no valid justifications for banning headscarves, women opposing it should also win on gender equality claims. This holds true even if the rule would ban all religious clothing and not just focus on headscarves. Even though it is true that there are some religions that require men to wear certain clothing, for example, the Jewish charmulke or the Sikh turban, currently the Muslim headscarf will be the religious clothing affected most clearly and in the greatest numbers by far.

Whereas Germany is very hard on women teachers wearing headscarves, there is virtually no demand to restrict pupils from wearing headscarves. The danger of pushing girls out of the public school system is too great. In other areas, however, surprisingly enough, administrative courts are very lenient about excusing Islamic girls from school activities. Islamic girls have been excused from sports class[64] and are permitted to stay home during class outings.[65] In my opinion this is wrong and dangerous. It is one thing to respect the right of adults, it is quite another to let children's parents keep girls from experiencing areas of life that society otherwise thinks are important. I would, therefore, be much stricter in ensuring that girls participate fully in school. Only through the exposure to the majority's lifestyle can girls be empowered to make their own choices.

16.5 Conclusion

The strong opposition against women with headscarves within the feminist community reminds me of the critique of 'white womanism'.[66] In the beginning of the (second) feminist movement of the twentieth century that took place in 1970s, the experience of white middle-class Western women was often (implicitly) seen as the general experience of all women. By now, it is widely accepted that discrimination does not take on a universal form.[67]

But this lesson seems to get lost when as far as religious Muslim women are concerned. In a way they are believed to possess 'false consciousness' (to use a term of the 1970s). To some feminists it seems their plight can rightly be forgotten, their discrimination ignored.

Religion has been one of the important instruments of patriarchy. For instance, traditionally, Christianity has justified and enforced the superiority of men over women on the basis of patriarchal interpretations of the bible. But religion also contains the potential for emancipation, and may give people strength to resist oppression; religious convictions have motivated important groups of participants in many liberation movements: in Latin America, in South Africa, in the Civil Rights movement in the US, in the German Democratic Republic.[68] In my opinion, religion should have a place in modern society and should not be banned to the private sphere. This applies to Islam as well. Of course, we have to fight against violence towards women or the suppression of women. But following religious rules, even when they look 'strange' to non-believers, has to be respected as long as it is the free choice of adults. The case of the headscarf does not even need a balancing of conflicting interest of religion and gender equality. In the case of the headscarf, religion and gender equality do not conflict but demand the same: women have the right to wear headscarves.

Notes

1 S Ateş (2006) *Große Reise ins Feuer. Geschichten einer deutschen Türkin*, Berlin: Rowohlt, pp 245–8; S Ateş (2004) 'Religionsfreiheit nicht auf Kosten von Frauen und Mädchen – Durchsetzung der Grundrechte und Selbstbestimmung', *STREIT*: 99–103; A Schwarzer (2006) 'Die Islamisten meinen es so ernst wie Hitler', interview with Alice Schwarzer, *Frankfurter Allgemeine Zeitung*, 4 July, available at www.faz.net/s/RubCF3AEB154CE64960822FA5429A182360/ Doc~EF6816D734A5C42A8A352CBB10367B7FA~ATpl~Ecommon~Scontent. html (accessed 20 September 2007); L Akgün, im Gespräch mit Alice Schwarzer (2003) 'Über das Kopftuch, Multikulti, den Zentralrat und die wahre Integration', *Emma*: 5, available at www.emma.de/658.html (accessed 20 September 2007); E Badinter (2002) 'Der verschleierte Verstand', in A Schwarzer (ed) *Die Gotteskrieger und die falsche Toleranz*, 2nd edn, Köln: Kiepenheuer & Witsch, pp 139–46.

2 Concerning gender equality and the German Constitution see generally B Rodríguez Ruiz and U Sacksofsky (2005) 'Gender in the German Constitution', in B Baines and R Rubio-Marin (eds) *The Gender of Constitutional Jurisprudence*, Cambridge: Cambridge University Press, pp 149–73.

3 The Constitution of the US, dating from 1787, includes the right to the free exercise of religion in the first Amendment since 1791. All attempts to amend the Constitution to include gender equality failed.

4 National decisions of German courts mentioned in this article are cited as follows: Decisions of higher courts are cited from the official law reports where available, such as the law reports of the Federal Constitutional Court *Bundesverfassungsgerichtsentscheidungen (BVerfGE)*, of the Federal Administrative Court *Bundesverwaltungsgerichtsentscheidungen (BVerwGE)* and of the Federal Labour Court *Bundesarbeitsgerichtsentscheidungen (BAGE)*. Other decisions of higher courts as well as decisions of courts of lower instances usually not published in official law reports are cited from generally accessible law journals. Most of the cited decisions are also published on the internet and are to be found by their reference numbers.

5 See for instance F Haug and K Reimer (eds) (2005) *Politik ums Kopftuch*, Hamburg: Argument; S Rademacher (2005) *Das Kreuz mit dem Kopftuch. Wieviel religiöse Symbolik verträgt der neutrale Staat?*, Baden-Baden: Nomos; A Weber (2004) 'Religiöse Symbole in der Einwanderungsgesellschaft', *Zeitschrift für Ausländerrecht*, 24: 53–60; S Baer and M Wrase (2003) 'Staatliche Neutralität und Toleranz: Das Kopftuch-Urteil des BVerfG', *Juristische Schulung*: 1162–6; G Britz (2003) 'Das verfassungsrechtliche Dilemma doppelter Fremdheit: Islamische Bekleidungsvorschriften für Frauen und Grundgesetz', *Kritische Justiz*: 95–103; SR Laskowski (2003) 'Der Streit um das Kopftuch geht weiter – Warum das Diskriminierungsverbot wegen der Religion nach nationalem und europäischem Recht immer bedeutsamer wird', *Kritische Justiz*: 420–44; U Sacksofsky (2003) 'Die Kopftuch-Entscheidung – von der religiösen zur föderalen Vielfalt', *Neue Juristische Wochenschrift*: 3297–301; N Janz and S Rademacher (2001) 'Das Kopftuch als religiöses Symbol oder profaner Bekleidungsgegenstand?, *Juristische Schulung*: 440–4; R Halfmann (2000) 'Der Streit um die "Lehrerin mit Kopftuch" ', *Neue Zeitschrift für Verwaltungsrecht*: 862–8; Ö Alan and U Steuten (1999) 'Kopf oder Tuch – Überlegungen zur Reichweite politischer und sozialer Akzeptanz', *Zeitschrift für Rechtspolitik*: 209–15; H Thomas (1998) 'Die Gefährdung der Allgemeinbildung durch das Kopftuch. Eine Replik', in I Gogolin *et al.* (ed) *Pluralität und Bildung*, Opladen: Leske & Budrich, pp 55–61.

6 VG Stuttgart (24 March 2000 – file no 15 K 532/99), *Neue Zeitschrift für Verwaltungsrecht*, 2000, 959–61, dazu insbesondere: E-W Böckenförde (2001)

'Kopftuchstreit auf dem richtigen Weg?', *Neue Juristische Wochenschrift*: 723–8; R Halfmann (2000) 'Der Streit um die "Lehrerin mit Kopftuch" ', *Neue Zeitschrift für Verwaltungsrecht*: 862–8, at p 209; N Janz and S Rademacher (2001) 'Das Kopftuch als religiöses Symbol oder profaner Bekleidungsgegenstand?, *Juristische Schulung*: 440–4, at p 440; U Häußler (2001) 'Muslim dress-codes in German State Schools', *European Journal of Migration and Law*: 457–74; S Mückel (2001) 'Religionsfreiheit und Sonderstatusverhältnisse – Kopftuchverbot für Lehrerinnen', *Der Staat*, 40: 96–127.

7 VGH Mannheim (26 June 2001 – file no 4 S 1439/00), *Neue Juristische Wochenschrift*, 2001, 2899–905; see especially: S Mückel (2001) 'Religionsfreiheit und Sonderstatusverhältnisse – Kopftuchverbot für Lehrerinnen', *Der Staat*, 40: 96–127, at p 96; J Rux (2001) 'Religiös motiviertes Kopftuch im öffentlichen Schuldienst', *Deutsches Verwaltungsblatt*: 1542–6; M Wittinger (2001) 'Kopftuchstreit auf europäisch, Aspekte des europäischen Grund- und Menschenrechtsschutzes', *Verwaltungsblätter für Baden-Württemberg*: 425–30.

8 BVerwGE 116, 359–364 (4 July 2002 – file no 2 C 21/01). Decision is discussed in detail especially by: G Neureither (2003) 'Kopftuch-BVerwG, NJW 2001, 3344', *Juristischen Schulung*: 541–4; L Michael (2003) 'Tragen eines islamischen Kopftuchs im Schuldienst', *Juristenzeitung*: 256–8; M Morlok and J Krüper (2003) 'Auf dem Weg zum "forum neutrum"? – Die "Kopftuch-Entscheidung" des BVerwG', *Neue Juristische Wochenschrift*: 1020–1; J Rux (2002) 'Der Kopftuchstreit und kein Ende', *Zeitschrift für Ausländerrecht und Ausländerpolitik*: 366–8; K Wiese (2003) 'Ablehnung der Einstellung als Lehrerin – Kopftuchstreit', *Zeitschrift für Beamtenrecht*: 39–41.

9 BVerfGE 108, 282–340 (24 September 2003 – file no 2 BvR 1436/02). See especially: S Baer and M Wrase (2003) 'Staatliche Neutralität und Toleranz: Das Kopftuch-Urteil des BVerfG', *Juristische Schulung*: 1162–6. R Dübbers and Z Dlovani (2004) 'Der Kopftuchstreit vor dem Bundesverfassungsgericht – ein Zwischenspiel', *Arbeit und Recht*: 6–11; J Ipsen (2003) 'Karlsruhe locuta, causa non finita', *Neue Juristische Wochenschrift*: 1210–13; I Gallala (2006) 'The Islamic headscarf: An example of surmountable conflict between Sharia an the fundamental principles of Europe', *European Law Journal*: 593–612; U Häußler (2004) 'Leitkultur oder Laizismus?', *Zeitschrift für Ausländerrecht*: 6–14; F Hufen (2004) 'Der Regelungsspielraum des Landesgesetzgebers im Kopftuchstreit', *Neue Zeitschrift für Verwaltungsrecht*: 575–8; G Neureither (2003) 'Ein neutrales Gesetz in einem neutralen Staat', *Zeitschrift für Rechtspolitik*: 465–8; J Rux (2004) 'Kleiderordnung Gesetzesvorbehalt und Gemeinschaftsschule', *Zeitschrift für Ausländerrecht*: 14–21; U Sacksofsky (2003) 'Die Kopftuch-Entscheidung – von der religiösen zur föderalen Vielfalt', *Neue Juristische Wochenschrift*: 3297–301; C Skach (2006) 'Religious Freedom-state neutrality-public order-role of international standards in interpreting an implementing constitutionally guaranteed rights', *American Journal of International Law*: 186–96.

10 BVerfGE 108, 282 (302 *et seq.*, 309 *et seq.*) (24 September 2003 – file no 2 BvR 1436/02).

11 BVerwGE 121, 140 (151) (24 June 2004 – file no 2 C 45/03).

12 Two more articles explicitly forbid discrimination on account of religious opinions (Art 3, para 3, Art 33, para 3).

13 BVerfGE 108, 282 (315 *et seq.*) (24 September 2003 – file no 2 BvR 1436/02).

14 The category of '*besonderes Gewaltverhältnis*' had traditionally been used for all areas where people were situated in a relationship depicting closeness and subordination to the state, such as prisons, schools – and public service: BVerfGE 33, 1 (14 March 1972 – file no 2 BvR 41/71) – prison. BVerfGE 34, 165 (6 December 1972 – file no 1 BvR 230/70); BVerfGE 47, 46 (21 December 1977 – file no 1 BvL 1/75, 1 BvR 147/75); BVerfGE 58, 257 (20 October 1981 – file no 1

BvR 640/80) – school. See also: K Hesse (1999) *Grundzüge des Verfassungsrechts der Bundesrepublik Deutschland*, 20th edn, Heidelberg: Müller Verlag, pp 144–7: W Loschelder (1982) *Vom besonderen Gewaltverhältnis zur öffentlich-rechtlichen Sonderbindung*, Cologne: Heymann.

15 This has been criticized: U Sacksofsky (2003) 'Die Kopftuch-Entscheidung – von der religiösen zur föderalen Vielfalt', *Neue Juristische Wochenschrift*: 3297–301, at p 3300; E-W Böckenförde (2004) 'Zum Verbot für Lehrkräfte in der Schule, ein islamisches Kopftuch zu tragen', *Juristenzeitung*: 1181–4, at p 1183.

16 BVerfGE 108, 282 [298] (24 September 2003 – file no 2 BvR 1436/02).

17 BVerfGE 108, 282 [313] (24 September 2003 – file no 2 BvR 1436/02).

18 Baden-Wuerttemberg, Bavaria, Berlin, Bremen, Hessen, Lower Saxony, North Rhine-Westphalia, Saarland.

19 Hessen and Berlin are the only states that ban headscarves for all public servants.

20 Baden-Wuerttemberg, Bavaria, Hessen, North Rhine-Westphalia, Saarland.

21 Lehrkräfte haben 'in Schule und Unterricht politische, religiöse und weltanschauliche Neutralität zu wahren; Insbesondere dürfen sie Kleidungsstücke, Symbole oder andere Merkmale nicht tragen oder verwenden, die objektiv geeignet sind, das Vertrauen in die Neutralität ihrer Amtsführung zu beeinträchtigen oder den politischen, religiösen oder weltanschaulichen Frieden in der Schule zu gefährden. Bei der Entscheidung über das Vorliegen der Voraussetzungen nach Satz 1 und 2 ist der christlich und humanistisch geprägten abendländischen Tradition des Landes Hessen angemessen Rechnung zu tragen' (§ 86, para 3, Hessisches Schulgesetz).

22 The position of a public advocate to the Hessian Constitutional Court is defined in the Hessian Constitution. The advocate is elected by the State Parliament. He or she is entirely independent and can intervene on behalf of the public in all cases before the Hessian State Constitutional Court. He or she can also start proceedings.

23 Staatsgerichtshof des Landes Hessen, 10 December 2007 – file no PSt 2016, available   at   www.staatsgerichtshof.hessen.de/migration/rechtsp.nsf/ 11CD3052759E452BC12573A9003649FB/$file/PSt_2016_Urteil.pdf (accessed 20 December 2007).

24 Staatsgerichtshof des Landes Hessen, 10 December 2007 – file no PSt 2016 (note 23), pp 21 *et seq.*

25 This would be the Verwaltungsgerichtshof Kassel.

26 Staatsgerichtshof des Landes Hessen, 10 December 2007 – file no PSt 2016 (note 23), pp 45 *et seq.* (Klein, Falk, Giani and von Plottnitz dissenting).

27 Staatsgerichtshof des Landes Hessen, 10 December 2007 – file no PSt 2016 (note 23), pp 47 *et seq.* (Klein, Falk, Giani and von Plottnitz dissenting); p 60 (Lange dissenting).

28 Staatsgerichtshof des Landes Hessen, 10 December 2007 – file no PSt 2016, pp 53 *et seq.* (Giani and von Plottnitz dissenting); p 60 (Lange dissenting).

29 Staatsgerichtshof des Landes Hessen, 10 December 2007 – file no PSt 2016, pp 33 *et seq.*

30 The VG Stuttgart (an administrative court on the lowest level) held that such a clause violated the equality of religions (7 July 2006 – file no 18 K 3562/05), *Neue Zeitschrift für Verwaltungsrecht*, 2006, 1444–7; Cf J Bader (2006) 'Gleichbehandlung von Kopftuch und Nonnenhabit?' *Neue Zeitschrift für Verwaltungsrecht*: 1333–7.

31 BVerwGE 121, 140 (151), (24 June 2004 – file no 2 C 45/03); see especially: S Baer and M Wrase, 'Staatliche Neutralität und Toleranz: Das Kopftuch-Urteil des BVerfG', *Juristische Schulung*: 1162–6; E-W Böckenförde (2004) 'Zum Verbot für Lehrkräfte in der Schule, ein islamisches Kopftuch zu tragen', *Juristenzeitung*: 1181–4.

32 Bayerischer Verfassungsgerichtshof (15 January 2007 – file no Vf 11-VII-05), *Bayerische Verwaltungsblätter*, 2007, 235–9.

33 BVerfGE 108, 202 (311) (24 September 2003 – file no 2 BvR 1436/02).
34 See (2006) 'Lehrer müssen Schülern ins Gesicht sehen', *Spiegelonline – Schulspiegel*, 28 April, available at www.spiegel.de/schulspiegel/0,1518,413819,00.html (accessed 8 January 2008).
35 (2007) *Spiegelonline*, 16 December, available at www.spiegel.de/schulspiegel/0,1518,523613,00.html (accessed 21 December 2007).
36 Negating the right to wear a headscarf: LG Dortmund (7 September 2007 – file no 14 (VIII Gen StrK), *Neue Juristische Wochenschrift*, 2007, 3013; affirming this right: LG Bielefeld (16 March 2006 – file no 3221 b E H 68), *Neue Juristische Wochenschrift*, 2007, 3014.
37 J Bader (2007) 'Die Kopftuch tragende Schöffin', *Neue Juristische Wochenschrift*: 2964–6, at p 2966.
38 BAGE 103, 111–23 (10 October 2002 – file no 2 AZR 472/01). See especially: N Hoevels (2003) 'Kopftuch als Kündigungsgrund', *Neue Zeitschrift für Arbeitsrecht*: 701–4; G Thüsing and D Wege (2004) 'Kündigungsschutz und Schutz vor rassischer Diskriminierung als Rechtsinstitute zur Sicherung der Religionsfreiheit in Deutschland und im Vereinigten Königreich', *Zeitschrift für Europäisches Privatrecht*: 404–23.
39 See D Schiek (2004) 'Just a piece of cloth? German courts and employees with headscarves', *Industrial Law Journal*, 33: 68–73 for a comparison focused on equality law.
40 For a current and very informative account of the role of the free exercise clause in the US see: K Greenawalt (2006) *Religion and the Constitution. Volume 1: Free Exercise and Fairness*, Princeton, NJ, and Oxford: Princeton University Press.
41 See JHH Weiler (2004) *Ein christliches Europa. Erkundungsgänge*, Salzburg: Pustet. The book has been translated into many European languages but not into English, Original: JHH Weiler (2003) *Un'Europa cristiana. Un saggio explorativo*, Milano: Rizzoli.
42 *Şahin (Leyla) v Turkey*, Application no 44774/98, 29 June 2004,(2005) 41 EHRR 8; see especially: I Gallala (2006) 'The Islamic headscarf: An example of surmountable conflict between Sharia an the fundamental principles of Europe', *European Law Journal*: 593–612; A Nieuwenhuis (2005) 'European Court of Human Rights: State and religion, schools and scarves', *European Constitutional Law Review*: 495–510; K Pabel (2006) 'Die Rolle der Großen Kammer des EGMR bei der Überprüfung von Kammer-Urteilen im Lichte der bisherigen Praxis', *Europäische Grundrechte Zeitschrift*: 3–11; C Skach (2006) 'Religious Freedom-state neutrality-public order-role of international standards in interpreting an implementing constitutionally guaranteed rights', *American Journal of International Law*: 186–96; A Weber (2006) 'Der Europäische Gerichtshof und das Kopftuchverbot an einer türkischen Universität', *Deutsches Verwaltungsblatt*: 173–4; ECHR, 15 February 2001, *Dahlab v Switzerland*, Application no 42393/98, ECHR 2001-V, p 429, for this see: H Goerlich (2001) 'Religionspolitische Distanz und kulturelle Vielfalt unter dem Regime des Art 9 EMRK', *Neue Juristische Wochenschrift*: 2862–3; B Schöbener (2003) 'Die "Lehrerin mit dem Kopftuch" – europäisch gewendet!', *Juristische Ausbildung*: 186–91; M Wittinger (2001) 'Kopftuchstreit auf europäisch. Aspekte des europäischen Grund- und Menschenrechtsschutzes', *Verwaltungsblätter für Baden-Württemberg*: 425–30. *Karaduman v Turkey* (3 May 1993 – Application No 16278/90). Concerning these decisions see: A Vakulenko (2007) 'Islamic dress in human rights jurisprudence: A critique of current trends', *Human Rights Law Review*, 7 September, doi:10.1093/hrlr/ngm024: 717–39.
43 The Jehovah's Witnesses have won this status only recently after a decision of the Bundesverwaltungsgericht (1 February 2006 – file no 7 B 80/05), *Neue Juristische Wochenschrift*, 2006, 3156–8.

44 BVerwG (8 March 1988 – file no 2 B 92/87), *Neue Zeitschrift für Verwaltungsrecht*, 1988, 937–8.

45 For instance: the Jehovah's Witnesses have been accepted as a corporation under public law only after the Federal Constitutional Court intervened, BVerfGE 102, 370–400 (19 December 2000 – file no 2 BvR 1500/97); originally, the Federal Administrative Court had denied their claim, see BVerwGE 105, 117–27 (26 June 1997 – file no 7 C 11/96).

46 Even though the German Federal Constitution (*Grundgesetz*) dates from after the Second World War (1949), the most important features concerning the treatment of religion have been incorporated from the Weimar Constitution (*Weimarer Reichsverfassung*) of 1919.

47 Arbeitsgericht (Labour Court) Düsseldorf (29 June 2007 – file no 12 Ca 175/07). The decision is not yet published, but available through Juris Online at www.juris.de or Beck Online at www.beck-online.de.

48 An ironic and very entertaining analysis of the case by R Ogorek (2008) ' "Gefährliche Mützen". Zum Urteil des ArbG Düsseldorf vom 29 Juni 2007 (Az: 12 Ca 175/07)', *myops*, 2: 4 *et seq.*

49 The problem of imposing 'Western' gender roles on Muslim communities in particular is being criticised by feminist researchers in different contexts (see N Markard (2007) 'Fortschritte im Flüchtlingsrecht? Gender Guidelines und geschlechtsspezifische Verfolgung', *Kritische Justiz*, 40: 373–89, at p 387 in the context of migration law, with further references). For a more detailed account of the relation of (post-)colonialism and enforcing 'Western' gender roles, which often coincides with unexpected exposure of feminist position by conservative politicians see C Ho (2007) 'Muslim women's new defenders: Women's rights, nationalism and Islamophobia in contemprorary Australia', *Women's Studies International Forum*, 30: 290–8.

50 See n 1 above.

51 This section is not meant to imply that the restrictions on women's rights in countries that adhere to some form of Islamisation can rightly be derived from the Quran. For a critical assessment of this see C Jones (1998) 'The status of woman in Islamic law', lecture on the occasion of the exhibition 'Meeting Arabia' at Goettingen, available at www.sub.uni-goettingen.de/ebene_1/orient/docs/womnislm.htm (accessed 8 January 2008).

52 On the other hand, some alleged oppression of women in immigrant communities is not always as clear cut as portrayed by mainstream discourses. Feminist writers rightly point to the possibility of conservative politicians defending women's rights for reasons unconnected with women's fates (see C Ho (2007) 'Muslim women's new defenders: Women's rights, nationalism and Islamophobia in contemprorary Australia', *Women's Studies International Forum*, 30: 290–8) Some have exposed the contradictory influences of some of the concepts cited above on individual lives (see P Pichler (2007) 'Talking traditions of marriage – Negotiating young British Bangladeshi femininities', *Women's Studies International Forum*, 30: 201–16, discussing how far phenomena acknowledged as 'forced marriage' in mainstream discourse are really pure force or rather results of communication within families, during which daughters are able to make their own decision on whom to marry). There are quite a few signs of specifically 'Muslim' forms of feminism that develop in diaspora communities (see AM McGinty (2007) 'Formation of alternative femininities through Islam: Feminist approaches among Muslim converts in Sweden', *Women's Studies International Forum*, 30: 474–85). At the same time, there are some actions, such as 'honour killings', that can never be accepted as culturally justified (V Meetoo and HS Mirza (2007) 'There is nothing "honourable" about honour killings: Gender, violence and the limits of

multiculturalism', *Women's Studies International Forum*, 30: 187–200). All these issues are beyond the reach of this chapter.

53 See for instance G Klinkhammer (2003) 'Moderne Formen islamischer Lebensführung. Musliminnen der zweiten Generation in Deutschland', in M Rumpf, U Gerhard and M Jansen (eds) *Facetten islamischer Welten. Geschlechterordnungen, Frauen- und Menschenrechte in der Diskussion*, Bielefeld: transcript, pp 257 *et seq.*; Y Karakasoglu (2003) 'Islam und Moderne, Bildung und Integration. Einstellungen türkisch-muslimischer Studentinnen erziehungswissenschaftlicher Fächer', in M Rumpf, U Gerhard and M Jansen (eds) *Facetten islamischer Welten. Geschlechterordnungen, Frauen- und Menschenrechte in der Diskussion*, Bielefeld: transcript, pp 272 *et seq.*; F Jessen and U von Wilamowitz-Moellendorff (2006) 'Wilamowitz-Moellendorff v. U, *Das Kopftuch – Entschleierung eines Symbols?*', Broschürenreihe herausgegeben von der Konrad-Adenauer-Stiftung e.V, Sankt Augustin/Berlin, available at www.kas.de//db_files/dokumente/zukunftsforum_politik/7_dokument_dok_pdf_9095_1.pdf?070807122758 (accessed 20 December 2007), in particular pp 23 *et seq.*

54 See the studies mentioned ibid.

55 G Britz uses the illustrative example of all the Christian teachers working part-time to further the careers of their husbands, G Britz (2003) 'Das verfassungsrechtliche Dilemma doppelter Fremdheit: Islamische Bekleidungsvorschriften für Frauen und Grundgesetz', *Kritische Justiz*: 95–103, at p 100.

56 J Dorbritz, A Lengerer and K Ruckdeschel (2005) *Einstellungen zu demographischen Trends und zu bevölkerungsrelevanten Politiken*, Wiesbaden, available at www.bib-demographie.de/info/ppas_broschuere.pdf (accessed 20 December 2007). Likewise, Infratest dimap ARD DeuschlandTREND März 2007, 3. 'Zwei Drittel halten Beruf und Kinder für schlecht vereinbar', available at www.infratestdimap.de/?id=39&aid=147#ue3 (accessed 20 December 2007): according to this survey 69 per cent (male/female) believe it would be best if the mother stays at home after birth as long as possible.

57 Staatsgerichtshof des Landes Hessen, 10 December 2007 – file no PSt 2016, 56–60, available at www.staatsgerichtshof.hessen.de/migration/rechtsp.nsf/ 11CD3052759E452BC12573A9003649FB/$file/PSt_2016_Urteil.pdf (accessed 20 December 2007).

58 *Griggs v Duke Power Co* 401 US 424 (1971).

59 See for instance Case C-96/80 *Jenkins v Kingsgate* [1981] ECR 911; Case C-170/84 *Bilka – Kaufhaus GmbH v Karin Weber von Hartz* [1986] ECR I-1607; Case C-171/88 *Rinner-Kühn v Spezialgebäudereinigung GmbH* [1989] ECR 2743.

60 T Loenen (1999) 'Indirect discrimination: Oscillating between containment and revolution', in T Loenen and PR Rodriguez (eds) *Non-Discrimination Law: Comparative Perspectives*, The Hague: Kluwer, pp 195–212; M Selmi (1999) 'Indirect discrimination: A perspective from the United States', in T Loenen and PR Rodriguez (eds) *Non-Discrimination Law: Comparative Perspectives*, The Hague: Kluwer, pp 213–22; D Schiek (2007) 'Indirect discrimination', in D Schiek, L Waddington and M Bell (eds) *Non-Discrimination Law*, Oxford: Hart Publishing; C Fuchsloch (1995) *Das Verbot der mittelbaren Geschlechtsdiskriminierung*, Baden-Baden: Nomos.

61 See for instance: BVerfGE 113, 1; 97, 35, 43; 104, 373, 393.

62 Council Directives 2000/43/EC, 2000/78/EC and 2002/73/EC: Art 2(2) in all the Directives.

63 These changes are explained in more detail by: D Schiek (2002) 'A New Framework on Equal Treatment of Persons in EC Law? Directives 2000/43/EC, 2000/78/EC and 2002/73/EC changing Directive 76/207/EEC in Context', *European Law Journal*, 8: 290–314, at pp 295–7; D Schiek (ed) (2007) *Allgemeines Gleichbehandlungsgesetz*

(AGG): ein Kommentar aus europäischer Perspektive, Munich: Sellier, § 3, no 24–8.

64 Decision of the Federal Administrative Court, BVerwGE 94, 82–94 (25 August 1993 – file no 6 C 8/91).

65 Decision of the Higher Administrative Court North Rhine-Westphalia (17 January 2002 – file no 19 B 99/02), *Neue Juristische Wochenschrift*, 2003, 1754–5.

66 See, e.g. A Rich (1979) *On Lies, Secrets, and Silence*, New York: Norton; E Spelman (1988) *Inessential Woman. Problems of Exclusions in Feminist Thought*, Boston, MA: Beacon Press; K Crenshaw (1989) 'Demarginalizing the intersection of race and sex: A black feminist critique of anti-discrimination law doctrine, feminist theory, and anti-racist politics', *The University of Chicago Legal Forum*: 139–67 (cited from the reprint in DK Weisberg (ed) *Feminist Legal Theory: Foundations*, Philadelphia, PA: Temple, pp 383–95; K Crenshaw (1991) 'Mapping the margins. Intersecitionality, identity politics, and violence against women of color', *Stanford Law Review*, 43: 1241–99.

67 C Weedon (1999) 'Race, racism and the problem of whiteness', in C Weedon (ed) *Feminism, Theory and the Politics of Difference*, Oxford, Malden, MA: Blackwell Publishers Ltd, pp 152–77. A Wing (ed) (1997) *Global Critical Race Feminism. An International Reader*, New York: New York University Press; AP Harris (1990) 'Race and essentialism in feminist legal theory', *Stanford Law Review*, 42: 581–616; For the German debate see B Stötzer (2004) *In Differenzen. Feministische Theorie in der antirassistischen Kritik*, Hamburg: Argument-Verlag; E Wollrad (2005) *Weißsein im Widerspruch. Feministische Perspektiven auf Rassismus, Kultur und Religion*, Königstein/Ts: Helmer; A Dietrich (2007) '*Weiße Weiblichkeiten*', Bielefeld: transcript.

68 See for the relation of Marxism and liberation theology for South America E Mendieta (ed) (2004) *Beyond Philosophy: Ethics, History, Marxism, and Liberation Theology*, Oxford: Rowman and Littlefield.

Bibliography

Aaltio, S (2002) 'Maahanmuuttajanaiset turvakotien asiakkaina', in R Nurmi and R Helander (eds), *Väkivalta ei tunne kulttuurisia rajoja. Maahanmuuttajanaisiin kohdistuva väkivalta Suomessa*, Naisiin kohdistuvan väkivallan ja prostituution ehkäisyhanke (1998–2002), Helsinki: Yliopistopaino, pp 49–54.

Abbott, D (2002) 'Teachers are failing black boys', *Guardian Unlimited*, 6 January, available at http://observer.guardian.co.uk/comment/story/0,,628287,00.html (accessed 14 January 2008).

Abrams, K (1990) 'Ideology and women's choices', *Georgia Law Review*, 24: 760–800.

—— (1994) 'Title VII and the complex female subject', *Michigan Law Review*, 92: 2479–540.

Aikio-Puoskari, U and Pentikäinen, M (2001) *The Language Rights of the Indigenous Saami in Finland – under Domestic and International Law*, Juridica lapponica 26, Rovaniemi: University of Lapland/Northern Institute for Environmental and Minority Law.

Akgün, L im Gespräch mit Alice Schwarzer (2003) 'Über das Kopftuch, Multikulti, den Zentralrat und die wahre Integration', *Emma*: 5, available at www.emma.de/658.html (accessed 20 September 2007).

Alan, Ö and Steuten, U (1999) 'Kopf oder Tuch – Überlegungen zur Reichweite politischer und sozialer Akzeptanz', *Zeitschrift für Rechtspolitik*: 209–15.

Alcoff, LM and Kittay, EF (2007) (eds), *The Blackwell Guide to Feminist Philosophy*, Malden, Oxford, Carlton: Blackwell Publishers.

Alibhai-Brown, Y (2001) *Who Do We Think We Are? Imagining a New Britain*, Harmondsworth: Penguin.

Altiparmak, K and Karahanogullari, O (2006) 'After Sahin: The debate on headscarves is not over', *European Constitutional Law Review*, 2: 278–83.

Amnesty International (2007) *Slovensko – Stále segregovaní, stále v nerovnom postavení, Porušovanie práva na vzdělanie romských dětí na Slovensku*, November, available at www.amnesty.cz/zpravy/Romske-deti-na-Slovensku-nemaji-rovny-pristup-ke-vzdelani (accessed 30 November 2007).

Andersen, A and Nielsen, R (2007) *Mainstreaming i juridisk perspektiv*, Copenhagen: Jurist- og \konomforbundets Forlag.

Andersen, A, Nielsen, R and Precht, K (2001) *Ligestillingslovene med kommentarer*, 4th edn, Copenhagen: Jurist- og \konomforbundets Forlag.

Anderson, B (1991 [1983]) *Imagined Communities – Reflections on the Origin and Spread of Nationalism*, 2nd reprinted edn, New York: Verso.

Anthias, F (1998) 'Rethinking social divisions: Some notes towards a theoretical framework', *Sociological Review*, 46: 506–35.

—— (2001) 'The concept of "social divisions" and theorising social stratification: Looking at ethnicity and class', *Sociology*, 35: 835–54.

—— (2006) 'Belongings in a globalising and unequal world: Rethinking translocations', in N Yuval-Davis, K Kannabiran and UM Vieten (eds) *The Situated Politics of Belonging*, London: Sage.

Anthias, F and Yuval-Davis, N (1983) 'Contextualizing feminism – ethnic, gender and class divisions', *Feminist Review*, 15: 62–75.

—— (1992) *Racialized Boundaries – Race, Nation, Gender, Colour and Class and the Anti-Racist Struggle*, London: Routledge.

Anttonen, A (1998) 'Vocabularies of citizenship and gender: Finland', *Critical Social Policy*, 18: 355–73.

Areheart, B (2006) 'Intersectionality revisited. Why Congress should amend Title VII to recognise intersectional claims', Express*O* Print series, paper 1289.

Arendt, H (1959) *The Human Condition*, New York: Doubleday Anchor.

Arnardóttir, OM (2003) *Equality and Non-Discrimination under the European Convention on Human Rights*, The Hague: Martinus Nijhoff Publishers.

—— (2007) 'Non-discrimination in International and European Law: Towards Substantive Models', *Nordisk tidsskrift for Menneskerettigheter*, 25: 140–57.

—— (2007) 'Non-discrimination under Article 14 ECHR – the Burden of Proof', *Scandinavian Studies in Law*, 51: 13–39.

Ashiagbor, D (1999) 'The Intersections between Gender and "Race" in the Labour Market: Lessons for Anti-discrimination Law', in A Morris and T O'Donell (eds) *Feminist Perspectives on Employment Law*, London: Cavendish, pp 139–60.

Asscher-Vonk, IP and Hendriks, AC (2005) *Gelijke behandeling en onderscheid bij de arbeid*, Deventer: Kluwer.

Ates, S (2004) 'Religionsfreiheit nicht auf Kosten von Frauen und Mädchen – Durchsetzung der Grundrechte und Selbstbestimmung', *STREIT*: 99–103.

—— (2006) *Große Reise ins Feuer. Geschichten einer deutschen Türkin*, Berlin: Rowohlt.

Aubert-Monpeyssen, T (2005) 'Principe "à salaire égal, salaire égal" et politiques de gestion des rémunérations', *Droit Social*: 18–30.

Austin, R (1989) 'Sapphire bound!', *Wisconsin Law Review*, 3: 539–78.

Auzero, G (2006) 'L'application du principe d'égalité de traitement dans l'entreprise', *Droit Social*: 822–5.

Axeli-Knapp, G (2005) 'Race, class, gender: Reclaiming baggage in fast travelling theories', *European Journal of Women's Studies*, 12: 249–65.

Bader, J (2006) 'Gleichbehandlung von Kopftuch und Nonnenhabit?', *Neue Zeitschrift für Verwaltungsrecht*: 1333–7.

—— (2007) 'Die Kopftuch tragende Schöffin', *Neue Juristische Wochenschrift*: 2964–6.

Badinter, E (2002) 'Der verschleierte Verstand', in A Schwarzer (ed) *Die Gotteskrieger und die falsche Toleranz*, 2nd edn, Köln: Kiepenheuer & Witsch, pp 139–46.

Baer, S and Wrase, M (2003) 'Staatliche Neutralität und Toleranz: Das Kopftuch-Urteil des BVerfG', *Juristische Schulung*: 1162–6.

Balibar, E (1991) 'Is there a neo-racism?', in E Balibar and I Wallerstein (eds) *Race, Nation, Class: Ambiguous Identities*, London: Verso.

Balog, K (2005) 'Equal protection for homosexuals: Why the immutability argument is necessary and how it is met', *Cleveland State Law Review*, 53: 545.

Barling, K (2007) 'Dying for an answer', *BBC London*, available at www.bbc.co.uk/london/content/articles/2007/04/17/kurt_bill_guns_feature.shtml (accessed 25 April 2007).

Barnard, C (2001) 'The changing scope of the fundamental principle of equality?' *McGill Law Journal* 46, 955–77.

Barnard, C. (2006) *EC Employment Law*, 3rd edn, Oxford: Oxford University Press.

—— (2007) 'Introduction', in C Barnard (ed) *The Fundamentals of the EU Revisited. Assessing the Impact of the Constitutional Debate*, Oxford: Oxford University Press.

—— (2007) 'Social policy revised in the light of the constitutional debate', in C Barnard (ed) *The Fundamentals of the EU Revisited. Assessing the Impact of the Constitutional Debate*, Oxford: Oxford University Press, pp 109–51.

—— (ed) (2007) *The Fundamentals of the EU Revisited. Assessing the Impact of the Constitutional Debate*, Oxford: Oxford University Press.

Barnard, C and Hepple, B (2000) 'Substantive equality', *Cambridge Law Journal*, 59: 562–85.

Barnes, R and Eicher, J (1992) (eds) *Dress and Gender: Making and Meaning in Cultural Contexts*, Providence, RI and Oxford: Berg.

Barth, F (1969) *Ethnic Groups and Boundaries: The Social Organisation of Cultural Difference*, Boston, MA: Little, Brown & Company.

Bauböck, R and Rundell, J (eds) (1998) *Blurred Boundaries: Migration, Ethnicity, Citizenship*, European Centre Vienna, Ashgate: Aldershot, pp 321–40.

Bayefsky, A (1990) 'A case comment on the first three equality rights cases under the Canadian Charter of Rights and Freedoms: Andrews Workers' compensation reference, Turpin', *Supreme Court Law Review*, 1: 503–34.

Beck, U (2000) 'The cosmopolitan perspective: sociology of the second age of modernity', *British Journal of Sociology*, 51: 79–105.

Bell, M (1999) 'The New Article 13 EC Treaty: A sound basis for European anti-discrimination law?', *Maastricht Journal of European and Comparative Law*, 6: 5–28.

—— (2000) 'Equality and diversity: Anti-Discrimination law after Amsterdam', in J Shaw (ed) *Social Law and Policy in an Evolving European Union*, Oxford: Hart Publishing, pp 157–69.

—— (2002) *Anti-Discrimination Law and the European Union*, Oxford: Oxford University Press.

Benhabib, S (2002) *The Claims of Culture: Equality and Diversity in the Global Era*, Princeton, NJ: Princeton University Press.

Berthou, K (2003) 'New hopes for French anti-discrimination law', *IJCLLIR*, 19: 109–37.

Berthoud, R (2002) 'Poverty and prosperity amongst Britain's ethnic minorities', *Benefits*, 10: 3–8.

Besson, S and Utzinger, A (2007) 'Introduction: Future challenges of European citizenship – facing a wide-open pandora's box', *European Law Journal*, 13: 573–90.

Beveridge, F and Nott, S (2002) 'Mainstreaming: A case for optimism and cynicism', *Feminist Legal Studies*, 10: 299–311.

Beveridge, F, Nott, S and Stephen, K (eds) (2000) *Making Women Count: Integrating Gender into Law and Policy-Making*, Aldershot: Ashgate.

Bielfeldt, H (2007) *Tackling Multiple Discrimination. Practices, Policies and Law*, Brussels: European Commission., September, available at http://ec.europa.eu/

employment_social/publications/2007/ke8207458_en.pdf (accessed 3 January 2008).

Blackwell, L (2003) 'Gender and ethnicity at work: Occupational segregation and disadvantage in the 1991 British census', *Sociology*, 37: 713–31.

Blomberg-Kroll, H (2004) 'Integration through work in a multicultural society? A study on elite groups debate on immigrants and the labour market in two Nordic welfare states', in V Puuronen, A Häkkinen, A Pylkkänen, T Sandlund and R Toivanen (eds) *New Challenges for the Welfare Society*, Joensuu: Yliopistopaino, pp 237–56.

Bobek, M, Boučková, P and Kühn, Z (eds) (2007) *Rovnost a discriminace*, Prague: Beck.

Böckenförde, E-W (2001) 'Kopftuchstreit auf dem richtigen Weg?', *Neue Juristische Wochenschrift*: 723–8.

—— (2004) 'Zum Verbot für Lehrkräfte in der Schule, ein islamisches Kopftuch zu tragen', *Juristenzeitung*: 1181–4.

Bodewig, C and Sethi, A (2005) *Poverty, Social Exclusion and Ethnicity in Serbia and Montenegro: The Case of the Roma*, Washington DC, available at http://web.worldbank.org/ (accessed 9 January 2008).

Boje, TP, Steenbergen van B and Walby, S (eds) (1999) *European Societies – Fusion or Fission?*, London, New York: Routledge.

Bonnard-Planke, L and Verkindt, P-Y (2006) 'Égalité et diversité: quelles solutions?', *Droit social*, 11: 968–80.

Bottero, W (2004) 'Class identities and the identity of class', *Sociology*, 38, 985–1003.

Bottois, B (2006) 'Le CV anonyme, un outil parmi d'autres au service d'une politique de la diversité', *Semaine Sociale Lamy*, 1287: 3.

Bourdieu, P (1999) *The Weight of the World: Social Suffering in Contemporary Society*, Cambridge: Polity Press.

Bradby, H (1999) 'Negotiating marriage: Young Punjabi women's assessment of their individual and family interests', in R Barot, H Bradley and S Fenton (eds) *Ethnicity, Gender and Social Change*, Basingstoke: Macmillan.

Brah, A (1996) *Cartographies of the Diaspora*, London: Routledge.

Brah, A and Phoenix, A (2004) 'Ain't I a woman? Revisiting intersectionality', *Journal of International Women's Studies*, 5: 75–86.

Bredal, A (2007) 'Den "spesielle" volden. Vold mot minoritetsjenter på sidelinjen', in K Storberget et al. (eds) *Bjørnen sover. Om vold i familien*, Oslo: Aschehoug, pp 56–61.

Breuilly, J (2000) 'Nationalism and the history of ideas', *Proceedings of the British Academy*, 105: 187–223.

—— (2001) 'The state and nationalism', in M Gubernau and J Hutchinson (eds) *Understanding Nationalism*, Cambridge: Polity Press, pp 32–52.

Bright, M and Hinsliff, G (2002) 'Bad teachers betraying black boys, says expert. National emergency feared if nothing is done', available at http://observer.guardian.co.uk/race/story/0,,632074,00.html (accessed 25 April 2007).

Britz, G (2003) 'Das verfassungsrechtliche Dilemma doppelter Fremdheit: Islamische Bekleidungsvorschriften für Frauen und Grundgesetz', *Kritische Justiz*: 95–103.

Brochmann, G and Hagelund, A (2005) *Innvandringens velferdspolitiske konsekvenser: nordisk kunnskapsstatus*, Oslo: Nordisk ministerråd (Nordic Council of Ministers).

Brown, C (2002) 'The Race Directive: Towards equality for all people of Europe?', *Year Book of EU Law*, 21: 195–217.

Brown, W (2000) 'Suffering rights as paradoxes', *Constellations*, 7: 230–41.

Browne I and Misra, J (2003) 'The intersection of gender and race in the labor market', *Annual Review of Sociology*, 29: 487–513.

Büchner, G and Janz, U (1991) 'Das verlorene Wir', *Ihrsinn,1991*: 3.

—— (1992) 'Die Qual der Moral', *Ihrsinn,1992*: 5.

Burri, S (2000) *Tijd delen. Deeltijd, gelijkheid en gender in Europees- en nationaalrechtelijk perspectief*, Deventer: Kluwer.

—— (ed) (2006) *Gelijke behandeling: oordelen en commentaar 2005*, Nijmegen: Wolf Legal Publishers.

Byrne, D (2005) 'Class, culture and identity. A reflection on absences against preferences', special issue of *Sociology*, 39: 807–16.

Cabinet Office (2002) *Ethnic Minorities and the Labour Market: Interim Analytical Report*, London: Cabinet Office.

—— (2003) *Ethnic Minorities and the Labour Market: Final Report*, London: Cabinet Office.

Cahn, C (2007) 'Birth of a nation: Kosovo and the persecution of pariah minorities', *German Law Journal*, 8: 81–94.

Caldwell, PM (1991) 'A hair piece: Perspectives on the intersection of race and gender', *Duke Law Journal*: 365–96.

Canada-Blanc, S (2006) 'L'égalité salariale et professionnelle: les femmes y parviendront-elles? A propos de la loi no 2006-340 du 23 mars 2006', *JCP G*: 870.

Caruso, D (2003) *Limits of the Classical Methods: Positive Action in the European Union after the New Equality Directives*, Boston University, School of Law, working paper no 03–21, available at www.bu.edu/law/faculty/scholarship/workingpapers/abstracts/2003/pdf_files/CarusoD090903.pdf (accessed 3 January 2008).

Castro R and Corral, L (1993) 'Women of colour and employment discrimination: Race and gender combined', *La Raza Law Journal*, 6: 159–173.

Chalmers, D (2001) 'The mistakes of the good European?', in S Fredman (ed) *Discrimination and Human Rights: the Case of Racism*, Oxford: Oxford University Press, pp 193–249.

Chege, V (2007) 'The interaction of race and gender in eu equality Law', in B Graue, A Mester, G Siehlman and M Westhaus (eds) *International-Europäisch-Regional*, Oldenburg: BIS-Verlag, pp 267–88.

Chew, PK (2007) 'Freeing racial harassment from the sexual harassment model', *University of Pittsburgh School of Law Working Paper Series*, No 54.

Chon, M and Arzt, D (2005) 'Walking while Muslim', *Law and Contemporary Problems*, 68: 225.

Chopin, I (1999) 'The Starting Line Group: A harmonised approach to fight racism and to promote equal treatment', *European Journal of Migration and Law*: 111–29.

Choudhry, S (2000) 'Distribution vs recognition: The case of anti-discrimination laws', *George Mason Law Review*, 9: 145–78.

Chtech Ombudsman's Report (2005) *Závěrečné stanovisko veřejného ochránce práv ve věci sterilizací prováděných v rozporu s právem a návrhy opatření k nápravě*, available at www.ochrance.cz/documents/doc1135861291.pdf (accessed 30 November 2007).

Cilliers, P (1998) *Complexity and Postmodernism: Understanding Complex Systems*, London: Routledge.

Collins, H (2003) 'Discrimination, equality and social inclusion', *Modern Law Review*, 66: 16–43.

Collins, PH (1986) 'The emerging theory and pedagogy of black women's studies', *Feminist Issues*, 6: 3–17.

——(2000) *Black Feminist Thought: Knowledge, Consciousness and the Politics of Empowerment*, New York: Routledge (first: Boston, MA: Univ Hyman, 1990).

——(2005) *Black Sexual Politics: African Americans, Gender and the New Racism*, New York: Routledge.

Commission de réflexion sur l'application du principe de laïcité dans la République (2003) *Rapport au président de la République*, 11 décembre 2003, available at http://lesrapports.ladocumentationfrancaise.fr/BRP/034000725/0000.pdf (accessed 8 January 2008).

Commission for Racial Equality (2003) *Race Equality and Public Procurement: A Guide for Public Authorities and Contractors*, London: Commission for Racial Equality.

Commission on Integration and Cohesion (2007) *Our Shared Future*, London: Department of Communities and Local Government.

Cormack, J and Bell, M (2005) *Comparative analysis of Anti-discrimination law in the 25 Member States*, Brussels: European Commission.

Cormack, J and Niessen, J (2002) 'Public procurement and anti-discrimination legislation', in I Chopin and J Niessen (eds) *Combating Racial and Ethnic Discrimination: Taking the European Legislative Agenda Further*, Brussels: Migration Policy Group.

Council of Europe (1998) *Gender Mainstreaming. Conceptual Framework, Methodology and Presentation of Good Practices*, Strasbourg, available at www.coe.int/t/e/human_rights/equality/02._gender_mainstreaming/099_EG(1999)03.asp (accessed 13 September 2007).

Craig, R (2006) 'The religious headscarf (hijab) and access to employment under Norwegian anti-discrimination laws', lecture for the Dr juris degree, February (unpublished).

Cremers-Hartman, E (2004) *Gelijke behandeling bij de arbeid in zes wetten. Een actueel overzicht van hoofdlijnen, overeenkomsten en verschillen*, Deventer: Kluwer.

Crenshaw, K (1989) 'Demarginalizing the intersection of race and sex: A black feminist critique of antidiscrimination doctrine, feminist theory and antiracial politics', *The University of Chicago Legal Forum*: 139–67 (reprinted in K Bartlett and R Kennedy (eds) (1991) *Feminist Legal Theory: Readings in Law and Gender*, Boulder, CO: Westview Press, pp 57–80 and in DK Weisberg (ed) (1993) *Feminist Legal Theory: Foundations*, Philadelphia, PA: Temple, pp 383–95).

——(1991) 'Mapping the margins: Intersectionality, identity politics, and violence against women of color', *Stanford Law Review*, 43: 1241–99 (reprinted in MA Fineman and R Mykitiuk (eds) (1992) *The Public Nature of Private Violence*, New York: Routledge).

——(1991) 'Race, gender and sexual harassment', *Southern California Law Review*, 65: 1467.

——(2000) *The intersectionality of race and gender discrimination*, draft paper, originally presented as the background paper for the Expert Group Meeting on Gender and Race Discrimination, Zagreb, Croatia, 21–24 November, available at www.wicej.addr.com/wcar_docs/crenshaw.html (accessed 4 January 2008).

Cudworth, E (2005) *Developing Ecofeminist Theory: The Complexity of Difference*, London: Palgrave.

Dale, A, Shaheen, N, Fieldhouse, E and Kalra, V (2002) 'Routes into education and employment for young Pakistani and Bangladeshi women in the UK', *Ethnic and Racial Studies*, 25: 942–68.

Daly, M (2005) 'Gender mainstreaming in theory and practice', *Social Politics: International Studies in Gender, State and Society*, 12: 433–50.

Danish Agency for Trade and Industry (2000) *The Relations of Banks to Women Entrepreneurs* 2000, available at http://videnskabsministeriet.dk/site/forside/publikationer/2000/the-relations-of-banks-to-women-entrepreneurs/ren.html (accessed 13 September 2007).

Däubler, W and Bertzbach (eds) (2006) *Allgemeines Gleichbehandlungsgesetz, Hand-kommentar*, Baden-Baden: Nomos.

Davies, P (1997) 'Posted workers: Single market or protection of national labour Law Systems?' *Common Market Law Review*, 24: 571–602.

Davydova, O and Heikkinen, K (2004) 'Produced Finnishness in the context of remigration', in V Puuronen, A Häkkinen, A Pylkkänen, T Sandlund and R Toivanen (eds) *New Challenges for the Welfare Society*, Joensuu: Yliopistopaino, pp 176–92.

De Búrca, G (2006) 'EU race discrimination law: A hybrid model?', in G De Búrca and J Scott (eds) *Law and New Governance in the EU*, Oxford, Portland, OR: Hart Publishing, pp 97–120.

De Búrca, G and Scott, J (eds) (2006) *Law and New Governance in the EU and the US*, Oxford, Portland, OR: Hart Publishing.

De Búrca, G and De Witte, B (eds) (2005) *Social Rights in Europe*, Oxford: Oxford University Press.

Dean, H (2002) 'Business versus families: Whose side is New Labour on?', *Social Policy and Society*, 1: 3–10.

—— (2002) *Welfare Rights and Social Policy*, Harlow: Prentice Hall.

Dein, S (2006) 'Race, culture and ethnicity in minority research: A critical discussion', *Journal of Cultural Diversity*, 13: 68–75.

Dench, S, Aston, J, Evans, C, Meager, N, Williams, M and Willison, R (2002) *Key Indicators of Women's Position in Britain*, London: Department of Trade and Industry.

Department for Communities and Local Government (2006) *Managing for Diversity: A Case Study of Four Local Authorities*, London: Department for Communities and Local Government.

—— (2007) *Improving Opportunity, Strengthening Society: Two Years On*, London: Department for Communities and Local Government.

Department for Education and Skills (2006) 'Priority review: Exclusion of black pupils "Getting it. Getting it right" ', available at www.standards.dfes.gov.uk/ethnicminorities/ (accessed 1 May 2007).

Department for Transport, Local Government and the Regions (2001) *Delivering Better Services for Citizens – A Review of Local Government Procurement in England*, London: Department for Transport, Local Government and the Regions.

Dietrich, A (2007) '*Weiße Weiblichkeiten*', Bielefeld: transcript.

Dijk, van P, Hoof, van F, Rijn, van A and Zwaak, L (eds) (2006) *Theory and Practice of the European Convention on Human Rights*, 4th edn, Antwerpen, Oxford: Intersentia.

Direction des relations du travail (2006) *La négociation collective en 2005*, Ministère de l'Emploi, Editions Législatives.

Dockès, E (2002) 'Equality in labour law: An economically efficient human right? Reflections from a French law perspective', *IJCLLIR*, 18: 187–96.

—— (2005) *Droit du Travail, relations individuelles*, Paris: Dalloz, coll. HyperCours.

—— (2005) *Valeurs de la Démocratie, 8 notions fondamentales*, Paris: Dalloz, coll. Méthodes du droit.

Dorbritz, J, Lengerer, A and Ruckdeschel, K (2005) *Einstellungen zu demographischen Trends und zu bevölkerungsrelevanten Politiken*, Wiesbaden, available at www.bib-demographie.de/info/ppas_broschuere.pdf (accessed 20 December 2007).

Dougan, M (2004) *National Remedies Before the Court of Justice: Issues of Harmonisation and Differentiation*, Oxford: Hart Publishing.

Douzinas, C (2002) 'Identity, recognition, rights or what Hegel can teach us about human rights?', *Journal of Law and Society*, 29: 379–405.

Dübbers, R and Dlovani, Z (2004) 'Der Kopftuchstreit vor dem Bundesverfassungsgericht – ein Zwischenspiel', *Arbeit und Recht*: 6–11.

Duclos, N (1993) 'Disappearing women: Racial minority women in human rights cases', *Canadian Journal Women and Law*, 6: 25–51.

Dworkin, R (2000) *Sovereign Virtue. The Theory and Practice of Equality*, Cambridge, MA: Harvard University Press.

Dwyer, C (1999) 'Veiled meanings: Young British Muslim women and the negotiation of differences', *Gender, Place and Culture*, 6: 5–26.

ECOHOST (2000) *Health needs of the Roma population in the Czech and the Slovak Republics. A Literature Review*, Final Report 2000, available at www.lshtm.ac.uk/ecohost/roma.pdf (accessed 5 March 2008).

Economic and Social Research Council (2005) 'Society today: Inequality in the UK', available at www.esrcsocietytoday.ac.uk/ESRCInfoCentre/facts/UK/index51.aspx?ComponentId=12699&SourcePageId=18134 (accessed 1 May 2007).

El Guindi, F (1999) *Veil: Modesty, Privacy and Resistance*, Oxford: Berg Publishers.

Ellis, E (2005) *EU Anti-Discrimination Law*, Oxford: Oxford University Press.

Ellis, J (1981) 'Sexual harassment and race: A legal analysis of discrimination', *North Dakota Journal of Legislation*, 8: 30–45.

ENAR (2006) Background Paper, ENAR Policy Seminar, Brussels, 6–7 October 2006, available at www.enar-eu.org/en/events/directives/backgroundpaper_EN.pdf (accessed 9 January 2008).

Equal Opportunities Commission (2003) *Facts About Men and Women in Great Britain 2003*, Manchester: Equal Opportunities Commission.

Erikson, E (1977) *Toys and Reasons*, New York: WW Norton.

ERRC (2004) *Stigmata: Segregated Schooling of Roma in Central and Eastern Europe*, Budapest, available at www.errc.org/cikk.php?cikk=1892 (accessed 8 January 2008).

—— (2007) *The Glass Box. Exclusion of Roma from Employment*, Budapest, available at www.ceeol.com/aspx/publicationdetails.aspx?publicationId=a46f1076-f8a4-45d0-8ef4-cf113f5a65d0 (accessed 5 March 2008), pp 9–10.

—— (2007) *The Impact of Legislation and Policies on School Segregation of Romani Children. A Study of Anti-Discrimination Law and Government Measures to Eliminate Segregation in Education in Bulgaria, Czech Republic, Hungary, Romania and Slovakia*, Budapest, available at www.ceeol.com/aspx/publication details.aspx?publicationId=a46f1076-f8a4-45d0-8ef4-cf113f5a65d0 (accessed 5 March 2008), pp 42–6.

Erridge, A and Fee, R (1999) 'Contract compliance: National, regional and global regimes', *Policy and Politics*, 27: 199–216.

Erridge, A and Gordon Murray, J (1998) 'Lean supply: A strategy for best value in local government procurement?', *Public Policy and Administration*, 13: 70–85.

Erridge, A and McIlroy, J (2002) 'Public procurement and supply management strategies', *Public Policy and Administration*, 17: 52–71.

EU Joint Monitoring and Advocacy Program/European Roma Rights Center (2004) *Shadow Report Commenting on the fifth periodic report of the Federal Republic of Germany Submitted under Article 18 of the United Nations Convention on the Elimination of All Forms of Discrimination against Women*, European Roma Rights Centre and Open Society Institute, 9 January 2004, available at http://lists.errc.org/publications/legal/CEDAW-Germany_Jan_2004.doc (accessed 5 March 2008).

European Commission (2004) *Equality and Non-Discrimination in an Enlarged European Union*, Green Paper, Luxembourg: Office for Official Publications of the European Communities.

European Commission (2006) *A Roadmap for Equality Between Women and Men 2006–2010*, COM(2006) 92.

European Commission (2007) *Special Eurobarometer 263: Discrimination in the European Union*, Brussels: European Commission.

European Commission (2007) *Tackling Multiple Discrimination. Practices, Policies and Laws*, Directorate-General for Employment, Social Affairs and Equal Opportunities, Unit G.4, Luxembourg: Office for Official Publications of the European Communities.

European Monitoring Centre on Racism and Xenophobia (2003) *Migrants, Minorities and Employment: Exclusion, Discrimination and Anti-discrimination in 15 Member States of the European Union*, Vienna: International Centre for Migration Policy Development (ICMPD) (on behalf of the European Monitoring Centre on Racism and Xenophobia (EUMC)), available at http://fra.europa.eu/fra/material/pub/comparativestudy/CS-Employment-en.pdf (accessed 4 March 2008).

—— (2005) *Racist Violence in 15 EU Member States – A Comparative Overview of Findings from the RAXEN NFP Reports 2001–2004*, April, available at http://fra.europa.eu/fra/material/pub/comparativestudy/CS-RV-main.pdf (accessed 9 January 2008).

—— (2006) *Roma and Travellers in Public Education*, May, available at http://fra.europa.eu/fra/index.php?fuseaction=content.dsp_cat_content&catid=43d8bc25bc89d&contentid=448ee6612aa4c (accessed 9 January 2008).

European Parliament (2005) Document A6-0148/2006: *Report on the situation of Roma Women in the European Union (2005/2164(INI))*, Committee on Women's Rights and Gender Equality, Rapporteur: L Járóka.

Evans, S M (1989) *Born for Liberty: A History of Women in America*, New York: The Free Press.

Favennec-Héry, F (2005) 'L'ANI relatif à l'emploi des seniors: un premier pas', *La Semaine Juridique Social*, 21: 1329.

—— (2006) 'Vers un ANI sur la diversité dans l'entreprise', *La Semaine Juridique Social*, 47: 1914.

—— (2007) 'Non-discrimination, égalité, diversité, la France au milieu du gué', *Droit social*, 1: 3–7.

Fee, R (2002) 'Contract compliance: Subnational and European influences in Northern Ireland', *Journal of European Social Policy*, 12: 107–21.

Fee, R, Maxwell, P and Erridge, A (1998) 'Contracting for services – A double jeopardy? An analysis of contract compliance in the context of European and UK social and public procurement policy', *Public Policy and Administration*, 13: 79–84.

Filadelfiová, J, Gerbery, D and Škobla, D (2007) *Report on the Living Conditions of Roma in Slovakia*, UNDP, Friedrich Ebert Stiftung.

Flynn, L (1999) 'The implications of Article 13 EC Treaty – after Amsterdam, will some forms of discrimination be more equal than others?', *Common Market Law Review*, 36: 1127–52.

Fraser, A (1992) *The Gypsies*, Oxford: Blackstone.

Fraser, N (2000) 'Rethinking recognition', *New Left Review*, 3: 107–20.

Fraser, N and Honneth, A (2003) *Redistribution or Recognition*, London, New York: Verso.

Fredman, S (1992) 'European community discrimination law: A critique', *Industrial Law Journal*, 21: 119–34.

—— (1994) 'A difference with distinction: Pregnancy and parenthood reassessed', *Law Quarterly Review*, 110: 106–23.

—— (1997) *Women and the Law*, Oxford: Clarendon Press.

—— (2001) 'Combating racism with human rights: The right to equality', in S Fredman (ed) *Discrimination and Human Rights: The Case of Racism*, Oxford: Oxford University Press.

—— (2001) *Discrimination and Human Rights. Essays in European Law*, Oxford: Oxford University Press.

—— (2001) 'Equality: A new generation?', *Industrial Law Journal*, 30: 145–68.

—— (2002) *Discrimination Law*, Oxford: Oxford University Press.

—— (2002) *The Future of Equality in Great Britain*, Manchester: Equal Opportunities Commission.

—— (2005) 'Changing the norm: Positive duties in equal treatment legislation', *Maastricht Journal of European and Comparative Law*, 12: 369–98.

—— (2005) 'Double trouble: Multiple discrimination and EU law', *European Anti-Discrimination Law Review*, 2: 13–21, available at http://ec.europa.eu/employment_social/fundamental_rights/pdf/legnet/05lawrev2_en.pdf (accessed 13 September 2007).

—— (2006) 'Transformation or dilution: Fundamental rights in the EU social space', *European Law Journal*, 12: 41–60.

—— (2007) 'Redistribution and recognition: reconciling inequalities', *South African Journal on Human Rights*, 23: 214–34.

Fredman, S and Spencer, S (2006) 'Delivering equality: Towards an outcome – focused positive duty', submission to the Cabinet Office Equality Review and to the Discrimination Law Review.

Fuchsloch, C (1995) *Das Verbot der mittelbaren Geschlechtsdiskriminierung*, Baden-Baden: Nomos.

Gallala, I (2006) 'The Islamic headscarf: An example of surmountable conflict between Sharia an the fundamental principles of Europe', *European Law Journal*: 593–612.

Gangaas, B (2006) 'Intersectionality as a challenge for the Equality and Anti-discrimination Ombud', presentation at seminar at the University of Oslo, 'Multiple discrimination and equality agendas: Intersectionality in practice', 4 December (unpublished, on file with the author).

Geddes, A and Guiraudon, V (2004) 'Britain, France and EU anti-discrimination policy; The emergence of an EU policy paradigm', *West European Politics*, 17: 334–53.

Gerards, J (2007) 'Chapter One: Discrimination Grounds', in D Schiek, L Waddington and M Bell (eds) *Cases, Materials and Texts on National, Supranational and International Non-Discrimination Law*, Oxford: Hart Publishing.

Gerards, JH (2002) *Rechterlijke toetsing aan het gelijkheidsbeginsel: een rechtsvergelijkend onderzoek naar een algemeen toetsingsmodel*, Maastricht: Universiteit Maastricht.

Gerards, JH and Heringa, AW (2003) *Wetgeving gelijke behandeling*, Deventer: Kluwer.

Gerards, JH, Vermeulen, BP and Zoontjes, PJJ (2007) *Gelijke behandeling: oordelen en commentaar 2006*, Nijmegen: Wolf Legal Publishers.

Gilbert, D (2003) 'Time to regroup. Rethinking section 15 of the Charter', *McGill Law Journal*, 48: 627–49.

Goerlich, H (2001) 'Religionspolitische Distanz und kulturelle Vielfalt unter dem Regime des Art 9 EMRK', *Neue Juristische Wochenschrift*: 2862–3.

Goffman, E (1990) *Stigma: Notes on the Management of Spoiled Identity*, London: Penguin.

Goldschmidt, JE (1993) *We need different stories. Een ander verhaal in het recht. Verhalen van verschil*, Zwolle: WEJ Tjeenk Willink.

Goldston, J (2005) 'European Court to address racism in landmark cases', *Open Society Justice Initative*, 28 February, available at www.justiceinitiative.org/db/resource2?res_id=102627 (accessed 9 January 2008).

Goodwin, M (2006) 'DH and Others v Czech Republic: A major set-back for the development of non-discrimination norms in Europe', *German Law Journal*, 7: 421–32.

Grabham, E (2006) 'Taxonomies of inequality: Lawyers, maps and the challenge of hybridity', *Social Legal Studies*, 15: 5–23.

Greater London Authority (2004) Increase black teacher numbers to improve education outcomes for black children, available at www.london.gov.uk/view_press_release-.jsp?releaseid=4304 (accessed 25 April 2007).

Greenawalt, K (2006) *Religion and the Constitution. Volume 1: Free Exercise and Fairness*, Princeton, NJ, Oxford: Princeton University Press.

Greer, S (2003) 'Constitutionalising adjudication under the European Convention on Human Rights', *Oxford Journal of Legal Studies*, 23: 405–33.

Gronow, J, Klemola, P and Partanen, J (1977) *Demokratian rajat ja rakenteet. Tutkimus suomalaisesta hallitsemistavasta ja sen taloudellisesta perustasta*, Porvoo: WSOY.

Gubernau, M and Hutchinson, J (eds) (2001) *Understanding Nationalism*, Cambridge: Polity Press.

Gunn, TJ (2004) 'Religious freedom and *laïcité*: a comparison of the United States and France', *Brigham Young University Law Review*: 419–505.

Haarakangas, T, Ollus N and Toikka, S (2000) *Väkivaltaa kokeneet maahanmuuttajanaiset – haaste turvakotipalveluille Suomessa*, Ministry of Social Affairs and Health, Publications on Equality 3.

Häkkinen, A and Tervonen, M (2004) 'Ethnicity, marginalization and poverty in the 20th century Finland', in V Puuronen, A Häkkinen, A Pylkkänen, T Sandlund and R Toivanen (eds) *New Challenges for the Welfare Society*, Joensuu: Yliopistopaino, pp 22–39.

Halfmann, R (2000) 'Der Streit um die "Lehrerin mit Kopftuch" ', *Neue Zeitschrift für Verwaltungsrecht*: 862–8.

Hall, S (2000) 'Conclusion: The multicultural question', in B Hesse (ed) *Un/Settled Multiculturalisms: Diasporas, Entanglements, Transruptions*, London: Zed Books.

Halpern, D (2005) *Social Capital*, Cambridge: Polity Press.

Hancock, I (2002) *We are the Romani people*, Hatfield: University of Hertfordshire Press.

Hannett, S (2003) 'Equality at the intersections: The legislative and judicial failure to tackle multiple discrimination', *Oxford Journal of Legal Studies*, 23: 65–86.

Harris, AP (1990) 'Race and essentialism in feminist legal theory', *Stanford Law Review*, 42: 581–616.

—— (1994) 'Foreword: The jurisprudence of reconstruction', *California Law Review*, 82: 741–85.

Harris, L (2000) 'Issues of fairness in recruitment processes: A case study of local government practice', *Local Government Studies*, 26: 31–46.

Hatzopoulos, V (2007) 'Why the open method of coordination is bad for you: A letter to the EU', *European Law Journal*, 13: 309–42.

Haug, F and Reimer, K (eds) (2005) *Politik ums Kopftuch*, Hamburg: Argument.

Haupert, A and Nicoara, M (2007) 'Roma activists assess the progress of the Decade on Roma Inclusion', available at http://demo.itent.hu/roma/portal/downloads/DecadeWatch/DecadeWatch%20-%20Complete%20(English;%20Final).pdf (accessed 5 December 2007).

Häußler, U (2001) 'Muslim dress-codes in German state schools', *European Journal of Migration and Law*: 457–74.

—— (2004) 'Leitkultur oder Laizismus?', *Zeitschrift für Ausländerrecht*: 6–14.

Havelková, B (2005) 'Equal opportunities for women and men: monitoring law and practice in the Czech Republic 2005', Open Society Institute Network Women's Program, available at www.soros.org/initiatives/women/articles_publications (accessed 5 December 2007).

—— (2006) 'Law and equality for men and women' in P Pavlik (ed) *Shadow Report on Equal Treatment and Equal Opportunities for Women and Men, 2006*, Open Society Fund Prague, available at www.osf.cz/en/ (accessed 8 October 2007).

—— (2007) 'Burden of proof and positive action in the Czech and Slovak Constitutional Courts', *European Law Review*: 686–704.

—— (2008) 'Challenges to the effective implementation of EC gender equality law in the Czech Republic – an early analysis', in K Arioli, M Cottier, P Farahmand and Z Küng (eds) *Wandel der Geschlechterverhältnisse durch Recht?*, Zürich: DIKE (forthcoming).

Héas, F (2007) 'Discrimination et admission de différences de traitement entre salariés', *La semaine juridique-Édition sociale*, 20 March: 11–14.

Hegel, GWF (1977) *Phenomenology of Spirit*, Oxford: Oxford University Press.

Held, D and Kaya, A (eds) (2007) *Global Inequality – Patterns and Explanations*, Cambridge: Polity Press.

—— (2007) 'Introduction', in D Held and A Kaya (eds) *Global Inequality – Patterns and Explanations*, Cambridge: Polity Press, pp 1–25.

Henrard, K (2007) 'The protection of minorities through the equality provisions in the UN Human Rights Treaties: the UN Treaty bodies', *International Journal on Minority and Group Rights*, 14: 141–80.

Hepple, B (1990) 'Discrimination and equality of opportunity – Northern Irish lessons', *Oxford Journal of Legal Studies*, 10: 408–21.

—— (2004) 'Race and law in fortress Europe', *Modern Law Review*, 67: 1–15.

Hepple, B, Choussey, M and Choudhoury, T (2000) *Equality: A New Framework: Report of the Independent Review of the Enforcement of UK Anti-Discrimination Legislation*, Oxford: Hart Publishing.

Herring, C and Collins, SM (1995) 'Retreat from equal opportunity? The case of affirmative action', in MP Smith and JR Feagin (eds) *The Bubbling Cauldron: Race, Ethnicity and the Urban Crisis*, Minneapolis, MN: University of Minnesota Press.

Hervey, T (2005) 'Thirty years of EU sex equality law: Looking backwards, looking forward', *Maastricht Journal of Comparative and European Law*, 12: 307–26.

Hervey, T and Shaw, J (1998) 'Women, work and care: Women's dual role and double burden in EC sex equality law', *Journal of European Social Policy*, 8: 43–63.

Hesse, K (1999) *Grundzüge des Verfassungsrechts der Bundesrepublik Deutschland*, 20th edn, Heidelberg: Müller Verlag.

Hibschannova, M (ed) (2007) 'Romové v České republice (1945–1998)', *Socioklub, Prague*: 102–4.

HMSO (1999) *The Stephen Lawrence Enquiry*, Cm 4262-1, London: Her Majesty's Stationery Office.

—— (2007) *The Equalities Review, Fairness and Freedom: The Final Report of the Equalities Review*, London: Cabinet Office.

Ho, C (2007) 'Muslim women's new defenders: Women's rights, nationalism and Islamophobia in contemprorary Australia', *Women's Studies International Forum*, 30: 290–8.

Hoevels, N (2003) 'Kopftuch als Kündigungsgrund', *Neue Zeitschrift für Arbeitsrecht*: 701–4.

Holli, AM and Kantola, J (2007) 'State feminism Finnish style: Strong policies clash with implementation problems', in J Outshoorn and J Kantola (eds) *Changing State Feminism*, Chippenham: Palgrave Macmillan, pp 62–81.

Holli, AM (1992) *Miehisestä tasa-arvosta kohti naisten käsitteellistä tilaa: Tasa-arvoasiain neuvottelukunnan tasa-arvopoliittinen diskurssi*, Helsinki: Helsingin yliopisto.

Holloway, L (2005) 'Carry on excluding', *Black Information Link*, 23 October, available at www.blink.org.uk/pdescription.asp?grp=7&cat=28&key=9798 (accessed 11 January 2008).

—— (2005) 'Fighting the powers that be', *Black Information Link*, 7 October, available at www.blink.org.uk/pdescription.asp?key=9758&grp=7 (accessed 14 January 2008).

—— (2007) 'One in ten', available at www.blink.org.uk/pdescription.asp?key=14284&grp=7&cat=28 (accessed 25 April 2007).

Holmes, E (2005) 'Anti-discrimination rights without equality', *Modern Law Review*, 68: 75–194.

Holtmaat, R (1992) *Met zorg een recht? Een analyse van het politiek-juridisch betoog over het bijstandsrecht*, Zwolle: WEJ Tjeenk Willink.

—— (1996) 'Alle dingen die opwaarts gaan komen ergens samen', *Nemesis*, 4: 125–31.

—— (1996) 'Deeltijdwerk, gelijkheid en gender. Een beschouwing naar aanleiding van de zaak Helmig inzake overwerktoeslagen voor deeltijdwerkers', *Nemesis*, 1: 4–17.

—— (1999) 'The issue of overtime payments for part-time workers in the *Helmig* case; Some thoughts on equality and gender', in Y Kravaritou (ed) *The Regulation of Working Time in the European Union; Gender Approach*, Brussels: Peter Lang, pp 411–44.

Holzleithner, E (2006) 'Mainstreaming equality: Dis/Entangling grounds of discrimination', *Transnational Law and Contemporary Problems*, 14: 927–57.

Hooks, B (1981) *Ain't I a Woman: Black Women and Feminism*, Boston, MA: South End Press (London: Pluto Press, 1982).

Horelli, L and Saari, M (2002) *Tasa-arvoa valtavirtaan: Tasa-arvon valtavirtaistamisen menetelmiä ja käytäntöjä*, Helsinki: Ministry of Social Affairs and Health.

Horner, K (2005) 'A growing problem: Why the federal government needs to shoulder the burden in protecting workers from weight discrimination', *Catholic University Law Review*, 54: 589–613.

Horsley, EM, Knudsen, SV and Aamotsbakken, B (eds) (2006) *Caught in the Web or Lost in the Textbook?*, STEF, IARTEM, IUFM de Basse-Normandie, Paris: Jouve.

Hoskyns, C (1996) *Integrating Gender: Women, Law and Politics in the European Union*, London: Verso.

Hufen, F (2004) 'Der Regelungsspielraum des Landesgesetzgebers im Kopftuchstreit', *Neue Zeitschrift für Verwaltungsrecht*: 575–8.

Hull, G, Scott, P and Smith, B (1982) *All the Women are White, all the Blacks are Men, But Some of Us are Brave*, New York: Feminist Press at CUNY.

Hussain Y and and Bagguley, P (2005) 'Citizenship, ethnicity and identity: British Pakistanis after the 2001 "riots" '; *Sociology*, 39: 407–25.

Hutchinson, DL (2003) 'Unexplainable on grounds other than race: The inversion of privilege and subordination in equal protection jurisprudence', *University of Illinois Law Review*: 615–700.

Ipsen, J (2003) 'Karlsruhe locuta, causa non finita', *Neue Juristische Wochenschrift*: 1210–13.

Jaakkola, M (2005) *Suomalaisten suhtautuminen maahanmuuttajiin vuosina 1987–2003*, Työvoimapoliittinen tutkimus, Työministeriö.

Jackson, JJ (1995) 'Race-based affirmative action: Mend it or end it?', *The Black Scholar*, 25: 30–42.

Jacobs, F (2007) 'Citizenship of the European Union – A legal analysis', *European Law Journal*, 13: 591–610.

Jacoby, J and Gotlinde ML (1990) 'Was "sie" schon immer über Antisemitismus wissen wollte, aber nie zu denken wagte', *Beiträge zur feministischen Theorie und Praxis*, 13: 27–95.

Janz, N and Rademacher, S (2001) 'Das Kopftuch als religiöses Symbol oder profaner Bekleidungsgegenstand?, *Juristische Schulung*: 440–4.

Jeammaud, A (2004) 'Du principe d'égalité de traitement des salariés', *Droit social*, 7/8: 694–705.

Jessen, F (2006) 'Wilamowitz-Moellendorff v. U, *Das Kopftuch – Entschleierung eines Symbols?*', Broschürenreihe herausgegeben von der Konrad-Adenauer-Stiftung e.V, Sankt Augustin/Berlin, available at www.kas.de//db_files/dokumente/zukunfts-forum_politik/7_dokument_dok_pdf_9095_1.pdf?070807122758 (accessed 20 December 2007), in particular pp 23 *et seq*.

Jewe, A (2004) *Constructing Equality: Identity and Intersectionality in Canadian and South African Jurisprudence*, MA dissertation, Cape Town.

John, G (2006) *Memorandum submitted by Gus John to the Home Affairs Committee*,

available at www.publications.parliament.uk/pa/cm200607/cmselect/cmhaff/181/
181we37.htm (accessed 20 July 2007).

Johnson, R (2005) 'Gender, race, class and sexual orientation: Theorizing the intersections', in G MacDonald, RL Osborne and CC Smith (eds) *Feminism, Law,
Inclusion: Intersectionality in Action*, Toronto: Sumach Press, pp 21–37.

Jokinen, A (2000) *Panssaroitu maskuliinisuus. Mies, väkivalta ja kulttuuri*. Tampere:
Tampere University Press.

Jones, C (1998) 'The status of woman in Islamic law', lecture on the occasion of
the exhibition 'Meeting Arabia' at Goettingen, available at www.sub.uni-
goettingen.de/ebene_1/orient/docs/womnislm.htm (accessed 8 January 2008).

Jones, C and Shorter-Gooden, K (2003) *Shifting: The Double Lives of Black Women in
America*, New York: Harper Collins.

Julkunen, R (1979) *Sosiaalipoliittinen uudistustoiminta 1960-luvulla Suomessa*,
Jyväskylä: Jyväskylän yliopiston yhteiskuntapolitiikan laitos.

—— (2007) 'Tasa-arvolaki kaksikymmentä vuotta', *Tasa-arvolaki 20 vuotta*, 1: 85–107.

Kahri, T and Vihma, J (1971) *Vuoden 1970 työsopimuslaki*, Helsinki: Weilin & Göös.

Kannabiran, K (2006) 'A cartography of resistance: the National Federation of Dalit
Women', in N Yuval-Davis, K Kannabiran and UM Vieten (eds) *The Situated
Politics of Belonging*, London: Sage, pp 54–71.

Karakasoglu, Y (2003) 'Islam und Moderne, Bildung und Integration. Einstellungen
türkisch-muslimischer Studentinnen erziehungswissenschaftlicher Fächer', in
M Rumpf, U Gerhard and M Jansen (eds) *Facetten islamischer Welten. Geschlechterordnungen, Frauen- und Menschenrechte in der Diskussion*, Bielefeld: transcript,
272–289.

Karst, K (1986) 'Paths to belonging: The Constitution and cultural identity', *North
Carolina Law Review*, 64: 303–77.

Keller, M (2002) 'La loi du 16 novembre 2001 relative à la lutte contre les discriminations', *Recueil Dalloz*: 1355.

Ketscher, K (2005) 'Etnisk ligebehandling, religionsfrihed og ligestilling mellem
kvinder og mænd – set i lyset af Føtex-sagen', *Ugeskrift for Retsvæsen*, 26: 235–43.

Killian, C (2003) 'The other side of the veil. North African women in France respond
to the headscarf affair', *Gender & Society*, 17: 567–90.

Kingsmill, D (2001) *The Kingsmill Review of Women's Pay and Employment*, London:
Cabinet Office, Department of Trade and Industry and Department for Education
and Skills.

Klinkhammer, G (2003) 'Moderne Formen islamischer Lebensführung. Musliminnen
der zweiten Generation in Deutschland', in M Rumpf, U Gerhard and M Jansen
(eds) *Facetten islamischer Welten. Geschlechterordnungen, Frauen- und Menschenrechte in der Diskussion*, Bielefeld: transcript, pp 257–71.

Knudsen, SV (2006) 'Intersectionality – a theoretical inspiration in the analysis
of minority cultures and identities in textbooks', in E Bruillard, M Horsley,
SV Knudsen and B Aamotsbakken (eds) *Caught in the Web or Lost in the
Textbook?*, STEF, IARTEM, IUFM de Basse-Normandie, Paris: Jouve, pp 61–76.

Koch, IE (2006) 'Economic, social and cultural rights as components in civil and
political rights: A Hermeneutic Perspective', *International Journal of Human
Rights*, 10: 405–30.

Koelman, SM (2005) *Algemene wet gelijke behandeling; Wet gelijke behandeling van
mannen en vrouwen, Wet gelijke behandeling op grond van handicap en chronische
ziekte, Wet gelijke behandeling op grond van leeftijd bij de arbeid*, Deventer: Kluwer.

Kokott, J (1998) *The Burden of Proof in Comparative and International Human Rights Law*, The Hague: Kluwer Law International.

Koldinská, K (2005) 'Contribution on the Czech Republic', *Bulletin*, 1: 22, available at http://ec.europa.eu/employment_social/gender_equality/legislation/bulletin_en.html (accessed 5 December 2007).

—— (2007) The reports of the Commission's Network of legal experts in the fields of employment, social affairs and equality between men and women and the Network's Bulletin 'Legal Issues in Gender Equality', available at http://ec.europa.eu/employment_social/gender_equality/legislation/bulletin_en.html (accessed 5 December 2007).

Komiteanmietintö (1970) A 8 *Naisten asemaa tutkivan komitean mietintö*, Helsinki.

Kontula, A (2005) *Prostituutio Suomessa*, Tampere: SEXPO Säätiö.

Kostakopoulou, D (2007) 'European Union citizenship: Writing the future', *European Law Journal*, 13: 623–46.

Kozol, J (2005) 'Still separate, still unequal. America's educational apartheid', *Harper's Magazine*, 311(1864): 41–54.

Králíková, A (2006) *Porušování lidských práv*, Praha: Gender Studies.

Kristková, V (2006) 'Právo na vzdělání – segregace romských dětí v základním školství', in *Zpráva o vývoji práv dětí v ČR v letech 2003–2005*, Liga lidských práv, Brno, available at www.llp.cz/_files/file/Zprava_deti.pdf (accessed 30 November 2007).

Kuusi, P (1961) *60-luvun sosiaalipolitikka*, Porvoo: WSOY.

Kymlicka, W (1995) *Multicultural Citizenship: A Liberal Theory of Minority Rights*, Oxford: Oxford University Press.

Kyntäjä, E (2004) 'The meaning of stigma for self-identication and psychological well-being amongst Estonian- and Russian-speaking immmigrants in Finland: A qualitative interview study', in V Puuronen, A Häkkinen, A Pylkkänen, T Sandlund and R Toivanen (eds) *New Challenges for the Welfare Society*, Joensuu: Yliopistopaino, pp 193–207.

Lacy, DA (2007) 'The most endangered Title VII plaintiff?' African-American males and intersectional claims', available at http://works.bepress.com/d_aaron_lacy/ (accessed 14 January 2008).

Landau, J (2005) 'Soft immutabilty' and "imputed gay identity": Recent developments in transgender and sexual orientation based asylum law', *Fordham Urban Law Review*, 32: 237–64.

Lanquetin, M-Th (2001) 'Le principe de non-discrimination', *Droit Ouvrier*, Mai: 186–93.

—— (2002) *La Double Discrimination à Raison du Sexe et de la Race ou de l'Origine Ethnique: Approche juridique, Synthèse du Rapport Final*, available at www.lacse.fr/ressources/files/etudesetdocumentation/syntheses/Lanquetin_02.pdf (accessed 13 September 2007).

—— (2006) 'L'égalité des rémunérations entre les femmes et les hommes, réalisée en cinq ans?', *Droit social*, 6: 624–35.

Lanquetin, M-Th and Grevy, M (2005) *Premier bilan de la mise en œuvre de la loi du 16 novembre 2001 relative à la lutte contre les discriminations*, final report, December, available at www.social.gouv.fr/IMG/pdf/etude_afem_122005.pdf (accessed 21 December 2007).

Laskowski, SR (2003) 'Der Streit um das Kopftuch geht weiter – Warum das Diskriminierungsverbot wegen der Religion nach nationalem und europäischen Recht immer bedeutsamer wird', *Kritische Justiz*: 420–44.

Leapman, B (2006) 'Three in four young black men on the DNA database', *The Sunday Telegraph*, available at www.telegraph.co.uk/news/main.jhtml?xml=/news/2006/11/05/nrace05.xml (accessed 17 December 2007).

Lehti, M and Aromaa, K (2002) *Trafficking in Human Beings and Illegal Immigration in Finland*, Helsinki: HEUNI Report Series No 38.

Lentin, A (2005) 'The intifada of the banlieus', *OpenDemocracy*, 17 November, available at www.opendemocracy.net/node/3037 (accessed 9 January 2008).

Levy, D and Sznaider, N (2002) 'Memory unbound – The holocaust and the formation of cosmopolitan memory', *European Journal of Social Theory*, 5: 87–106.

Lhernould, J-Ph and Martin, D (2007) 'Majoration d'assurance de l'article L. 351–4 du Code de la Sécurité sociale: fin programmée de la discrimination à l'égard des pères en matière de pension de vieillesse', *Droit social*, 3: 319–22.

Liga lidských práv (2007) *Sběr dat určujících etnickou příslušnost jako nástroj pro zjištění rozměru diskriminace romských dětí*, Brno.

Likestillings-og diskrimineringsombudet (undated) 'The Norwegian Equality Tribunal', available at www.diskrimineringsnemnda.no/wips/1416077327/ (accessed 23 November 2007).

—— (2006) *Praksis 2006*, Oslo: Likestillings- og diskrimineringsombudet.

—— (2007) 'Tilrettelegging av eksamen', 21 August, available at www.ldo.no/no/TopMenu/Uttalelser/2006/Kjonn/Tilrettelegging-av-eksamen/ (accessed 23 November 2007) (author's translation from the Norwegian original).

—— (2007) 'What does the Ombud do?', available at www.ldo.no/en-gb/TopMenu/Om-ombudet2/Information-in-english/What-does-the-Ombud-do/ (accessed 23 November 2007).

——(2007) 'Oppsigelse på grunn av hijab et multi-diskrimineunde' available at www.ldo.no/no/TopMenu/ultalelser/2007/oppsigelse-pa-grunn-av-hijab-er-multi-diskrimineunde (accessed 23 November 2007).

Loenen, T (1992) *Verschil in gelijkheid. De conceptualisering van het juridische gelijkheidsbeginsel met betrekking tot vrouwen en mannen in Nederland en in de Verenigde Staten*, Zwolle: WEJ Tjeenk Willink.

—— (1996) 'Holtmaat en *Helmig*, of: het trekken van verkeerde conclusies uit een verkeerd arrest', *Nemesis*, 4: 123–5.

—— (1999) 'Indirect discrimination: Oscillating between containment and revolution', in T Loenen and PR Rodriguez (eds) *Non-Discrimination Law: Comparative Perspectives*, The Hague: Kluwer, pp 195–212.

Loschak, D (1987) 'Réflexions sur la notion de discrimination', *Droit social*, 11 : 778–90.

Loschelder, W (1982) *Vom besonderen Gewaltverhältnis zur öffentlich-rechtlichen Sonderbindung*, Cologne: Heymann.

Loury, GC (2002) *The Anatomy of Racial Inequality*, Cambridge, MA: Harvard University Press.

Ludvig, A (2006) 'Differences between women? Intersecting voices in a female narrative', *European Journal of Women's Studies*, 13: 245–57.

Lustgarten, L (1989) 'Racial inequality and the limits of law', in R Jenkins and J Solomos (eds) *Racism and Equal Opportunities Policies in the 1980s*, 2nd edn, Cambridge: Cambridge University Press.

Lyon-Caen, A (1996) 'De l'égalité de traitement en matière salariale', *Droit Social*: 1013–15.

Maas, W (2008) 'The evolution of EU citizenship', in K McNamara and S Meunier (eds) *Making History European Integration and Institutional Change at Fifty: The State of The European Union*, vol 8, Oxford: Oxford University Press, forthcoming.

MacDonald, G, Osborne RL and Smith CC (eds) (2005) *Feminism, Law, Inclusion: Intersectionality in Action*, Toronto: Sumach Press.

MacKinnon, C (1988) *Feminism Unmodified. Discourses on Life and Law*, Cambridge, MA: Harvard University Press.

—— (1989) *Toward a Feminist Theory of the State*, Cambridge, MA: Harvard University Press.

Magdolenová, K (2006) *Postaveni rómskych žien na trhu práce na Slovensku*, Roma Press Agency, Košice.

Magnette, P (2007) 'How can one be European? Reflections on the pillars of European civic identity', *European Law Journal*, 13: 664–79.

Maguire, M (2005) 'Textures of class in the context of schooling: The perceptions of a "class-crossing" teacher', *Sociology*, 39: 427–43.

Mahlmann, M (2003) 'Religious tolerance, pluralist society and the neutrality of the state: the Federal Constitutional Court's decision in the headscarf case', *German Law Journal*, 4: 1099–116, available at www.germanlawjournal.com/ (accessed 8 January 2008).

Mahoney, P (1990) 'Judicial activism and judicial restraint in the European Court of Human Rights: Two sides of the same coin', *Human Rights Law Journal*, 11: 57–88.

—— (1998) 'Marvellous richness of diversity or invidious cultural relativism?', *Human Rights Law Journal*, 19: 1–6.

Makkonen, T (2002) *Multiple, Compound and Intersectional Discrimination: Bringing the Experience of the Most Marginalized to the Fore*, Institute For Human Rights Åbo Akademi University, available at http://web.abo.fi/instut/imr/norfa/timo.pdf (accessed 4 January 2008).

Markard, N (2007) 'Fortschritte im Flüchtlingsrecht? Gender Guidelines und geschlechtsspezifische Verfolgung', *Kritische Justiz*, 40: 373–89.

Markell, P (2003) *Bound by Recognition*, Princeton NJ: Princeton University Press.

Martin, Ph (1996) 'Droit social et discriminations sexuelles: à propos des discriminations générées par la loi', *Droit social*, 6: 562–8.

Martin, S, Hartley, K and Cox, A (1999) 'Public procurement directives in the European Union: A study of local authority purchasing', *Public Administration*, 77: 387–406.

Mason, D (2000) *Race and Ethnicity in Modern Britain*, Oxford: Oxford University Press.

—— (2003) 'Changing patterns of ethnic disadvantage in employment', in D Mason (ed) *Explaining Ethnic Difference: Changing Patterns of Disadvantage in Britain*, Bristol: The Policy Press.

Matsuda, M (1989) 'When the first quail calls', *Women's Rights Law Reporter*, 11: 7–10.

McCall, L (2005) 'Managing the complexity of intersectionality', *Signs: Journal of Women in Culture and Society*, 30: 1771–800.

—— (2005) 'The complexity of intersectionality', *Journal of Women in Culture and Society*, 35: 1771–800.

McColgan, A (2005) *Discrimination Law. Text, Cases and Materials*, Oxford, Oregon, OR: Hart Publishing.

McCrudden, C (1994) *Equality in Law between Men and Women in the European Community: United Kingdom*, Luxembourg, Office for Official Publications of the European Communities.

—— (2003) 'The new concept of equality,' *ERA Forum*, 4: 9–23.

—— (2003) *The New Concept of Equality*, Trier: Academy of European Law.

—— (2005) 'Thinking about the discrimination directives', *European Anti-Discrimination Law Review*, 1: 17–23.

—— (2007) *Buying Social Justice. Equality, Government Procurement and Legal Change*, Oxford: Oxford University Press.

McGinty, AM (2007) 'Formation of alternative femininities through Islam: Feminist approaches among Muslim converts in Sweden', *Women's Studies International Forum*, 30: 474–85.

McGlynn, C (2000) 'Ideologies of motherhood in European Community sex equality law', *European Law Journal*, 6: 29–44.

—— (2006) *Families and the European Union: Law, Politics, and Pluralism*, Cambridge: Cambridge University Press.

Meetoo, V and Mirza, HS (2007) 'There is nothing "honourable" about honour killings: Gender, violence and the limits of multiculturalism', *Women's Studies International Forum*, 30: 187–200.

Mendieta, E (ed) (2004) *Beyond Philosophy: Ethics, History, Marxism, and Liberation Theology*, Oxford: Rowman and Littlefield.

Merrills, J (1988) *The Development of International Law by The European Court of Human Rights*, Manchester: Manchester University Press.

Michael, L (2003) 'Tragen eines islamischen Kopftuchs im Schuldienst', *Juristenzeitung*: 256–8.

Mile, K (2004) 'Diskriminering av kvinner', in N Høstmælingen (ed) *Hijab i Norge – Trussel eller menneskerett?*, Oslo: Abstrakt forlag, pp 220–30.

Miné, M (2001) 'Les apports de la nouvelle loi à la lumière du droit communautaire', *Semaine Sociale Lamy*, numéro spécial 'Les discriminations dans l'emploi', 1055, 17 December, p 5.

Ministry of Social Affairs and Health (1995) *Inkerinsuomalaiset* (Ingrian Finns).

Mir-Hosseini, Z (1996) 'Women and politics in post-Khomeini Iran: Divorce, veiling and emergent feminist voices,' in H Afshar (ed) *Women and Politics in the Third World*, London, New York: Routledge.

Modood, T, Berthould, R, Lakey, R, Nazroo, J, Smith, P, Virdee, S and Beishon, S (1997) *Ethnic Minorities in Britain: Diversity and Disadvantage*, London: Policy Studies Institute.

Molle, W (2006) *The Economics of European Integration: Theory, Practice & Policy*, 5th edn, Aldershot: Dartmouth.

Monaghan, K (2007) *Equality Law*, Oxford: Oxford University Press.

Moon, G (2006) 'Multiple discrimination: Problems compounded or solutions found', *Justice Journal* 3: 86–102.

More, G (1999) 'The principle of equal treatment: From market unifier to fundamental rights?' in P Craig and G de Búrca (eds) *The Evolution of EU Law*, Oxford: Oxford University Press.

Moreau, M-A (1994) 'Congé de maternité. Obstacle à la notation. Absence de discrimination, Cour de Cassation (Chambre sociale 30 mars 1994 CNAVTS c/ Duchemin)', *Droit social*, 6: 561–2.

—— (1995) 'Egalité de traitement hommes/femmes. Congé de maternité. Absence de notation. Renvoi en interprétation de la directive du 9 février 1976. Cour de Cassation (Chambre sociale) 28 mars 1995 CNAV c. Thibault', *Droit social*: 1036–7.

—— (2002) 'Les justification des discriminations', *Droit Social*: 1112–24.

Morlok, M and Krüper, J (2003) 'Auf dem Weg zum "forum neutrum"? – Die "Kopftuch-Entscheidung" des BVerwG', *Neue Juristische Wochenschrift*: 1020–1.

Mückel, S (2001) 'Religionsfreiheit und Sonderstatusverhältnisse – Kopftuchverbot für Lehrerinnen', *Der Staat*, 40: 96–127.

Muir, H and Smithers, R (2004) 'Black boys betrayed by racist school system, says report', available at http://education.guardian.co.uk/racism/story/0,,1298791,00.html (accessed 25 April 2007).

Nátherová, J and Bučková, A (2006) 'Position of Roma women in Slovakia', speech delivered to the European Parliament, February, available in the Slovak language at www.rnl.sk/modules.php?name=News&file=article&sid=4498 (accessed 30 November 2007).

—— (2006) *Postavenie rómskych žien na Slovensku – minulost, súčasnost', budúcnost'*, a study prepared for the European Parliament, 19 May.

Neureither, G (2003) 'Ein neutrales Gesetz in einem neutralen Staat', *Zeitschrift für Rechtspolitik*: 465–8.

—— (2003) 'Kopftuch-BVerwG, NJW 2001, 3344', *Juristischen Schulung*: 541–4.

Nielsen, R (2006) 'EU law and multiple discrimination', *CBS Law Studies* WP 2006–01, available at http://cbs.dk/content/view/pub/38578 (accessed 13 September 2007).

—— (2004) *Gender Equality in European Contract Law*, Copenhagen: DJØF Publishing.

Nieuwenhuis, A (2005) 'European Court of Human Rights: State and religion, schools and scarves', *European Constitutional Law Review*: 495–510.

Nikula, P (2007) 'Samapalkkaperiaate vaikea pala alusta saakka', *Tasa-arvolaki 20 vuotta*, 1: 15–24.

Nordberg, C (2007) *Boundaries of Citizenship: The Case of the Roma and the Finnish Nation-State*, Helsinki: University Press.

Nousiainen, K (2005) 'Tasa-arvon monet kasvot: kansainvälisistä vaikutuksista Suomen tasa-arvo-oikeudessa', *Lakimies*, 7–8: 1188–209.

Nousiainen, K *et al.* (2004) *Kansalaisvaikuttamisen politiikkaohjelman sukupuolinäkökulman valtavirtaistamisselvitys*, Ministry of Justice, available at www.om.fi/uploads/9aad82q10c.pdf (accessed 11 December 2007).

Nurmi, R and Helander, R (eds) (2002) *Väkivalta ei tunne kulttuurisia rajoja. Maahanmuuttajanaisiin kohdistuva väkivalta Suomessa*, Naisiin kohdistuvan väkivallan ja prostituution ehkäisyhanke (1998–2002), Helsinki: Yliopistopaino.

Nussbaum, MC (2004) *Hiding from Humanity*, Princeton, NJ: Princeton University Press.

O'Cinneide, C (2003) 'Taking equal opportunities seriously: The extension of positive duties to promote equality', London: Equality and Diversity Forum/Equal Opportunities Commission, available at www.edf.org.uk/news/Cinneide %2026%20Nov.doc (accessed 5 December 2007).

—— (2007) 'The Commission for Equality and Human Rights: A new institution for new and uncertain times', *Industrial Law Journal*, 36: 141–62.

Office of the Deputy Prime Minister (2003) *Local Government Act 1999: Part 1 Best Value and Performance Improvement*, ODPM Circular 03/2003 (March), London: Office of the Deputy Prime Minister.

Ofsted (1999) *Raising the Attainment of Minority Ethnic Pupils*, available at www.

ofsted.gov.uk/publications/index.cfm?fuseaction=pubs.displayfile&id=771&type= pdf (accessed 25 April 2007).

Ogorek, R (2008) ' "Gefährliche Mützen". Zum Urteil des ArbG Düsseldorf vom 29 Juni 2007 (Az: 12 Ca 175/07)', *myops*, 2: 4 *et seq.*

Ollus, N and Haarakangas, T (2002) 'Väkivaltaa kokeneiden maahanmuuttajanaisten auttaminen – turvakotien kokemuksista palvelujen kehittämiseen', in R Nurmi and R Helander (eds) *Väkivalta ei tunne kulttuurisia rajoja. Maahanmuuttajanaisiin kohdistuva väkivalta Suomessa.* Naisiin kohdistuvan väkivallan ja prostituution ehkäisyhanke (1998–2002), Helsinki: Yliopistopaino, pp 55–69.

Ontario Human Rights Commission (2001) *An Intersectional Approach to Discrimination. Addressing Multiple Grounds in Human Rights Claims. Discussion Paper,* available at www.ohrc.on.ca/en/resources/discussion_consultation/Diss-IntersectionalityFtnts/view (accessed 13 September 2007).

—— (2005) *An Intersectional Approach to Discrimination: Addressing Multiple Grounds in Human Rights Claims, Discussion paper,* Queens Printer for Ontario, available at http://ohrc.on.ca/english/consultations/intersectionality-discussion-paper_1.shtml (accessed 4 January 2008).

Orton M and Ratcliffe, P (2003) *Working for an Inclusive Britain: an Evaluation of the West Midlands Pilot Project,* Sandwell: West Midlands Forum.

—— (2004) 'Race, employment and contract compliance: A way forward for local authorities?', *Local Economy,* 19: 150–8.

—— (2005) 'New labour ambiguity or neo-liberal consistency? Racial inequality in employment and the debate about contract compliance' *Journal of Social Policy,* 34: 255–77.

Osborne, RD (2003) 'Progressing the equality agenda in Northern Ireland', *Journal of Social Policy,* 32: 339–60.

Otto, D (1997) 'Rethinking the "Universality" of Human Rights Law', *Columbia Human Rights Law Review,* 29: 1–46.

Pabel, K (2006) 'Die Rolle der Großen Kammer des EGMR bei der Überprüfung von Kammer-Urteilen im Lichte der bisherigen Praxis', *Europäische Grundrechte Zeitschrift,* 3–11.

Panayotova, D (2002) 'Successful Romani school desegregation: The Vidin case', *Roma Rights,* 3–4: 44–51.

Parent-Thirion, A, Fernández Macías, E and Vermeylen, G (2007) *Fourth European Working Conditions Survey,* Dublin: European Foundation for the Improvement of Living and Working Conditions.

Patel, P (2001) 'United Nations: An urgent need to integrate an intersectional perspective to the examination and development of policies, strategies and remedies for gender and racial equality', address by Pragna Patel to the 45th session of the UN Commission on the Status of Women (CSW), available at www.un.org/womenwatch/daw/csw/patel45.htm (accessed 7 January 2008).

Pateman, C (1986) *Feminist Challenge: Social And Political Theory,* Sydney, London: Allen and Unwin.

—— (1989) *The Disorder of Women: Democracy, Feminism and Political Theory,* Cambridge: Polity Press.

Pay Equity Taskforce and Departments of Justice and Human Resources Development Canada (2004) *Pay Equity: A New Approach to a Fundamental Right,* Ottawa: Federal Pay Equity Task Force, available at www.justice.gc.ca/en/payeqsal/docs/ PETF_final_report.pdf (accessed 4 March 2008).

Pélissier, J, Lyon-Caen, A, Jeammaud, A and Dockès E (2004) *Les grands arrêts de droit du travail*, Dalloz.

Pelling, R (2005) 'Of Course it's ok to call another woman a hobnob-guzzling, lazy lard-arse', *Independent on Sunday*, 18 September.

Petrova, D (2001) 'Racial discrimination and the rights of minority cultures', in S Fredman (ed) *Discrimination and Human Rights: the Case of Racism*, Oxford: Oxford University Press, pp 45–76.

Phillips, A (1999) *Which Equalities Matter?*, Cambridge: Polity Press.

Phillips, T (2005) 'Running faster into the same brick wall', *Guardian Unlimited*, 31 May, available at http://education.guardian.co.uk/egweekly/story/ 0,,1495513,00.html (accessed 14 January 2008).

Phizacklea, A and Wolkowitz, C (1995) *Homeworking Women*, London: Routledge.

Phoenix, A (2006) 'Interrogating intersectionality: Productive ways of theorising multiple positioning', *Kvinder, Køn & Forskning*, 15: 21–31.

Pichler, P (2007) 'Talking traditions of marriage – Negotiating young British Bangladeshi femininities', *Women's Studies International Forum*, 30: 201–16.

Pierce, M (2003) *Minority Ethnic People with Disabilities in Northern Ireland*, Dublin: Equality Authority.

Pinkney, A (1984) *The Myth of Black Progress*, Cambridge: Cambridge University Press.

Platt, L (2005) *Migration and Social Mobility: The Life Chances of Britain's Minority Ethnic Communities*, York: Joseph Rowntree Foundation.

—— (2007) *Poverty and Ethnicity in the UK*, Bristol: The Policy Press.

Pohjanpää, K, Paananen, S and Nieminen, M (2003) *Maahanmuuttajien elinolot. Venäläisten, virolaisten, somalialaisten ja vietnamilaisten elämää Suomessa vuonna 2002*, Elinolot 2003:1, Helsinki: Tilastokeskus (Statistics Finland).

Pollack, MA and Hafner-Burton, E (2000) 'Mainstreaming gender in the European Union', *Journal of European Public Policy*, 7: 432–56.

Pothier, D (2001) 'Connecting grounds of discrimination to real people's experience', *Canadian Journal Women and Law*, 13: 37–73.

Powell, JA (2007) 'The race and class nexus: An intersectional perspective', *Law and Inequality*, 25: 355–428.

Prechal, S (2004) 'Equality of treatment, non-discrimination and social policy: Achievements in three themes', *Common Market Law Review*, 41: 533–51.

—— (2007) 'Direct Effect, Indirect Effect. Supremacy and the Evolving Constitution of the European Union', in C Barnard (ed) *The Fundamentals of the EU Revisited. Assessing the Impact of the Constitutional Debate*, Oxford: Oxford University Press, pp 35–69.

Prétot, X (2003) 'La conformité à la Constitution de la loi portant sur la réforme des retraites. Un décision bien peu convaincante', *Droit social*, 917.

Prins, B (2006) 'Narrative accounts of origins: A blind spot in the intersectional approach', *European Journal of Women's Studies*, 13: 277–90.

Pulma, P (2006) *Suljetut ovet: Pohjoismaiden romanipolitiikka 1500-luvulta EU-aikaan*, Helsinki: Suomalaisen kirjallisuuden seura.

Purporka, L and Zádori, Z (1999) *The Health Status of Roma in Hungary*, Budapest: World Bank Regional Office Hungary, NGO Studies, No 2.

Pylkkänen, A (2001) 'The responsible self: Relational gender construction in the history of Finnish law', in K Nousiainen, Å Gunnarsson, K Lundström and J Niemi-Kiesiläinen (eds) *Responsible Selves: Women in the Nordic Legal Culture*, Aldershot: Ashgate, pp 105–28.

Rademacher, S (2005) *Das Kreuz mit dem Kopftuch. Wieviel religiöse Symbolik verträgt der neutrale Staat?*, Baden-Baden: Nomos.

Raevaara, E (2005) *Tasa-arvo ja muutoksen rajat. Sukupuolten tasa-arvo poliittisena ongelmana Ranskan paritè- ja Suomen kiintiökeskusteluissa*, Helsinki: TANE Publications, Ministry for Social Affairs and Health, Council for Gender Equality.

Rao, N (2000) *Reviving Local Democracy*, Bristol: The Policy Press.

Ratcliffe, P (2004) *'Race', Ethnicity and Difference: Imagining the Inclusive Society*, Maidenhead: Open University Press.

Rawls, J (1971) *A Theory of Justice*, Oxford: Oxford University Press (2nd revised edn, 1999).

Razavi, S and Miller, C (1994) 'Gender mainstreaming: A study of efforts by the UNDP, the World Bank and the ILO to institutionalize gender issues', Occasional Paper No 4, UN Fourth World Conference on Women, Geneva.

Rebhahn, R (ed) (2005) *Gleichbehandlungsgesetz. Kommentar*, Wien: Springer.

Reed, AL (2005) 'The real divide', *The Progressive*, November, 69(11), available at http://progressive.org/?q=node/2660 (accessed 4 March 2008).

Rees, T (1998) *Mainstreaming Equality in the European Union: Education, Training and Labour Market Policies*, London: Routledge.

Reich, N (2001) 'Union citizenship – Metaphor or source of rights?', *European Law Journal*, 7: 4–23.

Reitman, O (2005) 'Multiculturalism and feminism – incompatibility or synonymity?', *Ethnicities*, 5: 216–47.

Rex, J (1996) 'Contemporary nationalism, its causes and consequences for Europe – A reply to Delanty', *Sociological Research Online*, available at www.socresonline.org.uk/ socresonline/1/4/rex.html (accessed 9 January 2008), p 1.

Reynosso, J (2004) 'Perspectives on the intersections of race, ethnicity, gender, and other grounds: Latinas at the margins', *Harvard Latino Law Review*, 7: 63–73.

Rich, A (1979) *On Lies, Secrets, and Silence*, New York: Norton.

Ringold, D, Orenstein, MA and Wilkens, E (2005) *Roma in an Expanding Europe. Breaking the Poverty Cycle*, Washington DC, available at http://web.worldbank.org/ (accessed 9 January 2008), p xiv.

Rongere, P (1990) 'A la recherche de la discrimination introuvable: l'extension de l'exigence d'égalité entre les salariés', *Droit social*, 1: 99–106.

Rooney, E (2006) 'Women's equality in Northern Ireland's transition: Intersectionality in theory and place', *Feminist Legal Studies*, 14: 353–75.

Roseberry, L (1999) *The Limits of Employment Discrimination Law in the United States and the European Community*, Copenhagen: DJØF Publishing.

Rothenberg, P (2003) 'Learning to see the interrelation of race, class and gender discrimination and privilege: implications for policy and practice', in *E-Quality-experts in gender en etniciteit*, Den Haag, pp 17–28.

Rovná, L (2003) referring to J Šiklová (Professor of sociology at the Charles University and a leading figure in gender studies in the Czech Republic), unpublished paper, presented at the Jean Monnet Conference on 'Gender Equality and the New European Union', Brussels, 4 March.

Ruiz, BR and Sacksofsky, U (2005) 'Gender in the German Constitution', in B Baines and R Rubio-Marin (eds) *The Gender of Constitutional Jurisprudence*, Cambridge: Cambridge University Press, pp 149–73.

Rundell, J (1998) 'Tensions of citizenship in an age of diversity: Reflections on territoriality, cosmopolitanism and symmetrical reciprocity', in R Bauböck and J Rundell (eds) *Blurred Boundaries: Migration, Ethnicity, Citizenship*, European Centre Vienna, Ashgate: Aldershot, pp 321–40.

Rux, J (2001) 'Religiös motiviertes Kopftuch im öffentlichen Schuldienst', *Deutsches Verwaltungsblatt*: 1542–6.

—— (2002) 'Der Kopftuchstreit und kein Ende', *Zeitschrift für Ausländerrecht und Ausländerpolitik*: 366–8.

—— (2004) 'Kleiderordnung Gesetzesvorbehalt und Gemeinschaftsschule', *Zeitschrift für Ausländerrecht*: 14–21.

Sacksofsky, U (2003) 'Die Kopftuch-Entscheidung – von der religiösen zur föderalen Vielfalt', *Neue Juristische Wochenschrift*: 297–301.

Sámi Parliament (2006) Memorandum of 15 December.

Scales-Trent, J (1989) 'Black women in the Constitution: Finding our place and asserting our rights', *Harvard Civil Rights-Civil Liberties Law Review*, 24: 10–44.

—— (1995) *Notes of a White Black Woman: Race, Colour, Community*, University Park, PA: Pennsylvania University Press.

Scarborough, C (1989) 'Conceptualising black women's employment experiences', *Yale Law Journal*, 98: 1457–78.

Schiek, D (2002) 'A new framework on equal treatment of persons in EC law? Directives 2000/43/EC, 2000/78/EC and 2002/73/EC changing Directive 76/207/EEC in Context', *European Law Journal*, 8: 290–314.

—— (2004) 'Just a piece of cloth? German courts and employees with headscarves', *Industrial Law Journal*, 33: 68–73.

—— (2005) 'Broadening the scope and the norms of EU gender equality law: Towards a multidimensional conception of equality law', *Maastricht Journal of European and Comparative Law*, 12: 427–66.

—— (ed) (2007) *Allgemeines Gleichbehandlungsgesetz (AGG): ein Kommentar aus europäischer Perspektive*, Munich: Sellier.

—— (2007) 'Implementing non-discrimination Directives – typologies for legal transplanting', *International Colloquia Europees Verzekeringsrecht – Colloques Internationaux de droit européen de assurance*, 5: 47–83.

—— (2007) 'Indirect discrimination', in D Schiek, L Waddington and M Bell (eds), *Non-Discrimination Law*, Oxford: Hart Publishing.

—— (2008) 'The European social model and the Services Directive', in U Neergaard, R Nielsen and L Roseberry (eds) *The Services Directive – Consequences for the Welfare State and the European Social Model*, Copenhagen: D\FV.

Schiek, D, Dieball, H, Horstkötter, I, Seidel, L, Vieten, UM and Wankel, S (2002) *Frauengleichstellungsgesetze des Bundes und der Länder – Kommentar für die Praxis*, 2nd edn, Frankfurt a M: Bund Verlag.

Schiek, D, Waddington, L and Bell, M (eds) (2007) *Cases, Materials and Texts on National, Supranational and International Non-Discrimination Law*, Oxford: Hart Publishing.

—— (eds) (2007) 'Introductory chapter: A comparative perspective on non-discrimination law', in D Schiek, L Waddington and M Bell (eds) *Cases, Materials and Text on National, Supranational and International Non-Discrimination Law*, Oxford: Hart Publishing, pp 1–23.

Schöbener, B (2003) 'Die "Lehrerin mit dem Kopftuch" – europäisch gewendet!', *Juristische Ausbildung*: 186–91.

Schwarzer, A (2006) 'Die Islamisten meinen es so ernst wie Hitler', interview mit Alice Schwarzer, *Frankfurter Allgemeine Zeitung*, 4 July, available at www.faz.net/s/ RubCF3AEB154CE64960822FA5429A182360/Doc~EF6816D734A5C42A8A352 CBB10367B7FA~ATpl~Ecommon~Scontent.html (accessed 20 September 2007).

Selmi, M (1999) 'Indirect discrimination: A perspective from the United States', in T Loenen and PR Rodriguez (eds) *Non-Discrimination Law: Comparative Perspectives*, The Hague: Kluwer, pp 213–22.

Sewell, T and Jasper, L (2003) 'Look beyond the street', *Guardian Unlimited*, 19 July, available at www.guardian.co.uk/comment/story/0,3604,1001151,00.html (accessed 11 January 2008).

Shachar, A (2001) *Multicultural Jurisdictions: Cultural Differences and Women's Rights*, Cambridge: Cambridge University Press.

Shanks, M (1977) 'The social policy of the European Communities', *Common Market Law Review*, 14: 375–83.

Shapiro, MR (2002) 'Treading the Supreme Court's murky immutability waters', *Gonzaga Law Review*, 38: 409–44.

Shaw, J (2004) *Mainstreaming Equality in European Union Law and Policymaking*, Düsseldorf: ENAR.

—— (2005) 'Mainstreaming equality and diversity in European Union law and policy', *Current Legal Problems*, 58: 255–312.

Shoben, EW (1980) 'Compound discrimination: The interaction of race and sex in employment discrimination', *New York University Law Review*, 55: 793–835.

Shorter-Gooden, K (2003) *Shifting: The Double Lives of Black Women in America*, New York: Harper Collins.

Siim, B and Skjeie, H (2007) *Tracks, Intersections and Dead Ends. Multicultural Challenges to State Feminism in Denmark and Norway*, August (unpublished, on file with the authors).

Silvera, R (2006) 'Les accords sur l'égalité de rémunération à la loupe', *Semaine Sociale Lamy*, 1264: 2.

Sjerps, I (1999) 'Effects and justifications – Or how to establish a prima facie case of indirect sex discrimination' in T Loenen and PR Rodrigues (eds) *Non-Discrimination Law: Comparative Perspectives*, The Hague: Kluwer Law International, pp 237–47.

Skach, C (2006) 'Religious freedom—state neutrality—public order—role of international standards in interpreting an implementing constitutionally guaranteed rights', *American Journal of International Law*: 186–96.

Skeggs, B (1997) *Formations of Class and Gender: Becoming Respectable*, London: Sage.

—— (2004) *Class, Self, Culture*, London: Routledge.

Skjeie, H (2007) 'Headscarves in schools: European comparisons', in T Loenen and J Goldschmidt (eds) *Religious Pluralism and Human Rights in Europe: Where to Draw the Line?*, Antwerp: Intersentia, pp 129–46.

—— (2007) 'Religious exemptions to equality', *Critical Review of International Social and Political Philosophy*, 10: 471–90.

Skjeie, H and Teigen, M (2007) 'Likestilling og minoritetspolitikk', *Tidsskrift for kjønnsforskning*, 31: 21–39.

Sloat, A (2004) *Legislating for Equality: The Implementation of the EU Equality Acquis in Central and Eastern Europe*, Jean Monnet Working Paper 08/04, New York.

Smith, AM (2001) *Nationalism – Theory, Ideology, History*, Cambridge: Polity Press.

Smith, PR (1991) 'Separate identities: Black women, work and Title VII', *Harvard Women's Law Journal*, 14: 21–75.

Spelman, E (1988) *Inessential Woman. Problems of Exclusions in Feminist Thought*, Boston, MA: Beacon Press.

Squires, J (2005) 'Is mainstreaming transformative? Theorizing mainstreaming in the context of diversity and deliberation', *Social Politics: International Studies in Gender, State and Society*, 12: 366–88.

Statistics Finland (2007) www.stat.fi/ajk/tiedotteet/v2007/tiedote_026_11_20en.html (accessed 11 December 2007).

Stenius, H (2003) 'Kansalainen', in M Hyvärinen, J Kurunmäki, K Palonen, T Pulkkinen and H Stenius (eds) *Käsitteet liikkeessä. Suomen poliittisten käsitteiden historia*, Tampere: Vastapaino, pp 309–62.

Stötzer, B (2004) *In Differenzen. Feministische Theorie in der antirassistischen Kritik*, Hamburg: Argument-Verlag.

Strand, VB (2007) 'Vern mot direkte og indirekte diskriminering etter norsk rett – et ensartet vern?', *Lov og rett*, 47: 131–53.

Streeck, W (1995) 'From market making to state building? Reflections on the political economy of European social policy', in S Leibfried and P Pierson (eds) *European Social Policy: Between Fragmentation and Integration*, Washington DC: Brookings Institution, pp 389–431.

Strickland, DS and Ascher, C (1992) 'Low-income African-American children and public schooling', in Philip W Jackson (ed) *Handbook of Research on Curriculum*, New York: Macmillan.

Sturm, S (2001) 'Second generation employment discrimination: A structural approach', *Columbia Law Review*, 101: 458–568.

Suonoja, K and Lindberg, V (2000) *Strategies of the Policy on Roma*, Helsinki: Ministry of Social Affairs and Health.

Taylor, BR (1991) *Affirmative Action at Work: Law, Politics and Ethics*, Pittsburgh, PA: University of Pittsburgh Press.

Taylor, C (1992) 'The politics of recognition', in A Gutmann (ed) *Multiculturalism and the Politics of Recognition*, Princeton, NJ: Princeton University Press.

Thomas, H (1998) 'Die Gefährdung der Allgemeinbildung durch das Kopftuch. Eine Replik', in I Gogolin *et al.* (ed) *Pluralität und Bildung*, Opladen: Leske & Budrich, pp 55–61.

Thompson, C, Syddall, H, Rodin, I, Osmond, C and Barker, DJP (2001) 'Birth weight and the risk of depressive disorder in late life', *British Journal of Psychiatry*, 179: 450–55.

Thüsing, G and Wege, D (2004) 'Kündigungsschutz und Schutz vor rassischer Diskriminierung als Rechtsinstitute zur Sicherung der Religionsfreiheit in Deutschland und im Vereinigten Königreich', *Zeitschrift für Europäisches Privatrecht*: 404–23.

Tobler, C (2005) *Indirect Discrimination. A Case Study into the Development of the Legal Concept of Indirect Discrimination under EC Law*, Antwerpen, Oxford: Intersentia.

—— (2005) *Remedies and Sanctions in EC Non-Discrimination Law*, European Commission: Brussels, available at http://p30029.typo3server.info/fileadmin/pdfs/Reports/Remedies_and_Sanctions/remedies_en1.pdf (accessed 3 January 2008).

Toivanen, R (2001) 'Saami in the European Union', in A Foellesdal (ed) Special Issue on Sámi Rights in Finland, Norway, Russia and Sweden, *International Journal on Minority and Group Rights*, 8: 303–23.

—— (2004) 'Anthropology and the paradox of rights in a multicultural context', in V Puuronen, A Häkkinen, A Pylkkänen, T Sandlund and R Toivanen (eds) *New Challenges for the Welfare Society*, Joensuu: Yliopistopaino, pp 107–23.

Tourain, A (1999) 'Conclusion – European sociologists between economic globalisation and cultural fragmentation', in TP Boje, B van Steenbergen and S Walby (eds) *European Societies – Fusion or Fission?*, London, New York: Routledge, pp 249–62

Tuori, K (2007) *Oikeuden ratio ja voluntas*, Helsinki: WSOY.

Tully, J (1995) *Strange Multiplicity*, Cambridge: Cambridge University Press.

Turner, ML (2001) 'The braided uproar: A defense of my sister's hair and an indictment of Rogers v American Airlines', *Cardozo Women's Law Journal*, 7: 115–62.

Twomey, B (2001) 'Labour market participation of ethnic groups', *National Statistics: Labour Market Trends*, 109: 29–42.

UNESCO (1950) 'The race question', UNESCO and its programme 3, UNESCO, publication 791, available at http://unesdoc.unesco.org/images/0012/001282/128291eo.pdf (accessed 4 March 2008).

United Nations Development Programme (2003) *Avoiding the Dependency Trap. The Roma Human Development Report 2003*, available at http://roma.undp.sk/ (accessed 23 September 2007).

United Nations Division for the Advancement of Women: Gender and Racial Discrimination (2000) *Report of the Expert Meeting*.

US Department of State (2003) *Victims of Trafficking and Violence Protection Act of 2000: Trafficking in Persons Report*, Annual Report 2003, available at www.state.gov/g/tip/rls/tiprpt/2003/ (accessed 26 June 2003).

Vakulenko, A (2007) 'Islamic dress in human rights jurisprudence: A critique of current trends', *Human Rights Law Review*, 7 September, doi:10.1093/hrlr/ngm024: 717–39.

Valentine, G (2007) 'Theorizing and researching intersectionality: A challenge for feminist geography', *The Professional Geographer*, 59: 10–21.

Veldman, A (1995) *Effectuering van sociaal-economisch recht volgens de chaostheorie*, dissertation, Utrecht.

—— (1996) 'De bescheiden functie van het juridisch gelijkheidsbeginsel. Het fundamentele verschil tussen juridische leerstukken en wetenschappelijke concepten binnen vrouw en recht', *Nemesis*, 2: 31–8.

Verkind, P-Y (2005) 'Changer le regard sur le travail des seniors après l'ANI du 13 octobre 2005', *Semaine Sociale Lamy*, 1234: 6–11.

Verloo, M (2006) 'Multiple inequalities, intersectionality and the European Union', *European Journal of Women's Studies*, 13: 211–28.

Vieten, U (2007) '*Situated Cosmopolitanisms: Notions of the Other in Discourses on Cosmopolitanism in Britain and Germany*, PhD thesis, University of East London (unpublished).

Vieten, UM (2002) 'Frauenförderpläne' in D Schiek, H Dieball, I Horstkötter, L Seidel, UM Vieten and S Wankel, *Frauengleichstellungsgesetze des Bundes und der Länder – Kommentar für die Praxis*, 2nd edn, Frankfurt a M: Bund Verlag, pp 126–138.

Vleuten van der A (2007) *The Price of Gender Equality: Member States and Governance in the European Union*, Aldershot, Burlington, VT: Ashgate.

Vleuten, van der A and Verloo, M (2006) 'Disappointing pioneers and surprising laggards: Understanding disparities between reputation and performance', paper presented at the Third Pan-European Conference of the European Consortium for Political Research Standing Group on the European Union, Istanbul.

Voas, D and Crockett, A (2005) 'Religion in Britain: Neither believing nor belonging', *Sociology*, 39: 11–28.

Walby, S (2007) 'Complexity theory, systems theory, and multiple intersecting social inequalities', *Philosophy of the Social Sciences*, 37: 449–70.

Walker, A (1982) 'One child of one's own: A meaningful digression within the work(s) – an excerpt, in GT Hull, PB Scott and B Smith (eds) *All Women are White, All Blacks are Men, but Some of Us are Brave*, New York: Feminist Press, pp 37–47.

Walker, TJE (2002) *Illusive Identity: The Blurring of Working-Class Consciousness in Modern Western Culture*, Lanham, MD: Lexington Books.

Wallace, CJ (1999) 'European integration and legal culture: Indirect sex discrimination in the French legal system', *Legal studies*, 19: 397–414.

Wallace, M (1982) 'A black feminist's search for sisterhood', in GT Hull, PB Scott and B Smith (eds) *All Women are White, All Blacks are Men, but Some of Us are Brave*, New York: Feminist Press, pp 5–12.

Wallace, SL (1999) 'Minority procurement: Beyond affirmative action to economic empowerment', *The Review of Black Political Economy*, 27: 73–98.

Weatherspoon, FD (1998) *African American Males and the Law*, Maryland, Boston, MA: University Press of America.

Weber, A (2004) 'Religiöse Symbole in der Einwanderungsgesellschaft', *Zeitschrift für Ausländerrecht*, 24: 53–60.

—— (2006) 'Der Europäische Gerichtshof und das Kopftuchverbot an einer türkischen Universität', *Deutsches Verwaltungsblatt*: 173–4.

Weedon, C (1999) 'Race, racism and the problem of whiteness', in C Weedon (ed) *Feminism, Theory and the Politics of Difference*, Oxford, Malden, MA: Blackwell Publishers Ltd, pp 152–77.

Wei, V (1996) 'Asian women and employment discrimination: Using intersectionality theory to address Title VII claims based on combining factors of race, gender and national origin', *Boston College Law Review*, 37: 771–845.

Weiler, JHH (2003) *Un'Europa cristiana. Un saggio explorativo*, Milano: Rizzoli.

—— (2004) *Ein christliches Europa. Erkundungsgänge*, Salzburg: Pustet.

Wentholt, K (1990) *Arbeid en zorg. Een verkenning vanuit het gelijkheidsbeginsel van de rechtspositie van werknemers met zorgverantwoordelijkheden*, Amsterdam: Universiteit van Amsterdam.

Wiese, K (2003) 'Ablehnung der Einstellung als Lehrerin – Kopftuchstreit', *Zeitschrift für Beamtenrecht*: 39–41.

Williams, A (2007) 'Respecting fundamental rights in the New Union: A review', in C Barnard (ed) *The Fundamentals of the EU Revisited. Assessing the Impact of the Constitutional Debate*, Oxford: Oxford University Press, pp 71–107.

Williams, F (2003) 'Contesting "race" and gender in the European Union', in B Hobson (ed) *Recognition Struggles and Social Movements: Contested Identities, Agency and Social Movements*, Cambridge: Cambridge University Press, Ch 5.

Williams, RR (1997) *Hegel's Ethics of Recognition*, Berkeley, CA: University of California Press.

Willmann, C (2006) 'Promouvoir le vieillissement actif: les modestes propositions des partenaires sociaux', *Droit Social*: 144–55.

Windisch-Graetz, M (2005) 'Probleme der mehrfachen Diskriminierung in der Arbeitswelt', *Das Recht der Arbeit (Wien)*: 238–43.

Wing, A (ed) (1997) *Global Critical Race Feminism. An International Reader*, New York: New York University Press.

Winston, JA (1991) 'Mirror, mirror on the wall: Title VII, section 1981 and the intersection of race and gender in the Civil Rights Act of 1990', *California Law Review*, 79: 775–805.

Wintemunte, R (2002) 'Religion vs. Sexual Orientation. A Clash of Human Rights?', *Journal of Law & Equality*, 2: 125–54.

Winter, B (2006) 'The great hijab coverup', *Off Our Backs*, 36: 38–40.

Wittinger, M (2001) 'Kopftuchstreit auf europäisch, Aspekte des europäischen Grund- und Menschenrechtsschutzes', *Verwaltungsblätter für Baden-Württemberg*: 425–30.

Wollrad, E (2005) *Weißsein im Widerspruch. Feministische Perspektiven auf Rassismus, Kultur und Religion*, Königstein/Ts: Helmer.

Woodiwiss, A (2006) 'The law cannot be enough: Human rights and the limits of legalism', in S Meckled-García and B Çali (eds) *The Legalization of Human Rights*, London: Routledge, pp 33–4.

Wrench, J (2007) *Breakthroughs and Blind Spots: Trade Union Responses to Immigrants and Ethnic Minorities in Denmark and the UK*, Oslo: Fafo.

Yuval-Davis, N (1997) *Gender & Nation*, London: Sage.

—— (2006) 'Intersectionality and feminist politics', *European Journal of Women's Studies*, 13: 193–209.

Yuval-Davis, N and Stoetzler, M (2002) 'Imagined boundaries and borders – a gendered gaze', *The European Journal of Women's Studies*, 9: 329–44.

Yuval-Davis, N and Werbner, P (eds) (1999) *Women, Citizenship and Difference*, London: Zed Books.

Yuval-Davis, N, Anthias, F and Kofman, E (2005) 'Secure borders and safe haven and the gendered politics of belonging: Beyond social cohesion', *Ethnic and Racial Studies*, 28: 513–35.

Yuval-Davis, N, Kannabiran K and Vieten, UM (eds) (2006) *The Situated Politics of Belonging*, London: Sage, pp 54–71.

Zack, N (2007) 'Can third wave feminism be inclusive? Intersectionality, its problems, and new directions', in LM Alcoff and EF Kittay (eds) *The Blackwell Guide to Feminist Philosophy*, Malden, Oxford, Carlton: Blackwell Publishers, pp 193–207.

Index